Gendering Modern Japanese History

D0881761

Barbara Molony *and*
Kathleen Uno, editors

Harvard East Asian Monographs, 251

Gendering Modern Japanese History

Barbara Molony *and*
Kathleen Uno, editors

Published by the Harvard University Asia Center
and distributed by Harvard University Press
Cambridge (Massachusetts) and London 2005

Printed in the United States of America

The Harvard University Asia Center publishes a monograph series and, in coordination with the Fairbank Center for Chinese Studies, the Korea Institute, the Reischauer Institute of Japanese Studies, and other faculties and institutes, administers research projects designed to further scholarly understanding of China, Japan, Vietnam, Korea, and other Asian countries. The Center also sponsors projects addressing multidisciplinary and regional issues in Asia.

Library of Congress Cataloging-in-Publication Data
Gendering modern Japanese history / Barbara Molony and Kathleen Uno,
editors. -- 1st ed.
        p. cm. -- (Harvard East Asian monographs ; 251)
    Includes bibliographical references and index.
    ISBN 978-0-674-01780-1 (hardcover : alk. paper)
    ISBN 978-0-674-02816-6 (paperback : alk. paper)
    1. Sex role--Japan--History. 2. Japan--History--1868– .   I. Molony,
Barbara. II. Uno, Kathleen. III. Series.
HQ1075.5.J3G44 2005
305.3'0952--dc22

                                                          2005013998

  ∞   Printed on acid-free paper

1st paperback edition: 2008
Last figure below indicates year of this printing
18 17 16 15 14 13 12 11 10 09 08

Acknowledgments

This project owes a great debt to the sixteen dedicated scholars who helped to bring it into being. The stimulating workshop in February 1997 permitted us to share our expertise in gender history and to critique one another's drafts. Following the workshop, the contributors all rewrote their chapters to link them to the others in the volume. Numerous individuals and departments at Santa Clara University lent both material and moral support to this project. The College of Arts and Sciences (which granted us its first Intellectual Community Grant), the Office of International Programs, the Markkula Center for Applied Ethics, and the Program for the Study of Women and Gender funded the opening workshop. Generous grants from Santa Clara's History Department and the Office of the Provost underwrote the editorial assistance of students Maki Kanimoto, Michelle Pritchard, and Kelly Greenwalt and Women's and Gender Studies Program Coordinator Rosa Guerra-Sarabia. Ann Beyer made all the arrangements for the workshop. We are also indebted to Professors Joby Margadant and Nancy Unger of Santa Clara University and Douglas Painter and Peter Gran of Temple University for their incisive comments. As always, Thomas Turley was a tremendous support.

Contents

About the Contributors   IX

Introduction   *Barbara Molony and Kathleen Uno*   I

I. Gender, Selfhood, Culture

1   Made in Japan: Meiji Women's Education   *Martha Tocco*   39

2   Thoughts on the Early Meiji Gentleman   *Donald Roden*   61

3   Commodifying and Engendering Morality: Self-Cultivation
    and the Construction of the "Ideal Woman" in 1920s Mass
    Women's Magazines   *Barbara Sato*   99

II. Genders, Bodies, Sexualities

4   "S" is for Sister: Schoolgirl Intimacy and "Same-Sex Love"
    in Early Twentieth-Century Japan   *Gregory M. Pflugfelder*   133

5   Seeds and (Nest) Eggs of Empire: Sexology Manuals/
    Manual Sexology   *Mark Driscoll*   191

6   Engendering Eugenics: Feminists and Marriage Restriction
    Legislation in the 1920s   *Sumiko Otsubo*   225

III. Gender, Empire, War

7   Making "Soldiers": The Imperial Army and the Japanese
    Man in Meiji Society and State   *Theodore F. Cook, Jr.*   259

8   Reading the Japanese Colonial Archive: Gender and
    Bourgeois Civility in Korea and Manchuria before 1932
    Barbara J. Brooks   295

9   Women's Deaths as Weapons of War in Japan's "Final
    Battle"   *Haruko Taya Cook*   326

    IV. Gender, Work, Economy

10 Gendering the Labor Market: Evidence from the Interwar
    Textile Industry   *Janet Hunter*   359

11 Sorting Coal and Pickling Cabbage: Korean Women in
    the Japanese Mining Industry   *W. Donald Smith*   393

12 Managing the Japanese Household: The New Life
    Movement in Postwar Japan   *Andrew Gordon*   423

    V. Theorizing Gender

13 The Quest for Women's Rights in Turn-of-the-Century
    Japan   *Barbara Molony*   463

14 Womanhood, War, and Empire: Transmutations of
    "Good Wife, Wise Mother" before 1931   *Kathleen Uno*   493

15 Toward a Critique of Transhistorical Femininity
    Ayako Kano   520

16 Feminism and Media in the Late Twentieth Century:
    Reading the Limits of a Politics of Transgression
    Setsu Shigematsu   555

Index   591

About the Contributors

BARBARA BROOKS is a professor of Japanese and East Asian history at the City College and the Graduate Center of the City University of New York. Author of *Japan's Imperial Diplomacy* (University of Hawai'i Press, 2000), she is currently working on a book on gender and marginality in the Japanese empire.

HARUKO TAYA COOK is co-author of *Japan at War: An Oral History* (New Press, 1992), and is completing a book for Viking tentatively titled *The War Within: The Japanese Experience of War, 1931–1945*. She is professor emerita at Fordham University Marymount College.

THEODORE F. COOK is a professor of Japanese history and director of Asian Studies at William Paterson University of New Jersey. He is co-author of *Japan at War: An Oral History*. He is completing a book on the Japanese people's experience during the Second World War in Asia and the Pacific and is writing a social history of the Japanese army.

MARK DRISCOLL, assistant professor of East Asian and International Studies at UNC-Chapel Hill, currently works on Japanese colonial-imperialism, focusing on sexuality, value, and the vampirization of difference. His monograph on colonial intellectual and propagandist Yuasa Katsuei will be published in 2005 (Duke University Press).

ANDREW GORDON is Lee and Juliet Folger Fund Professor of History at Harvard University. He has written on the history of labor and management in nineteenth- and twentieth-century Japan and on the politics of labor in the prewar era. He is currently studying Japan's twentieth-century emergence as a mass consumer society, with a focus on the sewing machine.

JANET HUNTER is Saji Professor of Economic History at the London School of Economics and Political Science. She obtained her DPhil. from Oxford, and subsequently taught at the University of Sheffield. She is the author of *Women and the Labour Market in Japan's Industrialising Economy* (Routledge Curzon, 2003).

AYAKO KANO is an associate professor in the Department of East Asian Languages and Civilizations at the University of Pennsylvania. Her publications include *Acting Like a Woman in Modern Japan: Theater, Gender, and Nationalism* (Palgrave, 2001).

BARBARA MOLONY, professor of Japanese history and former director of the Women's and Gender Studies Program at Santa Clara University, has published works on Japanese women's rights and gender theory. She is currently co-authoring (with Kathleen Molony) a biography of Ichikawa Fusae.

SUMIKO OTSUBO received her PhD from Ohio State University, where she completed her dissertation on "Eugenics in Imperial Japan: Some Ironies of Modernity, 1883–1945." Currently, she teaches at Metropolitan State University in St. Paul, Minnesota.

GREGORY M. PFLUGFELDER is an associate professor of Japanese history at Columbia University and author of *Cartographies of Desire* (UC Press, 1999). His work spans the premodern, early-modern, and modern periods, focusing on issues of gender and sexuality, body histories, and representations of monstrosity.

DONALD RODEN is a member of the History Department at Rutgers University and author of *Schooldays in Imperial Japan* (University of California Press, 1980).

BARBARA SATO is a professor of Japanese history and women's studies at Seikei University in Tokyo, Japan. She is the author of *The New Japanese Woman: Media, Modernity, and Women in Interwar Japan* (Duke University Press, 2003). Her present work explores lower middle-class and working-class women and their links to consumerism in the 1920s.

Setsu Shigematsu is an assistant professor of cultural studies in the Comparative Studies Department of Ohio State University. She is completing a book on the women's liberation movement in Japan and editing an anthology on militarism, gender, and feminism.

W. Donald Smith received his PhD at the University of Washington. His research has focused on Korean and women workers in the prewar Japanese coal mines, Japanese wartime labor mobilization, and Korean ethnic education in postwar Japan. He currently works for the U.S. government.

Martha C. Tocco received her PhD from Stanford University in 1995. She taught Japanese history for four years at UCLA and UC Irvine before changing careers. She is currently an independent scholar and first-grade teacher in Los Angeles, California.

Kathleen Uno is an associate professor of Japanese history and director of the Asian Studies Program at Temple University. Author of *Passages to Modernity* (University of Hawai'i Press, 1999), she has written extensively on "good wife, wise mother."

Gendering
Modern
Japanese
History

Introduction

Gender, as Joan Scott asserted in 1986, is a useful category of historical analysis.[1] In the last quarter century, gender has emerged as a lively area of inquiry for historians and other scholars. Gender analysis has suggested some important revisions of the "master narratives" of national histories—that is, the dominant, often celebratory, tales of the successes of a nation and its leaders.[2] These narratives, like all histories, are provisional and incomplete and, to varying degrees, reflect the changing material, discursive, and ideological contexts of their times.[3] To mention just two of the fields of history that had traditionally formed the core of national(ist) narratives—colonial history and political history—bringing in gender has begun to alter the dominant narratives in those fields.[4] Recent colonial studies examine such issues as gendered notions of expansion; virility among colonizers and colonized; and relations between men and women, women and women, and men and men on the colonial periphery. Because political histories look at the meanings of citizenship and participation, gender, like race and class, clearly has utility as a category of analysis.

While modern Japanese history has not yet been restructured by a foregrounding of gender, historians of Japan have, indeed, begun to embrace gender as an analytic category. Interested readers can barely keep up with the exciting new scholarship in the form of journal articles and monographs in both Japanese and Western languages. If the experience of previous turns in Japanese historiography is any guide— for example, in the 1950s and beyond, interest in the course of Japan's modern development led to the categorizing of historical patterns as stages of modernity, and interest in social groups defined by categories such as material circumstances, cultural identities, occupation, religion, or residence has complicated and enriched the master narratives of Japanese history—gender too will emerge as an important issue in redefining master narratives in modern Japanese history. This interdisciplinary volume attempts to ignite the process of redefinition by bringing together research by Western-trained historians of Japan and historically minded scholars in other disciplines.[5]

Problematizing gender in an anthology on modern Japanese history recognizes the stimulating developments in that field of scholarship.[6] A number of Japan scholars, including some of our contributors, have been engaged in research in women's history for over a decade, and are now producing works in the area of gender history. Gender history emerged from women's history outside the Japan field as well, although the sometimes rivalrous tension between women's history and gender history in other fields has not been replicated in Japan studies.[7]

This volume, which assembles articles on men as well as women, on theories of sexuality as well as on gender prescriptions, and on same-sex as well as on heterosexual relations, takes the position that history is gendered. To say that history is gendered is to make two interrelated claims. First, historians invariably, though perhaps unconsciously, construct a gendered notion of past events, people, and ideas. That is, we engender the past, creating ways of thinking about the past through our notions of gender (and other categories we take for granted) in the present. A gendered history, like any type of history, is an invention of historians. History attempts to view ideologies, discourses, practices, bodies, and institutions as both derived in part from notions of gender and, conversely, constantly reifying these notions.

Second, the assertion that history is gendered arises from the discovery and publication of evidence that societies, ideologies, and discourses in the past were ordered in varying degrees by notions of gender.[8] While gender was certainly not the only organizing principle in any given society—class, status, race, and various other factors have on many occasions trumped gender—people and institutions have often been implicated in the creation of gendered legal, social, cultural, political, and economic systems, institutions, and ideas. We do not believe that gender is an essential derivative of "biological" sex—indeed, "sex" is given definition through "gender"—but we do believe that laws, customs, ideologies, and the structures of societies, based as they have often been on the idea that gender is biologically determined, contribute to the social construction of gender. In other words, gender acts as if it is "real" despite being constructed and constantly redefined.[9] The articles in this collection address both of these claims, building on earlier efforts to incorporate gender perspectives into modern Japanese history.[10] Together these essays construct a history informed by the idea that gender matters because it was part of the experience of people in the past and because it often has been a central feature in the construction of modern ideologies, discourses, and institutions. Separately, each chapter examines how Japanese in former times (en)gendered their ideas, institutions, and society.

In the past several decades, there has also been notable interplay between history and other fields, as evidenced both by cooperative projects between historians and scholars in other disciplines and by the interest of these scholars in examining the hypotheses, concepts, and theories of other fields, especially anthropology, literary or cultural studies, and sociology.[11] This volume, then, a historical project in Japanese gender studies whose contributors represent social sciences, history, and cultural studies, reflects larger trends toward interdisciplinary exchanges in the fields of history and women's and gender studies.

This volume demonstrates that it is important for historians of modern Japan to continue to engage with research on gender. Modernity in Japan as elsewhere has encompassed changes in notions of gender and gender roles as well as economic, political, and cultural changes.[12] To understand Japan since the nineteenth century, especially the role of gender in its modern transformations, the authors of this volume aim to encourage cross-disciplinary dialogue around issues of gender among Japan specialists. Moreover, in order to advance the field of gender studies, it is important for historians of gender in Japan to exchange ideas with researchers pursuing cross-cultural approaches to gender and gender studies in other regions.

The time period covered by this book can be called the "long twentieth century," from the late nineteenth through the twentieth century. If, strictly speaking, scholars use "modern" to refer to the period 1868–1945 and popular writers use it to refer to Japan since 1868, the long twentieth century encompasses a longer "modern" period than these common definitions. The long twentieth century spans three commonly used eras of Japanese history: the final two decades of the Tokugawa (1603–1868), or early modern period; the modern[13] period (1868–1945); and the contemporary or postwar period (1945–present). As with most historical eras, these have been typically defined by political trends and events—decentralized, hereditary rule by samurai under the Tokugawa shogunate from 1603, followed by a centralized, civilian administration promoting national strength and imperial expansion under a strong monarch and constitution after 1868, and after World War II a centralized government under a revised constitution that relegated the emperor to a symbol of the state and outlawed resorting to war. A long twentieth century helps make gender changes in modern Japan more readily visible, because the continuities and changes that fascinate historians stand out more sharply in relief when observed in a longer time frame.

Modernity/Modernization in Japan

As a historical study, this exploration of gender in modern Japan also addresses modernity and its interpretations. Interpretations of modernity have influenced studies, including gender studies, of Japan and other parts of Asia and most of the rest of the world, due to similar concerns of historians and scholars in other disciplines. These issues include the formation of nation-states; the establishment of representative governments; the mobilization of mass participation in national affairs; the rise of industry along with associated changes in values, social life, and culture; the elimination or weakening of hereditary principles in occupations and leadership; and more recently, gender change. All of them are processes that have affected many regions of the globe for at least the last century or two.

Modernity studies of Japan do not by any means begin with this book, but as we shall see, modernity studies tracing gender change are relatively new. In fact, under the rubric of "modernization" studies, particular concerns related to "modernity" have long infused studies of Japan.[14] Modernization studies as well as the responses to that approach—visions of modernity that focus on radical political economy or the perspective of conflict, humanism, or victimization, on the one hand, or postmodern considerations of ambiguities and multiple identities, on the other—have had a significant impact on Japanese history and Japanese gender studies.

For most of the Cold War era (1946–1989), modernization theory was the dominant perspective in the United States informing studies of Japan and the rest of Asia as well as studies of Africa and Latin America. Although the modernization perspective was not monolithic even at its height from the 1950s to the 1970s, on the whole studies of this type presented a group of interrelated changes culminating in a society characterized by a capitalist economy and a representative government.[15] As the only non-Western industrialized country before the 1970s and one that was a Cold War ally of the United States, Japan was showcased as a model of industrial development, capitalism, and democracy in the competition between communist and free enterprise blocs for the loyalty of emerging nations. The discussion of history was often, though certainly not always, celebratory. The following quick introduction to Japan in the three eras of its long twentieth century is drawn from standard modernization sources. The absence of gender in this sketch reflects its relative neglect in modernization studies of Japan.

As Japan modernized in the late nineteenth century, rising educational levels, the flowering of textile and handicraft production, the spread of production for the market, a vibrant commercial economy, urbanization, migration, the importing of Western texts, institutions, and techniques, and the forced opening of diplomatic and trade relations with Western countries laid the foundation for the building of new infrastructures and a centralized, increasingly "modern" state. This permitted Japan to increase its military power, resulting in imperialism and domestic bureaucratization. In the early years of the modern period, officials and intellectuals initially stressed self-reliance and rising in the world over hereditary occupations and lifelong loyalty and deference by inferiors in return for benevolence by superiors. But Meiji-era leaders' fear that political movements rooted in popular rights (which these leaders saw as the masses' self-interest) would undercut an agenda designed to maximize national strength provoked them to revive earlier values of loyalty and filial piety in order to institute policies of obedience to superiors, repression of individual interests, and loyalty to the emperor.[16] The modern quest for national strength and security also led the Japanese to overseas wars and several waves of territorial expansion, including the acquisition of Taiwan (1895), the annexation of Korea (1910), the seizure of Manchuria (1931), and war with China, the United States, Great Britain, and their allies (1931–1945), including the occupation of much of the South Pacific and the Asian mainland (1937–1945).

Following defeat in the Pacific War, the Allied Occupation (1945–1952) dismantled the Japanese empire, abolished the armed forces, and implemented reforms in education, the constitution, civil code, family, and economy with the aim to demilitarize Japan and foster democratic institutions, ideologies, and attitudes. Industries, infrastructure, and housing stock lay in ashes, but Japanese will, know-how, and energy along with American procurements during the Korean War brought about economic recovery by 1955 and a position as the number two economy in the world by the late 1970s. Japan has gained recognition as an advanced economy and constitutional democracy, and Japanese consumer products and culture ranging from cars and advanced electronic devices to sushi, pop music, fashion, comic books, and DVD cartoons are in demand around the world. In contrast to the emphasis on continuities throughout the period under consideration in this volume, modernization studies foregrounded discontinuities between the pre- and postwar eras.

Rejecting the modernization approach that celebrated institutional development, progress, and the benefits of social change, historians, writing against the turbulent backdrop of the late 1960s antiwar and social protest movements, produced new studies of Japan that probed exploitation, resistance, and conflict.[17] Instead of touting Japan as a model of success for non-Western nations, these studies exposed the dark underside of economic and political changes, including their negative impacts on ordinary farmers and workers, women, and minorities. This triggered two trends that have continued from the 1970s to the present, a turn first to social history and then to cultural history. From these directions have emerged, since the mid-1970s, several streams of gender history, including, in roughly the following order, women's, men's, and sexuality studies.[18] The frontiers of Japanese modernity studies remain in social and cultural history. They include not only gender history and studies, but also the social and cultural histories of colonialism; the analysis of the social and cultural dimensions of Japanese modernism in elite society and popular culture; the interrogating of the links between race, ethnicity, identity, and citizenship; and tracking the particularities of individual as well as collective experience.[19] The articles in this volume take up all these issues, and view them through the lens of gender. They are also mostly in accord with a view expressed by Harry Harootunian that

see[s] modernity as a particular mode of experience that is not necessarily and only reducible to the empirical domain, as many historians have believed. Instead of examining the material transformation of Japanese society as an instance of some hypostatized conception of the social—the very subject and substance of social and political history—we need to read this episode not for the familiar story lines authorized by such historical narratives but rather as the production of experience that tried to catch hold of the moving present ("fleeting and fragmentary," as Baudelaire described the modern present) and thus give it meaning and direction.[20]

From the 1980s, ideas deriving from linguistic and critical theories have influenced Japanese historiography and Japanese gender studies, as some scholars have attempted to move beyond Japanese modernity or modernism and embraced postmodern approaches to what many see as the postmodern state and society.[21] However, as Harootunian and Miyoshi have pointed out, "as the term itself suggests, analyses of Japan as postmodern find it difficult to elude the earlier terms, conclusions, and debates of modernity and even modernization studies."[22] We have presented the historiographical categories of modernization studies, modernity studies, and postmodernism as distinct in this introduction, but all may be, in the end, interwoven in the interpretations of gender in modern Japan.

Studying Gender

Just as a fuller consideration of gender is beneficial to studies of Japanese modernity, learning from gender studies outside the Japan field offers new vistas on gender and processes of gender change in Japan's long twentieth century. Key issues in gender studies that help illuminate modernity studies are identity and linkages between gender and power. Recent gender theory highlights the relative neglect of individual experiences and, perhaps more tellingly, weaknesses in the conceptualization of identity in both modernization and modernity studies concerning Japan. Themes of gender construction and contestation have, in the last two decades, characterized research on gender in Japan. These themes play a major role in this volume, and they are joined by new approaches to gender studies that focus on identity (or subjectivity) and gender ambiguity.

In considering the relationship between gender and subjectivity or identity, it is possible to state that external labeling of gender may be at odds with self-identified gender, and those constructions of gender by other persons, groups, or society may be at variance with the perceptions and experiences of the individual. Individuals' identities are complicated by their multiplicity.[23] That is, individuals are constituted by a mix of characteristics derived from their gender(s), ethnicities, class, intermingling with others and their ideas, as well as other factors. Historical context also affects notions of individuals' identities; postmodern ideas of multiplicity differ from the modern emphasis on the unitary subject. In Japan's long twentieth century, individuals have constructed and experienced complex, fluid identities, while social institutions and the state have attempted to craft and enforce unitary constructions of gender. Social history and postmodern orientations lead us to question the success of these efforts to invent unitary gendered subjectivities. Indeed, throughout the long twentieth century, ambiguity has characterized notions of gender identity as well as gender norms. Variability in gender performance, including performance of sexuality in the early modern period, male and female androgyny in the 1910s–1920s, and female refusals in the 1990s of marriage, motherhood, and domesticity, reinforces the salience of ambiguity in constructions of gender. An examination of the Japanese case enriches the broader scholarship on genders, identities, and subjectivities and the role of contemporaries, historians, and subjects themselves in their construction.

"Gender" has not always been viewed as a constructed category describing relations of human beings. Historically, it came into use among Western feminists in the 1960s as a means of destabilizing "sex," which was seen as biologically determined and the basis for sex-difference-based discrimination.[24] "Gender" could be seen as a socially constructed notion with some attachment to sex.[25] That attachment was the basis on which different societies in various historical eras constructed different notions of gender. That is, sex was taken as the irreducible foundation on which all sorts of "cultural artifacts, specifically those of personality and behavior, [were] thrown or [were] superimposed."[26] Feminists who used "gender" in this way found that it satisfied the need to explain both commonalities and differences among women and encouraged the possibility of social transformation. As attractive as this view was, however, it was grounded in a kind of biological determinism and made unfounded transcultural assumptions about "women" and "men."[27] In its more egregious form, it made false universalizing claims about women transculturally and ahistorically; in its more modest form, it suggested that women's reproductive biology caused men and women to react in similar ways across many different cultures.

One way to avoid biological determinism is to reverse the relationship between "sex" and "gender." This is done by some feminist historians, most notably Joan W. Scott: "We cannot see sexual differences except as a function of our knowledge about the body, and that knowledge is not 'pure,' cannot be isolated from its implication in a broad range of discursive contexts."[28] Philosopher Judith Butler expresses this more boldly: "[S]ex is a gendered category."[29]

If "biological sex" is not the grounding for gender, it cannot stably ground gender identity either. How, then, does a gendered subjectivity or identity come into being?[30] Joan Scott's work on "experience" may be useful in addressing this question. She acknowledges that understanding one's identity as a subject permits one to speak from her or his "experience" and, in turn, for historians of difference to use a diversity of previously unheard voices as an exciting way to widen historical perspectives. Yet, at the same time, she notes the limitations of taking for granted the identity of those whose experience is being recounted, as it fails to question why subjects are able to speak or act—that is, have agency—and "precludes analysis of the workings of [the ideological] system and of its historicity; instead, it reproduces its terms."[31] Scott analyzes the problems that even well-intentioned historians of difference, studying the experiences of heretofore ignored groups, may face. Less charitably, identities may be defined for commercial reasons—consider the magazine publishers discussed in this volume by Barbara Sato—or defined for academic or other reasons—see the critics analyzed by Ayako Kano. More perversely, perhaps, identities may also be defined for political reasons by those in power. Part of the process of Japan's modernity from the late nineteenth century throughout World War II was the state's defining its power in relation to its subjects, and, as in modernizing states elsewhere, this included gender construction. Thus, as Kathleen Uno notes, "good wife, wise mother" ideology, developed and fostered as an important part of womanly identity, was closely bound with national needs over the course of seventy years of Japanese history. Even more ominously, Haruko Cook tells us that in 1944 Saipan women were given a false gendered "identity" in order to have them "speak," as it were, from a patriotic grave (false because it was constructed from misleading fragments of reality, and in quotation marks because it was not an identity claimed by any living, real woman).

Admittedly, allowing outside forces to define others' identities, then, is fraught with problems: what is the agenda of the definer? On the other hand, for political purposes it might seem highly useful to reify the gendered subject (that is, define woman as a category), as many women have done, for instance, in the course of organizing to identify, oppose, and negotiate with the processes that define them. Even though defining woman as a category will produce an essentialized subject, this is not, however, necessarily a problem for activists. Consider, for example, the Japanese men and women of the late nineteenth century who advocated rights for a set of people understood to occupy a subordinated group called women. As Barbara Molony indicates, women's rights were defined by a neologism, *joken,* whose presumed universality (to all women, that is) preserved social status disjunctions and hierarchies produced by identifications other than gender (e.g., class, regional origin, or ethnicity). Or consider the activism on behalf of women undertaken by Hiratsuka Raichō, as analyzed by Sumiko Otsubo. Ostensibly supporting all women against all diseased men, Hiratsuka's proposal ignored protection for some classes of women, particularly sex workers.

"Masculine" and "feminine" are conceived by some feminist historians and other theorists, possibly aware of the problems of essentializing, in terms of relations of power. But this perspective has limitations, too. As Jane Flax writes, "If subjectivity is constituted by pregiven categories like masculine and feminine, no individual subject can escape the effects of these categories. . . . [T]hese categories will continue to generate particular forms of subjectivity beyond the control of individuals."[32] If masculine is to feminine as powerful is to weak, things can look rather bleak both for progressive activists and for historians seeking to understand gender in the past. Positing a binary power relationship may undermine our understanding of gender in Japan. For example, although unequal power relations were embedded in the texts studied by early modern Japanese schoolgirls, Martha Tocco writes, they paled in significance to the empowering role of those texts' promotion of female literacy. Decades later, during the Taishō era, Otsubo notes, Hiratsuka and other feminists attempted to regulate male subjects and their sexuality.

It appears, then, that the concept of the gendered subject must be nuanced to be useful for understanding gender in Japan, as elsewhere. Perhaps the most notable need is to historicize notions of gendered identities. The importance of historical change is recognized in insightful introductions to each of the seven volumes of the 1994–1995 series *Nihon no feminizumu*. In the volume on "sex roles," Inoue Teruko's introduction takes up the issue of historical changes in sex roles and their effect on the formation of gender identity.[33] (Though we do not view socially constructed sex roles themselves as subjectivities or identities, their performance is, in many ways, analogous to the performance of gender.) In another introduction in that series, Ehara Yumiko stresses that "motherhood," rather than being simply an essential part of women's gendered identity, is constructed, institutionalized, and politicized.[34]

Wakita Haruko, one of the editors of another important collection, *Jiendā no Nihonshi*, places the (spatial) binary division of two sexes in the Meiji period. In her preface, she notes that this modern (*kindaiteki*) division created a public (man) / private (woman) dichotomy.[35] Janet Hunter, Andrew Gordon, Theodore Cook, and Donald Roden, in this volume, show us a much more permeable boundary between public and private. As Hunter notes, jobs came to be identified as either masculine or feminine, and, in turn, both employers and workers came to apply the gendered division of the workplace to individual workers' identities. Nevertheless, women's work, like men's, was in public, even if the public workplace was itself divided by gender. Gordon describes a significant moment in the evolution of gendered subjectivities in his analysis of the New Life Movement in postwar Japan. By virtue of their gender identity, women were to claim the home and men the workplace. Yet, the home was hardly private, nor were women seen as divorced from a public identity when they focused their performance of gender in the home. Cook shows us male schoolteachers in the Meiji era being called upon to act as "mothers" to help create the new Japanese male, a fascinating bridging of public and private spheres. Roden indicates that the public gentleman was, in part, a performance based on personal hygiene, a distinctly private behavior.

Unitary notions of gendered subjectivity are also called into question when we consider sexuality. Gregory Pflugfelder describes public worry about teenage girls' same-sex attachments in the early twentieth century. The critics of this anxiety argued that it reflected an improper focus on the girls' sexual identity. Mark Driscoll's analysis of Japanese sexologists' treatment of male and female sexualities shows the importance of fracturing and historicizing a unitary concept of sexuality; sexologists' work, done against a backdrop of discourse on modernity, colonialism, state building, military organization, and so on, influenced men's and women's sense of their gendered subjectivity. Setsu Shigematsu's depiction of the contemporary "ladies' comics" creator and artist Uchida Shungiku shows us a stunningly complex woman with a command of her sexuality that in no way fits into the stereotyped female norm.

If one part of the process of modernity was the reification of the gendered subject, often as a unitary subject for purposes of labeling and control, then the nuancing of the subject as one with multiple subjectivities parallels our unease with universalizing ideologies in the contemporary (postmodern) era. Inderpal Grewal and Caren Kaplan, in the introduction to their collection, *Scattered Hegemonies: Postmodernity and Transnational Feminist Practices,* write that, "We see postmodernism as a critique of modernist agendas as they are manifested in various forms and locations around the world."[36] Following up in her own chapter in the collection, Grewal notes that many feminists of color do not "share the position of the subject as individual (i.e., unitary and centered and created out of the binaries of Self–Other, Subject–Object) that has been part of the Western philosophical tradition."[37] Rather, Grewal calls for a multiple subject (which she calls the "collective subject") and reminds her readers that sharing a time and place does not mean that all women will share the same multiplicities.[38] (For example, all Japanese women of, say, 1900 did not share the same multiplicities.) In this volume, Donald Smith's chapter, which addresses Korean women in Japan, and Barbara Brooks's chapter, which examines nationality and citizenship of Japanese women in the colonies, support that insight.

The notion of "hybridity" may be a useful model for working with gendered subjectivity in Japan and elsewhere.[39] Although the concept was developed to address "the borrowing and lending across porous cultural borders,"[40] and generally has an activist sense of negotiating those flows rather than a passive sense of absorption by osmosis,[41] it can be helpful in understanding multiple subjectivities.

Metaphors of hybridity and the like not only recognize differences within the subject, fracturing and complicating holistic notions of identity, but also address connections between subjects by recognizing affiliation, cross-pollinations, echoes, and repetitions. . . . Instead of endorsing a drift toward ever greater atomization of identity, such metaphors allow us to conceive of multiple, interconnecting axes of affiliation and differentiation.[42]

This mode of analysis is particularly applicable to the topics addressed in this volume by Roden, Molony, Driscoll, Brooks, and Smith. As we have noted earlier, modernity in Japan involved state formation, the rise of industry, mobilization of mass participation in national affairs, changes in values, social life, culture, and identities, and interactions with non-Japanese in colonies and in Western countries. Modern manhood and womanhood in the Meiji era, as discussed by Roden and Molony, were strongly influenced by selected Western ideas of manhood or womanhood. To gain international respect, Japanese males should exhibit the qualities of modern English gentlemen; to gain respect as subjects at home, Japanese women might borrow from contemporary Western ideas linking personhood with modern education. At the same time, men and women were not unitary subjects created on Western models, but a shifting blend of characteristics that could be called on in different contexts. As Driscoll notes, discourse about sexualities was influenced by Western as well as Japanese ideas that were themselves affected by the course of Japan's modern development. Brooks and Smith discuss Japanese and non-Japanese both in the colonies and in metropolitan Japan. Shifting notions of gender in the two settings were the product of cross-pollination and both settings reinforced (in the case of colonial power) and undermined (in the case of gender) relations of power.

Structure of the Book

The essays in this book are organized into five sections that probe major themes in the field of gender studies, such as the construction of identities and sexualities; gender and imperial regimes; divisions of labor in households, economy, and society in general; and definitions and theories about gender, power, and the state. At the same time, the essays have implications for both new and classic issues in Japanese history in the long twentieth century—the shaping of modern and contemporary selfhood or subjectivities; the interpretation of cultural expressions of elite and ordinary Japanese; the policies, institutions, and ideas of imperialism and war and their impact on Japanese society; and gendered patterns of participation in economy, voluntary associations, polity, and culture. Each of these sections reveals that a consideration of gender can help to explicate the shaping of modern Japanese history.

Part 1: Gender, Selfhood, Culture

Genders and subjectivities intersect in complex ways. Notions of the self are not only generated by the subject or individual but also developed within historically changing discursive contexts that are influenced by state goals, the mass media, schools, and other institutions. These chapters address important issues in the construction of modern Japanese "masculinities" and "femininities," including changing assumptions about the educability of women, the demeanor and character of the modern gentleman, and the search for self-fulfillment of young middle-class women.

These chapters, which examine gender, selfhood, and culture, open new perspectives on Japan's transition to modernity. Early modern institutions of government, finance, foreign and domestic trade, education, law, social relations (particularly the status groupings required in the old regime), and the military were rejected in favor of new, often Western-modeled institutions. But modernity was also permanently embedded in the reconstructions of gender, the molding of the self, and the transformation of culture. Even before Japan developed such visible signs of modern strength as overseas colonies, Japanese modernizers were eager to develop men and women of "civilization and enlightenment" (*bunmei kaika*). These were code words for the creation of new subjects (in both senses of that word) whose modern acceptance of the "self" would make them, and Japan, deserving of Western respect. In a sense the new women and men were the cornerstone of modernity and, thus, one of the principal reasons for the West's growing, though still grudging, respect for Japan.

Martha Tocco's chapter in this volume contends that female education in the modern era was shaped by early modern Japanese ideals and practices, not just by imported Western notions. This revisionist view challenges notions of gender in Japan that overemphasize Western influence in the creation of modern schools for women. Donald Roden traces the evolution of gentlemanly ideals in Japan from their mid-nineteenth century moorings until the end of the nineteenth century. He explores transitions from the learned but rough warrior activists (*shishi*) in the last days of the shogunate to the refined gentleman and his coarser variants in the modern period. Roden's investigation of the qualities ascribed to the gentleman has particular relevance for the construction of manliness and the culture of gender in the middle class and above. Barbara Sato argues that self-cultivation (*shūyō*), a focus on personal success originally intended for men aspiring to upward mobility, was ardently embraced by many younger middle-class women who encountered the notion in popular books and magazines of the early twentieth century. Spurred by publishers seeking profits, the young women's desires for self-improvement lured them beyond the confines of domesticity and thereby promoted a certain degree of gender convergence. The new women's culture that emerged advocated attitudes and behavior somewhat at odds with good wife, wise mother (*ryōsai kenbo*), the state's expectation for women.

Part II: Genders, Bodies, Sexualities

As Thomas Laqueur in *Making Sex* (1990), Linda Nicholson in "Interpreting Gender" (1994), and many other scholars have shown, genders, bodies, and sexualities, and even that seemingly solid category, sex, are historically contingent. These chapters examine the continuing process of constructing genders, bodies, and sexualities in historical context.

In modern regimes, the articulation of appropriate sexualities and issues surrounding the body are often linked to power, and the case of Japan since the late nineteenth century is a good example. While Giacomo Puccini's 1904 opera, *Madame Butterfly,* presented the international power relationship of Japan to the United States in gendered terms that were almost a caricature in their theatrical starkness, nevertheless, the opera's contemporaries would have easily recognized the embodiment of the two countries as masculine (United States) and feminine (Japan). The control of sexuality and the body have been important concerns for leaders in Japan. No sooner had Japan opened its ports to international visitors than disease became an issue in foreign affairs. Some of those diseases, such as the cholera outbreak in the 1860s,[43] had nothing to do with sexuality, but some were linked to prostitution.[44] Successive Japanese governments, by involving themselves in the regulation of sexuality, clearly stated that definitions of sexuality were within the purview of the state. Official versions of sexuality as patriarchal and heterosexual were by-products of modernity. But the expanding public discourse of the modernizing state offered commercial media outlets, public pundits, and emerging feminist voices opportunities to weigh in on the topic of sexuality, and they introduced a broader spectrum of sexualities. As the articles here show, sexuality was discussed in many contexts, including the rise of female education, the movement of men and women throughout the empire and the potential for cross-cultural sexual contact, the developing concerns about race and sex, the modernization of the delivery of health, and the rise of female self-expression and feminist agency that contested the relationship of sexuality to power.

Gregory Pflugfelder analyzes the role of female sexuality in the emergence of the same-sex love (*dōseiai*) construct in discussions of the experiences of young women attending girls' schools in the early twentieth century. He explores some of the differences between female-female and male-male *dōseiai*, and considers their meaning in the gender system of modern Japan as a whole. Mark Driscoll analyzes the writings of three Japanese sexologists in the early twentieth century. He finds that these pioneering sexologists did not engage in wholesale adoption of prevailing

Western notions. He debunks conventional views that tolerance for male-male sexual practices in the early modern period was destroyed by the intrusion in the Meiji period of Western notions denigrating masturbation and same-sex sexual relations. Driscoll also argues that the construction of a ferocious male sexual desire demanding gratification was one of the reasons for the founding of army brothels and places the construction of notions of female sexuality in the context of Japanese colonialism. Otsubo examines the attempts of feminists of the New Woman Association (1919–1922) and their male supporters to gain passage of a eugenics law that would regulate the bodies of males seeking to marry by forcing them to undergo premarital tests for sexually transmitted disease and allowing women to break off engagements with infected men. Their direct approach to the legislative arm of the state to limit male sexuality challenged notions of unrestrained satisfaction of male heterosexual desire, female agency, and female exclusion from the state.

Part III: Gender, Empire, War

Imperialism and war often transform gender and society. These three authors consider crucial issues in the engendering of Japan's imperialist agenda and military development—including the formation of masculinity as the modern army evolved, gender and the formation of Japanese colonial societies, and shifting notions of womanhood under the stress of total war.

The building of an empire in the late nineteenth and early twentieth centuries accompanied Japan's quest for modernity. A modern army and navy were deemed essential to national security. Paralleling the shift in the role of the military was the shift in the meaning of manhood, as the nation went from concern about being a victim to inflicting imperialism on its own neighbors. Within a half-century of the founding of modern Japan, membership in the modern state had come to embrace certain masculine and military values. Numerous historians have treated Japan's expansionism in Asia, its changing diplomatic roles in Asia and in world arenas, the impact of world economic problems, the rise of nationalism and the demand for self-rule in colonies around the world, and the road to World War II. But none has brought in gender as a significant element in state-building through empire and war. These essays re-examine the last 150 years of history through the lens of gender and suggest new approaches to empire and imperialism. They look inward as well, analyzing the meanings of membership in the nation, and attempt to answer the question of whether inclusion was earned through military service, nationality, or sacrifice.

Theodore Cook examines the creation of the "soldier" in modern Japan and the ways in which gendered views of state service, citizenship, obligation, and rights emerged. He addresses the meaning of manhood in a nation first concerned about not being a victim of imperialism, then becoming an imperialist power itself. Modern conscription broke with the warrior tradition. Service in the modern army created new linkages between common men and the state and also facilitated social and sexual encounters outside the village. Despite the small number of men actually conscripted, the soldier became an important model for pre–World War II Japanese manhood. Barbara Brooks discusses gender in the colonial societies of Korea and Manchuria. Significantly, Japanese women outnumbered Japanese men on the frontier; Japanese colonial women were lauded as pioneers and were encouraged to marry Korean and Russian men in the early years; and single women were praised for working to support the empire. Brooks contrasts these patterns with European colonial experiences, while showing similarities in the patterns of interpenetration of colonial and metropolitan cultures. Gender was used as a tool of imperialist penetration by women on the borders at the same time that Japanese women in the colonies subverted gender and hybridized ethnicity. While some women negotiated their membership in the state, others were subject to manipulation. As Haruko Cook notes, the gendered rhetoric of nationality and citizenship could also be subject to manipulation. Cook explores the creation of the myth of women's self-sacrifice through death during the battle of Saipan in the summer of 1944. While women had been exhorted to a life of frugality, hard work, and bearing children during earlier phases of World War II, this new myth valorized women's dying in defense of the empire and became the basis for a new model of feminine behavior in the war's final stage. She raises the question of whether, by putatively "offering" their lives for the empire, women at last achieved a place in the imperial state equivalent to that of men.

Part IV: Gender, Work, Economy

Scholars who have dealt with the intersection of gender, work, and the economy have often arrived at one of two opposite and equally unsatisfying conclusions: that work is liberating in that it destroys gender differences; or that women in the economy are to be pitied. These three chapters advance discussion of gender far beyond those simple ideas. They suggest an increasing importance of gender in Japan's industrial economy as well as the mutual constitution of corporate needs, gender ascription, and, in the case of Smith's chapter, race and ethnicity, in the twentieth century.

The standard narrative of the development of the Japanese economy since the mid-nineteenth century is well known. The economy has been both lauded as an example of successful growth by a late developer and vilified as an example of growth at any cost. Studies of Japan's modernization have stressed the building of the infrastructure (media, communications, transportation, finance) in the early years of the Meiji period; the establishment of pioneering industries in mining, textiles, shipbuilding, and chemicals; the changing role of agriculture; the importance of the munitions sector; and the role of the government in supporting industrial and economic development. Studies of the decades following the end of the Meiji period have focused on Japan's need to negotiate its role in the larger and often hostile international arena and on the unequalizing effects of capitalist development on farmers, laborers, employers, and people under colonialism. In the postwar period, Japan was seen as enjoying the fruits of an economic miracle until the recession started in the early 1990s. Recovering from deep poverty, starvation, and a lack of housing in the first years after the war, Japan's economy grew by leaps and bounds for thirty years. Accounts of Japan's economic growth have taken for granted stages of modern development, but few have been informed by a deep analysis of the role of gender and its construction in the context of the economy. These three essays open new avenues of inquiry about gender. They consider the reification of stereotypes of men and women as workers as well as the negotiation and subversion of those stereotypes. They relate the success stories in the prewar and postwar eras to the fashioning of gendered roles in the family and the factory.

Hunter addresses the reasons for Japanese employers' increasing segmentation of the textile labor force by sex, age, and marital status during the early twentieth century and considers the generally over-looked employment patterns of men in that crucial industry. Further-more, she suggests long-term effects of the mutual constitution of gen-der-segregated employment patterns and gender ascription. Smith's analysis of the gender division of labor among Korean coal miners in Japan during the interwar period provides important lessons about the ways in which ethnic discrimination, gender stereotypes, cultural differ-ences, and the logic of capitalism interacted to shape the lives of indi-vidual workers. Gordon discusses the postwar New Life Movement, a set of loosely connected initiatives of government offices, women's groups, and corporations aimed entirely at women. He argues that the corporate manifestation of the movement naturalized a model of gen-der relations in which women of all social strata managed the home so that men could concentrate on the workplace.

Part v. *Theorizing Gender*

Both gender discourse and gender ideology have a long and changing history in nineteenth- and twentieth-century Japan. These four essays examine the assumptions and political agendas of critics, rights advo-cates, and segments of the state- and corporate-based economic inter-ests in theorizing gender in different historical eras.

This book is itself part of the interpretation of Japan and the dis-course on gender. We hope these essays will shed light and open up new avenues of investigation rather than channeling discussion in lim-ited ways. Participants in history, while often reflective about how they will be perceived by posterity, usually theorize primarily for political ends. Gender in Japan was theorized both by those who sought to tear down essentialist limitations on women's rights (while often preserving "woman" as a category for political reasons), and by those who used the power of the state to expand women's usefulness to the nation. In both cases, construction of gender was in conjunction with power.

Molony examines varying strains of "women's rights" (*joken*) and their similarities and differences with late nineteenth-century Japanese arguments for expanding men's inclusion in the state. She suggests how gender was embedded in notions of the state and society and was instrumental in the defining of "modernity" in the early twentieth century. Uno contends that there was a linkage between the state's female gender expectations and Japan's imperial expansion. *Ryōsai kenbo,* a synthesis of early modern wifehood and late nineteenth-century imported notions of motherhood, was established by the Education Ministry as a model of ideal womanhood in 1899 in the aftermath of the first Sino-Japanese War (1894–1895). Following each war that gained territory for the empire, a reassessment of the mobilization of women resulted in contested re-constructions of *ryōsai kenbo* that expanded norms of women's societal participation. Kano argues that a powerful strain in Japanese literary criti-cism of the 1980s incorporated transhistorical femininity ("some things about Japanese women never change") and reverse Orientalism ("Japan is uniquely different from the West"). These assumptions have operated as two wheels of a perpetual motion machine, driving and reinforcing each other. They have led to a denial of Japan's masculine aggression to-ward its neighbors as well as an antifeminist affirmation of the status quo of gender relations in Japan.

Shigematsu interprets the paradoxes of contemporary female sexual-ity and individual empowerment by looking at the work of Uchida Shungiku and its role in cultural production in the 1990s. She places Uchida's work and significance in the context of the last several dec-ades of feminism in Japan, from "women's liberation" in the 1970s through the promotion by the state and corporate interests of their own versions of feminism since the mid-1970s. While Uchida serves as a model for the type of sexual ambiguity highlighted in this volume and for the female transgression lauded by many feminists, Shigematsu notes that Uchida is also emblematic of the corporate world's com-modification of sex, of women who transgress gender boundaries for their own advancement, and of the state's emphasis on hard work as the route to individual success.

Conclusion

An analysis of gender enhances understandings of Japanese modernity. As the field of Japanese studies has turned away from modernization perspectives grounded in Cold War concerns valorizing capitalist soci-ety, institutions, and culture, modernity perspectives placing more em-phasis on themes of conflict, inequality, or exploitation as well as postmodern perspectives have come to the fore. Influenced by interpretations of modernity and the postmodern, this book aims to contribute to both social science and cultural studies of Japan by further historicizing gender construction, gender contestations, and gender ambiguity. In the preceding decades, a significant amount of research has emerged on gender construction and contestation in Japan's long twentieth century. However, gender ambiguity in Japan has been only lightly pursued.

If it can be said that deliberate state construction of male and female gender operated at a relatively low level in the early modern period, then current research suggests that on the whole that trend continued in the first several decades of the modern period. However, from about 1890, the Japanese government and its supporters made greater efforts to intervene in the construction of distinct male and female genders. Sexuality came under greater regulation, and heterosexuality was increasingly defined as normative for men and women. Despite contestation by individuals and groups and modifications by administrators and political leaders, especially during the mobilization for World War II, the continuities were probably greater than the changes in the official visions of woman as patriotic "good wife, wise mother" and man as servant of the state or loyal soldier. Nevertheless, to some extent gender expectations varied by class as well as ethnicity, race, and residence, that is, for Japanese and non-Japanese subjects at home and in the colonies.

Despite the demise of the wartime self-sacrificing soldier and mother, the legacy of public man and private or domestic woman has endured in the postwar period. Contemporary gender expectations are reflected in the attitudes and representations of the salaryman warrior, stoically enduring grueling overtime and spurning vacations to gain family income and prestige, increase corporate earnings, and raise the nation's exports, and of the housewife/mother lovingly yet efficiently managing all aspects of the household from budget and menus to cleaning, yardwork, childrearing, and perhaps even her husband.

However, even as boundaries of male and female gender were being delineated throughout the long twentieth century, they were continually being tested—especially those that created separate spheres or the paired binaries of public man/private woman often prominent in the agendas of modernity. From the 1880s until the twenty-first century, gender expectations have been contested by feminist movements and female workers' organizations and by individuals, including female and male students, educators and intellectuals, young and middle-aged women, and single and married women. Recent research reveals ongoing contestation of the postwar conventional wisdom about gender, e.g., domesticity as woman's primary destiny and performance of sexuality beyond heterosexual and marital sex.

While histories of women, men, and sexuality have deployed binaries of victimization and resistance used by Japanese men and women in their lived experiences and struggles, gender ambiguity has also been a characteristic of Japanese society and culture. In the early modern period, for example, there was no necessary one-to-one correspondence between sex and sexuality, whether in male-female sexual relationships or in same-sex liaisons. Furthermore, it was acceptable, indeed it was art for men to act as women on stage in the kabuki theatre; some even said that the female impersonators (*onnagata*) performed a more perfect femininity than could have been enacted by women had they been permitted to perform on the stage.

At the dawn of the modern era, as we have seen, the state attempted a greater differentiation of gender spheres while some men and women contested those moves. Thus, an unsung but salient characteristic of modernity has been continuing gender ambiguity. Multiple voices contributed to notions of gender, impeding the state's initiatives to define the masculine and the feminine to advance its nationalist agenda and blurring the boundaries between the two. Against state policies, individuals and organizations called for access to higher education for women, female suffrage, and continued acceptance of same-sex sexual relations. Desire for less rigid gender prescriptions has, at times, also slowed the progress of unified movements contesting the state. For instance, the classic debate, which occurred in Japan as elsewhere, between those who took a position of essentializing women as mothers and those who argued for women's rights irrespective of maternal roles hindered the emergence of a united feminist movement. At the same time, since the modern period, ambiguities derived from contestations, undefined attitudes and behaviors, and contradictions in policies and norms have provided space for men and women to perform their gender or sexuality in varying ethnic, class, or regional contexts. During the early Occupation years, moral chaos in the wake of defeat increased gender ambiguities. But by the 1970s, economic policies and industrial discipline attempted to reinscribe women's place as the home even as married women were allowed to enter the wage labor market under inferior conditions. In the late postwar period, boundaries between maleness and femaleness are again blurring—that is, there is again a swing toward gender ambiguity.

Indeed, in the long twentieth century, Japanese modernity has been characterized by oscillation between gender boundary construction and gender ambiguities. The ambiguities are particularly informative as they call into question binary models, e.g., the equations of woman/private/inside and man/public/outside. While research on the construction of gender norms by the state and other social actors as well as research on resistance to received norms has become established over the past several decades, the notion of gender ambiguity is relatively new and bears further exploration in Japan and elsewhere.

Barbara Molony and Kathleen Uno

Notes

1. Joan W. Scott, "Gender: A Useful Category of Historical Analysis," *American Historical Review* 91 (1986): 1053–1075.

2. Joan W. Scott, *Gender and the Politics of History* (New York: Columbia University Press, 1988), introduction; Joyce Appleby, Lynn Hunt, and Margaret Jacob, *Telling the Truth About History* (New York: Norton, 1994), chapter 6.

3. *The New Biography: Performing Femininity in Nineteenth-Century France*, ed. Jo Burr Margadant (Berkeley: University of California Press, 2000), introduction.

4. For works that have produced a new narrative on colonial history, see e.g., Mrinalini Sinha, *Colonial Masculinity: The "Manly Englishman" and the "Effeminate Bengali" in the Late Nineteenth Century* (Manchester, UK: Manchester University Press, 1995); Ann Stoler, *Carnal Knowledge and Imperial Power: Race and the Intimate in Colonial Rule* (Berkeley: University of California Press, 2002); and Anne McClintock, *Imperial Leather: Race, Gender, and Sexuality in the Colonial Contest* (New York: Routledge, 1995). On the reconfiguring of the meanings of rights and politics, see e.g., Carole Pateman, *The Sexual Contract* (Stanford, CA: Stanford University Press, 1988).

5. The interdisciplinary collaboration of this volume reflects a long tradition in the field of Japanese studies as well as recent trends in the fields of history and gender studies. Interdisciplinary collections in Japanese studies (in English) have abounded since the 1960s and 1970s. See e.g., the six-volume series on modernization, including *Changing Japanese Attitudes toward Modernization,* eds. John W. Hall and Marius B. Jansen; *The State and Economic Enterprise in Modern Japan*, ed. William W. Lockwood; *Aspects of Social Change in Modern Japan,* ed. Ronald P. Dore; *Political Development in Modern Japan*, ed. Robert E. Ward; *Tradition and Modernization in Japanese Culture*, ed. Donald Shively; and *Dilemmas of Growth in Prewar Japan*, ed. James W. Morley (Princeton, NJ: Princeton University Press, 1965–1971); *Postwar Japan as History*, ed. Andrew Gordon (Berkeley: University of California Press, 1993); *Mirror of Modernity: Invented Traditions of Modern Japan*, ed. Stephen Vlastos (Berkeley: University of California Press, 1998); and *Japan's Competing Modernities: Issues in Culture and Democracy 1900–1930*, ed. Sharon Minichiello (Honolulu: University of Hawai'i Press, 1998). Interdisciplinary volumes on specialized issues include, e.g., *Culture and Identity: Japanese Intellectuals during the Interwar Years*, ed. Thomas J. Rimer (Princeton, NJ: Princeton University Press, 1990); *Rude Awakenings: Zen, the Kyoto School, and the Question of Nationalism*, eds. James W. Heisig and John C. Maraldo (Honolulu: University of Hawai'i Press, 1995); and *Being Modern in Japan: Culture and Society from*

the 1910s to the 1930s, eds. Louise K. Tipton and John Clark (Honolulu: University of Hawai'i Press, 2000). Interdisciplinary anthologies on women include: *Proceedings of the Tokyo Symposium on Women*, eds. Merry I. White and Barbara Molony (Tokyo: International Group for the Study of Women, 1978); *Women in Changing Japan*, ed. Joyce Lebra et al. (Boulder, CO: Westview, 1976); *Recreating Japanese Women, 1600–1945*, ed. Gail Lee Bernstein (Berkeley: University of California Press, 1991); *Re-Imaging Japanese Women*, ed. Anne Imamura (Berkeley: University of California Press, 1996); *Japanese Women Working*, ed. Janet Hunter (London: Routledge, 1993); *Japanese Women: New Feminist Perspectives on the Past, Present, and Future*, eds. Kumiko Fujimura-Fanselow and Atsuko Kameda (New York: Feminist Press, 1995); *Gender and Japanese History*, eds. Haruko Wakita, Anne Bouchy, and Chizuko Ueno, 2 vols. (Osaka: Osaka University Press, 1999); and *Women and Class in Japanese History*, eds. Hitomi Tonomura, Anne Walthall, and Haruko Wakita (Ann Arbor: Center for Japanese Studies, University of Michigan, 1999). Publications such as *Stories by Contemporary Japanese Women Writers*, eds. and trans. Noriko Mizuta Lippitt and Kyoko Iriye Selden (Armonk, NY: M.E. Sharpe, 1982); *To Live and To Write: Selections by Japanese Women Writers 1913–1938*, ed. Yukiko Tanaka (Seattle, WA: Seal Press, 1987); *This Kind of Woman: Ten Stories by Japanese Women Writers 1960–76*, ed. and trans. Yukiko Tanaka (Stanford, CA: Stanford University Press, 1982); *Unmapped Territories: New Women's Fiction from Japan*, ed. Yukiko Tanaka (Seattle, WA: Women in Translation, 1991); Rebecca L. Copeland, *The Sound of the Wind: The Life and Works of Uno Chiyo* (Honolulu: University of Hawai'i Press, 1992); *The Woman's Hand: Gender and Theory in Japanese Women's Writing*, eds. Paul Schalow, Janet A. Walker, and Janice Brown (Stanford, CA: Stanford University Press, 1996); Hayashi Fumiko, *I Saw a Pale Horse* (Ithaca, NY: East Asia Program, Cornell University, 1997); Joan E. Ericcson, *Be a Woman: Hayashi Fumiko and Modern Japanese Women's Literature* (Honolulu: University of Hawai'i Press, 1997); Phyllis Birnbaum, *Modern Girls, Shining Stars, the Skies of Tokyo: Five Japanese Women* (New York: Columbia University Press, 1999); Rebecca L. Copeland, *Lost Leaves: Women Writers of Meiji Japan* (Honolulu: University of Hawai'i Press, 2000); *The Father-Daughter Plot: Japanese Literary Women and the Law of the Father*, eds. Rebecca L. Copeland and Esperanza Ramirez-Christensen (Honolulu: University of Hawai'i Press, 2001); and Jan Bardsley's "Discourse on Women in Postwar Japan: The Housewife Debate of 1955," *U.S.-Japan Women's Journal*, English Supplement, no. 16 (1999) make one hope for more collaboration between literary scholars and historians. Excellent multidisciplinary collections in women's/gender studies are too numerous to name, but a few are most helpful for scholars approaching this as a new field of inquiry. See e.g., *Buddhism, Sexuality, and Gender*, ed. José Ignacio Cabezón (Albany, NY: SUNY Press,

1992); *Feminists Theorize the Political,* eds. Judith Butler and Joan W. Scott (New York and London: Routledge, 1992); *Third World Women and the Politics of Feminism,* eds. Chandra Talpade Mohanty, Ann Russo, and Lourdes Torres (Bloomington: Indiana University Press, 1991); *Feminisms in the Academy,* eds. Donna C. Stanton and Abigail J. Stewart (Ann Arbor: University of Michigan Press, 1995); and *Feminist Contentions: A Philosophical Exchange,* eds. Seyla Benhabib, Judith Butler, Drucilla Cornell, and Nancy Fraser (New York and London: Routledge, 1995).

6. Currently Japanese gender studies lacks historical monographs treating both maleness and femaleness, but important directions are suggested by Donald Roden, "Taishō Culture and the Problem of Gender Ambivalence," in Rimer, *Culture and Identity,* 37–55; Robert J. Smith and Ella Lury Wiswell, *The Women of Suye Mura* (Chicago, IL: University of Chicago Press, 1982); and Jennifer Robertson, *Takarazuka: Sexual Politics and Popular Culture in Modern Japan* (Berkeley: University of California Press, 1997). Some works by social scientists discussing both genders in contemporary Japan include: Dorinne Kondo, *Crafting Selves: Power, Gender, and Discourses of Identity in a Japanese Workplace* (Chicago, IL: University of Chicago Press, 1990); Anne Allison, *Nightwork: Sexuality, Pleasure, and Corporate Masculinity in a Tokyo Hostess Club* (Chicago, IL: University of Chicago Press, 1994); Muriel Jolivet, *Japan: The Childless Society?* (New York: Routledge, 1997); and Yuko Ogasawara, *Office Ladies and Salaried Men* (Berkeley: University of California Press, 1998). Pioneering English language works on Japanese women's history include: Joyce Ackroyd, "Women in Feudal Japan," *Transactions of the Asiatic Society of Japan,* Third Series, 7 (Nov. 1959): 31–68; and Dee Ann Vavich, "Ichikawa Fusae: Pioneer of Woman Suffrage," *Monumenta Nipponica* 22, nos. 3–4 (1967): 402–436. Next followed works stimulated by the growth of Japanese social history from the mid-1970s, e.g., Lebra et al., *Women in Changing Japan;* Mikiso Hane, *Rebels, Peasants, and Outcastes: The Underside of Modern Japan* (New York: Pantheon, 1982); *Recreating Japanese Women,* ed. Gail Lee Bernstein (Berkeley: University of California Press, 1991); and Anne Walthall, *The Weak Body of a Useless Woman: Matsuo Taseko and the Meiji Restoration* (Chicago, IL: University of Chicago Press, 1998). Conjunctions of feminism and Japanese women's history resulted in writings such as: Sharon Sievers, *Flowers in Salt: The Beginnings of Feminist Consciousness in Modern Japan* (Stanford, CA: Stanford University Press, 1983); E. Patricia Tsurumi, "Female Textile Workers and the Failure of Early Textile Unionism in Japan," *History Workshop* 18 (Fall 1984): 3–28; Vera Mackie, "Feminist Politics in Japan," *New Left Review,* no. 158 (Jan./Feb. 1988); Mikiso Hane, *Reflections on the Way to the Gallows* (New York: Pantheon, 1988); E. Patricia Tsurumi, *Factory Girls: Women in the Thread Mills of Meiji Japan* (Princeton, NJ: Princeton University Press, 1990); Sharon H.

Nolte and Sally Ann Hastings, "The Meiji State's Policy toward Women, 1890–1910," in *Recreating Japanese Women, 1600–1945*, ed. Gail Lee Bernstein (Berkeley: University of California Press, 1991); Kathleen S. Uno, "Women and Changes in the Household Division of Labor," in Bernstein, *Recreating Japanese Women; Feminism and the State in Modern Japan*, ed. Vera Mackie (Melbourne, Australia: Japanese Studies Centre, 1995); Helen Hopper, *A New Woman of Japan: A Political Biography of Katō Shidzue* (Boulder, CO: Westview, 1996); Hélène Bowen Raeddeker, *Treacherous Women of Imperial Japan: Patriarchal Fictions, Patricidal Fantasies* (London and New York: Routledge, 1997); Vera Mackie, *Creating Socialist Women: Gender, Labour, and Activism, 1900–1937* (Cambridge: Cambridge University Press, 1997); Ayako Kano, *Acting Like a Woman in Modern Japan: Theater, Gender, and Nationalism* (New York; Houndmills [England]: Palgrave, 2001); and Vera Mackie, *Feminism in Modern Japan* (Cambridge: Cambridge University Press, 2003). Some pioneering works in men's history are: Donald Roden, *Schooldays in Imperial Japan: A Study in the Culture of a Student Elite* (Berkeley: University of California Press, 1980); Earl Kinmonth, *The Self-Made Man in Meiji Japanese Thought: From Samurai to Salaryman* (Berkeley: University of California Press, 1981); and Andrew Gordon, *Evolution of Labor Relations in Japan: Heavy Industry, 1850–1950* (Cambridge, MA: Harvard University Press, 1985), chapter 1. Later works on the history of men include many works on topics related to sexuality: Ihara Saikaku, *The Great Mirror of Male Love*, trans. Paul Schalow (Stanford, CA: Stanford University Press, 1990); Mikito Ujiie, "From Young Lions to Rats in a Ditch," in *Imaging/Reading Eros: Proceedings for the Conference, Sexuality and Edo Culture, 1750–1850*, ed. Sumie Jones (Bloomington: East Asian Studies Center, Indiana University, 1996); Tsuneo Watanabe and Jun'ichi Iwata, *The Love of the Samurai: A Thousand Years of Male Homosexuality*, trans. D. R. Roberts (London: Gay Men's Press 1989); Makoto Furukawa, "The Changing Nature of Sexuality: The Three Codes Framing Homosexuality in Modern Japan," trans. Angel Lockyear, *U.S.-Japan Women's Journal*, English Supplement, no. 7 (1994): 98–127; Gary Leupp, *Male Colors: The Construction of Homosexuality in Tokugawa Japan* (Berkeley: University of California Press, 1995); and Gregory Pflugfelder, *Cartographies of Desire: Male-Male Sexuality in Japanese Discourse 1600–1950* (Berkeley: University of California Press, 2000). Although works on the history of sexuality beyond male sexuality are few, see Smith and Wiswell, *The Women of Suye Mura*; Roden, "Taishō Culture"; Robertson, *Takarazuka; Choreographing History*, ed. Susan Leigh Foster (Bloomington: Indiana University Press, 1995); Ann Allison, *Permitted and Prohibited Desires* (Boulder, CO: Westview, 1996); Chizuko Ueno, "Collapse of Japanese Mothers," *U.S.-Japan Women's Journal*, English Supplement, no. 10 (1996): 3–19; and Sabine Frühstück, "Then Science Took Over: Sex, Leisure, and Medicine at the Beginning of the Twentieth

Century," in *The Culture of Japan Seen through Its Leisure,* eds. Sepp Linhart and Sabine Frühstück (New York: SUNY Press, 1998). See note 18 for references to later works and trends and additional works interpreting gender in contemporary Japan.

7. Tensions between women's and gender studies have emerged in various contexts. As Linda Nicholson notes in "Interpreting *Gender," SIGNS* 20, no. 1 (1994), destabilizing "woman" can lead to fear that politics in the name of "women" will not be possible. Sally Baden and Anne Marie Goetz, in "Who Needs [Sex] When You Can Have [Gender]?" *Feminist Review,* no. 56 (1997): 3–25, show that while academic feminists no longer contest "gender," some politically active women outside the academy, both on the right and on the left, reject thinking in terms of gender for different reasons. See also, for example, Gisela Bock, "Women's History and Gender History: Aspects of an International Debate," *Gender and History* 1 (1989): 7–30; Linda Gordon, "What's New in Women's History," in *Feminist Studies/Critical Studies,* ed. Teresa de Lauretis (Bloomington: Indiana University Press, 1986), 20–30; and Tanya Modleski, *Feminism Without Women: Culture and Criticism in a 'Postfeminist' Age* (New York and London: Routledge, 1991).

8. To be sure, people in the past did not necessarily view their societies as ordered by gender. "Gender" as an analytic category is a recent phenomenon. Initially used as a grammatical marker of categories, it was not limited to two (some languages have three or more), nor to femaleness and maleness alone. It has been applied by feminist scholars to societies in the last three decades.

9. The notion that "gender" is socially constructed is supported by the evidence offered by biologists that there are more than two "sexes." Biologist Anne Fausto-Sterling, in "The Five Sexes: Why Male and Female Are Not Enough," *The Sciences* 33, no. 2 (1993), notes that there are individuals with various combinations of "male" and "female" sex organs. Moreover, scholars in various disciplines have noted that widely diverse societies have preferred to operate with more than two genders. Sabine Lang, in "There Is More than Just Women and Men: Gender Variants in North American Indian Cultures," in *Gender Reversals and Gender Cultures,* ed. Sabrina Petra Ramet (London and New York: Routledge, 1996), 185, writes: "In most North American Indian cultures, there exist not only two genders, woman and man, but three or four: women, men, men-women, and women-men. This cultural construction of more than just two genders, the 'cultural expressions of multiple genders . . . and the opportunity for individuals to change gender roles and identities over the course of their lifetimes,' is referred to as *cultural variance.*" Lang cites Sue-Ellen Jacobs and Jason Cromwell, "Visions and Revisions of Reality: Reflections of Sex,

Sexuality, Gender and Gender Variance," *Journal of Homosexuality* 23, no. 4 (1992): 63. Some African societies also reject the notion that there are just two genders determined by genitals. See e.g., Ifi Amadiume, *Male Daughters, Female Husbands: Gender and Sex in an African Society* (Atlantic Highlands, NJ: Zed Books, 1987). For Southeast Asia, see e.g., *Bewitching Women, Pious Men: Gender and Body Politics in Southeast Asia*, eds. Aihwa Ong and Michael G. Peletz (Berkeley: University of California Press, 1995).

10. To our knowledge, the first session on Japanese women at a major North American conference was held at the annual meeting of the Association for Asian Studies in 1978. Since the mid-1980s, around a half dozen sessions on women, and more recently on masculinity and gender, have been held at every AAS meeting. Meetings of the American Historical Association since the late 1980s have usually included one or more sessions with papers on Japanese women and/or gender. The Berkshire Conference Program Committee has included a Japanese historian during the last four planning cycles, and several papers on Japanese gender topics are presented at each session.

Although the conferences and workshops at Washington, Michigan, and Princeton all contained "gender" in their titles, each focused on women alone. The 1993 *Journal of Japanese Studies* "gender symposium" likewise dealt only with women. Outside the Japan field, even the highly regarded *Engendering China*, ed. Christina Gilmartin et al. (Cambridge, MA: Harvard University Press, 1995), is overwhelmingly a collection of articles on women.

11. Works from social science, cultural studies, and activist perspectives that have aided historians' understandings of women's estate and their agency in advocating social change include Lebra et al., *Women in Changing Japan*; Susan Pharr, *Political Women in Japan* (Berkeley: University of California Press, 1981); Takie S. Lebra, *Japanese Women: Constraint and Fulfillment* (Honolulu: University of Hawai'i Press, 1984); Gail Lee Bernstein, *Haruko's World: A Japanese Farm Woman and Her Community* (Stanford, CA: Stanford University Press, 1983); Chizuko Ueno, "Origins of the Japanese Housewife," *Anthropological Quarterly* 55, no. 4 (1987): 444–449; Anne Imamura, *Urban Japanese Housewives: At Home and in the Community* (Honolulu: University of Hawai'i Press, 1987); Mary C. Brinton, *Women and the Economic Miracle: Gender and Work in Postwar Japan* (Berkeley: University of California Press, 1993); Sumiko Iwao, *The Japanese Woman: Traditional Image and Changing Reality* (Cambridge, MA: Harvard University Press, 1994); Glenda Roberts, *Staying on the Line: Blue-Collar Women in Contemporary Japan* (Honolulu: University of Hawai'i Press, 1994); Margaret Lock, *Encounters with Aging: Mythologies of Menopause in Japan and North America* (Berkeley: University of California Press, 1994); and many articles in *U.S.-Japan Women's Journal*, En-

glish Supplement. See note 18 for additional works and trends in cultural studies, social science, and activist perspectives.

12. Denise Riley, *Am I That Name? Feminism and the Category of "Woman" in History* (Minneapolis: University of Minnesota Press, 1988), sees the category of "woman" as connected to modernism. See also Joan Kelly, "The Social Relations of the Sexes," in *Women, History, and Theory: The Essays of Joan Kelly* (Chicago, IL: University of Chicago Press, 1984), 1–18; Mary Poovey, *Uneven Developments: The Ideological Work of Gender in Mid-Victorian England* (Chicago, IL: University of Chicago Press, 1988); and Barbara L. Marshall, *Engendering Modernity: Feminism, Social Theory, and Social Change* (Boston, MA: Northeastern University Press, 1994).

13. In popular writing, modern Japan often refers to both the modern and contemporary periods. Japanese historians generally distinguish between the modern and contemporary periods, but they too may refer to Japan during the era from 1868 to the present as modern Japan.

14. See for example, Marius B. Jansen, "Stages of Growth," *Japanese Studies in the United States*, Part I: *History and Present Condition*, Japanese Studies Series XVII (Tokyo: [Ann Arbor, MI]: Japan Foundation; Distributed by the Association for Asian Studies, 1988–1989), 27–68; Sheldon Garon, "Rethinking Modernization and Modernity in Japanese History: A Focus on State-Society Relations," *Journal of Japanese Studies* 53 (May 1994): 346–366; J. Victor Koschmann, "Introduction to the English Edition," in *Total War and "Modernization,"* eds. Yasushi Yamanouchi, J. Victor Koschmann, and Ryūichi Narita (Ithaca, NY: Cornell University East Asia Series, 1998), xi–xvi; and *The Postwar Developments of Japanese Studies in the United States,* ed. Helen Hardacre (Leiden ; Boston ; Köln: Brill, 1998). For Japanology, see for example, *Constructs for Understanding Japan,* eds. Yoshio Sugimoto and Ross Mouer (New York and London: Kegan Paul International, 1989); and Yoshio Sugimoto, *An Introduction to Japanese Society* (Cambridge: Cambridge University Press, 1997). Regarding other influences on interpretations of Japan, see Richard Minear, "Orientalism and the Study of Japan," *Journal of Asian Studies* 50 (1980): 507–517; *Othernesses of Japan: Historical and Cultural Influences on Japanese Studies in Ten Countries,* in *Monographien aus dem Deutschen Institut für Japanstudien der Philipp-Franz-von-Siebold-Stiftung,* eds. Harumi Befu and Josef Kreiner, Band. 1 (Munich: Iudicum-Verlag, 1995); and Tessa Morris-Suzuki, *Re-Inventing Japan: Time, Space, Nation* (Armonk, NY: M.E. Sharpe, 1998).

15. The original essay is John W. Hall, "Changing Conceptions of the Modernization of Japan," in Hall and Jansen, *Changing Japanese Attitudes,* 7–41. See also

the other five volumes of the Princeton modernization series cited in note 5; *Studies in the Institutional History of Early Modern Japan*, eds. John W. Hall and Marius B. Jansen (Princeton, NJ: Princeton University Press, 1968); and *Japan in Transition: From Tokugawa to Meiji*, eds. Marius B. Jansen and Gilbert Rozman (Princeton, NJ: Princeton University Press, 1985).

16. Carol Gluck, *Japan's Modern Myths: Ideology in the Late Meiji Period* (Princeton, NJ: Princeton University Press, 1985).

17. The following sample of works reflects what we are calling modernity studies—varied responses to modernization's approaches ranging from radical political economy to humanism, conflict perspectives, and modernism: John W. Dower, "Introduction," in Jon Halliday, *A Political History of Japanese Capitalism* (New York: Monthly Review Press, 1975), xx-xxxix; Hane, *Rebels*; *Conflict in Modern Japanese History: The Neglected Tradition*, eds. Tetsuo Najita and J. Victor Koschmann (Princeton, NJ: Princeton University, 1982); Herbert Bix, *Peasant Protest in Japan, 1590–1884* (New Haven, CT: Yale University Press, 1985); and Barbara Sato, *The New Japanese Woman: Modernity, Media, and Women in Interwar Japan* (Durham, NC: Duke University Press, 2003). Research on *modanizumu* can also be included in modernity studies; Sato (7–8) calls it "a neologism that combined the English *modern* with *ism*. In journalistic circles from approximately 1924 until the late 1930s, this 'modernism' became identified with the latest 'lowbrow' fads and fashions that were representative of the everyday. To be modern in Japan during the interwar years connoted being in the social vanguard of the age . . . but not that the commodification of daily life had its grounding in Western modernism, which indeed remained on the plane of 'high art.'"

18. Also see the references on women's history, men's history, gender history, and sexuality history in notes 6 and 11. Important recent scholarship on Japanese gender issues in the contemporary period includes: Fujimura-Fanselow and Kameda, *Japanese Women*; Joy Hendry, *Understanding Japanese Society* (London and New York: Routledge, 1995); *Voices of the Japanese Women's Movement*, ed. AMPO-Japan Asia Quarterly Review (Armonk, NY: M.E. Sharpe, 1996); Sandra Buckley, *Broken Silence: Voices of Japanese Feminism* (Berkeley: University of California Press, 1997); Mariko Tamanoi, *Under the Shadow of Nationalism: Politics and Poetics of Rural Japanese Women* (Honolulu: University of Hawai'i Press, 1998); Ochiai Emiko, *The Japanese Family System in Transition: A Sociological Analysis of Family Change in Postwar Japan* (Tokyo: LTCB International Library Foundation, 1997); *Queer Japan: Personal Stories of Japanese Lesbians, Gays, Transsexuals and Bisexuals*, eds. and trans. Barbara Summerhawk, Cheiron McMahill, and Darren McDonald (Norwich, VT: New Victoria Publishers, 1998); Robin LeBlanc, *Bicy-*

cle Citizens: The Political World of the Japanese Housewife (Berkeley: University of California Press, 1999); Helen Hardacre, *Marketing the Menacing Fetus* (Berkeley: University of California Press, 1999); Ruth Ann Keyso, *Women of Okinawa: Nine Voices from a Garrison Island* (Ithaca, NY: Cornell University Press, 2000); Tiana Norgren, *Abortion before Birth Control: The Politics of Reproduction in Postwar Japan* (Princeton, NJ: Princeton University Press, 2001); Nancy Rosenberger, *Gambling with Virtue: Japanese Women and the Search for Self in a Changing Nation* (Honolulu: University of Hawai'i Press, 2001); Karen Kelsky, *Women on the Verge: Japanese Women, Western Dreams* (Durham, NC: Duke University Press, 2001); Satoru Ito and Ryuta Yanase, *Coming Out in Japan: The Story of Satoru and Ryuta*, trans. Francis Conlan (Melbourne, Australia: Trans Pacific Press, 2001); and *Men and Masculinities in Japan: Dislocating the Salaryman Doxa*, eds. James E. Roberson and Nobue Suzuki (New York: Routledge/Curzon, 2003).

19. Preoccupation with modernity, or its converse, tradition, has not yet ended in Japanese studies, and can be seen as a result of reacting to modernizationist issues or interpretations. See for example, Gluck, *Japan's Modern Myths*; Stefan Tanaka, *Japan's Orient: Rendering Pasts into History* (Berkeley: University of California Press, 1993); Kevin Michael Doak, *Dreams of Difference: The Japanese Romantic School and the Crisis of Modernity* (Berkeley: University of California Press, 1994); Sheldon Garon, *Molding Japanese Minds: The State in Everyday Life* (Princeton, NJ: Princeton University Press, 1997); Louise Young, *Japan's Total Empire* (Berkeley: University of California Press, 1998); Miniciello, *Japan's Competing Modernities*; Vlastos, *Mirror of Modernity*; Kathleen Uno, *Passages to Modernity: Motherhood, Childhood and Social Reform in Early Twentieth Century Japan* (Honolulu: University of Hawai'i, 1999); Tipton and Clark, *Being Modern in Japan*, and Harry D. Harootunian, *Overcome by Modernity: History, Culture, and Community in Interwar Japan* (Princeton, NJ: Princeton University Press, 2000).

20. Harry Harootunian, *History's Disquiet: Modernity, Cultural Practice, and the Question of Everyday Life* (New York: Columbia University Press, 2000), xvii–xviii.

21. See for example, Stephen Heine and Charles Wei-hsun Fu, "Introduction: From 'The Beautiful' to 'The Dubious': Japanese Traditionalism, Modernism, Postmodernism," in *Japan in Traditional and Postmodern Perspectives,* eds. Stephen Heine and Charles Wei-hsun Fu (Albany, NY: SUNY Press, 1995), vii-xxi, and *South Atlantic Quarterly*, Special Issue: Postmodernism and Japan 87, no. 3 (1988).

22. Masao Miyoshi and Harry Harootunian, "Introduction," *South Atlantic Quarterly*, Special Issue: Postmodernism and Japan 87, no. 3 (1988): 396.

23. Kondo, *Crafting Selves*; and Rimer, *Culture and Identity*. Also note the multiple components of subjectivities.

24. Jane Flax, in "The End of Innocence," in *Feminists Theorize the Political*, eds. Judith Butler and Joan W. Scott (New York and London: Routledge, 1992), 454, has noted that feminists constructed gender categories as a way of analyzing power relations in their own cultures and experiences. Thus, gender relations may not be a "unitary relation present in all cultures."

25. This discussion borrows extensively from Linda Nicholson, "Interpreting *Gender*." Nicholson calls this the "coatrack" view of self-identity.

26. Ibid., 81.

27. Ibid., 82, 89.

28. Scott, *Gender and the Politics*, 2.

29. Judith Butler, *Gender Trouble: Feminism and the Subversion of Identity* (New York and London: Routledge, 1990), 7.

30. Even if one believes that two distinct sexes exist in nature prior to gender, we should recall that this idea, too, must be placed in its historical context. That is, until the late seventeenth century in the West, it was commonly believed that only one sex existed, and that women's sex was simply men's sex inverted. See Thomas Laqueur, *Making Sex: Body and Gender from the Greeks to Freud* (Cambridge, MA: Harvard University Press, 1990), 8.

31. Scott, *Gender and the Politics*, 25.

32. Flax, "The End of Innocence," 455.

33. Inoue Teruko, "Nihon no joseigaku to 'seiyakuwari,'" in *Seiyakuwari*, vol. 3, *Nihon no feminizumu*, eds. Inoue Teruko, Ueno Chizuko, and Ehara Yumiko (Iwanami shoten, 1995).

34. Ehara Yumiko, "Seido to shite no bosei," in *Bosei*, vol. 5, *Nihon no feminizumu*, eds. Inoue Teruko, Ueno Chizuko, and Ehara Yumiko (Iwanami shoten, 1995).

35. Wakita Haruko, "Jogen," in *Jiendā no Nihonshi*, eds. Wakita Haruko and Susan B. Hanley, vol. 1 (Tōkyō daigaku shuppankai, 1994), iii. In English, see also Uno, "Women and Changes," and her *Passages to Modernity*.

36. Inderpal Grewal and Caren Kaplan, "Introduction: Transnational Feminist Practices and Questions of Postmodernity," in *Scattered Hegemonies: Postmodernity and Transnational Feminist Practices*, eds. Grewal and Kaplan (Minneapolis: University of Minnesota Press, 1994), 2.

37. Inderpal Grewal, "Autobiographic Subjects and Diasporic Locations: *Meatless Days* and *Borderlands*," in Grewal and Kaplan, *Scattered Hegemonies*, 234. Grewal is focusing here mainly on the works of Gayatri Spivak and Norma Alarcón.

38. Inderpal Grewal, "Autobiographic Subjects," 240–241.

39. For more on hybridity, see Robert Young, *Colonial Desire: Hybridity in Theory, Culture and Race* (London: Routledge, 1995).

40. Rita Felski, "The Doxa of Difference," *Signs* 23, no. 1 (1997): 12.

41. Ien Ang, "Comment on Felski's 'The Doxa of Difference': The Uses of Incommensurability," *Signs* 23, no. 1 (1997): 62.

42. Felski, "The Doxa of Difference," 12.

43. Susan L. Burns, "Constructing the National Body: Public Health and the Nation in Nineteenth-Century Japan," in *Nation Work: Asian Elites and National Identities*, eds. Timothy Brook and Andre Schmid (Ann Arbor: University of Michigan Press, 2000), 20–21.

44. Sheldon Garon, "The World's Oldest Debate? Prostitution and the State in Imperial Japan," *American Historical Review* 98, no. 3 (1993): 710–733.

PART I

Gender,
Selfhood,
Culture

1 Made in Japan: Meiji Women's Education
Martha Tocco

Although it is now passé to argue that Tokugawa or early modern Japan (1600–1868) was stagnant, backward, and feudalistic, the period is still widely understood to represent the nadir in the status of Japanese women.[1] Yet there is much evidence to refute this understanding of Tokugawa women's history, and this evidence has important implications for the history of Meiji women's education.[2] Because a nationwide system of public institutions for women's education developed in Japan in the late nineteenth century, after the Meiji Restoration, many historians have focused discussions of the development of women's education on the Meiji period (1868–1912). But Japanese women's education did not begin then. The education of noble women had begun more than eight centuries earlier, and by the end of the Tokugawa period, the education of both samurai and affluent commoner women was a regular feature of the Tokugawa educational landscape.

After 1868, Japan's new government implemented the country's first centralized program of publicly sponsored education. The Meiji government couched its reform of education in an indictment of Tokugawa precedents; it based its blueprint for state-sponsored education primarily on Western educational practices, and it claimed American models as the basis for reshaping the formal education of Meiji women. Despite all this, in actuality, the government relied heavily on the Tokugawa educational infrastructure to deliver its educational program.

Tokugawa educational practices, which were shaped, in part, by Japan's adaptations of Neo-Confucianism, were inextricably bound up in Japan's asymmetrical gender system. For this reason, these practices have been labeled "indoctrination" and placed in opposition to the development of Japanese women's "modern" or "Western-style" education, which was adapted from late nineteenth-century American models. But, like their Tokugawa counterparts, late nineteenth-century American institutions also reflected that country's asymmetrical gender system; and America's understanding of female gender, which was heavily influenced by Protestant Christianity, was inscribed in American educational practice. Although the two gender systems and the educational traditions that developed within them differed, they also shared important common ground. Rather than competing, late-Tokugawa educational practices combined with American ones, and together they shaped the course of the development of women's education in the Meiji period.

Tokugawa Women's Education

It may never be possible to calculate the number of literate, educated women in Tokugawa Japan. Still, there is substantial *qualitative* evidence of women's education found in a diverse body of Tokugawa materials: philosophers' essays advocating women's education; the proliferation of moral guides for girls (*jokun*) from the mid-eighteenth century; the inclusion of sections for women's books in publishers' lists of offerings; the increase in the number of educational texts (*ōraimono*) written for women; and women's autobiographies that attest to the level of their education.[3] During the Tokugawa period, education expanded, education levels rose, and institutional development increased, as evidenced by the sustained growth in the number of local schools (*terakoya*) and private academies (*shijuku*). More and more parents sought greater education for their daughters as well as their sons, which increased enrollments in these two educational institutions.[4]

Traditionally, women had instructed young children, other women, and servants within the households. But by the nineteenth century, many women taught neighborhood children—boys as well as girls—in these local and private schools. Tokugawa women from both the samurai and commoner classes founded and managed *terakoya* and *shijuku* and employed other women there as teachers.[5] These women educators were able to find students whether they taught in castle towns or nearby cities. The increasing visibility of women from both samurai and commoner classes in the public role of teacher and school administrator shows that by the end of the Tokugawa period, teaching had become a suitable occupation for women as a gender group and not just for women of a certain social stratum.[6]

From the early 1800s, Japanese women increasingly received some kind of education, be it at home, in a village school, or in a private academy. The availability of education for Tokugawa women varied, however, according to class: affluent women had greater educational opportunities. Geography, region, and locale also presented barriers to women's education, and these barriers often proved to be more of an impediment than did social class.[7] The urban centers of Tokyo, Osaka, and Kyoto, for example, had a larger number of *terakoya* administered by women, higher ratios of girls' attendance at school, and higher numbers of women teachers.[8] Evidence suggests that in central urban areas almost all samurai women were literate and moderately to highly educated. Some cities and towns could boast relatively high numbers of educated women from a variety of classes, while, at the same time, there were rural villages and hamlets where seemingly no women and few men were educated.[9] In general, education was more widely available to women who lived in and around major cities and in the castle towns of the Tokugawa domains, but urban, suburban, and even rural middle-class women often acquired educations that went beyond the basics of literacy and moral training.[10]

Tokugawa Philosophical Canon and Women's Education

Aspects of Tokugawa philosophy fostered the expansion of women's education. Several rationales existed in the Tokugawa period in support of women's education, but the most common one concentrated on preparing women for domestic priorities after marriage; and to varying degrees, these priorities included a managerial and an ethical component. Japanese women's educations were similar on many points, and regardless of class, all educated women seemed to receive some foundation in Neo-Confucian ethical precepts. Although scholars have produced many studies of Tokugawa thought, ideology about women or women's education has not been studied systematically.[11] Because of this, Japan's versions of Neo-Confucianism have often been viewed in totalizing ways; that is, that the impact of Neo-Confucian thought on the status of Tokugawa women was devastating since Confucian tenets confined women within the family, subordinated their interests there, and proscribed their public participation in the political realm.

Tokugawa-period Neo-Confucian thought varied greatly, but in general it supported women's education.[12] Over the course of the period, several Neo-Confucian philosophers wrote essays on the importance of women's education and commanded parents not to neglect the education of daughters. Among them, Kaibara Ekiken (1630–1714) is often quoted in texts on Meiji women's history to provide evidence of the subjugated position of Tokugawa women and the inadequacies of their education. Yet, in his writings, Kaibara actually recommended that women be well educated.[13] It is one of the small injustices of history that this remarkable Confucian philosopher and humanist has for so long been associated with circumscribing women's education in the Tokugawa period. The cause for this misunderstanding rests with a Tokugawa-era morals text for women mistakenly attributed to Kaibara but actually of unknown authorship.[14] *Onna daigaku*, with Kaibara listed as author, is still regularly cited as evidence of the poor quality of women's education in the Tokugawa period. Unfortunately, Kaibara's pedagogical essay, *Nyoshi o oshiyuru hō* (Methods of teaching women), written in 1710 as part of his larger work *Wazoku dōjikun* (Precepts on Japanese customs for children), has received little attention.

In *Nyoshi o oshiyuru hō*, Kaibara instructed parents in the proper upbringing and education of girls.

> Boys go outside. They follow the guidance of their teachers, they learn from physical objects, they mix with their friends, and they learn the etiquette of the world with their eyes and ears. They do not learn only from their parents' instruction. The bulk of their education they gain through their eyes and ears. Usually, girls remain inside. They do not go out. In order to learn the etiquette of the world they must rely entirely on the instruction of their father and mother. Fathers and mothers who do not [teach] their daughters properly do not know [how] to love their children. To begin with, the education of girls should not differ from the education of boys.[15]

Boys have the opportunity to learn from the outside world, from teachers and from friends, and can offset unsuitable parental training. But, Kaibara cautions, since girls after the age of ten are not allowed the same freedom as boys, they have no opportunity to correct a faulty education. Therefore, Kaibara urged parents to be especially conscientious in the education of their daughters. He condemned the early eighteenth-century vogue among men to marry women solely on the basis of physical beauty and implored men to select brides on the basis of intellect and education.[16]

In his introduction to *Yamato zokkun* (Precepts for daily life in Japan), Kaibara briefly summarized part of his educational philosophy:

Thus for the sake of people who are so unfortunate as not to know Chinese characters, I have written in contemporary language about the principles that have been received from ages past. I would only ask that this book be made available for the instruction of husbands and wives who know nothing of worldly matters, and even that it be taught to small children who cannot distinguish beans from barley. I suppose that by trying to teach trivial things and making much use of the abbreviated script of the rustic Japanese of old I will become the laughingstock of scholars who have established a reputation in Confucian studies. But since I have committed myself to this task, I am not fearful of the criticism of others.[17]

Like many other Confucian scholars, Kaibara was a committed pedagogue. It is clear from this "Preface" that he wanted to educate men, women, and children and that he knew that men as well as women often had no education in Chinese characters. Therefore, he made a point of writing in the vernacular in order to reach as large an audience as possible.

Women's education benefited from these recommendations and from the value Tokugawa-era varieties of Neo-Confucianism placed on education as a means to self-cultivation. Not through prayer or meditation or good works but only through study could one acquire virtue—and for women as well as men, individual virtue led first to the stability of the family and ultimately to the stability of the country as a whole.

Written for Women: The Importance of *Jokun* and *Ōraimono*

Given such ideological support, moral guides directed at women proliferated over the course of the Tokugawa period. While the content of *jokun* has contributed to the negative image of the status of Tokugawa women and of their educations, the abundance of these texts can be interpreted in more than one way.[18]

More than anything else, education in Tokugawa Japan was about reading and writing, as students learned to master this complicated written language. By the late Tokugawa era, images of women reading and writing were everywhere—in the woodblock prints of famous artists, in the illustrations of popular novels, and in the pictures accompanying texts written for women. Throughout the Tokugawa period, these widely distributed texts provided an element of commonality to women's learning at a time when education was not standardized. During the course of their education and throughout their lives, educated Tokugawa women from both samurai and commoner classes often read the same moral guides. The tenets outlined in these eighteenth- and nineteenth-century guides drew heavily on Japan's adaptations of Neo-Confucian ethical principles for their instruction.[19] Although some historians of Japanese women criticize the content of *jokun*, the very existence of these texts, together with publication and republication records, substantiates the breadth and depth of Tokugawa educational traditions for women.

Tokugawa-period moral texts for women owed a large debt to Chinese Confucian didactic classics. Sometimes these texts were adapted wholesale from Chinese originals, which were rendered into vernacular editions directed at a female audience and used to teach morals and ethics to Japanese girls and women. The *Four Books for Women* (*Onna shishō*), for example, was adapted in this way.[20] In addition, Japanese philosophers, biographers, and novelists also authored new texts, which included moralistic biographies and novels; and often many of these, too, reflected the influence of Neo-Confucian philosophy. Many texts directed at women's moral and ethical training presented a straightforward adaptation of Chinese Confucian philosophy. Others, however, incorporated slightly different content and emphasized the importance of ethical and moral teachings for women's role as domestic managers after marriage, a role that gained new importance in the Tokugawa era.[21] This new type of guide dominated textbook publishing aimed at women for much of the Tokugawa period.[22]

While the content of women's moral texts has contributed to the negative image of the status of Tokugawa women and of their education, these texts were only one of several categories of books published for a female audience. *Joshi yō ōraimono*, a genre of basic textbooks written for women, was another. As a distinct category, *joshi yō ōraimono* have existed for women of the aristocracy since the late Nara period (710–784). Best translated as basic or introductory texts, the earliest *ōraimono* provided instruction in writing and conveyed general knowledge useful in the daily life of ordinary people.[23] The number, variety, and scope of these texts increased throughout the Tokugawa period, indicating an ongoing expansion of education beyond the narrow circle of nobility and military elites to commoner classes. Some texts were directed specifically at girls and women, others at boys and men, while many basic instructional writings often had no gender designation and were meant to be read by anyone. Furthermore, neither women nor men were restricted to reading gender-appropriate texts.[24]

Although more moral guides were published than any other category of text for women during the Tokugawa period, from the mid-seventeenth century, and increasingly from the beginning of the nineteenth century, the subjects of texts written for women gradually expanded and appealed to a wider audience. For example, the earliest guides to letter writing were limited to examples of formal correspondence, while later guides contained information on daily note writing and more popular epistolary forms, indicating an expansion of literacy into daily life. For the whole of the Tokugawa period, Ishikawa Ken catalogued 377 texts that he classified as moral texts. After 1789, however, the number of geography texts, a type of *ōraimono*, published for women outnumbered moral texts; and for some periods, the number of geography books issued for women was almost twice the number of moral texts.[25]

Onna Daigaku As One Example of Tokugawa *Jokun*

Onna daigaku was among the most widely published of Tokugawa *jokun*. Editions have been in print continuously since the early eighteenth century.[26] Most examinations of this and other *jokun* writings have focused on their content and overlooked other aspects of these texts. In the Tokugawa period, *jokun* were not simply used as moral tracts. *Onna daigaku*, for example, was designed to be used as a copy book to teach basic literacy. It was a primer for women in the reading and writing of

Chinese characters, and so its primary value was educational rather than philosophical.[27] Customarily, women's texts from earlier eras had been written in cursive syllabary. Because it was written in both *kana* sylla- bary and Chinese characters, and because almost all of those characters were glossed with additional *kana* syllabary (*furigana*) instructing the stu- dents in their proper Japanese reading, *Onna daigaku* and texts like it served to extend further the reading and writing skills of young Japa- nese girls. And by attaching Kaibara's name to this text, Tokugawa booksellers were able to launch not simply another morals text, but a primer that tutored girls from both samurai and commoner classes in Chinese characters.[28]

Despite their conservative tone, the widespread availability of texts like *Onna daigaku*, with their presumption of literacy, encouraged women's education. *Ōraimono* and *jokun* were published on thick Japa- nese paper in order to withstand the wear of repeated use. Filled with luscious illustrations, basic primers like *Onna daigaku takarabako* were lovely to behold. These sturdy, brightly colored editions, which often juxtaposed moral essays with grooming tips, classical poetry, and in- structions in geometry, were designed to be attractive to children, and they held the young reader's attention in ways that sober essays on mo- rality or pedagogy alone would not have done. By the mid-eighteenth century, textbooks for the education of girls and women were ubiqui- tous and on their way to becoming a permanent part of Tokugawa popular culture. By the end of the century, colorful anthologies of *jokun* were so popular that tiny models of them appeared among the appur- tenances in annual doll festival displays. Then in the early nineteenth century, an even wider variety of textbooks offering instruction in aca- demic subjects such as arithmetic and geography was available for use in girls' education. By the end of the Tokugawa period, more and more women were reading a diverse range of popularly published materials.

Over the course of the Tokugawa period, basic educational oppor- tunities became available to a growing number of women, and educa- tion became an important and increasingly common part of their lives. As mentioned earlier, the availability of education for women varied ac- cording to class and geographic area, and wealthy, urban women had greater educational opportunities. Female members of the nobility and of the daimyō class (feudal lords) lived in separate sections of their families' estates and were educated at home by their parents or by tutors. Ladies-in-waiting to both types of households were often selected on the basis of education, while at the same time, serving as a lady-in-waiting was one means of acquiring still higher education. Wealthy daughters from the commoner class were taught by parents or by notable scholars from the community, or they might be sent to board in the household of a scholar in a distant city if a desirable scholar was not available nearby. Village daughters from families of middle strata were educated in *terakoya* or *shijuku*, and some were also tutored privately. Whether education took place informally at home or in the neighborhood *terakoya* or *shijuku*, women's education shared a common canon and a common discipline required by mastery of the complexities of written Japanese. Family traditions and individual inclination determined Tokugawa women's higher education. When both converged, women received educations comparable to men of their class.

By the end of the Tokugawa period, few if any educators or philosophers argued that women should be ignorant and illiterate. In many cases where education was valued, it was valued for men and women from the same class, even though that did not mean that education was identical for men and women. Although women trained in Chinese (*kanbun*) and in the classics of Chinese literature might describe this aspect of their education as drawn from male traditions, facility with "men's learning" did not contravene gender boundaries to such a degree that women so educated were rendered social or educational pariahs. In fact, well-educated women, even ones that never bore children, as in the case of Kaibara Token, were lauded as models of exemplary wifely conduct.

Because education did not transgress the boundaries of their gender, most girls and women educated in the Tokugawa period did not have to study in secret. The content of their education was publicly acknowledged, and women with higher levels of education taught others without stigma. As a result, educated girls and women shared more than the content of their education, they shared a common process. Although some studied individually with tutors, many did not. Instead, they came together in school rooms or at their teachers' houses. There they joined their voices in recitation, endured the tedium of repetitious copying, and shared the difficulties of acquiring literacy with their peers. The educational process itself—the routines of women's education—was in many ways more important than its content, for it acknowledged women's educability to themselves and to society at large.

Meiji Women's Education and Its American Counterpart

When the Tokugawa period ended with the Meiji Restoration in 1868, the reform that followed obscured the importance of Japanese women's indigenous educational traditions. As Japan's new government looked to the West for the elements from which to form a national system of education, formal American models for women's education overshadowed informal domestic ones. Yet many of the reasons that Meiji government and education officials were able successfully to restructure Meiji women's education stemmed directly from the Tokugawa period. Tokugawa experience meant that many Meiji educators did not find the idea of educating women alien or threatening. Female education to serve the family had long been ideologically acceptable, being educated did not hurt a woman's marriagability, and going out of the home to study did not blemish her virtue.

A thorough-going condemnation of the Tokugawa system was central to the Meiji government's legitimacy, as well as to its reform programs, and this was true of the Education Ministry's efforts to recast Meiji education. For much of the late nineteenth century, Meiji reformers inside and outside government appeared to concur in America's negative views of Japanese institutions, which critics from every camp sought to root in the Tokugawa past. At that time, Japanese women's educational practices came frequently to be compared to American ones and to be measured against these in terms of the difference between the two systems, rather than their similarities.[29] Nevertheless, it is important to remember that in the early nineteenth century, the history of women's education in both countries shared core beliefs and principles.

First of all, America's education system grew out of the religious teachings of America's Protestant colonial religions, which initially restricted education beyond basic literacy to the male offspring of America's colonial settlers. In the eighteenth century, when Japanese women's education was based in part on popular versions of Neo-Confucianism, the education of white American women was also linked to religious duty. In most Protestant denominations at that time, men were responsible for civil and religious leadership, while women were to be obedient. To be obedient, however, women needed to be able to read the Bible in order to understand God's word and to sustain submissive female piety. Female piety required only that women be able to read; it did not require that they also be able to write. Yet, despite this distinction, many colonial girls and women learned to write as well as read. Colonial women's education was both encouraged and constrained by religious doctrine.[30] As in Japan, in America religious requirements and family decisions determined the direction and duration of daughters' educations until the end of the eighteenth century. For most of the next century, whether its sponsorship was private or public, American women's education developed in an informal and patchwork manner under the guidance of religious ideology inextricably tied to race and gender hierarchies.

In late eighteenth-century America, girls were educated at home or in private dame schools, which shared features with Tokugawa private academies. In contrast to the Tokugawa system, dame schools in America often mixed child care and education, blurring the distinction between school and family; in Japan, child care responsibilities could prevent a young Tokugawa girl from attending school. Because they enrolled whole families of siblings regardless of sex, dame schools were almost always coeducational. Some Tokugawa private academies were coeducational, but most were not, and even coeducational *terakoya* made an effort to seat boys and girls on opposite sides of the classroom.[31]

In the first half of the nineteenth century, American education expanded beyond a purely religious purpose into a strongly civic one. Early national rhetoric held mothers responsible for the early childhood education of republican sons. Under the impact of this ideology, girls flowed into American public primary schools in increasing numbers. Though many of these elementary schools were coeducational, girls' *public* elementary coeducation with boys remained controversial in America throughout the nineteenth century.

The gap between early nineteenth-century Japanese and American educational practice was even narrower at the level of women's secondary education. America's first public high schools began to take their place at the "summit of the urban school system" in the 1830s, but these were for a tiny student elite and almost always excluded girls.[32] Before the Civil War, women's formal secondary education was restricted to elites and was usually provided in private single-sex academies. About two hundred such female seminaries were founded between 1820 and 1860. Their curriculum of genteel accomplishments—musical performances, elocution, and painting, as well as religious training and a smattering of literature and history—would not have marked the young American gentlewoman as more learned than her Tokugawa counterpart.[33]

As in Tokugawa Japan, in nineteenth-century America it was not seen as self-evident, particularly for women, that formal institutionalized education within college walls was the only way to acquire higher learning.[34] By 1870, only eleven thousand women were enrolled in postsecondary institutions in the United States, and this number represented only seven-tenths of one percent (0.7 percent) of all American women aged eighteen to twenty-one.[35] Learned women both in midcentury America—who studied Latin and Greek—and in Japan—who learned Classical Japanese and *kanbun*—were likely to have received their education through informal means.

Some scholars of Japanese women's history measure the system for women's education that developed during the Meiji period not against this historical cross-cultural context, but rather in light of the views of Japanese reformers and feminists of the early twentieth century.[36] Following these critiques, they conclude that Japan's late nineteenth-century reform of women's education failed because it never incorporated, particularly at higher levels, the egalitarian promise presumed to have been imbedded in its American model. This conclusion assumes that American women's education in the 1870s, when it became a model for Japan's reforms, had gender equality as its mission. Yet, the educational recommendations American advisors and missionaries offered Japan in the 1870s were also based on an ideology of gender difference.

In the 1870s, American educators sought to convince the Japanese government to undertake the education of their own "race of enlightened mothers," and the educational policies they recommended for Japanese women grew out of a belief in women's special spiritual mission.[37] Just as American gender ideology constrained colonial women's education, it continued to constrain it, albeit differently, in the 1870s. Upon close examination, it can be seen that women's education in late nineteenth-century America had expanded within a system ultimately shaped by beliefs linking gender, religion, and education. This complex gender ideology, which argued for women's spiritual superiority, shaped women's education in late nineteenth-century America and formed the basis for the model that American advisors and reformers exported to Japan.

Conclusion

The education system that the Meiji state implemented was closely compatible with the "American model" offered to Japan by American advisors in the 1870s. The goal of the Meiji system was first and foremost universal elementary education aimed at producing law-abiding, productive, moral, and patriotic citizens. The state also offered limited education aimed at training youth of both sexes in gender-appropriate technical and vocational skills. Outside of teacher training, state-supported higher education was made available to only a small elite of future national leaders, presumed in both countries to be male. In the American model and in Japanese state educational policy, widespread public funding was limited to elementary education. State-supported secondary education accommodated gendered visions of male and female destinies, and focused some aspects of women's secondary education on their domestic roles. Public higher education was mandated almost exclusively for a small number of privileged males, leaving women's higher education almost entirely in private hands. Both systems encouraged women to train for domestic roles or for the vocation that represented an extension of their domestic roles—that of public schoolteacher.

In both the Japanese and American systems, coeducation was a controversial policy, especially after puberty. Although both systems stressed the moral/religious foundations of learning, the Japanese system differed from the American over whether ethical training should be based on Christian or indigenous moral traditions. Japan's late nineteenth-century American advisors were partisan advocates for a Christian morality they presumed offered "enlightened" views of women's place, but the moral content they sought for Japanese place, but the moral content they sought for Japanese education called attention to sexual conduct (monogamy, prostitution) rather than intellectual content. Most Meiji state educators were ambivalent about the sexual system of Christian morality, but were comfortable with a tradition-based ideology of women's education that called for educating women as mothers, an ideology that harmonized easily with American ideals of "republican motherhood."

Because public funding in both systems was usually reserved for elementary education, Japan's Education Ministry could only establish a few model institutions for women's secondary and eventually higher education. It is interesting to note that women educated in the Tokugawa period predominated in the new faculties of these institutions and that they were in charge of important areas of the curriculum: *kanbun*, Classical Japanese, and calligraphy. Male teachers who were hired were usually in charge of the "new" knowledge: Western-style mathematics and science. In America and Japan, late nineteenth-century state-supported secondary education accommodated gendered visions of male and female destinies and focused some aspects of women's secondary education on their domestic roles, much as Tokugawa-period education had done. With regard to women's secondary education, the Ministry of Education found it compatible with women's domestic roles, a determination that had resonance with both the Tokugawa past and late nineteenth-century America.

The Meiji government intended state-supported higher education to provide the nation with a few select males who would become the statesmen, scientists, and bureaucrats of the future. Women, who could not enter these professions in most other countries in the late nineteenth century, were not eligible for publicly funded university-level educations.[38] In Japan's new system, public higher education was mandated almost exclusively for a small number of privileged males.

Women's secondary and higher education in both systems owed a great deal to private initiative. The most important advances on both sides of the Pacific in terms of women's higher education were made outside the state sector. The Meiji state's fundamental commitment to women's basic educability provided ideological tools that could be used by private constituencies to shape and expand women's education. Because of the relative ease with which individuals could establish private academies—another legacy from the Tokugawa period that the Ministry of Education did not impede—educational reformers were able to supplement state offerings and partially rectify state omissions. Taking advantage of such official recognition, others were able privately to fund secondary and higher schools for girls and women. In the early Meiji period, a few institutions entered the new formal school system and extended Japan's tradition of higher education for women. As in America, the women educated in these institutions constituted an educated elite and represented just a fraction of the women age-appropriate to such education. Here official encouragement was important, but equally important was the latitude and the funding that allowed a diverse array of local and private educational ventures to grow. Again, even at the college level, both systems encouraged women to train for domestic roles or for the vocation of public schoolteacher; and this, too, was not a departure from acceptable Tokugawa-period gender roles or from late nineteenth-century American ones.

The Meiji state's promotion of girls' secondary education, as well as its limited support of women's higher education in normal schools and its tolerance of private institution building, provided a stable base from which a diverse cadre of dedicated educational reformers could press to expand women's education in several directions, and thereby continue, in a novel fashion, what their Tokugawa counterparts had begun over one hundred years before.

The success of Meiji educational policy directed at women resulted in part from compatibilities between Tokugawa and American educational practices. In many ways, the American influence on the development of Meiji women's education was significant *because* it reinforced Tokugawa practice in several areas and was a more palatable model in the early Meiji period than the largely discredited Tokugawa system. Although educational bureaucrats were loath to call attention to it, Tokugawa educational practice disguised as American practice permeated Meiji educational reforms. In the Tokugawa period, women had studied, taught, and managed schools of their own. They were the target audience for several types of books, including moral tracts and instructional texts. Many Tokugawa women went outside the home to study in classes with their peers. There they learned the rituals of copying and memorization, just as boys of their age did in their respective schools. Some daughters left their cities and villages to travel to larger cities such as Edo in order to learn more than they could at home. When they returned, these highly educated women were incorporated back into their families with no discernible stigma. These, then, are the Tokugawa educational practices that the Meiji state inherited; along with some Western innovations, it built its system for women's education upon them.

Notes

1. Much more needs to be known about the history of Japanese women before the term "nadir" can be applied accurately to one period over another. Clearly, the Tokugawa period does not represent the nadir for all women, although it probably represents a decline in inheritance for women from elite families. I am deeply suspicious that the term "nadir" can be used accurately because, in every culture, the "status of women" (itself a troublesome phrase) never changes in the same way and to the same degree for all women regardless of class or locale.

2. For examples of scholarship attempting to revise our interpretation of To-kugawa women's history, see *Recreating Japanese Women*, ed. Gail Lee Bernstein (Berkeley: University of California Press, 1991); and Sugano Noriko, "Shomin josei no kyōiku," in *Nihon joseishi*, eds. Wakita Haruko, Hayashi Reiko, and Na-gahara Kazuko (Yoshikawa kōbunkan, 1987), 150–155.

3. Ishikawa Ken, *Joshi yō ōraimono bunken mokuroku*, 1–13 (Dainihon yū benkai kōdansha, 1946); and Ishikawa Matsutarō, "*Onna daigaku* ni tsuite," in Kaibara Ekiken, *Muro Kyūsō*, vol. 34, *Nihon shisō taikei*, eds. Araki Kengo and Inoue Ta-dashi (Iwanami shoten, 1970/1985), 531.

4. Sugano, "Shomin josei," 150–155; Ishikawa Ken, *Terakoya* (Shibundō, 1960); Ronald Dore, *Education in Tokugawa Japan* (Berkeley: University of California Press, 1965), 252–270; and Richard Rubinger, *Private Academies of Tokugawa Japan* (Princeton, NJ: Princeton University Press, 1982). By mid-century, educational advisors in a few Tokugawa domains recommended establishing domain acad-emies for girls (*han jogakkō*) parallel to those for boys, and a few domains had begun to establish such academies. See "Kōtō jogakkō," in *Chūgakkō, kōtō-gakkō no rekishi*, vol. 3, *Gakkō no rekishi*, eds. Naka Arata, Uchida Tadashi, and Mori Takeo (Daīchi hōki shuppan, 1979), 79–85.

5. Ishikawa Ken, *Terakoya*; Dore, *Education*; and Sugano, "Shomin josei."

6. Hayashi Reiko, "Edoki no josei gunzō," in *Edoki josei no ikikata*, vol. 10, *Jin-butsu Nihon no joseishi*, ed. Enchi Fumiko (Shūeisha, 1977), 209–246. Sometimes, as for Tamura Kajiko, teaching represented a second career for women after they had served as ladies-in-waiting in daimyō castles or in the shogunal castle in Edo.

7. See Ishikawa Matsutarō's discussion of regional editions of *Onna daigaku*, in "*Onna daigaku* ni tsuite," 534–535.

8. Sugano, "Shomin josei," 150–155; and Dore, *Education*, 229, 257, 264.

9. Dore, *Education*, 205, *passim*.

10. Rural women's access to education depended upon family economics and the location of their home village. See Ann Walthall, "The Life Cycle of Farm Women," in Bernstein, *Recreating Japanese Women*, 46–50. Female literacy was lowest in the more remote areas of Tokugawa Japan.

11. See for example, studies by Tetsuo Najita, *Visions of Virtue in Tokugawa Japan: The Kaitokudō Merchant Academy of Osaka* (Chicago, IL: Chicago University Press, 1987); and Harry D. Harootunian, *Things Seen and Unseen: Discourse and Ideology in Tokugawa Nativism* (Chicago, IL: Chicago University Press, 1988), which contribute little to our understanding of ideology about Tokugawa women. In contrast, see Herman Ooms, *Tokugawa Ideology: Early Constructs, 1570–1680* (Princeton, NJ: Princeton University Press, 1985). While it is not central to his project, Ooms's analysis of the earliest stages of Tokugawa ideology has important implications for the history of gender in the Tokugawa period. His re-periodization of the rise in dominance of Tokugawa-era Neo-Confucian thought must occasion a reconsideration of its role in determining gender relations throughout the period. It calls into question the plausibility of continuing to assert that women's lives were shaped by one hegemonic discourse throughout the more than 250 years of Tokugawa governance. It is also clear from his study that female archetypes wielded important symbolic and cultural power in the early ideologies that were employed to legitimize Tokugawa rule: they occupied central symbolic positions in early Tokugawa Shintō philosophies, and they retained at least symbolic importance within the imperial family. His work suggests that systematic analysis of Tokugawa thought about women would elucidate other aspects of the Tokugawa polity.

12. Matsudaira Sadanobu seems to have argued that women should be literate and educated, but not to the same level as men because such excessively educated women would pose a danger to the state, while Yoshida Shōin argued that, given their role as mothers, *uneducated* women undermined the stability of the family and, by extension, the stability of the state.

13. For example, see Kaibara Ekiken, *Nyoshi o oshiyuru hō*, in *Yōjōkun—Wazoku dōjikun,* ed. and rev. Ishikawa Ken (Iwanami shoten, 1962).

14. For a discussion of text and authorship, see Matsutarō, *"Onna daigaku* ni tsuite,"* 531–545.

15. Kaibara, *Nyoshi o oshiyuru hō*, 264.

16. Ibid., 264–280.

17. Kaibara Ekiken, *Yamato zokkun*, trans. Mary Evelyn Tucker, in her *Moral and Spiritual Cultivation in Japanese Neo-Confucianism: The Life and Thought of Kaibara Ekiken (1630–1714)* (Albany: SUNY Press, 1989), 134.

18. *Onna daigaku*, published circa 1729, is reprinted in Kaibara, *Muro Kyūsō*, 202–227. For a discussion of text and authorship, see Matsutarō, "*Onna daigaku* ni tsuite," 531–545, in the same volume.

19. This chapter examines some of the influences of Neo-Confucian thought on women's education. The impact of other important intellectual traditions, for example Buddhism or Shintō, may have been equally great. Their influence on gender or education in the Tokugawa period has yet to be studied.

20. Ishikawa Matsutarō, "Joshi yō ōraimono," in *Nihon kyōkasho taikei: Ōraihen,* eds. Ishikawa Matsutarō and Ishikawa Ken, vol. 15 (Kōdansha, 1973), 1314.

21. Ibid., 11–18. Ishikawa Matsutarō connects the appearance of these new *jokun* to the Tokugawa-era consolidation of the family system. He argues that such consolidation was essential to the centralization of the Tokugawa state and that a specific type of married woman was essential for the consolidation of the family. Over the course of the Tokugawa period, his argument continues, the goal of women's education became the training of women as household managers (*shufu*), rather than as elegant, beautifully groomed, dilettante brides.

22. Matsutarō, "Joshi yō," 14–18, 46.

23. According to historian Ishikawa Ken, the term *ōraimono* was first used to refer to such educational texts in the latter half of the eleventh century. Prior to the twelfth century, women's education was largely restricted to noble women and initially consisted of instruction in music, poetry, and calligraphy—the three "R's" of elite women's education. The primary goal of this education was to prepare older girls and teenagers for marriage. With the rise of the military (*bushi*) class from the twelfth century, women's education expanded to include the women of Japan's new elite. See Ishikawa Ken, *Joshi yō ōraimono bunken mokuroku*, 1–10. In the Meiji period, such texts were renamed *kyōkasho* (textbooks) by the Ministry of Education (Monbushō). See Ishikawa Ken, "Hakko no kotoba," in *Ko ō rai*, vol. 1, part 1, *Nihon kyōkasho taikei ōraihen*, eds. Ishikawa Ken and Ishikawa Matsutarō (Kōdansha, 1968), 1–2.

24. *Nihon kyōkasho taikei ōraihen*, ed. Ishikawa Matsutarō, vol. 15, *Joshi yō* (Kōdansha, 1973), 12; and Ishikawa Ken, *Joshi yō ōraimono bunken mokuroku*, 1–2. Ishikawa Ken's and Ishikawa Matsutarō's brief assessment of pre-Tokugawa women's texts does not link women's educational practices to the history of women in earlier times. Several studies document aspects of Heian or Kama-

kura life in which elite women's education must have played a significant role. Most Heian-period histories note the pervasive influence elite women authors exerted on the production of classical literary forms. Kamakura-period historians have documented the importance of elite women's participation in almost every aspect of Kamakura institutional life through their extensive involvement in land transactions, their voluminous wills, and the numerous lawsuits they brought. Although they do not discuss elite women's education directly, scholarship by Jeffrey Mass, Hitomi Tonomura, and Haruko Wakita suggests that medieval elite women's educational practices went beyond beauty, arts, and social graces and had important application to elite women as fiscal and legal actors. See Mass, *Lordship and Inheritance in Early Medieval Japan: A Study of the Kamakura Sōryō System* (Stanford, CA: Stanford University Press, 1989); Tonomura, "Women and Inheritance in Japan's Early Warrior Society," *Comparative Studies in Society and History* 32 (July 1990): 592–623; and Wakita, "Marriage and Property in Premodern Japan from the Perspective of Women's History," *The Journal of Japanese Studies* 10, vol. 1 (Winter 1984): 77–99.

25. Altogether, from 1789 to 1868, publishers issued 178 volumes on geography while publishing only 165 morals texts. Between 1789 and 1829, 114 geography texts were issued versus 66 morals texts. Ishikawa Matsutarō, "Joshi yō," 46. For the Tokugawa period as a whole, however, *jokun* outnumbered any other single category of women's textbooks.

26. The exact date of *Onna daigaku's* initial publication and its authorship remain unclear. Still, most Japanese scholars now accept Ishikawa Matsutarō's evidence, given in his essay *"Onna daigaku* ni tsuite," that Kaibara Ekiken could not have been the author of this moral tract. It is also one of the first of these books to be translated into English in the late nineteenth century. For a late nineteenth-century English translation of *Onna daigaku* see Basil Hall Chamberlain, "Educational Literature for Japanese Women," *Journal of the Royal Asiatic Society of Great Britain and Ireland*, New Series, vol. 10, no. 3 (1878): 325–343. Chamberlain attacks the work ascribed to Kaibara in his article.

27. *Onna daigaku*, in Kaibara, *Muro Kyūsō*, 202–227.

28. Ishikawa Matsutarō, *"Onna daigaku* ni tsuite," 532.

29. It is interesting to note that in the late Tokugawa period, women's education was so firmly established in Japanese society that Dutch reports from that period include favorable evaluations of the status of Japanese women and the level of their educations. From the seventeenth through the mid-nineteenth century, the Netherlands was the only Western nation to have sustained contact with Japan. Members of exclusively male Dutch trading delegations re-

ported on Japanese culture. For example, see Philipp Franz von Siebold, *Manners and Customs of the Japanese* (New York: Harper and Brothers, 1841). The first reports from American diplomatic missions to Japan to appear in print in the United States were also generally approving. See S. B. Kemish, *The Japanese Empire: Its Physical, Political, and Social Condition and History with Details of the Late American and British Expeditions* (London: Partridge and Co., 1860). In America, this positive evaluation shifted after 1853. Then, Japan ceased to be the highly civilized *terra incognita* commended by the Dutch and became a dark, heathen Asian nation in need of American redemption. Still, the earlier Dutch evaluations substantiate the importance of women's education during the Tokugawa period.

30. See Tyack and Hansot, *Learning Together.*

31. For example, Tamura Kajiko's academy was coeducational.

32. Tyack and Hansot, *Learning Together*, 82.

33. Mabel Newcomer, *A Century of Higher Education* (New York: Harper & Brothers, 1959), 9.

34. American women were barred from admission to almost all of America's prestigious private colleges and universities until the late 1960s, by which time some of these institutions were close to three hundred years old, and most public colleges and universities had been coeducational for over eighty years.

35. Of this 11,000, those enrolled in four-year, A.B. degree–granting institutions numbered 3,000. Of this 3,000, approximately 2,200 were studying in America's private women's colleges. Although there were a few private colleges in America that had been coeducational since before the Civil War—in 1870 there were about forty such institutions—these only enrolled some 600 women. Finally, there were about 200 women enrolled in the eight state universities that, in 1870, admitted them. Another 3,000 women were enrolled in private academies that offered a curriculum more advanced than high school but below four-year college level, and the 5,000 women enrolled in normal schools were enrolled at a time when normal school education was not the equivalent of college education. An applicant for an elementary teaching position was considered highly qualified after one year of normal school, which was often simply an extension of the high school curriculum. See Newcomer, *A Century of Higher Education*, 19.

36. Some of these Japanese reformers whose work was available to historians were Shidzue Ishimoto, *Facing Two Ways: The Story of My Life* (Stanford, CA: Stanford University Press, 1984; originally published by Farrar and Rinehart in

1935), p. 38; Ai Hoshino, "The Education of Women," in Inazo Nitobe et al., *Western Influence in Modern Japan* (Chicago, IL: University of Chicago Press, 1931).

37. For typical examples of American advice on Japanese educational reform in the 1870s, see *Education in Japan: A Series of Letters Addressed by Prominent Americans to Arinori Mori*, ed. Mori Arinori (New York: D. Appleton, 1873).

38. Until 1897 there was only one nationally funded university in Japan, Tokyo Imperial University, and in 1877 it had 91 faculty members and 1,750 students, of whom 1,091 were in the preparatory course. State-supported university education included no women, but it also involved only a minuscule proportion of young adult males.

2   Thoughts on the Early Meiji Gentleman
Donald Roden

During his long career as early Meiji Japan's most celebrated educator, Fukuzawa Yukichi trumpeted the "upstanding and unsoiled gentleman" or the "gentleman of civilization" as his pedagogical ideal for a stable yet forward-looking nation-state.[1] Against a backdrop of political and social turmoil, often frightening to those who, like Fukuzawa, participated in public discourse, the gentleman offered a reassuring sense of the continuity of civilization. At the same time, the gentleman stood as a progressive force, reforming the image of Japanese public behavior both to allow space for the social civility necessary for measured change and to earn the respect of the Western nations the Meiji leadership so ardently wished to impress.

For Fukuzawa and other Meiji educators, the gentleman was made, not born, and thus emerged as a product of cultivation, much like the educated woman or the earliest visions of the "good wife, wise mother" that are addressed by Barbara Molony and Kathleen Uno later in this volume. As a cultivated ideal, the gentleman was of course susceptible to varying representations; and educators like Fukuzawa devoted considerable energy distinguishing what they regarded as the ideal gentleman from less desirable mutations. Such delineations assumed paramount importance because early Meiji educators believed that the properly cultivated gentleman would serve as the definitive model for masculine deportment within the Meiji elite, and that all young men of aspiration would eagerly embrace the refashioned gentleman as their exemplar. To a certain extent, the Meiji gentleman also proved important in the reconsideration of relations between the sexes, at least within the upper echelons of polite society, where the cultivated man supposedly could not exist without his cultivated feminine counterpart. As we shall see, however, the promise of a complementary gentility of form across gender lines remained largely unrealized throughout the early decades of Meiji.

The gentleman occupies a venerable place in the social history of education, not only in Japan but also in England, where a galaxy of critics, in some cases shaken by revolutionary events in France in much the same way as Fukuzawa was shaken by the Restoration struggles, latched onto the gentleman as a stabilizing anchor in turbulent times. Late eighteenth and early nineteenth-century English writers argued vigorously over the origins and education of the gentleman and sparked a protracted debate over the essential versus the nurtured contours of gentility. Because these notions both paralleled and informed Japanese thinking in the late nineteenth century, I turn briefly to their evolution.

Commentaries on the English Gentleman

In *Reflections on the Revolution of France* (1790), Edmund Burke issued one of history's most impassioned ideological defenses of social and political order under the trusteeship of an aristocratic corps of gentlemen. For Burke, the gentleman served a vital mediating function between the moral codes of late feudal chivalry and the demands of a modern political economy. In the broadest sense, we can say that the gentlemanly ideal had evolved in tandem with chivalry at precisely that time in the late feudal age when illiterate warriors began to assume the trappings of "civilization," relinquishing, as it were, the authority of the sword for that of the robe and accepting the ubiquitous dictum of William Wykeman, the fourteenth-century founder of Winchester, that "Manners makyth man."

This epic transition from sword to robe or from knighthood (in its pristine military sense) to bureaucratic officialdom propelled a refashioning of the battlefield codes of masculine courage and honor into a refined ethic of courtesy. This transformation facilitated more orderly, and certainly less lethal, human interactions while promoting the circulation of material goods. Thus, in Burke's view, the gentlemanly ideal stood on an equal plane with Christianity in accounting for both the rise of European civilization and the chivalric codes of social deference upon which that civilization rested: "Nothing is more certain, than that our manners, our civilization, and all the good things which are connected with manners, and with civilization, have, in this European world of ours, depended for ages upon two principles; and were indeed the result of both combined: I mean the spirit of a gentleman, and the spirit of religion." A society that forsook the gentlemanly spirit, therefore, was a society that had lost its moorings in historical tradition, a society without distinctions between good and mean people, a society that no longer deserved the title of "civilization."[2] Such was the case with the revolution that had erupted across the English Channel.

From a broad perspective, the celebration of an aristocracy of educated gentlemen, and the close association of that new aristocracy with the values of courtesy, public service, and conciliatory—as opposed to radical—reform, placed Burke at the forefront of an expansive cross section of late eighteenth- and early nineteenth-century writers, who reacted with alarm to what they saw as the egalitarian excesses of the French Revolution. As conceived by Burke, Macaulay, and other exponents of late eighteenth- and early nineteenth-century ideals of moderation and "civil prudence," the gentleman stood as a pillar of stability and order, an antidote to revolutionary brutality, who served as a "carrier of the civilization of centuries."[3] Yet while Whig historians led by Burke spoke with utter confidence about the "gentleman" as if the political ideal were set in stone, the fact remains that even within England, not to mention the United States or, as we shall see, Japan, the invocation of the gentlemanly ideal meant different things to different people. Even when writers used the same idioms for demarcating a gentleman from a rogue—courtesy, character, cultivation, and public spirit—they would not necessarily give equivalent weight to their common markers. Moreover, as the political and social ideal of gentility overlapped, inevitably, with the gendered ideal of manliness and manhood, a point that Burke himself recognized when he accused ungentlemanly barbarians for lacking "honor" and "manly pride," the possibilities for debate and controversy increased by several fold.

By the early nineteenth century, educators and moralists across western Europe and the United States paid homage to the gentleman as one who bears an elite status, accessible to all young men who perfected certain qualities of mind and demeanor, qualities that were rooted in the feudal aristocracy but that by the early 1800s had become increasingly subjected to embourgeoisement. To be sure, defenders of feudal blood legacies echoed Samuel Johnson in declaiming gentlemen as "persons distinguished by their birth from the vulgar,"[4] but theirs was an increasingly minority position among writers who celebrated the gentleman as a model for all social classes. Yet beyond the view that gentility represented lofty status which stood apart from simple birthright, moralists and social commentators were sharply divided over two distinct variants of the masculine ideal: the cultivated gentleman, often called the "fine gentleman" or what I shall call the gentleman of form, versus the "natural gentleman" or what I shall call the gentleman of essence.[5] Both models of gentility embodied the values of civic virtue, noblesse oblige, and social privilege. The cultivated gentleman of form perfected these sensibilities through education and the self-conscious application of social manners that advanced a "shame-threshold," to use Norbert Elias's phrase, among would-be gentlemen, inducing them to forsake indecorous behavior—spitting, sneezing, grunting, emitting wind—as inconsistent with their aspirations for status and power in polite society.[6] The primitive gentleman of essence, in contrast, drew more heavily upon an innate sense of moral rectitude, often coupled with a gendered endowment of masculine courage and valor that evoked memories of an earlier age of chivalry and battlefield prowess. In general the essentialist legacy of masculine honor and valor faded with the fall of feudal institutions and the rise of what Lawrence Stone has called a new "mode of life" and social breeding, which transformed former knights into men of elegant dress, literary attainment, and grace on the dance floor.[7]

The new gentility of form, to which Stone refers, attained its apotheosis in the figure of the "fine gentleman," first invoked and elaborately embellished by Lord Chesterfield in his famous mid-eighteenth-century *Letters to His Son*. For Chesterfield, the "fine gentleman" represented a supreme arbiter of good taste and fashion, a man of "an engaging, insinuating manner, an easy good-breeding, a genteel behavior and address," and above all, a champion in "the art of pleasing." Flattery was no sin in Chesterfield's view, for ingratiation with a soft voice, impeccable dress, and a delicate perfume signified the highest expression of a gentility that guarded against the "quick passions" of manhood. "Make yourself absolute master . . . of your temper and your countenance," Chesterfield cautioned, "whatever you may feel inwardly." In the epic battle against the eruptions of anger and passion, Chesterfield spoke not of an inner morality or lofty constellation of ideals, but rather of a "working morality," a practical manual for success in a social world that centered around "the graces" of speech, dress, and manner. "The manner of doing things is often more important than the things themselves," he argued, reiterating his persistent theme that form supersedes content.[8]

Although Chesterfield provided an enduring standard of gentlemanly behavior, his model did not survive without considerable debate and some modification during the Victorian age. In an apparent response to the Chesterfieldian vision of the gentility of form, Samuel Smiles stated that, "The gentleman is eminently distinguished for his self-respect. He values his character, not so much of it only as can be seen of others, but as he sees it himself; having regard for the approval of his inward monitor." The challenge for the educator, then, was to provide space for aspiring gentlemen to discover their "inward monitors," even at the risk of allowing them to vent their primal energies such as can be seen, for example, on the playing fields of the nineteenth-century public schools. Still, even Victorian critics stopped far short of a complete denial of the gentility of form and expected that the "true gentleman," to cite Smiles again, remain attentive to "the cultivation of manner" and "good-breeding."[9]

The arduous attempts by Victorian educators and critics to navigate between the gentility of form and gentility of essence bears a certain affinity to the debate over the masculine ideal in early Meiji Japan. As in Europe, Japan had deep historical roots in a tradition of feudal privilege and military élan. And like their European counterparts, Japanese educators faced the challenge of reconstituting the gentlemanly ideal as a desperately needed social anchor in a historical setting of social dislocation and political revolution. The Meiji Restoration did not unleash the wanton killing and destruction of the French Revolution, but it certainly sparked fears of anarchy and social breakdown among educators and critics who, like Edmund Burke, rallied around the gentleman as the only hope for orderly progress. Among the standard bearers for this resurrected vision of the gentleman were such enlightenment scholars as Nakamura Masanao, Mori Arinori, Fukuchi Gen'ichirō, and above all, Fukuzawa Yukichi, whose insights and pedagogy provide the focus for this essay.

The Gentlemanly Ideal in Japanese History

As an ideal of both pedagogy and political leadership, the gentleman was of course no nineteenth-century invention or simple adaptation of European or American models. The Confucian gentleman had been a fixture of Chinese civilization for more than two millennia, and pedagogical attempts in Japan to reconstruct a variation of the scholar-official date back at least to the founding of the Heian Academy (Daigakuryō) in the early eighth century. Perhaps the most striking early exemplars of the Confucian bureaucratic ideal were the scions of the Sugawara family, who, as Robert Borgen has argued, knowingly assumed the mantle of a Confucian gentleman: the literate, moralistic, and thoroughly dedicated public servant.[10] Although the Meiji architects of gentility, notably the First Higher Middle School's headmaster Kinoshita Hiroji, heaped praises on the Sugawara family, particularly Michizane, they regarded the "Heian gentleman" in general as a creature overburdened by form and underendowed with essence, all too susceptible to the whims of a literary dilettanti composed, to an alarming extent, of court ladies.[11] Determined to locate their vision of gentility within a more self-consciously masculine culture, the Meiji educators focused their attentions on the rise of the samurai gentleman through Japan's extended period of feudalism. Just as Burke proclaimed that the gentlemanly spirit sprung from knighthood and chivalry, so too did Nitobe Inazō, who was keenly aware of Burke's insights, locate the emergence of Japan's gentleman within what he called the "ascent of *bushidō*."[12] The distinctly evolutionary view of *bushidō* made clear, however, that gentility, while it must remain clear of the idle and effeminate dilettantism of the Heian courtiers, also required more than a simple re-enactment of the heroic and, in Nitobe's view, viscerally masculine exploits of early medieval warriors. Minamoto Yoshinaka was no gentleman by any stretch of the imagination, for the brute energy of a "wild boar warrior" proved meaningless unless harnessed and directed by grace and proper etiquette. Nitobe's "true gentleman," therefore, mediated between an untempered or instinctive gentility of essence and a cultivated or polished gentility of form. And although Nitobe spoke often of striking a balance between the two realms of "the rough" and "the gentle," his overall philosophy of education betrayed an undeniable bias for the cultivated gentility that sprang from the domestication of the samurai ethos during the Tokugawa period.

Throughout the seventeenth and eighteenth centuries, cultivated gentility, or "the pedagogy of cultivation," to use Weber's phrase, remained the central, though contested, principle for the education of the samurai class. In the view of a stream of Edo schoolmen, from Yamaga Sokō to Ogyū Sorai, the school existed not as a source for idealistic inspiration or intuitive self-discovery, but as an institution [*Catholic schools*] for building moral character according to clearly demarcated norms of external behavior, language, and demeanor. Most students attending either a recognized private or domain academy in the eighteenth century studied under what Dore calls "the heavy weight of ceremonial and of formal bureaucratic regulations," which served as a constant reminder that gentility required cultivation in a carefully choreographed regimen of learning and etiquette.[13] Herein lay the centerpiece of a gentility of cultivated form whereby manners defined the educated man, not the other way around. Although Sorai maintained that the seeds for gentlemanly virtue and talent remained a heavenly gift, the recognition and development of that gift required arduous training that centered upon the acquisition of concrete "ceremonial forms." In one of the summary prefaces for Sorai's famous *Instructions for Students,* a pedagogical manual for the cultivation of the gentleman, it is noted that, "The sages did not teach by means of theoretical terms and discussion; that they established forms and conditions of action and taught by means of these; and that students must follow these forms and conditions of action and thereby learn."[14] This externalized and thoroughly pedagogical view of gentility prompted Sorai's disciple Dazai Shundai to add: "Regardless of what is inside his heart, if someone adheres outwardly to the rules of proper conduct and does not violate them, he is a gentleman."[15] In other words, a student *learns* to be a gentleman through a program of forced habituation to concrete forms or etiquette; and the conspicuous display of those easily visualized forms in everyday life serves as a validation of cultivated status.

Like their counterparts in the Renaissance schools of Europe, the Edo schoolmen regarded the educated man as a creature of acquired affectation. The inculcation of this affectation required a pedagogy of strict discipline and grueling recitation of a nonvernacular language, the study of Classical Chinese serving as the functional counterpart to the study of Latin and Greek among gentlemen-in-training in the West. If spontaneity and humor remained in conspicuously short supply in the domain academies of the eighteenth century, it was only because Tokugawa educators regarded the project of gentlemanly cultivation as very serious business, inextricably intertwined with the health and stability of the existing political system. They fully accepted the fundamental principle that, to paraphrase the *Doctrine of the Mean*, when gentlemen avail themselves, government prospers, and when gentlemen step aside, government collapses. Cultivated gentility thus mirrored the Confucian faith in education as the supreme "socializing force" in the formation of a select group of superior men to serve as public servants within an established bureaucracy.[16]

Accordingly, by the eighteenth century the samurai class had experienced, in the words of Eiko Ikegami, "a remarkable transformation" in which "the instinctual search for glory on the battlefield through physical strength and endurance," what I have called the gentility of essence, gave way to an obsession over "style of dress or the seating arrangement in the castles" as defined by an elaborate hierarchy of etiquette (*rei*), or gentility of form. Yet the world of masculine instinct and primitive honor did not disappear completely. "The voice of the samurai's traditional ethos was muted," Ikegami argues, "but never totally silenced." This was true even within the discourses of illustrious *jusha*, including Sokō, Sorai, and Arai Hakuseki, each of whom voiced occasional, though by no means consistent, admiration for the unreflective values of courage and honor.[17] Still, the idealistic ethos of the medieval samurai had little room for expression within the portals of the domain academy, where strict adherence to the rules of external etiquette remained firmly in place.

But by the middle of the nineteenth century, an increasing number of private academies, many devoted to varying strains of Confucian and nativist idealism as well as to the martial arts and Dutch learning, offered a more free-flowing learning environment without the formalistic pedagogical routines and obsession with minute gradations in rank that prevailed in the domain academies. At Yoshida Shōin's Shōka Sonjuku or, for that matter, Ogata Kōan's Tekijuku, young men indulged themselves in an atmosphere of uninhibited male bonding and boyish primitivism. Shōin in particular insisted upon building a spiritual union among students and teachers; and toward that end he studiously avoided the imposition of any bureaucratic regulations regarding admission, promotion, evaluation, and even the scheduling of classes. [18] At Shōka Sonjuku, the young men ate from the same rice bowl, toileted in the same latrine, slept in the same cramped space with no concern for seating arrangements, clothes, or the niceties of social status. A similar gentility of essence flourished in Tekijuku, where Fukuzawa attended. He recollected how his fellow students cavorted together on hot summer days stripped to their loincloths or less.[19]

Such audacious breaches of the rules of propriety suggest more than the appearance of boys who discover the joys of acting boyishly. For the antics of young men jumping about without a stitch of clothing reflected not only rejection of the cultivated gentleman and his ponderously affected style, but also a broader political dissatisfaction with the bureaucratic regime whose very existence depended upon maintaining the rules of propriety. In this sense, many of the young men who flocked to the *bakumatsu* (1853–1868) private academies to indulge themselves in an informal setting of masculine camaraderie contributed to the broader political phenomenon of what H. D. Harootunian calls "secession."[20] The disaffection for a gentility of form and embrace of a gentility of essence converged indistinguishably with an angry detachment from the *baku-han* order. Just consider the behavior of the archetypal *shishi* (man of noble purpose) in the Restoration struggle. He was, as Marius Jansen so revealingly describes him, "brave, casual, carefree, took himself very seriously where 'first things' were concerned, and was utterly indifferent where they were not."[21] Casual, carefree, indifferent, irresponsible: these are precisely the qualities that distinguish a gentility of essence from a cultivated gentility of form. And these are the values, suggestive of a "primitive ethos," as Maruyama has phrased it, that hastened the overthrow of the *baku-han* order.[22]

Yet while primitivism and the gentility of essence provided much of the emotional fuel for the Meiji Restoration, the cultivated gentleman-bureaucrat, albeit in Victorian garb, survived the mid-nineteenth-century crisis even though his institutional protectors, notably the domain academies, did not. Pivotal to the gentleman's survival were the concerted efforts of a cadre of bureaucratic intellectuals known as enlightenment scholars (*keimō gakusha*), learned men who in many cases had benefited as much from bakufu patronage before the Restoration as they did from their advisory association with the new Meiji government. Among these, Fukuzawa Yukichi assumes special importance for reconstructing the ideal of the cultivated gentleman at its moment of greatest historical peril.

Fukuzawa Yukichi and the Reinvention of the Cultivated Gentleman

At first glance, Fukuzawa appeared unalterably opposed to the gentility of form as it had flourished during the Edo period. In the first essay in his *An Encouragement of Learning*, he attacked the fundamental intellectual premises of the pedagogy of cultivation: the study of classical language. "Learning does not essentially consist in such impractical pursuits as study of obscure Chinese characters, reading ancient texts which are difficult to make out, or enjoying and writing poetry. These dilettante literary pursuits may be quite a pleasant way of passing the time, but they hardly deserve all the praise which has been heaped on them in the past. . . ." Rather, Fukuzawa continued, "The object of one's primary efforts should be practical learning that is closer to ordinary human needs."[23]

Impracticality was not, however, the only cause for Fukuzawa's attack on classical learning. Of equal importance was his belief that arcane learning reinforced an ethic of privileged indolence at the top of society and self-deprecatory submission at the bottom, that education had served as "a tool of despotism." Throughout the Edo period, Fukuzawa lamented, schoolmen accepted the notion that "the more a scholar absorbs himself in his studies, the loftier he becomes, until he is ready to rise to the heavens. In contrast, ignorant farmers and merchants will grow ashamed of themselves until they want to hide themselves in a hole." Elsewhere Fukuzawa noted that, "Learning was entirely in the hands of the priests who stood more or less aloof from society. This I consider a disgrace to the cause of learning." To remedy this, Fukuzawa articulated his egalitarian plea in his Nakatsu school announcement of 1871: "Let us take the present change as a good opportunity to alter the old decrepit ways, abandon manmade nobility and stipends, and turn to depending on one's own body and mind for acquiring knowledge and skills to operate one's family business and build up one's own fortune."[24] One year later this view was incorporated into the preamble of the Fundamental Code of Education (Gakusei), which explicitly attacked "the evil tradition which looked upon learning as the privilege of the samurai" and called instead for an open system of education in which knowledge would be regarded as an amoral capital investment (*zaihon*) for individual self-improvement, regardless of hereditary background and, to an extent, gender. The framers of the code decried the lack of educational opportunities for women under the old regime as yet another "evil tradition," and in a supplementary policy statement proclaimed that "the way of humanity allows no distinctions between men and women."[25] In the same year as the issuance of the code, Fukuzawa visited several primary schools in Kyoto and was so impressed by the sight of children of both sexes studying together that he made this pronouncement upon departure: "These boys and girls will be the ones who will promote knowledge and virtue among commoners and lead them in acquiring their rights to debate civil problems publicly. These boys and girls will be the ones to work on their own to earn their living to insure their own independence and that of their families and thus to lay the foundation for national independence."[26] It would be hard to imagine the articulation of such a statement ten or even five years earlier. While the egalitarian promise of "no distinctions between men and women" would not be fulfilled, certainly not within the sanctuaries of higher learning, including Fukuzawa's academy, the initial proclamations of enlightenment scholars foreshadowed a new chapter in the history of education in Japan in which the discourse on the educated male would no longer take place in isolation from his feminine counterpart.

Clearly Fukuzawa subscribed, at least in part, to an ethic of competitive individualism and self-reliance that provided the philosophical basis for the drive for personal achievement (*risshin shusse*). Moreover, despite his gender-embracing remarks about the Kyoto primary schools, he viewed ambition and self-reliance as forces of an innate masculine energy, a gentility of essence, that invariably clashed with the artifices of status and ceremony. Accordingly, Fukuzawa loudly pronounced his distaste for foppery and even accepted the rowdiness of his earliest students at the Dutch language academy, the forerunner to Keiō, as a necessary antidote to effeminacy and sloth. He had no desire, he later explained, to turn his students into an effete corps modeled after the notorious dilettantes of the Edo period, *bunjin* scholars like Takizawa Bakin, Ota Nanpō, or Hiraga Gennai. Such elegant men of letters gave the appearance of "high-minded gentlemen" but "they indulged in idle literary pursuit" and thus forsook their overriding public duties.[27] In short, they represented extreme embodiments of artifice without substance. Having said this, I must quickly add that Fukuzawa's attacks on "manmade nobility" or exaggerated representations of the gentility of form only went so far. Just as Martha Tocco in this volume questions the iconoclastic underpinnings of Meiji educational reforms, so too one wonders whether Fukuzawa's broadsides against affected etiquette among Edo writers points to an instance of protesting too much. After all, cultivated gentility, in and of itself, was never really the problem for Fukuzawa. Rather it was the misrepresentation of that gentility by imposters or "false gentlemen" (*nise kunshi*)—men who in their exterior demeanor might look like gentlemen, at least part of the time, but who otherwise, when the opportunity avails itself, abandon their veil of respectability to act like rogues. Such was the case with impractical scholar-dilettantes like Nanpō and Gennai, but also certain uncritical proponents of Western studies whom Fukuzawa derisively dismissed as "teachers of enlightenment," philosophic fops who similarly failed to unite principle with conduct, form with substance.

At the same time, Fukuzawa applied the term "false gentleman" more generally to members of the *bushi* elite who had become masters of ingratiation and deception. At several points in *An Encouragement of Learning*, Fukuzawa Yukichi criticized the education and socialization of the samurai class for producing men who masqueraded as gentlemen but who fell far short of the Confucian models of righteousness and humanity. A "poisonous atmosphere" enshrouded the institutions of the Tokugawa regime, Fukuzawa argued, infecting retainers with the temptation for "swindling and subterfuge." On the surface vassals acted deferentially toward their overlords, but in reality they were merely "false gentlemen plated superficially with gold." While they gave every appearance of devoted service, underneath their gilded exteriors resentment smoldered like a ticking time bomb. And when the *bakumatsu* historical crises of economic and social strain ignited that bomb, all pretenses of gentility evaporated in what Fukuzawa described as a wave of "anarchy and lawlessness."[28] Ultimately, therefore, false gentility served as a thin cover for the worst forms of primitivism and brutality, embodied most dramatically in the carefree ideal of the *shishi*, which Fukuzawa regarded as a ghastly inversion of his vision of the gentleman.

Fukuzawa had every reason to recoil against the *shishi*. Between 1860 and 1867, he worked for the bakufu as a translator within the new offices of the foreign affairs commissioners (*gaikoku bugyō*). As a faithful government employee, he became a liege retainer with corresponding stipend, and deported himself, in the words of Albert Craig, as "a staunch supporter of the bakufu."[29] He also benefited enormously from the opportunities to travel with three successive bakufu-sponsored missions to the United States and Europe. No small wonder then that he presented himself as an inviting target for Restoration xenophobes, "lawless warriors" and "ruffians" as he described them, whom Fukuzawa quite understandably believed to be lurking in the shadows, ready to snuff out his life with one fell swoop of the sword. "It is not too much to have enemies who attack by means of words and epithets," Fukuzawa wrote in his autobiography after surviving at least three plots to take his life, "but to have enemies who would resort to violent means is a different matter. Nothing can be worse, more unsettling, more generally fearful, than this shadow of assassination. No one without the actual experience can really imagine it."[30]

Living under a continual threat of assassination until at least 1873, Fukuzawa not surprisingly denounced the carefree primitivism of the loyalist cause and the spillover of xenophobic terrorism into the new era of civilization and enlightenment. He firmly believed, as he later pointed out, that the improvement of social manners necessarily accompanied "the progress of enlightenment" and that no one should accept the immoral antics of those "illiterate ruffians" whose post-Restoration rampages would never have been accepted even during "the pitiable age of feudalism."[31] Obviously it was not simply his own personal safety that compelled Fukuzawa to lash out at masculine primitivism but the fear that "undisciplined behavior" might tear asunder the very fabric of the social order and reverse Japan's teleological course to civilization. Fukuzawa seemed to agree completely with Sugi Kōji that an age of turmoil required "a true statesman," that is, a gentleman, whose moderation and capacity for tolerance enabled him to restore peace and stability to the realm.[32] The rude and reckless "ruffians" who ruled the streets in the late 1860s and early 1870s had no such powers of self-restraint; they existed, again to invoke Elias's term, beyond the "shame-threshold," impervious to the "civilizing process."

Thus, for all of his dismay over the misrepresentations of the gentleman in *bakumatsu* society, whether in the guise of a quaint impracticality or a deceptive ingratiation that merely incubated the seeds of primitivism and brutality, Fukuzawa remained steadfastly committed to the conservative social ideal of leadership by men of broad learning and cultivated élan. Fukuzawa understood the exercise of raw ambition and self-reliance as the essence of masculine identity, but he also believed that the gentility of essence should not stand alone untempered by the external norms of proper etiquette and demeanor. In other words, the drive for material success converged with a cultivated sense of virtue, as Barbara Sato also notes in this volume, paving the way for a Meiji gentleman who would be both ambitious and decorous—indeed, had Fukuzawa had his way, more of the latter than the former. For the true gentleman, as Fukuzawa conceived him, would resist the surge of an uncontrollable, ill-mannered idealism associated with political extremists, primarily on the loyalist side but also among such diehard defenders of the bakufu as the Shōgitai and Byakkotai. More than ever before in Japanese history, Fukuzawa believed that young male elites must pay careful heed to a gentility of form that would establish once again the basis for a stable social and political order. And who would be the standard bearer for this reconstructed gentility? A corps of moderate educators and students known as "gentlemen of civilization" (*bunmei no kunshi*), an intriguing choice of words that captures both the forward-looking and backward-preserving thrust of Fukuzawa's pedagogy.[33] *Kunshi* was the accepted designation for the Confucian gentleman, and Fukuzawa's allegiance to such nomenclature, already bearing a hint of anachronism in the late 1860s and early 1870s, revealed the depth of his disenchantment with primitivism and the behavioral excesses of free-wheeling and decidedly uncultivated young men. Against the tide of disorder and violent impulse perpetuated by *shishi* activists and their self-anointed successors, Fukuzawa's gentleman, standing squarely in the rationalist Confucian tradition of a Sorai or Hoashi Banri, exemplified reason, deliberative judgment, respectability, and, of course, good manners at all times. Fukuzawa's relentless attacks on false gentility sprang, therefore, from a determination to clear the stage of what he regarded as misrepresentational historical baggage so that a true gentleman could reclaim his honored place and thereby continue a revered conservative tradition of the enlightenment of "fools" (*gujin*) from above.[34]

But Fukuzawa's masculine ideal did not merely mimic his historical prototype. He also assumed the mantle of an intellectual and social pioneer, a progenitor of a new body of universal learning and social mores that defined the highest stage of human existence, or what Fukuzawa and other enlightenment intellectuals called "civilization." Since by the middle of the nineteenth century, in Fukuzawa's view, the educated elites in western Europe and the United States had most successfully mastered the universal learning and mores of civilization, they would necessarily provide Japanese educators with new instructional models for decorum and scholarship. The understanding and dissemination of a distinctly cosmopolitan body of learning and, more importantly, social mores, and the belief that that body of information could be mastered by men of talent and energy, regardless of class background, distinguished Fukuzawa's "gentleman of civilization" from his historical antecedents in the Edo domain academies.

Ironically, or perhaps quite deliberately, Fukuzawa found much in the European sources for his "gentleman of civilization" that rescued certain components of the Confucian gentility of form at the same time that it reconfigured the gentleman in a way to meet the demands of an emergent nation-state. After all, the architects of the reformed nineteenth-century British public schools, to which Fukuzawa looked for inspiration at the time of the founding of Keiō Academy, had just completed the long and tortuous transformation of the English gentleman into a pedagogical icon, an increasingly middle-class master of a body of learning and social mores, rather than the hereditary scion of wealth or knighthood.[35] Throughout the latter Edo period, educators in both the domain and more importantly the private academies had moved similarly in the direction of the gentleman as a pedagogical invention rather than a birthright or simple manifestation of a particular class background. Led by Fukuzawa, however, early Meiji educators pushed this notion even further, while preserving the fundamental and universal principle of the gentlemanly ideal that "sweetness and light," to borrow Matthew Arnold's phrase, emanates exclusively from above.

The Pedagogical Challenge of Restoring Gentility of Form

As mentioned above, Fukuzawa protested vigorously against the misrepresentation of the gentleman in the Edo period as a mere dandy, a man of surface affectation without moral substance. He extended this argument in the opening years of Meiji by declaring repeatedly that the significance of "civilization" lay in its spiritual essence, not its external forms, and that a "gentleman of civilization," therefore, distinguished himself by his moral bearing rather than his physical trappings. Fukuzawa returned to this line of argument throughout his career whenever he encountered men who called themselves gentlemen but whose visible conduct fell short of an expected standard of moral behavior. The important point here is that even when Fukuzawa fretted over a disjuncture between form and substance, physical attribute and internal essence, he never allowed his vision of the gentleman to linger in a realm of moral subjectivity for very long. As a center for Western studies, the Keiō Academy, Fukuzawa later explained, distinguished itself from the beginning as a refuge for the "upstanding and unsoiled gentleman" (*hōsei seiketsu no kunshi*), whose exemplary deportment was obvious to all observers.[36] Intuition, sensibility, and atmospheric impressions were of little account in this emphatically empiricist and pedagogically centered view. In the wake of the violence and disruptions of the Restoration years, Fukuzawa had no interest in appealing to the idealistic impulses of his students. Expressive idealism, in Fukuzawa's view, invariably degenerated into a cult of heroic nonchalance (*gōki mutonchaku*), a distinctly masculine primitivism that posed a continuing danger to the gentlemanly ideal as he understood it.[37]

The fundamental challenge facing Fukuzawa and other bureaucratic educators of the early 1870s, then, was to thwart the expression of "masculine nonchalance," contain the juvenile urge for primitivism, and restore the gentleman of form through a reinvigorated and self-consciously cosmopolitan pedagogy that emphasized, in the Chester-fieldian tradition, the perfection of practical social graces and interactive social skills. The enlightenment intellectuals by no means ignored internal morality, but they rather optimistically believed that spiritual growth stood outside the realm of pedagogy and that inner morals would improve automatically with the advancement of knowledge and the apprehension of the etiquette and techniques of civilization.

Fukuzawa conducted his campaign for a new masculine gentility of form within two distinct yet overlapping pedagogical arenas: the first devoted to prescriptive literature for a wide audience of literate men and women; the second to higher education for the tiny academic elite who attended Keiō Academy. As to prescriptive literature, Fukuzawa argued vigorously for a revision and perpetuation of cultivated standards of dress and demeanor in a flurry of instructional texts that provided concrete tips to a generation of potential aspirants to gentlemanly status. An early example of such tracts, *Seiyō ishokujū* (Western clothing, food and homes, 1867), offered detailed advice to would-be gentlemen on the dos and don'ts of late Victorian dress and social manners; how one should never wear a suit without a collar or a top hat without a long coat (*zentsuruman kōto* to use Fukuzawa's term); how slurping should be avoided in the consumption of tea and soup; and how trousers or suspenders must be unbuttoned prior to elimination. Fukuzawa's cosmopolitan version of the cultivated gentleman would dwell in a world of finger bowls, chamber pots, and port wine (which should never be substituted with whisky or brandy at the dinner table).[38]

The attention Fukuzawa gave to such details suggests that carefully groomed appearances, crucial to the definition of cultivated gentility, assumed primary importance in his vision of the masculine ideal. The point was further underscored in Section 17 of *An Encouragement of Learning*, where Fukuzawa stressed the importance of sociability and likeability among educated young men. "A cheerful and lively countenance is one mark of a man of true virtue; in social intercourse it is most essential. A person's countenance is like the door to his home. To have a wide circle of friends and callers who feel welcome, one must first open one's gate, scrub clean the entrance, and show pleasure in their arrival." Unfortunately, Fukuzawa continued, "people nowadays go to the opposite extreme. They greet others with sour looks, in imitation of the pseudo gentleman, and are like people who put skeletons before their entrances and coffins before their gates. Who would want to call on them?"[39] Along with refashioning one's personal appearance (*yōbō*), Fukuzawa urged his young readers to perfect "the art of public speaking." Verbal fluency and eloquence, especially in organized public debate and oratory, assumed crucial importance in perfecting the skills of social interaction that underlay Fukuzawa's vision of the gentleman.

Throughout his prescriptive tracts that gave shape to the new gentility of form Fukuzawa repeatedly returned to his favorite themes of respectability and sociability, which he viewed as inseparable. Respectable dress and social demeanor invariably led to high levels of human association. When a man swaggered about in sloppy attire, thinking nothing about whether the space between his knees and hips was properly covered, or when he communicated with an ungentlemanly shout or belch, he in effect imprisoned himself in a truncated social space impenetrable to all but the crude and lowly. For this reason, Fukuzawa encouraged would-be gentlemen to join voluntary associations or social clubs in order to develop their "associational skills" (*kōsai jutsu*) with like-minded persons. The prototype for all early Meiji clubs, of which Fukuzawa was himself a prominent member, was the Meirokusha, an organization founded in 1873 so that "gentlemen of like mind" (*dōkō no shi*) might gather twice a month in the stylish rooms of Japan's most famous restaurant of Western cuisine, the Seiyōken.[40] There, the impeccably attired membership partook of an elegant lunch between a morning business meeting and afternoon lectures and discussions of political and social issues, many of which were subsequently published in the organization's journal, *Meiroku zasshi*. Other men's clubs, more social in their orientation, included the Kōjunsha, which Fukuzawa, along with Keiō faculty and alumni, founded in 1879–1880 as a sanctuary for "the opening of acquaintance among gentlemen" (*kunshi no majiwari o hiraki*) and the enhancement of "harmonious interchange."[41]

Although the social and academic clubs of the early Meiji period catered almost exclusively to cultivated men, Fukuzawa, like Mori Arinori, believed that the gentleman must ultimately extend the boundaries of sociability and respectability to encompass like-minded women. Fukuzawa fully accepted the proposition articulated by Samuel Smiles in *Self-Help* (widely available, as of 1871, in Nakamura Masanao's translation) that among "the many tests by which a gentleman may be known," how a man "conducts himself towards women" warranted special attention.[42] In his prescriptive articles on women and morality, Fukuzawa vociferously criticized the nonchalant behavior of men toward women, particularly in the sphere of the home where husbands routinely lorded over their spouses as if they were enslaved subjects. Such households appeared "more like a shed for animals than a home for human beings."[43] What concerned Fukuzawa about sexual hierarchy was not simply the mistreatment of women, although he palpably empathized with abused wives, but the savagery and total lack of character demonstrated by men who regarded their feminine partners as subjects. In other words, Fukuzawa saw an inviolate link between a marital relationship on the one hand and a man's claims to gentlemanly status on the other. "A righteous man in the outside world," he would argue, is necessarily a "good husband in the home."[44] And a good husband by definition had fully developed "associational skills" (*kosai jutsu*) that endowed his marriage with enlightening conversation and sharing of responsibility. Moreover, Fukuzawa strongly believed that men living by themselves in single-sex communities or as independent rovers could not fully develop their associational skills; that harsh prohibitions against women intermingling with men, except in debased places of assignation, had deleterious effects on male character. The time had come, Fukuzawa explained, to stop thinking of all interchange between men and women as "relations of the flesh." Rather, the advance of civilization heralded a new age when intellectual pursuit would supersede the passions of the body, and when young men and women would, quite naturally, "consult each other on intellectual problems, converse on literature and art, or simply enjoy a conversation or meal together." In order to encourage such lofty interchange, Fukuzawa prodded young gentlemen and ladies in training to take every opportunity to develop their associational skills, learn the etiquette of proper escort, dress, and conversation, and readily avail themselves of any opportunity to attend a garden party or afternoon tea.[45]

In his prescriptive writings during the 1870s and 1880s, Fukuzawa returned repeatedly to the theme of intellectual and spiritual association among educated men and women as the highest representation of a civilized gentility of form. Yet in early Meiji Japan such inspirational association across gender lines remained a utopian dream more than a working reality, and the fault for this sad situation, Fukuzawa noted, rested squarely upon the shoulders of uncultivated men who refused to abandon their instinctive proclivity for arrogant nonchalance.

At a party or at a gathering of relatives, all the men, without regard to age, take the seats of honor, and during the feast, the men do not even try to serve women. They expect women to serve them. They do not escort or help women when they leave, but they take it for granted when a woman kindly takes care of their outer garments and other clothing. Are not all these facts proof of the lack of etiquette on the part of men?[46]

To instill etiquette among men required more than a prescriptive manual on how to dress and escort a lady down the street. Rather, an aspiring gentleman could only achieve his goal with the help of a higher education that emphasized breeding as much as aptitude. For all of Fukuzawa's tributes to universal learning and achievement, he remained convinced that the attributes of a gentleman stemmed more from cultivation than natural selection. "It may be said that speech habits and appearance are inborn . . . ," Fukuzawa wrote in *An Encouragement of Learning,* "this may be true, but it turns out to be incorrect when we consider the principle of human intelligence and its development."[47] The perfection of speech and demeanor, Fukuzawa believed, required continual vigilance and training over an extended period of time; and the reconstructed school for higher learning provided the ideal setting for this important task. Thus Fukuzawa's private school, reopened as Keiō Academy in April of 1868, emerged as an experimental laboratory in the cultivation of the early Meiji gentleman.

In his inaugural address on the occasion of the reopening of his reconstructed academy, Fukuzawa conceived of Keiō as both a functional counterpart to the British public schools and a preserver of at least some of the genteel pedagogical traditions associated with the old bakufu academy, the Shōheikō. "We hope that like-minded gentlemen, lugging their books with them, will gather here from afar; that they will nourish their ability, increase their knowledge, relentlessly maintain correct deportment and manners and value friendship in all human relations."[48] In consecrating his school to "correct deportment and manners," Fukuzawa put the Keiō Academy in dialectical opposition to what he called a "revolutionary world" (*kakumei no yo*) marked by alarming uprisings within every sector of society. "In these dire circumstances," he explained in a second inaugural speech in July of 1868, "the gentlemen of our independent corporation will never change our objectives. We will preserve old things [*kyūbutsu*]; we will read the books we admire; we will pursue an honorable path; and we will study here day and night without altering our everyday routines."[49] Accordingly, as the Battle of Ueno raged within earshot of the campus, it was all business as usual at Keiō because there was "no connection between us and the scene of action."[50] Whereas the blood-spilling Restoration struggles attracted the unkempt, ill-mannered, and untrustworthy roughneck, Fukuzawa's academy remained a safe haven for the "upstanding and unsoiled gentleman."

Such a gentleman would not grace the campus of Keiō Academy, however, without considerable pedagogical intervention by Fukuzawa and his staff. Between 1868 and 1872, Fukuzawa launched an offensive against "rough and unmannerly" (*sobō murei*) behavior among his students with a veritable avalanche of injunctions against the very hallmarks of "masculine nonchalance": sword bearing, bellowing voices, swaggering postures, crude attire, and, above all, casual practices of elimination and sexual gratification. As Fukuzawa explained: "This academy is not simply a place for the reading of books; it is a place for establishing good standards of behavior. We intend therefore to abolish anything that smacks of vulgarity." He then went on to say this: "We shall, without fail, attend to all of the details of living, including table manners, the methods for urination and defecation, the arrangement of geta and umbrellas, and the handling of bedding and clothing."[51] In a similar vein, Fukuzawa attacked the roughneck fetish for sword bearing, which he courageously belittled as "a measurement of buffoonery," an utterly ludicrous custom in a "civilized and open country," and a threat to the new gentility of form that demanded respectability, cleanliness, and a well-kempt, nonthreatening demeanor. Inseparable from his disdain for the sword was Fukuzawa's revulsion for physical combat and vendettas (*katakiuchi*). In contrast to the death-defying *shishi* ideal, Fukuzawa stood out as a man who cared about living a good life and took every reasonable precaution to avoid unnecessary risk.[52]

Just how far Fukuzawa was willing to push his vision of the gentleman is suggested by his establishment, in 1872, of a special "office of clothing and tailoring" on the Keiō campus and his inauguration of a weekly Saturday clean-up day so that "not one speck of dust" would linger in any room on campus.[53] Fukuzawa's most exacting standards for cleanliness and good form were reserved for the school's lavatories, where "the methods for urination and defecation" deserved the "careful scrutiny" of every student. The goal here was to remove the most elemental of human functions from the primitive realm of masculine insouciance and transform it into a signifying emblem of civilization and enlightenment. The apparently immaculate state of the toilets at Keiō in the early 1870s, and the grace with which the students used them, remained a source of enormous pride for Fukuzawa, who invariably guided prominent visitors to the lavatories as a highlight of any campus tour. Indeed, before constructing public toilets at Shinbashi station, railway officials paid heed to the lavatories at Keiō, even though they had little hope of approaching the exemplary standards of Fukuzawa's students.[54]

Fukuzawa's obsession for cleanliness was more than just a campaign against particles of dust under a desk or a smear of waste on a toilet. Like Mori Ōgai, whose views are discussed by Mark Driscoll in this volume, Fukuzawa regarded sexuality as an untamed and potentially destructive reserve of masculine energy; yet he was far less forgiving than Ōgai and would countenance no display of overt sexuality within the campus confines. Although Fukuzawa may never have explicitly denounced masturbation, he emphatically insisted that upright morals govern both public and private conduct. Bodily injury through indulgence in "filth" (*fuketsu*), he warned, would surely arise in solitary pursuits as well as social intercourse.[55] More explicit were the injunctions against obscene graffiti, crude language, and displays of partial nudity. Intent on strict enforcement of such regulations, Fukuzawa routinely inspected the dormitory in search of any off-color scribble on a lamp shade or desk or lavatory wall. And woe onto the offender, who might find himself publicly chastised or, worse, booted out of the school.[56] Fukuzawa's in-loco-parentis policy extended beyond the campus as well. The headmaster grudgingly accepted prostitution as a necessary outlet, but he left little doubt as to his own expectation that a truly cultivated gentleman, like himself, would never frequent a brothel. So when errant Keiō students dared to spend the night in Shinagawa, Fukuzawa attempted to embarrass them publicly by setting out on horseback early in the morning in order to intercept the miscreants on their weary trek back to the campus.[57]

The strict standards of decorum that Fukuzawa imposed upon the campus community underscored the gap between respectable society within Keiō and the turbulence and debauchery that reigned outside. Any number of regulations at the school, regarding the closing of school gates and the prohibitions against casual entry onto the campus, seemed designed to keep the students away from the outside world. But Fukuzawa never conceived of the institution as a monastery, and beginning with his inaugural pronouncements of 1868, he continually stressed the public (*oyake*) rather than the private (*watakushi*) mission of the institution.[58] For Fukuzawa fully expected that the Keiō graduate, as a "gentleman of civilization" building upon the noblesse oblige of his Edo predecessor, would devote his adult life to public service broadly defined to include, along with government, journalism, education, and even business. Fukuzawa also expected his graduates to help articulate the crucial social issues that faced the nation and to become responsible molders of public opinion. But he also believed that arduous training and practice must precede the assumption of any role as public spokesman; and here we see a possible precedent for the linkage between women's learning (*jogaku*) and women's rights (*joken*) discussed in Barbara Molony's essay. Thus Fukuzawa organized a variety of debating societies and even, in the spring of 1880, a mock parliament so that students could hone their speaking skills in anticipation of their imminent forays into the outside world. In deference to the gentility of form, Fukuzawa invariably encouraged the perfection of style over the examination of content. According to one school chronicle, the organizers of the debate program at Keiō had no intention of swaying public opinion but rather concentrated on the techniques of speaking.[59] Student members of an early debating society called Kyōgisha also prided themselves on their "high collar" (*haikara*) dress and manners.[60]

Fukuzawa was certainly not the only educator or social critic to campaign for a new gentility of form during the early Meiji period, nor was Keiō the only training ground for the reconstructed masculine ideal.

Nakamura Masanao at Dōjinsha and Niijima Jō at Dōshisha shared many of Fukuzawa's views of etiquette and respectability, along with his disdain for the swaggering ethos of the untamed ruffians who settled their disputes with a sword or fist rather than rational debate. Nakamura in particular proclaimed that "the realization of gentlemen" (*kunshi no jōju*) remained the highest priority in his academy; and he harnessed regulations similar to those imposed at Keiō in the pursuit of that goal.[61] Moreover, in his rendition of Samuel Smiles's *Self-Help*, Nakamura gave special attention to discussions of the Victorian gentleman, whom he recast as "*shinsei no kunshi*," a true gentleman marked by his attention to exterior manners (*gaibō no reigi*). This ideal was a close approximation, as Earl Kinmonth suggests, to the cultivated ideal that shaped the translator's pedagogy from his days on the faculty of the Shōheikō Academy. The complexities of Nakamura's language, which made little concession to vernacular expression, further obfuscated any hints of the gentility of essence that Smiles may have intended and thereby insured an audience restricted to the highly literate.[62] More emphatic ideological support for the gentility of form emanated from a translated rendition of the archetypal text from the English archives of polite learning: Chesterfield's *Letters to His Son*. Translated by Nagamine Hideki and published consecutively in 1875 and 1878 under the title *Chishi kakun* (Mr. Chesterfield's house rules), the Japanese version of the text emphasized precisely those selections from Chesterfield's original that reinforced Fukuzawa's admonitions against masculine nonchalance, crude language, and vulgar appearance. Nagamine, for example, repeatedly turns to the Chesterfieldian homilies that virtue (*tokugi*) and intelligence (*saichi*) mean nothing without proper bearing (*giyō*) and dress; that one judges a gentleman by the company he keeps and the ability to ingratiate that company with punctilious attention to the social graces. Straying from the letter but not the spirit of Chesterfield's text, the Nagamine rendition, in a seamless blend of Confucian and Augustan traditions, warns its readers to refrain from spitting when drinking tea and to adjust their manner of speaking in accordance with the status of their listener as either a "little person"(*shōjin*) or "gentleman" (*kunshi*).[63]

Of course, beyond the pedagogical tracts of a Fukuzawa, or the translated works of Samuel Smiles and Lord Chesterfield, the new gentility of form drew obvious support from government leaders, at both the national and prefectural levels, who supported the ban on sword bearing, pushed for new dress codes, and enacted prohibitions against public nudity and careless practices of elimination on urban streets. An important distinction must be made here, however, between the new standards of *civic gentility*, which now applied to all classes, and *exemplary gentility* expected of high government officials and their trainees at elite institutions of higher learning like Keiō. It was civic gentility that applied to the class-breaking standards for recruitment and deportment that Theodore Cook discusses in his essay; and, in theory at least, Fukuzawa, as Cook notes in his essay, argued for a universal army that would draw upon a broad social spectrum. But Fukuzawa did draw clear lines between the realms of civic and exemplary gentility; he spoke out vigorously for the granting of conscription exemptions to distinguished students at the nation's private institutions for higher learning.[64] An exemplary gentleman, as he suggested in *An Encouragement of Learning,* did not need a policeman with a club telling him where and where not to go to the bathroom. Such threats applied to "lowly folk" (*genin*) who, as of 1871 and with very few exceptions, were also denied entrance to the Keiō campus.[65] Moreover, the exemplary gentleman stood on a pedestal above and beyond the disorders and vulgarities that afflicted early Meiji society. Recall an impeccably attired Fukuzawa conducting business as normal at Keiō while the canon exploded in the Battle of Ueno. Or consider the case of Fukuzawa's former colleague in the translation bureau of the bakufu, Fukuchi Gen'ichirō, whose legendary quest for sartorial perfection extended to his underwear that were, as James Huffman tells us, so elegant that a Parisian servant mistook them for dining napkins.[66] Kobayashi Kiyochika's famous 1885 portrait of Fukuchi reporting on the Satsuma Rebellion perhaps did as much as any written source in projecting the image of the new Meiji gentleman as an unsullied paragon of elegance and form in a disordered world. In the foreground stands a bespectacled Fukuchi, resplendent from head to toe in exquisitely tailored haberdashery, squeezing a walking stick under his arm, calmly taking notes while infantrymen fight it out in the background under clouds of billowing smoke.

Conclusion: The Contested Fate of the Early Meiji Gentleman

Fukuzawa Yukichi's vision of the Meiji gentleman clearly broke new ground at the same time that it preserved and indeed rejuvenated a longstanding pedagogical tradition of cultivation and proper form. In emphasizing the qualities of oratorical eloquence, cheerful sociability across gender lines, and self-reliance in a world of competitive individuals, Fukuzawa, Nakamura, and other enlightenment pedagogues charted a new course in the historical construction of the educated man in modern Japan. Wittingly or not, under the theoretical rubric of associations between men and women, the enlightenment liberals opened a new sexual dialogue that problematized and therefore underscored the constructability of both manhood and womanhood. Simultaneously, Fukuzawa's "gentleman of civilization" was clearly conceived in the Confucian tradition of noblesse oblige, cultivated breeding, and enlightened guidance from afar, a tradition that dovetailed quite conveniently with Whiggish—most especially Burkean—strains of European conservatism. For Fukuzawa, as with Edmund Burke, the reconfigured gentleman provided the ideal model to counteract the strains of revolutionary idealism, restore social order, and launch an incremental crusade for the progressive development of the individual and the state.

Yet whether the gentleman adopted the guise of moderate social reformer or conservator of past values, he appeared in the eyes of Fukuzawa's detractors, at both ends of the political spectrum, as a man of form rather than substance. Despite Fukuzawa's denunciations of "false gentlemen," his pedagogical reforms at Keiō gave clear priority to externals: how one spoke rather than what one happened to say; how one appeared on the surface rather than what mysterious feelings lay hidden beneath the skin. The enemies, after all, what Fukuzawa called the "bloodthirsty young warriors," those idealistic heirs to the *bakumatsu shishi*, were men of unadulterated essence; men who shouted when they felt like shouting, brawled when they felt like brawling, relieved themselves when they felt like relieving themselves. They had little sense of self-restraint and no desire to appear any differently from how they felt. In waging a relentless campaign against this man of essence, Fukuzawa pushed his "gentleman of civilization" perilously close to a realm of artifice inhabited by dilettantes, dandies, or men who were so preoccupied with their style of dress, their modes of discourse, their ability to vacate a lavatory without leaving a telltale odor that they robbed themselves of any sense of internal integrity.

Not surprising then that Fukuzawa's "gentleman of civilization" became the object of ridicule and attack almost as soon as he made his entrance on the historical stage. In *Aguranabe* (1871), Kanagaki Robun makes a mockery out of the new gentility of form by presenting a perfumed clotheshorse who justifies his predilection for beef stew by invoking the views of Fukuzawa.[67] A more wicked depiction of Keiō's headmaster appeared on the pages of the notoriously derisive *Marumaru chinbun,* whose cartoonists, in 1877, reconfigured Fukuzawa as a groveling frog ready to leap in any direction according to the fashions of the day.[68] During the course of the 1870s and especially the 1880s, unflattering characterizations of the civilized gentleman as a scheming imposter assumed the form of a stock feature of Meiji literature. Who can forget, from *Ukigumo,* Futabatei Shimei's piercing depiction of Honda Noboru with his Turkish fez, walking cane, and smartly tailored appearance? For Noboru the acquisition of gentility is an act of imitating the gestures and speech of that "worthy gentleman" who is his supervisor in a government office. "He copied the gentleman's speech and gestures and even assumed the way he cleared his throat and his manner of sneezing."[69] The cult of flattery and smart, yet calculated, appearance drew howls of protest from "unenlightened" roughnecks like Shōyō's Kiriyama Benroku, from *Tōsei shosei katagi,* who lashed out at the genteel style of his more cultivated school friends. "It's no good the way all of you are carried away by luxuries. Why, back home we used to catch rabbits in the mountains, skin them, boil them, and eat them up. How shameful that guys around Tokyo are so soft . . . I guess they think it's their manly duty to primp themselves up in fluffy gowns." In defiance of the perceived effeminacy of his fellow students, Kiriyama proudly dons a kimono of coarse duck cloth that reeks of dirt and perspiration, refuses to ride in a rickshaw, and uses his fist rather than a knife to sever a watermelon. His language is gruff and direct; and he is horrified at the idea of making the kinds of social concessions that Fukuzawa expected of would-be gentlemen, especially in their associations with young women.[70]

To an extent, the tensions between a cultural primitivism represented by Kiriyama Benroku and a cultivated gentility represented by Honda Noboru reflect a growing gap in the 1880s between a bureaucratic power elite in Tokyo and a disillusioned culture of young men who, as students or journalists, had no direct access to the metropolitan centers of authority. In the political novels of the 1880s, the moderate activists, who work within the developing structure of parliamentary politics, usually adhere to the gentility of form as constructed by enlightenment educators like Fukuzawa, while the radical revolutionaries, men like the loud-mouthed and hard-drinking Takeda in Tetchō's Setchūbai, project the image of an unabashed roughneck.[71] This is not simply a figment of literature. From the atavistic League of the Divine Wind to the popular rights rebels on Mount Kaba, violent insurrectionists expressed their disdain for the Meiji government by invoking the language of a visceral and a wholly uncultivated manliness, or gentility of essence, that often manifested itself in open defiance of "civilized" etiquette and a dismissive attitude toward women. Evidence of the latter enraged Fukuda Hideko as she confronted the boisterous revelry of her fellow conspirators in the Osaka Incident. Still, she preferred men of essence—"heroic men" (*gōketsu*), as she put it—and was certainly no admirer of Fukuzawa's "gentleman of civilization."[72]

Yet cultural primitivism and the cult of manliness that resurfaced, especially in the 1880s, was by no means limited to a handful of violent rebels; nor did the attack on the gentility of form emanate exclusively from outside the institutions of state or the narrow circles of bureaucratic intellectuals. Several of Fukuzawa's colleagues in the Meiroku Society voiced their concern that, in the words of Nishimura Shigeki, writing in 1875, "wise persons in the upper classes, detesting barbarism, . . . establish excessively detailed regulations for the correction of customs and the proprieties, and they punish all manner of things such as baring the legs and urinating in public."[73] Similarly Katō Hiroyuki and Sakatani Shiroshi worried that the new codes of gentlemanly sociability placed too many limits on masculine self-expression.[74] Men should not have to worry about the smoke they exhaled, the liquor they consumed, the noises they emitted simply because they happened to be in the presence of women from their own social class.

Such concerns, although clearly not shared by Fukuzawa, Mori Arinori, or Nakamura Masanao, did, however, reflect the thinking of at least two of the leading oligarchs, notably Saigō Takamori, whose dismay over the gentility of form contributed to his defection from the government, and more significantly Kuroda Kiyotaka. On the surface, Kuroda stood out as a model gentleman of form. No other oligarch looked more dapper in frock coat and top hat or demonstrated such consummate grace on the ballroom floor.[75] But Kuroda was not entirely at home in his guise as the impeccably dressed and mannered bureaucrat, and much preferred the active, physical life of galloping on horseback through the frontiers of Hokkaido or matching his forearm strength with a sumo wrestler.[76] Unlike the carefully manicured Ōkubo Toshimichi or Kido Kōin (Takayoshi), Kuroda clearly saw himself as more a gentleman of essence than of form and as such he felt he had every right to go on a drinking rampage whenever the hearty spirit moved him. On such occasions, Kuroda the impeccably attired and well-mannered gentleman turned quickly into Kuroda a wholly uncivilized and half-crazed bully. In January of 1875, after witnessing one of Kuroda's episodes of getting "raving drunk," Kido complained loudly about his fellow oligarch's egregious behavior.[77] But neither his warnings nor those of other colleagues had any discernible influence. For on the night of March 28, 1878, Kuroda beat his frail, sickly wife to death in a drunken rage.[78] The incident never received a formal investigation and had no apparent effect on Kuroda's continuing prominence as a high official and future prime minister (1888–1889).

Miyake Setsurei once remarked that Kuroda Kiyotaka was certainly no gentleman. But the fact remains that he was often identified as such, at least when he stepped onto the ballroom floor; and Fukuzawa Yukichi retained a remarkably amicable relationship with the sometimes gruff and monstrously abusive oligarch even after the murder of his wife.[79] In part one can explain this seemingly odd pairing as a result of Fukuzawa's selective evaluation that narrowly focused on Kuroda's well-tailored appearance, his impeccable manners when greeting foreign emissaries, and his consistent advocacy of higher education for women.[80] But the issue is not quite that simple. For one suspects that especially after 1880, when the new sobriquet for the gentleman (*shinshi*) assumed the ever more pejorative connotation of an effeminate, spineless fop, and when vociferous critiques of the gentility of form surfaced on campuses around the country, including Keiō, Fukuzawa felt his original vision of cultivated gentility could no longer be sustained. He had never, of course, wanted his "gentleman of civilization" to be mistaken for an irresolute dandy; but that is in effect what happened.

To remedy this situation, Fukuzawa felt increasingly compelled during the 1880s and 1890s to imbue his "gentleman of civilization" with a clearer sense of masculine essence, reflected, for example, in his vigorous advocacy of athletic competition among his students and his increasingly aggressive expressions of nationalism.[81] At the same time, he backed away from an 1888 proposal to open a women's college within Keiō.[82] The maintenance of the university as a male bastion, the flag-waving before and during the Sino-Japanese war, and the continuing friendship with Kuroda provided Fukuzawa with a certain ideological cover as he attempted to keep his detractors off guard and struggled, sometimes courageously and sometimes not, for that elusive mean between cultivated form and uninhibited essence. The "gentleman of civilization," of course, leaned unmistakably toward the former, toward proper decorum and respectability and sociability across gender lines, but he did so without complete renunciation of what Fukuzawa regarded as a potentially dangerous, yet undeniably masculine, disposition for bold resolution, direct expression, and boisterous camaraderie. For all of his caution and occasional inconsistency, Fukuzawa Yukichi broke new ground in the discussion of gender in Meiji Japan. Recalling in his autobiography an incident from the early 1860s, Fukuzawa tells how he and another samurai, upon passing each other on a dark narrow street, suddenly took flight like a pair of "frightened cowards." [83] Few men of his time, certainly not Theodore Roosevelt or Charles Kingsley, would have taken such marvelous delight in a story about running away from a fight.

Notes

I would like to acknowledge that this essay would never have been written without the generous encouragement and continuous support of Barbara Molony and Kathleen Uno.

1. Ishikawa Mikiaki, *Fukuzawa Yukichi den,* vol. 1 (Iwanami shoten, 1932), 626–627; Ishikawa Mikiaki, *Fukuzawa Yukichi den,* vol. 4 (Iwanami shoten, 1932), 165; Fukuzawa Yukichi, *Fukuzawa Yukichi zenshū,* vol. 20 (Iwanami shoten, 1958–1964), 12; Nagao Masanori, *Fukuzawa Yukichi no kenkyū* (Kyoto: Shibunkaku shuppan, 1988), 185. For related phrases, see Fukuzawa Yukichi, *Fukuzawa Yukichi zenshū,* vol. 15 (Iwanami shoten, 1958–1964), 533.

When Fukuzawa spoke of "the gentleman," especially within pedagogical settings, he used the venerable Chinese compound *kunshi,* a designation for the educated man that was deeply rooted in the Confucian classics. (The Chinese rendering of *kunshi* is *junzi.*) Despite the archaic resonance of the term, especially in an iconoclastic age of "civilization and enlightenment," Fukuzawa invoked the ideal of the gentleman as *kunshi* in order to express continuity with Edo scholastic traditions. Other early Meiji educators, including Nakamura Masanao and Kinoshita Hiroji, shared a similar terminological preference for the gentleman as *kunshi.* But the term held less attraction for social critics and journalists, who, especially after 1885, gave currency to another term to identify the gentleman, notably *shinshi.* Far from a lofty pedagogical construct, *shinshi* evoked more pejorative connotations of a smooth operating dandy or a well-tailored but decidedly self-interested politician. See, for example, Carol Gluck's discussion of the "gentlemen of the Diet" (*gikai no shinshi*) and John Pierson's discussion of Tokutomi Sohō's "country gentleman" (*inaka shinshi*) in Carol Gluck, *Japan's Modern Myths* (Princeton, NJ: Princeton University Press, 1985), 67–71; and John Pierson, *Tokutomi Sohō* (Princeton, NJ: Princeton University Press, 1980), 191–192, 207–208. Still, the gentleman as *shinshi* never took hold as a pedagogical construct in the education of the nation's elite: During his later life, Fukuzawa invariably used the term derisively, often in reference to shady businessmen, and reserved *kunshi* for exemplary scholars and students. (See, for example, "Shinshi no enkai," in Fukuzawa, *Fukuzawa Yukichi zenshū,* vol. 15, 489–491.) Indeed students at the First Higher School, the nation's premier preparatory institution, proudly declared their dormitory an exclusive residence for self-governing *kunshi* long after Fukuzawa's death. See *Kōryōshi,* ed. Dai ichi kōtō gakkō kishukuryō (Dai ichi kōtō gakkō, 1925), 49. Since the completion of this essay in the fall of 1998, the following three English-language works have been published and deserve the reader's attention: Sally A. Hastings, "A Dinner Party Is Not a Revolution: Space, Gender, and Hierarchy in Meiji Japan,"

U.S.-Japan Women's Journal, English Supplement, no. 18 (2000): 107–132; Norio Tamaki, *Yukichi Fukuzawa, 1835–1901: The Spirit of Enterprise in Modern Japan* (New York: Palgrave, 2001); and Jason G. Karlin, "The Gender of Nationalism: Competing Masculinities in Meiji Japan," *Journal of Japanese Studies* 28, no. 1 (2002): 41–77. Karlin's essay is especially relevant, as he juxtaposes the early Meiji gentleman, whom he identifies as an archetype of a cosmopolitan and "feminized masculinity," with the roughneck and decidedly nativist manliness of the young political activists, or *sōshi,* of the late Meiji period. This juxtaposition certainly dovetails with the distinctions between a "gentility of form" and a "gentility of essence," which are discussed in my essay. In general, however, Karlin is much more interested in the emergence of the gentleman as *shinshi,* especially in the 1880s and 1890s, than the gentleman as an idealized pedagogical construct (*kunshi*) within the history of late Tokugawa and early Meiji education. Thus the significance of Karlin's essay extends beyond Fukuzawa, who receives only brief mention, to the broader issue of "how questions of national identity were articulated in the idiom of gender," something which is not addressed within the more limited scope of this essay.

2. Edmund Burke, *Reflections on the Revolution in France,* in *The Writings and Speeches of Edmund Burke,* ed. L.G. Mitchell, vol. 8 (Oxford, UK: Clarendon Press, 1989), 129–130. For more on Burke, see J. G. A. Pocock, *Virtue, Commerce, and History* (Cambridge: Cambridge University Press, 1985), esp. 194–212; and George Watson, "Burke's Conservative Revolution," in *Edmund Burke,* ed. Daniel E. Ritchie (New Brunswick, NJ: Transaction, 1990), 75–88.

3. Joseph Hamburger, *Macaulay and the Whig Tradition* (Chicago, IL: University of Chicago Press, 1976), 184, 261–262. Also Watson, "Burke's Conservative Revolution," 82.

4. Quoted in Edwin Harrison Cady, *The Gentleman in America* (1949; reprint, New York: Greenwood Press, 1969), 9.

5. For this discussion I have been influenced by Cady, *The Gentleman in America,* esp. 52–61. See also *From Max Weber: Essays in Sociology,* eds. H. H. Gerth and C. Wright Mills (New York: Oxford University Press, 1958), 426–427.

6. Norbert Elias, *The Civilizing Process* (Oxford, UK: Blackwell Publishers, 1994), esp. 110–111, 130–131, 492–498.

7. Lawrence Stone, *The Crisis of the Aristocracy* (Oxford, UK: Clarendon Press, 1965), 50–51.

8. Earl of Chesterfield, *Letters to His Son,* vol. 1 (Washington, DC: M. Walter Dunne, 1901), 9–10, 13, 26, 66, 72, 169, and 180–181. For more on Chesterfield, see

Temple Scott, *Lord Chesterfield* (Indianapolis, IN: Arthur Zinkin, 1929), esp. 35–39, and Robin Gilmour, *The Idea of the Gentleman in the Victorian Novel* (London: George Allen, 1981), chapter 1.

9. Samuel Smiles, *Self-Help* (New York: Thomas Y. Crowell, 1884), 408–413.

10. Robert Borgen, *Sugawara no Michizane and the Early Heian Court* (Cambridge, MA: Harvard University Press, 1986), esp. 8, 39–40, 69–71.

11. I have discussed the career of Kinoshita Hiroji in *Schooldays in Imperial Japan* (Berkeley: University of California Press, 1980), esp. 53–64.

12. Nitobe Inazō, *The Works of Nitobe Inazō*, vol. 1 (Tokyo University Press, 1972), 282–285. The discussion of Nitobe draws upon my essay "Toward Remaking Manliness," in *Nitobe Inazō*, ed. John H. Howes (Boulder, CO: Westview, 1995), 133–156.

13. R. P. Dore, *Education in Tokugawa Japan* (Berkeley: University of California Press, 1965), 83.

14. Richard H. Minear, "Ogyū Sorai's *Instructions for Students*: A Translation and Commentary," *Harvard Journal of Asiatic Studies* 36 (1976): 18; see also 9, 38, and 41. The phrase "ceremonial forms" comes from Samuel Yamashita's insightful essay, "Nature and Artifice in the Writings of Ogyū Sorai," in *Confucianism and Tokugawa Culture,* ed. Peter Nosco (Princeton, NJ: Princeton University Press, 1984), esp. 146–147.

15. Quoted in Maruyama Masao, *Studies in the Intellectual History of Tokugawa Japan* (Tokyo University Press, 1974), 246.

16. This phrase comes from Joseph R. Levenson and Franz Schurmann, *China: An Interpretive History* (Berkeley: University of California Press, 1969), 64. See also Roden, *Schooldays in Imperial Japan*, 14–19.

17. Eiko Ikegami, *The Taming of the Samurai* (Cambridge, MA: Harvard University Press, 1995), 276, 268, 320; and Maruyama Masao, "Chūsei to hangyaku," in *Kindai Nihon shisōshi kōza*, ed. Itō Sei et al., vol. 6 (Chikuma shobō, 1960), esp. 387–397.

18. On the building of a "spiritual union," see Hirose Yutaka, *Yoshida Shōin kenkyū* (Shibundō, 1943), esp. 327, 371–374. I discuss other details about Shōin's role as an educator in my dissertation, "Schooldays in Imperial Japan," PhD dissertation, University of Wisconsin, 1975; see also Richard Rubinger, *Private Academies of Tokugawa Japan* (Princeton, NJ: Princeton University Press, 1982), 191–207.

19. Fukuzawa Yukichi, *The Autobiography of Yukichi Fukuzawa*, trans. Eiichi Kiyōka (New York: Columbia University Press, 1966), 59–61; also Rubinger, 131.

20. Harry Harootunian, "Ideology as Conflict," in *Conflict in Modern Japanese History*, eds. Tetsuo Najita and J. Victor Koschmann (Princeton, NJ: Princeton University Press, 1982), esp. 40–41.

21. Marius B. Jansen, *Sakamoto Ryōma and the Meiji Restoration* (Princeton, NJ: Princeton University Press, 1961), 98.

22. Maruyama, "Chūsei to hangyaku," 387.

23. For this composite translation, I have drawn upon Fukuzawa, *An Encouragement of Learning*, trans. David A. Dilworth and Umeyo Hirano (Sophia University Press, 1969), 1–2; and Carmen Blacker, *The Japanese Enlightenment: A Study of the Writings of Fukuzawa Yukichi* (Cambridge: Cambridge University Press, 1964), 51. Blacker's book remains the definitive intellectual biography of Fukuzawa in the English language.

24. The above quotations are all taken from *Fukuzawa Yukichi on Education: Selected Works*, ed. and trans. Eiichi Kiyooka (University of Tokyo Press, 1985), 62, 81, 105–106.

25. Quoted in Hirota Masaki, "Bunmei kaika to josei kaihōron," in *Kindai*, vol. 4, *Nihon joseishi*, ed. Joseishi sōgō kenkyūkai (Daigaku shuppankai, 1982), 9. On the Fundamental Code of Education, see Roden, *Schooldays in Imperial Japan*, 21–22.

26. Kiyooka, *Fukuzawa Yukichi on Education*, 78.

27. *An Outline of a Theory of Civilization*, trans. David A Dilworth and G. Cameron Hurst (Sophia University Press, 1973), 66.

28. The above quotations are taken from Fukuzawa, *An Encouragement of Learning*, 72–74, 95; see also Kiyooka, *The Autobiography of Yukichi Fukuzawa*, 141–142.

29. Albert M. Craig, "Fukuzawa Yukichi: The Philosophical Foundations of Meiji Nationalism," in *Political Development in Modern Japan*, ed. Robert Ward (Princeton, NJ: Princeton University Press, 1968), 103.

30. Kiyooka, *The Autobiography of Yukichi Fukuzawa*, 142, 225.

31. Fukuzawa Yukichi, "Nihon danshiron," in Fukuzawa Yukichi, *Fukuzawa Yukichi zenshū*, vol. 5 (Iwanami shoten, 1958–1964), 624.

32. Sugi Kōji, "The True Statesman," in *Meiroku zasshi: Journal of the Japanese Enlightenment*, trans. William Reynolds Braisted (Cambridge, MA: Harvard University Press, 1976), 131–132.

33. Fukuzawa, *Fukuzawa Yukichi zenshū*, vol. 20, 12; Masanori, *Fukuzawa Yukichi no kenkyū*, 185.

34. Earl Kinmonth convincingly argues this point in "Fukuzawa Reconsidered: *Gakumon no susume* and Its Audience," in *Journal of Asian Studies* 37, no. 4 (1978): 677–696.

35. "It is presumed that Fukuzawa took the English public schools as the model for his Keiō Gijuku," argues Kiyooka in *Fukuzawa Yukichi on Education*, 18. See also *Keiō Gijuku hyakunenshi*, ed. Keiō Gijuku jukushi hensanjo, vol. 1 (Keiō Gijuku, 1958), 245.

36. Ishikawa, *Fukuzawa Yukichi den*, vol. 1, 626–627, and Ishikawa, *Fukuzawa Yukichi den*, vol. 4, 165.

37. See, for example, Fukuzawa, "Hinkōron," in Fukuzawa, *Fukuzawa Yukichi zenshū*, vol. 5, 553.

38. Fukuzawa Yukichi, "Seiyō ishokujū," in Fukuzawa, *Fukuzawa Yukichi zenshū*, vol. 2 (Iwanami shoten, 1958–1964), 187–209, esp. 195; see also Julia Meech-Pekarik, *The World of the Meiji Print* (New York: Weatherhill, 1986), 64–71.

39. Fukuzawa, *An Encouragement of Learning*, 111.

40. See Braisted, *Meiroku zasshi*, xvii–xxiii; and *Meiji keimō shisōshū*, ed. Ōkubo Toshiaki, in *Meiji bungaku zenshū*, vol. 3 (Chikuma shobō, 1967), 406.

41. *Kōjunsha hyakunenshi*, ed. Tomita Masafumi et al. (Kōjunsha, 1983), 15.

42. Smiles, *Self-Help*, 420–421.

43. Fukuzawa, *An Encouragement of Learning*, 53. For an interesting parallel discussion of the issues addressed in this paragraph, see Mikiso Hane, "Fukuzawa Yukichi and Women's Rights," in *Japan in Transition*, ed. Hilary Conroy (Rutherford, NJ: Fairleigh Dickinson University Press, 1984), 96–112.

44. Fukuzawa, "Nihon danshiron," 625.

45. The passages are taken from Fukuzawa's essay "On the Association of Men and Women," which is found in *Fukuzawa Yukichi on Japanese Women*, trans. Eiichi Kiyooka (University of Tokyo Press, 1988), esp. 110–111, 115, and 126.

46. "On Japanese Women, Part Two," in Kiyooka, *Fukuzawa Yukichi on Japanese Women*, 68.

47. Fukuzawa, *An Encouragement of Learning*, 111.

48. Keiō Gijuku jukushi hensanjo, *Keiō Gijuku hyakunenshi*, 258; for an alternative translation, see Kiyooka, *Fukuzawa on Education*, 19.

49. Keiō Gijuku jukushi hensanjo, *Keiō Gijuku hyakunenshi*, 264–265.

50. Kiyooka, *The Autobiography of Yukichi Fukuzawa*, 210.

51. Ishikawa, *Fukuzawa Yukichi den*, vol. 1, 760–761; and Keiō Gijuku jukushi hensanjo, *Keiō Gijuku hyakunenshi*, 351–352.

52. Ishikawa, *Fukuzawa Yukichi den*, vol. 1, 641; Tamaki, *Yukichi Fukuzawa, 1835–1901,* 90. During the tumult of the 1860s and early 1870s, Fukuzawa "lived as discreetly as possible," and even asked his carpenter to construct a trap door in his residence so that he could escape from would-be intruders. See Fukuzawa, *The Autobiography of Yukichi Fukuzawa*, 143, 226.

53. Keiō Gijuku jukushi hensanjo, *Keiō Gijuku hyakunenshi*, 389.

54. Ishikawa, *Fukuzawa Yukichi den*, vol. 1, 758, and Keiō Gijuku jukushi hensanjo, *Keiō Gijuku hyakunenshi*, 352.

55. Keiō Gijuku jukushi hensanjo, *Keiō Gijuku hyakunenshi*, 352.

56. Ishikawa, *Fukuzawa Yukichi den*, vol. 1, 619 and 775; Keiō Gijuku jukushi hensanjo, *Keiō Gijuku hyakunenshi*, 344, 351–352; and Kiyooka, *The Autobiography of Yukichi Fukuzawa*, 212–213.

57. The interception custom is discussed in Iwabuchi Tatsuo, *Inukai Tsuyoshi* (Jiji tsūshinsha, 1958), 19.

58. Keiō Gijuku jukushi hensanjo, *Keiō Gijuku hyakunenshi*, 257; Kiyooka, *Fukuzawa on Education*, 15–16.

59. Keiō Gijuku jukushi hensanjo, *Keiō Gijuku hyakunenshi*, 449.

60. Ibid., 675–681, esp. 679.

61. See Takahashi Masao, *Nakamura Keiu* (Yoshikawa kōbunkan, 1966), 127; see also 122–123.

62. At least this was the case during the 1870s and 1880s. See Earl H. Kinmonth, *The Self-Made Man in Meiji Japanese Thought* (Berkeley: University of California Press, 1981), esp. 34, 42; I have also drawn upon the complete list of chapters, along with subheadings, and partial reproduction of the Nakamura translation, *Saikoku risshihen,* in *Nihon kyōkasho taikei: kindaihen,* ed. Kaigo Tokiomi, vol. 1 (Kōdansha, 1961), esp. 23.

63. Nagamine's rendering of selections from Chesterfield's tract can also be found in Kaigo, *Nihon kyōkasho taikei*, 430–484. See especially 437–440 for above references. My thanks to Itō Yutaka for his suggestion that the character *chi* in the title represents Nagamine's makeshift rendering of Chesterfield's name.

64. In 1880, Fukuzawa criticized the government for granting draft dispensations to young men in public institutions of higher learning, but not to their counterparts at Keiō and other private colleges. Ishikawa Mikiaki, *Fukuzawa Yukichi den*, vol. 2 (Iwanami shoten, 1932), 759–761.

65. Fukuzawa, *An Encouragement of Learning*, 39; and Keiō Gijuku jukushi hensanjo, *Keiō Gijuku hyakunenshi*, 344, 384.

66. James L. Huffman, *Politics of the Meiji Press: The Life of Fukuchi Gen'ichirō* (Honolulu: University of Hawai'i Press, 1980), 79.

67. Kanagaki Robun, *Aguranabe*, in *Meiji shoki bungakushū*, in *Nihon gendai bungaku zenshū*, eds. Itō Sei et al., vol. 1 (Kōdansha, 1969), 6–7; also discussed in Donald Keene, *Dawn to the West* (New York: Henry Holt, 1984), 19–20.

68. *Manga zasshi hakubutsukan*, ed. Shimizu Isao, vol. 1 (Kokusho kankōkai, 1986), 15–16.

69. Marleigh Grayer Ryan, *Japan's First Modern Novel* (New York: Columbia University Press, 1965), 198, 245, and 247.

70. Tsubouchi Shōyō, *Tōsei shosei katagi*, in *Nihon no bungaku*, vol. 1 (Chūō kōronsha, 1971), 74; see also Roden, *Schooldays in Imperial Japan*, 27–28.

71. Suehiro Tetchō, "Setchūbai," in *Nihon kindai bungaku taikei*, ed. Yamada Yūsaku, vol. 2 (Kadokawa shoten, 1974), esp. 355–360, 382–386.

72. Fukuda Hideko, *Warawa no hanseigai* (Iwanami shoten, 1958), 53; Mikiso Hane, *Reflections on the Way to the Gallows* (Berkeley: University of California Press, 1988), 43–44.

73. Nishimura Shigeki, "Government Ethics are Not Separate Paths," in Braisted, *Meiroku zasshi*, 382.

74. Ibid., 376–379, 392–399.

75. Iguro Yatarō, *Kuroda Kiyotaka* (Yoshikawa kōbunkan, 1977), 241–242.

76. Iguro Yatarō, *Tsuiseki Kuroda Kiyotaka fujin no shi* (Sapporo: Chusei Insei, 1986), 22–26. Kuroda's thirst for adventure and his masculine rivalry with the

American advisor Horace Capron is discussed in my article "In Search for the Real Horace Capron," in *Pacific Historical Review* 55 (November 1986): 549–575.

77. *The Diary of Kido Takayoshi*, trans. Sidney Devere Brown, vol. 3 (University of Tokyo Press), 124.

78. Iguro, *Tsuiseki Kuroda Kiyotaka*, esp. 58–62.

79. Iguro, *Tsuiseki Kuroda Kiyotaka*, 68–71; Kiyooka, *The Autobiography of Yukichi Fukuzawa*, 258.

80. On Kuroda's early advocacy of women's education, see Sharon L. Sievers, *Flowers in Salt: The Beginnings of Feminist Consciousness in Meiji Japan* (Stanford, CA: Stanford University Press, 1983), 12.

81. On Fukuzawa's growing insistence in the 1880s that Japan remove itself from Asia, see Kimitada Miwa, "Fukuzawa Yukichi's 'Departure from Asia,'" in *Japan's Modern Century*, ed. Edmund Skrzypczak (Tokyo; Rutland, VT: Sophia University and Charles Tuttle, 1968), 1–26.

82. See Keiko Fujiwara's "Introduction" to Kiyooka, *Fukuzawa Yukichi on Japanese Women*, xiv.

83. Kiyooka, *The Autobiography of Yukichi Fukuzawa*, 235–238.

3 Commodifying and Engendering Morality: Self-Cultivation and the Construction of the "Ideal Woman" in 1920s Mass Women's Magazines

Barbara Sato

Whether it was on a moving train or a crowded bus, among young factory workers or among office girls during their breaks, women's magazines had become highly delectable reading for women in the 1910s. Such publications were devoured and savored to such an extent that by the 1920s they claimed over one million of the total sales of Japanese magazines.[1] The images of women in the articles reflected the complex relationships affecting women's lives and their status both at home and at work. The growth of a modern print culture, which in the early twentieth century included magazines like *Jogaku sekai* (Women's higher school world, 1901) and *Fujin sekai* (Women's world, 1906) that were geared to the tastes of women's higher school students and heavily colored with fiction, formed the underpinning for the new media form to be reckoned with.

One notable characteristic of these women's magazines was the large number of articles on the ways in which women could achieve self-development or selfhood, referred to at the time as *shūyō*, or self-cultivation. In the August 1907 issue of *Fujin sekai*, one young reader wrote: "In my search for personal fulfillment, I succeeded in overcoming what I thought were insurmountable family problems." In the June 1919 issue of *Fujokai* (Woman's sphere, 1910), another reader related: "Working in an elementary school office taught me the joy of life and perseverance." A sickly young woman, whose letter was published in the February 1920 issue of *Fujokai*, wrote: "The special issue on *shūyō* [October 1920] detailing the countless hardships other women endured gave me the will to persevere." Although this reader described herself as "someone without much formal education," she stressed that "reading in general, and more specifically, women's magazines have altered my life." Educators and intellectuals like Hatoyama Haruko and Nitobe Inazō encouraged women in articles with such titles as "Self-Cultivation Suitable for Our Times" and "Women Can Improve Their Characters through Self-Cultivation."[2] During the 1910s and 1920s, the media—particularly with the growth of mass women's magazines—became a vehicle for a popularized version of self-cultivation that fueled the desires and anxieties of middle-class women, and, to a degree, of lower-class women. An analysis of the process by which the self-cultivation discourse emerged in journalism offers an assessment of the impact of the changes in popular morality and clarifies the shifts in gender articulated in the 1920s.

The Tokugawa-period (1603–1868) text, *The Great Learning for Women* (*Onna daigaku*), and the state-constructed "good wife, wise mother" (*ryōsai kenbo*) ideology of the late 1890s supported an ethical system based on "tradition," "civilization," and "state-building," and designed to control the lives of women. In the first three decades of the Meiji period, from the 1860s to the 1890s, when almost all intellectual resources were directed toward the formation of the nation-state, the official morality for women was crafted in intellectual discourses and, after 1872, in women's education as well, especially through classes devoted to morals training (*shūshin*).[3] Yet, in addition to this modern official morality, a popular morality that promoted people's everyday spiritual needs was also developing. By the late 1910s and into the 1920s, popular notions of women's morality emerged, accompanying a surge in circulation of women's magazines. As mass women's magazines became an integral component of media culture—in part because editors introduced a variety of genres that appealed to a wider and more diverse readership—discourses of a more popular morality came to the forefront.[4]

In a 1963 article, literary critic Nakajima Kenzō cogently argued that the Russo-Japanese War (1904–1905) and World War I stand out as major watersheds in prewar Japanese history.[5] This has since become the prevalent view among social historians. In the wake of Japan's victory over Russia, disillusionment ensued. Concerns of state were challenged by a concern for the individual that facilitated a transformation in mentality as well as a reconfiguration of gender roles. Within a year of the Great Earthquake of 1923, a rising consumerism, referred to as *modanizumu* (modernism), was visible. Among other things, this 1920s consumerism represented a desire for private fulfillment, particularly for the middle-class urban woman whose space existed mainly within the context of the home.[6]

Self-cultivation, achieved in part through reading, represented the ideal for a middle-class persona. In addition, some working-class women, like the factory worker who waited excitedly for her monthly issue of *Fujokai*, were fixing their gaze on the next rung of the social and cultural ladder.[7] For these women, reality meant coping with a "divided sense of self," to borrow from Stuart Ewen.[8] Ewen's study of lower middle-class consumerism in England from 1870 to 1914 suggests that one factor that held the lower middle class together was "their desire to ape the gentility of their superiors."[9] In Japan, self-cultivation also promised upward mobility and individual success. A popularized form of self-cultivation symbolized the preoccupation that women (and also men) of different backgrounds and classes shared for a lifestyle characterized by personal desire and ambition.

Most readers of mass women's magazines identified with the middle class (*chūryū kaikyū*) in 1920s Japan. In the eyes of many intellectuals at the time, middle-class identity was based less on income and family status and was related more to educational background. Graduation from a four-year women's higher school or normal school, also considered a higher school, earned a young woman middle-class status. (Because prewar educational policies prohibited girls from admission to middle schools after completing elementary school, girls' higher schools enjoyed prestige among young women eager to further their education.) As more mass women's magazines discussed topics like employment options, training required for jobs, and monthly salaries, the prospects for employment and advancement assumed increasing relevancy for young women. These topics were all related to the new *shūyō* discourse emerging in journalism, and the increasing importance of this discourse parallels the changes in popular morality and gender in the 1920s.

From *Risshin shusse* to *Shūyō*: A Male Success Ethic for the Masses

The late political theorist Maruyama Masao, caught up in the spirit of democratization after World War II, interpreted the drastic changes in the early Meiji years as a release from the rigid moral standards governing the Tokugawa era. Maruyama saw the early Meiji era as a time when Japanese people were at last beginning to voice their private wants and needs.[10] However, we should remember that the impact of any cultural or political transformation is uneven and far more gradual than it might appear in hindsight. The restrictions that had guided the lives of the public at large did not disappear overnight. Nevertheless, in the 1870s the enlightenment intellectuals (*meirokusha*) sought to create a set of norms befitting a modern nation. First, they emphasized the need for a secular morality that would meet the demands of a society in flux. Interestingly, their model envisioned freedom and morality as interdependent and intrinsically related. The concern for morality, spirituality, and ethics was not limited to the enlightenment intellectuals. The majority of other intellectuals and the general public shared similar views.

Interest in morality in various forms, including some quite different from those envisioned by the early Meiji secularists, continued to inspire Japanese throughout the pre–World War II era and into the postwar years. Indeed, the idealism Japanese militarists exhibited during the Fifteen-Year War (1931–1945) is common knowledge. Until Japan's defeat in 1945 a large part of the public agenda centered on raising the moral consciousness of the Japanese people. Two weeks after the acceptance of the Potsdam Declaration (July 26, 1945), Prime Minister Higashikuni Naruhiko declared that "one hundred million apologies" (*ichioku sōzange*), penance for losing the war, should be offered to the emperor. Higashikuni admitted that the failure of state policy had precipitated Japan's defeat. But of even greater importance for him was the breakdown in national morality.[11] The barometer for measuring the fate of the nation was thus linked to the level of morality of its citizens even after the Fifteen-Year War had ended.

Individuals' perceptions of morality and spirituality were intertwined with national ethics. This connection between personal success and morality was evident since the early years of Meiji.[12] As social mobility increased and the desire to "rise in the world" (*risshin shusse*) presented a viable option for privileged men, self-cultivation came to be seen as a key to a man's personal success. *Risshin shusse* held out a new ideal of masculinity. Enlightenment intellectual and educator Nakamura Masanao's (1832–1891) adaptation in 1871 of the English writer Samuel Smiles's (1812–1904) book *Self-Help* (*Saikoku risshi-hen*) ranked alongside Fukuzawa Yukichi's (1835–1901) *Encouragement of Learning* (*Gakumon no susume*, 1872) in popularity. *Self-Help* guided men on how to live successfully in a modern society and stressed the importance of contributing to the well-being of that society.[13] The reference to "character ethics" made by Smiles reflected the change of direction in the culture of masculinity of middle-class British young men, a change motivated by ideals based on personal achievement. Historian Earl Kinmonth, who referred to *Self-Help* as the "holy book," commented:

In character ethics, accomplishment and advancement were the products primarily of individual virtues of character: hard work, diligence, frugality, perseverance, attention to detail, and so forth. Developing these virtues was a task for the individual himself, and they and his performance were depicted as the sole factors determining achievement and advancement.[14]

For enterprising young men, a superior standard of personal morality became a requisite for getting ahead. Their determination did not spring from religious and spiritual obligations, but rather from a commitment to a secular morality that revered success in everyday life. Seen from this dimension, personal achievement was not contradictory to the welfare of the state. It was integrally connected to it.

From the early twentieth century, the concept of self-cultivation found expression not only in *shūyō*, but also in the word *kyōyō*. In the vernacular, the terms took on markedly dissimilar nuances. *Shūyō* is rarely used today. When it is, it is associated with practical, pedestrian values like "perseverance" (*nintai*) and "stick-to-it-iveness" (*ganbaru*). *Kyōyō*, on the other hand, lacks the practicality of *shūyō*. Although *kyōyō* is occasionally used somewhat cynically in reference to a knowledgeable but spiritually empty person, as in the expression *kyōyōshugi na ningen*, most often *kyōyō* connotes the positive features identified with sophistication and intellectual accomplishments found in phrases like "the well-educated person" (*kyōyō ga takai*) or someone "overflowing with knowledge" (*kyōyō ga afurete iru*).

Until the late Meiji period, references made to *shūyō* and *kyōyō* link *shūyō* with the growth of a strong sense of national consciousness. The term *kyōyō*, however, gained substance with Taishō-period (1912–1926) intellectualism and individualism.[15] In explaining the similarities and differences of these terms, some scholars have argued that originally *shūyō* and *kyōyō* served a dual purpose that underscored the significance of character building (*jinkaku kōjō*). A distinction between the two terms emerged in the 1920s when *shūyō* and *kyōyō* came to fulfill different needs. At that time, *shūyō* satisfied the ideal for self-cultivation prevalent among middle-class people, while *kyōyō* was associated with the ethical principles that regulated the ideals of a particular group of elite male higher school (*kyūsei kōkō*) students (equivalent to first and second year university students).[16] The separation of the terms in the 1920s, however, does not necessarily reflect a complete break or disconnectedness in the two concepts.

In short, the *shūyō* and *kyōyō* terminology that would become encoded with new class and gender ideals developed alongside the Meiji period's *risshin shusse* notion of popular morality. Although disparities between *shūyō* and *kyōyō* have been debated from the point of view of the words' uses and class implications, gender-based differences and, more importantly, the interconnection with *risshin shusse* have remained unexplored.[17] Most women in the Taishō era were not counted among the social elite, and academically rigorous higher schools were limited to men.[18] However, state pressure and moral and, to some degree, economic considerations convinced an increasing number of parents that formal education was an advantageous part of their middle-class daughter's upbringing. The aspirations embraced by women thus became conceptualized in the practical aspects of the *shūyō* discourse that took on a new power of expression in magazines like Masuda Giichi's *Fujin sekai*, Tsugaya Masashi's *Fujokai*, and Ishikawa Takeyoshi (Takemi's) *Shufu no tomo* (Housewife's companion, 1917). In considering the relationship of middle-class women to self-cultivation, one of the first questions to be raised is why women ardently embraced *shūyō* when it was symbiotically linked to the notion of a Meiji-period *risshin shusse* male ethic. What kinds of gratification did these women envision for themselves, and what role did *shūyō* play in fulfilling their expectations?

In a state with carefully delineated gender roles, men were prodded to climb the social ladder to success. Most women fell outside this "success" paradigm: they did not envision climbing to social fame and monetary success as an option either for themselves or their female companions. Be that as it may, this articulated gender difference did not dampen women's devotion to *shūyō*. Rather, it supports the contention that acquiring further education and gaining new expertise made women better equipped to deal with everyday life even if they did not use their skills in the workplace.[19] Indeed, women's yearning for self-cultivation was rooted in common dreams about who they could become—hopes that beckoned just as strongly as those of their male counterparts. The late literary critic Maeda Ai was one of the first to recognize the appeal *shūyō* held for women in Japan during the 1910s and 1920s. Maeda labeled it the "love child" (*shiseiji*) of *risshin shusse*. However, Maeda did not distinguish between *risshin shusse*, *shūyō*, and *kyōyō*.[20] An examination of the *shūyō* discourse, particularly the discursive prose found in mass women's magazines and books that promoted self-cultivation, opens the way for a re-evaluation of the relationship that existed between these concepts from the Meiji period. *Risshin shusse* encompasses the public values of status, personal dedication to state, society, or social groups (i.e., family, workplace, or regional ties); *kyōyō* implies a male-centered erudition; and self-cultivation for women is a variant aspect of *shūyō* that emerged in full force in the 1920s, and sought a new habitus that afforded women spiritual guidance in their private lives.

The Emergence of a *Shūyō* Discourse for Men in Popular Magazines

Although Fukuzawa Yukichi's and Samuel Smiles's books often enjoyed the acclaim of a privileged group of readers, it was not until after the Sino-Japanese War (1894–1895), with the increase in magazine publishing, that a reading public of considerable proportion took root in Japan.[21] Two publishing companies, Jitsugyō no Nihonsha (1897) and Kōdansha (1911), paved the way for the circulation of popular books and magazines that would reach mass proportions.[22] Both companies saw *shūyō* as a vital concept for augmenting sales. Nevertheless, it was the high quality, general interest magazine *Taiyō* (The sun), put out in 1895 by rival firm Hakubunkan (1887), that boasted over 100,000 in circulation after marketing its first issue.[23] *Taiyō*'s critiques of current events and developments in the business world, its analyses of political affairs, its family column, and its coverage of the arts all contributed to its staggering circulation figures. How, then, did *Jitsugyō no Nihon* (Business Japan), which started publication two years later, and which was unable to match Hakubunkan's circulation for several years, finally surpass Hakubunkan's sales by the end of the Meiji period?[24]

Despite its inferior editorial know-how and smaller capital base, the answer lies in Jitsugyō no Nihonsha's aptitude for reaching a more general audience—the new social class of less-educated male readers. The magazine instilled in its readers the vision of a powerful connection between social success and self-cultivation that could be realized from reading. Articles like "The Basis for Character Building" ("Jinkaku shūyō no kiso"; in *Jitsugyō no Nihon*, March 1907) and "How to Put Forth One's Best Effort in Life" ("Ikanishite yo o wataru bekika"; in *Jitsugyō no Nihon*, July 1908) fostered a sense of pride of self in its male readers and helped make the transition to achievement possible. Indeed, Jitsugyō no Nihonsha's triumph rested in appealing to those men who felt left behind in the Meiji-period *risshin shusse* rhetoric on advancing in the world—men eager not to be relegated to the margins of "modern" social achievement.

In 1911, Jitsugyō no Nihonsha published *Shūyō* (Self-cultivation) by renowned Tokyo University professor Nitobe Inazō. The book was an overnight success and went through more than one hundred printings. Nitobe thereafter contributed articles to every issue of *Jitsugyō no Nihon*. His book elaborated on the numerous letters he had received from devoted readers. A grocery store clerk, a young medical student, a restaurant owner, a trading firm manager whose greatest wish was to transfer to a more prestigious company, and students who failed the entrance exams for middle school, all solicited his help and laid bare their individual problems. The common thread in their letters was the appeal for advice to help them redefine their options. The unusualness of a university professor contributing regularly to a popular magazine of *Jitsugyō no Nihon*'s caliber prompted Nitobe to write "Why I Became an Edito-

rial Advisor" ("Yo wa naze Jitsugyō no Nihonsha no henshū komon
to naritaruka") for the January 1909 issue. Nitobe asserted that a moral
responsibility kept him from abandoning the magazine's readers who
were at differing stages in their quest to climb the ladder of success. Indeed, Nitobe implied that the decisions that his readers had to resolve
were decisions that shaped the lives of most people. Nitobe's academic
background did not deter him from presenting a pessimistic view of
higher education. He chose to locate success within the context of self-
cultivation, which he believed presented an optimistic approach for
fulfillment.

On the first page of every issue of *Jitsugyō no Nihon,* editor and publisher Masuda Giichi (1869–1949) made a personal attempt to reach his
audience through a column devoted to *shūyō.* The column focused on
the theme of the secret of success in life for young men. It convinced
readers that men in their position could indeed cope with life's frustra-
tions and tensions, and that a viable way did exist out of their morass.
The column enjoyed such popularity that in 1912 it appeared in book
form as *Young Men and Self-Cultivation (Seinen to shūyō),* complete with
sections on "How to Build One's Self-Restraint" ("Kōkishin wa ikanishite shūyō subekika") and "How to Strengthen Your Will" ("Ishi wa
ikanshite kyōko ni subekika"). In 1943, even though publishers were
hampered by the paper shortage caused by the war, the book underwent its 124th and final printing.[25] Masuda, who had featured in *Jitsugyō
no Nihon* advertisements such as "The Smiles of Japan," continued his
appeal for self-cultivation in other books. "How to Get Ahead" ("Gun
o nuku michi"), "Guidance for Young Men on Rising in Society"
("Seinen shusse kun"), and "The Basis for Self-Advancement" ("Risshin no kiso") are a few examples. Masuda invariably sprinkled words
like "perseverance" (*nintai*), "effort" (*dōryoku*), "positiveness" (*sekkyo-
kusei*), and "sincerity" (*seijitsu*) throughout his writings, underscoring his
determination to adopt those ideals that stressed high ethical and moral
standards for upward achievements. He relied heavily on success stories
to elucidate his points, but his stories focused on ordinary people, differing from some publicists who preferred to introduce well-known
figures like the entrepreneur Shibusawa Eiichi (1840–1931). Masuda's editorial explains the social need for articles and books on *shūyō* in the following manner:

I am often told that people receiving a higher education and concentrating in specialized areas of study know almost nothing about practical matters. They lack the ability to cope with everyday problems and are short on common sense. Since I have received numerous letters from readers seeking a way to deal with these problems, no doubt there is some truth to their claims. The way I see it is that education today tends to be too academically oriented. Teachers forget to teach students about the art of living and self-cultivation [*shūyō*] in order for them to make a success of their lives. If educated people are plagued by these worries, I can imagine what shop clerks, factory workers, and farmers are enduring.[26]

Indeed, Masuda's genius as an editor entailed using self-cultivation as a way to keep his male readers at the center of a morality that offered an alternate means to social ascent. Although *Taiyō* prided itself on its circulation figures, like other magazines of the period that had preceded it, *Taiyō* catered to a highly select intellectual reading audience.[27] Masuda's invocation of the pitfalls in an unduly academic education and the weight he placed on the merits of self-cultivation implies that the academic level of his readers was far below those of *Taiyō*. *Jitsugyō no Nihon*'s readers indeed perceived "higher education" from a more practical standpoint—a middle-school level. Masuda's cynical evaluation of the "merits" of orthodox learning that left one unqualified to cope with life's practicalities provided solace to young men who only had the equivalent of an elementary or higher elementary school education. In actuality, these young men were in no position, financially or otherwise, to enter middle school. Behind Masuda's words was the implication that young male readers in this category should not be disheartened and were still in a position to idealize "success" (*seikō*) outside the educational network.[28]

Jitsugyō no Nihon, Masuda's brainchild and originally called *Dai Nihon jitsugyō gakkai*, started out by offering mail-order correspondence courses aimed at these aspiring students with no school affiliation. The company magazine invested its energy in publishing middle-school lectures in abridged form, joining several other companies that jumped on that bandwagon in the 1890s.[29] Sociologist Takeuchi Yō has pointed out that mastering the middle-school curriculum on one's own proved an overwhelming task for most young men. In fact, most students abandoned their studies in midstream.[30] Masuda's disappointment with this first endeavor served as the impetus for launching the magazine *Jitsugyō no Nihon.* But Masuda did not abandon his intended audience, focusing on those young men who craved social prominence but lacked "proper" academic credentials.

Part of *Jitsugyō no Nihon*'s appeal lay in its ability to help readers reinterpret their "inadequacies." Masuda preached the benefits of self-cultivation to accomplish this task, while he denounced as useless an education that left one unprepared for the real world. Although *Jitsugyō no Nihon* turned away from the mail-order correspondence business within a year, its initial entry into that area of work, albeit temporary, no doubt influenced Masuda's decision to appeal to readers overlooked by other magazines. By the late nineteenth century, Jitsugyō no Nihonsha had superceded Hakubunkan as the leading magazine publisher.[31]

Former prime minister Okuma Shigenobu, in a speech delivered at the 10th anniversary celebration of Jitsugyō no Nihonsha's founding, remarked with tongue in cheek: "With his constant preaching about success, no one has reaped the benefits of success more than Masuda Giichi!"[32] The success story Masuda held out for his readers, however, was slightly ambiguous and lacked the clarity in the call for self-advancement in the slogan *risshin shusse.* At a time when advancing in the world was measured by earning high school and university diplomas, acquiring a high government post or a promising executive position in a reputable company, or joining the ranks of professionals as either a doctor or lawyer, Masuda pushed for rather more modest accomplishments. He extolled the joys, for example, of owning a small business—which may have offered little more than the chance for financial security and an easier lifestyle. Masuda's notion of success suggested an ability to turn obstacles into incentives. *Jitsugyō no Nihon*'s wide circulation legitimized and embraced the aims, desires, and possibilities of a group of middle- and lower middle-class men from the grocery store clerk on down to the unsuccessful student, making a virtue of a necessity.

Kōdansha's founder, Noma Seiji (1878–1938), followed a path much like that of Masuda, and he reaped even greater acclaim than Masuda in the world of publishing. When Noma's magazine, *Kōdan kurabu* (Storytelling club), came out in 1911, the advertisements promised "fun," "interesting," and "beneficial" (*tame ni naru*) reading. Three years later, *Shōnen kurabu* (Boys' club) relied on the same words to attract youthful readers. Both magazines enjoyed immediate popularity, which led

Noma to publish *Omoshiro kurabu* (Interest club) in 1916. Targeting women readers, *Fujin kurabu* (Women's club) appeared in 1920, followed by *Shōjo kurabu* (Girls' club) in 1923, a magazine that Noma considered complementary to his magazine for boys. In all his publications, Noma's endorsement of self-cultivation and his criticism of Japan's educational system as the sole means for getting ahead were even more emphatic than Masuda's. Eager to expand on Masuda's brand of *shūyō*, Noma took pains to portray self-cultivation as an important cultural practice that transcended gender and background. He made sure that his columns devoted to self-cultivation, whether in the mass women's magazine *Fujin kurabu*, the later general interest magazine *Kingu* (King, 1925), or his many books, exuded a sense of excitement for both men and women.

In the May 1925 issue of *Kingu*, Noma discussed his criteria for an ideal wife and husband. He emphasized that while "*shūyō* keeps a wife abreast of the latest happenings in the world, she should exude an air of freshness and innocence and be a good speaker and listener. . . . A husband must be in tempo with the times. Still, he is faithful and kind, and knows how to direct his wife unobtrusively. . . ." Noma was implying that self-advancement entailed making use of one's resources. His conception of *shūyō* constructed the image of a symbiotic family that observed accepted rules and observations. In an article in the same issue titled "Let's Make the Great Leap Together" ("Konzen ittai no daiya-kushin"), one reader exuberantly commented that in five short months the *shūyō* Noma introduced in *Kingu* changed his life. In particular, he was referring to *Kingu*'s practice of printing success stories of famous people—*meishi no shūyōdan*. The reader added that *Kingu* was "more interesting than reading a novel."[33] All Noma's publications made sure to stress Kōdansha's link to the emergent new middle- and lower-class popular morality:

What must one do to become a person of extraordinary greatness? It does not depend on knowledge acquired in a classroom. Being morally upright forms our characters. Most people wrongly assume that knowledge and learning are our guiding lights. Conceptualizing education in that way was a big mistake made from Meiji through Taishō. . . . Learning is necessary. Knowledge is necessary. But before we reach that stage in our development, we have to become good people. The moral person will know the value of knowledge and learning. The individual is the one who counts.[34]

The personal assets that Noma hailed epitomized Kodansha's strategy for success. Noma's autobiography *My Life up to Now* (*Watashi no hansei*) was required reading for Kodansha's new employees.[35] Words like "knowledge," "teaching," and "morals" certainly were not unfamiliar to people who subscribed to the *shūyō* ethic. But Noma had the knack of convincingly drawing on ideals that also suggested alternative approaches to a better life. Noma disputed the view that individual good fortune combined with money undermined the character ethic inherent in self-cultivation. He persuasively articulated that outdated, incompatible ethics for getting ahead left no room for viable changes in styles of living. Noma's brand of self-cultivation had great appeal as it provided a new twist. His philosophy and organizational energy clearly reached a peak with *Kingu*'s publication, famous as the first magazine to sell 1,000,000 copies in its very first printing.

Crossing Gender Boundaries: The Self-Cultivation Debate and Women

Like many contrivances in a "modern" society like Japan, discourses surrounding self-cultivation did encompass gender-based differences. Placed in the context of the getting-ahead-in-the-world ideal, self-cultivation was a propelling force for a broadened but overwhelmingly male audience. And yet, this very discourse became a special attraction in women's magazines from the early 1900s.[36] Once again, Masuda played a leading role, showing the same talent he had for attracting male readers to *Jitsugyō no Nihon*, by wooing and winning over women readers to *Fujin sekai*. Although Masuda and later Noma appropriated many ideas from educators and moralists, Masuda was the earliest among the editor-publishers to grasp the potential in a direct tie between self-cultivation and women, and he lost no time in making *shūyō* a prominent feature of his own magazine. Within three years of its founding, *Fujin sekai* had surpassed *Jogaku sekai*, Hakubunkan's best-selling women's magazine, and sold twice as many copies as its equivalent for men, *Jitsugyō no Nihon*, which, of course, was also an advocate of *shūyō*.[37] Employing tactics similar to those he had used at *Jitsugyō no Nihon*, Masuda challenged Hakubunkan's authority a second time.

While *Jogaku sekai*'s readership consisted mainly of higher school students, *Fujin sekai* branched out and included a new consumer audience—the housewife (*shufu*). Space was devoted to articles and helpful information on the home and family (*katei kiji*). A mélange of articles on food, clothing, and other domestic concerns appeared in conjunction with articles on self-cultivation and was written in easily understandable prose for young women with the equivalent of an elementary or higher elementary school education in addition to higher school graduates.[38] An article by woman educator Hatoyama Haruko, "The Kind of Bride I Would Like for My Son," was featured with selections like "The Unique Character of Atomi Women's Higher School," and readers' contributions like "How I Devised a Way to Make Use of Leftover Remnants of Material" and "A Wife who Understood Her Husband's Wish to Change Jobs."[39] The *shūyō* Masuda advocated in *Fujin sekai* and *Jitsugyō no Nihon* supported an alternative to the education that people received in the classroom. But particularly in the case of women, Masuda believed that dedication to self-cultivation presented women with far more viable and practical possibilities than the limited educational opportunities available in schools. In Masuda's opinion, as was the case with Noma, the virtues of *shūyō*, while not gender-bound, were to be put to different use by women and men.

It is said that young women educated under today's educational system tend to be egotistical, pompous, and extremely self-indulgent. These are traits that women should be made aware of and correct. Women need to have a sense of who they are, but at the same time they must be responsible to their families, conscious of their positions at home, mindful of what is expected of them as women and know their place in society. Women should ask themselves whether or not they have reached that stage of self-cultivation where they can recognize their own weak points and strong points.[40]

Masuda proposed *shūyō* for men as a way to deal with impracticalities in the school curriculum. But for women, impracticality was surpassed by his belief that formal school training actually had a deleterious effect on young women's sense of morality. Masuda's conception of self-cultivation—be it the pursuit of training for homemaking or taking lessons in flower arrangement and tea ceremony (*hanayome shūgyō*)—afforded an appropriate means to counteract the egotism and distorted thinking in women that resulted from their having received a formal education. As *shūyō* crossed gender boundaries to appeal to women, it appeared to possibly conflict with the requirements posed by the prevalent good wife, wise mother ideology—but this was not the case across the board. *Shūyō* could also be used in a discourse that was essentially conservative, and even reactionary.

Masuda's engagement in the *shūyō* discourse for women came precisely when the concept of the middle-class "home" (*katei*) was being debated and taking root in Japan in the early 1900s.[41] The emphasis on the modern family as a unit in Japan was one consequence of the internalization of the "civilization and enlightenment" trends popularized in the early 1870s that garnered support from the introduction of Western lifestyles. Indeed, in the 1840s Alexis de Tocqueville claimed that the concept of the American family provided a set of values that gave social and political order to life.[42] Nevertheless, given this historical context, Japan's endorsement in 1891 of Prussian advisor Herman Techow's proposal for a civil code was designed to keep patriarchal values alive. Under a paternalistic system, the morality that determined a harmonious home celebrated a wife's subservience to her husband and precluded a highly developed female ego. British historian Sylvia Walby describes the notion of male power as an essentialist one, which assumes something in maleness that determines the position of power.[43] Simply stated, patriarchy sanctions a social system that men control.

While the elementary school was literally pulling girls out of their homes, Masuda attempted to place them back in the home to become proper, moral women. For Masuda, since a woman's natural place remained in the home, being overly egotistical would hinder her in accomplishing household tasks. Skillfully and rationally running the home was not considered an obligatory task that a wife performed for her husband, but rather was premised on the belief that by "satisfying her husband, a woman found self-fulfillment."[44] Taking care of one's appearance did not imply a wife's extravagance, but rather an awareness of personal hygiene. Masuda defined women by nature as "submissive, all-enduring, and self-denying." The reason that his *shūyō* narrative made frequent mention of a woman's "innate disposition" (*tensei*) and her "calling (mission) in life"(*tenshoku*) was that, for him, the prime significance of self-cultivation was for women to discover the "essence" of womanhood.

When Masuda enjoined women "to refrain from angering their husbands and to take pains to please them and satisfy their wants," the *shūyō* he promoted was encoded with a commonly voiced male-centered sense of expectation instructing women on how to live self-sacrificing and helpful lives.[45] Masuda was adhering to a social notion of what he saw as a woman's modern identity. His ethical principles, however, sounded like the Victorian-period ideology of poet Coventry Patmores (*The Angel in the House*, 1854) and writer John Ruskin, who claimed in his 1864 "Sesame and Lilies" lecture that "a man ought to know any language or science he learns thoroughly; while a woman ought to know the same language and science only so far as may enable her to sympathize in her husband's pleasure, and in those of his best friends." In the July 1919 issue of *Fujin kōron* (Women's review), one male lawyer expressed contempt for Masuda's view and tried to show the incompatibility of this outdated interpretation of self-cultivation for married women in modern Japan:

Marriage in the true sense of the word means that a man and woman must love each other and become one mentally and physically. They have to help each other, continue to be diligent in their practice of self-cultivation (*shūyō*), and contribute to the development of world civilization. Traditional marriages in our country were completely opposed to these objectives. Frankly speaking, the reason a woman married had nothing to do with the man, but with the family (*ie*).[46]

When one considers the widespread support that a magazine like *Fujin sekai* received from its readers, however, in addition to the more "conservative" aspects of self-cultivation, the complexities of *shūyō* for women become apparent. In one issue, a young graduate of a women's higher school, whose parents tried to hide their outcaste (*buraku*) roots, questioned whether a determined will (*shūyō*) was enough to overcome her shame and give her confidence to live openly in society. Writer Kagawa Toshihiko counseled this woman and assured her that by continuing to practice *shūyō* she would transcend petty prejudices.[47] In the same issue another young woman, who followed in the footsteps of her older sister and became an actress, lamented the fact that the community ostracized them for choosing an alternative life course. Although the older sister was described as a beauty and the pride of the neighborhood as a young woman, by pursuing a career in the theater, she ruined her chances for marriage. Neither sister regretted her choice, but their socially unacceptable careers left them open to unfounded criticism and filled them with anxiety. The poet Yosano Akiko advised the sisters to rise above the gossip and praised them for following their artistic callings.[48] Kagawa and Yosano both negated gender distinctions that defined personal relations, but neither could radically change public opinion in women's favor.

If the *shūyō* discourse, as exemplified in *Fujin sekai*, had merely been an expression of the psychological endurance required to survive the realities of everyday life, *shūyō* could never have held sway over women for a period of several decades. In fact, from Taishō through early Shōwa, *shūyō* came to comprise an even more important agenda for young women. One reason is that trends formerly associated primarily with Taishō culturalism spilled over to middle-class young women. Contrary to Masuda's vision, some middle-class women subscribed to a life outside of the home precisely because of their engagement with self-cultivation. In a supplementary pamphlet put out by the popular women's magazine *Fujin kurabu,* the complexities of *shūyō* are evident:

By nature you share the innate gift of having been born women, but the question is how to cultivate that celestial gift. Women can achieve sophistication through self-cultivation [*kyōyō*]. If we are attentive to the spiritual aspects of self-cultivation, we gradually will learn to curb our egos and to become more flexible individuals able to cope with various situations. Even if we do not think of ourselves as fully liberated, at least we will be able to enjoy a semblance of freedom, equality, and harmony with our husbands, parents-in-law, and our neighbors. In every area—from personal hygiene to cleanliness at home—women naturally will master useful and rational ways without experiencing untoward emotional stress.[49]

The reference to "sophistication" made in this 1928 supplement reflected an elite image of the home as a product of the "modern" nation-state. For some young women, gender-based differences in morality within the home acted as a conduit for attaining a higher-class identity and, in this regard, attracted young women who aspired to improve their social status.[50]

However, obstacles in coping with the realities of everyday life, like the relationship with one's mother-in-law and husband, bore testimony to the psychological dilemmas to be dealt with.[51] The notion of self that editors like Tsugawa Masashi, who took over *Fujokai* in 1913, and Ishikawa Takeyoshi (Takemi), who founded *Shufu no tomo*, exerted on the *shūyō* discourse took on special significance. The tactics undertaken by both men to find ways that readers could relate to their publications gave new meaning both to self-cultivation and to the function of women's magazines. Through the use of the *shūyō* discourse, both men helped carve out a specific space that women could call their own.

When Tsugawa first took over *Fujokai*, the overpowering strength of *Fujin sekai*'s circulation led him to believe, on several occasions, that he was fighting a losing battle in the marketplace.[52] Inspired by Masuda, he too turned to *shūyō* to sell more magazines. More than just a case of skillful borrowing, Tsugawa transformed the concept of self-cultivation to include a new aspect: active reader participation. As he remarked: "Every woman should consider herself a member of the editorial board."[53] A Fukuoka (western Japan) resident and devoted reader of *Fujokai* spoke of *shūyō* as "my moral support," that which "prepared me for the responsibilities of a career in midwifery." Because of reading and her membership in *Fujokai*'s club, the All-Japan Women's Self-Cultivation Society (Dai Nihon fujin shūyōkai, described below), which she described as "ongoing and life-long," she had the courage to examine her personal feelings, thus making her sympathetic to the needs of the women she serviced in her professional working life.[54] Self-cultivation was central to this young woman's identity. However, the philosophical and religious concepts that had a pivotal place in most intellectuals' discourses were inconsequential in the *shūyō* she subscribed to. Instead of underlining the otherworldly character of self-cultivation, she and other young women like her reconstructed *shūyō* to meet their individual circumstances.

In another case, a woman from the provinces who graduated at the top of her class at a women's higher school but who had had no marriage offers because of her ill-favored looks, remarked that reading magazines like *Fujokai*, coupled with a love for books, sustained her "in the darkest moments." The emotional stability she received from *shūyō* helped her persuade her parents of the benefits of moving to Tokyo where she could further her studies and obtain a coveted diploma in midwifery. "Compared to the salaries some young women in the capital receive, midwifery is hardly a lucrative profession. Nevertheless, I have enough material possessions, and I am emotionally rich."[55]

A woman reporter who visited Tokyo's first women-only employment agency expressed surprise that in 1926 few young women sought employment as domestics, and only four applicants opted for 130 positions as bill collectors. In contrast, as many as 281 young women vied for 89 openings as office girls, which satisfied their yearning for socially acceptable jobs before marriage. Moreover, employers advertised for middle-class young women with bookkeeping skills and a good knowledge of the written language, and preferred higher school graduates.[56] Holding a job figured as a particularly advanced form of self-cultivation that wove a common thread in the greater scheme of life for some middle-class women. With the encouragement of creative editors like Tsugawa and Ishikawa, by the early 1920s *shūyō*, along with entering society as a professional working woman, was the ideal for the construction of the middle-class woman.

Even if most middle-class women believed in male superiority, that did not stop some women from drawing attention to the inequities in the family system or from aspiring to a marriage based on love. The phrase current at the time, "unity of body and soul" (*rei niku itchi*), conveyed an image of love and marriage that was consistent with *shūyō* thought.[57] A letter printed in the readers' column of *Fujokai* focuses on the lack of legal redress for women in marital matters. The writer details the experience of a friend's sister who lost her virginity to a man who promised to marry her, but reneged without any hesitation when his parents voiced opposition. The victim, cast aside by her lover, also suffered the wrath of her authoritarian older brother. In the brother's role as head of the family, he chastised his sister for defaming the family name and forbade her from returning home. Here, the readers' column served as the venue where the reader/contributor could voice concerns about the treatment of women. Access to space in a "cherished" monthly magazine that many readers called "their closest friend" provided personal support and a sense of empowerment, however slight. This contributor gained comfort knowing that she was informing other young women about the pitfalls of emotional naïveté and rash decisions in a society where chastity was a paramount virtue for women. Because the law provided limited recourse, she looked to *shūyō* for inspiration and asserted that "mental resolve plays a valuable role in a woman's well being."[58] In short, *shūyō* offered her a social identity.

Another *Fujokai* reader entered her arranged marriage "naive and ignorant" and "a believer in the teachings in *The Great Learning for Women*." However, after several years of tacitly enduring the humiliation of her children and herself at the hands of her debauched husband, she exposed his escapades and revealed her own expectations for married life. What she formerly attributed to "the proclivities of men in their late thirties and forties" became unforgivable when she discovered that her husband had impregnated a twenty-two-year-old niece who married suddenly thereafter to hush up the scandal. Although she described her circumstances as "more extreme than other women's," she articulated her frustration with "the destiny a wife is expected to abide by."[59] Other women also turned to advice columns, which served as a more useful forum than "traditional" sources like the family for providing guidance in coping with grievances. Despite the fact that many men at that time accepted men's philandering and engaging geisha as natural and not immoral, this reader's appeal reveals her longing for a more equal marital relationship.[60] She was calling into question the assumption that sexual promiscuity was a masculine natural right, both before and after marriage.

The problem, however, went beyond virtue. Increasingly, women voiced their anxieties about married life and so-called "appropriate" gender values that dictated their positions vis-à-vis their spouses. By disavowing the arbitrary authority of their husbands, indirectly they were questioning the tenets of the Meiji Civil Code that legally limited wives' rights.[61] Their almost total lack of legal power left women with uncertainty in their lives. In the above examples a link can be seen between *shūyō* and its relationship to love and marriage. Women were applying the notion of *shūyō* to help shape their perceptions of their private lives and advance options for the future, and for some this meant moving beyond the confines of the home.

Within three months of assuming control of *Fujokai*, Tsugawa launched the *shūyō* reader's club, initially named the All-Japan Women's Self-Cultivation Society, and changed in 1923 to the Self-Cultivation Society for *Fujokai*'s Beloved Readers (*Fujokai* aidokusha shūyō-kai). Sounding extremely authoritative and confident, Tsugawa declared:

"Every article in my magazine, *Fujokai*, presents the best possible opportunity for achieving *shūyō*."[62] At frequent gatherings held all over Japan, the Self-Cultivation Society reminded its members of their moral needs and attempted to advance a social ideal that was within their reach. Socializing at these meetings with their idols—figures like Hato-yama Haruko, Nitobe Inazō, Tsuda Umeko, Tsugawa Musashi—women felt a sense of belonging to the "we" rather than the "other." This is apparent in readers' letters: "Tsugawa-sensei, I will never forget your words"; "Listening to Hatoyama-sensei is the highlight of my year."[63] Be that as it may, for the magazines, another rationale for establishing a *shūyō* society was to increase the magazine's readership. Since the magazine had no fixed subscription system, a society of this sort, if successful, would assure the constant sale of magazines. Richard Ohman describes late nineteenth-century magazines in America as "commodities" that conferred "distinction."[64] One might say the same for mass women's magazines in Japan in the twenties.

Ishikawa Takemi also took great pride in boasting about the special relationship that existed between *Shufu no tomo* and its readers. Reminiscent of Noma's strategy, Ishikawa opined that "unlike other magazines, a close bond of mutual trust and friendship joined us to our readers. . . . For me, it was as if every woman reader was my friend."[65] Excerpts from readers' letters published in *Shufu no tomo* are revealing: "How can I ever express how I have benefited from all the instructive articles published in each issue.";[66] "Please help guide someone like me who is lacking in *shūyō*."[67] Ishikawa and Tsugawa both attempted to construct a surrogate family relationship that was bolstered by a kind of community formed by the readers.[68]

Thus, Masuda both secularized and engendered morality by articulating a man's *shūyō* and a differing woman's *shūyō*. The popularized version of *shūyō* for men placed their dreams outside the home and oriented them toward worldly success, even if limited, thereby affirming their push for middle-class identities. Women, on the other hand, were placed—and eventually actively placed themselves—within the home in their effort to become "modern." Tsugawa and Ishikawa, borrowing Masuda's tactics, made their magazines into women's forums for the popularization of *shūyō*. In the process, the *shūyō* ideal helped fuel the spread of consumerism.

Conclusion

The *shūyō* discourse, which reverberated first through the pages of male-centered magazines like *Jitsugyō no Nihon* and later in women's magazines like *Fujin sekai* in the early 1900s and in *Fujokai* and *Shufu no tomo* from the 1910s, proposed a morality for women consistent with that of a patriarchal nation-state. Yet, unlike classes in ethics training (a required part of the school curriculum for girls and boys from the elementary years until after the Fifteen-Year War), *shūyō* for young women was not imposed from above. Rather it may be described as a discourse that editors and publishers incorporated into their magazines and women actively incorporated into the practices of their everyday lives. The numerous advertisements sprinkled throughout most mass women's magazines, which boasted of readerships in the hundreds of thousands and the benefits derived from reading their particular publications, no doubt helped construct a femininity that cultivated both the desires and anxieties of these new female readers. By the 1920s women from both middle- and lower middle-class families relished the plethora of *shūyō*-related articles that sought to prepare them for marriage or entry into the workplace or inspired them to strive for a higher social status or more satisfying lives. It was they who became the subscribers of mass women's magazines.

Indeed, many young women's desires were compounded with anxieties. Some of the most commonly voiced complaints came from middle-class working women who were concerned that the physical exhaustion accompanying long hours on the job would prevent them from pursuing *shūyō*. Romance is the subject of Janice Radway's book *Reading the Romance*, but her analysis of "reading" is helpful in addressing "the question of determination," which was an integral part of women's desire to embrace the notion of self-cultivation in Japan. Radway makes the point that "romance reading buys time and privacy for women even as it addresses the corollary consequence of their situation, the physical exhaustion and emotional depletion brought about by the fact that no one within the patriarchal family is charged with *their* care."[69] In the 1920s, Japanese women who had not been in the habit of reading turned to books and magazines for consolation and self-development. Reading itself became a form of consumption, and women served as the chief agent of this activity. In Stuart Ewen's words: "One of the most available routes to satisfaction is consumption. While the preponderant work structures of consumer capitalism often bear the fruits of frustration, the images of consumerism continually acknowledge the desire for freedom, the freedom to desire."[70] Examining the varied genres of mass women's magazines in Japan that increased yearly prompts one to call this the age of a "reading revolution."

As a multi-layered "revolution," reading necessitated expanded literacy, more free time, extra spending money, and innovative techniques for mass printing among its many components. Robert Darnton suggests that in order to understand the motivation for reading one must "learn more about the ideals and assumptions underlying reading in the past."[71] When considered from the vantage point of Neo-Confucianism during the Tokugawa period, the act of reading was not so much a means of attaining knowledge, but rather a way to develop and reveal one's true ethical character. The strategies used by publishers like Masuda, Noma, Tsugawa, and Ishikawa to enhance their respective businesses involved the commodification of women's middle-class desires and anxieties. For these publishers, *shūyō* functioned as a key word for winning over wider classes of women readers.

The rise of a consumer society found women turning to the "bourgeois" women's magazines that offered them a chance to achieve their desires and overcome their anxieties through *shūyō*. Socialist feminist Yamakawa Kikue expressed disappointment when she saw, first-hand, women workers at a printing factory, less educated and materially less fortunate than their middle-class sisters, delighting in magazines like *Fujin kurabu* and *Shufu no tomo* over lunch and after work. She and other like-minded intellectuals attached pejorative labels to these magazines.[72]

The hardships that these women endured and the tedium that was the reality of their lives were real. Yet, in the case of these factory women, judging from their avid consumption of mass women's magazines, their concerns were not rooted in social activism but in more "traditional" (*dentōteki*) and personal issues: love and marriage. They, too, had come under the *shūyō* spell. In fact, the popularization of *shūyō* helped these women negotiate an ideal that promised upward mobility and personal success, an ideal that had little to do with ideological beliefs. Without exaggerating the importance of self-cultivation, the type of *shūyō* manifested in women's popular magazines, particularly in the 1920s, held out a standard of personal success that for women was comparable to that held out to men.

Male-dominated publishing companies could not force women to follow publishers'/editors' views, but they could use their power to manipulate women readers. For all the valiant intentions of Masuda, Noma, Tsugawa, and Ishikawa, their main aim was commercial—to sell magazines. In spite of this, women readers, through reading and writing, were attempting to assert their claims for female agency. Although their options were limited, some middle-class women decided voluntarily on the basis of their experiences the extent to which self-cultivation offered them the resources needed for self-improvement. From the early twentieth century, when the notion of social fluidity began to take root, *shūyō* became a cultural resource for the formation of a middle-class woman's identity. Michel de Certeau points out in *The Practice of Everyday Life*: "the binominal set production-consumption can often be replaced by its general equivalent and indicator, the binominal set writing-reading."[73] Indeed, de Certeau's respect for the autonomy of the reader/consumer resonates with particular significance throughout this chapter in Japan's history. This equation defines the enthusiasm with which many women in the 1920s embraced the *shūyō* discourse.

Notes

1. See Minemura Toshio, "Kigyō fujin zasshi kettai ron," in *Sōgō jānarizumu kōza*, vol. 5 (Naigaisha, 1931), 203–277. Japanese publishing companies did not make their circulation figures public. The figures that were given out tend to be unreliable. Several companies reported in 1931 that *Shufu no tomo*'s monthly circulation was 600,000 with a rate of 0.5–1 percent in unsold, returned magazines (*henpinsei*). *Fujin kurabu* reported 350,000 and a return rate of 25 percent; *Fujin kōron* 200,000 and a return rate of 15 percent; and *Fujin sekai* 120,000 with a 45 percent return rate. According to *Seventy-Year History of Business Japan (Jitsugyō no Nihonsha nanajūnenshi)*, put out in 1967 by Jitsugyō no Nihonsha, the company claimed that *Fujin sekai*'s readership was over 250,000 in 1909.

2. The above-mentioned quotes appear in the order they are cited in the text: Reader's article, "Gyyakkyō yori seikō shitaru fujin no jitsurei kidan," *Fujin sekai*, August 1907, vol. 2, no. 9, 70–76; Reader's letter, Kyōko from Hokkaido, "Dōryoku de konnichi no kōfuku o eta onna kyōmuin no seikatsu," *Fujokai*, June 1919, vol. 19, no. 6, 69–71; Reader's letter, Nobuko from Saga, *Fujokai*, October 1920, vol. 22, no. 4, 197; Hatoyama Haruko, "Jidai ni tekiō seru shūyō," *Fujokai*, February 1920, vol. 21, no. 2, 2–7; Nitobe Inazō, "Shūyō de jinkaku o kitaeta fujin," *Fujin sekai*, November 1918, vol. 13, no. 5, 10–15. Contributors usually included only their given names, but they tended to list the region where they came from.

At the time, women factory workers generally were not considered middle class. However, an elementary school education was sufficient for reading popular women's magazines and some factory workers also submitted letters to magazines like *Fujokai* and *Shufu no tomo*. They submitted fewer letters than higher school graduates, but working-class women also conveyed appreciation to the magazines for giving them hope. Some women described *shūyō* as a way to raise their class status. See e.g., Ichizawa Ya'ichi, "Aichi-ken shibu taikai no ki," *Fujokai*, March 1920, vol. 21, no. 3, 186–187; and Yamazaki Sawa, "Rōdō fujin no seikatsu," in *Fujokai*, March 1920, vol. 21, no. 3, 49–53.

3. Kawashima Jirō et al., *Gendai shūshin kyōiku taikan* (Nankōsha, 1929); Kusaba Hiroshi, *Shogakkō shūshin kyōyōho* (Sansei shobō, 1933), 19. See also Martin Colcutt, "The Legacy of Confucianism in Japan," in *The East Asian Region: Confucian Heritage and Modern Adaptation,* ed. Gilbert Rozman (Princeton, NJ: Princeton University Press, 1993), 149.

4. *Shufu no tomo no gojūnen* (Shufu no tomosha, 1967), 14; Tsugawa Masashi, "Fujin zasshi no henshū," in *Sōgō jānarizumu kōza*, vol. 10 (Naigaisha, 1931), 56–57.

See also Barbara Sato, *The New Japanese Woman: Modernity, Media, and Women in Interwar Japan* (Durham, NC: Duke University Press, 2003), 80–89.

5. Nakajima Kenzō, *Jigazō,* vol. 2 (Heibonshsa, 1963).

6. Sato, *The New Japanese Woman,* 32–37. See also Warren I. Susman, *Culture as History: The Transformation of American Society in the Twentieth Century* (New York: Pantheon Books, 1984), 63.

7. Reader's letter, *Fujokai,* October 1918, 97.

8. Stewart Ewen, *All Consuming Images: The Politics of Style in Contemporary Culture* (New York: Basic Books, 1987), 78–101. Stuart Ewen reinforces the findings of others scholars when he remarks that in "an urban industrial world, traditional hierarchical patterns of work and family life were disintegrating, and new promises of economic opportunity were fueling the imagination . . . ," in Ewen, *All Consuming Images,* 62–63.

9. Geoffrey Cossick made this assumption. On the same issue, see also Christopher P. Hosgood, "Mrs. Potter's Purchase: Lower Middle-Class Consumerism and the Sales, 1870–1914," in *Gender, Civic Culture, and Consumerism: Middle-Class Identity in Britain, 1800–1940,* eds. Alan Kidd and David Nicholls (Manchester, UK: Manchester University Press, 1999), 146–147.

10. Maruyama Masao, "Nihon ni okeru jiyūshiki no keisei to tokushitsu," *Senchū to sengo no aida* (Misuzu shobō, 1976), 303–304.

11. Higashikuni Naruhiko, interview in *Asahi shinbun,* August 29, 1945.

12. Carol Gluck, *Japan's Modern Myths: Ideology in the Late Meiji Period* (Princeton, NJ: Princeton University Press, 1985), 210.

13. In 1908, a book with a similar message to that of *Self-Help* came out in Japanese. See Iguchi Chūji, *Nihonjijōron* (Naigai shuppan kyōkai, 1908).

14. Earl H. Kinmonth, *The Self-Made Man in Meiji Japanese Thought: From Samurai to Salary Man* (Berkeley: University of California Press, 1981), 12–13.

15. Karaki Junzō, *Gendaishi e no kokoromi* (Chikuma shobō, 1949), reprinted in *Showa bungaku zenshū,* vol. 28 (Dai Nihon insatsu, 1989), 17–25.

16. Tsutsui Kiyotada, *Nihongata "kyōyō" no unmei: Rekishi–shakaigakuteki kōsatsu* (Iwanami shoten, 1995), 2, 32.

17. Karaki, *Gendaishi,* 17–25; Tsutsui, *Nihongata,* 85, 88; Takeuchi Yō, *Risshin shusse to Nihonjin* (Nippon hōsō shuppan kyōkai, 1996), 162.

18. See chapters by Martha Tocco and Barbara Molony in this volume. In 1872, the Ministry of Education fixed compulsory education at four years. In 1879, it was reduced to sixteen months during the decentralization of education. In 1881, it increased regardless of gender to three years, and then reverted back to the original four years. By 1906, six years of schooling was compulsory. Although girls' options for further education narrowed considerably after that, they could seek admission to a women's higher school (*kōtō jogakkō*). Like the boys' middle school (*chūgakkō*), higher school went from grades 7 to 11. However, qualitatively, the differences between the two were great.

19. Hani Makoto, "'Jiyū gakuen' no seiritsu," in Hani Makoto, *Kyōiku sanjūnen* (1933), reprinted in *Kyōiku*, ed. Mitsui Tametomo, vol. 4, *Nihon fujin mondai shiryō shūsei* (Domesu shuppan, 1983), 544–561; Yamada Waka, "Shufu no chikara," in *Shōwa fujin dokuhen, Katei hen*, vol. 23 (1927), reprinted in *Seikatsu*, ed. Morioka Hideko, vol. 7, *Nihon fujin mondai shiryō shūsei* (Domesu shuppan, 1984), 76–81; Hani Makoto, "Katei to nōritsu," in *Hani Makoto chōsakushū*, vol. 3 (1928), reprinted in *Seikatsu*, ed. Morioka Hideko, vol. 7, *Nihon fujin mondai shiryō shūsei* (Domesu shuppan, 1984), 181–185.

20. Maeda Ai, *Maeda Ai chosakushū*, vol. 2 (Chikuma shobō, 1989), 191.

21. Ogawa Kikumatsu, *Nihon shuppankai no ayumi* (Seibundō shinkōsha, 1962), 12. In Japan the term "best seller" did not exist until the 1950s. See Ueda Yasuo, *Besto sera-kōgengaku* (Media paru, 1992), 7.

22. *Kōdansha no ayunda gojūnen: Meiji–Taishō hen* (Kōdansha, 1959).

23. Suzuki Sadami, "Hakubunkan bunka," *Hōsho gekkan*, no. 170, November, 1999, 2–29; Suzuki Sadami, "Sōkanki Taiyō ronzetsuran o megutte," in *Nihon kenkyū*, no. 15 (Kyoto: Kokusai Nihon bunka kenkyū sentā, 1995), 64; and Barbara Sato, "'Sōgōka sareta' zasshi ni okeru jendā-no hyōshō-Taiyō 'Kateiran o megutte,'" in *Nihon kenkyū*, no. 17, 273–283. Early Shōwa critic Kimura Tsuneyoshi discussed Hakubunkan's contributions to late Meiji publishing in his article "Nihon zasshi hattatsu–shi, part 2," in *Sōgō jānarizumu kōza*, vol. 5 (Naigaisha, 1931), 250–252.

24. Hashimoto Motomu, *Nihon shuppan hanbaishi* (Kōdansha, 1964), 66–67.

25. Masuda Giichi, *Seinen to shūyō* (Jitsugyō no Nihonsha, 1912), 321. See also Susman, *Culture as History*, 281.

26. Masuda, *Seinen to shūyō*, preface.

27. A comparison of the table of contents of *Taiyō* and *Jitsugyō no Nihonjin* provides ample proof of the differences in reading classes targeted by each magazine.

28. Masuda, *Seinen to shūyō*, 65, 152–153.

29. Ogawa, *Nihon shuppankai no ayumi*, 111–118.

30. Takeuchi Yō, *Risshin, kugaku, shusse: Jukensei no shakaigaku* (Kōdansha gendai shinsho, 1991), 152–154.

31. Hashimoto, *Nihon shuppan hanbaishi*, 67.

32. Ibid., 66–67.

33. Noma Seiji, "Konzen ittai no daiyakushin!!" *Kingu* 1, no. 5 (May 1925): 296–297.

34. Noma Seiji, *Taiken o kataru* (Dai Nihon yūbenkai kōdansha, 1930), 2.

35. Degawa Samio, *Kiseki no shuppan ō–Noma Seiji to Henrii Rūsu* (Kawadeshobō, 2000), 240. See also Noma Seiji, *Watashi no hansei* (Chikuma shobō, 1936). A new analysis of the literature is offered by Satō Takumi, *'Kingu' no jidai: Kokumin taishū zasshi no kōkyōsei* (Iwanami shoten, 2002). Satō describes a correlation between Noma's techniques and those used in radio programming.

36. According to Margaret Beetham, from the early nineteenth century in Britain, women's magazines "offered both amusement and instruction." Christianity was the moving force behind these magazines, which "sought to fulfill the role of guide to conduct which was already established as central to female reading." By the twentieth century, however, instruction rather than entertainment became the mainstay of women's magazines in Britain. Margaret Beetham, *A Magazine of Her Own? Domesticity and Desire in the Woman's Magazine, 1800–1914* (London: Routledge, 1996), 24, 54.

37. Hashimoto, *Nihon shuppan hanbaishi*, 67.

38. Since one copy of *Jogaku sekai* sold for 20 sen, equivalent to approximately 400 yen in today's currency, it was expensive reading for the average young woman. Nevertheless, the magazine remained in circulation until 1925. According to Fukuda Sumiko, *Kōtō jogakkō shiryō shūsei: Kōtō jogakkō no kenkyū*, vol. 2 (Ōzorasha, 1999), 29, in 1898 only about 1 to 2 percent of girls continued their education beyond elementary school. At that time, approximately 8,500 girls were enrolled in women's higher schools located throughout the country.

In the United States, approximately 3 percent of American women were high school graduates by 1885 (Washington, DC: Historical Statistics of the U.S.

Department of Commerce, 1976, 379) and 1.9 percent between the ages of 18 and 21 were enrolled in college; Barbara Miller Solomon, *In the Company of Educated Women: A History of Women and Higher Education in America* (New Haven, CT: Yale University Press, 1985), 64; this is quoted in Helen Damon-Moore, *Magazines for the Millions: Gender and Commerce in the Ladies' Home Journal and the Saturday Evening Post, 1880–1910* (Albany, NY: SUNY Press, 1994), 41.

39. Hatoyama Haruko, "Watakushi wa waga ko no tanemi ikanaru yome o motomuraka" [The Kind of Bride I Would Like for My Son], in *Fujin sekai*, September 1908, vol. 3, no. 10, 18–23; Reader's contribution, "Tokushoku aru Atomi jogakkō no bifū" [The Unique Character of Atomi Women's Higher School], in *Fujin sekai*, January 1915, vol. 10, no. 1; Reader's contribution, "Furui kire o atarashiku tsukau kufū," [How I Devised a Way to Make Use of Left-over Remnants of Material], in *Fujin sekai*, December 1918, vol. 13, no. 14, 92–93; and Reader's contribution, "Otto no tenshoku o rikai shita fujin" [A Wife Who Understood Her Husband's Wish to Change Jobs], in *Fujin sekai*, December 1918, vol. 13, no. 14, 118–120.

40. Masuda Giichi, *Fujin to shūyō* (Jitsugyō no Nihonsha, 1928), 37.

41. Muta Kazue, *Senryaku toshite no kazoku: Kindai Nihon no kokumin kokka keisei to josei* (Shinyōsha, 1996), especially chapter 3.

42. Alexis de Tocqueville, *Democracy in America*, vol. 1 (New York: Vintage Books, 1945), 315. In de Tocqueville's words: "There is certainly no country in the world where the tie of marriage is more respected than in America or where conjugal happiness is more highly or worthily appreciated"; "But when the American retires from the turmoil of public life to the bosom of his family, he finds in it the image of order and peace"; "[T]he American derives from his own home that love of order which he afterwards carries with him into public affairs."

In her study of the American family in an upper New York State community in approximately the same period, Mary Ryan comments: "The vaunted autonomy and egotism of the nineteenth-century male was not a monument to self-reliance. Quite the contrary, it was conceived, cultivated, pampered, and protected within a revitalized American home. . . . Their story is not a dramatic case of upward mobility but rather a sustained battle to maintain middle-class occupations for themselves and their children." Mary Ryan, *Cradle of the Middle Class: The Family in Oneida County, New York, 1790–1865* (Cambridge: Cambridge University Press, 1981), 184.

43. Sylvia Walby, *Theorizing Patriarchy* (London: Oxford University Press, 1990), 20.

44. Masuda, *Fujin to shūyō*, 37.

45. According to Michel Foucault in his discussion of classical texts on marriage, "marriage required a particular style of conduct, especially insofar as the married man was the head of the family, an honorable citizen, or a man who aspired to exercise over others an authority that was both practical and moral." Michel Foucault, *The History of Sexuality: The Care of the Self*, trans. Robert Hurley, vol. 3 (New York: Vintage Books, 1988), 147.

46. Yamawaki Gen, "Musume chūshin no jiyū kekkon nare," *Fujin kōron*, July 1919, vol. 4, no. 7, 30.

47. Advice to reader by Kagawa Toyohiko, "Sekken no tsumetai soko o aruite yuku warera no mure," *Fujin sekai*, October 1924, special issue, vol. 9, no. 10, 36–45.

48. Advice to reader by Yosano Akiko, "Geijutsu e no akogare to ane no endan," in *Fujin sekai*, October 1924, special issue, vol. 9, no. 10, 62–66.

49. Noma Seiji, "Shōwa fujin shin bunko," *Fujin kurabu*, January 1928, vol. 9, no. 1. Here I argue that Noma is using *kyōyō* synonymously with *shūyō*.

50. Maeba Nakachiko's *Josei hōkan* (Ai no jigyōsha, 1935) is an example of a popular book that many young women who coveted a higher social status, but lacked "culture and refinement," turned to for concrete advice. Topics included etiquette, the ability to use proper language in different social situations, tips for making a good marriage, learning to handle family relations, preparing nutritious and tasty menus, cleaning aids, and beauty techniques. Maeba worked her way up at Matsuya Department Store and later joined the staff of the magazine *Fujin sekai*. Social critic Nii Itaru highly recommended Maeba's book for the "new modern young woman."

51. Kōgyoku Joshi (pen name), "Tsuma no shintoku," *Taiyō*, vol. 4, no. 1, January 1898, 162–165. According to Helen Damon-Moore, in the United States, many writers wrote of similar adjustment difficulties experienced by young women following college graduation. *Ladies' Home Journal* editor Edward Bok viewed the changes as having a stressful effect on women. Damon-Moore cites Katherine Roich's article "The College-Bred Woman in Her Home" as one of many articles that discuss these problems. (Katherine Roich, "The College-Bred Woman in Her Home," *Ladies' Home Journal* [April 1899], 14), in Damon-Moore, *Magazines for the Millions*, 88.

52. Tsugawa Masashi, *Koete kita michi* (Fujokaisha, 1930), 287–289.

53. For Tsugawa's comment, see *Fujokai*, March 1923, vol. 27, no. 3, 129.

54. Supplement, *Fujokai*, September 1924, vol. 30, no. 3, 315–330.

55. Mitsuko, "Yōsō no minikuisa kara happun shite sanba ni," *Fujokai*, March 1928, vol. 37, no. 3, 82–86. See also the survey *Shokugyō fujin ni kansuru chōsa*, ed. Tōkyō–shi shakaikyoku, which contains data collected in 1922 and published in 1924 for figures pertaining to working women's favorite magazines. In 1925, this survey was published under the title *Fujin jiritsu no michi* and printed in *Kindai fujin mondai meicho zenshū zokuhen*, vol. 7 (Nihon tosho sentā, 1982), 109–114.

56. Akita Sumire, "Shoku o motomete jōkyō sen to wakaki hitobito e–fujin shokugyō shōkai jo no kinkyo," *Fujokai*, March 1928, vol. 37, no. 7, 104–105.

57. Kuriyagawa Hakuson, "Ren'ai to jinsei," *Fujin kōron*, June 1922, vol. 7, no. 6, 25–31; Kagawa Toyohiko, "Ren'ai to tamashi no shikkan," *Fujin kōron*, January 1928, vol. 13, no. 1, 13–16.

58. Reporter, "Hōritsu mondai," *Fujokai*, April 1928, vol. 37, no. 8, 351.

59. Reader's letter, Teruko from Kyoto, "Shinseki no musume ni haramaseta otto no fugyōseki," *Fujokai*, April 1928, vol. 37, no. 8, 169–172.

60. A helpful commentary for examining the place of gender from the perspective of the partnership between a husband and wife is Leonore Davidoff and Catherine Hall, *Family Fortunes: Men and Women of the English Middle Class, 1780–1850* (London and Chicago: Hutchinson and University of Chicago Press, 1987).

61. For more on wives' rights in the Meiji era, see Barbara Molony's chapter in this volume.

62. Tsugawa, *Koete kita michi*, 290. Maeda Ai, *Maeda Ai chosakushū*, 160–161, offers a comparison of the *Shufu no tomo* and *Fujokai* readers' clubs.

63. See e.g., Reader's letter, Mitsuko from Tokyo, *Fujokai*, June 1918, vol. 17, no. 6, 142; Reader's letter, *Fujokai*, May 1924, vol. 19, no. 5, 269; Reader's letter, *Fujokai*, September 1924, vol. 20, no 3, 334; and Reader's letter, *Fujokai*, January 1928, vol. 27, no. 1, 334.

64. Richard Ohmann, *Selling Culture: Magazines, Markets, and Class at the Turn of the Century* (London and New York: Verso, 1996), 174–175.

65. Ishikawa Takeyoshi (Takemi), *Waga ai suru katei*, first published in 1942, reprinted in *Ishikawa Takeyoshi zenshū*, vol. 1 (Ishikawa bunka jigyōzaidan, 1980), 236.

66. Reader's letter, "Shijō kurabu," *Shufu no tomo*, February 1920, vol. 4, no. 2, 157–158. Similar examples can be found in *Fujokai* and other mass women's magazines.

67. Reader's letter, *Shufu no tomo*, October 1919, vol. 3, no. 10, 135.

68. American journalist Edward Bok, who became the editor of *Ladies' Home Journal* (1883) in 1889, which he later claimed was the "largest bully pulpit in the world," shared views similar to those of Tsugawa and Ishikawa regarding reader participation. The "moral vision" he cultivated for his readers was known as "simple living," which represented his ideal for women in a "modern" world. See Jennifer Scanlon, *Inarticulate Longings: The Ladies' Home Journal, Gender, and the Promises of Consumer Culture* (London: Routledge, 1995), 50–51.

In Britain, "the domestic women's magazine has always offered an illusion of security to women readers" over how to define "womanliness" by assuming a "connection between domestic and feminine virtue" and, from the 1890s, "explicitly offering itself to its readers as a 'friend.'" See Ros Ballaster, Margaret Beetham, Elizabeth Frazer, and Sarah Hebron, *Women's Worlds: Ideology, Femininity and the Woman's Magazine* (London: Macmillan Press, 1991), 106–107.

69. Janice Radway, "Reading the Romance," in *Studying Culture*, eds. Ann Gray and Jim McGuigan (London and New York: Edward Arnold, 1993), 70–71, and Janice Radway, *Reading the Romance* (Chapel Hill: University of North Carolina Press, 1984).

70. Ewen, *All Consuming Images*, 103.

71. Robert Darnton, "History of Reading," in *New Perspectives on Historical Writing*, ed. Peter Burke (University Park: The Penn State University Press, 1994), 152.

72. Yamakawa Kikue, "Gendai fujin zasshi ron," *Shinchō*, June 1928, reprinted in Yamakawa Kikue, *Yamakawa Kikue shū*, vol. 5 (Iwanami shoten, 1982), 129. Tokuda Shū, Nii Itaru, and Miyake Yasuko were among the intellectuals who joined Yamakawa in this roundtable discussion denouncing mass women's magazines.

73. Michel de Certeau, *The Practice of Everyday Life* (Berkeley: University of California Press, 1984).

PART II
Genders, Bodies, Sexualities

4 "S" is for Sister: Schoolgirl Intimacy and "Same-Sex Love" in Early Twentieth-Century Japan
Gregory M. Pflugfelder

In recent decades, scholars have explored some of the various forms of love and friendship that emerged over the course of history in all-female educational institutions around the world. Schoolgirls in England around the turn of the twentieth century called intense emotional ties among their classmates (or alternatively between students and teachers) by such names as "raves," forming attachments that, according to the historian Martha Vicinus, "simultaneously satisfied the desire for intimacy and individuality, independence and loyalty."[1] Diaries, letters, and memoirs attest to similar relationships in the United States—for example, the phenomenon of "smashing" at nineteenth-century women's colleges as described in a pathbreaking article by Nancy Sahli.[2] That such cultures of schoolgirl intimacy are not limited to a Euro-American context is apparent from the 1970s ethnographic research of Judith Gay on "mummy"/"baby" bonds in the African kingdom of Lesotho.[3]

In early twentieth-century Japan, as in England, America, and elsewhere around the globe, postprimary institutions of education, including girls' schools (*jogakkō*) provided the setting for ardent emotional attachments among large numbers of young females.[4] This essay offers a historical introduction to a phenomenon that was widely known or experienced by Japanese of that era. By contrast, few of their grandchildren have much knowledge of it today. The term "S" (*esu*), for example, is nowadays more likely in Japan to evoke images of "S/M" (sadomasochism) than it is of the swooning schoolgirls that it did just a half-century ago. Nevertheless, many older women can still vividly recall their own experiences of schoolgirl "sisterhood." The present essay draws primarily upon published sources, but has been enriched by interviews with seven girls' school graduates, ranging in age from their sixties to their eighties at the time of our conversations in the early 1990s.

Girls' schools no longer exist in the pre-1947 legal form under examination in the following pages, and even the memories of their graduates have been overlaid by subsequent layers of personal struggle and historical change. I do not pretend, therefore, that historians can ever fully recover the affective culture of early twentieth-century girls' schools. Instead, this essay focuses on the ways in which the practices and desires of schoolgirls took on meaning in the discourses of others, as well as in the recollections of ex-schoolgirls themselves. The early decades of the twentieth century witnessed a vociferous debate among diverse cultural authorities over proper and improper forms of schoolgirl intimacy. These contentious and often contradictory discourses do not allow us reliably to reconstruct schoolgirl experience—although they may occasionally illuminate it in their crossbeams—yet they are nonetheless valuable to the historian because they bear testimony to the changing significances of female love and sexuality within the larger social landscape of early twentieth-century Japan.

Endearing Words

By all accounts, schoolgirl intimacy in early twentieth-century Japan involved a good deal of talking. Through speech, intimate feelings were transformed into words, and words had in turn the capacity to evoke powerful emotions and desires. Few schoolgirl conversations have come down to us in their original, spoken form. It is possible, however, to use published accounts, supplemented by personal interviews, to reconstruct—if imperfectly—the terminology used by schoolgirls when they spoke about their own relationships.

Quoting a female educator, a 1911 newspaper article informed readers that students at contemporary girls' schools called "passionate love" (*netsuai*) among their classmates by a variety of names.[5] At Atomi Girls' School (founded 1875), one of the oldest private schools for girls in Japan, students reportedly spoke of *goshin'yū*, or "intimate friends."[6] The largely aristocratic students at the female division (established 1877) of the Peers' School (Gakushūin), on the other hand, allegedly favored *ohaikara*, a word deriving from the English "high collar"—in the sense of "stylish."[7] By contrast, their counterparts at Ochanomizu Girls' School (established 1890)—the only national, as opposed to prefectural, secondary school for girls at the time—were said to feel *onetsu,* meaning "fever" or "passion." At one or more of Tokyo's four prefectural girls' schools (founded between 1888 and 1907), meanwhile, the preferred designation was reputedly *ome.* Its etymology is not certain but it possibly derives from a combination of the elements *o* and *me,* meaning "male" and "female."[8] Finally, the educator credited students at an unnamed private school with having formed the neologism *odeya,* which prefixed the honorific *o-* to a transliterated form of the English word "dear."[9]

A magazine writer, commenting on the above report, expressed incredulity that such a diverse vocabulary had put down roots among the country's schoolgirl population.[10] For the abundance of such words implied the currency of practices and feelings that, in the minds of many adults in the early twentieth century, were beginning to take on a new, and often alarming, set of connotations. The above expressions all manifested the power of schoolgirls to define themselves and their cohorts in their own terms—a power that adult authorities preferred to keep in their own hands. That journalists took note of this vocabulary is a boon, however, for historians, since the words they recorded capture something of the meaning that student intimacies carried within the conceptual universe of schoolgirls.

For schoolgirls or college women in early twentieth-century Europe and America, the associations of a term such as "fever," the Japanese character for which literally signifies "heat," might well have struck a chord of recognition. Various terms in the Anglo-American student vocabulary—"rave," "pash" (for passion), "smash"—registered a similarly ardent emotional intensity, as did Romance-language equivalents such as the Italian *fiamma,* which means "flame" (a term used also in England).[11] Likewise, just as Atomi schoolgirls spoke of "intimate friends," pedagogues at early twentieth-century Dutch convent schools referred to "particular friendships" (*bijzondere vriendschapen*), suggesting that observers in both school contexts situated these relationships along an affective continuum that included "ordinary" friendship as well.[12] Two features of the Japanese schoolgirl vocabulary that are more peculiar to their linguistic environment also deserve mention. Several of the terms listed in the 1911 article incorporated the honorifics *o-* or *go-*, which have no precise European analogues. In addition to suggesting that the relationships referred to enjoyed a respected place in schoolgirl culture, the use of honorifics was a marker of feminine, and especially upper-class, speech within a linguistic system that was deeply classed and gendered. A similar sense of cultural capital and socioeconomic privilege is echoed in Japanese schoolgirls' use of English words such as "high collar" and "dear." However radically transformed from their original pronunciations, these words point to the European-language education restricted to girls' schools and other elective institutions, which were largely inaccessible to daughters of working-class families.

The ostensible diversity of student vocabulary may indicate that cultures of schoolgirl intimacy were relatively localized around the close of the Meiji era, each school constituting something of a world unto itself.[13] In 1911, 250 "higher girls' schools" existed in Japan, enrolling a combined student population of 64,809.[14] Schoolgirls, particularly those fortunate enough to attend the well-established and prominent institutions with which the "female educator" claimed familiarity, often developed a sense of allegiance to their school that lasted long after graduation. During the time that they attended girls' school (anywhere from two to eight years), the girls' primary social world and the horizon of their day-to day activities existed within the school's gates, especially in the case of those students who boarded in adjacent dormitories. The vocabulary of schoolgirl intimacy might thus vary easily from school to school even within the relatively narrow boundaries of Tokyo, which was the site of all the institutions that the article explicitly named.

In paradoxical fashion, greater signs of lexical uniformity may be detected by the 1920s and 1930s, even as girls' schools and their students continued to multiply rapidly. A word that does not appear on the 1911 journalist's list—"S"—had come into common use at girls' schools across the country by this time. I will hereafter use "S"—in the Latin alphabet, as it was frequently graphicalized during the period—as a generic signifier for schoolgirl intimacy. In doing so, I follow the practice of many Japanese schoolgirls and members of the general public in the early twentieth century.[15] As British sexologist Havelock Ellis (1859–1939) wrote about a contemporary Italian equivalent, Japanese schoolgirls used "S" to designate "both the beloved person and the friendship in the abstract."[16] "S" stood as an abbreviation for the English word "sister," which schoolgirls employed also in such transliterated forms as *shisutā* and *shisu* ("sis"). Although the expression does not appear to have been directly borrowed from English usage, it carried, like the previously mentioned *ohaikara* and *odeya,* a certain Westernized cachet and corresponding aura of privileged knowledge. Beginning in the 1920s, the term "S" also became widely diffused through the mass media, a fact that doubtless accounts in part for its geographical spread and standardization among schoolgirls themselves. By the late 1930s, the word had become sufficiently naturalized among schoolgirls—as well as being familiar to many outsiders—that one woman who attended girls' school during that period, Tokiko, remembered with embarrassment that she once had to ask her father about its etymology.[17]

This lexical history was still vivid in the memories of two women whom I interviewed in the summer of 1992, both alumnae of Akita City's prefectural girls' school (founded 1900). Toshi had entered in 1922 and graduated in 1926, while Hideko attended from 1927 to 1932.[18] Toshi recollected that the prevalent term among her classmates was *ome*—the same expression that prefectural girls' school students in Tokyo reportedly used more than a decade previously. Hideko also knew and used the expression *ome* during her early years at the same institution, but recalled that it had fallen out of fashion by the time she graduated. It had by that time been replaced by "S," which sounded more "chic" (*kakkō ii*). Hideko conjectured that part of the appeal of the new term derived from its association with a geographically broader schoolgirl culture with which her classmates grew familiar through their reading of nationally distributed girls' magazines (*shōjo zasshi*).[19]

The apparent shift from *ome* to "S" in the usage of Akita City schoolgirls suggests a more complicated relationship between these two terms than has hitherto been proposed. Jennifer Robertson, an anthropologist, has provocatively analyzed the two expressions as emblematic, respectively, of "heterogender" and "homogender" constructions of same-sex intimacy.[20] To the extent that the term *ome* conveyed, at least in some early twentieth-century print sources, a sense of masculine/feminine dichotomy, while "S" implied a relationship between same-gender siblings, this is undoubtedly true. Yet we must also take

into account the possibility that the usage of outsiders may have differed from that of schoolgirls themselves. Toshi and Hideko recalled
that in the institution they attended schoolgirls used the terms interchangeably. According to both women, there was little sense of a
"butch/femme" division of roles among the couples to whom they and
their schoolmates applied the term *ome,* nor was its presumed derivation
from "male" and "female" something that they themselves were aware
of at the time. In Hideko's conceptual lexicon, "S" was not an antonym
of *ome* but a synonym that came to replace it over the course of her
schoolgirl career. Instead of a dichotomy, the lexical distinction between *ome* and "S" represented for her a diachronic process, involving
changing interregional cultural dynamics.

At the Urawa girls' school in Saitama prefecture (founded 1896),[21]
some students may have used the term without being aware of a connection with the English word "sister," like Tokiko, who entered the
institution in 1937. Yet without a doubt, the metaphor of sisterhood was
a recurring trope in the language of Japanese schoolgirls.[22] This sense
of sorority registers itself not only in the English-derived *shisutā* and
shisu, but in such older indigenous designations as *ane* (elder sister) and
imōto (younger sister), which schoolgirl couples frequently used in addressing one another both in speech and in written correspondence.

On a related note, the historian Carroll Smith-Rosenberg has characterized entry into school in nineteenth-century America as the point at
which a "young girl began to move outside the matrix of her mother's
support group to develop a network of her own." Smith-Rosenberg
hypothesizes that earlier socialization by female relatives, and in particular by mothers, impressed itself on the form that friendship took
among American schoolgirls, in which one partner might assume the
"nurturing role of pseudo-mother," and the other the "dependency role
of daughter."[23] This mother/daughter dynamic finds more recent and
obvious lexical expression in the "mummy"/"baby" ties of Lesotho.
Japanese schoolgirls' preference for the sororal rather than the mater-
nal/filial kinship metaphor that is found among their American and Lesotho counterparts is thus striking from a comparative perspective.

The social dynamics and valences of sisterhood are not universal,
but instead vary according to historical and cultural context. It is necessary to remember that most indigenous kinship terms for sister or

brother in Japanese specify the position of one sibling relative to others with respect to age. The fictive sisters who constituted the "S" pair thus participated in what was widely conceived as an unequal relationship— a relationship in which role asymmetry was structured according to age difference, in which the senior person enjoyed the superordinate position, and whose hierarchy of elder and younger was permanent and inflexible.[24] We should not assume that, when Japanese schoolgirls chose a sororal rather than a maternal metaphor, it was because sisterhood represented for them an egalitarian ideal of the sort that the feminist catchphrase "Sisterhood is global," rooted as it is in Western historical understandings of kinship, presupposes. Rather, the Japanese idiom of sisterhood could accommodate relationships of nurturing and dependency just as easily as the maternal trope identified by Smith-Rosenberg.[25]

One of my interviewees, Toshi, conjectured, like Smith-Rosenberg did in a different context, that earlier family ties left a decisive imprint on schoolgirl attachments. It was only natural, Toshi suggested, that upon entering the unfamiliar environment of the girls' school a younger student might wish to form a bond with an older and more experienced one, much as she may have looked up to an elder sister or sisters at home. Both print sources and personal interviews indicate that schoolgirl couples were often of slightly different ages, and belonged to different grades in school. One girls' school graduate whom I interviewed, Emiko, recollected that the "ideal" couple consisted of girls separated by about two years or grades.[26]

The sororal metaphor used by Japanese schoolgirls thus incorporated a sense not only of solidarity, but of hierarchy and difference. Still, by no means should the resonances of the word "S" be understood as harsh or authoritarian. Among the salient characteristics of the vocabulary discussed above were its focus on the affective aspects of the relationship and its connotations of emotional intensity and warm trust— "fever," "dear one," "intimate friends," and so forth. Not all twentieth-century observers spoke, however, of schoolgirl intimacies using terms of endearment. The remainder of this essay examines in turn the discourses of three groups of outsiders—sexologists, journalists, and feminists—who had a great deal to say on the subject of schoolgirls during the early twentieth century. Although all three groups shared a privileged status as adults and as published opinion leaders, the terms in which they discussed schoolgirl intimacy reflected perspectives that differed significantly from one another as well as from that of students. Outside the walls of the girls' school, the whispers and laughter of schoolgirls often drowned amid the clamor of these adult voices.

Same Difference: Sexological Constructions

Like the institution of the girls' school, the science of sexology was a recently arrived presence on the cultural landscape of early twentieth-century Japan. [27] A variety of discourses had claimed authoritative knowledge of sexuality during the Tokugawa period (1600–1868). From the late nineteenth century, however, the erotic realm came increasingly to be regarded as the domain of medical experts who had been trained in scientific principles and taxonomies that, albeit first systematized in the West, were deemed to hold a universal validity. In Japan as elsewhere, the emergence of sexology as a discrete and coherent branch of scientific knowledge was by no means a smooth or even process, and encountered opposition and obstacles in many quarters. Even so, its impact upon popular understandings of female-female intimacy in Japan was swift and far-reaching. Through the writings of sexologists, by the early decades of the twentieth century even many who were not medical experts came to hold that intimate relationships between females—epitomized by "S" ties among schoolgirls—manifested a form of "sexual perversion" (*hentai seiyoku*) known as "same-sex love" (*dōseiai*).

As I have argued elsewhere, the concept of "same-sex love" had little meaning for Japanese before the late nineteenth century.[28] Although earlier discourses allowed the possibility of erotic desires and practices taking place between males or between females, Japanese sources do not articulate the idea that female-female and male-male eroticism constituted analogous and fundamentally related phenomena—one of the theoretical underpinnings of the "same-sex love" construct—before the late Meiji period. The Tokugawa erotic lexicon featured various words to describe sexual interaction between females, yet this vocabulary remained·distinct from the much more rich, more standardized, and widely circulating one that surrounded male-male erotic relations. [29] Only with the emergence of new medical understandings of sexuality in the late nineteenth century did a language come into being that permitted male-male and female-female forms of eroticism to be spoken of in the same terms. The neologism *dōseiai* dates, strictly speaking, from around the 1910s, but its cognate *dōsei no kōsetsu* or "same-sex intercourse" appears as early as an 1890 forensic-pathology text by Shimizu Sadao.[30] The "same sex" (*dōsei*) element of the new formulation made explicit that what was most important in determining the nature of a given sexual interaction was not the category to which the erotic object belonged per se, but rather whether the sexes, classed according to genital dimorphism, of the participants were the same as or different from each other. Male-male and female-female combinations came to be perceived as intrinsically related because both failed to embody the norm of "cross-sex love" (*iseiai*) upheld by the emerging science of sexology, which defined human erotic capacities as existing primarily for the purposes of reproduction.

Even among medico-scientific authorities, male and female forms of "same-sex love" did not immediately gain equal recognition. Shimizu Sadao revealed his androcentrism, for example, when he defined "same-sex intercourse" as synonymous with anal intercourse (*keikan*)—implicitly between males.[31] Forensic pathologists of the Meiji period, who were among the earliest medical experts on "same-sex love," devoted far less attention to female-female than to male-male sexual practices. This was not only because the use of coercion or involvement of minors that would subject them to prosecution under the post-1880 criminal code were relatively rare, but also because physical evidence of these practices was, by forensic pathologists' own admission, not so easy to detect clinically.[32] Meiji discursive authorities also inherited the masculinist textual legacy of the still recent Tokugawa past, in which female-female relations occupied less conspicuous a place in the realm of cultural representation than male-male eroticism—or the "way of youths" (*shudō*)—and were virtually ignored in legal and medical sources. The emergence in the late nineteenth century of the new sexological model, with its theoretical equation of male and female "same-sex love," played a key role in elevating the visibility of female-female erotic relations within the social imaginary, and accorded them for the first time in the history of Japanese erotic discourses an integral place within authoritative cultural mappings of sexuality.

Within just a few decades, female "same-sex love" appeared to sexological authorities to be ubiquitous. In 1920, the prominent sexologist
Sawada Junjirō listed the "classes" of women among whom it was
known to take place as follows: students, factory workers, nurses, aristocratic ladies, unmarried daughters, married women and concubines,
widows, convicts, maids at inns and restaurants, shop clerks, clerical
workers, koto teachers, actresses, geishas and prostitutes, and nuns.[33]
Few, if any, women would not have fit into one or more of these categories. Among the above groups, however, Sawada viewed the phenomenon as most prevalent among girls' school students—so much so
that schoolgirls and "same-sex love" appeared "virtual concomitants"
(*tsukimono*) of each other. More specifically, Sawada noted that the incidence of "same-sex love" was concentrated around the second and
third grades of girls' school, when students were likely to be between
thirteen and sixteen years of age.[34] Sawada's observations contrasted
sharply with the view expressed twenty years previously by the forensic
pathologist Ishikawa Kiyotada that female "same-sex love" occurred
most frequently among prostitutes.[35] Over the space of two decades,
schoolgirls had come to occupy a conspicuous—if by no means reputable—place in the sexological imagination.

In explaining "same-sex love" among schoolgirls, Japanese sexologists relied heavily on the work of their European and American colleagues, who had begun compiling a vast medical literature on "homosexuality" in the latter part of the nineteenth century. Whatever its local
name, sexologists believed "same-sex love" to share a universal essence
that was constant across cultures and eras, constituting a phenomenon
that they as scientists were best equipped to understand and possibly to
eradicate. By documenting that "same-sex love" existed in Japan as in
the West, Japanese sexologists sought to demonstrate the universal validity of the medico-scientific constructs that they introduced to their
colleagues and to the general public, and thereby to legitimate the
knowledge to which they claimed privileged access. Wherever possible,
they supplemented foreign descriptions of sexological categories with
native examples. This was not difficult in the case of male "same-sex
love," since Japanese history and literature furnished a rich and continuous written record of male-male eroticism stretching back more
than a millennium. By contrast, it was contemporary accounts of

schoolgirl culture that offered the most readily available and best documented examples of "female same-sex love," no doubt because of their sheer number and ease of access.

Sexology embraced a range of viewpoints, and sexologists were not always in agreement with one another. Regarding the causes of "same-sex love," for example, considerable debate surrounded the relative importance of congenital and acquired factors, just as it continues to do among Western authorities on "homosexuality." Habuto Eiji (?–1929), one of the most widely read sexologists in early twentieth-century Japan, felt that while it was common for preadolescent girls to experience a "feeling of love" toward a close friend or a teacher of the same sex, this tendency might indicate a "hereditary element of mental disease" if it lasted into puberty. The latter phenomenon occurred, according to Habuto, in "extremely many" cases.[36] Congenital etiologies like Habuto's typically stressed the presence of "masculine" traits in one of the partners, not only in behavioral or psychological terms but often physiologically. They drew heavily upon the trope of "sexual inversion" that had been elaborated by such nineteenth-century Western authorities as Richard von Krafft-Ebing (1840–1902).[37] Yet even the sex counselor Shimada Hiroshi, who leaned toward the acquired view, assumed that schoolgirl couples typically consisted of one girl who took on the "male" role and another who acted as the "female."[38] In assuming gender polarity to be an intrinsic part of erotic exchange, Shimada, Habuto, and many of their colleagues revealed their fundamentally heteronormative biases.

Other sexologists, however, acknowledged that intimate schoolgirl ties were usually followed by "normal" marriage to a man, and that few schoolgirls exhibited overtly masculine characteristics. They therefore adopted the opinion, which had found earlier articulation by Havelock Ellis, that "same-sex love" among schoolgirls was typically acquired, situational, and temporary. The forensic pathologist Takada Giichirō (1886–?), for example, refused to believe that the "protagonists" (*hiroin*) of various publicly reported scandals involving *ome* in girls' schools were invariably manlike, or that they possessed congenitally diseased personalities, as the viewpoint of Krafft-Ebing implied. Rather, Takada understood *ome* to be the resort of "graceful [*yūbi*] females who turned to it because of inadequate sexual lives."[39] According to Takada and other supporters of this acquired view, segregation from the opposite sex was sufficient cause for "same-sex love" to thrive in girls' schools, just as it reputedly flourished in other male-scarce environments such as textile mills, penitentiaries, convents, nurses' quarters, and venereal hospitals for prostitutes. Such a perception echoed the earlier observation of American physician R. N. Shufeldt that "Female boarding schools and colleges are the great breeding grounds of artificial homosexuality."[40] It also fueled arguments for coeducation, a measure that many sexologists in early twentieth-century Japan viewed as salutary for the psychosexual development of young females as well as males, although it was not until after the Pacific War that it became widely implemented.

To say that "same-sex love" was acquired was not the same as saying that it was benign. While a number of sexologists were willing to admit that intimate relationships between schoolgirls might be less pathological than other forms of "same-sex love," they nevertheless predicted dire consequences for the parties involved when the relationships progressed too far. How far was too far? For authorities such as Habuto and Komine Shigeyuki (1883–1942), it was the initiation of physical relations that marked the danger point.[41] Shimada, on the other hand, saw the formation of masculine and feminine roles as cause for worry in itself.[42] If intimacy exceeded permissible limits, schoolgirls supposedly risked a wide range of misfortunes that early twentieth-century experts attributed to "same-sex love," including vaginal cramps, frigidity, "withering of the genitals" (*in'i*), sterility, neurasthenia, insanity, masculinization of muscular and cell structure, suicide, murder, and other types of criminal behavior.[43] Nor was the imagined harm limited to the individual: one 1913 sexological tract identified "same-sex-love" in girls' schools as a "principle cause of declining birth rates in civilized nations."[44]

Such dire prognoses provided a rationale for sexologists to codify and to publicize the supposed symptoms of "same-sex love" among schoolgirls. Taking a cue from the Italian team of Obici and Marchesini, a psychiatrist and a psychologist respectively, Japanese experts drew up elaborate checklists to aid parents, educators, and other interested parties in distinguishing "same-sex love" from ordinary friendship.[45] According to this symptomatology, the true nature of a relationship lay encoded in such seeming trivia as hairstyle and hair ornaments. If two girls wore their hair alike, it was a mark of excessive affection; if one of them bobbed her hair, it might indicate sexual relations.[46] Since taking portraits together was a common schoolgirl practice, the girls' manner of being photographed likewise offered a text of their intimacy, available for sexological deciphering. If "love" (*ren'ai*) was involved, one girl allegedly remained standing while the other sat (a common arrangement in male-female wedding portraits even today); by contrast, mere friends adopted the same pose.[47] Curiously, in the case of coiffure, sameness functioned as a sign of danger, while in the example of the photographic pose it was difference that was alarming. Notwithstanding such inconsistencies, Sawada assured his readers that, "These things are immediately visible to the eyes of those with experience, but to those with none, they cannot easily be apprehended."[48]

The experience claimed by male sexologists was obviously not first-hand knowledge, but consisted rather in a pastiche of stereotypes that sexology itself helped to disseminate. Habuto, for example, depicted "same-sex love" among schoolgirls and female factory hands in a manner that is homogenizing to the point of caricature.

As love between the female couple begins to heat up, their letters start to read like love notes [between males and females], which they send under pseudonyms for no reason. They have their photographs taken often. They wear the same hairstyle, hair ornaments, and so forth. They count meeting at school (in the case of schoolgirls) or at the factory (among factory hands) as their greatest pleasure. They leave the house early, visit each other inordinately, and stroll hand in hand in parks and at shrine and temple fairs. They exchange meaningful smiles on almost any occasion. Their conversations are invariably long, and they scribble their partner's name in their books and notebooks.[49]

Still, the sociologists Takebe Tongo (1871–1945) and Washio Hiroshi (1892–1951) noted that, despite such pleasures, the couple was always aware they were "committing something forbidden."[50]

Part of what branded "same-sex love" as forbidden was the criticism of sexologists themselves. Earlier Japanese discourses—whether religious, ethical, medical, or legal—had seldom explicitly condemned excessive intimacy between females. When female-female intimacy had received cultural (or more accurately, male) attention, it was typically for the purpose of erotic titillation or of humor. The proliferation of sexological commentary on "same-sex love" that began in the late Meiji period helped not only to place intimate bonds between females within the public spotlight, but to imbue them with a suspect aura as part of the domain of sexuality—the domain to which sexology held claim as an authoritative science. From the perspective of the general public, what made "S" seem an intrinsically sexual phenomenon was perhaps not so much the practices and desires of schoolgirls themselves, with which only a minority of adults had direct familiarity, as the fact that sexologists chose to speak and write about them in the first place. Although sexological authorities varied in the degree to which they characterized schoolgirl relationships as either pathological or harmless, their discussions of the subject almost inevitably surfaced in connection with the question of "sexual perversion," which had clearly negative, and obviously sexual, connotations. Here, the neighbors of "same-sex love" included such newly coined notions as sadism, masochism, fetishism, and zoophilia, which the taxonomic practices of sexologists brought into alarming proximity with the prim confines of the girls' school.

At the same time, evidence that schoolgirl attachments involved sexual activity, or of the form it took, was not easy to produce. Sawada imagined a "stepladder" by which the physical element of "same-sex love" increased with the age of the schoolgirl. Sexual relations, he maintained, did not usually occur until after the age of fifteen or sixteen, reaching a peak frequency at "twenty and eighteen."[51] The ostensible scientificity of such statistics—the source of which Sawada saw no need to provide—masked the inherent difficulty that sexologists faced in asserting authoritative knowledge of activities that were, by their own account, carried out in secret. Sexologists imagined sexual practices between schoolgirls as encompassing, at least in some cases, genital activity. This is evidenced by the comments of Habuto, who alleged that an autopsy, performed seventeen years prior to his writing, upon a drowned pair of girls' school graduates had revealed the sexual organs of both to be "extremely devastated"—closer to those of "prostitutes," he maintained, than of "virgins."[52] A similar claim of privileged vision into the innermost recesses of schoolgirl sexuality may be found in an anecdote, related by at least one sexologist as "fact," that workers who were renovating a certain school dormitory in Tokyo had found hidden within its ceilings and floorboards an abundant cache of dildos—instruments that popular sources had associated with both autoerotic and female-female sexual practices since the Tokugawa period.[53] Such allusions were about as far as prewar sexologists dared go in specifying the presumed nature of sexual activity among schoolgirls, not only because of the difficulties of empirical verification, but for fear of violating rigid obscenity laws that the state had imposed on publishers since the 1880s. By the same token, the existence of censorship prompted sexologists to resort more readily to insinuation, and afforded their audiences greater scope for lurid inference.[54]

Others within the sexological community were inclined to believe that "same-sex love" manifested itself among the majority of girls as a form of "romance," in the words of Shimada, whose physical expression went no further than a kiss, or according to another authority, a gentle caress (*aibu*).[55] So long as it did not escalate any further or last indefinitely, some experts came to hold that "same-sex love" might even qualify as a healthy phenomenon within the context of female adolescence. The sexologist and social activist Yasuda Tokutarō (1898–1983), for example, regarded "same-sex love" among schoolgirls not as a sign of physiological defect but as a "normal" (*jōtai*) phase in the development of the female libido. In Yasuda's interpretation, "same-sex love" figured as a harmless form of adolescent "love play" (*ren'ai yūgi*), or as a "preliminary step" to a future career in "cross-sex love."[56] Similarly, the psychoanalyst Ōtsuki Kenji (1891–1977) described intense attachments between young females as a "practice run" (*yokō enshū*) for future male-female relations.[57] Such constructions of "same-sex love" as a necessary and even beneficial stage in psychological development became increasingly common during the 1930s and 1940s, reflecting the growing influence of Sigmund Freud, one of whose early translators was Ōtsuki himself. This view nevertheless took for granted that "cross-sex love" was the only legitimate outcome of the developmental process, and that "same-sex love" remained a form of "perversion" in the event that it outlasted adolescence.

While not all sexologists countenanced the notion that schoolgirl "same-sex love" was normal, many found it more palatable than its schoolboy equivalent. Like girls' schools, boys' schools (that is, all-male middle schools and higher schools) figured prominently in the landscape of so-called sexual perversion that early twentieth-century sexologists charted.[58] Although schoolboys and schoolgirls employed separate vocabularies to designate intimate relations among their peers— suggesting that they probably saw little in common with each other's experiences—sexologists routinely assigned both to the category of "same-sex love." Even sexologists, however, had to acknowledge that significant differences existed between the two cultures of student eroticism, and between the manifestations of male and female "same-sex love" more generally. Virtually all authorities agreed, for example, that relationships between schoolboys were more likely to involve a physical dimension than those of their schoolgirl contemporaries. Embedded in this perception was the sexological belief that sexual desire sought release more straightforwardly in males than in females, the presumption being that females were burdened with a complex emotional makeup not readily accessible to rational male understanding. Shirai Kiichi, in a work on adolescent psychology, stated in no uncertain terms that "same-sex love" between males living in dormitories or other settings, who were deprived of contact with females, contained little of the "mysterious" (*shinpiteki*) and "platonic" (*puratonikku*) character of female "same-sex love," instead consisting mainly of the "congress of flesh and flesh, in other words, anal intercourse."[59] Similarly, elements of coercion surfaced much more frequently in sexological accounts of schoolboy "same-sex love" than they did in corresponding descriptions of schoolgirls.

These representational strategies may or may not have reflected actual differences in the social organization of schoolboy and schoolgirl cultures, which deserve further exploration. Yet, they undoubtedly served to reassure many ordinary readers, as well as sexologists themselves, that familiar gender distinctions prevailed even in the "mysterious" world of "same-sex love," and that in the end sexual sameness could never entirely erase sexual difference. Notwithstanding the theoretical equivalence of male and female "same-sex love" in the medicoscientific paradigm, the characteristics that sexologists assigned the two were in many cases diametrically opposed. According to Sawada, for example, "same-sex love" in males was "positive" (*sekkyokuteki*) and "yang" (*yōsei*), in females "negative" (*shōkyokuteki*) and "yin" (*insei*); in males, it was "deep and narrow," in females "shallow and broad."[60]

Yasuda wrote simply that "same-sex love" in females was "feminine to a fault" (*doko made mo onnarashii*).[61] While such characterizations were hardly models of analytic rigor, they helped to legitimate the sexological view of the two sexes as incommensurable opposites. At the same time, they reinforced popular gender stereotypes by endowing them with the supposedly unimpeachable authority of science.

Paradoxically, in describing schoolgirl relationships, sexologists and other male writers borrowed tropes from the world of the boys' school, with which they possessed greater personal familiarity, and which had a history of textual representation stretching back as far as the late nineteenth century. When Yasuda wrote of married women who had spent their time in girls' school "chasing . . . beautiful young girls" (*bishōjo o sakan ni oimakutta*), or when a certain girls' school principal referred to "upper-grade students sending love notes to pretty and sweet lower-grade students, or else seeking their acquaintance through a third person," they were invoking images already stereotypical within a boys' school context.[62] Such characterizations took for granted that the initiative in forming intimacies came from the senior party, as was conventionally imagined to be the case among schoolboys. The elderly girls' school graduates whom I interviewed, on the other hand, recalled that in fact the reverse dynamic prevailed just as often, if not more frequently. Among published male writers, the novelist Hamao Shirō (1896–1935) was one of the few to posit a fundamental gender difference in this respect, claiming that "whereas love advances [*kyūai*] usually come from the senior person in male same-sex love, in females they more often are directed upward from the junior one." Hamao explained the discrepancy, however, by stating that "females prefer to be loved rather than to love," thus implying that, despite the supposedly reversed polarities of the relationship, age hierarchy prevailed insofar as the senior party enjoyed the position of privilege.[63]

According to many sexologists, female and male "same-sex love" differed not only qualitatively but also quantitatively. As the early decades of the twentieth century progressed, "same-sex love" was gendered increasingly as a female phenomenon. The psychiatrist Kure Shūzō (1865–1932) was already in the minority in 1920 when he asserted that it occurred more commonly in males. Kure based this view not on empirical evidence, but on the belief that "sexual desire" (*seiyoku*)—by which he meant an instinct to mate with the opposite sex—constituted the "foundation" of the female character, making girls and women less likely to deviate from the "goal" of reproduction.[64] By 1935, however, Kure's fellow sexologist Yasuda could assert with little hesitation that "same-sex love" in the present day and age had become virtually a female "monopoly" (*dokusen*). By way of evidence, Yasuda cited frequent press reports describing suicides of pairs of females, as well as the apparent prevalence of "S" relationships in girls' schools. Conversely, Yasuda believed "same-sex love" to be on the decline among schoolboys, for whom its appeal had allegedly been diminished by the spread of "modern institutions of entertainment."[65] His historical narrative painted "same-sex love" as a formerly male bastion that had fallen into female hands as part of a more general advance of women in post–Restoration society. Yasuda thus drew attention to broader changes in gender relations and to issues of feminism, which the last section of this essay will consider in greater detail. At the same time, Yasuda's reference to media reports of scandal highlighted the important role that newspapers and magazines played in furnishing material for sexological assessments of contemporary social pathology. It was not only the diagnostic pronouncements of medico-scientific authorities but also the sensationalizing narratives of journalists that focused public attention on the intimate lives of schoolgirls.

Schools for Scandal: Journalistic Constructions

From their debut in the 1870s, girls' schools and their students attracted a degree of journalistic attention far out of proportion to their actual numbers. Just as the institutional architecture of the girls' school offered material witness to the rapid changes occurring in Meiji society, the figure of the schoolgirl, with her distinctive code of dress—perhaps even jauntily riding a bicycle—provided journalists with a conspicuous embodiment of the "new" Japan and a rhetorically useful, if deeply ambiguous, symbol of the nation's budding womanhood. As Honda Masuko has vividly described, the schoolgirl entered the cultural stage greeted by "envy and aspiration" on the one hand, and "derision and contempt" on the other.[66] Journalists found much to criticize in her appearance, behavior, and various intrusions into masculine domains of learning and pleasure, yet at the same time garnered profits by circulating images of her among a reading public that was ever eager for a glimpse behind the gates of educational privilege.

Prior to the twentieth century, journalistic representations of the girls' school seldom focused attention upon intimate relations among their students. Rather, it was the fear that young females who had been loosed from traditional forms of familial and community supervision might engage in premature and dangerous interaction with males that was foremost on the minds of critics. Even as Meiji journalists accused the schoolgirl of arrogating "masculinity" and of indulging in "decadence," they typically saw these qualities as manifested in her precocious involvement with the opposite sex rather than in her behavior toward other females. Anxiety over illicit male-female relations was the other side of the coin, as it were, of the proclaimed goal of secondary education for females, which was to train girls for their future role as "good wives and wise mothers" (*ryōsai kenbo*).[67] It also distinguished the schoolgirl from her schoolboy counterpart, whom journalists and popular writers began criticizing considerably earlier in the Meiji period for his sexual misbehavior with fellow male students as much as for his pursuit of male-female eroticism.

From around the turn of the twentieth century, public perceptions regarding the propriety of relations between schoolgirls began conspicuously to change. Traces of this process may be found in the humor magazine *Kokkei shinbun* (Funny times; 1901–1908). A 1902 issue of the magazine offered readers, by implication male, a list of topics that they might use in starting conversations with strangers (also implicitly male) on a train. Among the proposed icebreakers was the following: "I hear that love between females [*onna dōshi no ren'ai*] is popular in Tokyo lately. What's that all about? Is it like the '*toichi-haichi*' that once got written up in one of the Osaka rags?"[68] Another article in the same issue cited the girls' school as the institutional source of such "pernicious fads" (*akufū ryūkō*). It placed the blame in part upon an incident earlier that year in which a government-approved reader for schoolgirls had been found to contain a passage from a Tokugawa literary work that made passing reference to Yotsumeya, a store in Edo that specialized in dildos, aphrodisiacs, and other erotic paraphernalia.[69]

The humorous context in which it appeared notwithstanding, the imaginary train discussion suggests that schoolgirl relationships were in

1902 a timely, if still somewhat unfamiliar, subject for men to talk about. In the magazine's construction, "love between females" constituted a suitable and even recommended topic of conversation within the quintessentially public setting of the train, along with more conventional opening lines such as "Do you have a match?" Activities that went on ostensibly "between females" became public—and in large part male—knowledge through the agency of journalism, whether in the guise of newspapers (for example, the disreputable if unspecified "Osaka rag"), or of magazines such as *Kokkei shinbun*, which disseminated the information to an even broader national audience. Journalists possessed the authority not only to determine what was newsworthy, but to brand certain cultural phenomena as "fads," thereby implying that their incidence was actually growing.

Equally suggestive is the attempt of our perplexed man on the train—a stand-in, I would argue, for a larger masculine reading public—to make new conceptual connections within the realm of female love and sexuality. The imaginary passenger is already familiar with the notion of *toichi-haichi*, a slang expression of either Tokugawa or Meiji origin and uncertain etymology used to designate sexual interaction between two females. *Toichi-haichi* appeared usually in reference to the milieu of prostitutes and geishas, and stories of such activities taking place between professional entertainers, or between them and female patrons, occasionally surfaced in the columns of Meiji newspapers.[70] The train passenger is depicted as confused, however, about how to integrate his existing knowledge with information that he has acquired more recently. What was the connection between "love" and genital acts between females? Was what happened in Tokyo the same thing that happened in Osaka? Could the feelings and practices of prostitutes and schoolgirls be related despite their positions at opposite ends of the social ladder? Tellingly, the speaker never wonders whether there might be any relationship between "love between females" and "love between males."

The train scenario illuminates a broader circuit of knowledge. Journalism provided a medium for the ostensibly private intimacies of schoolgirls to circulate far beyond the confines of the girls' school, becoming an object of consumption and taking on a new range of public meanings. Typically, schoolgirl relationships entered this circuit of knowledge in connection with a scandal, prompting journalistic commentary that was deliberately sensationalistic and that encouraged various reader inferences regarding schoolgirl culture in general. News stories flowed easily from one publication to another, just as the *Kokkei shinbun* article drew upon and added new inflections to the earlier reportage of the unspecified "Osaka rag." Newspaper and magazine accounts also served as an important source of knowledge for nonjournalistic authorities, including sexologists and feminists, as well as general readers.

One prototypical scandal involving schoolgirl intimacy occurred in 1911, near the very end of the Meiji period. Early in the morning of July 26, the bodies of two young females, tied together at the hips with a pink waistband, were discovered awash near the town of Itoigawa on the Oyashirazu coast of Niigata prefecture.[71] Police identified the dead couple as Sone Sadako and Okamura Tamae, twenty-year-old graduates of Tokyo's Second Prefectural Girls' School. In subsequent days, newspaper readers would learn many more details of the two girls' relationship, which their fellow students were said to have regarded as a conspicuous case of *ome*, and for which a teacher had reprimanded them on more than one occasion. It was reported that the pair continued to visit each other almost daily in the year following their graduation, leading the father of one of them to insist that they limit the frequency of their meetings. Arrangements were proceeding at the same time for Sone's marriage. Evidently unhappy with either of these prospects, Sone and Okamura slipped out of their homes and journeyed to the Oyashirazu coast (curiously, the place name literally means "Parents Not-Knowing"), where they spent part of their last days together sightseeing. On the night of the 25th, leaving behind a small sum of money at the inn where they had stopped for a rest and a meal, they leapt into the Japan Sea, weighting their sleeves with stones.

In staging their joint suicide, Sone and Okamura followed a long tradition of death performance known as *shinjū*, meaning "what is in the heart." During the early Tokugawa period, the term had referred to a variety of bodily practices that a person might use to demonstrate the sincerity of his or her feelings toward another person, ranging from writing vows in blood or cutting one's hair, to more extreme acts such as flesh-piercing or cutting off a finger.[72] By the eighteenth century, *shinjū*, along with its synonym *jōshi*, or "death out of passion," came more specifically to denote various forms of self-inflicted death, including not only joint suicides, but also solitary suicides and suicide-murders. *Shinjū* served in Tokugawa literature and drama as a conventional recourse for ill-fated lovers, whose fatal act gave visible and permanent expression to otherwise illicit ties and emotions. Long after the Tokugawa period had ended, *shinjū* continued to function as a mutual demonstration of loyalty as well as a form of self-representation toward others.

The exact thoughts of Sone and Okamura in their last days of life, we will never know. Yet through their actions, the couple made "what is in the heart" available for reading. It seems significant, for example, that upon purchasing ferry tickets the pair identified themselves as "Tanaka Mitsu (24) and Tanaka Kiku (22)," their shared name implying a more literally sororal—note the age difference—or perhaps a conjugal, bond. That Sone and Okamura cared about the impression they would make after their deaths may be surmised from the money that they left for the staff at the inn, politely wrapped in white paper and signed "Two Pine Needles" (*matsu no ha futari*) in elegant calligraphy. Pine needles, it should be noted, typically grow in pairs joined at the base. Finally, the pair's familiarity with a longer tradition of "death out of passion" is clear from their act of binding their bodies together with a sash before taking their leap into posterity, as *shinjū* couples often did in literature as well as in contemporary newspaper reports.[73]

Journalistic representations of the incident, too, observed well-established formulae. The itinerary of the couple's journey toward death (what on the bunraku or kabuki stage would have been called a *michiyuki*), the scenic locale of their suicide, the meticulous descriptions of their clothing—decidedly "smart" (*koiki*), in the words of one newspaperman—had all been familiar components of *shinjū* narrative since the Tokugawa period. Journalists pulled at readers' heartstrings with such poignant observations as, "When it was seen that one of the two young ladies was carrying in her pocket a cute doll, onlookers could not help covering [their teary eyes] with their sleeves." Some newspapers reproduced a photograph that Sone and Okamura had posed for together—both standing and with similar hairstyles, incidentally. The physical appearance of the couple likewise dominated written accounts, one reporter enthusiastically referring to them as "beauties" (*bijin*) no less than six times. Headlines unanimously labeled the incident a *shinjū* or *jōshi*, and one borrowed a toponymic formula common on the Tokugawa stage to dub it the "Itoigawa *shinjū*."

What made the "Itoigawa *shinjū*" fascinating reading for the early twentieth-century public was as much a matter of class as it was of gender. Joint suicides between females, or between males, were not a new phenomenon, although it was not until the early twentieth century that "same-sex suicide" came to be understood as a discrete category of behavior with a distinct psychology.[74] In the medium of the *kawaraban*, a hand-carved newssheet that served as a Tokugawa precursor to the newspaper, a joint suicide by three young females appeared, complete with woodblock illustrations, as early as 1847.[75] In 1873, a similar incident was reported in one of the first mechanically printed dailies established after the Restoration.[76] By the closing years of the Meiji period, all-female *shinjū* were staple journalistic fare: the social researcher Ōmichi Kazuichi (1871–?) counted no less than eighteen reported incidents between February 1908 and November 1910.[77] Many participants in these *shinjū* hailed from marginalized socioeconomic backgrounds, with factory workers, prostitutes, and maids accounting for at least half of Ōmichi's statistics. A decade later, the sociologists Takebe and Washio described joint suicides among female factory workers with searing candor as a sign of "our nation's industrial development."[78] And indeed, even as the remains of Sone and Okamura were being returned to their parents in 1911, another pair of females, a sixteen- and a seventeen-year-old factory hand from Nagano prefecture, was jumping from Azuma bridge in downtown Tokyo in an unsuccessful attempt to end their lives.[79]

Although one newspaper (*Kokumin shinbun*) reported the two incidents on the same day, and even on the same page, editors did not allot nearly so much space to the story of these factory workers as to that of their upper-class counterparts. Whereas the former were proletarian migrants from the countryside who had absconded from the mill to which they had been contracted by their families and taken jobs as live-in housemaids in Tokyo, the latter had grown up in affluent circumstances in the capital as the daughters of high-salaried professionals and students. Newspapers underscored the high socioeconomic status of the two "young ladies" (*reijō*) by relating such details as the fact that one wore a ruby ring and carried a silver watch on a chain. Readers of such articles likely aspired, if they did not already belong, to a similarly comfortable social rank, so that tragedy among the elite, notwithstanding its material and educational privileges, elicited a greater amount of curiosity than the sufferings of the underclass, which may have seemed tautological.

The Itoigawa *shinjū* provoked extensive commentary across a wide range of publications. Over the course of the following month and a half, the weekly women's periodical *Fujo shinbun* (Woman times; 1900–1942) carried no less than five articles dealing with the incident and the issues that it raised, including a front-page editorial and opinions from such diverse authorities as a physician, a girls' school graduate, a principal, a married woman, a psychologist, a recent returnee from the West, and a military man.[80] Shimanaka Yūzō (1881–1940), a sometime reporter for *Fujo shinbun*, conceded that treating this particular topic in detail might seem of questionable propriety, given that the journal counted schoolgirls among its main readers. Yet inasmuch as the magazine served as an "organ" for specialists in female education, he felt it part of the journal's mission to publish "research" on this "grave problem."[81] In this way, the Itoigawa *shinjū* helped to spark a much broader public conversation on female-female intimacy, familiarizing readers of *Fujo shinbun* and other periodicals not only with such insider vocabulary as *ome* and *odeya*, but with emerging sexological terminology. Prominent among the latter was the notion of "same-sex love," which, in one form or another, featured conspicuously in the title of all but one of the five *Fujo shinbun* articles.

The impact of the Sone/Okamura suicides and their reinscription in the new language of sexology were visible also in publications that boasted a broader readership than *Fujo shinbun*. About a month after the incident, Kuwatani Teiitsu, a journalist accustomed to writing about business topics, cited recent newspaper coverage of the affair to launch a tirade titled "Frightful Inverted Sexual Desire between Females" in the monthly magazine *Shin kōron* (New review; 1904–?).[82] His article appeared in a special issue on "sexual desire" that was the first of its kind among general-circulation journals. Over the next three decades, sexologists repeatedly cited the Sone/Okamura affair as a classic example of "female same-sex love," not only in journal articles but in their published monographs. It was Sone and Okamura whom Habuto Eiji, in his 1928 book quoted earlier, charged with possessing less than virginal genitals, and whom his colleague Takada Giichirō in the same year must have remembered among the more feminine "protagonists" of schoolgirl scandal.

The reactions of ordinary readers to these discursive reformulations of female-female intimacy are more difficult to gauge. One hint may be found, however, in the joke (*hitokuchibanashi*) column of the Tokyo daily *Miyako shinbun*. Shortly after the two suicide incidents, a Tokyo resident by the name of Watanabe submitted the following contribution: "Party A: Did you hear about that *shinjū* between females? Party B: I guess they did it because they couldn't get married."[83] In presenting the imaginary conversation as a joke, Watanabe implied that B's interpretation of the situation was facile to the point of being ludicrous: everyone knew, Watanabe seems to have assumed, that suicides between females did not follow the same principles as those that occurred between men and women, and that marriage was by definition a cross-sex affair. Ironically, however, sexologists, journalists, and other authorities were beginning to take the joke's scenario seriously just around this time. A number of experts now claimed that female-female intimacy ran precisely the risk of developing to the point of constituting an illegitimate form of marriage—what *Fujo shinbun* called the "female married couple" (*onna fūfu*)—and that love suicides were one of the potential consequences of such ill-fated unions.

By 1911, the language of sexology had begun to appear regularly in newspaper and magazine headlines, and journalists described such relationships as Sone and Okamura's using words like "inverted sexual desire," "unnatural love," and "same-sex love." Over the course of the following decade, the term "same-sex love" would gradually become standardized in its simplified form of *dōseiai*. Furukawa Makoto, a sociologist, has suggested that the character "love" (*ai*) in *dōseiai* endowed the notion with a "spiritual" tinge that derived primarily from prevailing understandings of female-female rather than male-male intimacy, since popular discourse associated the latter more with physical acts than with the emotional faculties.[84] Yet the fact that the early twentieth-century press typically publicized female "same-sex love" in connection with "same-sex suicide" and other forms of scandal helped to suffuse this particular "love" with a sense of distinct, and possibly mortal, danger.

Experts did not always understand or explain the exact relationship of "same-sex love" and "same-sex suicide." Published accounts abounded in conjecture and contradiction, since the emotional state of *shinjū* participants expressed itself more through deeds than by words, and suicide notes were not always available. Out of a sample of seventeen cases of female "same-sex suicide," Takebe and Washio identified eight in which they suspected that "same-sex love" had played some part, but noted that published reports gave "no precise facts clearly [indicating] that same-sex love was the cause," nor that the suicides had "despaired that their relationship was about to be severed."[85] Different newspapers were known to provide conflicting versions of the same incident. In one 1915 case involving two schoolgirls, for example, a certain paper reported the motive for suicide as "same-sex love," and another as both parties' recent "disappointment in [cross-sex] love."[86] In creating these etiologies of female "same-sex suicide," journalists and sexologists drew not only on contemporary scientific notions, but also on older folk constructs, such as the venerable adage that "fellow sufferers commiserate with each other" (*dōbyō aiawaremu*), or the popular perception of females as naïve creatures more apt than males to sacrifice themselves out of sympathy for or obligation to another, or the supposed proclivity among young females toward "despairing of the world, whether because of poverty, being unfairly blamed for something, disappointment in love, or some other cause."[87] The exact point at which such ethically valued qualities as sympathy and sensitivity ended and an undesirable "same-sex love" began, few authorities could state definitively.

The "vows of sisterhood" (*shimai no chigiri*) that *Fujo shinbun* cited as the basis for "same-sex suicide" were not limited to schoolgirls.[88] Indeed, schoolgirls constituted at most a distinct minority among all cases of female "same-sex suicide" during the early twentieth century. According to data compiled by the sexologist Komine Shigeyuki, 39 participants could be identified from newspaper reports appearing between 1927 and 1941 as schoolgirls, although the author conjectured that many more students were subsumed under such categories as "daughter" or "young woman" (*musume*) or among the unidentified.[89] By contrast, fac-

tory work produced at least 80 female participants in "same-sex suicide" over the same period, according to Komine's statistics, while
nursing accounted for 39, domestic service 34, and various erotic-
service professions (*baishō*) no less than 145.[90] As with Sone and Okamura, the relatively high socioeconomic status of schoolgirls garnered
them a disproportionate amount of press attention. Some authorities
noted differences between schoolgirl suicides and those among other
social groups. Yasuda claimed, for example, that "same-sex suicide"
among schoolgirls often resulted from an idealized (*puratonikku*; literally,
"platonic") vision of "same-sex love" that prompted girls to seek death
while they were still young and beautiful.[91] Other motivations reported
were more obviously peculiar to a school environment, such as being
scolded by a teacher, or concluding a suicide pact in order to protest
the departure of a favorite principal.[92]

By the time Yasuda wrote in 1935, "same-sex suicide" among schoolgirls and other groups of females was again a hot topic in the press—or
as Yasuda himself put it, a "phenomenon of the age" (*jidaiteki genshō*).
According to Komine, nearly half of the 342 cases of female "same-sex
suicide" reported between 1927 and 1941 occurred between 1932 and 1935,
coinciding with the trough years of the Great Depression.[93] While the
economic downturn hit working women more directly than the daughters of the elite, schoolgirls became caught up, at least rhetorically, in
the popular imaginary of the growing national and imperial crisis. Contemporary journalists touted as emblematic of the times the phenomenon of "Mount Mihara disease" (*Mihara-yama byō*)—a rash of suicides,
by both males and females, singly and in pairs, whose dramatic venue
was an active volcano on the island of Ōshima, some seventy miles
southwest of urban Tokyo.[94] Favorite sites for suicide were subject to
fads, the most popular combining a reputation for natural beauty (recall
Sone and Okamura's sightseeing excursion along the Oyashirazu coast)
with a folk notoriety as the abode of gods (*shinigami*) who beckoned the
world-weary to their deaths.[95] It was during the turbulent opening years
of the Great Depression and of the Fifteen-Year War that the fiery crater of Mount Mihara, which boasted unparalleled scenery, relative ac-
cessibility from the capital, and the possibility of almost instantaneous
death, enjoyed its heyday among would-be suicides. So alluring seemed
its mortal beacon during the summer of 1933 that the Salvation Army

opened a counseling office at its foot, as well as at Shimoda, an embarkation point for ferries heading there, in order to discourage those beset with personal difficulties from attempting a one-way climb up its slopes.[96]

Schoolgirls were among those who felt the pull of Mount Mihara.[97] Among the visitors to Mount Mihara earlier in the same year were Matsumoto Kiyoko and Tomita Masako, both enrolled in Tokyo's Jissen Girls' School (founded 1899). While some reporters described the episode as a failed "same-sex suicide," the story that eventually prevailed was that Matsumoto had intended from the start to perish alone, and had not revealed her plan to Tomita until they reached the summit. Tomita chose not to jump, but she cast her lot in with her classmate at least symbolically by donning one of the straw sandals that Matsumoto had shed before taking her fatal leap and by throwing one of her own clogs into the crater. The periodical press gave extensive coverage to the "bizarre" (*ryōki*) case, characterizing Matsumoto as an esthete (*tanbishugisha*) who was "extremely fond of literature," and solicited reactions to the event from prominent cultural figures.[98] The litterateur Kikuchi Kan (1888–1948) expressed his opinion that only females could truly comprehend the psychology of the incident, just as most males, he alleged, found perplexing the imported film hit *Maedchen in Uniform* (Girls in uniform; 1931), which depicted a scandal surrounding student-teacher relationships in a German girls' school. The female writer Yoshiya Nobuko (1896–1973), on the other hand, maintained that it was typical of adolescent girls to harbor a "fascination with death" (*shi e no akogare*), a theme that emerges often enough in her own work. In evidence throughout journalistic coverage of the incident was a discursive link between literary tendencies, "same-sex love," and death that had become well entrenched by the 1930s, and that received confirmation in the work of sexologists—who were, after all, newspaper readers—as well.[99]

Mount Mihara was not the only backdrop for "same-sex suicide" during the 1930s, although it was certainly one of the most spectacular. Similarly notorious was the scandal that followed the suicide of Kaneda Ai and simultaneous attempted suicide of Eguchi Yuki, who each swallowed sleeping pills with whiskey and set out to drown themselves in Lake Biwa one night in April 1934.[100] Eguchi had graduated in the previous year from the Kyoto Girls' Higher Specialty School (founded 1920), and thereafter found employment teaching literature at another girls' school in the same city. Her schoolmate Kaneda had graduated only in the previous month, and was under pressure from her stepfather to be married. Scandal deepened several months after the incident, when Uruki Hiroshi (1903–1936), a popular motion-picture actor, published a steamy account of his secret affair with the late Kaneda in the prominent women's magazine *Fujin kōron* (Woman's review; 1916–), a dashing publicity photograph immodestly splashed across the article's first page. According to Uruki, it was not Kaneda's desolation at being parted from her ex-schoolmate Eguchi that had triggered her suicide, but rather the termination of their own cross-sex romance.[101] This alternate narrative of events did not prevent Komine in his 1940s study from unequivocally identifying the cause of the episode as "same-sex love."[102]

Jennifer Robertson further explores the dramatic overtones of "same-sex suicide" and "same-sex love" in her provocative examination of the culture of all-female musical theater in twentieth-century Japan, represented most famously by the Takarazuka (founded 1913) and Shōchiku (1921) Revues. As Robertson points out, prewar journalism placed the world of the all-female revue in close rhetorical proximity with that of the girls' school. For one thing, schoolgirls were a conspicuous presence among the revue's fan constituency. And like the girls' school, the revue theater gave birth to several notorious incidents of "same-sex suicide," among them the widely publicized 1935 suicide attempt of Saijō Eriko, a Shōchiku performer, and Masuda Fumiko, the daughter of a wealthy Kyoto family.[103] According to Robertson, "Widespread press and magazine coverage [of incidents like the Saijō/Masuda suicide attempt] facilitated the public intertextuality of lesbian practices and acts (both successful and unsuccessful) of double suicide, although the majority of actors in these incidents were but names and statistics without faces."[104]

In a further example of intertextuality, media stereotypes of the flamboyant revue star and her devoted schoolgirl admirer flowed beyond the boundaries of journalism to inflect the writings of early twentieth-century sexologists. Both Ōtsuki Kenji and Komine warned parents in the same breath of adolescent girls' tendency to exchange "saccharine" (*amattarui*) letters with friends—evidently a reference to "S" practices—and to participate "audaciously" in fan cliques (*dōsururen*) for such idols as Mizunoe Takiko (1915–), a leading player of masculine roles. What linked these forms of behavior, according to the two sexologists, was their relatively benign function as temporary substitutes for "cross-sex love," which could not be consummated safely until reaching a suitable age for marriage. Difficult though such adolescent enthusiasms might be for adults to stomach, the wisest strategy, in the opinion of Ōtsuki and Komine, was to remain alert for any signs of physical involvement, and otherwise to "look on while pretending not to see."[105] Whether it was journalists, sexologists, or parents, the eyes of adults found little rest when it came to the topic of schoolgirl intimacy.

Sisters Divided: Feminist Constructions

What meanings did schoolgirl "sisterhood" acquire for men and women who were active in the early twentieth-century feminist movement, and how did they interpret its significance within the broader context of gender and age relations? Yasuda, a radical among sexologists, expressed feminist as well as socialist sympathies when he wrote of the "twofold oppression"—in other words by patriarchy and by capitalism—that Japanese women had risen to challenge in the twentieth century, not only through organized activism, but also by wresting the practice of "same-sex love" away from "male dictatorship." Fukushima Shirō (1874–1945), the founder of *Fujo shinbun*—the publication over which he presided for more than four decades and that offered a forum and a journal of record for more moderate elements within the women's movement—provides another example of male involvement in early twentieth-century feminism. Both Yasuda and Fukushima portrayed schoolgirl intimacies in a generally benign light, refuting the aspersions that harsher male critics, whether among the ranks of sexologists or of journalists, had placed upon them. Yasuda, for example, despite his own training as a physician, rejected the view that "same-sex love" among schoolgirls stemmed from "physiological defect." Instead he stressed the importance of social factors, such as the constitution of the bourgeois household and the historical decline of patriarchy. He also found evidence for the latter in schoolgirls' appropriation of masculine speech patterns, which seemed to be on the rise. According to

Yasuda, even scientists, with all their medical expertise, could neither easily distinguish between "normalcy" and "perversion" in the sphere of schoolgirl relations, nor more generally between female "friendship" and "same-sex love."[106]

For Fukushima, by contrast, a clear distinction between good and bad varieties of schoolgirl intimacy was not only possible, but necessary. After the Sone/Okamura story broke in 1911, Fukushima penned an editorial in which he sought to shield the majority of schoolgirls from the journalistic fallout by propounding just such a dichotomy. "Same-sex love" among females, Fukushima maintained, could take one of two forms. The first was "pure friendship" (*junzentaru yūai*) of an "ardent" and only mildly "pathological" (*byōteki*), albeit platonic, character. The second was the "female married couple," also known as *ome*, whose relationship was based on physical bonds. Whereas the former supposedly occurred between two individuals similar in age, background, and personality, the latter required that one partner be "masculine" and "controlling." According to Fukushima, schoolgirl intimacies, including Sone and Okamura's, typically fell into the former category, despite the lurid interpretations imposed upon them by a scandal-hungry press. Fukushima did not, however, entirely condone the former type of relationship, since it might escalate into fanaticism and suicide. He instead called upon educators to direct the constructive "enthusiasm" (*netsujō*) that fueled it into more "suitable" channels.[107]

Feminist women, too, were of more than one mind on the subject of schoolgirl intimacy, as well as of "same-sex love," and displayed similarities to as well as differences from their male counterparts. In 1921, for example, a prominent literary journal published the contrasting views of the writer Yoshiya and Kamichika Ichiko (1888–1981), a journalist, feminist activist, and postwar parliamentarian, under the title "Two Women Look at Same-Sex Love." Like Fukushima before her, Kamichika drew a primarily moral distinction between emotional and physical aspects of "same-sex love." She found "no particular reason to condemn" purely emotional attachments, but maintained that sexual involvement brought "both spiritual and physical corruption for the individual." In Kamichika's view, females who engaged in "same-sex love" merely lacked the "courage" and "energy" that were necessary to form a "healthy" and "free" relationship with the opposite sex. Such types, she believed, were to be found in greatest numbers in the dormitories of "religious schools."[108] By contrast, Yoshiya selected a more lyrical approach, writing a paean to the uplifting qualities of love itself. "There is nothing shameful about loving someone, nor about being loved by someone," she declared simply but boldly. In Yoshiya's opinion, one of the greatest failings of girls' school education was that it devoted far too little attention to the fostering of this all-important emotion.[109] Like Yasuda, Yoshiya stressed the positive value of intimate relationships between schoolgirls, whereas Kamichika and Fukushima sought only to absolve certain of their manifestations as opposed to others.

Despite the difference in Kamichika's and Yoshiya's positions, the two women shared a subjective identification with schoolgirls that remained rare among their counterparts of the other sex. Kamichika, for example, reserved the severest blame in her essay for girls' school educators who failed to ascertain the true nature of a particular relationship—in other words, whether it was physical or purely emotional—before causing irreparable harm to the individuals involved. Such "ignorance" on the part of school authorities, in Kamichika's opinion, was a form of "evil" in itself.[110] In a similar vein, Yoshiya criticized pedagogues and moralists for branding "love" among schoolgirls as "dirty" and "unnatural"—or as they were wont to characterize it, a "first step on the path of decadence." Such an attitude on the part of adults, Yoshiya charged, led girls all too often to mistrust their own feelings and hence to smother the "beautiful and tender nature with which they have been divinely blessed."[111] In this way, Kamichika and Yoshiya cast themselves not only as foes of gender oppression, but as allies of schoolgirls against uncomprehending adults of both sexes. Their sense of solidarity with schoolgirls stemmed in part from their own educational backgrounds, both having recently attended girls' school.[112]

Each in her own way, Kamichika and Yoshiya also betrayed a discomfort over the physical dimensions of intimacy between females. Kamichika made it clear that only male-female eroticism could constitute a "healthy" sexuality. From her perspective, the struggle for "freedom" in sexual relationships had as its proper target not social restrictions against "same-sex love," but rather the various obstacles that fettered the individual in her "courageous" pursuit of the opposite sex.

Kamichika caused great scandal in 1915 by venting her libidinal passions so freely as to stab her male lover, the anarchist Ōsugi Sakae (1885–1923), after he entered into an affair with her feminist comrade Itō Noe (1895–1923), and she may have counted herself among such brave souls. For Yoshiya, too, sexuality was a deeply personal issue. Since at least 1918, Yoshiya had been involved in a series of romantic relationships with other women, the physical aspects of which she rarely disclosed apart from private letters. Public acknowledgment of her relationship with Monma Chiyo, with whom she began living in 1926, depended, according to one biographer, upon the polite fiction that the couple were simply "two schoolgirls," or later, "author and secretary."[113] Given the personal stakes involved, it is not at all surprising that Yoshiya chose to gloss over, if not necessarily deny, the physical dimensions of "same-sex love" in her 1921 article. Whatever she believed the erotic nature of schoolgirl intimacies to be (or not to be), it is telling that she, unlike Kamichika, felt it best not to raise the issue of sexuality at all.

The views of Kamichika and Yoshiya help illustrate some of the diversity, as well as the difficulty, with which the "new women" of the era confronted the emerging sexological construct of "same-sex love." The tension that inhered in this relationship burst into the open as early as the days of the Bluestocking Society (Seitōsha; founded 1911), among the period's most controversial feminist organizations.[114] One of many charges that a hostile press leveled against the iconoclastic Bluestockings was that their activities extended to the erotic pursuit of females by other females. In July 1912, for example, Tokyo newspapers reported that the society's cofounder Hiratsuka Raichō (1886–1971) and two younger members, Otake Kōkichi (1893–1966) and Nakano Hatsu (1886–1983), had recently made an excursion to the Yoshiwara brothel district. After arriving by rickshaw, the party was said to have engaged the services of a geisha named Eizan, who was reputedly a girls' school graduate, and they spent the night at an upscale teahouse.[115] While some of those involved would subsequently defend the outing as an educational expedition, it was easy for contemporary newspaper readers to infer that Bluestockings were brazen pleasure-seekers who coveted the conventionally masculine privilege of hiring female erotic entertainment. All the more so when Otake was quoted as saying that she considered redeeming Eizan's contract. Nor was negative reaction confined to antifeminists: shortly after the incident Yasumochi Yoshi (1885–1947), the other Bluestocking cofounder, penned a letter to Hiratsuka, later published in the society's journal *Seitō*, in which she voiced a moralistic disapproval of the trio's "frivolous" foray to a known den of vice.[116]

Controversy also surrounded the relationship between Hiratsuka and Otake. The conspicuous intimacy that existed between the writer and the artist assumed a public profile during the summer of 1912, as each avowed her affection for the other in the pages of *Seitō*.[117] Both women referred repeatedly to Otake's role in the relationship as that of *shōnen*, a word that literally meant "boy," but in contemporary schoolboy slang more specifically applied to the junior partner (conventionally the sexual object) in a male-male erotic couple. The age and gender nuances of the term presumably alluded to the fact that Otake, at nineteen, was seven years younger than Hiratsuka; that she was unusually tall, and unrestrained in her movements and speech; that her unconventional mode of dress, like that of several other Meiji female artists, incorporated masculine elements; and that her nickname of Kōkichi or Beniyoshi had a virile, or androgynous, ring. Within the literary culture of the day, a certain amount of strategic advantage lay in evoking a boys' school, rather than a girls' school, trope. By appropriating a male-male erotic vocabulary descended from the Tokugawa "way of youths," the couple laid claim to a longstanding tradition of same-sex intimacy that enjoyed more positive, or at least more conventional, recognition in educated circles than that which currently surrounded schoolgirl attachments. This was particularly true in the wake of the previous year's Sone/Okamura suicides. By the same token, since the sexological equation of male-male and female-female attraction had only recently emerged onto the discursive landscape, at least one newspaper reporter interpreted the metaphor all too literally. He informed readers that Hiratsuka was currently lavishing her affections on a "beautiful boy" (*bishōnen*) of twelve or thirteen years of age with whom she had allegedly been spotted strolling the evening streets of Tokyo, he wearing a "darling" schoolboy cap.[118]

By the end of 1912, Hiratsuka had distanced herself from Otake and entered into a romantic affair with Okumura Hiroshi (1889–1964), a male artist with whom she began living in 1914. Only after Otake married the potter Tomimoto Kenkichi (1886–1963) in 1914 and, like Hiratsuka, began raising children would the two women's relationship again grow cordial.[119] As scholars such as Iwami Teruyo, Kurosawa Ariko, and Yoshikawa Toyoko have chronicled, Hiratsuka's attitude toward her former involvement with Otake, and toward "same-sex love," underwent significant changes over the years.[120] Even though Hiratsuka had boasted of Otake as her *shōnen* in *Seitō* in 1912, she had only once employed the sexological term "same-sex love" in connection with their relationship.[121] Yet by the time she published her autobiography in 1971, Hiratsuka felt the need to include a nearly page-long denial that she, unlike Otake, had acted out of "same-sex love." Hiratsuka insisted that she had been drawn only to Otake's "uniquely individual charms," and been prompted by a certain sense of "mischievousness." She invoked a rigid sexological binary in maintaining that the intensity of her subsequent ardor for the male Okumura furnished unmistakable proof that her feelings for Otake did not constitute "same-sex love."[122] Hiratsuka's strikingly defensive rhetorical stance—what Kurosawa has described as her attempt to legitimate her sexual "normalcy" by differentiating herself from a "pathological" other, in this case Otake—poignantly reveals the stigmatizing power that the "same-sex love" construct would acquire over the course of the twentieth century.[123]

Hiratsuka's interest in sexology deepened after her estrangement from Otake.[124] Particularly influential was her association with the sexologist Ogura Seizaburō (1883–1941), whom Hiratsuka met in 1913, and who was to become the only regular male contributor to *Seitō*.[125] In the pages of the journal, feminism and sexology quickly became familiar, if not always comfortable, bedfellows. One example of the new collaboration was the publication of an abridged chapter from Havelock Ellis's *Studies in the Psychology of Sex* (1897–1928), titled "Sexual Inversion of Females," in the journal's April 1914 issue.[126] The translator of the piece was the later women's suffrage activist Sakamoto Makoto (1889–1955), who chose to maintain a respectable distance from the controversial topic by writing under a pseudonym. Hiratsuka, in her role as *Seitō* editor, penned a preface in which she explained that the work was one that Ogura had recommended when she had asked for informative reading on "same-sex love," and justified her curiosity about the subject in the following way:

One often hears that same-sex love takes place in the dormitories of girls' schools, but I myself never saw nor experienced such a thing, so I only half believed it. I used to have no interest in the problem [of same-sex love] whatsoever. [Nevertheless] I have become very much interested in this problem after my acquaintance in the recent past with a certain woman—a woman who would appear to be almost congenitally a sexual invert. I spent about a year as the object of that woman's love. Prompted in this way to think about various things, I came to want to know more about this problem.[127]

Few readers of *Seitō*—or, for that matter, of contemporary newspaper gossip—would have failed to surmise that the woman to whom Hiratsuka alluded must be her former "boy" Otake, who had quit the society after a tumultuous year in its inner circle.[128]

Seitō was not the only feminist publication to play a role in spreading sexological knowledge of "same-sex love." After quitting the Bluestockings, Otake herself founded a short-lived women's literary magazine named *Safuran* (Saffron; 1914). This competitor journal began serializing an abridged translation of *The Intermediate Sex* (1908) by the British sexologist and socialist visionary Edward Carpenter (1844–1929) about a month after Ellis's views on "sexual inversion" appeared in *Seitō*.[129] Like his countryman and contemporary Ellis, Carpenter was deeply interested in the phenomenon of "same-sex love," but adopted in his book a more radical political stance. Appropriately enough, the translator of the work was Yamakawa (known at the time as Aoyama) Kikue (1890–1980), who was still on her way to becoming a prominent socialist-feminist critic. However, when Yamakawa republished her translation in book form several years later, it was with the caveat that she did not necessarily endorse all of Carpenter's opinions.[130] Kamichika offers a provocative summation of these questionable views. In Kamichika's paraphrase, Yamakawa had explained to her that Carpenter believed "same-sex love" to be more "spiritual" than "cross-sex love," and further maintained that, "by steering it in a good direction, one of the partners can [positively] influence and guide the other."[131]

That the writings of two prominent Western authorities on "same-sex love" should have appeared in close succession in the pages of rival feminist journals can hardly have been a coincidence. Kamichika, who was one of the editors of *Safuran*, wrote that she first learned of Carpenter's views in a conversation she once had with Yamakawa on the topic of "same-sex love," whereafter she decided to commission a translation.[132] It is not clear whether the original conversation, or the subsequent commission, transpired in direct response to Hiratsuka's disparaging, if veiled, remarks about Otake, and/or from Ellis's somewhat less positive evaluation of "same-sex love," in the recent issue of *Seitō*, but these possibilities cannot be ruled out. Given the fact that Kamichika and Otake were not only coeditors but close friends, it seems likely that personal considerations were somehow involved. In 1921, Kamichika would refer to "two, or possibly three" female acquaintances who had allowed her to witness at first hand the supposed physical and spiritual ravages of "same-sex love."[133] In 1915 she was more vague, writing only that the "sexual intermediates" of whom Carpenter spoke had "recently begun to surface in Japan, and among certain people this has become a problem."[134]

The near-simultaneous translations of Ellis and Carpenter reflected the growing feminist attention to what contemporary journalists and social critics had begun to dub the "sexual problem." Published debates among feminist leaders over such aspects of sexuality and reproduction as chastity, abortion, prostitution, and motherhood punctuated the 1910s, with Hiratsuka and Yamakawa among their most outspoken participants.[135] Within the existing scholarship on the Japanese women's movement, debates about these issues have come to enjoy a high profile. Yet far less attention focuses on the feminist debate about what both Hiratsuka and Kamichika defined as the "problem" of "same-sex love." For early twentieth-century feminists, "same-sex love" was a multivalent signifier, conveying in some cases new possibilities of solidarity and in others strategic liabilities. Since the strengthening of bonds between women was a fundamental part of feminist coalition-building, those who opposed women's efforts to organize themselves would label excessive intimacy between females as symptomatic of a pathological physiology or perverted psychology, lending useful scientific ammunition to their rhetorical armory. Antifeminists rarely hesitated to claim this diagnostic privilege even when they were not themselves doctors. In Japan, as in America and Europe, various observers connected the rise of the women's movement with an ostensible rise of "same-sex love" among the female population. The physician Ōtsuka Shinzō, for example, characterized the "new woman" as a species of congenital "pervert" whose masculine bodily structure, gait, and clothing visibly betrayed an abnormal constitution, as did her alleged taste for the color blue (perhaps as in Bluestockings?).[136] Feminist women who remained unmarried or who lived together were especially vulnerable to the charge that they preferred "same-sex love" to "normal" relations with men. It is not surprising that when it came to the controversial issue of "same-sex love," many feminists remained on the defensive.

In this way, the notoriety for "same-sex love" that schoolgirls had acquired in early twentieth-century journalism and sexology posed not only an intellectual problem for feminists, but again one of strategy. Although schoolgirls may have supported the women's movement in significant numbers, organized feminism was primarily an adult activity. Nevertheless, feminists commonly regarded the girls' school as part of their special domain of authority, since the demand for educational opportunities had been an integral part of the women's movement from its earliest days. Moreover, the fact that many feminists had once attended girls' schools made it easy for them to interpret criticisms of schoolgirl behavior as an attack on the broader community of educated females to which they themselves belonged. Individual feminists responded to the sexological and journalistic vilification of schoolgirl intimacy in diverse ways. So wide was the feminist spectrum of opinion on this subject that it could embrace, at one end, a positive, if qualified, endorsement of "same-sex love" among schoolgirls, and at the opposite extreme, calls for its total eradication.

One of the most remarkable and fervent expressions of the former position may be found in a 1922 essay by Furuya Toyoko (1880–?). Furuya, a mission school graduate, had in 1903 become the first female to pass the Ministry of Education's English certification exam, and went on in 1917 to found the Furuya English Academy for Girls, based in Osaka.[137] Her 1922 article, "The New Meaning of Same-Sex Love in Female Education," appeared originally in the women's journal *Fujin kōron*, and was republished in 1923 as part of a multiauthored anthology of writings on love and sexuality.[138] In her essay, Furuya painted a stark contrast between "same-sex love" as it was found in "modern civilization" and that of "feudal times." Before the Meiji era, Furuya argued, "same-sex love," both male and female, had been a "sordid" (*shūaku*) affair, its female manifestations found chiefly among ladies-in-waiting (*goten jochū*) in the women's quarters of the warrior elite or among Buddhist nuns in the cloister, who succumbed out of loneliness or temptation to "base passion" (25). By contrast, "same-sex love" in its "modern" form had the potential to "purify" and to "beautify" the individuals involved, thereby enriching their emotional lives and contributing toward their education (26). In the opinion of Furuya, "same-sex love" of this latter variety required neither encouragement nor prohibition; its appearance was simply "one of the characteristics of contemporary civilization," which had expanded opportunities for social contact and tended toward the refinement of human feelings (29).

The "modern" incarnation of "same-sex love," Furuya continued, had already taken firm root in the girls' school. When it occurred between a student and her teacher, she maintained, it led schoolgirls to exert themselves and to compete with one another in order to emulate their beloved mentor, and was all the more effective pedagogically because in front of a member of her own sex a young female need not feel the same sense of embarrassment that she might when faced by a male instructor (26–27). Likewise, when "same-sex love" occurred between two students, it supposedly helped to soften the mechanical quality of institutionalized learning and to foster the development of the emotions and of the personality. As such, Furuya claimed, it was a necessary component of a "new culturalistic education" (*kyōikuteki shin bunkashugi*). A further beneficial "side effect" of "same-sex love," she hastened to point out, was that schoolgirls whose minds were preoccupied in this way would have little attention to spare for the blandishments of young male "delinquents" (28). Given the rich emotional life and intellectual attainments of present-day schoolgirls, it was virtually unthinkable, in Furuya's view, that they should indulge in "base passion," which is to say, genital interaction, so that to associate "same-sex love" with "lewdness" was a "thing of the past" (27–28).

The idealized pedagogical role that Furuya assigned to "same-sex love" in her article bore the unmistakable imprint of the aforementioned Edward Carpenter, a familiarity with whose work other contemporary writers on "same-sex love," such as Yoshiya, also acknowledged.[139] However, Furuya maintained a critical stance toward Carpenter's notion of an "intermediate sex," which implied that at least one of the partners in "same-sex love" possessed the attributes of the opposite gender. In Furuya's view, "same-sex love" occurred just as easily when two individuals were similar in temperament as when one was masculine and the other feminine, the latter case representing only one of many possible variations (29). For Furuya, "same-sex love" was a subjective desire that could be experienced by anyone, and not the characteristic of a minority group.

Furuya's essay captures a historical moment when the concept of "same-sex love" could still convey a remarkably positive meaning in the realm of public discourse, or at least when some could imagine the possibility of rescuing its signifying power from the hands of critics.[140] Kurosawa has written, in a related context, of "another possible modernity"—a vision of the future in which female-female intimacy would enjoy a prominent and respected position, yet that in the end did not easily find its realization.[141] Furuya's essay offers a further instance of such an alternate vision.[142] It is important to note, however, that, even though Furuya envisioned new possibilities for "same-sex love," her vision imposed distinct boundaries and limitations. Conspicuous among them was Furuya's consignment of physical interaction between females to the realm of the "barbarous" or "semicivilized"—an abject and "sordid" other that had to be repudiated in order for true modernity to be achieved.

At the other end of the spectrum were those feminists who denied the value of "same-sex love" in any of its forms. This was the position of Tozuka Matsuko, who, like Furuya, remains a regrettably obscure figure in standard histories of the women's movement. In 1920, Tozuka joined with the socialist feminist Yabe Hatsuko (1895–1985) and Miyazaki Setsuko to form the Red Thought Society (Sekisōsha), records of which are unfortunately sparse. According to *Fujo shinbun*, by focusing its attention on such issues as marriage and sexual desire, the group offered an "inner-directed" (*naimenteki*) alternative to the more outwardly political—and therefore historiographically more famous—New Women's Association (Shin fujin kyōkai), founded in 1919.[143]

In 1924, Tozuka published a lengthy book on "love education" (*ren'ai kyōiku*), a subject that she believed to merit an important place in the girls' school curriculum.[144] One of the primary missions of Tozuka's "love education" was to "rescue" schoolgirls from the "dangers of same-sex love," which she defined as one of the main forms of "incorrect love" (15).

> Same-sex love needlessly wears out soul and body. If the couple's emotions get carried away, a gloomy feeling will enter their bright lives like the dismal skies of December, and take all the vitality out of their existence. When considered from another perspective, [same-sex love] defiles the sanctity of the correct love with which they shall be blessed in the future, and violates the purity of their unknown lover-to-be's affection. (16)

Tozuka urged educators to offer instruction that was "kind" and that drew on the teacher's personal experiences, yet would also be grounded in "sexual knowledge based on profound scientific principles" (15–16).

Rather than simply warning schoolgirls about the dangers of "incorrect love," Tozuka urged teachers to go a step further and provide them with an understanding of "correct love," which could only take place between a man and a woman. In the context of her time, she was a sexual radical in that she saw positive benefit, rather than danger, in imparting knowledge of male-female erotic fulfillment to adolescent females. More often during this period, adult authorities strove to keep such notions out of the heads of schoolgirls, whom they regarded as highly susceptible by virtue of their age and gender to the wiles of "delinquents," and whose destinies as "good wives and wise mothers" youthful indiscretion might endanger. Nor did Tozuka limit male-female sexual relations to the context of marriage, which in its current legal form she believed to enslave women (67–68). Whatever the legal status of the couple, Tozuka emphasized the need for equality and mutual understanding between the two partners, so that a male-female relationship in which one party "ignored the will" of the other constituted for her a form of love no less "incorrect" than "same-sex love" itself (17–18). Tozuka claimed that one individual's romantic involvement with two or more persons at the same time was just as improper (21–24). Finally, Tozuka labeled as "incorrect" not only relationships between men and women that were primarily physical, but also those "spiritual" male-female romances in which sexuality held no place, which she went so far as to describe as "perverse" (18–21).

Tozuka's vision of "correct love" between pairs of mutually committed and sexually active men and women shared much in common with the new ideal of "companionate marriage" that was being advocated at the time by influential feminists in Europe and America.[145] In citing "scientific principles" (*gakuri*) to extol male-female monogamy and to discredit all other forms of love and sexuality, Tozuka echoed the views, for example, of such British feminists as Marie Stopes (1880–1958), whose best seller *Married Love* (1918) appeared in Japanese translation— and was promptly banned—in the same year that Tozuka published her own tract.[146] The sociologist Akagawa Manabu has argued that, by the 1920s, the "eroticization of sexual behavior in [male-female] marriage" had emerged as a significant theme within Japanese discourses on sexuality. Simultaneous with this process, he notes an intensification in the social regulation of other forms of erotic behavior, conspicuous among them "same-sex love."[147]

Although Furuya's exaltation of "same-sex love" stood at an opposite pole from the condemnation of her contemporary Tozuka, both women were united in the belief that scientific knowledge would advance, rather than hinder, the achievement of feminist goals. Many early twentieth-century feminists shared this faith, feeling drawn to sexology because it promised to cast the ostensibly objective light of science upon the realm of gender relations, and thereby to delegitimize the various cultural and moral traditions that stood in the way of social change. In an era where science seemed synonymous with progress, there were few who questioned whether sexological knowledge might not reinforce gender roles just as easily as ameliorate them, nor what influence feminists actually had in setting scientific agendas. It is all too easy to forget, for example, that the same Hiratsuka Raichō so often honored as a pioneer of Japanese feminism was, as Sumiko Otsubo discusses elsewhere in this volume, also the Hiratsuka who warmly embraced the emerging science of eugenics.

Coda: Girl Trouble

By incorporating such constructs as "same-sex love" into their working vocabulary, early twentieth-century feminists tacitly accepted sexologists' authority to set the terms of public debate on the nature of their intimate feelings. Meanwhile, schoolgirls continued talking about "sisterhood" in a language of their own creation. According to some women with whom I spoke, the term "S" survived well into the 1950s and 1960s, even in the coeducational schools that sexologists had hoped would stamp it out.[148] Nevertheless, the elaborate expressions of endearment used by early twentieth-century schoolgirls are today all but unintelligible to the female student population, which is much more likely to use such terms as "same-sex love" and "lesbian" (*rezubian*), if not the latter's pejorative stepsister *rezu*. Sexological understandings of love and friendship, in other words, have gained a currency no longer limited to specialists or even to adults, forming one of the cornerstones of contemporary common knowledge in the Japanese archipelago. Just as the earlier decades of the twentieth century saw the private words of schoolgirls move into a larger realm of public discourse, the language of outsiders now finds a home within the schoolyard.

Among some of the older women whom I interviewed in 1990 and 1992, a significant gap separated their own understanding of schoolgirl intimacy and the unsavory implications placed upon it by various commentators. What seemed to have most lingered in their minds after more than a half-century was a sense of youthful enthusiasm and of emotional richness. I was often struck by the candor, sometimes the perceptible pleasure, with which these women, who had married after graduation and now had children and grandchildren, shared their personal recollections of "S"—a phenomenon that sexologists and others had begun to stigmatize as "same-sex love" even in their own time. This gap in perceptions serves as a useful reminder that adult authorities possessed only a limited power to shape the experiences, and the subsequent memories, of schoolgirls, and that the discourses of outsiders can never fully capture the meanings that "S" held for its participants.

What the contending views of sexologists, journalists, and feminists highlight unequivocally is the heightened profile of relationships between females in public discourses of the twentieth century. Females had long interacted in meaningful ways with one another, yet masculinist rhetoric had traditionally paid minimal attention to such relationships, choosing to elaborate on the interactive possibilities of males with females, or of males with other males. The proliferation of girls' schools from the Meiji period onward placed large numbers of females not only in close proximity with one another, but also before the eyes of a broader public audience. Being nationally accredited institutions, girls' schools derived special significance from the fact that they were intended to provide young females with sanctioned models of social behavior. As young females in schools and other settings emerged onto the civic landscape of the nation-state, the ways in which they interacted with one another received greater scrutiny from adult authorities, and came to occupy a prominent place in serious public debate. What forms relationships between them took, which were "proper" and which "improper," and what significance they held for society at large, became questions asked more frequently and more audibly.

Public discourses on schoolgirl intimacy had both a regulatory and a contestational aspect. By representing some forms of interaction as legitimate and stigmatizing others, adults sought to influence the behavior of young females and to bring it in line with their own expectations and ideals. Even though their attempts did not always succeed, the vociferousness of their pronouncements bore witness to the anxieties that the emergence of such female public institutions as the girls' school and such identities as the schoolgirl had provoked throughout the larger society. In the case of male commentators, the desire to have a critical say over the affective lives of schoolgirls was sharpened by the fact that, by virtue of their sex, they were necessarily outsiders to the world of the girls' school and to the possibility of sharing in its intimate pleasures. In this sense, the sexological and journalistic vilification of "S," and of "same-sex love" among females more generally, may be seen as an effort to assert male control over female behavior and emotions in an age when women and girls were enjoying new forms of autonomy. Feminist attempts to steer schoolgirl culture, meanwhile, rested not so much on an assumption of gender superiority as on the hierarchical privilege that adults conventionally claimed over the young.

Each constituency spoke out on the topic of schoolgirl intimacy not only with a view toward regulating student conduct, but also as a means of asserting its authority against other discursive contenders. Sexologists found in "S" a native manifestation of a phenomenon concerning which they, as experts in a new scientific discipline, claimed privileged knowledge. Journalists pursued profits by turning the private dealings of schoolgirls into public information. Feminists challenged many of the assumptions of male critics, yet were by no means united in their own critiques of schoolgirl culture and of "same-sex love." This discursive fray did not result in a consensus on the significances and dangers of female-female intimacy, but, through its very clamorousness, helped keep the schoolgirl at the forefront of early twentieth-century debate on gender and sexuality.

It is a position she continues to hold today. For anyone familiar with the Japanese popular press, television, or motion pictures, the figure of the schoolgirl—now commonly referred to as a "female high school student" (*joshi kōkōsei*)—remains as conspicuous a presence as ever. Little matter that she is more likely now to attend a coeducational rather than a single-sex school, or that student fashions have changed markedly from a half-century ago. Public controversy in the last decade has come to focus primarily on her relations with adult males (as in the much criticized phenomenon of *enjo kōsai* or dating for money), but her function as an emblem of worrisome sexuality is inherited from the schoolgirls of her grandmother's generation. Adults still gravely and self-importantly debate the improprieties of young female behavior, finding in student culture convenient ammunition for their own discursive battles. Today as yesterday, schoolgirls stand largely at the sidelines, more often spoken about than listened to.

Notes

The author wishes to thank the Japan Fund of Stanford University for a grant that allowed him to conduct interviews in Japan in the summer of 1992; the seven women whom he interviewed in 1990 and 1992 (one in the United States and six in Japan), whom this essay refers to by given name alone in consideration of their privacy; and Yoshiko Fredisdorf, Itonaga Masayuki, and Saori Kamano for related assistance. He is grateful also to Terry Castle, Peter Duus, Laura Engelstein, Estelle Freedman, Yukiko Hanawa, Earl Jackson, Barbara Molony, Julie Rousseau, Barbara Sato, Satō Kazuki, Martha Tocco, Kathleen Uno, and the other contributors to and anonymous readers for this volume for their critiques of the project in its various stages.

1. Martha Vicinus, "Distance and Desire: English Boarding-School Friendships," in *Hidden from History: Reclaiming the Gay and Lesbian Past,* eds. Martin Bauml Duberman, Martha Vicinus, and George Chauncey, Jr. (New York: NAL, 1989), 215. I follow Vicinus's practice in uniformly referring to young females of various ages as girls, even as I recognize that the expression "girl" has historically facilitated a wide range of infantilizing and discriminatory practices. "Girl" functions in this essay as a rough equivalent for *shōjo*, which in early twentieth-century Japan designated "unmarried girls and women, [meaning] literally, a 'not-quite-female' female" (Jennifer Robertson, *Takarazuka: Sexual Politics and Popular Culture in Modern Japan* [Berkeley: University of California Press, 1998], 65).

2. Nancy Sahli, "Smashing: Women's Relationships before the Fall," *Chrysalis* 8 (Summer 1979): 17–27. For another American example, see Katy Coyle and Nadiene Van Dyke, "Sex, Smashing, and Storyville in Turn-of-the-Century New Orleans: Reexamining the Continuum of Lesbian Sexuality," in *Carryin' On in the Lesbian and Gay South,* ed. John Howard (New York: New York University Press, 1997), 54–72.

3. Judith Gay, "'Mummies and Babies' and Friends and Lovers in Lesotho," *Journal of Homosexuality* 11, nos. 3/4 (Summer 1985): 97–106. On "platonic love" among schoolgirls in early twentieth-century China, see Ping-Ying Hsieh, *Autobiography of a Chinese Girl: A Genuine Autobiography,* trans. Tsui Chi (London: Allen, 1943), 76–81.

4. "Girls' school" refers here mainly to single-sex institutions of secondary education for females, both public and private, which from 1899 were legally classified as *kōtō jogakkō* or "higher girls' schools," and were equivalent to boys' middle schools (*chūtō gakkō*). More advanced education was available to fe-

males at teachers' training colleges, "specialty schools" (*senmon gakkō*) such as Japan Women's University, and a handful of predominantly male universities. See Ann M. Harrington, "Women and Higher Education in the Japanese Empire (1895–1945)," *Journal of Asian History* 21, no. 2 (1987): 169–186, and Martha Tocco's contribution to this volume. Female students at all postprimary educational levels were colloquially called *jogakusei*, a term I translate here as "schoolgirl."

5. "Bō onna kyōikuka iwaku," *Kokumin shinbun*, 31 July, 1911, 2.

6. According to another newspaper, the term was used by schoolgirls at Gakushūin. See "Toka jogakkō fūbunki," pt. 4, *Yomiuri shinbun*, 17 February 1907, 3.

7. The word appears as *ohakarai* in the original *Kokumin shinbun* report, as well as in various subsequent sexological tracts drawing upon it, but I have followed Akashi Shigetarō (*Danjo ryōsei no ai* [Hidaka yūrindō, 1912], 30) in emending it to *ohaikara*, a more intelligible candidate. For a related usage, see the 1910 letter from an Osaka schoolgirl ("Hana no Ō") quoted in Satō (Sakuma) Rika, "'Kiyoki shijō de gokōsai o': Meiji makki shōjo zasshi tōshoran ni miru dokusha kyōdōtai no kenkyū," *Joseigaku* 4 (1996): 141. ("I know who your S is. The two of you are so *haikara*.")

8. An employee at one of these schools (quoted in "Osorubeki dōsei no ai," *Yomiuri shinbun*, 31 July 1911, 3) suggested that *ome* might alternatively derive from *omedetō*, a phrase meaning "congratulations." Some slang authorities (e.g., Higuchi Sakae, *Ingo kōsei no yōshiki narabi ni sono goshū* [Osaka: Keisatsu kyōkai Ōsaka shibu, 1935], 89) allege that it is a contraction of *omekake* or "concubine." Early twentieth century sources also attest the forms *omesan* (adding the honorific and personalizing suffix -*san*), *omegokko* ("playing at *ome*"; Ubukata Toshirō, *Meiji Taishō kenbunshi* [Chūō kōronsha, 1978], 101); *ometome* (Kitagawa Seijun and Fujisawa Morihiko, *Shikijō shisō no kaibō* [Ryūseidō, 1913], 240), and *omega* (Ōtsuka Shinzō, *Josei igaku* [Asakaya shoten, 1922], 41).

9. Another newspaper article ("Jogakusei," pt. 9, *Tōkyō asahi shinbun* [hereafter *Asahi*], 13 March 1913, 5) attributed the expression *odeya* to Gakushūin students.

10. Kuwatani Teiitsu, "Senritsu subeki joseikan no tentō seiyoku," *Shin kōron* 26, no. 9 (September 1911): 35.

11. Havelock Ellis, *Sexual Inversion*, vol. 1, *Studies in the Psychology of Sex*, 2nd ed. (Philadelphia: Davis Co., 1908), 243, and Vicinus, "Distance and Desire," 215.

12. Marieke Hilhorst, "Attitudes and Experiences Concerning 'Particular Friendships' at Convent Boarding Schools for Girls (The Netherlands 1920–1965),"

paper delivered at "Homosexuality? Which Homosexuality?" Conference, Free University of Amsterdam, 15–18 December 1987.

13. Nevertheless, the image of one word per school that the 1911 account paints is almost certainly too neat, as the conflicting newspaper reports cited in notes 6 and 9 underscore.

14. The equivalent figures ten years earlier (1901) were 70 schools and 17,540 students. By 1921, these figures rose to 580 schools and 176,808 students; by 1931, to 980 schools and 362,625 students; by 1941, to 1126 schools and 617,281 students. For useful statistics, see Monbushō, *Gakusei hyakunenshi: shiryō hen* (Teikoku chihō gyōsei gakkai, 1972), 484–487.

15. The precise geographic origin of the term and the course of its spread are not entirely clear. Already in 1910, the expression was familiar to some students at the Osaka prefectural girls' school in Shimizudani (established 1900; see Satō, "Kiyoki shijō," 141). Students, both male and female, in early twentieth-century Japan habitually formed new slang words by taking the initial Roman letters of European terms and giving them a Japanized pronunciation—so that *eitchi* or *etchi* (H), for example, was schoolgirl jargon for "husband," while *emu* (M) was schoolboy argot for "money" (or, among schoolgirls, for one's "menses"). See Higuchi, *Ingo kōsei*, 45, 77, 78.

16. Ellis, *Sexual Inversion*, 243.

17. Tokiko, interview, 8 October 1990. Tokiko attended girls' school in Urawa, Saitama prefecture, from 1937 to 1942.

18. Toshi and Hideko, interview, 15 August 1992.

19. A longer version of this essay deals in greater detail with the various interconnections between girls' magazines and "S" culture. See Gregory M. Pflugfelder, *Queer Archipelago: Historical Explorations in Japanese Gender and Sexuality* (forthcoming).

20. Robertson, *Takarazuka*, 68–70.

21. Tokiko, interview, 8 October 1990.

22. On the metaphor of sisterhood as used among geisha, see Lisa Crihfield Dalby, *Geisha* (Kodansha International, 1983), 4.

23. Carroll Smith-Rosenberg, *Disorderly Conduct: Visions of Gender in Victorian America* (New York: Oxford University Press, 1986), 66–67.

24. On the use of sibling metaphors in the context of male-male erotic

relationships, see my "Women, Youths, and Men: Male-Male Eroticism and the Age/Gender System of Tokugawa Japan," in *The Problem with Boys,* ed. Gilbert Herdt (Chicago, IL: University of Chicago Press, forthcoming).

25. Honda Masuko nevertheless maintains that "S" relationships functioned in psychic terms as a re-1creation of the mother-daughter bond, and of a "primordial union" that preceded subject-object relations. See her "'S': taai naku, shikamo kongenteki na ai no katachi," *Imāgo* 2, no. 8 (August 1991): 68–73.

26. Emiko, interview, 21 February 1990. Emiko attended Ōin Girls' School in Tokyo from 1935 to 1940.

27. On the emergence of sexology in Japan, see Sabine Frühstück, *Colonizing Sex: Sexology and Social Control in Modern Japan* (Berkeley: University of California Press, 2003), and also her "Managing the Truth of Sex in Imperial Japan," *Journal of Asian Studies* 59, no. 2 (2000): 332–358.

28. Gregory M. Pflugfelder, *Cartographies of Desire: Male-Male Sexuality in Japanese Discourse,* 1600–1950 (Berkeley: University of California Press, 1999).

29. See my forthcoming *Queer Archipelago.*

30. Shimizu Sadao, *Jitsuyō saiban igaku* (N.p.: Eimeikan, 1890), 312.

31. Ibid.

32. See for example, Ishikawa Kiyotada, *Jitsuyō hōigaku* (Nankōdō, 1900), 427. On constructions of female-female sexuality in Meiji law, see Pflugfelder, *Cartographies,* 176–177.

33. Sawada Junjirō, *Shinpi naru dōseiai,* 2 vols. (Kyōekisha shuppanbu, 1920), 2: 140.

34. Ibid., 2: 141.

35. Ishikawa, *Jitsuyō hōigaku,* 427. An even earlier forensic pathology textbook (Katayama Kuniyoshi et al., <*Zōho kaitei*>*Hōigaku teikō,* vol. 1 [Shimamura Risuke, 1891–1897], 194) cited female convicts as the most typical practitioners of "Tribadie" (*toribaji*).

36. Habuto Eiji, *Fujin sei no kenkyū* (Jitsugyō no Nihonsha, 1921), 338.

37. On the inversion trope, see Pflugfelder, *Cartographies,* 255–258.

38. Shimada Hiroshi, *Joseiten* (Seibundō, 1928), 498–499.

39. Takada Giichirō, *Tōseijutsu* (Hakubunkan, 1928), 104–105.

40. Quoted in Carroll Smith-Rosenberg, "Discourses of Sexuality and Subjectivity: The New Woman, 1870–1936," in *Hidden from History*, 271 (also in her *Disorderly Conduct*, 280). Similarly, the Japanese psychiatrist Sakaki Yasusaburō (1870–1929) referred to dormitories as "factories of same-sex love" (*dōseiai no seizōjō*; *Seiyoku kenkyū to seishin bunsekigaku* [Jitsugyō no Nihonsha, 1919], 182).

41. Habuto, *Fujin sei no kenkyū*, 339, and Komine Shigeyuki, *Dōseiai to dōsei shinjū no igakuteki kōsatsu*, in Komine Shigeyuki and Minami Takao, *Dōseiai to dōsei shinjū no kenkyū* (Komine kenkyūjo, 1985), 80.

42. Shimada, *Joseiten*, 499.

43. "Dōsei no ai no kenkyū," *Fujo shinbun* (hereafter *FS*), no. 586 (11 August 1911), 4; Katō Bimei, *Kore dake wa kokoroeoku beshi* (Seibundō, 1934), 46–47; and Murata Tenrai and Saitō Masaichi, *Seiyoku to jinsei* (Bunkodō shoten, 1912), 114.

44. Kitagawa and Fujisawa, *Shikijō shisō*, 244.

45. Ellis, *Sexual Inversion*, 245; Kuwatani, "Senritsu subeki," 37; Sawada, *Shinpi*, 2: 137–140; and Takebe Chikugo and Washio Hiroshi, *Fūzoku mondai*, vol. 11, *Gendai shakai mondai kenkyū* (Tōkasha, 1921), 203–204.

46. Sawada, *Shinpi*, 2: 137.

47. Ibid., 138. In a like vein, see Akashi, *Danjo ryōsei no ai*, 18. Kawamura Kunihiko discusses the role of photography in schoolgirl culture in *Otome no inori: kindai josei imēji no tanjō* (Kinokuniya shoten, 1993), 126–132.

48. Sawada, *Shinpi*, 2: 140.

49. Habuto, *Fujin sei no kenkyū*, 339.

50. Takebe and Washio, *Fūzoku mondai*, 204.

51. Sawada, *Shinpi*, 2: 142. The exact significance of the latter figures is obscure, but they are perhaps meant to denote the ages of senior and junior partners in a couple.

52. Habuto Eiji, *Fujin seiyoku no kenkyū* (Shichōsha, 1928), 287.

53. Komine, *Dōseiai to dōsei shinjū*, 22, 152, 231. Komine referred to the school in question as the "highest seat of learning for females" (*joshi no saikō gakufu*), a designation often given at the time to Japan Women's University or, alternatively, to the Tokyo Women's Higher Normal School (founded 1890).

54. A 1910 newspaper article ("Jogakusei," pt. 9) reported that schoolgirls used the terms *Suma-ura* ("Suma Bay"—a toponym celebrated in classical literature)

and *toppu* (possibly from the English word "top," as in the toy) to refer to "corrupt practices" (*heifū*), whose evidence might be found concealed in dormitory trunks and desk drawers, but left the exact nature of the sexual acts involved up to the imagination of readers. After censorship of erotic expression eased under the American Occupation of 1945–1952, published details of sexual practice grew more explicit. One 1949 text (Nishimura Isaku and Shikiba Ryūzaburō, *Gakusei to sei kyōiku* [Kensetsusha], 209–210) specifically cited mutual masturbation (*sōgo onanī*) as the pinnacle of physical involvement among schoolgirls.

55. Yasuda Tokutarō, "Dōseiai no rekishikan," *Chūō kōron* 50, no. 3 (March 1935): 151, and Shimada, *Joseiten*, 498.

56. Yasuda, "Dōseiai," 150.

57. Ōtsuki Kenji, *Ren'ai seiyoku no shinri to sono bunseki shochihō* (Tōkyō seishin bunsekigaku kenkyūjo, 1936), 228.

58. On schoolboy eroticism, see Pflugfelder, *Cartographies*, 212–225, and on schoolboy culture more generally, Donald Roden, *Schooldays in Imperial Japan: A Study in the Culture of a Student Elite* (Berkeley: University of California Press, 1980).

59. Shirai Kiichi, *Seinenki danjo no shinri* (Meguro shoten, n.d. [preface 1920]), 237.

60. Sawada, *Shinpi*, 2: 130.

61. Yasuda, "Dōseiai," 150.

62. Mushimei Sanjin, "Dōsei no ai ni tsuite," *FS*, no. 590 (8 September 1911), 3, and Yasuda, "Dōseiai," 151.

63. Hamao Shirō, "Dōseiai kō," *Fujin saron* 2, no. 9 (September 1930): 137.

64. Kure Shūzō, "Dōsei no ai," *Fujin gahō*, no. 177 (October 1920): 26–27.

65. Yasuda, "Dōseiai," 150.

66. Honda Masuko, *Jogakusei no keifu: saishoku sareru Meiji* (Seidosha, 1990), 8.

67. On "good wife, wise mother" ideology, see also Kathleen Uno's essay in this volume.

68. "Tetsudō sharyō waryō," pt. 1, *Kokkei shinbun*, no. 30 (15 June 1902), 19.

69. "Kinji zappō," *Kokkei shinbun*, no. 30 (15 June 1902), 18. For details of the "Yotsumeya incident," see the serial article "Monbushō no Yotsumeya jiken," *Yorozu chōhō*, 26 April–5 May 1902, 2.

70. For more on *toichi-haichi*, see Pflugfelder, *Queer Archipelago* (forthcoming).

71. Details of this incident are drawn from the following articles: "Bō onna kyōikuka iwaku"; "Ichigen ichigen," *Miyako shinbun*, 31 July 1911, 2; "Itoigawa shinjū," *Miyako shinbun*, 31 July 1911, 5; "Kijō manroku," *Chūgai shōgyō shinpō*, 31 July 1911, 4; "Nireijō aiyōshite Echigo ni jōshi su," *Kokumin shinbun*, 30 July 1911, 4; "Osorubeki dōsei no ai," in *Yomiuri shinbun*, 31 July 1911; "Reijō dōshi no jōshi," *Yorozu chōhō*, 31 July 1911, 3; "Suishi seru nibijin," *Tōkyō nichinichi shinbun* (hereafter *Nichinichi*), 31 July 1911, 5; and "Suishi seshi nireijō," *FS*, no. 586 (11 August 1911), 2.

72. See Lawrence Rogers, "She Loves Me, She Loves Me Not: *Shinjū* and *Shikidō Ōkagami*," *Monumenta Nipponica* 49 (1994): 31–60.

73. In another suicide involving two schoolgirls, the date of which is unclear, the participants demonstrated their familiarity with *shinjū* conventions by each secreting within her sleeve a lock of the other's hair. See Komine, *Dōseiai to dōsei shinjū*, 197.

74. On male-male *shinjū*, see Iwata Jun'ichi, "Nanshoku shinjūron," *Hanzai kōron* 2, no. 12 (December 1932): 70–79, and Komine, *Dōseiai to dōsei shinjū*, 202–228.

75. *Kawaraban shinbun: Edo Meiji sanbyaku jiken,* ed. Nishimaki Kōsaburō, 4 vols., *Taiyō korekushon,* no. 5 (Heibonsha, 1978) 1: 129.

76. "Kōko sōdan," *Nichinichi,* 8 July 1873, 1.

77. Ōmichi Kazuichi, *Jōshi no kenkyū* (Dōbunkan, 1911), appendix 1, 3–80. This figure excludes suicides between sisters, as well as triple suicides, each of which Ōmichi classified separately.

78. Takebe and Washio, *Fūzoku mondai,* 205.

79. For reportage, see "Nishōjo idaite nyūsui," *Yomiuri shinbun*, 30 July 1911, 3; "Onna aiidaki minage su," *Yamato shinbun*, 30 July 1911, evening edition, 4; "Onna dōshi no dakiai shinjū," *Tōkyō niroku shinpō*, 30 July 1911, 5; "Onna dōshi no shinjū," *Miyako shinbun*, 30 July 1911, 5; "Onna dōshi no shinjū," *Nihon*, 30 July 1911, 3; "Onna no dakiai shinjū," *Chūō shinbun*, 30 July 1911, evening edition, 2; "Onna no dakiai shinjū," *Yorozu chōho*, 7 July 1911, 3; "Ryōjo aiidakite Azumabashi yori tōshin," *Hōchi shinbun*, 30 July 1911, evening edition, 4; "Tetsudō to tōshin jōshi," *Chūgai shōgyō shinpō*, 30 July 1911, 4; "Wakai onna no dakiai shinjū," *Kokumin shinbun*, 30 July 1911, 4; and "Wakaki onna dōshi no shinjū," *Nichinichi*, 30 July 1911, 5.

80. "Dōsei no ai," *FS*, no. 586 (11 August 1911), 1; "Dōsei no ai no kenkyū"; Mushimei Sanjin, "Dōsei no ai ni tsuite"; Shimanaka Yūzō, "Dōsei no koi to sono jitsurei," *FS*, no. 587 (18 August 1911), 4; and "Suishi seshi nireijō."

81. Shimanaka, "Dōsei no koi."

82. Kuwatani, "Senritsu subeki," 35. In the same issue, the recent incidence of "*jōshi* between females" also received mention in Boson Inji's "Seiyoku mondai no rinkaku" (*Shin kōron* 26, no. 9 [September 1911]: 35).

83. "Dokusha bungei," *Miyako shinbun*, 5 August 1911, 6.

84. Furukawa Makoto, "The Changing Nature of Sexuality: The Three Codes Framing Homosexuality in Modern Japan," trans. Angus Lockyer, *U.S.-Japan Women's Journal*, English Supplement, no. 7 (1994): 115.

85. Takebe and Washio, *Fūzoku mondai*, 205–206.

86. Ishizumi Harunosuke, *Seiteki fujin hanzai kō* (Onko shooku, 1927), 261–266.

87. See for example, "Dōsei no ai," *FS*, no. 586 (11 August 1911), 1, and Habuto, *Fujin sei no kenkyū*, 340.

88. "Dōsei no ai," *FS*, no. 586 (11 August 1911), 1.

89. Komine, *Dōseiai to dōsei shinjū*, 153. The leading known cause, according to Komine, was "same-sex love," which allegedly provided a motive for 12 of the deaths. Komine could identify only four schoolgirl participants in "same-sex suicide" from 1873 to 1926 (257), although he was working with spotty data. Komine also counted sixty-five schoolgirl participants in "cross-sex suicide" (*isei jōshi*) between 1872 and 1934, not including thirty-four who had attempted it but were unsuccessful (152). It should be noted that Komine's figures include some cases from colonial territories in China, Korea, and Taiwan.

90. Komine, *Dōseiai to dōsei shinjū*, 117, 121, 125, 129, 137, 140, 145.

91. Yasuda, "Dōseiai," 152.

92. "Jogakusei no dōsei shinju," *Nichinichi*, 27 November 1929, 2; Komine, *Dōseiai to dōsei shinjū*, 153, 154, 155; and "Shi o motomete," *FS*, no. 1648 (10 January 1932), 16.

93. Komine, *Dōseiai to dōsei shinjū*, 174.

94. I have taken the phrase "Mount Mihara disease" from "Mihara-yama ni jinji sōdan," *FS*, no. 1721 (4 June 1933), 2.

95. Komine, *Dōseiai to dōsei shinjū*, 173, 229–230.

96. "Mihara-yama ni jinji sōdan."

97. For another scandal involving Mount Mihara, schoolgirls, and "same-sex suicide," see Komine, *Dōseiai to dōsei shinjū*, 154; "Shūnen ni shima wa maneku," *Miyako shinbun*, 31 January 1934: 13; and "Tōkyō-wan no namima e," *Asahi*, 31 January 1934, 11.

98. For reportage and commentary, see Fukushima Teiko, "Mittsu no jogakusei jiken," *FS*, no. 1707 (26 February 1933), 8; "Jogakusei dōsei shinjū," *Asahi*, 14 February 1933, 7; "Jogakusei ga nageta futatsu no uzumaki," *Asahi*, 16 February 1933, 5; "Jogakusei no ryōki jisatsu," *Asahi*, 15 February 1933, 11; "Mihara kakō de jisatsu," *FS*, no. 1706 (19 February 1933), 2; "Shi o nozomu kanojo ni kangen shita ikka," *Asahi*, 16 February 1933, evening edition, 2.

99. Writing of a 1928 case involving two schoolgirls, for example, Komine postulated a chain of events leading from "addiction to novels" to "same-sex love" and finally to "same-sex suicide" (*Dōseiai to dōsei shinjū*, 154).

100. For reportage, see "Biwa-ko de shi o ou," *Ōsaka mainichi shinbun*, 8 April 1934, evening edition, 2; "Kosui ni minage," *Ōsaka asahi shinbun*, 8 April 1934, 2.

101. Uruki Hiroshi, "Dōsei shinjū no iinazuke Aiko," *Fujin kōron* 19, no. 6 (June 1934): 312–319.

102. Komine, *Dōseiai to dōsei shinjū*, 154–155, 167–168.

103. The Saijō/Masuda incident is discussed in Yukiko Hanawa, "Inciting Sites of Political Interventions: Queer 'n' Asian," *Positions* 4, no. 3 (1996): 471–472; Robertson, *Takarazuka*, 191–197; and Jennifer Robertson, "Dying to Tell: Sexuality and Suicide in Imperial Japan," *Signs* 25, no. 1 (1999): 1–6, 16–19.

104. Robertson, "Dying to Tell," 27.

105. Komine, *Dōseiai to dōsei shinjū*, 80; Ōtsuki, *Ren'ai seiyoku*, 228. For a photograph of Mizunoe, popularly known as Tāki, see Robertson, *Takarazuka*, 149.

106. Yasuda, "Dōseiai," 146–152.

107. "Dōsei no ai."

108. Kamichika Ichiko, "Dōsei ren'ai no tokushitsu," *Shin shōsetsu* 26, no. 1 (Jan. 1921): 74–78.

109. Yoshiya Nobuko, "Aishiau kotodomo," *Shin shōsetsu* 26, no. 1 (Jan. 1921): 78-80.

110. Kamichika, "Dōsei ren'ai," 78.

111. Yoshiya, "Aishiau kotodomo," 80.

112. It was not beyond the capacity of some men as well to express similar allegiance with schoolgirls. As Frühstück (*Colonizing Sex,* 70, and "Managing the Truth of Sex," 342) discusses, the radical sexologist Yamamoto Senji (1889–1929) criticized girls' school administrators' handling of "same-sex love" on identical grounds.

113. Wada Naoko, "Nihon no senpai rezubiantachi," in *Onna o aisuru onnatachi no monogatari, Bessatsu takarajima,* no. 64 (JICC shuppankyoku, 1987), 78. In 1957, Yoshiya legalized the couple's union by adopting Monma as her daughter. For biographies of Yoshiya, see Jennifer Robertson, "Yoshiya Nobuko: Out and Outspoken in Practice and Prose," in *The Human Tradition in Modern Japan,* ed. Anne Walthall (Wilmington, DE: Scholarly Resources Books, 2002), 155–174; Tanabe Seiko, *Yume haruka Yoshiya Nobuko: akitomoshi tsukue no ue no ikusanga,* 2 vols. (Asahi shinbunsha, 1999); and Yoshitake Teruko, *Nyonin Yoshiya Nobuko* (Bungei shunjū, 1982). See also Hiromi Tsuchiya Dollase, "Reading Yoshiya Nobuko's 'Yaneura no nishojo': In Search of Literary Possibilities in *Shōjo* Narratives," *U.S.-Japan's Women's Journal,* English Supplement, nos. 20–21 (2001): 151–178.

114. For histories of the Bluestockings, see Nancy Andrew, "The Seitōsha: An Early Japanese Women's Organization, 1911–1916," *Papers on Japan* 6 (1972): 45–67; Horiba Kiyoko, *Seitō no jidai: Hiratsuka Raichō to atarashii onnatachi, Iwanami shinshu,* no. 15 (Iwanami shoten, 1988), and Ide Fumiko, *Seitō no onnatachi* (Kaien shobo, 1975). Other useful works include *Seitō o yomu,* ed. Shin feminizumu hihyō no kai (Gakugei shorin, 1998), and *Seitō o manabu hito no tame ni,* eds. Yoneda Sayoko and Ikeda Emiko (Sekai shisōsha, 1999).

115. On the Yoshiwara outing, see Hiratsuka Raichō, *Genshi, josei wa taiyō de atta: Hiratsuka Raichō jiden,* 4 vols. (Ōtsuki shoten, 1971–73), 2: 373–376; "Iwayuru atarashiki onna," pt. 2, *Kokumin shinbun,* 13 July 1912, 4; "Onna bunshi no Yoshiwara asobi," *Yorozu chōhō,* 10 July 1912, 3; and "'Seitōsha' no koro: Meiji Taishō shoki no fujin undō," pt. 1, *Sekai,* no. 122 (February 1956): 129.

116. Hiratsuka Raichō, "Marumado yori," *Seitō* 2, no. 8 (August 1912): 78.

117. See for example, "Henshūshitsu yori," *Seitō* 2, no. 7 (July 1912): 110; Hiratsuka, "Marumado yori," 76–108; and Otake Kōkichi, "Aru yoru to, aru asa," *Seitō* 2, no. 6 (June 1912): 114–118.

118. "Iwayuru atarashiki onna." For contemporary images of the *bishōnen*, see Pflugfelder, *Cartographies*, 225–230.

119. For biographies of Otake, see Takai Yō and Orii Miyako, *Azami no hana: Tomimoto Kazue shōden* (Domesu shuppan, 1985), and Watanabe Sumiko, *Seitō no onna: Otake Kōkichi den* (Fuji shuppan, 2001).

120. Iwami Teruyo, "Hiratsuka Raichō: mō hitotsu no koi," in *Seimei" de yomu nijisseiki Nihon bungei,* ed. Suzuki Sadami (Shibundō, 1996), 65–73; Kurosawa Ariko, "1912–nen no Raichō to Kōkichi: 'Josei kaihō' to rezubianizumu o megutte," in *Bungaku: shakai e chikyū e,* ed. Nishida Masaru tainin taishoku kinen bunshū henshū iinkai (San'ichi shobo, 1996), 309–327; and Yoshikawa Toyoko, "'Josei dōseiai' to iu 'yamai' to jendā," in *Jendā no Nihon kindai bungaku,* eds. Nakayama Kazuko, Egusa Mitsuko, and Fujimori Kiyoshi (Kanrin shobō, 1998), 111–117.

121. Hiratsuka, "Marumado yori," 89.

122. Hiratsuka, *Genshi,* 2: 388.

123. Kurosawa, "1912–nen," 310.

124. For another aspect of Hiratsuka's involvement with sexology, see Sumiko Otsubo's essay in this volume.

125. Hiratsuka, *Genshi,* 2: 541–544.

126. Havelock Ellis, "Joseikan no dōsei ren'ai," trans. Yabo [Sakamoto Makoto], *Seitō* 4, no. 4 (April 1914): furoku, 1–24.

127. Ellis, "Joseikan," 1.

128. Ellis's chapter described various forms of "sexual inversion" among females, including the "ardent attachments" of schoolgirls. In the author's view, the phenomenon could be "found in all countries where girls are segregated for educational purposes," and its symptoms were "on the whole, singularly uniform" (*Sexual Inversion*, 131 [Ellis, "Joseikan," 12]). However, according to Ellis, such "girlish devotions" were usually little more than an acquired and temporary aberration brought on by isolation from the opposite sex—a qualification that made Hiratsuka's diagnosis of her former admirer as being not situationally but instead "congenitally" inclined toward "sexual inversion" all the more striking.

129. Edward Carpenter, *Chūseiron*, trans. Aoyama Kikue, pts. 1–3, *Safuran* 1, no. 3 (May 1914): 1–22; 1, no. 4 (June 1914): 130–153; and 1, no. 5 (July 1914): 55–76.

130. Sakai Toshihiko, "Hashigaki," in trans. Sakai Toshihiko and Yamakawa Kikue, *Josei chūshinsetsu/Dōseiai* (Arusu, 1919), 2.

131. "Henshūshitsu nite," *Safuran* 1, no. 3 (May 1914): 157–158.

132. "Henshūshitsu nite," 157–158.

133. Kamichika, "Dōsei ren'ai," 77.

134. "Henshūshitsu nite," 158.

135. For useful sourcebooks, see *Shiryō: bosei hogo ronsō,* ed. Kōuchi Nobuko, *Ronsō shirīzu,* no. 1 (Domesu shuppan, 1984); and *Shiryō: sei to ai o meguru ronsō,* ed. Orii Miyako, *Ronsō shirīzu,* no. 5 (Domesu shuppan, 1991). On the significance of these debates, see Iwabuchi Hiroko, "Sekushuariti no seijigaku e no chōsen: teisō datai haishō ronsō," in Shin feminizumu hihyō no kai, Seitō *o yomu,* 305–331; Iwazaki Shōko, *"Seitō* ni okeru sekushuariti no mondai teiki," in Yoneda and Ikeda, *Seitō o manabu hito no tame ni,* 125–141; and Muta Kazue, *Senryaku to shite no kazoku: kindai Nihon no kokumin kokka keisei to josei* (Shin'yōsha, 1996), chapter 5.

136. Ōtsuka, *Josei igaku,* 40.

137. During the 1920s, Furuya would become a prominent figure in various Kansai-based women's organizations. For biographical information, see Furuya Toyoko, *Kyōran kara fukkatsu e,* ed. Kōbe sekai renpō no ie (Osaka: Ningen kagakusha, 1955); Furuya Toyoko, *Onna no shōzō* (Asahi geinō shuppan, 1962); Furuya Toyoko, "Sōan no ichinichi," *FS,* no. 2612 (17 December 1939), 8; and "Han Taiheiyō fujin kaigi ni tsuite," pt. 7, *Yomiuri shinbun,* 21 March 1928.

138. Furuya Toyoko, "Dōseiai no joshi kyōikujō ni okeru shin igi," *Fujin kōron* 7, no. 8 (Summer 1922): 24–29, republished in *Sei to ren'ai no kenkyū,* ed. Satō Hisashi (Nihon shoin shuppanbu, 1923), 295–305. Subsequent quotes are from *Fujin kōron,* with page numbers in parentheses.

139. Yoshiya, "Aishiau kotodomo," 79–80.

140. For at least another decade, some women continued to use "same-sex love" to refer to an idealistic and altruistic loyalty to one's own gender. For example, when the women's suffrage activist Wazaki Haru (1885–1952) launched a campaign in Akita City in 1930 to reform married men who kept concubines, she described her motive as "same-sex love" (see "Yo no danjo in uttau," newspaper clipping in the private files of Wazaki Masayuki). I have written about Wazaki and Akita suffragism in *Seiji to daidokoro: Akita-ken joshi sanseiken undōshi* (Domesu shuppan, 1986). On "same-sex love" and suffragism, see my

"Senzen seiji bunka no jendāka: 'fujin sanseiken' saikō," in *Kakudai suru modaniti*, vol. 6, *Iwanami kōza kindai Nihon no bunkashi*, ed. Yoshimi Shun'ya (Iwanami shoten, 2002), 63–114.

141. Kurosawa, "1912–nen," 326.

142. Furuya was not alone in the early 1920s in being able to imagine an integral and valued role for "same-sex love" as part of the trajectory of modernity. Elsewhere, I have introduced a 1921 magazine essay by Ozaki Shirō (1898–1964), who foresaw a corresponding reevaluation of male-male bonds, and who was likewise familiar with the work of Carpenter. Ozaki Shirō, "Bishōnen no kenkyū," *Kaihō* 3, no. 4 (1921): 539–540. See also Pflugfelder, *Cartographies*, 307.

143. "Naigai zappō," *FS*, no. 1038 (11 April 1920), 8. Biographical information on Tozuka is scarce. In 1930, she authored *Kindai Nihon jokenshi* (Kōgyokudō), a history of women's rights.

144. Tozuka Matsuko, *Ren'ai kyōiku no kisoteki kenkyū, Fujin kyōiku kenkyū sōsho*, no. 1 (Seirindō shoten, 1924). Subsequent quotes are from this source, with page numbers in parentheses.

145. On this ideal, see Christina Simmons, "Companionate Marriage and the Lesbian Threat," *Frontiers* 4, no. 3 (Fall 1979): 54–59.

146. Margaret Jackson, "'Facts of Life' or the Eroticization of Women's Oppression?: Sexology and the Social Construction of Heterosexuality," in *The Cultural Construction of Sexuality*, ed. Pat Caplan (London: Tavistock, 1987), 64–67; and Marie Stopes, *Kekkon'ai*, trans. Yaguchi Tatsu (Asakaya shoten, 1924).

147. Akagawa Manabu, *Sekushuariti no rekishi shakaigaku* (Keisō shobō, 1999), 193–202.

148. Itonaga Masayuki kindly arranged a meeting for me, on 23 September 1990, with several women who had attended secondary schools during these years.

5 Seeds and (Nest) Eggs of Empire: Sexology Manuals/Manual Sexology

Mark Driscoll

All I did was jerk-off the whole time.

> —Miyatake Gaikotsu in 1892 after his release from a two-year
> prison sentence for pornography when asked, "How
> did you pass the time when you were in jail?"

Men, Become Longer and Stronger in No Time at All!

> —Advertisement for penis extension in Japanese colonial
> newspaper, *Manshū nichi nichi shinbun*, March 19, 1924

Hysteria is often used to describe women. Like the word 'emotional,' it is not at all an insulting word; rather it is a way of showing respect for the special characteristics of women.

> —*Chōsen kōron*, June 1916

Michel Foucault has argued that through the patterned discursive excitation of the "four great strategic unities"[1] of the masturbating youth, hysterical woman, perverse adult, and Malthusian couple, a regime of sexuality was installed as the new instrument of power in late eighteenth- and nineteenth-century Europe. Through the partial overturning of the older regime of alliance—the "homeostatic" system of marriage and kinship anchored by the patriarchal family—the deployment of sexuality was liberated from the conservative functions of reproduction and social maintenance. What Foucault calls the insistent "singular imperialism" (33) of the regime of sexuality "had its reason for being, not in reproducing itself, but in proliferating, innovating, annexing, creating, and penetrating bodies" (106), increasing pleasure and sensations through its "mobile, polymorphous, and contingent techniques of power" (105). Although the deployment of alliance is anchored by the family through juridical structures of power—and here I would suggest the homologues of the *ie* system and *ryōsai kenbo* in Japan (see Kathleen Uno's essay in this volume)—the regime of sexuality is disseminated through the nonjuridical networks of sexology, psychology, and journalism.

Within these Foucaultian protocols, the famous Meiji (1868–1912) and Taishō (1912–1926) sexologist, pornographer, and journalist Miyatake Gaikotsu (1867–1955) retrofits the modern regime of sexuality. In interviews and in his own popular magazines in the years that followed his release from prison after violating the censorship laws, Gaikotsu continually defied the state authorities by insisting that instead of obeying their erotophobic juridical code that delineated a conservative regime of filial relationships, he would continue to follow the common-sense notions of obscenity and sexual expression held by most men in Japan.[2] Outfitted with fabulous accessories like his notorious penis-shaped pipe and showing off knowledge of both European sexual science and the history of Japanese sexuality, he became famous hypothesizing that the development of the modern Japanese state was established by *repressing*[3] nonreproductive libidinal energies and forcing them to hide behind shut sliding doors (*fusumas*). Nevertheless, as one of the contradictory effects of Gaikotsu's crusade of speaking the truth to power about sexuality, those shut *fusumas* would soon be flung wide open and domestic interiors blinded by the flood lights and search warrants of a new science; a powerful sexual science whose pioneers included the pop sexologist Gaikotsu himself. Alongside the deployment of alliance anchored by the reproductive family of the patriarchal father and "good wife, wise mother"—whose injunctions the performatively "cocky" Gaikotsu would wage a thirty-year war against—there developed a parallel "deployment of sexuality" thanks to the efforts of sexologists, psychiatrists, and sex-positive journalists like Gaikotsu. One of the effects of this multiplication, magnification, and extension of the power of sexuality is visible in the second citation above, some thirty years after the beginning of Gaikotsu's crusade.

The large paid advertisement in the colonial *Manshū nichi nichi shinbun* (Manchuria daily newspaper) published in Dalian, China, is a popular type of sexual improvement ad that incites heterosexual desire by employing familiar technical terms from Japanese sexology. These kinds of ads appeared frequently in the colonial newspapers and differed slightly from ads in *naichi* (metropolitan) magazines and newspapers published inside Japan in that the regulative ideal of orthosexuality was not assumed to be reproductive, monogamous marriage. In Dalian, as everywhere in the Japanese colonies, a healthy sex life for men free from what the ad calls the "bad habit of masturbation" (*akushū onani*) and "debilitating sexual neurasthenia" (*seiteki shinkei suijaku*) would begin for most Japanese men by hygienically following the advice in the colonial newspaper's weekly column called "Using the Red-Light District" (*karyūshi*). This column featured advice on sex clubs, bars, and the brothels where female sex workers—Russian, Chinese, Korean, and Japanese—in Dalian could be cheaply purchased as commodities. And the colonial male could heed the commendation of the ad for more "rewarding sex with healthy and medically examined sex workers" without suffering the social stigma against prostitution that was appearing with increasing force inside Japan. Adamantly opposed to the mounting worldwide pressure against prostitution and the bourgeois married women who sponsored its prohibition in Japan, bureaucrats and capitalists in the colonies oversaw a deployment of sexuality that overwhelmed the ideology of family. This defeat of the conservative norms of family alliance by the regime of sexuality reached the point where Japanese sex workers were often regarded as the brave pioneers of imperial capitalism and the centerpieces in the system of prostitution that was for the most part considered indispensable to the establishment of a civilizing empire.[4] In the periphery of Japan's empire then, sexology-smart advertising warned men about the dangers of masturbation, claiming not that it was dangerous in and of itself, but that it would interfere with the pursuit of more pleasurable sex defined as robust heterosexual intercourse. And in metropolitan Japan, Gaikotsu was one of many public figures wielding both old and new theories of sexuality and sexology, and who advocated the alleviation of what they perceived to be the repressive attitude toward sexuality of the Meiji and Taishō states.

But wait just a minute. It has been considered one of the fundamental axioms of historiography on modern Japan that the science called sexology (*seikagaku* or *seiyokugaku* in Japanese) had clearly demarcated "Western" origins. The great majority of essays and books written in English and Japanese are grounded in this presupposition.[5] Euro-

American sexology has been almost unanimously invoked as the repressively erotophobic force that violently interrupted the pre-Meiji utopia of permissiveness in Japan and then led the way in establishing a racialized eugenics as the sexological ground for Japanese ultranationalism. This premodern utopia is claimed to have enjoyed first, the social and moral permissiveness that is invariably evidenced through the invocation of the pure and grand tradition of Japanese homophilia, and second, an indigenous symbolic regime that was supposedly free from the "Western" sexological injunction that individual identities be coerced to follow exclusively and uniformly from the sexual acts of those individuals. The pillaging of this "Japanese" utopia of free love is said to have been brought about primarily through the "copying" of homophobic, erotophobic, and misogynist European codes like "homosexual," "hysteria," and "masturbation" by Japanese sexological modernists.

For example, in what is considered one of the best recent volumes on modern sexuality in Japan—purportedly employing a Foucaultian methodology—we read in Kawamura Kunimitsu's *Sekushuarite no kindai* (Modern sexuality) about the ways in which a seventeenth- and eighteenth-century indigenous Japanese discourse that stimulated and elicited polymorphous pleasures for men and women, and indulgently pampered reproductive women with "natural" gynecology, was "penetrated," "annihilated [*danzetsu shita*] . . . and overwhelmed by Western science and sexology."[6] Kawamura further claims that "Western" sexology was the monocausal agent for all of the degenerate phobias of modern Japan, ranging from masturbation and hysteria to the preference for male children (78–79). He writes that the first Japanese translations of these "Western" texts in 1875 completely severed modern Japan from its Tokugawa past where erotic pleasure and desire were ostensibly free from a Westernological regime that stigmatized individual identities based solely on the invented categories of the perverse: hysterical women, masturbating youth, and nonreproductive adults (46, 63). Kawamura claims that the modernization of Japan was the logical effect of the repressive hypothesis, although, for Kawamura, this repression is spatialized, with an undifferentiated "West" responsible for repressing an indigenous Japanese pleasure principle. This blame-the-West discourse asserts that those popular sexologists and psychiatrists in Japan slavishly imitated and copied Western sexology's repressive coding of nonreproductive sexuality as "unnatural" (*fushizen*) and "abnormal" (*ijō*) (73). The effects of this imperialism were so invasive that Japanese uteruses themselves were claimed by Kawamura to have been violently "colonized by Western science" (*Seiyō kagaku ni shokuminchika sareru shūkyū*) (78).

Likewise, in an authoritative new work on modern Japanese sexology, Sabine Frühstück deploys colonialism as a metaphor to install what Gayatri Spivak calls a "Euroteleological"[7] determination to Japan's sexological modernity. Insisting that uniquely European notions of "normative sex" were much later "translated into cultural practices in an effort to 'colonize' the sex and sexuality of the Japanese populace,"[8] Frühstück falls into the trap of flagging all non-Western experience of modernity with what I call the "Three Ls": local, late, and lacking with respect to an imagined full and transcendent European precedent. Frühstück informs us in a totalizing fashion that "Japanese tradition was denounced as uncivilized, and the authority of Western culture in general and of Western science in particular was emphasized" (11) in the development of sexological modernity in Japan. In my reading, her impressive scholarship is undercut by claiming, like Kawamura, an adherence to Foucault while refusing the critique of the repressive hypothesis that is the centerpiece of Foucault's *History of Sexuality*. As a result, by her insistence on the "repression and liberation of sex throughout Japan's modern history," Frühstück contravenes the Foucauldian recommendations that "excitation" not be apprehended as "repressive colonization" and "extension and proliferation" as "freedom" (5).

Acknowledging only the metaphoric importance of coloniality, historiographical accounts of sexological modernism in Japan like those of Kawamura and Frühstück fail to acknowledge either the constitutive force of Japanese colonial-imperialism (which, as Leo Ching argues, was largely grounded on its *difference* from Euro-American colonialism[9]) on Japanese sexology or the underanalyzed ways in which Japanese sexologists and historians of sexuality refused and resisted the Eurocentrism of what Depesh Chakrabarty calls the schema of "first in Europe and then elsewhere."[10] The structure adduced by both Kawamura and Frühstück of assigning a pure Euro-American origin to modern sexology and sexual science creates crucial erasures and displacements.

The following excavation of those elisions and displacements will try to show that while Europeans stigmatized and condemned the central categories of sexological modernism—masturbation, hysteria, and homoeroticism—in Japan, sexologists not only did not follow the Europeans' moral condemnation, but in important cases, overturned it to the extent of valorizing the categories. That is to say that rather than another repetition of the tropology of the "Three Ls" and "first in Europe and then elsewhere," I want to demonstrate some of the ways Japanese thinkers produced sexological categories markedly different from the ways these categories were inflected in Europe. As Japanese colonial-imperial ideologues insisted on Japan's difference from Euro-American colonialism, the provincializing and anti-Europe rhetoric of much sexological discourse in Japanese was logically constitutive of that differential specificity of Japan's colonial-imperial modernity. When inserted into the historical-material contours of colonial-imperialism, this more active, constitutive mode of sexological discourse in Japan can furthermore be understood as an enthusiastic participant in the *global* project of developing sexological and criminological social science, a project that received important contributions from commentators in Mexico City, Buenos Aires, and Shanghai, places not usually considered to belong in or to the "West."

Even when we relax the "provincializing Europe"[11] strictures of postcolonial critique and history somewhat and grant a provisional temporostructural priority to certain aspects of European sexological thought, poststructural thought can still offer a *caveat lector.* The protocols of contemporary critical theory hold that every material articulation has been enabled by the constraining force of that which preceded it, what Judith Butler calls "enabling constraints."[12] European "sexology manuals" were translated and read in Japan starting around 1875, thereby functioning as one element in the modernizing impulse of Japanese sexology and an ever present component of the new regimatics of a "deployment of sexuality." Parts of this emerging field were constrained, to be sure, by a European fore-structure, but because the new articulation and re-inscription of sexology discourse in Japan was temporally and spatially different from its predecessor, the historically specific ways in which it was *manually* handled in its own historical chronotope can be shown to have been equally as enabling as the "constraining force" (i.e., European sexology, but also Japanese, South Asian, and Chinese premodern and early modern discourse on sexuality) that preceded it. Poststructural theory helps to highlight the process whereby European sexology, when it was not being dismissed outright as erotophobic Christian propaganda, as was frequently the case, was differentially inscribed in a historically material, *hands-on* mode of "manual sexology" in the composition of Japanese sexology texts.

Returning to postcolonial theory's recommendation that we read Japanese sexology as inextricably embedded in a project of colonial-empire, I argue that at the level of both form and content, late Meiji and Taishō sexology can be shown to have produced texts in many ways *antithetical* to those of mainstream European sexology. With the requirements for successful imperial consolidation more (in the works of Mori Ōgai and Tanaka Kōgai) or less (in the works of Mina-kata Kumagusu) in mind, Japanese sexology will be shown to have been imbricated in both the historically unprecedented deployment of Japanese female sex workers as the "first wave" in capitalist empire in Asia and the equally unprecedented presence of socially powerful and unmarried women in the colonial cities.[13] The content of these texts will be shown to have deconstructed and reconstructed three of the four "strategic unities" of the regime of modern sexuality. First, the category of the masturbating male youth was important in the production of an exuberantly libidinalized heterosexual masculinity requiring an extensive network of scientific prostitution for its satis-faction (Ōgai, Tanaka). Second, the production of the category of hysteria in Japanese sexology had many contradictory effects includ-ing the identification of a physically powerful, intensely independent, and emotionally unstable woman with erotic demands often satisfied homoerotically or outside of heterosexual marriage (Tanaka).[14] Third, there was an enabling ambivalence toward whether or not the "per-verse" (*hentai*) was normative and universal. For example, Minakata Kumagusu highlighted the historic Japanese practices of male-male love in order to link them with other similar practices in China, Okinawa, and ancient Greece. At the level of form, these texts dem-onstrate a striking eclecticism and polyphony, frequently citing the au-thor's own case histories, previous sexological texts written in many languages, psychoanalytic theory, and philosophies of eroticism from Indian, Chinese, Daoist, and ancient Greek and Roman traditions.

For me, the formal polyphony is as interesting as the frequent refusals and contraventions of European sexological phobia. In a different context, the literary critic Franco Moretti has called those representations that formally employ different languages and multiple citational voices "world texts."[15] These modernist texts are unconcerned with any one national culture, but invoke the world and the desire for empire by the "supranational dimension of their represented space." Moretti's Marxist analysis emphasizes that although these polyphonic world texts are written in the semiperiphery of world capitalism, they narrativize empire by enfolding multiple voices into their own textual logic, refusing the tight confines of the homogeneous nation-state.

In Japanese literary history, Mori Ōgai (1862–1922) is considered the founder of the modern "I-Novel." However, under his family name of Rintarō, he performed double duty as a chief scientific and medical expert. After four years studying hygiene, medicine, and psychiatry in Germany in the 1880s he quickly advanced in the military's scientific hierarchy, finally serving as surgeon general from 1907 to 1916, a period when the Japanese victory in the Russo-Japanese War of 1904–1905 and the annexation of Korea brought the Imperial Army enormous national and international prestige. Foucault has argued convincingly that sexuality should not be considered the Master-signifier for a solid mass of immutable chromosomal determinants, but rather the "set of effects produced in bodies, behaviors, and social relations by a certain deployment" of a "complex political technology."[16] A crucial element of the "complex political technology" of Japanese imperialism was Mori's definitive text on modern Japanese hygiene, *New Hygiene Compilation* (*Eisei shinpen*). He first published a short hygiene textbook called *Army Hygiene Manual* (*Rikugun eisei kyōtei*) in 1889 for use by military doctors exclusively, but his *Eisei shinpen* was meant to both replace the earlier manual for doctors and to be used by nonmilitary doctors throughout Japan and the colonies. *Eisei shinpen* was released in five separate editions in 1897, 1899, 1904, 1908, and 1914. The first was largely a translation with commentary of Max Rubner's *Lehrbuch der Hygiene* (1890) done by Mori with assistance from Nakayama Toichirō, and at 942 pages was immediately the authoritative source on modern hygiene in Japan. Subsequent editions featured material previously published in Mori's own medical journal *Eisei shinshi*, which included both independent studies done by him and more translations of the newest European hygiene research. With the second edition of *Eisei shinpen* the translations of European works took on the character of a general introduction to a theme within which Mori would introduce European scientific theories, then critically examine them through "global" knowledges drawn from a breathtaking image reservoir that deftly moved from ancient Greek and Roman sources to Hindu and Zoroastrian science and philosophy, and inevitably concluded with Japanese and Chinese science and medicine. Mori drew on his reading ability in Latin, German, Chinese, and English to offer a novel and startling synthesis of global knowledge on hygiene and the body. If ever there was a case of Japanese sexology *not* blindly "copying the West," then this would be it.[17]

As we glimpse the confident world textual vision that subtends his central discussions of sexology in *Eisei shinpen*, its historical impact should not be underestimated. *Eisei shinpen* appeared in two different issues: one for the military and one for more general use as the definitive textbook on hygiene in Japanese universities, although the differences disappear with the publication of the 1908 edition. The piece that I will discuss is called "Sexual Development" ("Seiiku"), and its final version, written in 1912, should be considered one of the most important documents in the construction of modern sexological hygiene in Japan and for that reason alone demands critical analysis. However, because the document served as the main text on sexual hygiene in the Japanese Imperial Army until 1945, it seems more crucial to begin to understand the ways in which this text operated as the scientific ground for the political technology of sex for Japanese soldiers during the Fifteen-Year War of 1931 to 1945, whose effects would include but should not be limited to the coerced sexual slavery of between 150,000 and 200,000 East Asian "comfort women."

"Seiiku" was published first in 1912 and was included in the final 1914 version of *Eisei shinpen*. More than any other genre definition, it is a text of comparative sexology. Mori translated and introduced central German sexology texts—including early essays by Freud—and also wrote his own. He begins this text with an introduction to the central themes in the German sexology texts of Karl Lowenfeld and Richard von

Krafft-Ebing and dryly presents their classic erotophobia. Against what he claims is the Europeans' frequent advocacy of "absolute abstinence"[18] as the best way to maintain psychosomatic health, Mori ends the four-page discussion with his opinion that "I want to make it clear that I consider sexual intercourse to be of no harm at all to someone in good health" (117). As the first fifteen pages or so are concerned with general sexual "maturation" including puberty, masturbation, the first experience of intercourse, and so on, Mori employs his standard mode of broad overview style, ranging from the most contemporary discourse of European sexology to Classical Chinese and ancient Greek sources. He presents quotes from Latin doctors, Zoroastrian classics, and Confucius, as well as scientific charts of the average age of puberty in India, Iran, Paris, London, Okinawa, colonized Taiwan (where Mori's own team of researchers gathered the data), and Tokyo. The taxonomic obsession is startling and seems to undergird his desire for objectivity and global "truth," a truth distinct from what he suggests is the false universalizing of European sexology. For him, contemporary European sexology's phobia about erotic pleasure is "strongly overstated" (121). With the exception of his support for Freud, Mori consistently contravenes the accepted European sexological axioms concerning the purported dangers of sexuality.

The next major section of the piece, "Male Sexual Abstinence and Control" ("Otoko no seiyoku yokusei"), initializes a discussion of what Mori translates from the German sexual "*Abstinenz*" and renders into Japanese as *seiyoku yokusei*. *Yokusei* is usually rendered as restraint or control, but it is significant that Mori translates sexual abstinence into the Japanese for sexual regulation or sexual moderation. The implication is that any mode of sexual moderation or censoring would be considered sexual abstinence. It would be a mere minor troping if he did not follow this translation with an objective insistence about the rarity of this type of human male who follows the path of sexual abstinence: "Its number is extremely low" (115). Then he paraphrases Andrej Gyurkovechky by claiming that those who excessively and/or exclusively masturbate are so inconsequential that they are "not even worth wasting time discussing at all" (121); in other words, masturbation is hardly the kind of social problem that European sexology has made it out to be.

Next, he connects "sexual abstinence" (in Mori's view, "restraint" or "control") to sexual repression and claims that it is the basis of all sexual dysfunctions. He concludes this paragraph with a paraphrase of the sexologist Wilhelm Lallemand who theorized that this type of sexually repressed male has "from the beginning, been unable to have successful coitus." So Mori concludes this section by essentializing a sexually repressed male type who excessively masturbates—only because he is unable to achieve heterosexual intercourse—and links this failure to the paucity of opportunities for heterosexual intercourse.

In the next paragraph, the impotent masturbating male is read against a type that is nominated as the "healthy and strong male," characterized by his "violent, furious [*mōretsu zen'yoku*] natural desire." What I would like to foreground in my analysis here is that Mori is not quoting or citing any other sources in this section, but is producing his own binary. He goes on to hypothesize that serious sexual problems arise when this "extremely violent/ferocious natural desire" (*shizen'yoku wa hanahada mōretsu ni shite*) is repressed. The qualification of this "natural desire" as "furious" or "ferocious" is significant. I propose the translation of this crucial adjectival rendering of the supposed naturalness of Japanese masculine desire as "ferocious" rather than "violent," because ferocious carries the sense of an animal urge always out of control, as well as articulating the kernel of the libido theory that he had been deploying with increasing frequency since he read Freud's *Three Essays on the Theory of Sexuality* in 1907 or 1908. Mori argues that since "it is a very difficult thing for healthy men to repress their sexual desire," and the opportunities to "realize this desire are everywhere" (125), the proper role for sexual hygienists and scientists is to regulate and provide frequent opportunities for the satisfaction of this ferocious heterosexual desire. Mori is very clear in his warning that this violent desire should not be restricted, because the negative effects of sexual repression on men outside of normative heterosexuality should be obvious, and again "are not even worth talking about." Mori's disavowal here—"not even worth talking about"—is meant to emphasize the obvious deleterious effects of excessive sexual repression in Western Europe, which he warns of again in his conclusion. Here he is marking off his more natural and rational analysis from the irrationality of Christian and European sexological attitudes that praise complete sexual repression.

But what about other ways of checking this ferocious heterosexual animality? Can they be considered effective? Mori asks these questions rhetorically and then grudgingly admits that there are some who control their ferocious heterosexuality "through religious constraints," and there are some who control their innate heterosexual ferocity through "hygienic concerns," fearing "infectious diseases." Nevertheless, he concludes, "cases where desire is actually limited by moral or aesthetic considerations are extremely rare" (115). So he concludes by surmising that normal heterosexual boys need to fornicate ferociously rather than relying on religious, moral, or health censors, and that scientists should acknowledge what Mori insists on calling the nature of this desire (*sei*) and provide rational outlets for its animal satisfaction.

One would expect suppositions like this to be supported by the standard scientific supplements—empirical data, graphs and charts, and so on—but unlike the other essays that surround this one in the final version of *Eisei shinpen,* there are few scientific surveys featuring empirical data, and of course, Mori possesses no empirical evidence for his suppositions about what he calls sexual abstinence. Seemingly out of desperation, he quotes the second-century Roman doctor Clerus for support, followed by a Classical Chinese source. Thus, sexual abstinence is defined by Mori as the affliction of those unfortunate few who have failed at the game of coitus and have to rely on masturbation as a substitute for heterosexual intercourse. The only fortunate thing about the male masturbating type is that there are very few men who are possessed by this nature. And one cannot help wondering if he won't deal with the question of promiscuity, as he here naturalizes an abundance of heterosexual intercourse, while dismissing solitary masturbators who situate themselves harmlessly outside of the heteronormative gaze of hygienic science.[19]

A few pages later he takes up the theme of promiscuity only to quickly shift the discussion to masturbation, once again questioning the validity of European sexology's platitudes against excessive eroticism: "The damage done by promiscuity to the body [*inkō no shintai o gaisuru koto*] has been written about since ancient times" (121). He then cites the Tannhaeuser legend and admits that legends that warn against promiscuity and sexual relations altogether are common. But he wants to caution against the legends' hyperbole and against the sex-negative attitude of ancient Greek and Roman doctors, claiming that their "discourse is exaggerated" (*ōō kono fudeo kōtai*). Furthermore, Mori contends that the degree of contemporary phobia concerning promiscuity is "not inferior to [that of] former people." That is to say, the unscientific erotophobia of the ancients is roughly equaled by the contemporary European sexological discourse on the frequency of erotic practice. Over and against a simplistic disparaging of exorbitant heterosexual intercourse, European doctors would be well served to look closer and more scientifically at their moral and religious condemnation of human sexuality, he advises. Therefore, Mori suggests that European sexology and sexual science can be shown to have not advanced at all from an earlier irrational, premodern, and Christian erotophobia.

Mori then asks: "How can one define what is excessive and what is moderate in sexual intercourse? Surely this is a difficult thing to ask and a difficult thing to answer. In considering men's ability to have sexual intercourse, one should factor in the significant differences among race, age, character, and hygienic state [*kenkō jōtai*]." He advises that these things should be taken into account before one decides what is appropriate and what is excessive. He then discusses at length various religious traditions' suggested amounts of sex per month to show how infrequent they are compared to his own recommended rate of intercourse. The rates range from once a week in Zoroastrianism, to twice a month in some Jewish sects, and with further variation by occupation, he again concludes with an opinion that contravenes European sexology discourse by recommending that intellectuals, bureaucrats, and educated people should be encouraged to have more sex than workers and uneducated people.

As Mori is trying to specify a norm for Japanese soldiers and male citizens that differs from world historical norms, he implies that Japanese ethnic or racial characteristics, hygiene standards, and education levels have advanced to such a degree that an extremely high level of heterosexual intercourse—four to five times a week—should be the norm for male Japanese civilians and soldiers. This is a bold critique of the most advanced European and North American attitudes on sexuality at that time, which have come to be identified as a hydraulic and economic model of sexuality, whose calculus holds that the higher the degree of civilization the higher the amount of sexual repression needed to sustain that civilizational level. Therefore, in technologizing high normative rates of intercourse for civilized and educated men, Mori opposes the racist projection of highly sexed "primitive people" in the European sexual schema that configured relations with different modes of Otherness in the age of modern imperialism. We should be careful, however, before congratulating Mori for anything like a liberationist humanism. Very far indeed from a deferential mimicry of European superiority and its so-called "science of sexuality," Mori demonized Europe in the name of a more enlightened Japanese colonial-imperialism and established an eroticized norm that would be deployed with increasing frequency in the 1930s.

Several pages later, "Sexual Development" treats the theme of masturbation directly and typologizes the practitioners of this incomplete form of eroticism. In a long section subtitled "Masturbation," the text offers a few clinical definitions of masturbation before editorializing that it is simply "that which does not rely on sexual intercourse, but is experienced instinctually like intercourse" (124). Another short definition is followed by a seeming logical leap that declares, "there are some people in the world who think that masturbation is an unfortunate evil of modernization. Horses and monkeys in particular don't know about masturbation, but then it is already known by the most inferior races of humans."

Mori then provides a short history of masturbation among world civilizations that begins in ancient Greece and Rome where, he claims, it was rarely practiced because those great empires encouraged high levels of sexual intercourse. As masturbation becomes widespread in early modern society because of "aggressive competition" (*kyōsō mōretsu*), which in turn leads to the breakdown of traditional marriage patterns, Mori suggests that the contemporary problems surrounding marriage make him fearful that the number of people who masturbate has increased. It is striking that East Asia and the Middle East are absent from this world history of masturbation. Their exclusion may imply that masturbation is a specifically modern European phenomenon that arose with the beginnings of market capitalism in early modern Europe, a fate avoided by Asian civilizations. By avoiding this evil of modernization, Imperial Japan is completing the circle of world history through the return to the classical infrequency of masturbation in ancient

Greece and Imperial Rome. Different from the abjection of masturbation hegemonic in European sexology—an abjection reiterated by some Japanese sexologists like Yamamoto Senji[20]—Mori locates several of the causes of masturbation within Euro-American capitalism and Christian civilization, provincializing them and offering a healthier East Asian approach as the universal standard.

I have already suggested that Mori's essay contributed greatly to the political technology of a masculinized and heterosexualized male libido. After the gloss on autoeroticism, "Seiiku" ends predictably with a ringing endorsement of sex work through a discussion of the positive benefits to civilization of a scientifically controlled and organized system of female prostitution. Here, Mori strongly naturalizes prostitution, calling it a "fact of civilization [*kanmei no jujitsu*] that has existed for all eternity [*eikyū sonzai*]" (135). Dehistoricizing prostitution and simultaneously heterosexualizing it allows the articulation of female sex work as natural, civilized, and enlightened. Mori struts his scientific commitment to controlling the negative effects of prostitution and regulating it hygienically, and concludes that "people" (*ningen*) will benefit from a rationally planned and scientifically managed system of prostitution. It is safe to assume that by "people" Mori is denoting the ferociously libidinalized men of Japan's colonial empire.

Tanaka Kōgai (1875–1944) is considered one of the three important popular sexologists of Taishō Japan (the other two are Habuto Eiji and Sawada Junjirō, whose work I do not address in this chapter). As their journals and books were the most commercially successful, the three are the culprits most often singled out for flooding the Japanese mass media with the erotophobia copied from European sexology.[21]

Tanaka began his sexology journal *Hentai seiyoku* (Perverse sexuality) in 1921, and along with the longer versions of his arguments published annually in his popular sexology books, he quickly became one of the main sources of popular information on hysteria, S/M, and autoeroticism in Japan.[22] Together with the publication of his controversial sexology work from 1919, he became famous for his sexological journalism and collections of metapsychological essays[23] written in the late 1920s and 1930s when he retired from his medical practice as a neurologist and stopped writing popular sexology. His essays on the history of sexuality and popular fashion treated positively themes like the hybrid origin of the Japanese race, intermarriage between colonizer Japanese and colonized East-Asian ethnicities, the East Asian tradition of powerful and intense women he called "female supremacism" (*josei yūetsushugi*), and histories of Japanese vampirism, S/M, ESP, and cannibalism. His intellectual investment in these issues can be explained in part by his tenure in colonial Taipei as the Japanese doctor in charge of instructing Taiwanese medical trainees in hygiene and pathology from 1897 until his transfer to Osaka University as professor of medicine in 1906.[24] However, return to the homeland did not rid him of the lifelong advocacy of the Japanese colonial policies he helped disseminate as a chief doctor in Taipei: mixed marriages, the hybrid origins of Japanese ethnicity from five Asian ethnicities,[25] and, like Mori, the insistence on a scientifically controlled, yet extensively deployed, system of prostitution.

Like Mori Rintarō, Tanaka was a persistent critic of European sexology and what he called its "Christian moralizing." In his popular 1923 text *Women and Passion* (*Josei to aiyoku*), which was reprinted nine times in three years, Tanaka began his long discussion of prostitution (*baishō seidō*) with a stinging critique of Krafft-Ebing's famous denunciation of sex work as the "thorough poisoning of civilization."[26] Rather than the poisoning of civilization, Tanaka contends that a controlled system of prostitution supported every major empire in Asia and Europe. Even the origin of the Christian empire defended by German sexologists like Krafft-Ebing can be traced back to a system of prostitution (296) where Jesus Christ himself was served by female sex workers. According to Tanaka, this proves the "hypocrisy of Christian countries" all over the world who "curse Japan as the number one country in the world for prostitution" (292). In doing so, European critics perpetrate a "deluded sense of the animalistic sexual instinct [*honnō*] of humans" and a distorted view of "the erotic drives [*shōdō*] that modern civilization and material culture have increasingly incited" (308, 297). Because "behind all humans are drives that can't be repressed," Tanaka claims that "the more that the state attempts to repress them, the more wild they'll become" (304). He finds proof of this in his historical reading of the always unsuccessful attempts to eliminate sex work in ancient Rome, Syria, and Japan during the Tokugawa Tempo Reforms. In finally refus-

ing the repressive hypothesis, Tanaka calls for the "scientific management of the drives," claiming that without erotic pleasure there can be
no "joy in life" and no rational forms of civilization.

This notion of the directing and guiding of human drives also
grounds Tanaka's discussions of male masturbation, this time featured
in a 1922 text called *The Dark Regions of Human Sexuality* (*Ningen no seiteki
ankokumen*). Again disagreeing with what he calls the "exaggeration"[27]
of the negative effects of masturbation by European sexual science, he
claims that "for healthy people, there is no danger in masturbation" and
that there is "no connection between psychic illness and masturbation"
(37), although masturbation should not be allowed to substitute permanently for the "pleasure of sexual intercourse" (33). Here we have
the same critique of European erotophobia as in Mori, where a secular
and non-Christian awareness of the intensity of the sexual instincts and
drives of men leads to the call for their "scientific" management and
satisfaction through state-controlled channels.

Although his discussions of female masturbation and orgasm were
completely censored in *Ningen no seiteki ankokumen*,[28] we know from his
other texts that Tanaka's obsession with women's sexuality and
women's power does not translate into much concern for the mechan-
ics of female erotic pleasure. Although he treats female sexuality in
many of his texts, *Josei to aiyoku* features his most sustained discussion.
Predictably, half of the text treats the theme of female hysteria. He
leads into the discussion of hysteria with what he calls the "democratic"
way in which men and women become sexually aroused through the
stimulation of a plurality of erogenous zones (*hatsujōtai*) (11). Tanaka
frames his opening discussion of hormones and erogenous zones by
firmly opposing his "scientific" discussion against popular misconcep-
tions of women's physical and emotional weakness, many of which
originated in European sexology: "It's fundamentally erroneous to regard women's sexuality as weaker than men's" (10–11). Then he takes
the next ten pages of *Josei to aiyoku* to insist on the scientific fact of
there being no direct relation between women's reproductive function
and sexual desire. "Even among women forty-five and fifty years old,
sexual desire remains very high . . . even where there is no reproductive
capability there is an excess of sexual desire" (15, 18). Tanaka highlights
this division between reproductive function and what he calls both sex-

ual desire (*seiyoku*) and drive (*shōdō*) with examples from both his own practice and European case studies of older women marrying much younger men with no intention of reproducing, such as reports of women over fifty-five in Ireland who enjoy active sex lives (15). He goes so far as to demonstrate that marriage is debilitating for women's erotic lives, that unmarried women have more rewarding erotic lives, and "because most women feel nothing at all erotically toward their husbands" (23), they try to conceal this because of social pressure.

Nevertheless, Tanaka concedes that women's strong sexuality may be one factor contributing to the pathology of nymphomania, where women visit male sex workers called "*ryokan no bōi*" and frequently carry out acts of "perverse sex" (*tōsaku seiyoku*), either alone, with other women, or with men. Hysteria is sometimes the cause and sometimes an effect of this kind of perversion, writes Tanaka. When sexual drives are too strongly repressed, the somatic effects are clearly hysterical, yet when drives get too out of control, this state can lead to hysteria as well (25, 27). Tanaka elaborates that although the complications surrounding menstruation are too often cited as the only source of hysteria, when combined with the reality of inequality between the sexes in modern society, these two causal factors together can explain most cases. Here, although Tanaka was previously careful not to conflate the reproductive function with erotic drives, he begins to attribute the instance of women's excessive and "supernatural" behavior to irregularity in menstruation (31). Even though he initially claimed that hysteria was limited to cases of too little desire (*fukanshō*), frigidity (*seiyoku reitan*), or excessive desire (*seiyoku kōshinbyō*), for five pages or so he locates the source of hysterical symptoms with the instinctual biological pressures around reproduction. These include paralysis, hallucinations of uterine "wandering," an extraordinary physical strength, the inability to remain in one place, and loss of speech and memory.

Tanaka could have taken the opportunity to expose the impossible double bind (see Setsu Shigematsu's essay in this volume), which holds that women are always too cold or too hot vis-à-vis male equanimity. Instead he disavows the contradiction of what Sarah Kofman locates in Freud as the masculinist projection of both a stronger *and* weaker sexuality[29] and displaces it onto the contemporary sociopolitical problem of the inequality between men and women: "Men and women were equal in primitive society but in our modern age women have become men's plaything [*ganrōbutsu*]" (32). Inequality between the sexes, in turn, is a result of the capitalist division of labor. Tanaka theorizes that, following the class structure, "Men gradually took control of the means of production and the status of women became lower and lower until they came to be treated like animals. Now they have given themselves over to wearing makeup and accessories. All that women are left with today is to be bought and sold by men who hold all the financial power" (32). Compared to the democracy of primitive societies where women had economic, sexual, and political power, Tanaka claims that the reactionary character of modern gender inequality has naturally produced hysterical women, and just as naturally, has led to the "women's liberation movement" as the only hope of returning modern society to the democracy of relations between the sexes of earlier times.

However, Tanaka continues, the Japanese women's liberation movement has also produced an unfortunate rise in lesbianism and "women wanting to become like men" (38), therefore contributing to their refusal to have children. The Japanese women's liberation movement, which Tanaka saw previously as an answer to the misogynistic social conditions causing hysteria, is now seen as exacerbating the spread of hysteria because part of women's natural role as mother and wife is being denied. The situation is said to be so dire that some experts considered 50 percent of women living in Japan to be hysterics. After ending a long discussion of hysteria's purported causal relation to women killers, shoplifters, necrophiles, and sadists (103, 105), Tanaka opines that the contemporary situation of hysterical (though powerful and "supernaturally strong") women was actually like that of ancient East Asia, where women were religious and political leaders and powerfully erotic at the same time (112). At a time when there was intermixing between the five ethnicities in East Asia, which produced the current ethnoracial makeup of the Japanese, hysterics had "overwhelming power" that made them respected and feared like authoritative priestesses (113). According to Tanaka's genealogy, the appearance of independent and powerful women "started in the ancient East, then was imported into Greece, where it found its way into ancient Rome" (114). Suppressed by Christianity, powerful women reemerged as the witches of feudal Europe, only to then be transformed into the hysterics of European sexology.[30]

If the subject positions for women in late Meiji and Taishō Japan were bracketed by the polarities of "good wife, wise mother" (see Kathleen Uno's essay in this volume) at one end, and the hysteric at the other, what I have been binarizing as the regime of family alliance and the regime of sexuality, respectively, then central figures of popular sexology must be linked to the latter. In the colonies, however, with the noticeable absence of a state discourse of "good wives, wise mothers"[31] to act as the Other to hysteria, the stigmatized sexological depiction of hysterical women as rebellious, nonreproductive, and economically and erotically independent from men, paradoxically contributed to the partial valorization and even role model status for such Japanese women living in Korea, Taiwan, and Manchuria. Even the purported emotional instability and hypersensitivity of hysteria were positively valorized as conditions retrofitted for the shifting emotional state that facilitated identification with the colonized Other.[32]

The production of a stigmatized and etiologized norm of women in metropolitan Japan—what Judith Butler calls the "girling of the girl"[33]—had, in the colonies, the effect of contributing positively to a widespread discourse about Japan's colonial empire being primarily the "business of women," who, when compared to men, were often said to be "better at languages, business, and the management of empire."[34] Although Tanaka invokes colonial women who fit this description only sporadically in his texts, his discourse performs a double operation that at once pathologizes women while claiming there was a time in East Asia where proto-hysterics enjoyed social and economic equality with men as they contributed to a multiracial empire. Judith Butler has demonstrated the ways in which the materialized effects of the deployment of the regulative norms for gender and sexuality sometimes will fall opposed to the expressed intent of the norm itself.[35] In Tanaka and in the colonial print media of the 1910s and 1920s, although the sexological deployment of the category of hysteria in Japanese sexology was for the most part pathologizing and stigmatizing, its omnipresence in the hugely popular sexology magazines and books both in Japan and in the colonies[36] partially accounts for Japanese women outnumbering Japanese men in the main colonial cities; for a more than 50 percent unmarried rate for women over 18; and for a divorce rate three times higher than inside Japan.[37] The historically material, *manual handling* of sexology manuals in Japan was an obvious contribution to this phenomenon.

Because of their purported characteristics as independent, adventurous, and erotically and emotionally unpredictable, Japanese women in the colonies were subjectivized by a metaphorics of birds who had left the nest of Japan. Depending on whether their hatching process was successfully completed in the imperial periphery, they were destined either to be imperial success stories or to fall into a life of drugs, lesbianism, or sex work. Whether they were seen as paragons of empire or not, however, they were inevitably characterized as ornithic wanderers (*rurō*), drifters (*nagaremono*), and masterless and lordless warriors (*rōnin*) who had left the nest (*sudachi*). The *Manshū nichi nichi shinbun* and the colonial monthly *Chōsen kōron* (Korea digest) frequently ran feature articles for the most part praising colonizer women who had wandered. A six-part series in *Manshū nichi nichi shinbun* called "Sudachi" (Leaving the nest) featured Arata Suhako, described as a young, beautiful, unmarried hair salon owner who was a "model for Japanese capitalism in northern China."[38] Saibu Shizuko, a professional pianist who performed regularly in Dalian concerts and bars, was also "beautiful, unmarried and carefree . . . this prominent member of Manchuria's music world left the nest as soon as possible."[39] However, the same series carried a story of an unnamed beautiful college graduate who, not wanting to settle down to a boring life as a mother in Japan, went to the continent with high hopes only to end up in Dalian's red-light district. The concluding article warns that "there is no way to predict whether a young woman is ready to leave the nest or not,"[40] and that the colonies hold out both opportunity and danger for these women. Defined as money that is stored and saved, if these "nest eggs" are spent too soon in the colonies, it will be bad both for the accumulation of capital and for the reproduction of imperial children.

A 1916 essay from *Chōsen kōron* called "What are Men Looking for in Women?" asserts that some men in the colonies are looking for independent, unpredictable women and that if this is called "hysteria" then that should be something that is respected, not despised.[41] A May 1913 article from the same journal features a "hysterical woman" who had come to the colonies and wound up involved in illegal financial schemes. Describing her as a "hussy [*hakuren*] of a new woman"—

narcissistic, short-haired, and as masculine as any man—the writer invokes a stream of sexological adjectives to define her state as "wandering" and "drifting" and then concludes that this type of woman can either do very well in the colonies or end up in a brothel.[42] It is no coincidence that identifications like these of hysterical women in the colonies as "drifting" and "wandering" matched the etiology of hysteria described in the Japanese sexology discourse. Often employing the definition from Plato's *Timaeus*, hysteria was nominated as the disease of the "wandering womb" (*ryūryū shikyū*) and the "womb revolting" (*shikyū bōdō*).[43] In this way, the discourse on hysteria can be read as both cause and effect of the wandering and drifting nest-leavers who made significant contributions to empire both in valorized (judge, capitalist entrepreneur, artist) and stigmatized (sex worker, drug dealer, lesbian) modes.

Gregory Pflugfelder's authoritative monograph, *Cartographies of Desire: Male-Male Sexuality in Japanese Discourse, 1600–1950,* addresses some of the issues on male homoeroticism that I make here as well. Male homoeroticism was the last category in Foucault's "strategic unities of the deployment of sexuality" and also one that was purportedly annihilated by the invasion of European sexology. To discuss homoeroticism, I need to introduce some writings by Minakata Kumagusu, whom I mention earlier in this chapter. Although Minakata was considered an important sexologist and cultural anthropologist in late Meiji and Taishō Japan, and published frequently in the sexology and ero-guro-nonsense journals, his work has rarely been discussed within the contours of sexology in the 1910s and 1920s. The narrow framework frequently employed in contemporary works on modern Japanese sexology cannot encompass the breadth, wit, and erudition of Minakata's writings on eroticism and anthropology. More than even Mori and Tanaka, Minakata completely disqualifies the historiographic paradigm of a Japanese sexology that is said to have done nothing more than "copy" or "import" its erotophobia from the "West." For Minakata, the "West" never existed as a universal that "Japan" or the "East" needed to be particularized against. Instead, he was a lifelong critic of what he construed as the bogus universalizing of European classificatory sciences.

Perhaps it was only Minakata who could critique this Eurocentrism, as there was arguably no other social and natural scientist writing anywhere in the world in the 1910s and 1920s who could match his erudition and knowledge of world religion, anthropology, and the multiple histories of sexuality. His writings on sexuality combined a thorough and critical knowledge of European classical scholarship on the history of the body with Tibetan, Hindu, Chinese Buddhist, and Japanese scholarship, along with his own contributions to world anthropology and sexology gained from his travels and fieldwork.

Recent historical revisions have insisted that Minakata should be regarded as one of the three or four dominant intellectual figures in Japan in the 1920s.[44] Minakata became well known to a mass readership in Japan on the strength of his knowledge of both European science and philosophy and esoteric Buddhism and Chinese philosophy, as well as for his own mythic life which encompassed travel to the United States and Latin America—where he worked in a circus for two years—and life in London and Paris for ten years. After studying in London and Paris and publishing the first essays on botany, natural history, and philosophy by a Japanese in European academic journals, his gradual conversion during this time to the philosophy and practice of Daoism and Shingon Buddhism brought him into an increasingly antagonistic relationship to the purported universality of European science, philosophy, and anthropology. Minakata came to theorize that for anything like a universal (what he called a "cosmic" [*seken uchū*]) logic to be possible, his version of "the storehouse of the East"—including Daoism, Hinduism, and Buddhism—had to be mined.[45]

Minakata, who lived in London and researched at the Natural History Museum there from 1891 to 1900, closely followed the scandal that surrounded the trial of Oscar Wilde. Having been deeply in love with a male teenage friend for years, he began to develop his own sexological system that was firmly opposed to the pathologization of homoerotic men he saw grounding the heteronormativity of both the sex/gender system of Victorian England and German sexology. Extremely well read in the new European sexology and cultural anthropology, he developed what he called a "New Age" syncretic system, combining the best from Asian and European sexology and erotics. He advanced iconoclastic theories on masturbation, incest, pornography, and the proper eroticospiritual training for children, but it was his theories and global knowledge of male homoeroticism that brought him to the attention of younger scholars in Japan after 1927.

Minakata's knowledge of Chinese, ancient Greek, and Buddhist homoerotic history as well as his own anthropological investigations of Japanese homoeroticism enhanced his reputation as the most important theoretician of sexual anthropology in Japan by the early 1920s. His growing importance resulted in a two-decades-long clash with Yanagita Kunio and his new discipline of *minzokugaku* (Japanese folk studies). Minakata argued that Yanagita's *minzokugaku* was too bourgeois and did not pay sufficient attention to the body and sexuality. Partly influenced by Bronislaw Malinowski's lectures at the London School of Economics, but also drawing on his familiarity with some of Emile Durkheim's early theory, Minakata became convinced of the importance of sexuality in ritual. He argued that ethnographic investigation meant going out into the field and doing participant observation of the material rituals of a particular group. In his ethnographic studies Minakata seemed to relish erotic and exuberant experiences, often referencing all-night parties in his field notes. In the 1920s he opposed what he called the "lazy-chair [*anraku isu*] anthropology" of Yanagita to his own fieldwork methodology, which he claimed was more like ethnographic cruising.[46] Minakata insisted that the erotic pleasure in observation could not be disavowed and, once accepted, the erotics grounding any ethnographic practice would begin to dissolve the wall between observer and observed.

Although he had written often about male homoerotic philosophy and practice, his mature theory of the different historical modes of homosocial and homoerotic love between men was developed and nurtured in the late 1920s with his three-year participation in Edogawa Rampo and Iwata Jun'ichi's Nanshoku Kenkyūkai (Study group on male homoeroticism). Although Minakata rarely attended the lectures, parties, and discussion groups sponsored by the group, in his published correspondences with Iwata and other group members he developed his often-misunderstood notion of pure vs. impure love.[47] Feeling strongly that Iwata's groundbreaking work on the history of homoeroticism and *nanshoku*[48] in Japan would be read as overemphasizing physical sex in his treatment of male sex workers and samurai boyfriends, he tried to expand the signifying field of *nanshoku* by adding several elements to it. First, he insisted that in medieval Europe, ancient Greece, and the samurai tradition of *bushidō*, rather than a same-sex relation based on erotic attraction, there was a privileging of what he called "*jō no otokomichi*."[49] The Chinese character voiced *jō* in Japanese is usually rendered as "pure" and is found in things like Shintō water rituals to signify "ritually cleansed." *Otokomichi* is used by Minakata to signify a Japanese premodern sense of feudal ethics through its literal translation "the way of men," as well as standing for his translation of "chivalry." What he means by this is a paramilitary loyalty to one's comrades that involves serving one's seniors sexually and politically. Minakata privileges this "way of men" over Iwata's beloved *nanshoku*: "Pure love [*jōai*], which is often exemplified in *otokomichi*, and impure love [*nanshoku*] are completely separate things."[50] Minakata uses the character for pure, *jō,* before the character for love, *ai,* to get what I translate as "pure love." "A different thing altogether"(*betsu no mono*), he says, is "*fujōai*" (impure love), a term he creates by simply placing the fricative *fu* before the Japanese for "pure love," *jōai.* Here it is interesting that although he located the paradigm of impure love in Japanese *nanshoku,* he insists that pure love is extremely rare in Japan: "I know of only one indigenous text that treats the issue of 'pure love.' As far as I'm concerned it is nothing but the way of friendship [*yūdō*], central among the ethical relationships, so it is unnecessary to cite anything other than the Chinese Confucian notion of the five ethical relationships [*gorin gojō*]."[51] Ten years earlier, he located the paradigm case of pure love in ancient Greece, and in the mid-1930s he would situate it in Tibet.

What appears to be a fundamental anthropological binary was in fact a very subtle intervention into the debate on male homoeroticism and male sexuality. Although this binary has been read as diametrically opposed by Japanese commentators, the relationship was actually much more complex. Minakata simply wished to displace the hegemony of *nanshoku* from the center of discussions about Japanese male homoeroticism. Against the enclosure of this homoeroticism through a Eurocentric particularization of Japan, he wanted to homologize the tradition of *nanshoku* to the other great world traditions and demonstrate its archetypicality. To do this, he did not simply Platonize and de-eroticize the feudal ethic of the "way of men," for, as he emphasized

later, the ethic of the way of men includes both pure and impure in it:
"One can expect that in whatever time or whatever place the pure and
the impure appear together and that one knows that as there is always
the pure within the impure, there is always the impure inside of the
pure [*jōari fujōari, jō ni shite fujō kaneshimo arishi to shiraru*]."[52]

This undecidability of pure/impure should be read as ontologically
constitutive of all male bodies, replacing the tendency to purge the
body of its impurity. Minakata sees this impurity as fundamental for the
subject, and moreover, that which connects it to different bodies. In
addition to noting the imbrication of the relation of self/Other in the
pure/impure interlacing, Minakata also highlighted the ways in which
human men are made of constituent parts of: (1) *kokoro* (heart, compas-
sion); (2) *ishi* (will, drive), and (3) *seishin* (spirit). He recommended male
homoeroticism as the practice best suited to combine these three things.

His evidence for the fit of homoerotic men with these three crucial
elements of heart, spirit, and drive came from ancient Greece and, in
particular, from his reading of Plato's *Symposium*. He discovered in that
text something he found to be close to Tibetan religious and erotic
practice: the simultaneous emphasis on the sacred (*shinsei*) and the profane.[53] Although Minakata found the ecstatic unification of these opposites in collective rituals to be a universal element, he thought that only
in ancient Greek homoerotic culture and in Tibetan culture were the
sacred and the profane sustained by a corresponding philosophical
practice. As David Halperin would argue similarly sixty years later,[54]
Minakata did not think that there was a discrete notion of "homosexuality" in Greek erotic culture, but rather a constellation of different
forces, chief among them the force of philosophical love. However,
this philosophical practice was itself split into what he called the "pornographic" (*shunga*) and the "ideal" (*kannen*). This strange fusing of opposites culminated in an ethics of community that both "worshipped
the pornographic" and "meditated on the ideal"—an ideal he claimed
was closest to the cosmic universal, which he in turn recommended for
future male homoerotic societies.

Recent scholarship in Japan has shown that this fascination and
privileging of male homoerotic sociality was instrumental in the early
period of the anthropological "discovery" of Okinawa.[55] Two years before Yanagita and Origuchi Shinobu's research identified Okinawa as a

wellspring of Japanese archaic practices, Minakata exchanged letters and thoughts with the Okinawan ethnographer Matsuyoshi Yasuo on the centrality of *nanshoku* to the indigenous customs of Okinawa. According to the Japanese historian of anthropology Kamisaka Jirō, Yanagita heard about the exchange that had been going on between Minakata and the Okinawan scholar and, furious, set out eighteen months later with the intention of disproving Minakata's obsession with what Yanagita called the sociality of "lust" (*kōshoku*). Minakata, through his pioneering curiosity and research on Okinawa, merely wanted to foreground male homoeroticism in Okinawa as one more example of its universality extending from ancient China to classical Greece to Tokugawa Japan. Yanagita, like some historians of Japanese sexuality, wanted to quarantine Okinawa and set it up as a preserve, free from the contagion of the "West."

Michel Foucault locates sexuality as a "grid of intelligibility" that organizes and regulates perceptions and practices through what he calls the four "strategic unities" of hysteric, masturbating youth, queer adult, and Malthusian reproductive man and wife. I've looked at the first three of these categories to demonstrate that the processes generating them by Japanese sexology necessarily differed materially and historically from their production in European sexology. Moreover, the production of these strategic unities had very different effects in the periphery of empire than they did in the metropolitan center, so much so that reversals and revalorizations of categories stigmatized inside Japan materialized in the colonies. In criticizing contemporary historians of Japanese sexuality, I have argued that the history of modern Japanese sexuality must be read through the history of Japan's colonial-imperialism. Only through this reframing can historical sense be made from these reversals and revalorizations of stigmatized sexual subjectivities.

Notes

I'd like to thank Barbara Brooks, Brett de Bary, Ayako Kano, Barbara Molony, Kotani Mari, Ann McNight, Diane Nelson, Naoki Sakai, Barbara Sato, Yuki Terasawa, Kathleen Uno, and Keith Vincent for comments on different versions of this paper.

1. Michel Foucault, *The History of Sexuality: An Introduction*, trans. Robert Hurley (New York: Vintage, 1978), 103. Further citations will appear in the text.

2. Yoshino Takao, *Miyatake Gaikotsu* (Kawade bunkō, 1992), 162.

3. I am referencing the theory of the "repressive hypothesis" most famously elaborated by Sigmund Freud in his 1908 "'Civilized' Sexual Morality and Modern Nervous Illness," in *Sexuality and the Psychology of Love* (New York: Macmillan, 1963), and in his 1920 text *Beyond the Pleasure Principle* (New York: Basic Books, 1962). Briefly, the assumption is that modern capitalist civilization demands high levels of sexual repression, and the energy from that repression is then economically sublimated into "higher" modalities of sociopolitical development and civilization. One of the obvious effects of this is the sense that sexual activity *tout court* is always "against" sociopolitical power, and that it necessarily refuses power's injunction to repress an essentialized libido. Foucault's dramatic overturning of what he considered this generally accepted "repressive hypothesis" begins from the proposition that sexuality is not a stubbornly innate force that civilization needs to repress. Rather, it is that which is "immanent to power" and is not "an exterior domain to which power is applied, that on the contrary it is a result and instrument of power's designs." Foucault warned that "we must . . . abandon the hypothesis that modern industrial societies ushered in an age of increased sexual repression" in Foucault, *The History of Sexuality*, 49, 152.

4. Japanese imperialism did not simply project an exotically erotic "Orientalism" onto the Asian continent and Korean peninsula. These areas were materially constructed as sexualized and heterosexualized utopias for Japanese men. There is no better way to apprehend this than to look at the colonial newspapers from Seoul, such as *Keijo nippō* (Seoul daily report), and Dalian's *Manshū nichi nichi shinbun* (Manchuria daily newspaper). Research on these two newspapers and the journals published in the colonies from 1911–1930 showed evidence of the massive deployment of Japanese, Chinese, Russian, and Korean sex workers in the Empire some twenty-five years before the Japanese military's violent mobilization of military "comfort women." See also Song Youn-ok, "Japanese Colonial Rule and State-Managed Prostitution: Korea's Licensed

Prostitutes," in *positions* 5, no. 1 (Spring 1997): 171–218, and Barbara Brooks's groundbreaking piece in this volume. On the frequently invoked predication of Japanese sex workers as the crucial first step in the developmental stage (*hatten dankai*) of Japanese capital expansion in Asia, see *Manshū nichi nichi shinbun,* April 18, 1924, 7, where the writer argues that first there are women sex workers, then male workers, followed by small, then large capital industries. The author identifies sex workers as the indispensable "pioneering sacrifices" (*senkuteki giseisha*) of Japanese imperial capital. For an example of the many times that the notion of the sex worker as exemplifying the first wave for Japanese capitalist imperialism appeared in the Korean colonial newspapers and monthlies, see *Keijo nippō,* May 23, 1919, 3, where Japanese female sex workers are claimed to be leading the imperial advance into Southeast Asia. In this regard it is significant that although Japan voted to join the International Convention for the Suppression of the Traffic in Women and Children at the Second League of Nations in 1925, it did not agree to apply the law to its colonies and mandates in China, Korea, Taiwan, and the South Pacific.

5. The most recent is Gary Leupp's *Male Colors,* where the "dramatic" shift in attitudes toward male-male sex from celebration and acceptance to gradual shame is said to be caused by "homophobia" imported from the West. Leupp, *Male Colors* (Berkeley: University of California Press, 1997), 202. The same problem is evident in Japanese scholarship in Saeki Junko's *Bishōnen zukushi* (Heibonsha, 1992). For useful correctives, see *Sekushuarite no shakaigaku,* ed. Ueno Chizuko (Iwanami shoten, 1996), and Fujime Yuki, *Sei no rekishigaku* (Fuji shuppan, 1997).

6. Kawamura Kunimitsu, *Sekushuarite no Kindai* (Kōdansha, 1996), 40. The last line of the Japanese reads: "Seiyōgaku ya sekusorogī ni attō sarete itta." Further citations will appear in the text.

7. Gayatri Chakravarty Spivak, *A Critique of Postcolonial Reason: Toward a Critique of the Vanishing Present* (Cambridge, MA: Harvard University Press, 1999), 153.

8. Sabine Frühstück, *Colonizing Sex: Sexology and Social Control in Modern Japan* (Berkeley: University of California Press, 2003), 1. Further citations will appear in the text.

9. Leo Ching, *Becoming "Japanese": Colonial Taiwan and the Politics of Identity Formation* (Berkeley: University of California Press, 2001).

10. Dipesh Chakrabarty, *Provincializing Europe: Postcolonial Thought and Historical Difference* (Princeton, NJ: Princeton University Press, 2000), 8.

11. This is a reference to Dipesh Chakrabarty's book cited above.

12. Judith Butler, *Bodies That Matter: On the Discursive Limits of "Sex"* (New York: Routledge, 1993).

13. The *Manshū nichi nichi shinbun,* October 2, 1919, 1, reports a Mantetsu census for that year of 26,135 men and 22,260 Japanese women living in Dalian and suggests that Japanese women rather than men were the majority in the northern Chinese city of Harbin. Mantetsu statistics for far northern Manchuria in 1915 give 1543 Japanese women against only 769 men. The *Manshū nichi nichi shinbun,* Sept. 7, 1920, gives the Japanese population living in Manchuria in 1919 as 73,440 men and 69,149 women. Population figures reported yearly in the *Keijo nippō* show roughly 90,000 Japanese men to 80,000 women in Korea at around the same time. However, the large numbers of unregistered women sex workers in the Chinese and Korean cities, coupled with the fact that most of the censuses were based on people *in families* (and there was consistently a 50 percent unmarried rate for Japanese women over 18 in colonial cities in the 1910s and 1920s, which means that they frequently were not counted in population censuses, although always employed), leads most commentators to the conclusion that the Japanese population in colonial urban areas during the first ten-year period of Korean colonization (1910–1920) and northern Chinese settlements from the same period had either an equal division of men and women or a majority female colonial population. See, for example, the *Manshū nichi nichi shinbun,* March 30, 1924, 2, where a long feature article claimed that independent Japanese women refused to settle for married life in the Japanese countryside and were moving in disproportionate numbers to the colonial cities in the attempt to be economically independent.

14. This will strike some readers as insufficiently sensitive to the ways in which the "scientific" gynophobia of male sexologists contributed to violence against powerless women. As this was certainly the historical case and forced hysterectomy was legal for certain types of women criminals in the 1920s and 1930s, the widespread use of the category of hysteria operated—sometimes contradictorily, sometimes not—to produce clearly identifiable representations of strong, rebellious women adamantly refusing the ideology of "good wife, wise mother." Although at times against the express intent of the law, the deployment of this kind of representation of Japanese women in the colonies—who, following the definition of hysteria as a mode of wandering or fleeing the domesticated space of Japan—via the deployment of sexuality, contributed to the presence of strong women who played significant imperial roles as policewoman, businesswoman, and even judge in the colonies. (The Japanese woman Minamoto Hatsuko was given a judgeship in Seoul in May 1924, and

two other women would follow her in the colonial capital.) Although the sexological category of hysteric was a "bad" stigmatizing label that obviously produced widespread externalized and internalized gynophobia, as Judith Butler has argued, the deployment of the regulatory ideals of power will often have contradictory effects when used by the regime of sexuality and when materialized in bodies. Although much of the discourse on hysteria was intensely misogynist, at least part of what it did was make available a discourse about women who *by nature* refused the ideology of "good wife, wise mother." To reiterate, one of the constitutive effects for Japan's colonial-imperialism was that this discourse of hysteria made the colonies a place where this category and the qualities that constituted it would for a time be dramatically unstigmatized and even valorized.

15. Franco Moretti, *Modern Epic* (London: Verso, 1996), 2. Unfortunately, Moretti's aggressive Eurocentrism disqualifies his own book from consideration as a "world text."

16. Foucault, *The History of Sexuality*, 127.

17. Frühstück only mentions the early Euromimetic texts from 1889 and 1897 and ignores the later work that features criticisms of Euro-American sexology and medicine. See *Colonizing Sex*, 34.

18. "Seiiku," in *Mori Ōgai zenshū*, vol. 32 (Iwanami shoten, 1973), 114. Further citations will appear in the text.

19. As Ōgai was trained in Chinese as well as Latin and ancient Greek medicine, he would have been aware of the radical shift he was helping to produce from a discursive regime that emphasized moderation and temperance in erotic affairs, to a Foucaultian excitation of heterosexual desire in the name of a newly technologized Japanese heterosexual male essence, or *sei*.

20. See, for example, Yamamoto's 1924 article "Onna ni taishite seikyōiku 2," *Tsūzoku igaku* 2: 39–41.

21. Kawamura, *Sekushuarite no kindai*, 151. For a more measured and useful essay on the topic that also claims that these three are the main popularizers of sexological discourse in Japan, see Furukawa Makoto, "Rennai to seiyoku no daisan teikoku," *Gendai Shisō* 21, no. 7 (1993): 110–127.

22. There has been nothing at all published on Tanaka in Japanese except for one sentence in Furukawa and the citation of Furukawa in Kawamura's text. I've read all of his available works in the Diet Library in Tokyo, but only in a

postwar reprint of his best-selling 1939 sexology/ero-guro-nonsense text *Ki, mezura, aya* (Strange, weird, outrageous) (Hōmeidō shoten, 1953) is there much biographical information on him, but only one paragraph. Gregory Pflugfelder's *Cartographies of Desire: Male-Male Sexuality in Japanese Discourse, 1600–1950* (Berkeley: University of California Press, 1999) contains the first serious mentions of Tanaka, although these are for the most part limited to his writing on male homoeroticism.

23. See Tanaka Kōgai, *Shinshidan shinwa* [New history, new myth] (Tōgakusha, 1934), as well as his *Ki, mezura, aya.*

24. Tanaka went to Germany for one year to study pathology and hygiene sometime around 1900, and then went to Manchuria for the Russo-Japanese War in 1904.

25. The locus classicus of this is Oguma Eiji, *Tanitsu minzoku shinwa no kigen*, (Shinyosha, 1995).

26. Tanaka Kōgai, *Josei to aiyoku* (Osaka: Okugō shoten, 1923), 271. Further citations will appear in the text.

27. Tanaka Kōgai, *Ningen no seiteki ankokumen* (Osaka: Okugō shoten, 1922), 38. Further citations appear in the text.

28. Approximately thirty of the three hundred pages are completely censored and occasional phrases in other parts of the text have been deleted as well.

29. Sarah Kofman, *The Enigma of Woman: Woman in Freud's Writing*, trans. Catherine Porter (Ithaca, NY: Cornell University Press, 1985), 68–71.

30. This genealogical conflation of nineteenth-century hysteria with witchcraft resonates with currents in 1970s French feminism. See Hélène Cixous and Catherine Clément, *The Newly Born Woman*, trans. Betsy Wing (Minneapolis: University of Minnesota Press, 1986).

31. The first mention of "good wives, wise mothers" I came across in the *Keijo nippō* was an article of April 9, 1925, 2, whose lead line asked, "Is it time to think about applying the 'good wife, wise mother' policy to the colonies?"

32. *Keijo nippō*, September 8, 1921, 4.

33. Butler, *Bodies That Matter*, 7.

34. *Manshū nichi nichi shinbun*, October 16, 1921, 3. See also the Dalian monthly *Tairiku* (Continent) of March 1920 with articles like "The Superior Qualities of Japanese Women," as well as monthly features in the *Keijo nippō* in the late 1910s and early 1920s called "Japanese Women and Colonialism"; see *Manshū nichi ni-*

chi shinbun, for example, October 8, 1921, 4. In a *Manshū nichi nichi shinbun* feature of Sept. 21, 1921, 3, Japanese women claimed that they could open the huge frontier from north China to Mongolia all by themselves! A two-part series in the same newspaper on women and capitalist development declares bluntly in the first installment that "women are better capitalists than men in the periphery." *Manshū nichi nichi shinbun*, April 16–17, 1922, 3.

35. Judith Butler, *The Psychic Life of Power* (Stanford, CA: Stanford University Press, 1997).

36. There's abundant evidence proving that sexology was very popular reading material on city buses and trains in Japan in the 1920s. On the popularity of sexological books and journals (which were advertised heavily in the colonial papers and sold publicly in Dalian and Seoul) in the Manchurian cities, see *Manshū nichi nichi shinbun*, April 11, 1924, 2.

37. *Manshū nichi nichi shinbun*, Nov. 18, 1920, 4. The divorce rate in Dalian for Japanese was three times what it was in Japan in 1920, according to a *Manshū nichi nichi shinbun* feature of March 8, 1921, where Japanese colonial women are said to push for divorce as soon as any small problem arose. I'm suggesting that sexology was one factor in a structure of overdetermination that must include political-economic factors as well.

38. Ibid., March 27, 1924, 1.

39. Ibid., April 6, 1924, 3.

40. Ibid., April 10, 1924, 3.

41. *Chōsen kōron*, June 1916, 78.

42. Ibid., May 1913, 112.

43. Aoyagi Arioshi, *Shinseiyoku tetsugaku* [Philosophy of the new sexuality] (Kabusha, 1922), 235–236. See as well Nozoe Atsuyoshi's long discussion of the history of hysteria in Japan and Europe—including the "wandering womb" phenomenon, in *Josei to hanzai, Kindai hanzaigaku zenshū*, vol. 4 (Bukyōsha, 1929). The most important writer and clinician of hysteria was the so-called "Jean Martin Charcot" of Japan, the *hentaigakusha*, psychoanalyst, and ero-guro-nonsense writer Nakamura Kokkyo. Based on his research and case studies at his own center for hysteria from 1924–1935, Nakamura wrote several books and essays for the women's journals on hysteria, the most famous being his *Hisuteri-no ryōhō* [Treatment of Hysteria] (Shufu no tomosha, 1932), and his early 700-page review book *Saiminjutsu kōgi* [Lectures on Hypnosis] (Nihon seishingakkai, 1920). In his three-part series on hysteria called "Treatment of the Hys-

terical Patient" in *Shufu no tomo*, April, May, and June 1930, he cites the classical definition of hysteria as "wandering womb"; see the April installment, 234–241. Nakamura's own case studies featured patients who spoke Korean and Chinese, although they had never been to the colonies or studied the languages.

44. See especially the popular text by Nakazawa Shinichi, *Mori no Barokku* (Sakariba Shobō, 1993).

45. Ibid., 72.

46. Ibid., 49.

47. See the special issue of *Bungaku, Minakata Kumagusu tokushū*, Winter 1997, 84–96.

48. *Nanshoku* is the Japanese voicing of the Chinese character for "male" (*nan*) and the character for "passion or color" (*shoku*).

49. Minakata Kumagusu, *Jō no sekusuoroji*, vol. 3, *Minakata Kumagusu Korekushon*, ed. Nakazawa Shinichi (Kawade, 1991), 366.

50. Ibid., 317.

51. Ibid., 316.

52. Ibid., 320.

53. Ibid., 362.

54. David Halperin, 100 *Years of Homosexuality: and Other Essays on Greek Love* (New York: Routledge, 1990).

55. *Asahi shinbun*, April 5, 1997, 4.

6 Engendering Eugenics: Feminists and Marriage Restriction Legislation in the 1920s

Sumiko Otsubo

Unregulated male heterosexuality faced a formidable challenge from the short-lived but influential feminist group the New Woman Association (Shin fujin kyōkai, NWA) between 1919 and 1922. Hiratsuka Raichō (1886–1971), one of the NWA's founders, had come to embrace eugenics, the science of improving the human race by better breeding, as a way of strengthening Japan's racial stock. But Hiratsuka proposed a gendered regulation of bodies, seeking to control male sexuality and access to marriage through testing men for venereal diseases,[1] while assuming the bodies of women not in the sex trades would likely be free of the sexually transmitted diseases she saw as destructive to the Japanese population. Thus, she viewed male and female bodies as dimorphic where disease was concerned.

Hiratsuka's notion of eugenics foregrounded gender, but her plan of attack strongly challenged established gender norms. As Mark Driscoll shows in an essay in this collection, men were believed to have more powerful sexual desires that need not be regulated by the state.[2] Others at the time argued that regulation should take the form of control of female sexuality through brothels.[3] Hiratsuka's struggle to enact legislation requiring premarital testing of men for syphilis flew in the face of men's privilege of unregulated sexuality. Moreover, by working with the Diet, the legislative arm of the state, Hiratsuka placed women squarely in politics. While continuing to be denied the right of franchise during the time in which Hiratsuka led the NWA, she and her colleagues worked through the Diet as if they were, in a sense, part of the state. This, together with their bold assertion of female agency, constituted another challenge to gender norms. This essay examines NWA publications, autobiographies of its leaders, parliamentary documents, contemporary magazine articles, and other sources in an attempt to analyze Japan's first organized effort, led by women, to establish a eugenic legal context for marriage.

After the term eugenics was coined by Francis Galton (1822–1911) in 1883, the idea spread to many parts of the world. Japanese language studies on eugenics in Japan, though limited in number, exist; and they demonstrate that eugenic ideas were quite widespread in Japan in the early twentieth century.[4] Japanese eugenic ideas often modified Western notions, which had negative racial implications for the Japanese. For example, Naruse Jinzō, who in 1901 founded the Japan Women's College, a leading institution of higher education for women, was chagrined by the prescribed "inferior" status of Japanese in Western discourse. Nevertheless, Naruse continued to adhere to many other eugenic principles; he was able to accept them by shifting emphasis, around the turn of the century, from "race" to "gender."[5] This chapter explores another shift in the early 1920s whereby women—previously marginal to most public Japanese discourse—asserted themselves as biologically "fitter" than men in Japanese eugenic discourse for the first time and in a very remarkable way. Ironically, Naruse's former student led this movement, which unsettled the eugenic gender roles he had prescribed.

Hiratsuka Raichō: Developing Eugenic-Feminist Consciousness

Hiratsuka Raichō worked to establish a eugenic law prohibiting men infected with venereal disease from marrying. Although the same association's effort to revise the Police Regulation Law (*Chian keisatsu-hō*), which banned women from engaging in political activities, has been well studied by historians as an important aspect of Japan's women's suffrage movement,[6] its campaign against venereal diseases has been largely neglected as a subject of in-depth analysis. Furthermore, none of the existing studies fully explores Hiratsuka's activities in the context of the history of eugenics in Japan.[7] Some works dealing with the NWA's anti-V.D. legislative effort are much more concerned with such issues in women's history as motherhood, equality vs. difference, or women's wartime collaboration with the state.[8]

Hiratsuka attained the highest level of education available for women in her day she graduated from the Japan Women's College in 1906. Following a notorious suicide attempt, Hiratsuka embraced feminism and founded the often controversial literary magazine *Seitō* (Bluestocking). Many decisions she made in her personal life were equally controversial. She rejected the existing marriage system and began practicing "cohabitation" with a young painter in 1914. Her daughter and son were therefore illegitimate.

Hiratsuka's experience of being pregnant, giving birth, and raising children made the works of the Swedish feminist Ellen Key (1849–1926), who advocated the protection of motherhood based on eugenic reasoning, particularly appealing to her. Many of Key's works were available in Japanese translation. Hiratsuka herself published the translation of Key's *Love and Marriage* in 1913 and *The Renaissance of Motherhood* in 1918. Key extolled eugenics in *The Renaissance of Motherhood* (1914):

During all these passionate conflicts about sexual morality, we are, on the whole, quietly and constantly advancing in regard to the elevating of future generations. . . . Further advance may be recognized in the fact that many women and men now break an engagement of a marriage when they find out that either party suffers from some hereditary disease. Increasingly numerous are the men and women who abstain from erotic relationships when they know themselves victims of such heredity. To be sure the great majority are still ignorant, or unscrupulous, in regard to the commands of eugenics. But public opinion is fast developing in this respect and is already beginning to influence conventions, which in turn will influence the laws.[9]

Eugenic ideas resonated with Hiratsuka's conceptions of feminism. Earlier in the decade, she had launched the Seitō movement by daringly stating that "in the beginning [*genshi*], women were in fact the sun." This feminist manifesto thus suggested the ancient identification of women with Nature and underscored the prominence of the imperial ancestor, the Sun Goddess, in the national origin myth. In contrast to women in the ancient period, Hiratsuka lamented, Taishō women had a diminished status. Key's vision for the rebirth of motherhood through eugenic enlightenment was, therefore, attractive to Hiratsuka, who began to seek ways to scientifically legitimize her feminist effort to reclaim the lost power and prestige of women. Hiratsuka began translating the word "race" into the more temporal Japanese term *shuzoku* (racial stock or lineage) instead of the spatial *jinshu* (race) by 1919.[10] The concept of "racial stock" was useful for linking Japanese women past, present, and future.

Hiratsuka began her quest for scientific ways to reclaim women's lost status by evaluating post–World War I social conditions for women in Japan. Even before the war, many young Japanese women from poor farm families throughout the country had been recruited to work in textile factories. Crammed into dormitory rooms, working long hours with inadequate rest, and ill-nourished by company cafeteria food, these women and girls were easy victims of tuberculosis.[11] Because they returned to their village homes to recuperate or die, some thought they were slowly sterilizing the once healthy rural population. After actually observing the miserable working conditions of factory women in Nagoya, Hiratsuka, like Key, called for state protection of motherhood using eugenic arguments. In a famous four-person series of polemical essays, Hiratsuka debated the state's role in economic support of mothers with feminist poet Yosano Akiko, socialist feminist Yamakawa Kikue, and maternalist feminist Yamada Waka.[12]

Debate alone did not satisfy Hiratsuka; she wanted to apply Key's eugenic ideology to society. According to Key's *Mutterschutz* (motherhood protection) *Idee*, it would be possible to discourage the "unfit" from procreating by legally regulating marriage. Ruth Bré, another leading member of Germany's Alliance for Motherhood Protection, "urged that health certificates be required as a condition for marriage and that the laws concerning contagious disease should be changed."[13] It appears that Hiratsuka soon realized, however, that applying this kind of negative eugenic law to factory women would hurt their chances to marry and reproduce. The action could jeopardize women rather than help them. Although she did not abandon eugenics, she had to shift her focus.

While her ideas derived at times from other feminists' theories, what distinguished Hiratsuka from other sympathizers with feminist causes was her capacity to put ideas into action. Together with Ichikawa Fusae

(1893–1981), who had been a local newspaper correspondent in Nagoya and had taken Hiratsuka to investigate the working conditions of factory girls in the area's textile mills, Hiratsuka organized the New Woman Association in late 1919. Responding to Hiratsuka's request, another alumna of Japan Women's College, Oku Mumeo, soon joined the two as the third leader of the group. Their association focused attention on two issues: revision of the Police Regulation Law, which prohibited women from engaging in political activities, and enactment of a law to prevent men infected with venereal diseases from getting married, based on eugenic reasoning.[14] The second cause was undoubtedly a manifestation of Hiratsuka's commitment to Key's *Mutterschutz Idee*, though modified to reflect Hiratsuka's concern for avoiding harm to infected factory workers. Instead of promoting a negative eugenic law against women with tuberculosis, Hiratsuka now decided to target men with venereal diseases.

At the time, social problems like tuberculosis, venereal diseases, leprosy, criminality, prostitution, and alcoholism were known as "racial poisons" in Western eugenic discourse.[15] Though some of them were infectious, rather than hereditary, these poisons, believed to be passed from one generation to another, were deemed harmful in their effect on racial stocks and treated biologically (inclusive of eugenics). The prevention of venereal diseases and tuberculosis was considered the top priority of health policy in post–World War 1 Europe, notably in France.[16] The spread of V.D. in the military and cities was a growing concern in Japan as well.[17]

Politicization of Venereal Diseases

Hiratsuka decided to submit a petition to the 42nd Imperial Diet session in December 1919.[18] Having studied the existing marriage restriction laws against the venereally diseased in such countries as Mexico, Norway, and different states in the United States, she wrote a petition draft. She then sought advice from legal experts. One of them was a civil law professor at Tokyo University, Hozumi Shigetō (1883–1951). Taking professional advice into consideration, Hiratsuka's original petition read as follows:

A Petition Regarding Marriage Restriction against Men with Venereal Diseases

Petition Items

We humbly request that you add the following clauses in an appropriate place of the marriage regulations of Chapter 3, Collateral Relatives, Civil Law Code.

• A man who is currently infected with venereal diseases is not allowed to marry.

• A man who wants to marry must prove that he is not infected with venereal diseases by submitting to his prospective wife a health certificate prepared by a physician.

• This document with a marriage registration document must be submitted to a family registration officer [*kosekiri*].

• If it is revealed after marriage that a husband has concealed the fact of his infection with venereal diseases, the marriage can be annulled.

• If a husband becomes infected with venereal diseases or a wife is infected with them through her husband, a divorce can be requested by the wife.

• If a wife is infected with venereal diseases by her husband, she is entitled to request that he pay her living and medical expenses until she is completely cured, as well as an appropriate amount of compensation.[19]

The NWA appended three reasons for its submission of the petition. This explanatory material, together with the petition draft, was printed and sent out to other reform activists and intellectuals by late January 1920. Over two thousand endorsed the proposal with their signatures and seals.[20]

At that time, petitions could become law by following a multistep process: submission by a Diet member to his House's petition committee; discussion and vote on adoption by that committee; submission to the entire House as a legislative proposal; and voting in both Houses.

Hiratsuka asked Miyake Shō to present the petition to the House of Peers and prevailed on Tomita Kōjirō and Yamane Masatsugu (1857– 1920) to sponsor it in the House of Representatives.[21] While Miyake was a pathology professor at Tokyo University, Yamane was a forensic medical expert. Both were Western-trained in medicine and interested in the promotion of public health issues. While Yamane had been active in the suppression of such "racial poisons" as venereal diseases, alcohol, and nicotine, Miyake had recognized the potential role of women in hygiene. In fact, he taught classes at Hiratsuka's alma mater, Japan Women's College, in its early years.[22] The two men seemed well-suited indeed to support the NWA's anti-V.D. campaign in the national assemblies.

These Diet members suggested that Hiratsuka revise her petition's justification for an anti-V.D. law. They particularly urged her to elaborate on why the proposed law should only restrict men.[23] She did. Her revised explanation consisted of four major points. The first emphasized the serious degenerative impact of the spread of venereal diseases to "civilized societies." Her first point called from a racial stock hygienic (*shuzoku eisei*) perspective for responsible action by the state to stop the further spread of V.D. After pointing out the existence of V.D. prevention laws in the United States and Europe, it lamented the paucity of such laws in Japan. The term "civilized societies" was used as a synonym for the West, while Japan was depicted as a country on the border between "civilized" and "uncivilized" societies. Japan's negligence in controlling these diseases contrasted with the progressive laws enacted by "civilized" nations.[24] Thus, Hiratsuka was able to make use of legislators' consciousness of Japan's image in Western eyes as a method of persuasion.

The second part of the rationalization referred to the ongoing crusade against V.D. in Japan and distinguished it from Hiratsuka's campaign. While the official effort to suppress V.D. through the Health and Hygiene Investigation Committee (Hoken eisei chōsakai) was not gender-specific, Hiratsuka's movement was a gender-specific attempt to prevent husbands from bringing the diseases home. Yet none of the Western anti-V.D. laws that Hiratsuka had studied were as gender-specific as her plan was.[25] As a matter of fact, most treated men and women equally. Exceptions were laws in two American states, North Dakota and Oregon. North Dakota subjected to marriage restrictions all potential spouses, male and female, in unions where the bride was under forty-five years of age and, therefore, presumed fertile. In contrast, the Oregon state law issued on February 16, 1913, required only men to prove they were not infected with V.D. by submitting a health document prepared by a certified physician.[26] The majority of the Western marriage restriction laws that Hiratsuka's group examined were egalitarian on the basis of gender. To make a medical check of reproductive organs feasible in Japan, Hiratsuka picked a gender-specific Oregon law—which was by no means typical of the marriage restriction laws she had studied—as a model and modified it.

Her rationalization for the petition contained quantitative and qualitative reasons for restricting men. Hiratsuka noted men's more frequent sexual indulgence, which often caused family tragedies related to V.D. In addition to providing statistical data supporting this claim, Hiratsuka argued against testing women for cultural reasons. For women, a gynecological check in these circumstances had the connotation of rape or loss of virginity. She suggested that most females with venereal diseases were prostitutes; V.D. was thus class- and location-specific.[27]

Finally, she stressed the eugenic significance of the proposed law; the protection of housewives and their children would improve the quality of the nation (*kokumin*) and strengthen national power (*kokuryoku*). It would also serve the racial stock, viewed as an obligation of both men and women.[28]

Initial Parliamentary Debate

The NWA's first parliamentary attempt went reasonably well, and the Lower House Second Petition Committee seriously discussed the anti-V.D. proposal. On February 23, 1920, Hiratsuka's petition was introduced by a member of the House of Representatives, Arakawa Gorō. Like Tomita, Arakawa belonged to the majority party, the Kenseikai. He summarized the petition drafted by the NWA, emphasizing its eugenic goals, and requested that the committee adopt the petition. Representative Saitō Kiichi responded negatively to Arakawa's request. A medical doctor, Saitō belonged to the opposition party, Rikken Seiyūkai (hereafter Seiyūkai). He noted that many more men became infected with venereal diseases after marriage, so that restricting marriage in the way that the NWA proposed would not achieve the expected goal. He also criticized the petition for imposing health testing only on men because he believed many poor women, who earned their family's living by prostitution, had V.D. as well. However, he concluded that some kind of measures were necessary and suggested further study.

The chief of the Home Ministry's Bureau of Public Health (without a vote in the committee), Ushio Keinosuke, explained that the government had also been concerned with the issues raised by the petition. After presenting the official research plans against V.D., Ushio noted that important questions had to be answered: Should women be exempt from the medical check? Are doctors able to make a reliable diagnosis? If a divorce were to result from this law, would it not have a negative impact on Japan's traditional family system? In the United States, Ushio continued, marriage restriction laws prevented not only people with V.D. from marrying, but also those who had mental diseases or who had committed serious crimes. There were also sterilization laws restricting the ability of the unfit to procreate. Like Saitō, Ushio called for more careful research before taking any action against the diseases.

Ultimately the committee decided to send the petition to the House as a documentary reference (*sankō sōfu*).[29] While not adopted, it had been discussed as a serious matter, rather than dismissed as a frivolous petition proposed by radical women with no knowledge of hygiene or parliamentary procedures. Significantly, no one questioned its eugenic goals. What provoked discussion, however, was its method. In particular, committee members reacted against the gendered aspect of Hiratsuka's plan since this might affect the life of many men, perhaps including themselves. Prior to the NWA's anti-V.D. campaign, most enthusiasts publicly promoting eugenic causes had been highly educated middle-class men exposed to Western scientific knowledge. They had never been in a position where they themselves might be considered "unfit" and subject to restrictions, at least within Japan. Realizing their endangered place in this plan, Saitō tried to replace Hiratsuka's men-unfit/women-fit ideas with middle-class-fit/lower-class-unfit notions. In this way, middle-class males could escape possible classification as eugenically unfit.

The petition never made it to the main floor of the Diet, however, as Prime Minister Hara Takashi dissolved the Diet the next day for reasons unrelated to the eugenics petition. In spite of the disappointing interruption, the petition movement enjoyed much media attention. As expected, many men expressed antipathy. Many articles, by men and women, were published in the next several months in response to the

NWA's petition against V.D. The authors (and magazines) included Yosano Akiko (*Taiyō*), Yamada Waka (*Fujin to shinshakai*), Endō Kiyoko (*Hōchikoku*), and Hozumi Shigetō (*Tōyō gakugei zasshi*, *Hentai shinri*, and *Fujin no tomo*).[30]

Dissolution of the Diet gave the NWA much needed time to better organize itself before the Diet reassembled in summer 1920. In that first session since the dissolution, the NWA asked Arakawa Gorō (Kensei-kai), Nemoto Shō (Seiyūkai), and other members to submit their antivenereal disease petition to the Lower House on June 30.[31] On July 12, Nemoto introduced the petition to the committee in charge. Nemoto was a veteran representative who since 1901 had persistently submitted a bill to restrict minors from drinking. He was a leader of a Christian temperance group and had worked closely with reform-minded Christian women both in the United States and in Japan.[32] Unlike Arakawa, who had introduced the petition by emphasizing the eugenic reasons in February, Nemoto stressed the gender issue—he believed that existing laws and social institutions served men's interests rather than women's. He implied that adopting the NWA's V.D. restriction would correct such social injustice.

Perhaps this was a persuasive argument for Nemoto, whose values were based on Christian morality. But other Diet members were put off by it. For example, Matsushita Teiji asked Nemoto to define the venereal diseases. Matsushita was a former medical professor at Kyoto University with extensive training in Germany in the fields of hygiene and bacteriology. Following Nemoto's response, Matsushita medically defined V.D. He dismissed Nemoto's as well as the NWA's explanation as amateurish. He also raised a question whether a medical check by a physician would yield any useful information. In his opinion, a medical check would be useful only if the venereal disease were advanced. He maintained, however, that even physicians could not always tell whether one is infected with chronic V.D. or not. Matsushita thus discredited the petition scientifically.

Nemoto, however, tried to regain legitimacy. But his request for support was not answered in the way he had hoped. Other members joined the discussion and expressed negative views toward the petition. Takada Unpei, for instance, openly displayed a male-chauvinistic attitude:

I believe [the petition] is being proposed by some women who want to revise the fifth clause of the Police Regulation Law. If we adopt this, it will lead to a predominance of women over men [*joson danpi*], allowing any woman, even those with V.D., to marry without restrictions while men are restricted in marrying. As I think this is such a selfish petition, I choose not to support it.

This emotional rather than rational response may have been representative of many men in Japan. Representative Asaka Chōbei contended that these "kinds of restrictions exist in Western nations. These, however, are individualistic countries in which women predominate over men. By contrast, ours is a country that maintains the [patriarchical] family system." Representative Shimizu Ichitarō was an observer and did not have a vote in the committee. He nevertheless supported the ideas expressed by Takada and Asaka: "I believe if we adopt this petition the number of divorces will be innumerable in Japan. Since this would cause a great marriage revolution . . . I hope you will not adopt it."

Except for the presenter, Nemoto, no one supported the petition, and it was rejected at the Lower House committee level.[33] The primary reason for its rejection was its gendered aspect, requiring only men to submit a medical certificate before marriage. While Matsushita questioned the petition as scientifically unsound, others such as Takada and Asaka all tried to emphasize Japanese women's proper role. As in the previous parliamentary session, none of the objections focused on the petition's eugenic arguments. The authority of international eugenic discourse is said to have reached its peak during the early interwar years. The NWA's lobbying on behalf of a eugenic marriage restriction law embodied the progressive and scientific spirit of a time in which discourse embraced democracy (*minshushugi*), reform (*kaizō*), and life (*seimei*).[34] Western eugenics was associated with fundamental reforms of human society; such concepts as progress, modernity, and civilization were not something that the educated in Japan could easily dismiss in 1920.

Earlier that day (July 12, 1920), before the rejection in the Diet committee of the NWA's eugenics petition, the association's petition to revise the Police Regulation Law had been adopted by the same committee.[35] As a result, the NWA was busy drafting a bill that was to be discussed in the Lower House. This prevented them from taking the time and energy to submit an anti-V.D. petition to the Upper House.[36] Thus, as in the previous 42nd session during which the Diet was dissolved, the V.D. prevention proposal failed to be discussed in the House of Peers petition committee.

Public Response

With the mixed results of their petition efforts, Hiratsuka and other feminists continued to maintain their focus and actively pursue their goal. They successfully sponsored a formal lecture series that summer.[37] One of the featured speakers was Hozumi Shigetō, the civil law expert, who upheld the basic idea of eugenic marriage regulations.

To popularize their ideas, the group began publishing *Josei dōmei* (Women's alliance) in October 1920. Many female teachers in public schools throughout Japan responded to these efforts. They corresponded with the activists in Tokyo, participated in regional seminars, subscribed to the journal, and began organizing local branches of the NWA in their own areas. In November, however, prefectural authorities in Hiroshima suppressed a group of teachers who tried to form a local association.[38] The so-called Hiroshima incident was well covered by influential national newspapers, including *Asahi* and *Kokumin*.[39] Although this event scared many local teachers from active participation in the NWA, it also helped disseminate information on the NWA's efforts to institute a eugenic marriage restriction law. In addition, the association announced its plan to organize a marriage rejection alliance against men with venereal diseases (Karyūbyō danshi kyokon dōmei).[40] The plan called for women's voluntary but active commitment to eugenic principles by refusing to marry men with V.D. The controversial voluntary program became a popular topic in the Taishō media. Monthly magazines like *Chūō kōron* and *Kaizō*, both popular among educated people, devoted much space to leading intellectuals' views of eugenics.

Many writers acknowledged that this movement raised public awareness of eugenic principles. For example, social hygienist Teruoka Gitō viewed the rejection alliance favorably. He believed that the NWA's anti-V.D. law campaign and the marriage rejection alliance would have a positive impact on the fate of the racial stock by elevating the sexual and marital morality in Japan. Teruoka was particularly impressed by the fact that, unlike most social movements in Japan, Hiratsuka's efforts appeared soundly based on scientific and quantitative data.[41] A medical historian, Fujikawa Yū, commented on the marriage rejection alliance from a reproductive hygienic (*seishoku eisei*) perspective. Considering the widespread existence of sexual relations outside of marriage, he wrote, the alliance might not make a significant difference in society. Yet he saw the movement as meaningful in that awakened women called for sexual desire hygiene (*seiyoku eisei*).[42]

Some questioned the female-centered nature of the alliance and offered an alternative. A Buddhist social critic, Takashima Beihō, suggested that both men and women should reject marriage to anyone with undesirable health problems including tuberculosis and mental diseases.[43] Honma Hisao, translator of Ellen Key's *Younger Generation*, expressed a similar view.[44] Like Takashima and Honma, Christian social reformer Abe Isoo proposed an expanded eugenic measure that encouraged both men and women to refuse to marry the venereally diseased. He differed from Takashima and Honma because, from a reformist perspective, he believed some problems would require gender-specific approaches, while others would not. He thought women should reject men who drank, for instance, since alcoholism also had a dysgenic effect.[45]

There were other critics who saw the alliance as a class issue. For example, the anarchist Itō Noe—the only female critic except Hiratsuka Raichō given a voice in *Kaizō* and *Chūō kōron*—criticized the movement because it separated middle-class women from their lower-class sisters. Itō, who had once worked for Hiratsuka in the Bluestocking movement, fiercely criticized Hiratsuka, claiming that she selfishly intended to protect the women of her class while alienating other women who were forced to do sex work because of family poverty.[46]

A Marxist literary critic, Eguchi Kiyoshi, agreed with Itō on the class matter. Eguchi opposed the alliance, arguing that Hiratsuka's call for "motherhood protection" contradicted her effort to improve women's status in Japan. He believed that women's liberation could not be attained through an emphasis on gender difference. Thus, he criticized the *Mutterschutz Idee* as a hindrance to the emancipation of women. He argued that it assumed that women needed to be protected, thereby admitting that women were inferior to men.[47]

The engendered nature of the women's alliance against men with V.D. provoked a response from the media, which contributed to the dissemination of eugenic thought in Japanese society. Carefully examining the kinds of support and criticism they received, the feminist leaders revised the petition for the next Diet session with the help of Hozumi Shigetō and Ōsawa Kenji (1852–1927), a professor of physiology at Tokyo University.[48] As a result, the new petition was less charged gender-wise and more inclusive in that women would have to submit a health certificate if required, and common-law marriages without legal sanction (*jijitsukon*) could also be covered. The new petition was sent out for signatures and seals. This time, they received support from about 2,500 people including 1,000 men.[49]

End of the Campaign

Rather confident with these preparations, the NWA submitted the revised petition to the 44th regular session of the Imperial Diet. On January 29, 1921, the Lower House members, Arakawa, Chūma Okimaru, and Kagawa Yasutada of the Kenseikai party, and Nemoto of the Seiyūkai party, submitted the petition on behalf of the NWA.[50] Arakawa and Nemoto had been involved with the petition in previous sessions, and the female lobbyists were successful in recruiting Chūma and Kagawa, two representatives with medical backgrounds. At the February 7 petition committee meeting, Chūma presented the case to the other committee members. He explained that this petition had been rejected in the previous session because of its gender bias, so the petitioners revised it to make it more egalitarian. He used the authority of the medical profession by saying that he, as a medical practitioner, had often witnessed tragedies caused by widespread venereal diseases. Their profound negative impact not only on contemporaries but also on the future population demanded that the Diet take prompt preventive measures. He further explained the modifications: Rather than requiring a man to show the medical document directly to a prospective bride or her family, the new plan proposed that he acquire a license from a municipal office by submitting documentation to them. Women were not required to do the same; but if asked by a future husband, the prospective wife would have to supply the health document. Chūma also mentioned that the revised petition tried to improve its effectiveness by requiring the submission of the medical document from common-law couples.

Following Chūma's introduction, Kagawa expressed his support by emphasizing the prevalence of these diseases among the general population and their dreadful dysgenic effect on descendants. One member renewed opposition based on cultural differences between the West and Japan. Chūma intelligently pointed out that any parent could benefit from this plan because it would protect his or her own daughters. He also pointed out that recent progress in medicine made it easy to cure V.D.[51] Although there was an opinion that the proposed plan was not yet gender-neutral, the general atmosphere of the committee discussions started out on a positive note.

Further deliberations one week later were less promising. Supporter Arakawa emphasized the eugenic purpose of the petition to protect the state (*kokka*) and the racial stock—or the ethnic nation (*minzoku*)—from degenerating.[52] But some committee members were still unhappy about the fact that men and women had different medical certificate requirements and suggested that there might be other ways to control the spread of V.D. Others raised questions about how long a medical document would be valid. Arakawa reminded the members that details could be adjusted after this petition was adopted and asked them to judge it based on eugenic principles. In the end, the petition was rejected in the Lower House committee by a narrow margin.[53] Despite the disappointing result, the members of the association expressed gratitude for the serious discussions.[54]

Nevertheless, the members of the NWA remained optimistic for other reasons. Their other petition, which addressed the Police Regulation Law, appeared to be achieving success. The petition was adopted and forwarded from the committee level to the representatives and peers. Although the Lower House passed it, the Upper House rejected the plan on the last day of the session, March 25, 1921.[55] This was a major blow to the whole feminist movement led by the NWA because their energetic but overworked leaders lost focus. Hiratsuka, strained physically, psychologically, and financially, fell ill. The association's organ *Josei dōmei* began apologizing for the delay of proposed articles because Hiratsuka was unable to write.[56] Her illness was so serious that she had to withdraw from public activity. Personal relations among the leaders—especially between Hiratsuka and her fellow founder Ichi-kawa—turned sour. As a result, Ichikawa resigned as a director of the association in June 1921.[57] Thus, the group lost its two most experienced members and their ability to draft new petitions, lobby, publish the journal, and manage the financial and clerical matters of the association.

Remaining members did continue their efforts, however. The association announced its intention to submit three petitions, including the revised anti-V.D. proposal, in the 45th Diet session; they were supposed to submit it in early January and ask familiar Diet members, Miyake Shū (House of Peers) and Nemoto (House of Representatives), to present the case.[58] In spite of this rather concrete plan, no Diet records report discussion on the matter. Neither Hiratsuka, Ichikawa, nor Oku Mumeo recorded the outcome then or later.

Apparently, the remaining members of the association prioritized other petitions. One of these was the revision of the petition of the Police Regulation Law.[59] The revision was passed and members celebrated when the law came into effect in May. It was a significant first step for female suffrage in Japan. But the association continued disintegrating without strong leadership. Hiratsuka, still recuperating away from Tokyo, decided to disband the New Woman Association by the end of 1922.[60]

Unlike the petition for the revision of the Police Regulation Law, the petition to revise the Civil Law to restrict men with venereal diseases from getting married never passed. No other member of the NWA had been so determined to promote this eugenic cause for women. After all, it was an embodiment of Hiratsuka's personal commitment to Ellen Key's motherhood ideology. This movement, Japan's first organized effort to establish a eugenic law, is nonetheless suggestive in different ways.

Significance in Women's History

Students of women's history would stress the feminist perspective of the initiative, generally seeing the wartime prenatal policy associated with the 1940 National Eugenics Law as evidence of state efforts to objectify the female body to reproduce more babies and better "fit" children. Historian Sheldon Garon correctly points out that "when it comes to scholarship on women's movements and women in politics, the history of Japanese women has, for the most part, been written in terms of resistance to state power and ideology."[61] This image of the "objectified" female body and "victimized" women does not reflect the eugenic movement by women during the Taishō period. Contrary to the prevailing view, this particular case shows that women actively chose to influence state policy by strategically appropriating certain aspects of eugenic rhetoric. The scheme of formulating the eugenic marriage restriction law in this organized manner was unprecedented, and at least some men followed the example set by women.

It also shows that Hiratsuka's feminism was Janus-faced. While questioning differential treatment of men and women in a political and legal arena on one hand, she acknowledged the importance of physical differences between men and women on the other. Glorifying the female ability to bear and nurture children, she called for state protection for women in the name of eugenics. Her use of "motherhood protection" ideology, pushing women to the "traditional" female sphere, may be seen as counterproductive by some people who narrowly define feminism as women's effort to attain equality. Yet, I see clear continuities in her commitments to women's causes linking her Bluestocking literary movement, revision of the Police Regulation Law effort, and the marriage restriction law campaign against men with venereal diseases.

Hiratsuka consciously used the temporal term "*shuzoku*" hoping to remind Taishō women of the close relationship with Nature and sociopolitical power and prestige once enjoyed by women in the beginning of Japanese history. She also changed her focus from factory women suffering from tuberculosis to housewives suffering from their husbands' V.D. Some Western countries had adopted eugenic marriage laws restricting individuals with tuberculosis from marrying. It seems that Hiratsuka deliberately avoided targeting women factory workers. Instead she concentrated on another gender-specific "racial poison" harmful to the general population, venereal diseases. The fact that she "engendered" eugenics appears to indicate that her ultimate objective was the improvement of women's well-being, not the improvement of the racial stock per se. She failed to recognize that V.D. was, in fact, doubly "engenderable": While she saw middle-class housewives as "fit" and their husbands as "unfit," her opponents saw men as "fit" and prostitutes as "unfit." Hiratsuka refused to include prostitutes in her category of "women" by marginalizing them as a minority. V.D. was thus not only gender-specific but also a class-specific "racial poison."

Considering that Hiratsuka was situated at the cross section of women's issues and eugenics, it is also intriguing that she never addressed other issues such as the biological-deterministic notion of female criminality prevalent in Western eugenic discourse.[62] She used eugenic rhetoric rather selectively, making eugenics her strategy but not her objective. She exploited the eugenics discourse to attack unregulated male sexuality that caused physical and emotional sufferings of women. In this sense, if we are to call her a feminist, we have to recognize the duality of a feminism that was concerned with women's equality with men as well as their differences from men.

Hiratsuka's use of a eugenic rationale may cause difficulty in interpreting her life, at least for some. She seemed determined to question norms imposed by all levels of authority—whether it be her father, Japan Women's College, government officials, or society as a whole. Why, then, did she sanction state power to protect mothers? Hiratsuka was interested in solving a very specific women's problem (*fujin mondai*): Middle-class women suffered from venereal diseases brought into the home by their husbands. As Barbara Molony points out, the motherhood ideology of European origin was not very different from the *ryōsai kenbo* or "good wife, wise mother" ideology endorsed by the Japanese state.[63] Both stressed women's "difference" from men as mothers and wives, and they both tried to give significance to women's childbearing and nurturing roles at home. The fundamental differences between the two rests on the basis of the eugenic notions and the new sexual ethics of the motherhood ideology. Hiratsuka did openly criticize the *ryōsai kenbo* ideology.[64] Yet, the paradox of Hiratsuka's sudden glorification of state power suggests that she sensed that the juxtaposition of the two ideologies was the most effective way to win over the public support for her eugenic effort.[65]

The Context of Eugenic Ideas and Movements in Japan

To appreciate the implications of this first organized eugenic movement in Japan even further, we should situate it in the context of a series of eugenic movements in prewar Japan. From this perspective, Hiratsuka's campaigns are mutually consistent. First, her college education at the Japan Women's College was significant. Naruse Jinzō, the school's founder, emphasized the usefulness of physical education: he claimed that active exercise would improve the size and capacity of relatively small- and weakly-built Japanese women. As early as 1892, he expressed his interest in "race improvement" (*jinshu kairyō*) in his diary.[66] He noted the importance of providing women with proper scientific knowledge in health, since physically "fit" women would be more likely to produce "fit" children (future soldiers and mothers). He read such imported works as *Race and Sex: Some Aspects of Social Betterment* and *The Task of Social Hygiene* by the socially radical eugenicist Havelock Ellis. The parts he underlined indicate that Naruse was attracted to the idea of social and human betterment by euthenics or positive eugenics.[67] By linking women to the Meiji government's slogan, "Enrich the nation, strengthen the army" (*fukoku kyōhei*), he was trying to legitimize his effort in higher education for women.

Physiologist Ōsawa Kenji also taught at the Japan Women's College. Hiratsuka entered the college in 1903 and took Ōsawa's physiology classes.[68] Ōsawa later helped improve the NWA petition in 1920. When the Japan Society for the Prevention of Venereal Disease (Nihon karyūbyō yobōkai) was established by Yamane Masatsugu (a representative who supported Hiratsuka's anti-V.D. petition) and others in 1905, Ōsawa assumed the group's vice chairmanship.[69] By 1909, he began supporting the Christian representative Nemoto Shō's temperance legislative effort.[70] In his writings, Ōsawa promoted positive eugenic marriage between the "fit" while regulating dysgenic marriage and articulated the idea of requiring health documents for legal marriage.[71] Besides Ōsawa, the college's lecturers included other notable eugenic enthusiasts.[72]

Among students, Hiratsuka's contemporary at the college, Arai Tsuru (1886–1915), went to study psychology at Columbia University in the United States. There she was supervised by Professor Edward Thorndike (1874–1949), a committed eugenicist. After she received her PhD, she returned to Japan and translated the book *Hereditary Genius* by the founder of eugenics, Francis Galton.[73] The early history of Japan Women's College shows that the institution stressed the significance of women's reproductive and nurturing abilities and tried to make them more valuable by providing a sophisticated level of science education. One suspects that Naruse's extraordinary interest in women's issues and race improvement had some impact on the evolution of Hiratsuka's thinking.

Nagai Hisomu (1876–1957), a Tokyo University physiology professor, succeeded Ōsawa as a lecturer at the Japan Women's College in 1921. He would later found Japan's most prominent and credible eugenic organization, the Association of Race Hygiene (Minzoku eisei gakkai),[74] in 1930. This organization would lead efforts to enact the 1940 National Eugenics Law (*Kokumin yūsei-hō*). The traditional account of how this sterilization law came into effect largely ignores the Japan Women's College network and the preceding effort by the NWA to enact an antivenereal disease law.[75] What Hiratsuka proposed was not sterilization but a marriage regulation law. Yet both sterilization laws and marriage regulation laws are forms of negative eugenics, discouraging the unfit from procreating. It is reasonable to ask whether there were any direct lines of continuity between the feminist movements of the early 1920s and the enactment of the National Eugenics Law in 1940.

Actually there was a significant connection. Hozumi Shigetō, who had advised Hiratsuka on revision of the anti-V.D. law petition, with Nagai Hisomu established the National Marriage Guidance Society (Kokumin kekkon hodōkai) in the mid-1920s. This group intended to promote "rational" marriage and to encourage a higher level of sexual morality among the Japanese. To join the society, one was required to submit a health document certifying that he or she was eugenically fit. In 1935, Nagai organized the Japan Society for Popularization of Eugenic Marriage (Nihon yūsei kekkon fukyūkai), hoping to involve more women in the eugenic cause.

Second, among women there was a renewal of the anti-V.D. marriage restriction campaign in 1930. Prominent female leaders who were against birth control—Yamada Waka, Takeuchi Shigeyo, and Kōra Tomiko, as well as Hiratsuka Raichō, who had returned to Tokyo in 1923—formed a new organization called the Motherhood Education Association (Bosei kyōiku kyōkai). Though many details are unclear, one of its aims was to prohibit people infected with venereal diseases from getting married.[76]

Third, Diet members who had supported the NWA's antivenereal disease campaign later submitted eugenic bills that were to lead the way for enactment of the 1940 National Eugenics Law. For example, Chūma

Okimaru proposed a eugenic marriage restriction law to the 58th Imperial Diet in May 1930.[77] Diseases to be restricted under this plan included V.D., mental diseases, alcoholism, tuberculosis, and leprosy. Representatives Arakawa Gorō and Yagi Itsurō (1863–1945), who would introduce sterilization bills to the Diet in the 1930s, supported Chūma's proposal. As we have seen, Arakawa had introduced Hiratsuka's plan to the House petition committee in 1920 and 1921 and Chūma had done so in 1921. Following news of the 1933 Nazi sterilization law, Arakawa submitted a eugenic sterilization bill (Arakawa plan) to the Diet committee in 1934 (the 65th Diet session) and 1935 (the 67th Diet session). When he introduced the Ethnic National Eugenics Protection Bill (*Minzoku yūsei hogo-hō an*) on March 6, 1934, Arakawa acknowledged the continuity by stating, without specifically referring to the NWA campaign, that he had been studying the issue of eugenic legislation for more than ten years.[78] He later cooperated with Nagai Hisomu's Association of Race Hygiene.[79]

Conclusion

Integrating the women's reform effort against venereal diseases into the history of eugenics, eugenic thought, and eugenic movements gives us a new perspective. There are three possible reasons why this movement has not been treated as a legitimate eugenic movement in the existing history of eugenics in Japan: Hiratsuka's petition was gender biased; men were reluctant to acknowledge the women's initiative; and venereal diseases by 1920 had already been proven to be infectious rather than genetic in origin.

Perceived gender bias was the principal reason for the effort's failure. But as some have pointed out, the engendered nature of the movement attracted media attention and thus, ironically, helped to expose eugenic ideas to a wider public.[80] It might be fair to say that Hiratsuka had a greater impact on the popularization of eugenic principles than scholars who had published either scholarly or popular books on eugenics. Public awareness about eugenics was one of the factors that led to the enactment of the 1940 National Eugenics Law. The ramifications of the women's reform effort were not insubstantial. What is important is that Hiratsuka for the first time identified "(middle-class) women" with the "biologically fit" status while reducing men to the "biologically unfit" status by problematizing venereal diseases. Prior to her organized effort, eugenics popularizers had been educated middle-class men who saw themselves as "mentally and physically fit." Hiratsuka unsettled the existing gender hierarchy by upsetting the boundary between the "biologically desirable" and "biologically undesirable."[81]

A second reason for the existing historiographic biases is that male activists were unwilling to acknowledge that women in fact pioneered the organized legislation effort to enact a eugenic law. For example, though Arakawa Gorō was proud of his longtime commitment to the cause of eugenic legislation, he did not want to attribute his involvement in the cause to Hiratsuka and her supporters.

The third reason is more complicated. Let us remember the definition of "eugenics": the science of improving human stock by controlling heredity. Until fairly recently, existing literature on Japanese eugenics was inclined to see eugenics primarily as a precursor of genetics. As historian of science Matsubara Yōko suggests in her 1996 work, scholars possessing today's more sophisticated genetic knowledge tend to see the early twentieth-century interest in the "hereditary" nature of infectious diseases as scientifically crude.[82] This may have contributed to the underrepresentation of nonhereditary diseases in the history of eugenics.

Hiratsuka's plan for an anti-V.D. law was clearly based on the negative eugenic premise of scientific thinking in her day. Social historian Fujino Yutaka, in his 1993 study of the history of Hansen's disease (leprosy) control in Japan, also points out that this disease was a target of various negative eugenic regulations—quarantine, marriage restriction, and sterilization—even long after it was proven to be infectious rather than genetic in nature.[83]

Indeed, "inclusive eugenics," which does not exclude "racial poisons" caused more directly by germs and environment than by genes, was a staple of prewar eugenic legislative efforts. Not only Hiratsuka's proposals in the 1920s, but many eugenic plans drafted by legislators like Chūma and Arakawa in the 1930s were also inclusive. During wartime, however, a group of medical professionals briefly overshadowed inclusive eugenics by successfully passing the genetically restricted National Eugenics Law in 1940. Inclusive eugenics was soon revived by postwar reformers, such as feminist Katō Shizue, in their endeavor to recast the 1940 law into the 1948 Eugenics Protection Law.[84]

Unlike its twin sibling, the revision of the Police Regulation Law, the NWA's marriage restriction legislative campaign in the Taishō era has remained relatively obscure because it failed to achieve its goal. Yet, precisely because it was one of the earliest examples of women's own initiative politicizing their own bodies, particularly their reproductive abilities, Hiratsuka's eugenic effort deserves more recognition. Considering the fact that the Maternal Body Protection Law replaced the Eugenics Protection Law in 1996 as a result of feminist criticism against certain elements in the latter, self-awareness of women's bodies is a key concept bridging various important and sometimes ideologically conflicting prewar and postwar feminist movements.[85]

Notes

1. Diseases like syphilis, gonorrhea, and chancre were commonly known as "*karyūbyō*" (red-light district diseases) in Taishō Japan (1912–1926). In most cases, however, I translate the term as "venereal diseases" (sometimes abbreviated as "V.D.") in this essay because "venereal diseases" was the term specifically used in the Western "racial poisons" discourse at that time. For extensive discussion on venereal diseases in Japanese history, see Sabine Frühstück, *Colonizing Sex: Sexology and Social Control in Modern Japan* (Berkeley: University of California Press, 2003), 17–54.

2. Regarding male sexuality, see Mark Driscoll's essay in Chapter 5 of this volume.

3. See for example, Sheldon Garon, "The World's Oldest Debate? Prostitution and the State in Imperial Japan, 1900–1945," *American Historical Review* 98, no. 3 (1993): 710–732, and Fujime Yuki, "Kindai Nihon no kōshō seido to haishō undō," *Shūkyō to minzoku shintai to seiai*, vol. 1, *Jendā no Nihonshi*, eds. Wakita Haruko and Susan B. Hanley (Tokyo daigaku shuppankai, 1994), 461–491.

4. For a brief but interdisciplinary survey of research on eugenic science, thought, and movement in Japan, see the second half of Suzuki Zenji, Matsubara Yōko, and Sakano Tōru, "Tenbō: yūseigaku kenkyū no dōkō III; Amerika oyobi Nihon no yūseigaku ni kansuru rekishi kenkyū," *Kagakushi kenkyū*, no. 194 (1995): 97–106. Recently published works not dealt with in the above essay include: Fujino Yutaka, "Hisabetsu buraku," in *Iwanami kōza Nihon tsūshi*, vol. 18, *Kindai (3)*, eds. Asao Naohiro, Amino Yoshihiko, Ishii Susumu, Kano Masanao, Hayakawa Shōhachi, and Yasumaru Yoshio (Iwanami shoten, 1994), 135–167; Fujino Yutaka, "Yūsei shisō to minshū: Ikeda Shigenori to yūsei undō," *Minshūshi kenkyū*, no. 49 (May 1995): 41–60; Fujino Yutaka, "Kindai Nihon no Kirisuto-kyō to yūsei shisō," *Kirisuto-kyō shigaku*, no. 49 (July 1995): 1–20; Fujino Yutaka, "Buraku mondai to yūsei shisō," *Buraku kaihō kenkyū*, no. 100 (October 1994): 124–142; Fujino Yutaka, "Nihon fashizumu to byōsha, shōgaisha: danshu to gyakusatsu," *Kikan sensō sekinin kenkyū*, no. 12 (Summer 1996): 48–55; Katō Shūichi, "Aiseyo, umeyo, yori takaki shuzoku no tame ni: Ippu ippu sei to jinshu kairyō no seijigaku," in *Kōza sei o kangaeru*, eds. Ōba Takeshi, Hasegawa Mariko, and Yamazaki Kaoru, vol. 3 (Senshū daigaku shuppankyoku, 1997), 201–246; Matsubara Yōko, "Meiji-matsu kara Taishō-ki ni okeru shakai mondai to 'iden,'" *Nihon bunka kenkyūjo kiyō*, no. 3 (1996): 155–169; Matsubara Yōko, "Minzoku yūsei hogo-hō an to Nihon no yūsei-hō no keifu," *Kagakushi kenkyū*, no. 201 (1997): 42–50; Matsubara Yōko, "'Bunka kokka' no yūsei-hō: Yūsei hogo-hō to *Kokumin yūsei-hō* no dansō," *Gendai shisō* 25, no. 4 (April 1997): 8–21;

Sugiyama Takeshi, "Senzen Nihon no yūsei shisō: sono ronri to rinri," *Karada no kagaku*, no. 191 (November 1996): 75–80; and Tomiyama Ichirō, "Kokka to iu gihō: jinshu kara kokumin e," *Kokka (jiko) zō no keisei*, no. 4, *Edo no shisō* (July 1996): 119–129.

5. Sumiko Otsubo Sitcawich, "Eugenics in Imperial Japan: Some Ironies of Modernity, 1883–1945," PhD dissertation, Ohio State University, 1998, 36–88.

6. For instance, see Matsuo Takayoshi, "Taishō-ki fujin no seijiteki jiyū kakutoku undō: Shin fujin kyōkai kara Fusen kakutoku dōmei e," in *"Josei dōmei" kaisetsu, sōmokuji, sakuin* (Domesu shuppan, 1985), 21–83.

7. Science historian Saitō Hikaru sees the use of eugenic theories by non–life scientists like Hiratsuka as an indication of how popularized eugenic ideas had become by the late 1910s. See his "<Nijū-nendai, Nihon, yūseigaku> no ichi-kyokumen," *Gendai shisō* 21, no. 7 (1993): 134.

8. See for instance, Kobayashi Tomie, "Kaisetsu," in *Bosei no shuchō ni tsuite*, vol. 2, *Hiratsuka Raichō chosakushū*, ed. Hiratsuka Raichō chosakushū henshū iinkai (Ōtsuki shoten, 1983), 411–423; Suzuki Yūko, *Haha to onna*, vol. 1, *Joseishi o hiraku* (Miraisha, 1989), and in the same series, vol. 2, *Yokusan to teikō* (Miraisha, 1989); Tachi Kaoru, "Kindai Nihon no bosei to feminizumu: bosei no kenri kara san'iku-ken e," in *Bosei kara jisedai ikuseiryoku e: umisodateru shakai no tame ni*, eds. Hara Hiroko and Tachi Kaoru (Shin'yōsha, 1991), 3–39; Ishizaki Shōko, "Seishoku no jiyū to sanji chōsetsu undō: Hiratsuka Raichō to Yamamoto Senji," *Rekishi hyōron*, no. 503 (March 1992): 92–107; Hirota Masaki, "Kindai erīto josei no aidentitī to kokka," in *Shutai to hyōgen shigoto to seikatsu*, vol. 2, *Jendā no Nihonshi*, eds. Wakita Haruko and Susan B. Hanley (Tōkyō daigaku shuppankai, 1995), 199–227; Yoneda Sayoko, "Hiratsuka Raichō no 'sensō sekinin'-ron josetsu," *Rekishi hyōron*, no. 552 (April 1996): 45–56; Ehara Yumiko, "Yūsei shisō to feminizumu: Ichinokawa ronbun o megutte," in *Seishoku gijutsu to jendā*, vol. 3, *Feminizumu no shuchō*, ed. Ehara Yumiko (Keisō shobō, 1996), 340–347; and Fujime Yuki, *Sei no rekishigaku* (Fuji shuppan, 1997). Hiroko Tomida's biography of Hiratsuka focuses on the NWA activities in chapter 6 without referring to eugenics at all. See Hiroko Tomida, *Hiratsuka Raichō and Early Japanese Feminism* (Leiden and Boston: Brill, 2004), 263–330.

9. Ellen Key, *The Renaissance of Motherhood* (New York and London: G.P. Putnam's Sons, 1914), 80.

10. For example, see Hiratsuka Raichō, "Fujin rōdō mondai to shuzoku mondai" and "Sengo no fujin mondai: Fujin rōdō mondai to shuzoku mondai," *Shakai kaizō ni taisuru fujin no shimei*, vol. 3, *Hiratsuka Raichō chosakushū*, ed. Hi-

ratsuka Raichō chosakushū henshū iinkai (Ōtsuki shoten, 1983), 21–26, 35–39. Despite its title, the former article (first published in 1918) used the term *jinshu,* while the latter (published in 1919) used *shuzoku* in the text consistently. At the time, different translating terms for eugenics and race hygiene existed. For example, *Fujin eisei zasshi* used *jinshu kaizengaku* (1916), *shuzoku kaizengaku* (1916), *shuzoku eisei* (1916), and *minzoku eisei* (1919). For more on varieties of competing translations, see Suzuki Zenji, *Nihon no yūseigaku: Sono shisō to undō no kiseki* (Sankyō shuppan, 1983), 77 and 88. See Hirota Masaki's discussion on Hiratsuka's temporal or historical vision of the *shuzoku* community. Hirota, "Kindai erīto josei," 220–221 and 222–223. The terms *shuzoku, jinshu,* and *minzoku* are often translated into "race." Yet, taking historical contexts into account, Kevin M. Doak demonstrates that some Japanese intellectuals clearly distinguished these terms. Thus, these terms deserve careful translations in order to convey original nuance. See for example, his "What is a Nation and Who Belongs?: National Narratives and the Ethnic Imagination in Twentieth-Century Japan," *American Historical Review* 102, no. 2 (1997): 283–309.

11. E. Patricia Tsurumi, *Factory Girls: Women in the Thread Mills of Meiji Japan* (Princeton, NJ: Princeton University Press, 1990), 169–173.

12. See Kōuchi Nobuko, *Shiryō bosei hogo ronsō* (Domesu shuppan, 1984).

13. Katherine Anthony, *Feminism in Germany and Scandinavia* (New York: Holt, 1915), 89.

14. Barbara Molony discusses earlier efforts to pursue women's rights in Chapter 13 of this volume.

15. Nancy Leys Stepan, *"The Hour of Eugenics": Race, Gender, and Nation in Latin America* (Ithaca and London: Cornell University Press, 1991), 63–101; Paul Weindling, *Health, Race and German Politics between National Unification and Nazism, 1870–1945* (Cambridge and New York: Cambridge University Press, 1989), 170–188; and Daniel J. Kevles, *In the Name of Eugenics: Genetics and the Uses of Human Heredity* (New York: Alfred A. Knopf, 1985), 92–93.

16. See the Chief of Home Ministry's Bureau of Public Health Ushio Keinosuke's view in "Seigan iinkai dai-ni bunkakai giroku (sokki) dai-yonkai," in *Dai yonjūnikai, Teikoku Gikai Shūgiin iinkai giroku, Taishō 8, 9–nen,* reprinted in *Teikoku Gikai, Shūgiin iinkai giroku* (hereafter abbreviated as *TGSIG*), vol. 23 (Kyōto: Rinsen shoten, 1983), 617.

17. Frühstück, *Colonizing Sex,* 17–54.

18. Hiratsuka Raichō, "Karyūbyō danshi kekkon seigen-hō seitei ni kansuru sei-

seigan undō," *Josei dōmei*, no. 1 (October 1920; reprint, Domesu shuppan, 1985): 30.

19. Hiratsuka, "Karyūbyō danshi," 30–31.

20. Ibid., 31.

21. Ibid.

22. Tsuji Isao, "Nihon joshi daigaku sōritsu tōji no kyōin soshiki ni kansuru kenkyū," *Nihon joshi daigaku kiyō (Ningen shakai gakubu)*, no. 3 (1992): 40.

23. Hiratsuka, "Karyūbyō danshi," 31.

24. Conversely, there was an expression: "Civilization is syphilization." V.D. usually spread rapidly in urban settings and in the military. Since urbanization and military conscription were attributes of Western-style modernity—industrialization and imperial expansion—one might argue that the prevalence of the sexually transmitted diseases in Japan was a sign of modernity. The paradox that V.D. could be seen as both uncivilized and modern resembles the paradox of prostitution in China at the same period. See Gail Hershatter, "Modernizing Sex, Sexing Modernity," in *Engendering China: Women, Culture, and the State*, eds. Christina K. Gilmartin, Gail Hershatter, Lisa Rofel, and Tyrene White (Cambridge, MA and London: Harvard University Press, 1994), 147–174. See also Frühstück, *Colonizing Sex*, 17–54.

25. The NWA's Social Study Group headed by Hiratsuka examined the marriage restriction laws of several U.S. states, plus Norway, Germany, and Mexico. It also looked at a law plan drafted by a female parliament member in Czechoslovakia and reports presented at the 17th V.D. prevention conference in Germany. See Shakaibu kenkyūkai, "Karyūbyō kekkon seigen ni kansuru Ōbei shokoku no genkō hōrei," *Josei dōmei*, no. 3 (December 1920): 44–47. See also Hiratsuka Raichō, "Karyūbyō to zenshugakuteki kekkon seigen-hō," *Josei dōmei*, no. 2 (November 1920): 37.

26. Shakaibu, "Ōbei hōrei," 44–45.

27. About the notion of a wife's likely undiseased status, see Chapter 14 by Kathleen Uno in this volume.

28. Hiratsuka, "Karyūbyō danshi," 31–32.

29. For petition committee discussions at the 42nd Imperial Diet session (1919–1920), see *TGSIG*, vol. 23, 616–617.

30. Hiratsuka, "Karyūbyō danshi," 31–32.

31. Ibid., 35.

32. Katō Junji, *Miseinensha inshu kinshu-hō o tsukutta hito: Nemoto Shō den* (Nagano: Ginga shobō, 1995); and Rumi Yasutake, *Transnational Women's Activism: The United States, Japan, and Japanese Immigrant Communities in California, 1859–1920* (New York: New York University Press, 2004).

33. "Seigan iin daiichi bunkakai giroku (sokki) dai-ikkai," in *Dai yonjūsan-kai, Teikoku Gikai Shūgiin iinkai giroku, Taishō 9–nen,* in *TGSIG,* vol. 25 (1984), 325.

34. For example, see "Tokushū: Taishō seimei shugi," *Bungei* (Fall 1992): 245–321.

35. *TGSIG,* vol. 25, 322–323; Ichikawa Fusae, "Chian keisatsu-hō dai-gojō shūsei no undō (Chū)," *Josei dōmei,* no. 2 (November 1920): 26–27. Ichikawa mistakenly recorded that the petition for the revision of the Police Regulation Law was adopted on July 16th.

36. Hiratsuka, "Karyūbyō danshi," 36.

37. Hiratsuka Raichō, *Hiratsuka Raichō jiden: Genshi josei wa taiyō de atta* (hereafter *Genshi*), vol. 3 (Ōtsuki shoten, 1973), 108–109; and Ichikawa Fusae, *Ichikawa Fusae jiden: Senzen hen* (Shinjuku shobō, 1974), 78.

38. As for the so-called Hiroshima incident, see *Josei dōmei,* no. 4 (January 1921) and no. 5 (February 1921): 33–40.

39. Hiratsuka, *Genshi,* 152.

40. Hiratsuka, "Karyūbyō to zenshugakuteki," 41; Hiratsuka Raichō, "Karyūbyō ni taisuru kekkon seigen-hō to kyokon dōmei ni tsuite," *Kaizō* (February 1921): 118–128.

41. Teruoka Gitō, "Minzoku eisei no risō to yūseigakuteki shuzoku kaizen no risō," *Kaizō* (February 1921): 97–102.

42. Fujikawa Yū, "'Seishoku eisei' no shakaiteki kenchi kara," *Chūō kōron* (February 1921): 49–50.

43. Takashima Beihō, "Otoko mo mata onna ni taishite kyokon no kenri ari," *Chūō kōron* (February 1921): 52–55.

44. Honma Hisao, "Otoko no tachiba to shite," *Chūō kōron* (February 1921): 55–61.

45. Abe Isoo, "Kyokon Dōmei wa danjo ryōsei ni saiwai su," *Chūō kōron* (February 1921): 70–77.

46. Itō Noe, "Chūsan kaikyū fujin no rikoteki undō: Fujin no seiji undō to Shin fujin kyōkai no undō ni tsuite," *Kaizō* (February 1921): 103–110.

47. Eguchi Kiyoshi, "Kyokon dōmei no zehi," *Chūō kōron* (February 1921): 61–69.

48. Hiratsuka, "Karyūbyō to zenshugakuteki," 35–41. Hozumi's view toward eugenics and marriage restriction laws can be observed in his "Yūseigaku to kon'in-hō," *Tōyō gakugei zasshi*, no. 462 (March 5, 1920): 7–22. Ōsawa Kenji's article expresses his disappointment upon learning of the rejection of the anti-V.D. law petition. See Ōsawa, "Karyūbyō danshi kekkon seigen-hō hiketsu no fujōri," *Josei dōmei*, no. 3 (December 1920): 47–48. It was reprinted from the journal *Sei* (November 1920).

49. For the statistical information of petition supporters, see Ichikawa Fusae, "Sanshu no seigan no chōinsha chōsa hōkoku," *Josei dōmei*, no. 5 (February 1921): 41–44.

50. "Dai yonjūyon Gikai to kyōkai no undō," *Josei dōmei*, no. 5 (February 1921): 1.

51. "Seigan iin dai-ni bunkakai giroku (sokki) dai-nikai," in *Dai yonjūyonkai, Teikoku Gikai Shūgiin iinkai giroku, Taishō 9, 10-nen*, in *TGSIG*, vol. 28 (1984), 118–119.

52. Ibid., 137.

53. Ibid., 137–139; "Giin no karyūbyō kekkon seigen ni tsuite no tōron," *Josei dōmei*, no. 6 (March, 1921): 38–46. There were three members in favor in the eight-member (including the chair) committee. See "Dai-sankai," *TGSIG*, 127, 139, and Ichikawa Fusae, *Ichikawa Fusae jiden*, 90.

54. "Giin no karyūbyō kekkon seigen ni tsuite no tōron," *Josei dōmei*, no. 6 (March, 1921): 46.

55. Ibid. Also see Hiratsuka, *Genshi*, 158–160.

56. For example, see "Henshūshitsu yori," *Josei dōmei*, no. 6 (March 1921): 78; Hiratsuka Raichō, "Goaisatsu," *Josei dōmei*, no. 7 (April 1921): 61; "Henshūshitsu yori," *Josei dōmei*, no. 7 (April 1921): 65; and "Hiratsuka Raichō-shi no kōkaijō," *Josei dōmei*, no. 8 (May 1921): 15.

57. Ichikawa Fusae, *Ichikawa Fusae jiden*, 96–98.

58. *Josei dōmei*, no. 12 (January 1922): 1–8, 51.

59. Ibid., 98; and Hiratsuka, *Genshi*, 164–167. The petition to revise the Police Regulation Law was discussed and adopted by the House of Representatives Committee on February 6, 1922. See "Seigan iin dai-ni bunkakai giroku (sokki) dai-nikai," in *Dai yonjūgokai, Teikoku Gikai Shūgiin iinkai giroku, Taishō 10, 11–nen,* in *TGSIG*, vol. 32 (1985), 82. It was sent to the regular session of the House of Representatives and then to the House of Peers. Both Houses passed the bill and the Police Regulation Law was finally revised in favor of women in 1922. Regarding the process, see the association's new leader Sakamoto Makoto's "Chikei dai-gojō shūsei undō no gairyaku," in *Josei dōmei,* no. 14 (June 1922): 5–12.

60. Hiratsuka, *Genshi*, 203–210.

61. Sheldon Garon, "Women's Groups and the Japanese State: Contending Approaches to Political Integration, 1890–1945," *Journal of Japanese Studies* 19, no. 1 (1993): 6. Katō Shūichi also questions the view that "motherhood" was imposed on women by the state. See Katō, "Aiseyo," 10.

62. For example, see David G. Horn, "This Norm which Is Not One: Reading the Female Body in Lombroso's Anthropology," in *Deviant Bodies: Critical Perspectives on Difference in Science and Popular Culture*, eds. Jennifer Terry and Jacqueline Urla (Bloomington and Indianapolis: Indiana University Press, 1995), 109–128.

63. Barbara Molony, "Equality versus Difference: The Japanese Debate over 'Motherhood Protection,' 1915–50," in *Japanese Women Working*, ed. Janet Hunter (London and New York: Routledge, 1993), 125–126, 129. Iwahori Yōko also pays attention to the paradox of the affinity between the *ryōsai kenbo* ideology and the modern (Western) family ideals. See her "Meiji chūki Ōka shugi shisō ni miru shufu-zō no keisei: '*Jogaku zasshi*' no seikatsu shisō ni tsuite," in *Shutai to hyōgen shigoto to seikatsu*, 459–486. For more on the *ryōsai kenbo* ideology, see Kathleen Uno's chapter in this volume.

64. See for example, Hiratsuka Raichō, "Meiji matsunen yori Taishō shotō no waga fujin mondai (1915)," *Hiratsuka Raichō chosakushū*, vol. 2, 109; "Inoue Tetsujirō-shi no ryōfu kenpu o nanzu (1918)," *Hiratsuka Raichō chosakushū*, vol. 2, 343–349; and "Sengo no fujin mondai," *Hiratsuka Raichō chosakushū*, vol. 3, 35–36.

65. Hiratsuka's comparison of ancient women with the Sun Goddess is another example of this paradox and juxtaposition. This feminist strategy was succeeded by Takamure Itsue. Ehara Yumiko points out that, in order to be included in mainstream discussions, the politically dominated sometimes have to borrow logic shared by the dominant. Thus the former's expressions may not reflect what they actually think and may contain contradictory factors.

See her "Yūsei shisō to feminizumu," 344–345. A similar point is made by Oguma Eiji and Kōno Nobuko about Takamure. See Oguma Eiji, *Tan'itsu minzoku shinwa no kigen: <Nihonjin> no jiga-zō no keifu* (Shin'yōsha, 1995), 198, and Kōno Nobuko, "Onna to nashonarizumu," *Jōkyō*, no. 59 (January 1996): 35.

66. See *Nihon Joshi Daigaku sōritsusha Naruse sensei*, ed. Watanabe Eiichi, rev. ed. (Ōfūkai shuppanbu, 1948), 114.

67. The Naruse Memorial Hall of the Japan Women's University in Tokyo holds Naruse Jinzō's personal book collection.

68. Hiratsuka, *Genshi*, vol. 1 (Ōtsuki shoten, 1971), 144. For discussion about Ōsawa Kenji and eugenics, and connections between Ōsawa and Hiratsuka, see Sumiko Otsubo, "The Female Body and Eugenic Thought in Meiji Japan," in *Building a Modern Nation: Science, Technology and Medicine in the Meiji Era and Beyond*, ed. Morris Low (New York: Palgrave Macmillan, forthcoming).

69. "Nihon seibyō yobō kyōkai setsuritsu no riyū," in *Igaku (2)*, vol. 25, *Nippon kagaku gijutsushi taikei*, ed. Nihon kagakushi gakkai (Dai-ichi hōki shuppan, 1967), 151–152.

70. "Ōsawa igaku hakushi miseinensha kinshu hō-an o sansei su," *Kuni no hikari*, no. 192 (1909): 5.

71. Ōsawa Kenji, *Tsūzoku kekkon shinsetsu* (Ōkura shoten, 1909).

72. Botanist Yamanouchi Shigeo, psychologist Matsumoto Matatarō, and social hygienist Koya Yoshio are a few examples. See Sumiko Otsubo, "Between Two Worlds: Yamanouchi Shigeo and Eugenics in Early Twentieth Century Japan," *Annals of Science* 60 (2003): 1–27; and Matsumura Hiroyuki, "'Kokubō kokka' no yūseigaku: Koya Yoshio o chūshin ni," *Shirin* 83, no. 2 (March 2000): 272–302.

73. It was published in 1916 under the name Haraguchi (her husband's last name) Tsuruko. For details about her life, see *Haraguchi Tsuruko: josei shinrigakusha no senku*, ed. Ogino Izumi (Nagano: Ginga shobō, 1983).

74. The association did not use the term *jinshu*, but this is the official English name. Having attained foundation status in 1935, it became Minzoku eisei kyōkai.

75. A recent work, Matsubara Yōko's "Minzoku yūsei" is an exception.

76. "Sanji seigen hantai-ha ga Bosei Kyōiku Kyōkai setsuritsu," *Yūseigaku*, no. 76 (June 1930): 34. Hiratsuka joined a group promoting birth control (Nihon sanji chōsetsu renmei) in 1931. This behavior appears contradictory.

77. "Showa gonen gogatsu tuitachi teishutsu, kengi dai-nijūhachigō, taikanja kekkon seigen-hō seitei ni kansuru kengi-an," in *57–58 Teikoku Gikai Shūgiin jōsō kengi dōgi shitsumon 1929–30*, 1–5 (Kokuritsu Kokkai Toshokan); "Taikanja no kekkon seigen-hō," *Yūseigaku*, no. 76 (June 1930): 31; and Fujino Yutaka, *Nihon fashizumu to iryō: hansen byō o meguru jisshōteki kenkyū* (Iwanami shoten, 1993), 37.

78. "Kenkō hoken-hō chū kaisei hōritsu-an hoka ikken iinkai giroku (sokki), dai-hachikai," in *Dai-rokujūgokai, Teikoku Gikai Shūgiin iinkai giroku, Showa 8, 9–nen*, in *TGSIG*, Microfilm, Reel 15 (Kyōto: Rinsen shoten, 1991), 2.

79. Yoshimasu Shūfu, "Waga kuni yūsei undō no enkaku," in *Yūseigaku no riron to jissai: Toku ni seishin igaku to no kankei ni oite* (Nankōdo, 1940), 216–217.

80. For example, Representative Chūma Okimaru noted the extensive media coverage and academic as well as popular response to the anti-V.D. marriage restriction law petition, see "Seigan iinkai dai-ni bunkakai giroku (sokki) dai-nikai," *TGSIG*, vol. 28, 119. Hiratsuka herself commented that her plan often provoked unnecessary opposition from men just because it was submitted by women. See Hiratsuka, "Karyūbyō to zenshugakuteki," 37.

81. Other examples of unsettling established gender roles in Taishō Japan are discussed in Jennifer Robertson, "Gender-Bending in Paradise: Doing 'Female' and 'Male' in Japan," *Genders*, no. 5 (Summer 1989): 50–69, and Donald Roden, "Taishō Culture and the Problem of Gender Ambivalence," in *Culture and Identity: Japanese Intellectuals during the Interwar Years*, ed. J. Thomas Rimer (Princeton, NJ: Princeton University Press, 1990), 37–55.

82. Matsubara, "Meiji-matsu," 163.

83. Fujino, *Nihon fashizumu to iryō*, esp. 29–54 and 236–254.

84. Matsubara, "Minzoku yūsei" and "Chūzetsu kisei kanwa to yūsei seisaku kyōka: Yūsei hogo-hō saikō," *Shisō*, no. 886 (April 1998): 116–136.

85. See Tachi Kaoru, "Nihon no feminizumu riron: Hiratsuka Raichō ni okeru 'bosei' to feminizumu o chūshin ni," in *Onna no me de miru*, vol. 4, *Kōza joseigaku*, ed. Joseigaku kenkyūkai (Keisō shobō, 1987), 274–280. Some contemporary feminists criticize ecological feminism precisely because it is reminiscent of eugenic feminism. See for example, Suzuki Yūko, *Yokusan to teikō*, vol. 2, *Josei-shi o hiraku* (Miraisha, 1989), 42.

PART III

Gender,
Empire,
War

7 Making "Soldiers": The Imperial Army and the Japanese Man in Meiji Society and State

Theodore F. Cook, Jr.

The noted Japanese screenwriter Hirosawa Ei, thinking back to his childhood, recalled a moment in 1931, at the time of the Manchurian Incident that began the Fifteen-Year War, that seemed to capture his own youthful image of Japan's soldiers:

I remember the three soldier-boys who were billeted at our home overnight at about that time, a private first class who had a red shoulder patch with three stars, and two privates with two stars each. They were on military maneuvers. I got really excited. I was so swept up in my admiration for soldiers as a young boy. They interlaced their rifles so skillfully, making a tripod by the door. I timidly approached those Type-38 rifles and saw the chrysanthemum crests on them. "That shows they were bestowed on us by the Emperor," one of the soldiers told me.

Soldiers had a unique smell, a mixture of sweat and leather. When they removed their uniform blouses, white, crystallized maps from dried perspiration were on their khaki undershirts. I stared at them in surprise. From their sunburned faces, from smiles showing white teeth, came an explanation, "We've been marching since dawn." The next morning, still in darkness, the three soldiers snapped to attention, formally saluted my father and me, and declared loudly, "Thank you for your kindness." They left with quick steps. Through the morning mist I could hear the sounds of their unit marching off.[1]

For Hirosawa, and so many youths of his day, the soldier embodied Japan and what it meant to be a Japanese man. As visualized by a man who would go on to make films in and about war, it was an image that never left him. In it, we can see the ambiguous tensions between hard work and duty, between good humor and discipline, and the near awe of a young boy at these visitors to his world. That, as a Japanese youth, he would one day be one of the soldiers was not yet firmly established in Hirosawa's mind, perhaps, but already planted was the notion that his future was somehow bound up with these men in khaki.

To be a soldier—not a samurai warrior of the leadership caste, but a common soldier, an "every*man* in uniform"—was a central part of the conscript/soldier/reservist/veteran "life-course" that universal conscription and frequent warfare would make normative for male Japanese for much of a century. While a gender distinction in military service was certainly not new in the Meiji era (1868–1912), the extension of conscription obligation (in theory at least) to the entire able-bodied members of one gender contributed directly to the gendering of political participation and leadership; while at the same time, literary and other cultural images of soldiers emerged so that "man as soldier" came to be a representation of at least one key dimension of "the Japanese" at the beginning of the twentieth century.[2]

How the military system of Japan was conceived and constructed from the beginning of the Meiji era is a good place to observe the way gender roles were linked to the definition of the active citizen (or subject). Preparation for assuming the role of "soldier" was one of the foundations of mass education for boys, and avoidance of conscription a key variable for some in choosing to become their teachers. This helped create a notion of the rights of men tied to military service, sacrifice, and heroism. In the course of the first forty years of the history of the Imperial Army and Navy, roles essential to the support for soldiers serving in peacetime and in war were developed and assigned primarily to the female gender: raising sons to be soldiers; lamentation, sorrow, and mourning for lost soldiers; and making a place for veterans, or former soldiers, in their communities. Although implications for broadening political democracy were inherent in universal conscription, the modern virtues of manhood and citizenship did not emphasize the independent exercise of political rights. In prewar Japan, military service or other efforts for the nation did not underwrite political participation. Male suffrage remained restricted by high property qualifications until 1925, while women, despite their complementary service to the nation at home in domestic roles and in public through philanthropic and income-earning work, did not gain the vote until after the Second World War.

Meiji Japan's New Model Army

Despite a long tradition of military service and governments dominated by men from the *bushi,* or warrior, class in the centuries before the overthrow of the Tokugawa shoguns, known widely outside Japan as the "Age of the Samurai," the Meiji Emperor's new army and navy had no true antecedents in Japanese history. The Imperial Japanese Army and Navy, created in the 1870s, were new institutions entrusted with tasks and responsibilities in a domestic and international environment without parallel in Japan's history. Unlike nineteenth-century Western European armies, Japan's armed forces did not emerge slowly as part of the transformation of aristocratic governmental institutions from patterns of military organization tied to traditions of feudal obligation.

The very newness of the Imperial Japanese Army and Navy— originality and lack of encrusted tradition and impeding "norms"—is their most distinctive feature, and was so recognized at the time of their creation. Unlike the German officer-corps, which Michael Howard once observed was "fighting a desperate rearguard action against the Spirit of the Age" in the nineteenth century, Japan's new army considered itself to be the embodiment of the spirit of a new age.[3] It was a prototype for the total transformation of Japan into a nation capable of taking a place on the world stage. This spirit of transcending tradition through organization and technology required a transformation of the Japanese people, especially its men. The photograph of Japan's young monarch, clad in the Western-style uniform of a field marshal, a beard just beginning to appear on his jaw, was an image that symbolized innovation. It demonstrated a martial spirit and a desire to rid the country of the loathsome constraints of the unequal treaties forced on the country by superior Western military force in the 1850s. Young Japan was now to be portrayed not as a perfumed Mikado, but as a belligerent man arrayed in the symbols used to endow Western monarchs with emblematic competency and dynastic virility.

The Meiji government founded its military policy on a concept revolutionary for Japan—that all Japanese, of whatever class, would be called on to serve in their country's military. The imperial edict of November 28, 1872, announcing the "re-introduction" of conscription, referred to a supposed "heritage" of Japanese military service to their country.[4] That this "universal" excluded women was implicit and did not need to be spelled out. Looking back to ancient Japan—the source of so many images in early Meiji years—the edicts evoked a supposed time "when all men were soldiers." That this had never really been the case—the new institutions being created in these early days of Meiji were brand new and only vaguely similar to the militias and "armies" of earliest Japanese history and bore little resemblance to institutions in the time of the shoguns—seemed not to trouble the drafters of the ordinances and documents. What they were engaged in was inventing a tradition to justify institutions that they believed were essential to their ability to hold power and their hopes to guarantee Japan's survival. The old *bushi* (many nascent Meiji oligarchs themselves sprang from this warrior class) were portrayed as usurpers of power, and their privileges now were to be swept aside. The ordinance promised "the hereditary distinction between the soldier and the farmer will be done away."[5] Although uniting more than 250 former feudal domains behind one central government was a daunting task in itself, the problem of winning the support of the people for the notion of military service to that state would prove even more difficult. The ordinance had to present a rationale for imposing on Japanese commoners an obligation for military service not required of them for over ten centuries.

The needs of the Meiji government for internal policing and the minimal needs for coastal defense could probably have been met by a continued reliance on the hereditary military class; there were certainly enough former *bushi* in need of employment in the early 1870s. Many of the members of the warrior class had valuable experience at routine tasks with a military dimension—but adopting such a policy would not have brought foreign acknowledgment that Japan had embarked on a new course; neither would it have put the entire resources of the nation at the disposal of the new government; nor would it have removed the privilege to bear arms from a class with an ancient tradition of usurping civilian authority. Getting the broad base of the people to serve the state was an explicit objective of the new government. The conscription ordinance was presented as an "obligation" of all people—that is, men—to serve the state, in keeping with the practices of the advanced nations.

No one in the world is exempt from taxation with which the state defrays its expenditures. In this way, everyone should endeavor to repay one's country. The Occidentals call military obligation "blood tax," for it is one's repayment in life-blood to one's country. When the state suffers disaster, the people [Kokumin] cannot escape being affected. Thus, the people can ward off disaster to themselves by striving to ward off disaster to the state. And, where there is a state, there is military defense; and if there is military defense, there must be military service. It follows, therefore, that the law providing for a militia is the law of nature and not an accidental man-made law. As for the system itself, it should be made after a survey of the past and the present, and adapted to the time and circumstance.[6]

It was precisely the phrase "blood tax" that raised problems. It was anything but obvious to the mass of the Japanese public in the early years of Meiji that they owed such loyalty to any government, whether headed by a daimyo, a shogun, or an emperor. There is little evidence that anyone was seeking a "right to bear arms," unless it was those rambunctious members of the former warrior class who advocated immediate foreign military adventure—especially an invasion of Korea. The controversy over conscription, especially the possibility that the new soldiers could be sent abroad, to Korea or Taiwan, was one of the first great domestic issues to threaten to unseat the new Meiji government. And one of the major objectives of the new army's first assignment was protecting the position of the Japanese leaders who founded the new military establishment.[7]

It seemed imperative to channel Japan's development and create up-to-date military institutions capable of defending Japan against all threats, and so began the transformation of Japanese men to fit the new armed forces. The ultimate goal proved far beyond the country's resources, with the most profound effects on Japan's political, economic, and social development. Yet, that course won lavish praise from the Western nations, and not only from those like the French who were paid by the new government to train their troops.[8] Emory Upton, an American army officer visiting Japan in 1875, liked what he saw even at that early date. "The sudden transition of Japan from ancient to mod-

ern civilization, which will ever be the marvel of history, is nowhere
more conspicuous than in the army."[9] The one area in which he felt it
necessary to criticize the Japanese troops was where they seemed to
have "fallen into the swinging of arms and slovenliness of marching,
once so admired in the French army, but so utterly in contrast to the
precision and steadiness of the English and German soldiers." That fact
was not trivial to the Civil War veteran, because Upton believed precision was the secret to success in modern war: "The recent modifications in tactics require increased individuality among the men, and this
individuality, it has been shown by experience, can only be developed
by rigid discipline and steadiness when in ranks."

Men in uniform, marching in line during drill, under iron discipline,
were men being prepared for their new role in modern war. Whether a
new masculinity was in Upton's mind or not is difficult to say, but there
is no doubt that he saw the once "effeminate" Japan becoming a power
to be reckoned with. In marked contrast to China, which he visited after Japan, Upton said Japan displayed all the signs of a nation on the
rise, and he credited this to the Japanese government, although Japan's
new leaders had only just begun to implement ideas and ideals of conscription as they understood them. For Upton, at least, the prognoses
for Japan were excellent. "Already," he wrote, "she has reaped the reward of her foresight. The foundations of her government . . . are set-
tling down to the rock; insurrections, before ripening into rebellion,
have been promptly stamped out." (The Satsuma Rebellion of 1877 was
still ahead.) Moreover, "her success in Formosa and Corea give evidence that Japan, no longer contented with progress at home, is destined to play an important part in the history of the world."[10]

Soldiers and the New State

Advocates of conscription saw universal military service as a means
to effect dramatic change in society as a whole. Yamagata Aritomo
(1838–1922), who would come to be most responsible for the development of Japan's military institutions, argued in favor of the adoption
of a conscript army and the integration of the new government's military requirements with the needs of the people for an education. He
wrote in 1872:

If boys enter grammar school at six, middle school at thirteen, and graduate at nineteen, after which from their twentieth year, they spend a few years as soldiers, in the end all will become soldiers and no one will be without education. In due course, the nation will become a great civil and military university.[11]

Not only was the military development of Japan endorsed enthusiastically, but the writings and speeches of civil servants such as Nishi Amane (1829–1897), who was charged with many of the nuts and bolts tasks of military administration of the early Meiji army, reveal a belief that struggle and warfare were both essential in the process of creating civilization.[12] This interpretation of history was shared by many in the "Civilization and Enlightenment" era in the 1870s when the progress of Japan was seen as closely linked to the adoption of foreign ways and practices. Addressing an audience interested in military affairs at the end of the 1870s, Nishi claimed that since Commodore Matthew C. Perry sailed his squadron of American naval ships into Edo Bay in 1853 to present the Tokugawa shogun with demands that Japan be opened to trade and commerce, events "demonstrate that neither international law nor treaties of amity are sufficient to protect Japan's national interests . . . that which preserves our independence is our army and navy."[13] If Japan did not strengthen its military forces, Nishi foresaw a bankrupt country—its ports reduced to sites for slave auctions—"suffering the fate of Poland." [14] In Nishi's opinion, economic development should not take precedence over establishing a powerful military force. "Strengthen the army" was *just as* essential as "enrich the country" in the rich country, strong army (*Fukoku kyōhei*) prescription for national development.[15]

There is little doubt that Meiji leaders faced a real foreign threat. The humiliation of treaty ports, unequal treaties, the close proximity of the Western exploitation of China, and the clear superiority of European military science had to be faced every day. Yet, it did not necessarily follow that the kind of military needed to meet that threat was a national conscript army. This was one of the great paradoxes for the Meiji government. Soldiers were vital for a state to survive, to prevent a coup from abroad or an easy overthrow by rebellion. Soldiers were also critical symbols of a people's will and capacity to maintain their independence. But how could a poor country afford soldiers?

Nishi Amane drew on his own personal and institutional perspective to formulate the issue: *If* "War preparations do not constitute something to be employed after blood has flowed and corpses have piled up," *but* rather had their effect "before the sound of rifles is heard or the flash of gunpowder is seen," *then* a country wishing to maintain an army had to devote itself to their preparation long before they were needed. Nishi saw it "in the course of events" that "it is our fate today to grasp the plow with the right hand and the rifle with the left. . . . Though we be farmers, artisans, or tradesmen, we must also be soldiers." While Nishi saw distinctions between civilian and military society, it does not appear that he gave much weight to what individual Japanese may have thought about becoming soldiers.[16]

In 1880, Toyama Shōichi (1848–1900) wrote a small book titled *Managing the Perplexity of Popular Rights,* in which he declared:

The conscription ordinance is something that makes parents separate from their beloved children and little women separate from their beloved men. Unless a person who tries to stay in a steady job pays 270 yen [the fee for exemption from conscription], he cannot avoid entering the military.[17]

Despite conscription's terrible impact on the common man's home and family, Toyama felt his colleagues who were among advocates of People's Rights were mistaken in their belief that conscription was necessarily the enemy of eventual achievement of rights by the people: "The conscription system," he asserted, "should be the thing most hated by those who consider it too early for the people to elect a parliament."[18] Showing an extraordinary appreciation of the power conscription *might* play in the creation of popular society, Toyama's logic built on the very concerns and interests most cherished by Japanese families in the early years of the conscription system. At first, Toyama suggested, farmers' sons—the conscripts—resented being forced into the army,

but once they entered the barracks and mingled with many other soldiers, devoted themselves day and night to military matters, walked around the city streets in the company of others during their off-duty hours, became enamored of the maids working in public baths, became acquainted with the newly established archery booths, developed a taste for *shamonabe,* learned to dance the *kappore,* and day by day learned the ways of the city, their memories of their homes gradually dimmed.[19]

More than anything else, this was the core of rural apprehension—the loss of a son for years in a far-off military garrison. The erstwhile village boy might see his home less favorably, or as Toyama put it, "A woman, whom he thought 'the beauty,' . . . whom he loved, and with whom he had talked about becoming husband and wife, now seems ugly . . . " while men "who have shot their guns at Saigo Takamori at Shiroyama [i.e., fought for the government side against the rebels in 1877] . . . cannot go back to carrying night soil."[20]

Perhaps in expectant optimism, Toyama predicted that the experience altered the conscript soldier's whole political outlook: "Those who were illiterate when they left their homes learned to read and write while in the service, and not a few read newspapers like the *Chōya* and *Hōchi*, which advocate People's Rights, and radical magazines like *Fusō shinshi* and *Kinji hyōron*." But it was not only a man's political awareness that was piqued. Even more critically, once a soldier had experienced military life he became unfit for the life he had led before going in the service:

When they finish their period of enlistment and return to their homes, their minds are no longer those of the clodhopper they had been a few years ago. They can no longer bear to collect night soil and carry honey buckets on their shoulders. But rice does not descend from heaven, and they cannot avoid collecting night soil, and carrying honey buckets. For this reason, there are few who accept their lot and who are satisfied.[21]

Back in the village—at least in Toyama Shōichi's fantasy—this man, with his military background and newfound confidence, would be in no mood to accept things as they were, or as he put it, "A man who has urinated by the side of the [city] street [while a soldier] and beaten up a policeman who criticized him for it, . . . is not the same man who once viewed prefectural officials as demi-gods."[22] The result would be that when the conscript returned to his village, "It is rare for him not to assert People's Rights and advocate liberalism. There, it is rare [for such a man] not to wish to lead bamboo spear and flag bearers, or to be like Ōshio Heihachirō."[23] In time, Toyama warned, the strength of such men "will reach a level to be feared. This is what should most concern politicians who believe it is too early for a popularly elected legislature."[24] To institute universal military service, in Toyama's view, was to sanction the granting of People's Rights, the essential aim of the "Freedom and People's Rights Movement" that was so powerful a force in the Meiji era from 1874 until the first general election under the new Constitution in 1890.[25] It was also, by unspoken implication, to take the young male of the village into a new world, separate from that of his nonconscripted brothers and completely divorced from that of girls and women. It would provide him not only with the idea of his rights in a world beyond the village, but also afford him a means to see that they were not withheld from him. To conscript a man was necessarily to empower him.

Despite the grandiose plans, the ideal of "universality" was not actually implemented in the years when dreams and fears were at the core of discussions on popular rights. Indeed, actual numbers would seem to demonstrate that, in practice, those who believed service in the army would be a way to foster either People's Rights or military competence— let alone national education and transformation—were grossly exaggerating actual effects. Yet, it must also be noted that such advocates were usually exercising their imaginations on a longer time frame than next year's budget. Universal service foundered on the rocks of the government's economic weakness and a realization that, for practical reasons, the army could not embrace the entire male population. The Imperial Army itself was small; it had a peacetime footing of only some 33,000 men on the eve of the Satsuma Rebellion. Active-duty call-ups were only a small share of the total men eligible to serve. Instead of a *levée en masse*, Japanese conscription merely nibbled around the edges of the manpower pool. In 1888, just before a major reform of the regulations took effect, of 427,846 military-age males in a population of 39,607,224, the government conscripted only 20,115 eligible men for active duty that year, or just 4.7 percent. The next year, conscripts inched over 5 percent. It wasn't until after the Sino-Japanese War of 1894–1895, when the number of divisions in Japan's regular army was doubled, that actual conscripts exceeded 10 percent of men eligible for conscription.[26]

Conscripts in the early Meiji era were hardly a representative cross section of the New Japan's manpower. In fact, they more closely resembled the press-gang collected soldiers who had once served the British crown than the "embodiment of the nation" touted in idealized Prussian or French descriptions of a "nation in arms."[27] Their educational level was abysmally low, and the exemptions incorporated in the

conscription law itself excluded many who would have held the strongest economic positions in the countryside—first sons, heirs, important
personages, those who could purchase exemption—so they were also
the poorest of the poor in the villages.[28] For example, most soldiers
taken into the army in 1884 came from the countryside, as best as can
be determined from the generalized data official records provide. In
1884, of the 59,033 newly entering soldiers, agriculture was the occupation of 46,758, or 79.2 percent. No breakdown by type of agriculture—
tenant farmer, owner-cultivator, laborer—appears in the records, and,
unfortunately, there is no way to easily make such determinations.[29] In
1891, two years after the new conscription ordinance had extended service and limited many exemptions, nearly 27 percent of all new enlistees
were illiterate, while another 34 percent were rated as capable of only
limited reading and calculation. Graduates of elementary school and
those who tested as equivalent to elementary school graduates comprised only about 28 percent. Only 11 percent tested at the level of
higher elementary school.[30] Even at the end of Meiji, after the Russo-
Japanese War, and on the eve of the First World War, only 3.82 percent
of first-class conscripts were classified above the middle school grade
educational level in 1909. This increased to only 4.5 percent in 1910.[31]

In the years before the Sino-Japanese War broke out in 1894, the
army certainly did become an agent for the introduction of many West-
ern-oriented technical and social developments.[32] To become a soldier
meant to be measured by height, by weight, and by common characteristics and standards. This system of physical ratings established by the
military authorities put men into categories that would determine their
military careers. Was a man Class A or Class B? Was he physically fit,
did he have a serious physical flaw? Was he in any way "defective," or
did he differentiate from the norm? The ratings influenced their personal lives as well, as the exam provided data to the "folks back
home."[33] A man passed through the physical was certified healthy by
his government. He was, at least at the moment he took the enlistment
exam, free of loathsome skin conditions and dreaded diseases such as
tuberculosis or venereal disease.

If it is true, as some scholars of the military and society suggest, that
the soldier in developing countries is in some crucial ways a modernized man, then it is important to understand what everyday dimensions

of "modernity" he encounters.[34] For the first time, in early Meiji, conscripted villagers were removed from their land or small towns, were grouped together, thrown into a world that few could have imagined. Beds, trousers, and shoes were some of the things that were new to them, as were beer, cigarettes, bread, and in some cases, newspapers. The spread of all these owed much to the conscript's time with the regimental colors. A nationwide telegraph system and the fostering of heavy industry, and such supporting industries as canning, wool spinning, and boot making were all tied directly to the new military's needs.[35] Military budgets, military settlements in Hokkaidō, and concerns for military morale all loomed larger and larger. In many respects, social habits such as wearing trousers and shoes, drinking beer, smoking cigarettes, eating military meals incorporating meat, were spread by military service among conscripts, creating new social and habitual separations between genders, and giving new "masculine" behaviors currency.

Of course, in the end, a few years in the army did not turn every son of the countryside into a man who felt himself capable of emulating Ōshio Heihachirō in leading a rebellion. The thought that it *might* did not elude Japan's leaders, however. Arguments ensued over the benefits, dangers, and potential merits of taking men of all classes into the army. Such a debate is familiar to any student of the history of European conscription. In France, for example, the armed masses were to be feared, especially if they were without the control of a strong central authority.[36] Military service might be exacted as the natural price of citizenship, but it was deemed wise not to excessively tax the sensibilities or careers of those most essential to the maintenance of bourgeois order, whether from love of the Republic, or concern for stability. In Germany, there were many who feared that arms in the hands of reservists, led by reserve officers of bourgeois background and radical tendencies, could even lead to revolution.[37] Concern among contemporaries that service in the Prussian forces was so harsh that it would turn even the most patriotic German against his Kaiser, led to efforts to temper the severity of discipline. As military service became more universal and civilian reserve call-up for annual maneuvers and training exercises became a more regular feature of the German man's life, the German army adjusted to accommodate its civilian officers, albeit reluctantly.[38] John

Gooch has argued that in Italy the followers of Garibaldi posed a threat in the development of the Italian monarchy's military "tradition," and in the 1860s it was feared that popular enthusiasm, expressed in volunteers for the army, could lead to pressure to expand the electorate, then standing at only 2 percent.[39] Moreover, the Italian conscription system was used to weld formerly disparate kingdoms and governments into one nation by avoiding district service (i.e., keeping men of a region together for both mobilization and training) as practiced in Germany.[40]

The issue of honor and of duty to country, asserted in the early Meiji years as the natural "re-establishment of tradition," was increasingly personalized in Japan in the 1880s. The military institutions indoctrinated recruits with the belief that their military service was to their emperor first. *The Imperial Precepts for Soldiers and Sailors*, issued in 1882, incorporated these notions directly, of course, but the question of who would control His Imperial Majesty's government—an oligarchy or an elected assembly—was still open to debate in those years. While the conscious identification of military service and social change motivated much of early Meiji military policy, conservatives also wanted to exploit the principle of military service to advance their notion of the imperial ideology. Placing the army above politics, and tied directly to the "Throne," as enshrined in the German Constitution and practiced by Bismarck, seemed increasingly preferable in their eyes to a politicized armed citizenry.[41]

A central question of what the army would be used for remained open for a long time. While the Japanese army might teach discipline, order, respect for authority, punctuality, and patriotism, as armies were purported to do in Europe, it was not absolutely clear what the army itself was intended to accomplish in the strictly military field. Was it an army of defense of the people, or even a force of last resort in the case of invasion, or was it an instrument of the state, to be wielded in Clausewitzian fashion by Japanese statesmen? As we have seen, Nishi Amane offered a view readily accepted by most government authorities, but the proponents of People's Rights, who were working to encourage more popular participation in early Meiji government, seem to have been reluctant to conclude that conscription and a standing army were linked. The state's notion of "manhood," in which a soldier was part of a military institution created by and embodying the state, at the command of the emperor, was quite different from the People's Rights position that a citizen's manhood was confirmed by rights derived from his individual participation in the vital institutions of the state, especially through military service.

An editorial published under the name "Yoshida Tata" in the *Chōya* newspaper, appearing March 22, 1873, advocated the abolition of the *Rikugun jōbihei*, the standing army of that day. While acknowledging that there might be a need for a standing navy and an Imperial Guard, he argued that the peacetime army should be voluntary: "A small nation's military system should avoid a standing army and should have an army only for wartime." He maintained that the economic costs of the military were simply too great and that Japan should abolish the peacetime standing army and create a system where everyone was in the army in wartime.[42] An editorial writer in the same paper argued in 1879 that the main body of the military should be volunteers, and that the country should resort to conscription only if there was a shortage of soldiers. Voluntary service was declared to be the best system, since "that sense of duty needed for military service was lacking in Japan." The editorial writer even maintained that the best use of people was to employ them in the fields where they most want to be of service and not to force men to serve in the military against their will.

Since the work of the military is different from that of other people, the people seek to avoid it, looking for hundreds of exemptions and ways out. Therefore those who enter the military should be drawn to military affairs by their own nature and should want to devote themselves to military matters. . . . In this way one achieves a strong soldiery. . . . This helps create the vitality of the state.[43]

This was a terrible indictment of the qualities of Japanese men and of the very notion of demonstrating patriotism through military service; it had the potential to serve as a clarion call to others to bring about a transformation of spirit. It also expressed the counterargument to conscript service by partially supporting the old samurai notion of a dedicated class of warriors and imparting to them the highest motivations of service.

A major problem for advocates of Freedom and People's Rights in the military sphere was their inability to differentiate clearly between the army capable of aggression abroad and the army dedicated to national defense.[44] Even Nishi Amane had difficulty chartering a course—for "a country the size of Japan"—between the extremes of adventurism ("Russianism" as he called it) and what he considered its opposite, "Ryūkyūism," which he saw as the pacifism of the people and government of Okinawa when Japan had just incorporated that nominally independent Kingdom—long dominated by outside forces—into the Japanese empire. Indeed, the military conceptions of People's Rights advocates such as Nakae Chōmin (1847–1901) and Fukuzawa Yukichi (1835–1901) drew extensively on the French literature on conscription that emphasized a linkage between universal military service and popular, even universal, manhood suffrage. The "right to serve" in the military was a corollary to the notion of a right to play a part in the process by which that service was exacted and the causes for which service was required.

Nakae Chōmin's study of the militia, *Dochakuhei ron,* advocated the complete adoption of a militia rather than a conscript army (*chōheisei*) system. His proposal is almost unique among arguments at the time. Most advocates of People's Rights felt that the process of providing exemptions from service stood in the way of creating a people's army (*kokumingun*), or what was called the "nationalization of the military."[45] The People's Rights' faction did not really differentiate between a people's army to defend the civil revolution and the motherland and the conscript army used for foreign action.[46] Appearing in *Shinonome shinbun* between May 16 and May 18, 1888, the essay shows that although Chōmin could not justify the abolition of military forces in light of the international situation at large, he did advocate the elimination of the standing army and its replacement with a militia. To him that would be the true completion of the effort to create a nation-in-arms:

It is often said that a standing army is the People's duty, but in reality, the sons of those who have rank, those who have money, do not serve. Those who bleed in the face of the enemy are the sons and brothers of the common people. Can we call this "equal duty"? Gathering several tens of thousands of animals together, feeding them in camps, and spending tax money paid for by the people's hard labor. . . . Can we say that is economical?[47]

Nakae Chōmin envisioned a military experience very different from Yamagata Aritomo's notion of a "civil and military university" cited earlier. Chōmin's farmers would put aside their tools and scholars would lay down their books on training days. They would go forth to learn how to shoot rifles and exercise in the techniques of defending the nation. Then they would return home to resume their everyday work after a few days. Through this process, Nakae Chōmin believed, "all men will achieve a love of nation and learn that the smell of gunpowder is not necessarily loathsome. . . . This is close to the principle of a popular ethic of equality." He also asked a question vital in those financially difficult times for Meiji Japan: "Isn't it also close to the principle of economics?"[48]

Fukuzawa was particularly concerned with "fairness" in conscription. He advocated a special military service tax to be levied on those exempted from service. The money would then be paid as compensation, in order to equalize the financial and physical burden on those unfortunate enough to be caught in the web of conscription.[49] At the same time, Fukuzawa was willing to praise the law of December 28, 1883, that terminated many of the exemptions and deferrals that had been available under the early conscription laws. But he raised a crucial point army men had been reluctant to address: "The reason why people dislike conscript service is not necessarily because it is hard labor, and not necessarily out of a fear of death or injury in the event of war. The reason they do not find conscription pleasant is their dislike of base or lowly service. Up to this point members of the upper social classes have avoided active-duty service, while the poor, lowly people have gone on active duty."[50] To Fukuzawa, further conscription revision also seemed a good opportunity for the upper class, the rich, and the noble to aid the military:[51] "When sons and brothers of good families go into the military," he confidently predicted, "military service will become honored service and will encourage the people to serve."[52]

These ideas were still part of a current of thought that considered it important for individuals to share the burden of military service equally. Few questioned whether there should be military service of any kind. Nakae Chōmin did call for a purely defensive military, it is true, but his was almost a solitary voice. If the issue of the military relationship between the state and the male citizen was subject to intense debate in France, it can hardly be surprising that it was equally up in the air in Japan, where the realities of war were far less clearly ingrained in the popular consciousness, and where threats to national security seemed at least as much economic and political as they did military. Efforts to keep discussion of military service founded on the premise that Japan's very existence was linked to the status of the army and navy continued to consume military figures as they sought justification for their ever-growing demands on scarce state resources. In 1882, referring to Russia indirectly as a threat, Yamagata warned that Japan needed to become a "veritable floating fortress"; it was clear that Japan's military policy was still tied to the need to insure that the central government's authority ran "to all corners of the state *in the spirit of steadfast valor*" (emphasis added), to assure that Japan would not "again" be threatened from "nations in the immediate vicinity."[53] Making Japanese both subjects to the state and capable of defending it were central goals, but these goals required putting the manpower of the state at the army's disposal.

War and Soldiers

To many observers, foreign and domestic, the Sino-Japanese War confirmed the wisdom of the Meiji elite and displayed to the world that Japan was a nation ready to stride the stage as a leading actor. It was the Japanese people's enthusiasm for the war that was the most obvious sign of Japan's elevation to the jingoism and aggressive fervor, which seem to have been so characteristic of full membership in the first rank of nations.[54] The Chinese enemy was denigrated; cries for Chinese blood abounded. Vivid images in the colorful *nishikie* woodblock prints, which flooded Tokyo and brought the action of the war to the streets and into the parlors of the people, showed ordered, disciplined, immensely brave and noble Japanese forces sending the unruly Qing rabble scurrying. Toyama Shōichi, the erstwhile Popular Rights advocate quoted above, became a member of the House of Peers in 1890. (He would go on to become president of Imperial University in Tokyo.) Toyama claimed to have written one of the more popular ditties of the war and expressed his delight that "at last the nation had come to recognize the importance of war songs." According to Donald Keene, Toyama's song, "Advance Men of Japan" ("Yuke Nihon danji"), "contains some of the most sensational anti-Chinese sentiments [seen in the Sino-Japanese War]. He calls the Chinese 'evil monsters,' 'burglars,' 'wolves,' 'the enemy of our wives, the enemy of our sisters and daughters,' and urges that 'the pure blood of the divine land not be defiled by the beasts of the enemy country.'"[55]

As Keene noted in a characteristically understated way, "These are rather strong views for a man who four years earlier had considered Chinese and Japanese to be 'elder and younger brothers.'"[56] Those lyrics also construct Japanese masculinity around dislike of monstrous foreigners and the defense of Japanese women and children.

At the same time, new images of Japan and the Japanese soldier were pressed forward in the wild competition to capture the country's imagination. Serial publications like Tokutomi Roka's (1868–1927) *Dream Tale of the Sino-Japanese War* (*Nisshin sensō yumemonogatari*) started up in the newspaper *Yomiuri shinbun* in September 1894, only a month after war was declared. It was soon followed by Izumi Kyōka's (1873–1939) *Reserve Soldier* (*Yobihei*). Both reached large audiences. At first, the Japanese officer leading his men into battle seemed the new Heroic Image, but very quickly it was the Japanese enlisted men who were made darlings of the press, the new popular theater, and the printmakers. Few attracted the attention of the world more than "Shirakami Genjirō, Bugler in the Line," glorified in Classical Chinese, modern Japanese poetry, and even in the English verse crafted by Sir Edward Arnold in London in November 1894. Although the supposed bugler Shirakami turned out not to have been the man poets made him out to be, and was replaced in the textbooks of generations of Japanese schoolchildren by Kiguchi Kohei ("a first-class private of identical attributes" in Donald Keene's memorable phrase), the position of the lowly private as hero, suffering to do his duty with all the loyalty and devotion of a classical warrior, giving no thought to self or glory, was firmly established in the popular mind.[57]

Victories, national unity, heroism, and duty were the images that the war conveyed, and these are often cited to show the transformation of Japan's *mentalité*.[58] Yet of about 240,000 men deployed to the theater of war, 13,488 men died in the war with China, most from disease. These "blood taxes," and the additional costs of the bloody expedition to newly won Taiwan after the Treaty of Shimonoseki, were the first down payments on Manchuria.[59] Such unpleasantness as a massacre of prisoners and civilians in Port Arthur, after the city was captured in November, did little to impede the general acclaim that settled on Japanese arms in the Western press, especially in the Anglo-Saxon world.[60] In triumphing over China, Japan had gone far toward winning European recognition of their "special nature" among Asian peoples.

Confidence also rose in the Japanese military.[61] Both the West's acclaim and the confidence in the Japanese military were clear in a draft presented to the General Staff Headquarters in September 1895 that including the warning, "As a result of our victory over China, the Powers have focused their sights on the East, and the day of reckoning for the East is rapidly moving closer."[62] The country embarked on a major expansion of its army and navy. Deciding how to pay for it led to great governmental and Diet controversy.[63] Less open discussion occurred about whether the far larger slice of Japanese manpower to fill these new divisions should be able to determine for themselves, through their elected representatives, their country's course.

The "Imperial Man" (*Teikoku danshi*): Toward "A Nation Dressed in Arms"

How was the expanded army to be manned? Would it be possible to handle the greater demands that larger annual conscript classes would place on the army itself in peacetime? Such questions were at the heart of a genre of widely circulated publications aimed at potential soldiers, reservists, and their families. These publications allow us a glimpse into the army's evolving views of the emerging place of soldiers in Meiji society in the critical years of transition between the end of the war with China in 1895 and the outbreak of war with Russia in 1904.

An editorial in *Military Affairs Magazine* (*Heiji zasshi*) in 1896 took umbrage at the popular propensity to indulge in euphoria over Japan's victory over China, but thought the people should simultaneously rush to support the government's Diet requests for huge increases in military expenditures in the wake of the Sino-Japanese War and the Triple Intervention by France, Germany, and Russia, which had "robbed" Japan of the Liaodong Peninsula. "Military armaments are," the editorial proclaimed, "a matter of concern for the people, and they are a responsibility that must be shouldered by the whole people," and went on to say:

Therefore, the soldier is representative of the whole people, and the duties of the nation are the duties of the soldier. The soldier's responsibility is the state's responsibility, but today, the honor of the soldier is not matched by the honor of the nation.

The magazine deeply deplored this situation and declared, "The soldier must bear a heavy responsibility, but the people do not have the will. Our people's military thought is shriveling."[64]

Addressing the Dai Nippon kyōikukai, an association of school-teachers from across Japan, meeting in Tokyo in 1897, Lieutenant Colonel Tōjō Eikyō (1855–1913) reminded his audience:

As you are well aware, the merits and demerits of the People are directly related to the values of the army, and the values of the army are closely related to [the values of] the state. Thus, the training of the nation is in your hands . . . educators of the nation. You, who are in charge of the children younger than middle school, are the mothers who produce the army. Of course, I know every Kokumin [person] you train does not become a military man, . . . but from the military's point of view, you are the mothers who bear the army.[65]

Warming to his theme, Colonel Tōjō filled the circle opened by Yamagata Aritomo in 1872 by a simple formulation:

The training of the people . . . is like the education of a preparatory school for the school we call the army. Therefore, it is vital that you educators of the people know the educational methods used by the army, which is the main school. It is the duty of the preparatory school to educate [the people] in such a way that they can be educated easily when they arrive at this main school.

Yet the army fell short of Colonel Tōjō's ideal in 1897, since, as he said, "The raw material of the military"—the Japanese people—were lacking "orderly thought." That "orderliness" was an essential element of the discipline he wished to instill. "I would not say that they are the worst in the world. . . . But they are quite inferior to the people of the European Great Powers." Indeed, in his eyes, the Japanese, as a people, demonstrated an array of bad habits—tardiness, bringing horse-pulled carts where forbidden, and scribbling graffiti—offenses proven by the fact that notice boards had to be put up to warn against such behavior. "These are minute things," he said, "but they indicate that the people do not have discipline."[66]

This lack of discipline was potentially ruinous for the army, Colonel Tōjō asserted: "If you gather men who have been raised without discipline, then real military discipline cannot be created." Of such things is defeat born, he argued. "As Napoleon said, the strength of an army is the product of its strength in soldiers and speed." Although invoking the French emperor first, Tōjō had examples closer to hand in mind: "Whoever utilizes time effectively, wins. The defeat of China in 1894–95 was, I think, a result of the Qing's inability to use time well. They waited until our army marched on them and surrounded them. . . . The Japanese people [remain] very lax about time in their minds and I can state clearly that the Japanese people are not [yet] suited to war."[67] The only solution seemed to be a militarization of the entire society to ensure that the individual recruit received the required discipline *before* he was trained as a soldier. Here we may see how "social planning" and education were directly linked to military training and war-fighting capability in the pre-1914 era.

The Sino-Japanese War, and the warlike atmosphere of challenge that proceeded from the war, were buttressed by strong institutional support and effort and produced some positive effects, or so some officers thought in retrospect: "The military thinking of the Imperial People [*Teikoku kokumin*] has made great progress since operations in China," declared Army Infantry First Lieutenant Numano Yoshio in 1898. "I was very impressed by what I observed of the new soldiers of Meiji 29 [1896] on the day they entered the service, in their language, their behavior and their appearance." In comparison with earlier conscript classes he had seen—where more than half would have come in with their hair long and three or four out of ten might have been dressed in wild or unusual clothes—virtually all turned out in what the lieutenant considered the proper way. "Some even try to look like military men—striking military postures—and others seem to understand what military life is about. Their manner toward their superiors was correct and their language under control. I was deeply moved by that."[68]

Changes were observable in the country at large as well. Numano praised the men's communities, as villages and hamlets celebrated the departure of new soldiers with honors and prayers for their futures, accompanied by the encouragement and support of elementary schoolteachers and their students. The lieutenant wrote that the soldiers could feel the trust of the *Kokumin*, which strengthened their will to devote themselves to the heavy responsibilities of the state. "Thus, they understand that to avoid call-up is a shame and know that wearing a sword is the privilege of each Man of the Empire [*Teikoku danshi*]."[69] At last, Fukuzawa's prediction seemed to have come true. *Danshi* was now defined as imperial and "male." At the same time, the male was now also called a *danshi*. I would agree with Greg Pflugfelder who suggested that the whole notion of *danshi*, this category of male gender, does not really come into existence before the emergence of institutional contexts like the army and schools. In Edo-period institutions, the male was not a unified subject, but rather was fractured by class and age. In early Meiji, this fracturing continued with such things as the exemption from conscription made for eldest sons of families and the possibility of purchasing an exemption. Fractures within the category of maleness came to be institutionalized, and the fracture became less pronounced over time. Thus, the army played a vital role in the birth of the category of "male."

How had this situation come about? Lieutenant Numano asserted that an answer was to be found in the efforts made at educating the Japanese people, as he retold the oft-repeated story about the comment made by Chief of the Prussian General Staff Helmuth von Moltke when he entered Paris in the war of 1870–1871. The Prussian commander, it was said, attributed the defeat of France not to French arms, but to their textbooks, while "the power that led Germany to victory was not the power of the officers, rather it was the power of elementary schoolteachers." Lieutenant Numano declared that now Japan "is a nation where arms [*bu*] are respected and is a nation of universal conscription. Whether [one is a] military man or not, there should only be one center."[70] It was clear to him where this center lay. Quoting the Tokyo Prefectural Educational Association, he said, "'Teachers are the font of patriotism, and Japanese teachers are the core.'"[71] "As in Sparta and at Cambridge University," military-style sports build character, and "Military-style training arms the nation and leads them to become a nation dressed in arms [*busō teki kokumin*]." Such achievements have taken time, the lieutenant reported: "In the summer of 1887 the magazine *Kyōiku jiron* criticized military-style drill by normal school students, I am sorry to say, but today military thought has risen and is heading toward [creating] a nation with [truly] universal conscription. I am very pleased by that."[72]

Transformation of Japanese men into perfect conscripts and soldiers was not yet complete. The factors that Colonel Tōjō saw as proof that

Japanese society lacked discipline posed major challenges for internal military administration. The varied experiences of the men drafted into the annual conscript classes—their behavior in the ranks and their run-ins with the locals of the garrison towns—seemed a throwback to the problems that Toyama Shōichi had perhaps been hoping would develop twenty years earlier. For one thing, soldiers taken into the regiments bombarded their families back home with requests for money. *Finances of Privates in Barracks* (*Zai'eikan heisotsu no hiyō*), published in August 1901 in the city of Sendai, tried to address this difficulty by presenting purportedly differing views on the issue of whether families should answer their loved one's pleas. A "Guard Battalion Commander" wrote that although the conscripts themselves did not mind serving, many of the parents of his new soldiers complained bitterly. He cautioned delicately against supplementing the men's pay, since "Newly inducted soldiers are sincere and innocent but when they come to towns, what they hear and see is quite different from what they have known before and their desires are stimulated." A "Second Lieutenant Aoto" warned that when parents or brothers of privates sent money they were "leading them to delinquency," by which he meant the *furyō machi*, the "pleasure quarters" of the town.[73]

While Japan still did not approach France or Germany in the share of the population conscripted or trained, the attention of the military bureaucracy did confront enormous social difficulties as the annual intake of conscripts grew to meet the ever-increasing requirements for manpower. To take just one example, the Army Medical Department reported to the Army Ministry its efforts in coping with the problems caused by venereal diseases associated with the red-light districts that ringed Japan's military cantonments.[74] While noting that Japan's rate of 64.12 cases per 1,000 men in the Imperial Army (6.412 percent) in 1897 was not as appalling as the British Army's 139.7 cases per 1,000 (13.97 percent), or Italy's 90.10 per 1,000 (9.01 percent), Japan still ranked third highest among ten countries for which statistics were published.[75] Contracting sexually transmitted diseases after conscription was a threat to the bodies of men who had now been entrusted to the state and became a matter of great concern for all in the army who cared about preserving and training a healthy instrument of state policy.

Back in 1884, Fukuzawa Yukichi had written that people looked down on the military and despised military service because of the status of military men. The authors of *Requirements for an Infantryman* (*Hohei suchi*)—a 1903 privately printed "review manual" for the man about to be called into the service or facing recall with the reserves—proudly asserted that "The military man now belongs to the premier class of society, bearing the heavy responsibility of the military man, wearing the same insignia on his uniform as the Great Field Marshal Emperor, and bearing the colors of regiment *X*."

Emphasis on the connection with the emperor—the very heart of internal army and navy education, especially since the publication of *Imperial Precepts for Soldiers and Sailors* in 1882—was tempered by anxiety lest the vaunted soldier be contaminated by the society outside the army. Despite two decades of incantation of the precepts, the internal military regulations were just as zealously presented. Judging from what army leaders thought it essential to remind infantrymen to obey, the rules must have been flaunted in 1903 just as frequently as they had been in earlier days.[76] If Toyama Shōichi back in 1880 had envisioned an army of reading, swaggering, rebellious soldiers discovering their citizenship in camp and returning home changed men, ready to lead rebellions for their rights, a soldier who heeded the lessons of *Requirements for an Infantryman* less than two decades later would be a man isolated from "the civilian outsiders," living a minutely regulated life, cut off from books and newspapers. There would be no radical *Shoya* newspaper proclaiming popular rights to that model soldier. Reality seemed to see the soldier as seeking to escape the constraints of the barracks in a realm of sanctioned activities approved, or at least tolerated, by both the army and the sponsoring civilian communities.

Nonetheless, male discipline before and after induction had improved, the stature of military service, conscripts, and veterans had risen, and army values had begun to infuse the educational system during the Meiji era. As Kathleen Uno writes in this volume, when the Ministry of Education created a separate track in secondary education for girls, with an emphasis on domestic training of future wives and mothers for the sake of the nation, that institution "intervened conspicuously in the process of gender construction." For men, military service, a calling long seen as an upper-class masculine preserve, had by the end of the century become a rite of passage for non-elite young Japanese men, especially the strongest boys from the countryside, and was supported by a system of military drill and preliminary training at school that expanded during the next four decades.

Conclusion

The Japanese soldier came close to achieving acceptance as a comrade-in-arms of Western soldiers during Japan's first joint operations with Occidentals during the North China Incident of 1900, better known as "the Boxer Rebellion." It took the Anglo-Japanese Alliance of 1902 and the Russo-Japanese War to bring Japan to the same plateau as Western nations, though it is unlikely that Western officers ever accepted their Japanese counterparts as their social, not-to-say, "racial" equals. Sir Ian Hamilton (1853–1947) considered the Japanese infantry he saw in Manchuria during the Russo-Japanese War to be the finest non-British infantry in the world: "This Japanese army shows conscription at its best—a comparatively small number, picked out of several hundreds of thousands for physical fitness and aptitude at certain necessary trades. The army is the cream of the nation." Hamilton then completed his thought ironically, quoting the then popular ditty, "How different from us, Miss Beale and Miss Buss," thereby putting Japan's soldiers on a level above Britain's own.[77]

The Japanese army overcame the Russian defense of Port Arthur in a bitter siege and after the huge land battles culminating in Mukden in 1905. Japan survived its first encounter with a Great Power, but at terrible cost. According to the army's medical service, 46,423 men were classified as war dead (*senshi*), and 153,623 were wounded.[78] The horror of the fighting was captured in Sakurai Tadayoshi's memoir *Nikudan*, translated and published in 1912 as *Human Bullets: A Soldier's Story of Port Arthur*, and was closer than Hamilton's memoir to an actual picture of modern war. *Nikudan* also seemed to feed an adoration of the "spirit of the offensive," abroad no less than in Japan.[79] The myth of Japan's triumph over enemy numerical superiority through *Yamato damashii*—the indomitable spirit of the Japanese race—was born from the bodies sacrificed at Port Arthur.

The idea that soldiers should go to the slaughter on command was not universally accepted in Japan, of course. The oft-quoted poem by Yosano Akiko (1878–1942), addressed to her brother in the army, seems today an example of the unwavering spirit of one woman against the militarism of her age:

> O no, my brother; no, you must not die.
> Let the damn fortress of Port Arthur fall
> Or let it stand, what difference can it make
> To merchant folk who are not called to cramp
> Their lives in patterns cut for samurai?
>
> O no, my brother; no: you must not die
> Can it be true that, while the Emperor
> Remains himself immune from risks of war,
> He urges others on to kill their kind
> And, calling death in battle glorious,
> Sends them to die the deaths of savage beasts?
> If, as it is, the Emperor's heart is noble,
> How could such thoughts find lodgment in his mind?
>
> O youngest brother, not in senseless war
> Can you, nay, may you, throw your life away.[80]

Yet views critical of the madness of war, and the futility of the common soldier's place in it, did little to impede military expansion.

Despite awareness of the relationship between conscription and the male citizen's rights in other modern countries, Japan's military leaders eschewed the notion that the military service demanded by the state was a confirmation of the soldier's claims to a role in setting state policy. Thus Japan's military turned elsewhere for the source of political legitimacy. Japan's young men, after all, were never able to become "citizens" in the French sense. They paid their tax in blood, they gave themselves up to their country's service, but they never became the acknowledged foundation of the state, nor did the state profess that it served their wishes. As imperial subjects under what has been called "imperial democracy," rather than as politically active citizens bearing arms, the men of Meiji in their role as soldiers were incorporated into the state.

As we now know, the emergence of a Japanese military establishment that defined service as obedience and loyalty without rights of political participation, and manhood as jingoism and protection of Japan and its women in the Meiji era, was, in the end, hardly less disastrous for the peoples of Asia than it was for Japan's population. East Asia, where Japan's efforts to win a place at the table of the Great Powers had led Japanese statesmen to seek security, if not hegemony, bore the brunt of Japan's military aggression. An overseas empire was carved out in the name of the imperial state. Governments in the coming decades trod a path of ruthless exploitation well marked out by the "successful" Great Powers. At home, a new model had been created. Government attempts to use military service and martial organization to build up the Japanese nation-state profoundly affected Japanese society. In particular, the educational system sought to instill political awareness, a foundation for a popular sense of nationhood and patriotism centered on military service. The search for effective means to channel popular energies into loyalty to the political, economic, and social institutions fostered by many leaders of the Meiji government bore fruit. Their objective was not to create a "new man," or even a citizen fired in the crucible of war. The goal was to mold loyal subjects and obedient soldiers, and not citizen-soldiers filled with political zeal to defend their own rights and privileges.

By 1914, military leaders had come to see their army as the embodiment of the nation, almost a fulfillment of Yamagata Aritomo's goals of forty years earlier. In a letter to General Terauchi Masatake (1852–1919) in 1913, General Tanaka Giichi (1863–1929) wrote:

[I]f we think toward the future and correctly guide reservists, who will number three million in another six or seven years, and the nation's youth, we can control completely the ideals of the populace and firm up the nation's foundations. By continuing to promulgate educational orders . . . we can permeate education and the local government with the ideal that good soldiers make good citizens.[81]

Implicit in this vision was the notion that the leaders could then wield that instrument themselves, pointing to their oaths of office to confirm that they were acting "in the best interests of the state and people, under the command of the emperor."

Japanese political life was now gendered by ties to military service. Women in Japan would have to play roles as imperial subjects in "separate spheres." As Haruko Taya Cook shows in this volume, when a new role for women was required by a desperate state seeking to save itself from the consequences of its failed war in the final year of the Second World War, women's deaths were raised to the level of the soldiers who had "died for their emperor."

Notes

1. "I loved American movies," in Haruko Taya Cook and Theodore F. Cook, *Japan at War: An Oral History* (New York: The New Press, 1992), 241.

2. Spectacular progress has been made in recent years by scholars looking at the development of images and patterns of masculinity. See Joanna Bourke, *Dismembering the Male: Men's Bodies, Britain, and the Great War* (Chicago, IL: University of Chicago Press, 1996), 11. Also Leonard V. Smith, "Masculinity, Memory, and the French World War 1 Novel: Henri Barbusse and Roland Dorgeles," in *Authority, Identity and the Social History of the Great War,* eds. Frans Coetzee and Marilyn Shevin-Coetzee (Providence, RI and Oxford: Berghan Books, 1995), 251–274; George L. Mosse, *The Image of Man: The Creation of Modern Masculinity* (New York and London: Oxford University Press, 1996); R. W. Connell, *Masculinities* (New York: Polity Press, 1996); and Graham Dawson, *Soldier Heroes: British Adventure, Empire and the Imagining of Masculinities* (London and New York: Routledge, 1994), especially his first chapter, "Soldier Heroes and the Narrative Imagining of Masculinities," 11–26, have been particularly useful. My focus here is the institutional "frame" of "the soldier" itself in the Meiji era conceptualization of both the male subject and the "Japanese man." I hope here to lay a foundation and pose questions to assist future work linking the making of the notion of the soldier to such vital issues as gendering "Japanese citizenship" and the creation of a modern typology of "heroes."

3. Michael Howard, "Introduction," in Karl Demeter, *The German Officer-Corps in Society and State, 1640–1945* (London: Weidenfeld and Nicolson, 1965), viii–ix. It is important to realize that the struggle between "progressive" and "conservative" ideals within the German army was fought firmly within a concept of a state structure based on Prussia, which was stable and recognized, although the German Empire itself had only been born in 1871.

4. The Conscription Ordinance (*Chōheirei*), issued November 28, 1872. See the annotated text in Yui Masaomi, Fujiwara Akira, and Yoshida Yutaka, *Guntai heishi* [The military and soldiers] (Iwanami shoten, 1989). See 69–90 for the text and forms associated with the Conscription Ordinance issued by the Army Ministry in January 1873. The "standard" English translation of the Official Notice or Instructions to the Conscription Ordinance is probably Ryusaku Tsunoda, Wm. Theodore DeBary, and Donald Keene, *Sources of Japanese Tradition*, vol. 2 (New York: Columbia University Press, 1964), 196–198. (Tsunoda et al. used the text in Tokutomi Iichirō, *Kōshaku Yamagata Aritomo den* [Biography of Yamagata Aritomo], vol. 2 (Yamagata Aritomo Kō Kinen Jigyōkai, 1933), 194–196.)

5. Ibid.

6. Ibid. Translation in Tsunoda et al., *Sources*, 197–198.

7. The story of the implementation of the conscription law and the struggle against it have been told many times elsewhere, but the baseline history remains Matsushita Yoshio, *Chōheirei seitei shi* [History of the establishment of the conscription system] (Satsuki shobō, 1981; orig. edition 1943), as supplemented and expanded by his *Meiji gunseishi ron* [A study of the history of the Meiji military system], 2 vols. (Yūhikaku, 1956). For a shorter treatment, see Ōe Shinobu, *Chōheisei* [The conscription system] (Iwanami shoten, 1981). Two works in English have unique perspectives: Gotarō Ogawa [T. Takata], *Conscription System in Japan* (New York: Oxford University Press, 1921), a remarkable work carried out under the support of the Carnegie Endowment for International Peace, and the seminal E. H. Norman, *Soldier and Peasant in Japan: The Origins of Conscription* (Vancouver: University of British Columbia, 1965; orig. edition 1943). See Tokutomi, *Kōshaku Yamagata*, 200–205, cited by Roger F. Hackett, *Yamagata Aritomo in the Rise of Modern Japan, 1838–1922* (Cambridge, MA: Harvard University Press, 1971), 62.

8. Shinohara Hiroshi, *Rikugun sōsetsushi: Furansu Gunji Komondan no Kage* [History of the founding of the army: The shadow of the French military advisory group] (Liburopto, 1983). See also, Ernst L. Presseisen, *Before Aggression: Europeans Prepare the Japanese Army* (Tucson: University of Arizona Press, 1964).

9. Emory Upton, *The Armies of Asia and Europe* (1878; reprint, New York: Greenwood Press, 1968), 11.

10. Ibid., 12.

11. Yamagata Aritomo in "Opinion Favoring a Conscript Army," his second major proposal, following his earlier one in February 1872. Matsushita, *Chōheirei seitei shi*, 121. Partial English translation in Hackett, *Yamagata Aritomo*, 65.

12. Thomas R. H. Havens's discussion of Nishi's views in "Civil and Military Society," *Nishi Amane and Modern Japanese Thought* (Princeton, NJ: Princeton University Press, 1970), especially 191–221, led me to the *Heifuron*, a collection of Nishi's military lectures delivered between 1878 and 1881 and published in the *Naigai heiji shinbun*. References here are to the text of *Heifuron*, in *Nishi Amane zenshū*, ed. Ōkubo Toshiaki (Munetaka Shobō, 1966), 18–96, cited hereafter as *NAZS*. See also Umetani Noboru, *Meiji zenki seijishi no kenkyū: Meiji guntai no seiritsu to Meiji kokka no kansei* (Miraisha, 1963), 59.

13. Nishi, *Heifuron*, *NAZS*, 35.

14. Ibid., 35–36; Havens, *Nishi Amane,* 196.

15. Nishi, *Heifuron, NAZS,* 51–54. See Richard J. Samuels, *Rich Country, Strong Army: National Security and the Technological Transformation of Japan* (Ithaca, NY and London: Cornell University Press, 1994).

16. Ibid., 54, 63 [Havens, 196–197]. See also Nishi Amane's "The Moral Conduct of Soldiers," in *Heika tokkō, Heika tokkō, NAZS,* 3–17.

17. Toyama Shōichi [or Masakazu], *Minken benwaku* [Managing the perplexity of popular rights] (Tokyo: n.p., 1880), reprinted in *Jiyū minken* [Freedom and people's rights], vol. 5, *Meiji bunka zenshū* [Collected works of Meiji culture], ed. Yoshino Sakuzō (Nihon hyōronsha, 1927), 221–229, with a commentary, 30–33. Toyama had studied overseas before the 1868 Restoration and had served in the government before 1872. After becoming a member of the House of Peers in 1890, he became president of Tokyo University in 1897. He is perhaps best remembered as a leading force in the creation of modern Japanese poetry. Nobutake Ike, "War and Modernization," in *Political Development in Modern Japan,* ed. Robert E. Ward (Princeton, NJ: Princeton University Press, 1968), 189–211, makes several references to this 1880 work; Ike's translations are credited below.

18. Toyama, *Minken benwaku,* 227.

19. Ibid., 228. *Shamonabe* was a duck dish of great rarity for a country boy, while the *kappore* was a wild dance.

20. Ibid.

21. Ibid. Translation from Ike.

22. Toyama, *Minken benwaku,* 228.

23. Ōshio Heihachirō (1793–1837), a lower-level *bushi* who led the rebellion in Osaka in 1837, in the waning days of the Tokugawa bakufu. Motivated by the Wang Yangming school of Confucianism, which he taught, Ōshio sought change by direct action and offered a dangerous precedent of rebellion led not by peasants but by disgruntled members of the samurai class itself.

24. Toyama, *Minken benwaku,* 228.

25. See the excellent discussion of the "Freedom and People's Rights Movement" in Marius B. Jansen, *The Making of Modern Japan* (Cambridge, MA: Harvard University Press, 2000), esp. 383–387.

26. *Naikaku Tōkei kyoku* [Cabinet Statistical Bureau], *Dai-Nihon teikoku tōkei nenkan* [Great Japanese Empire Statistical Annual] (Tōkei kyōkai, 1882–1920), *Rikugunshō tōkei nenpō* [Army Statistical Yearbook] (Rikugunshō, 1914), and

Ogawa, *Conscription System in Japan*, 39–41, 46–48. For example, in 1897, 401,952 men were examined for conscription (of the 477,555 men in that draft cohort), and 48,264 were inducted.

27. Takashi Fujitani, *"Kindai Nihon ni okeru kenryoku no tekunorojii: guntai, chiho, shitai"* [Technologies of power in modern Japan: the military, the local, the body], trans. Umemori Naoyuki, in *Shisō* 845 (November 1994): 163–176.

28. See discussion of what Sasaki calls a "class military organizing principle" (*kaikyū teki guntai hensei gensoku*) in Sasaki Takaya, "Nihon gunkokushugi no shakaiteki kiban," *Nihonshi kenkyū* (71): 61–83.

29. *Nihon teikoku teinenkan* for 1884 cited in Kikuchi Kunisaku, *Chōhei hihi no kenkyū* [Research on conscription evasion] (Tatekaze shobō, 1977), 28.

30. *Kōtō shō gakka* graduates 4.10 percent, equivalent to that 7.25 percent, *jinjō shō gakka* graduates 10.61 percent, equivalent to that 17.29 percent, some capability in reading, writing, and calculating on paper (*yomikaki hissan o nasumono*) 34.14 percent, completely illiterate 26.61 percent. See Yui et al., *Guntai heishi*, 473–474.

31. Ogawa, *Conscription System in Japan*, 155. Despite the enormous expansion of the annual intake of soldiers in the coming decades, by the end of the Meiji period, the educational level of entrants actually improved. See the *Rikugunshō tōkei nenpō* [Army Statistical Yearbook] (Rikugunshō, 1914) for the vast array of data collected on soldiers each year, and Kikuchi, *Chōhei hihi*, 33. It is not clear whether these percentages refer to the entire population of tested potential conscripts or only those entering the service, as the figures are not clearly identified according to Kikuchi.

32. See D. Eleanor Westney, "The Military," in *Japan in Transition: From Tokugawa to Meiji*, eds. Marius B. Jansen and Gilbert Rozman (Princeton, NJ: Princeton University Press, 1986), 192–194. For a later era, see Edward J. Drea, "In the Army Barracks of Imperial Japan," *Armed Forces and Society* 15, no. 3 (Spring 1989): 329–348.

33. Cook and Cook, *Japan at War*. Nohara Teishin, a soldier first drafted in 1935, described his joy at being classed at the top: "I swaggered a lot, I guess. Though the whole town was praised for getting ten A's." His military experience in China is related in "A Village Boy Goes to War" (*Japan at War*, 29–35).

34. See Lucien Pye, "Armies in the Process of Political Modernization," in *The Role of the Military in Underdeveloped Countries*, ed. J. J. Johnson (Princeton, NJ: Princeton University Press, 1962), 80.

35. See Morimoto Masuda, *Armaments Industries of Japan* (Concord, NH: The Rumford Press, 1922); Giichi Ono, *War and Armament Expenditures of Japan* (New York: Oxford University Press, 1922); and Ushisaburo Kobayashi, *War and Armament Loans of Japan* (New York: Oxford University Press, 1922), on the impact of military expenditures on Meiji society.

36. Eugen Weber, *Peasants into Frenchmen* (Stanford, CA: Stanford University Press, 1976).

37. Frederick Engels and Karl Marx, on the other hand, even hoped that this might be the case and saw potential benefit in the subversion of the Prussian officer corps and army from within. See Michael Howard, *War in European History* (Oxford: Oxford University Press, 1976), 109.

38. F. E. R. & H. E. R., *Military Life in Prussia: The Soldier in Time of Peace*, trans. F. W. Hackländer (London: Sampson Low, Marston, Low, & Searle, 1873).

39. John Gooch, *Army, State and Society in Italy, 1870–1915* (New York: St. Martin's Press, 1989), 11–13. Flight from conscription, especially from Sicily abroad, helped lead to a law in 1888 to prevent men under age thirty-two from leaving Italy, without effect. Kiernan, "Conscription and Society in Europe," 150–151.

40. Charles Martel, *Military Italy* (London: Macmillan and Co., 1884), 62–95.

41. Ōzawa Hiroaki, "Emperor versus Army Leaders: The 'Complications' Incident of 1886," in *The Emperor System in Modern Japan*, ed. Banno Junji, in *Acta Asiatica*, vol. 59 (Tōhō Gakkai, 1990), 1–17, has demonstrated that the emperor's personal opinions and desires were not always the winners when he went up against the unified views of his advisors.

42. "Yoshida Tata," *Chōya shinbun*, March 22, 1873, in Yui et al., *Guntai heishi*, 130–131. The editors of the collection have been unable to determine the true identity of Yoshida Tata, but speculate that he may have been a reader whose letter was used as an editorial.

43. "Aoki Tadasu," *Chōya shinbun*, August 9, 1879, in Yui et al., *Guntai heishi*, 132.

44. Thomas Havens has stated that "Nishi's position thus encompassed the two domestic aspirations of early Meiji Japan: to establish a powerful and wealthy independent state and to join the world family of nations. But it is uncertain whether he fully anticipated or supported the late Meiji drive for expansion on the Asiatic mainland," Havens, *Nishi Amane*, 197. While it is true that he does not assert direct continental ambitions, it seems clear to me that the thrust of Nishi Amane's arguments was in the classic Spenserian school,

which states that if a nation was not to find itself the victim of aggression, it must itself be on the hunt.

45. Nakae Chōmin, *Dochakuhei ron*, originally appearing in *Shinonome shinbun*, May 16 and May 18, 1888, quoted in Yui et al., *Guntai heishi*, 139–145.

46. See Yui et al., *Guntai heishi*, 472.

47. Nakae Chōmin, *Dochakuhei ron*, May 18, 1888, in Yui et al., *Guntai heishi*, 142.

48. Ibid., 142–143. Of course, Nakae Chōmin's 1887 *San suinin keirin mondō*, translated by Nobuko Tsukui as *A Discourse by Three Drunkards on Government* (New York and Tokyo: Weatherhill, 1984), raised many of the arguments for and against strong armies in the context of international relations through the words of Nakae's characters. Mr. Champion set the course.

49. Fukuzawa Yukichi (compiled by Nakagamigawa Hikōjirō), *Zenkoku chōhei ron*, Meiji 17, January (Iida Heisaku, 1884), sold by Keiō gijuku shuppansha. 4–19.

50. Ibid., 44.

51. Ibid., 45.

52. Ibid., 46. There were men who came to see military service as practically a prerequisite to a right to political participation, perhaps even taking a position as extreme as science fiction writer Robert J. Heinlein did in his *Starship Troopers* in the wake of the Second World War.

53. Hackett, *Yamagata Aritomo*, 87–88. See Tokutomi, *Kōshaku Yamagata*, 816.

54. See Donald Keene's marvelous assessment of the impact of the war on Japanese culture, "The Japanese and the Landscapes of War," *Landscapes and Portraits: Appreciations of Japanese Culture* (Tokyo and Palo Alto, CA: Kodansha International, 1971), 259–299.

55. *Chuza sonkō*, vol. 11, 271. Quoted in Keene, "The Japanese and the Landscapes of War," 268. See *Rikukai gunka zenshū* [Complete collection of army and navy war songs], 24–25, also in Keene.

56. Toyama's song was entitled "Battōtai" [The Drawn Sword Unit]. Keene, "The Japanese and the Landscapes of War," 268, 296*n*31.

57. Ibid., 276–279.

58. See Stewart Lone, *Japan's First Modern War: Army and Society in the Conflict with China, 1894–95* (London: St. Martin's Press, 1994), for an excellent overview of the war with special attention to Gifu prefecture. Chapter 3, "The Soldier's Experience," 51–77, takes a stab at the way the war was fought.

59. *Nihon no sensō—tsukai to dētā* (Hara shobō, 1982), Data 1. "Only" 1,417 were killed in combat.

60. See Trumbull White, *The War in the East: Japan, China, and Korea* (Philadelphia, PA and Chicago, IL: J. H. Moore, 1895), 595–609, who detailed the massacres as reported by eyewitnesses among the press. See also Mutsu Munemitsu, *Kenkenroku: A Diplomatic Record of the Sino-Japanese War, 1894–1895*, trans. Gordon Mark Berger (Princeton, NJ and Tokyo: Princeton and Tokyo University Presses, 1982), 74–75.

61. Banno Junji, *Meiji kenpō taisei no kakuritsu* (University of Tokyo Press, 1971), 103, translated by J. A. A. Stockwin as *The Establishment of the Japanese Constitutional System* (London and New York: Routledge, 1992), 86.

62. The full text of "Reasons for an Army Build-up," an opinion paper dated September 1895 in *Hisho ruisan zaisei shiryō*, vol. 2 (Hisho ruisan kankōkai, 1935), 81–82, is cited in Banno, *Meiji kenpō*, 103 [86].

63. Ibid., 104–106 [88–89].

64. Editorial, "Gunji shisō ishuku" [The withering of military thought], *Heiji zasshi* [Military affairs magazine], no. 5, October 20, 1896, 1–2. *Heiji zasshi* was well received by leading newspapers when it appeared in 1896. It was acclaimed for filling a gap in coverage and for addressing directly issues that were consuming the attention of the Diet in the wake of the Triple Intervention and the demands for army and navy expansion. The September issue carried favorable comments from such papers as *Mainichi shinbun, Yomiuri shinbun, Kokumin shinbun, Tokyo shinbun*, and local papers from Nemuro to Kyoto.

65. Tōjō Eikyō, "Rikugun kyōiku to kokumin kyōiku to no kankei" [The relationship of army education and national education], *Heiji zasshi*, no. 11, February 8, 1897, 5–11. Tōjō continued, "In peacetime, the army is one huge school, but the reason the army keeps this unproductive army in peacetime, investing enormous financial resources, is that in wartime it's not possible to have (such a school). . . . In peacetime, the army is preparing for its departure for war . . . 80 to 90 percent of its energy is used for education. . . . The commander is responsible for educating his subordinates. For military men—officers, noncommissioned officers, and private soldiers—their time on active duty is a time for study."

66. Tōjō Eikyō, "Rikugun kyōiku to kokumin kyōiku to no kankei—zoku" [The relationship of army education and national education—continued], *Heiji zasshi*, no. 13, March 1897, 5–6.

67. Ibid., 6.

68. Numano Yoshio, "Kokumin no gunji shisō ni tsuite" [On the people's military thought], *Heiji zasshi*, no. 9, January 10, 1898, 15.

69. Ibid.

70. Ibid., 15–16. This tale is told again and again in the context of addressing the army's reasons for affording exemptions from active duty, and short-term service to teachers enrolled in the normal schools. It points to the German victory over France in 1871 as proof positive for the case.

71. Military-style drill and training (*heishiki kyōren*) at the normal schools (*shihan gakkō)* also had been advocated by Mori Arinori, and was implemented as a part of the Education Ministry's plans, with the extensive influence of Katsura Tarō. This system has been extensively studied by Kikuchi, *Chōhei hihi no kenkyū*, 458–464. A six-week active duty system (*rokushū kan gen'ekihei seidō)*, first implemented in January 1889 and firmly established in the November revision of the conscription law, as a critical part of the program of nation-building, was implemented outside of the normal requirements for military service and became the foundation for spreading an ideal of military training throughout society at large.

72. Numano, *Heiji zasshi*, no. 9, January 10, 1898, 17–18. He singled out the country of Montenegro as a country displaying unusual foresight in adopting this policy, and praised Germany, France, and Russia as well. Mochida Yukio, *Gunpuku o kiru shimintachi; Doitsu gunkokushgi no shakai shi* [Civilians dressed in uniform: a social history of German militarism] (Yūhikaku, 1983) is one of the more comprehensive studies of the process of the spread of these practices in Germany.

73. Anonymous, *Saieikan heisotsu no hiyō* [Finances of privates in barracks] (Sendai: Shōbukan, 1901), 6, 9.

74. *Rikugun ni okeru karyū byō* [Venereal disease in the army], ed. Rikugunshō (Rikugunshō, 1908).

75. Ibid., 10–11.

76. Anonymous, *Hohei suchi* [Requirements for an infantryman] (N.p.: Shōbido, 1903), frontmatter, 53, 75–87.

77. Sir Ian Hamilton, *A Staff Officer's Scrap-Book During the Russo-Japanese War*, vol. 1 (New York: Longmans, Green & Co., [1906]), 9–10. One of the most thorough eyewitness accounts of the war, it is by the man who would command the British-ANZAC debacle at Gallipoli in 1915.

78. These numbers are even more frightful if examined in detail, for they indicate that 12.41 percent of all men who went into action were killed, and an additional 41.08 percent were wounded, for total casualties of over half. See *Rikugun gun'i gakkō no 50 nenshi* [Fifty-year history of the Army Medical School], quoted in Ōhama Tetsuya, *Tennō no guntai* (Hanbai kyōikusha Shuppan Saabisu, [1978]), 139–140.

79. Sakurai Tadayoshi, *Human Bullets: A Soldier's Story of Port Arthur* (Teibi Publishing, 1912). *Nikudan* first appeared in Japanese in 1906. It has recently been reissued in yet another English edition as *Human Bullets: A Soldier's Story of Port Arthur / by Tadayoshi Sakurai;* with an introduction by Count Okuma; translated by Masujiro Honda; edited by Alice Mabel Bacon; introduction to the Bison books edition by Roger Spiller (Lincoln, NE: University of Nebraska Press, 1999).

80. Quoted in Atsumi Ikuko and Graem Wilson, "The Poetry of Yosano Akiko," *Japan Quarterly* 21, no. 2 (April–June 1974): 184. A complete translation of the poem, one that takes a creative tack in expressing the young sister's emotions at the thought of the devastation her brother's death would bring to her merchant family, appears in Maruyama Masao, *Thought and Behavior in Modern Japanese Politics,* trans. Ivan Morris (Oxford: Oxford University Press, 1963), 154–156.

81. Quoted in Inoue Kiyoshi, *Taishō no seiji to shakai. Inoue Kiyoshi hen* [Politics and society in the Taishō period] (Iwanami shoten, 1969), 369. Also translated in Richard J. Smethurst, *A Social Basis for Prewar Japanese Militarism: The Army and the Rural Community* (Berkeley: University of California Press, 1974), vii.

8 Reading the Japanese Colonial Archive: Gender and Bourgeois Civility in Korea and Manchuria before 1932

Barbara J. Brooks

As we have begun to explore the colonies as more than sites of exploitation but as "laboratories of modernity," the genealogical trajectories mapping what constitutes metropolitan versus colonial inventions have precipitously shifted course.

—Ann Stoler, *Race and the Education of Desire*[1]

Most modern Japanese historians have been no less at fault than their European counterparts in separating their narratives or analyses of metropolitan society from their understanding of its larger context in empire. Perhaps we should be even hastier in seeking to bridge the gap, given the obvious impacts of Japan's colonial experience on the metropole both before and after World War II. Several milestones of the history of modern Japan point to a submerged story of Japanese colonialism and its culture. For example, given the proximity of offshore territories, relatively large movements of peoples back and forth between metropole (*naichi*) and periphery (*gaichi*) caused tensions in the polity, which is indicated in the visible historical narrative by the aftermath of the 1923 earthquake and reprisals against Koreans in Japan.[2] Other milestones include the importance of empire in domestic politics in the heyday of Taishō democracy (1912–1932) and in mass mobilization for war in the 1930s; the intensity of Japan's assimilationist mission in its colonies (those acquired before 1931, primarily Taiwan and Korea); the present day repercussions of Japan's expansion and wartime atrocities as its many victims and their supporters call for reparations and justice; and the contested memory of the wartime era in its diverse manifestations. Japan's period of empire was brief compared to European experiences of empire, but far more intense. Any cultural analysis is also complicated by the simultaneous processes the Japanese (and their colonial subjects) were undergoing: that of "civilization and enlightenment" (*bunmei kaika*), or rapid formation of characteristics of (Western) modernity, including the creation of a bourgeoisie out of whole cloth, as it were. This development occurred at the same time that Japan struck out to formulate its colonial policies and shape the nature of colonial society, an ongoing process not strictly imitative of the Western example as it gained its own momentum. Without a doubt, gender also lies at the heart of these processes of modernity and imperialism.

This essay focuses on the Japanese colonial community in Korea and Manchuria (China's Northeast provinces, known as Manshū to Japanese) prior to 1932 and offers a preliminary view of its dynamics of gender, both within what appears at first glance to be a remarkably insular community of the colonized, at least in Korea, and at the points of its porous interface with the surrounding peoples. While Japan's legal and administrative systems differed in methods of imperialism across Korea and Manchuria,[3] in a cultural sense the Japanese community embraced both regions as empire without always paying heed to the niceties of international law.

The Seoul-based journal *Chōsen oyobi Manshū* (Korea and Manchuria), which served as a mouthpiece for the life and dreams of the colonial community, represented these cultural bounds of empire both graphically and imaginatively in its pages. At the same time, perhaps just as importantly, the journal was an integral and productive part of a colonial site of modernity that must be examined not for comparison to metropolitan sites but for an understanding of how such imperial and metropolitan sites and their discourses were mutually constituted. Ann Stoler has made the case that many of the discourses or technologies encoding European bourgeois sexuality and racism in the late nineteenth century were prefigured in the preoccupations of colonial society, perhaps arising from its more immediate and ongoing fears and confrontations with colonized "others."[4] In the telescoped history of Imperial Japan, such judgments may be hard to make, but, in analogous fashion, we can easily understand that modernity, or even *modanizumu*, occurred simultaneously in Tokyo, Osaka, Seoul, Dairen, Shanghai, Taipei, and other imperial urban centers, and imagine that new trends in disparate ports fed each other in an age of rapid communications and relatively short distances. In short, historians can no longer neglect the dynamism of these offshore sites of *Japanese* cultural production.

Chōsen oyobi Manshū (*COM*) began its life in 1908 as a journal titled *Chōsen*, published in Seoul by a bookstore owner and two colleagues. The following year one of them, Shakuo Kyokuhō, took over as sole owner and editor and ran the journal from within his new company, Chōsen zasshisha. Kyokuhō (many of his editorials bear only this given name) was the son of a temple family in Bizen, Okayama, who graduated in philosophy from Tetsugakkan (later Tōyō daigaku) and came to Korea in 1900. In January 1912, Kyokuhō renamed the journal *Chōsen oyobi Manshū*, reflecting his own as well as his readership's desire to link the burgeoning Japanese community in Manchuria and Manchuria's new economic opportunities to their own. The journal ran 398 issues from 1908 to 1941.[5] Early on, *Chōsen* had pledged:

This journal, without tiring of explaining the true meaning of our rights to protect Korean people or refusing to defend to the world our policy toward Korea or our colonial government, nevertheless takes a position of unsparing criticism of our national government and the colonial authorities.[6]

Under Kyokuhō's strong editorial hand, many of the journal's articles concerning the colonial government (from 1910, the Chōsen sōtokufu) and interviews with its leaders were openly accusatory or critical, largely on the basis that these authorities did not act in the best interests of the *naichi* community.[7] The journal's criticisms and its other explorations could not go too far; the colonial authorities held an arbitrary power of censorship in contrast to the publishing laws of metropolitan Japan, and as early as October 1916 they suspended the distribution of that month's issue altogether.[8] Echoing the imperial chauvinism of treaty port and colonial communities elsewhere, many of *COM*'s articles openly expressed a desire to consolidate and expand the imperial order and the status of colonizers in it.[9] Kimura Kenji characterizes its readership in Korea, judging from its editorial point of view, as based in "a strata that formed lower levels of Japanese society in Korea, located farther from the benefits of policy within Korea."[10] But this readership in Korea also helped stimulate the production of thousands of articles concerning daily life in Seoul and throughout an extended region (as far as Inner Mongolia), which provides scholars with a wealth of sources from which to construct an ethnography of colonial society.

The journal did not simply represent or reflect a community of Japanese people in Korea and Manchuria. In 1909, its distribution of 24,000 broke down geographically as follows: Seoul, 7,000; elsewhere in Korea, 8,600; Japan, 7,200; Taiwan, 840; and China, 360.[11] A casual perusal of the journal quickly reveals that it was a forum for discussion for people in Japan, China, Korea, and even Taiwan. A question-and-answer feature toward the end of the journal solicited inquiries about business, tourist, job-seeking, and other opportunities on the continent from readers in diverse parts of Japan. A caustic series of editorial comments and articles about the colonial government in a late 1915 issue prompted a response in a long article by a resident of Tokyo in February 1916.[12] Business and bureaucratic leaders in Japan and elsewhere consumed articles on raw materials, agricultural products, projected engineering and industrial products, and other developments in Korea and Manchuria. Articles on colonialism and colonial policy abound: some explicitly compare colonial Taiwan and Korea, while others discuss European colonialism, as in a two-part series on Cecil Rhodes and South Africa.[13] Articles by well-known Japanese writers, including Yoshino Sakuzo, Torii Ryūzō, Shiratori Kurakichi, Inukai Tsuyoshi, and ministers to China such as Yoshizawa Kenkichi and Gotō Shimpei, contribute to an overall impression of national, imperial community.

The editor and the colonial community represented in *COM* asserted themselves and their region of the empire as integral to the Japanese polity in a variety of ways. Although critical or fearful of the colonial government's stated policies of assimilation, impatience was sometimes expressed that Korea had not yet been brought under the Meiji constitutional rule, or, in other words, that it had not yet achieved *naichi* status. Even in the wake of the Manchurian Incident, in 1932 the journal published an article calling for the extension of the homeland, suffrage for Koreans, and even the election of Korean representatives to the Diet.[14] Particularly in the 1920s, articles such as "The Relationship of the Korean Labor Problem to Workers in Japan, Korea, and China" and "The State of Hygiene in Japan, Korea, and Manchuria as Viewed by International Sanitary Engineers" asserted the commonality of these regions of empire.[15] Numerous articles profiling colonial officials and large trading company branch heads as they arrived and departed from Korea or Dairen emphasized the fluidity of this community from *naichi* to *gaichi*.

Both in the 1910s and 1920s, articles concerning elections in Japan profiled "candidates" from Korea or Manchuria who had won or lost in both provincial and Diet elections. Such men apparently ran from districts in the metropole region while still considering themselves residents of Korea or Manchuria (one was described as a "colonial nouveau riche" or *narikin*) and presumably ran on platforms reflecting their imperial connections and ambitions. In 1914 when only one of five such candidates from Korea won, and that one "only from Pusan," *COM* described this as an affront (by *naichi* Japanese) to the Korean colonial community: "it's not just the individual candidates' reputations that are damaged, it's as if the whole community of Japanese people in Korea were made ridiculous [*baka ni sareta yo*]."[16]

Proximity to the metropole played a large role in creating the colonial community as a living extension of the homeland. In Seoul, if a member of the Japanese community was very ill, relatives from Japan proper might come quickly to nurse him or her, or he/she might quickly be moved to a hospital in Fukuoka. Given the insistence of the policy of assimilation and the promise of eventual union under the constitution, some Japanese in these pages insistently asserted their importance as an integral fragment of the Japanese national community. Korea, for example, was repeatedly described as analogous to Ireland when writers called for Diet representation from the colony.[17] Their journal as well as other evidence supports the conclusion that the cultural construction of the limits of empire, or rather perhaps of the imagined community, implicitly and explicitly embraced these offshore settlements. The people of *COM* together did not represent the official version of colonial society, nor did they much respect its official geopolitical limits. Rather, the journal is their voicing of a popular imperialism, emanating from a point closest to the colonial encounter itself, which naturalized and domesticated that encounter and its cultural manifestations for broader imperial consumption.

Gendered Constructions: Japanese Women at the Edges of Empire

Feminist attempts to engage the gender politics of Dutch, French, and British imperial cultures converge on some strikingly similar observations; namely that European women in these colonies experienced the cleavages of racial dominance and internal social distinctions very differently than men precisely because of their ambiguous positions, as both subordinates in colonial hierarchies and as active agents of imperial culture in their own right.

—Ann Stoler, "Carnal Knowledge and Imperial Power"[18]

Japanese imperialism in northeast Asia stands out in comparison to other imperial experiences for the overwhelmingly large numbers of women who often preceded Japanese men to arrive in disparate parts of the region, and whose population distribution was far more far-flung and interior. Just as significantly, Japanese settlers articulated clear views about the gendering of the colonizing enterprise. To quote from *COM*: "In contrast to the tendency for many Japanese men to want to concentrate together, Japanese women are the forerunners of Japanese people's development, in the invasion and struggle in every terrain."[19] In a very real sense, Japanese sex workers and women in the "entertainment" business, or as they are better known in Japanese, *karayuki-san* (literally, "one who goes to China") or *joshigun* (literally, "female warriors"), the latter term exclusively used in this journal, were the pioneers of this frontier.[20]

Japan's worldwide export of impoverished women into the flesh trades from the 1860s into the 1920s has received scholarly attention, although the popular historian Yamazaki Tomoko, in a series of works beginning in the late 1960s, deserves the greatest credit for postwar revival of the story of untold numbers of destitute Japanese women who came to inhabit brothels located in places as disparate as San Francisco, Dairen, Shanghai, Borneo, Rangoon, and South Africa. Her most famous work relied on oral histories (conducted in the 1960s) of a few surviving women who had worked in Sandakan, North Borneo, and bequeathed a valuable record of the voices of *karayuki-san* themselves. Yamazaki's work, however, in its geographic focus on Southeast Asia and occasionally the United States, has consistently underestimated the enormity of the numbers of women who went to Northeast Asia along the cheapest and easiest route, by steamer from Japanese ports to Pusan (Korea), Vladivostok, or Dairen, and then along the burgeoning rail network that fanned out into Manchuria and Siberia.[21]

In the 1880s, the writer Futabatei Shimei (1864–1909) wrote an essay extolling the efforts of Japanese "women in drinking establishments," or prostitutes, on the Russian frontier. Not only would such Japanese women convert Russians to the ways of Japanese life, but these efforts would stimulate demand for Japanese goods that would vastly increase trade. Already, he stated, *katsuobushi* (dried bonito flakes) exports to Russia had increased dramatically because of this phenomenon. Some Japanese women had even married well and become upper-class wives of Russians, and were introducing Russian society to the idea that high-class goods could only be obtained from Japan.[22] The modern historian Hara Teruyuki has discussed the large numbers of Japanese women arriving in Russian Siberia from the 1880s to the early twentieth century as a natural occurrence in a colonizing, frontier Russian society of mostly male Russian settlers.[23] The image of the tragic but courageous Japanese woman of the night, in the far reaches of empire, is reproduced over and over again in the pages of *COM*, often replete with biographical sketches and other vignettes. For the most part, writers here honor the sacrifice of their respectability for the sake of empire.

Official records partly document the uncommon presence of women from the metropole in an early colonial community.[24] In Vladivostok in 1884, for example, records indicate 276 resident Japanese women versus 119 Japanese males, a highly unusual ratio in comparison to any other national group. In other expatriate communities, men outnumbered women by a factor of at least three times or more. In 1915, a Foreign Ministry breakdown of resident Japanese in Manchuria by profession listed 7,122 women, with women in the entertainment business claiming the top numbers of all Japanese "professions" in the cities of Harbin and Tsitsihar.[25] Statistics published in *COM* for the city of Harbin from 1907 to 1914 show a steadily increasing proportion of Japanese women to men, ending with 897 women to 578 men. Elsewhere in the far north of Manchuria (the area of the Chinese railway) for 1915 there were 1543 Japanese women to 769 men.[26] Kimura gives the official employed Japanese population of Korea in 1910 as 171,543, divided between 92,751 men and 78,792 women.[27] Sheer numbers alone were not an indication of the level of settled or "respectable" population. This is indicated by the fact that such statistics were always accompanied by numbers for households (in Korea in 1910, 50,992 households), and consuls noted with satisfaction their growing household numbers in treaty port communities. But it is more than evident that these official numbers do not account for an unregistered and floating population of people, especially women, who are not considered "resident" but are nevertheless there.

Statistics on the presence of "anomalous" or "unaccompanied" Japanese women in Korea, Manchuria, Inner Mongolia, and Siberia fade in comparison to the overwhelming anecdotal evidence.[28] In the early days of the Japanese settlement of Manchuria after the Russo-Japanese War, it was said that for every lodging room available in Manchuria, there was a (Japanese) woman attached.[29] A 1916 *COM* article by a Dairen reporter on "Yaponskii madamu" described the good business enjoyed by *joshigun* in northern Manchuria and Siberia by saying that they were a "*Manshū meibutsu*" (local product of Manchuria).[30] Writers in the journal refer to the presence of Japanese women in prostitution and *mizushōbai* (the "water trade," a euphemism for all varieties of bar hostesses, prostitutes, madams, mama-sans) in Korea, China, and Russia, and these women are often a featured part of the voluminous travel writings. A writer of an account of Inner Mongolia in January 1917, for example, devoted a whole section to prostitutes in Mongolia with details on two brothels in Zhengjiadun that employed around thirty Japanese women for Chinese clients, and wrote in amazement that "it is the custom there that Chinese and Mongolian men visit houses of pleasure openly in broad daylight, so the establishment is closed at night," a phenomenon unseen in other red-light districts (*karyūkai*) of the world.[31]

Other writers dwelt more explicitly on the perceived advantage for Japanese imperialism of the presence of these scattered women. One writer, worrying about the competitive cultural influences of single female Anglo-American missionary teachers in remote areas of China, remarked that at least their dispersal could not compare with that of *joshigun,* who presumably offered competing visions of the virtues of Japanese civilization.[32] In the wake of the Manchurian Incident, one fascinating piece discussed how Japanese women were important contributors to Japan's success in occupying Manchuria, because the great weakness of many powerful Chinese warlords in the region was their fondness for Japanese concubines. The article goes on to profile numerous Japanese women who were "number one" among various powerful military men's household women and discusses how such women were responsible for the Japanese governesses and schoolteachers that imparted Japanese education to the children of these households.[33] Occasional detailed profiles of such women leap out vividly from these pages. For example, in January 1928 an article titled "Women Adrift and Hopelessly Lost on the Continent" profiled three such cases based on the writer's recent and lengthy trip to China. The first, a beautiful but extremely troubled young woman in Harbin, showed up around 3 a.m. in a bar where the writer and a Japanese friend were drinking vodka and gin. Her unseemly behavior and her intimate embrace with a Russian at the next table prompted the two Japanese men to get up to leave the establishment, and the writer to comment, "When the woman Hitomi Kinue appeared as the only competitor bearing the Japanese flag among 160 foreign athletes at the Swedish Olympics, that virtue and beauty was one side [of Japanese women], but [this girl] is the offensive and ugly side." His comment, with its identification of Japanese womanhood with the nation, resonates with the sentiments of European imperialists or even Chinese patriots who viewed the disgrace (or violation) of their own women by foreigners (or subalterns) as a blow to national dignity and prestige. But the writer went on to amend his view into one of keen pathos when the woman stopped him and confessed her loneliness and longing to return to Japan, though she refused offers of money to aid her in finding a new life. The writer departed Harbin, but months later a letter from his friend arrived informing him of this girl's suicide. The second profile described a Japanese dancer of great popularity in Dairen (at the Cafe Lily), who left for the big time of Shanghai as the Manchurian port life became constricting (and she ran into trouble with the Japanese police). The third dealt with the double suicide in Shanghai of two women, one of whom had tried and failed, despite a patron's backing, to start a new life running a beauty shop in Dairen.[34] Although this essay does not champion these women's roles in imperialism, its pathos and sentimentality toward these marginalized but sensitive women contrast with stereotypical European moral condemnations of similar women's roles. Japanese male writers in *COM* characteristically boasted of the glory of their colonial red-light districts, particularly in Seoul and Dairen, and frequently contributed fictionalized accounts of their encounters there or portraits of *karyūkai* denizens.

The latter pages of almost every issue of *COM* feature articles for and about women; within these pages is a whole taxonomy of *Japanese* sex workers, geisha, and other women in the entertainment business of Korea and Manchuria. In December 1912, for instance, an article on the methods of recruiting Japanese prostitutes from newly arriving women in Seoul laid out in detail all the machinations, middlemen, and costs involved from start to contract, as well as how to reproduce a complete contract. The article also pointed out that an additional illegal contract, kept in a locked safe, further constrained the women. All involved were *naichi* people. The story begins with the complicity of lodging owners who immediately telephone the go-between agency (*kuchi-ireya*) to set up meetings with establishment proprietors as the women check in. Contracts included specifications for such practicalities as who paid and how much was paid for bedding, clothing, and make-up for the women. Women had to undergo medical certification and trial runs with the customers before receiving such contracts. The article is replete with information on the proprietors' rating of prostitutes by their provenance (Osaka and Chūgoku are best) and their age (they average from seventeen to twenty-five; at twenty-eight they are almost done for, and only 10 percent of *naichi* prostitutes were "adorably" under the age of eighteen).[35]

Geisha also received attention. An article of February 1912 deplored the decline of the geisha in Seoul due to the lack of appreciation on the part of resident Japanese bureaucrats and gentlemen, insisting that, for geisha now, "what was more important than learning the tiresome *shamisen* and singing was using their spare time to study methods of birth control."[36] This gloomy outlook seems to have been unwarranted; only a few years later another article on geisha in Seoul profiled several accomplished women by name, place of employment, and short biographies.[37]

Japanese colonial authorities in Korea and the Kantō leased territory (an early Japanese colony in Manchuria) established systems of licensed prostitution and pleasure quarters in cities that echoed such arrangements in the metropole.[38] In colonial Korea, more than half of licensed

prostitutes were *naichi* women.[39] These numbers alone suggest the colonial regime's investment in controlling the large presence of Japanese
women on the continent; contemporary critics in Korea labeled the system "an overseas development policy" for Japan, and Japanese sex
workers were named as the frontline troops of colonial policy.[40] In the
same vein, a Shanghai critic of Japanese prostitution in China alleged
that the Japanese "used sexual desire to numb other peoples."[41] In 1932,
a *COM* article looked retrospectively at "twenty-five years of Seoul's
pleasure quarters," roughly estimating that there were for that year and
specific to that quarter, 750 Korean to 1,250 Japanese women in several
categories of sex workers.[42]

Kimura has discussed how the majority of Japanese who found their
way to Korea in the early period of settlement were hard-pressed after
losing their basis of livelihood at home or having it severely threatened.[43] Certainly the story of the impoverished women who became sex
workers supports this view, but in a larger sense the transferral of all
kinds of ordinary or poor people from *naichi* to Korea had dramatic
consequences for the gendered society that came into being, at least in
comparison to other colonial cultures. For in Korea, and in Seoul in
particular, bourgeois Japanese seemingly had no need for subordinate
colonized servants, mistresses, everyday merchants, or for Koreans to
perform almost every type of daily service. All their needs were met by
naichi Japanese. A series of articles in *COM* profiled all the pawnshops,
masseuses, midwives, carpenters, hairdressers, and the like, giving figures for numbers of Korean vs. *naichi* tradesmen.[44] The writer Yasuoka
Shōtarō, in his postwar memoir of Shōwa experience, recollected his
childhood household in Seoul (c. 1926) and the two maids, Haru and
Yuka, employed by his mother:

When I consider this, the point is not just that such labor was so inexpensive,
but that it shows what large numbers of Japanese had come to Korea. At the
time, it was not yet twenty years since the annexation of Korea, and yet Japanese
people had built within Korea a complete society inhabited only by Japanese.[45]

Perhaps most dramatically, such terms as *Chōsen nyobō*, *Senzuma*,
Kanzuma (terms that translate as "Korean wife"), or *Manzuma* ("Manchurian wife") did not refer to Korean women cohabiting with Japanese men, but rather, Japanese women of a questionable character who

came to live with Japanese men of the bureaucracy or trading companies, who, just as they do today, typically left behind their wives and children, the latter remaining in their permanent homes in the metropole. Articles that defined and satirized these women are noteworthy for their ambivalence.

A February 1912 article titled "A Study of 'Korean' Wives" began by defining a "Korean" wife as "a kind of mistress"—a *naichi* woman who maintained an "imitated married couple" relationship with a *naichi* man who had an official wife back in Japan. Most were aged about twenty to twenty-three, but were not prostitutes—they were "promoted" maids. The men, the article suggests, were also straitlaced to begin with, and in their search of good servants they might have gone through old women, *naichi* manservants, and Korean boys before turning to young women from home (most were from Kyūshū). Then they would succumb to these women's charms because "over here, the rules of virtuous conduct are not as strict as in the *naichi*." The article concluded that for the women this could be the start of a life on the streets, and celebrated those steadfast girls who refused such relationships, saved their money, and returned home to marry well and live happily.[46]

Other articles were not as serious or sympathetic as this one. Most of them ridiculed the *Senzuma* or *Manzuma* for her love of luxury, her spendthrift nature, and her grasping and shrewish ways. In May 1918 a Dairen reporter began a series titled "The Diary of *Manzuma* Harue," which related the fictional follies of one such mistress.[47] In an article deploring the love of ostentatious fashion and extravagance among Japanese women in Seoul, the *Senzuma* became a major culprit in influencing other *naichi* women.[48] Another writer repeated the lyrics of a popular song about a tearful parting at Pusan as a man returned home, sarcastically adding that this sentiment was fine but did not indicate how expensive such a parting was for the errant husband.[49] In an ever-recurrent series on prominent Japanese administrators and businessmen and their habits in sake and women, the terms *Senzuma* and *Manzuma* are not explicitly mentioned, but many of these men are described as being attached to *naichi* maids in their households, who are "about age thirty," and so on.[50] While in European colonies early colonizers are noted for their open concubinage or marriage with native women, Japanese men on the continent often chose Japanese female sojourners as companions. The contemporary colonial discourse about such women that depicts them as materialistic, pampered with cosmopolitan colonial luxuries, and partaking of an incipient café culture in the colonies, bears a telling resemblance in its way to the later metropolitan focus on that exciting and ephemeral figure, the "modern girl."[51]

If women were geographically at the edge of empire and also domestically surrounding and succoring the Japanese men of empire in the latter's heroic labors, they were also present at the greatest boundary of all: that between colonizer and colonized. In August 1912 *COM* began a series titled "Japanese-Korean Love Stories of Men and Women" that ran seven or eight times over a few years, and featured biographical accounts of mixed Japanese-Korean couples in Seoul along with their courtship and details about their extended families. Nearly all of the stories involved Japanese women who were married to or living with Korean men; most were *nai-ensai*, or "common law wives," because in this way they retained metropolitan registration (citizenship), and their children retained their mother's Japanese surname and metropolitan registration.[52] In 1925 another article profiled some Japanese men who had formally married Korean women, after lamenting the slow pace of intermarriage (*sōgo kekkon*, in its early years) that could produce "an age of no discrimination between Koreans and Japanese, even in blood."[53] Adoption, often a by-product of uxorilocal marriage, conferred even more beneficial privileges on Korean men marrying into Japanese families. In 1923 one Japanese writer described with pride how he had arranged the marriage of a Korean graduate of Sapporo Agricultural College to the single daughter of a former samurai (*shizoku*) family. With the wedding, the young man at once became a "superlative [*rippa na*] *naichi* Japanese and a nobleman!"[54] Thus, both marriage and adoption, on investigation, prove that the boundaries between colonizer and colonized were anything but fixed or stable, as elsewhere in the colonial world.

The Korean colonial government stood out among global colonial governments for its promotion of intermarriage as part of the policy of assimilation. After 1937 the government actually offered monetary rewards; by its own account 1,200 marriages had been achieved by that year.[55] In 1935 a detailed article in *COM* laid out the official statistics for intermarriages from 1923 on. Among officially married couples in 1935, approximately 600 were Japanese men married to Korean women and over 400 were Japanese women married to Korean men. The article acknowledged that many married relationships were never reported to the authorities (implicitly, primarily those between Japanese women and Korean men), however, and estimated these other liaisons would swell the official numbers by a factor of four or five. In its conclusion, the author stated that without being pessimistic about the future rates of intermarriage in Korea, only a good deal of time could bring about similar rates of increase of intermarriage between Chinese and Japanese in Manchukuo.[56] Later, the Manchukuo government also promoted intermarriage. A 1936 *COM* piece even describes a school that was established in Harbin, Manchuria, with the sole mission of training Chinese women to become wives of Japanese settlers.

The great model for subject peoples in the region was intermarriage among the East Asian royal families. Japanese policymakers forced the intermarriage of members of both the Korean and Manchu royalty to members of the Japanese imperial family (albeit the latter were at some distance from the emperor). And, though it is easy to speculate that the majority of Korean-Japanese unions were of lower- or working-class people, royal and elite class examples of intermarriage demonstrate that the colonizing regime had at least hoped for more marriage alliances between native and *naichi* elites. This type of intermarriage pattern would have echoed some of the early European colonizing experiences.

Japanese colonial policies of assimilation were founded on the belief that the Japanese people were themselves formed from a mixture of diverse ethnicities over time, with the core Japanese "forever assimilating surrounding ethnic groups without losing their own identity."[57] The colonial drive to assimilate was strongest in Korea, fueled in part by the belief, buttressed by modern Japanese archaeologists and anthropologists, that Koreans and Japanese shared the same ancestors (*dōsōron*); colonization of Korea would return the "branch" family of Koreans to the "main" branch of the Japanese. Kyokuhō was highly critical of assimilation in his editorials and articles, although he often couched his approach as gradualist in comparison to that of the government, and he did not specifically discuss the policy of approval of intermarriage. One article he published did, taking up the issue of intermarriage and mixed-blood offspring with an interesting twist. The author argued that since

Koreans had long ago in pre-Heian Japan (before 700 AD) intermarried with Japanese, there was no necessity for further mixing of the two peoples' blood. He next listed the known Japanese surnames associated with Korean ancestry, and then proceeded to list dozens of Japanese of these surnames who were resident in Seoul, even giving their addresses, in order to emphasize that there was no fundamental difference for the government to pursue between *naichi* and Korean residents.[58]

Significantly, in contrast to European colonial societies, Japanese colonialism could produce no true creolization or *métissage*. No mixed-blood class sprang up to further complicate and splinter the structure of the colonizer's societal ranks. Ann Stoler and others have written at length of the evolution of creole communities from an early period of liberal or even dependent relations with European colonized communities (largely male) to nineteenth-century efforts to completely close the boundaries of European and mixed-blood communities. Although linked to an emerging class structure where the colonial bourgeoisie sought to separate itself from "poor whites," mixed-blood people were far more threatening or degenerate by nature.

They were the "enemy within," those who might transgress the "interior frontiers" of the nation-state, who were the same but not quite, potentially more brazen in their claims to an equality of rights with "true" Europeans, but always suspect patriots of colonial rule.[59]

In East Asia, at least, no colonial structure of racism emerged based on shades of color.

Perhaps the greatest insight of the emerging scholarship on gender and the culture of European colonialism has been the significance of the colonial regime's control of sexuality in the attempt to forge boundaries between colonizers and colonized. Japan offers another case, where access to women by males—whether colonized men to metropolitan women or metropolitan men to colonizer women—did not become a determining factor in the colonial order of subjects. Women did not come to serve as "markers" around which colonialism's taboos (sometimes laws), aligned with powerful discourses of sexuality, constructed the politics of inclusion and exclusion. Nevertheless, as perhaps indicated by the rather low real numbers for intermarriage cited above, for the most part Japanese colonizers and

Korean/Chinese subjects dwelt in worlds separated by other kinds of powerful discourses. The following sections of the paper will offer some preliminary considerations about what those might be.

Bourgeois Civility and the Japanese Colonial Community

Colonial politics locked European men and women into a routinized protection of their physical health and social space in ways that bound gender prescriptions to the racial cleavages between "us" and "them."

—Ann Stoler, "Carnal Knowledge and Imperial Power"[60]

Scholars of the culture of European colonialism have focused a great deal of attention on tracing "discourses on morality and sexuality through empire and back to the making of the interior frontiers of European nation-states."[61] The pages of *COM* abound with such discourses, often weighted with the authority of modern medicine or new "scientific" and professionalized disciplines, that were at once contributing to the ongoing construction of Japanese bourgeois society in the colonial setting as well as at home.

One can use *COM* as a text to look at one important gendered project, the raising of *naichi* children in the colonial setting. The absence of any discourse on the pernicious evils of native servants stands out, but concerns about schools for Japanese children loom large, and are intertwined with conflict over the colonial government's hopeful intention of establishing Korean-Japanese integrated schools. Even within an article extolling the need for true integration, in recounting a school's success in bringing in a Korean student, one author dwelt on how this was made easier after bathing him and cleaning up his "dirtiness."[62] Japanese children attended segregated schools, but many small *naichi* communities bore the expenses of running them, giving rise to accusations that the colonial government provided better school facilities (and other facilities) for Korean children and "abandoned" poor Japanese in Korea's interior.[63]

In a December 1916 *COM* article the principal of the Dairen higher girls' school discussed educational issues for the more than 600 *naichi* female students in Manchuria who were enrolled in schools above the primary level. Education for Japanese girls in the colonies, he insisted, was not made distinctive by its need so much for different texts or principles, but because of the challenges of being in the colonies:

In order to prevent the loss of Japanese womanly virtue and beauty and the slide into a materially deprived state of civilization that appears gradually among Japanese girls who have lived for long years in the colonies, I believe that in the treatment of this disease, it is even more important to have conservative training and strict institutions.[64]

Such ideas about shoring up Japanese values in nurturing women were inherent also in Kyokuhō's strident and articulate concerns that the assimilation policy could not work: his concern was that, rather than Koreans becoming "Japanized," Japanese would wind up "Koreanized." In his view, this was already taking place, as proved by the lax character and laziness of so many Japanese in Korea.[65] Such cultural anxieties betray that Japanese colonial culture, in a way similar to what scholars have demonstrated for the European cases, was not as confident and self-assured as often assumed. It was fraught with awareness of its own tenuous nature and precarious boundaries, in a fashion that made discourses asserting "Japanese" values all the more driven.

The journal's pages reveal many threads of arguments or discourses that placed the Japanese family at the center of an assertive formation of a discursive space of Japanese colonial culture. Medical invocations and elaborations were pre-eminent. Articles written by doctors at the Sōtokufu's premier hospitals warned of diseases prevalent on the continent. Especially in the winter, discussions concerned diseases to which children were particularly vulnerable; cited statistics indicated the vastly higher incidence of illnesses such as scarlet fever, whooping cough, mumps, and the dreaded typhus among *naichi* as opposed to Korean residents. An article on the care of newborn infants, written by the doctor who headed the Seoul Women's hospital, was entirely couched in rational terms of science and medicine and included statistics on body temperatures at birth and early weight gains.[66] Members of the community, including one woman who expressed horror at the sight of poor and unhygienic Koreans consuming hospital wastes that could pass disease, occasionally published lurid accounts of illness and their own and family members' treatment at the colonial government's hospitals, which were outposts of modern medicine. Doctors warned of the dangers of venereal disease and gave statistics for its rates in *naichi* and other colonial territories; Korea's rates were comparatively better than even the metropole's. Medicalization lent itself in alarming ways to some efforts to distinguish the Japanese people as physically distinct from Koreans and Chinese. One doctor published a long series on his painstaking comparative measurements of body parts and skull sizes of Japanese, Chinese, and Korean people, while another carried out dozens of measurements concerning the nature of hair growth (some of it measured in submillimeters) on these East Asian peoples as compared to Europeans.[67] *COM* readers at home and in the *gaichi* found the perils and *cordon sanitaire* of colonial life both authoritatively defined by biomedicine and its Japanese practitioners.

Attention to the colonial climate was closely related to some of the medical discourses. *COM* featured special sections devoted to "avoiding the heat" in August and "avoiding the cold" in winter.[68] In one special, "Families and Summer Vacations," *naichi* residents of Seoul and Dairen responded to questions both about what to do during the summer vacations and whether taking them was even a good idea, particularly for schoolchildren.[69] A doctor instructed how to keep children warm and prevent colds in the cold winter.[70] In another issue, a special section that questioned officials and businessmen of the colonial community about how to inspire *naichi* Japanese to remain permanently in Korea produced responses praising the beauty of the Korea summer and the fact that hot springs resorts were not far away in Manchuria. The journal often favorably compared the suitability of the northeast continental climate to that of Taiwan, sometimes in the remarks or writings of *naichi* people who had previously lived there.

Men of power in the colonial community also often articulated good wife, wise mother ideals (*ryōsai kenbo*).[71] Kyokuhō also devoted many pages of one issue to responses from men about their ideal woman, and not surprisingly the men mostly praised these virtues, as well as a dislike for women who were too "Western" or otherwise showy in appearance.[72] Occasionally writers held up the Japanese *ryōsai kenbo* ideal as a model for women in Korean and Chinese societies. Significantly, Kyokuhō interviewed and profiled many Japanese women married to important men of the community, and their high attainments in education, foreign language abilities, and accomplishments in artistic areas seemed a source of pride for the community. His good wives and wise

mothers seemed uncharacteristically learned and refined. An article titled "Studies of Seoul's Female Doctors," for example, detailed the careers and families of the five qualified women doctors in a city of about
30,000, "Koreans and Japanese included." Of them, only one was still
practicing medicine after marriage.[73]

Finally, the most distancing discourse of all was a prejudicial one
against Koreans. *COM* did feature occasional articles by Koreans, including a few analyzing what was wrong with common discriminatory
terms, in a gesture of response to or recognition of this prejudice, but
discriminatory readings of Korean cultural attributes abound. Many, although not all, Japanese authors casually used such derogatory slang
terms for Korean people and things in discussing almost every topic.
Kyokuhō himself wrote an article about the "world's highest murder
rates" that prevailed among Korean women after learning the surprising statistics from the appropriate colonial office. Adulterous Korean
women murdered their husbands, he concluded, because early age of
marriage in Korea brought on impotency in men that forced the
women into such crimes.[74] Branding Korean women murderers and
emasculating colonized men in this way was only one example of manifest prejudicial assertions that helped create a discourse that elevated
the *naichi* community from the colonized as it simultaneously pulled it
together in a homogenizing discourse of modernity.

Women and Modernity in Japanese Colonial Society

Of all the Japanese colonial sites in Northeast Asia, Seoul was a jewel
of modernity. Particularly at the center of the Japanese business and
shopping district around the South Gate (Nandaimon), the architecture of the Japanese banks, trading companies, the Mitsukoshi department store, and the branch shops of fashionable Ginza retailers
all contributed to an impression of up-to-date urban sophistication.
Running into the South Gate square, the bustling avenue of Hon-
machi-dōri rivaled the metropole's flashy shopping streets, such as the
Motomachis of Kobe and Yokohama.[75] Japanese colonial culture embraced the material trappings and urban infrastructure of modernity
as confident signs of the value of their endeavors. Indeed, as late-
comers and non-Western aspirants to high levels of modern sophistication, by the 1890s Japanese had come to distinguish the superiority of

their culture, society, and economy from all their Asian neighbors in these terms.

In the *naichi*, women's roles as agents of modernity in the household and private life were viewed with far less ambivalence than their emerging roles in the public, as they, too, moved to fill the countless new lower-level jobs of the modern sector. In contrast, in the pages of *COM* and in the context of the achievements of the colonizers among a subordinate people, Japanese women's jobs are unambiguously celebrated for their contribution to such modernity. An article on telephone operators discusses the details of 101 *naichi* girls between the ages of thirteen and nineteen who worked at the telephone exchange, praising them for their quickness and courtesy and that "they never lose sight of the fact that this is the work of our nation."[76] Articles on "women in *hakama* [men's kimono]" profiled many different kinds of Japanese female office workers and even ticket takers in train stations.[77]

Several articles go much further than that. A February 1920 article, for example, titled "*Naichi* women and the women of Manchuria," began with a discussion of the rights now advocated by women's groups in Japan that included the right to assemble, to vote, and to obtain equality with men in cases of divorce. After rejecting their politics as "impossible for now given the national sentiment" and despairing that such women will ever "act like women," the writer goes on to assert that the Japanese women of Manchuria are the truly "liberated women," working as hard and as many hours as they do to accomplish their jobs. He went on to profile a group of women in Dairen, headed by the widow Nakajima, who planned to open a women's savings bank where everyone, from investor down to the lowest clerk, will be female.[78] Another article began with the same protest against women's rights and then turned to demonstrate that women in Seoul were far ahead: the author provided detailed biographical sketches of five strong-willed single women who, he says, contributed greatly to the life of Japanese women in Seoul through their independent jobs, in such fields as education and nursing.[79] Another writer profiled the true "new woman" (*atarashii onna*) abs a prostitute he had known in Dairen who had become a Christian convert. When he ran into her several years later, she had transformed into a crisp and professional nurse in Tokyo, though she confessed that her shame over her past prevented her from marriage.[80]

Fujii Chōzō, the school principal from Dairen, lamented that the families of his students had no ancestral graves nearby and that most were from lesser branch families with no Buddhist altars (*butsudan*) in their homes. He was just as distressed that his 150 pupils had family registration locations (*honsekichi*) from almost all prefectures of Japan so that none had been raised within the bounds of tradition as represented in regional languages and customs.[81] Large numbers of articles dwelt on the range of regions in Japan from which the population of the colonial community had come. To the conservative schoolmaster this distancing from tradition was a negative force leading to the degeneration of the colonized. Such uprooting and reassembling in the colonies, however, played its role in the creation of the bonds of Japanese ethnic and national identity and the reshaping of traditional roles for purposes of modernity.

Wittingly and unwittingly *COM* promoted the continent as a place of new opportunities for women. An article in 1933 broke down statistics concerning employment of women (both Japanese and Korean) from a Seoul government employment office, with jobs including housework, nursing, department store clerks, telephone operators, office work, café waitressing, and prostitution. The article noted that, for *naichi* women, while many applicants to available positions were turned down, it had to be recognized that competition for jobs in Korea was nowhere near as fierce as that back home.[82] Surely this article helped promote the continuing surge of marginal Japanese women to the continent during times of economic stress at home during the 1930s. In contrast to bright, even welcoming articles about metropolitan women and employment, several articles deplored the large numbers of Japanese young men or *seinen* who ventured to Korea for work and opportunity.[83] Young, proletarian (*rumpen shiki*), metropolitan youths, it was alleged, were apt to fall into gangs and other organized criminal activities. Thus, unlike European colonial culture where single white women (such as missionaries and schoolteachers) were often despised by the bourgeois elites, here single Japanese were showcased and sentimentalized. In the process of praising them as *naichi* agents of colonial modernity even in their new public roles, the journal promoted a positive discourse of the changing roles of women across the empire.

   The culture of Japanese colonialism in Northeast Asia, like that of other colonialisms, was shot through with contradictory impulses. Perhaps the most outstanding tension of all was between the official Japanese mission to assimilate and the growing quest, felt by many Japanese across the empire, for a clearer, national Japanese identity. Despite this, the fluid, unstigmatized status of Japanese women in colonial society was consistent into the 1930s. I have tried to suggest that boundaries between colonizer and colonized were more particularly policed by powerful discourses of hygiene, biomedicine, modernity—discourses, of course, drawn straight out of the repertoire of those instilled into the Japanese masses by the modernizing Meiji state in the second half of the nineteenth century.[84]

Conclusion

In their early phase, European colonial cultures had far more porous boundaries and fewer white women. As their realms of empire expanded to their territorial limits and stabilized, larger numbers of European women arrived and with them came a closing of previously porous boundaries between colonizers and colonized. European men could no longer maintain native concubines, and racialization played its role in casting adrift mestizo communities that now became endogamous. Within the colonies, rigid discourses of behavior and hygiene also circumscribed the lives of women and their bourgeois families.

   Japan offers a different case of twentieth-century colonialism. During the empire's phase of vigorous expansion, women from Japan played remarkable roles in reaching the geographic and cultural edges of empire. The writers and readers of *COM* were an ardent expansionist group, and in a fashion that resembled Japanese schemers in Manchuria, who claimed Korean settlers as compatriots to better establish their own numbers and claims to control of the region, the people of *COM* greedily enlisted images of these marginal Japanese women, particularly *joshigun,* and asserted their imperialist roles. If women in their most marginal roles were agents of empire, in others they were agents of empire's most alluring accomplishment, modernity. Japanese sought to prove the modernity of their colonial sites to their home au diences, to the colonized, and to critics from other colonial experiences. While many of the "working women" (*shokugyō fujin*) romantically depicted in the journal were young and expected retirement prior to entering their *ryōsai kenbo* phase, they still challenged stereotypes for a wide range of readers. And stories of the single job-holding woman, commingled with stories of "anomalous" women in the entertainment business, were powerfully suggestive of the growing autonomy of Japanese women. Here, seemingly discordant images of women—as *joshigun*, as *ryōsai kenbo*, and as *shokugyō fujin*—were all deployed in the service of empire.

Notes

This work was supported (in part) by a grant from The City University of New York PSC-CUNY Research Award Program.

1. Ann Laura Stoler, *Race and the Education of Desire: Foucault's History of Sexuality and the Colonial Order of Things* (Berkeley: University of California Press, 1995), 15.

2. The 1923 reprisals must be linked to the Japanese press, both domestic and colonial, and other responses to the March 1919 uprising in colonial Korea and its long aftermath, in a process of the spread or importation of the prejudicial fear of the colonized from *gaichi* to *naichi*. See my "Peopling the Japanese Empire: Koreans in Manchuria and the Rhetoric of Inclusion," in *Japan's Competing Modernities,* ed. Sharon Minichiello (Honolulu: University of Hawaii Press, 1998), 25–44.

3. Direct colonial rule in Korea and a differing direct colonial rule in the leased territory of the Kantōshū, where the city of Dairen was situated, and along the South Manchurian rail corridor; indirect rule, centered on the semicolonial office of the Japanese consulate, in the rest of Manchuria.

4. Stoler, *Race and the Education of Desire*, 7. In general, I am arguing that to fully understand modern Japan we must also work from the offshore archive, an endeavor largely ahead of us. By "offshore archive" I especially mean those sources produced outside the *naichi*. Such spatial sites correlate with a variant but critical process of "Japanese" identity formation (as well as producing far more mundane takes on policy formulations, political views, etc.).

5. Kimura Kenji, *ZaiChō Nihonjin no shakaishi* (Miraisha, 1989), 154, 200. Kimura devotes a chapter to an analysis of another journal, *ManKan no jitsugyō*. He uses *COM* as a comparison in his discussion of the other journal, which ceased publication in 1914.

6. *COM*, September 1908.

7. In the context of Manchuria, that community was often extended to include "our compatriots" (*dōhō*), Koreans resident in Manchuria. See my "Peopling the Japanese Empire." Authors in the journal represent a range of Japanese (very occasionally Korean) people, including women, resident in Korea, Manchuria, and the *naichi*. Like many contemporary journals, though, the majority of articles, especially concerning everyday life or travel accounts, were signed with pseudonyms or phrases like "a reporter from Dairen," "a student," or more literary terms.

8. Kyokuhō responded by speeding up the release of the next issue, replete with a full page, large print protest of the authorities' action. While in general he published the titles of articles the censors had withheld from circulation (notably concerning *futei Senjin* or "recalcitrant Koreans"), in this instance none of the titles of articles in the forbidden issue were listed. In the late 1920s, Japanese journalists in Korea and China submitted petitions to the Japanese government calling for similar rights of publication as in the *naichi*. See Brooks, *Japan's Imperial Diplomacy: Consuls, Treaty Ports and War in China, 1895–1938* (Honolulu: University of Hawaii Press, 2000), chapter 3. Michael Robinson has also argued that press controls over the Korean-owned (as opposed to Japanese-owned) press prefigure those adopted in Japan after 1925 in "Colonial Publication Policy and the Korean Nationalist Movement," in Ramon Myers and Mark Peattie, *The Japanese Colonial Empire, 1895–1945* (Princeton, NJ: Princeton University Press, 1984), 314–315.

9. On chauvinism of treaty port residents, whom Mark Peattie has likened to the French *colons,* see Brooks, *Japan's Imperial Diplomacy,* chapter 3. COM interviewers were remarkably hostile whenever they encountered Japanese consuls in Manchuria.

10. Kimura, *ZaiChō Nihonjin no shakaishi,* 168. *ManKan no jitsugyō* was closely associated with colonial authorities and came to publish a version in Korean as well.

11. Kimura, 156, based on *Kankoku tōkanfu tōkei nenpyō,* 1909.

12. "Kyokuhōron o tsūjite mitaru Chōsen," *COM,* no. 103, February 1916, 18–23.

13. "NanA no kaitakusha Seshiru Rōji," *COM,* no. 139, January 1919, 76–81, and following issue.

14. *COM,* February 1932.

15. "Chōsen rōdō mondai to nai Sen Shina rōdōsha to no kankei," *COM,* March 1926, 18–23, and "Kokusai eisei gijutsukan no mitaru naichi Chōsen oyobi Manshū no eisei jōtai," *COM,* June 1926, 26–29.

16. "Chōsen yori oideshi kōhosha," *COM,* no. 95, April 1914, 38. "Manshū kara kotoshi no fusen ni daigishi kōho to shite utte deru hitobito," *COM,* no. 243, January 1928, 69–71. It is important to realize that in prewar as well as postwar Japan there have been no residency requirements for candidacy. For the impact on women candidates in postwar Japan, see Sally Hastings, "Women Legislators in the Postwar Diet," in *Re-Imaging Japanese Women,* ed. Anne Imamura (Berkeley: University of California Press, 1996), 271–300.

17. "Chōsen to kenpō," *COM*, no. 102, June 1916, 33–35, and many other articles. The contemporary shift in Irish patriot goals from emphasis on representation in the United Kingdom to the fight for independence was not lost on the *COM* authors. In the 1920s they openly discussed this in comparison to the March 1919 Independence movement. But they still claimed the relevance of Ireland as a model for Korea; clearly they identified their own roles with that of the English architects of UK rule.

18. Ann Stoler, "Carnal Knowledge and Imperial Power: Gender, Race, and Morality in Colonial Asia," in *Gender at the Crossroads of Knowledge: Feminist Anthropology in a Postmodern Era,* ed. Micaela di Leonardo (Berkeley: University of California Press, 1991), 55–56.

19. Here the term *joshi* is used for "women," and the discussion takes place in a larger discussion of *joshigun,* a term Kenkyūsha translates as "Amazonian troops," but that is better translated as *karayuki-san* (a term not used in *COM*). *Joshigun* is actually a reference to a classical Tang poem that celebrated a division of female troops created by one emperor. From an internal reading of *COM*, it is doubtful that it has negative connotations. By 1940, the term pops up in reference to female office workers in Seoul who are giving their best to the war effort. "Manshū no Nihonjin," *COM*, no. 70, May 1913, 169.

20. On Japanese prostitutes worldwide, note Ronald Hyam, *Empire and Sexuality: The British Experience* (Manchester, UK: Manchester University Press, 1990), 142–143, 150–151.

21. Yamazaki Tomoko, *Ajia josei kōryū shi* (Chikuma shobō, 1995), 17–41, and the translation of her book, *Sandakan Brothel No. 8: An Episode in the History of Lower-class Japanese Women* (Armonk, NY: M.E. Sharpe, 1999). Her chief informant in the latter, Osaki, spent over a decade in Borneo as a prostitute (sold there at the age of ten), and returned to her village in southern Japan. Later, in her late 20s, she moved to Mukden, Manchuria, to a job as a bar hostess (a step up as she no longer had debts to pay off), married a Japanese there in 1932, and lived with her family in a sturdy Korean-style house until 1945. After the surrender, Osaki and her family, like so many other Japanese residents of Manchuria at the end of the war, had a harrowing escape back to Japan in the face of Chinese and Russian reprisals against Japanese rule.

22. Futabatei Shimei, "Shūgyōfu," quoted in Kanō Mikiyo, "Manshō to onnatachi," 203–204.

23. Hara Teruyuki, *Shiberia shuppei: kakumei to kansho, 1917–1922* (Chikuma shobō, 1989), 8–12.

24. On European limits on migration of white women to colonies, the resulting systems of concubinage with native women, and the ratios of white men to women in the European colonial world, see Stoler, "Carnal Knowledge," 57–62. "European demographics in the colonies . . . were enormously skewed by sex . . . [I]n the late nineteenth and early twentieth centuries, the number of men was, at the very least, double that of the women, and sometimes exceeded the latter by twenty-five times," 61–62. In Tonkin (Indochina) in 1931, there were 14,085 European men to 3,083 women.

25. Kanō Mikiyo, "Manshū to onnatachi," in *Iwanami kōza: kindai Nihon to shokuminchi*, vol. 5 (Iwanami shoten, 1993), 203, 205–206.

26. "HokuMan ni iru hōjin no sanpu jōtai," *COM*, no. 92, March 1915, 36–37. The article notes that in the far north of Manchuria Russians welcomed Japanese women as domestics and child caretakers.

27. Kimura, *ZaiChō Nihonjin no shakaishi*, 12.

28. The phrase "anomalous women" is borrowed from the work of Eileen Scully on American prostitutes in treaty port China. She has reconstructed their lives from probate documents and other legal proceedings in the American court system in China. See Eileen Scully, "Prostitution as Privilege: The Shanghai 'American Girl' of Treaty Port China," *International History Review* 20, no. 4 (1998): 855–883.

29. Fukuda Minoru, *Manshū Hōten Nihonjinshi* (Kenkōsha, 1975), 76.

30. "Yaponskii madamu: HokuMan yori Roryō no Nihon joshigun," *COM*, no. 113, December 1916, 148–153.

31. "Mōko zakkan," *COM*, no. 112, November 1916, 63–66.

32. "Chinese education in Manchuria," *COM*, no. 113, December 1916.

33. "Jihen no kage ni = Nihon josei," *COM*, no. 306, May 1933, 103–105.

34. "Tairiku o nagare tadayofu aware na josei," *COM*, no. 243, January 1928, 92–99.

35. "Keijō no geishōgi baibai hō," *COM*, no. 89, December 1914, 100–106.

36. "Keijō geigi wa masumasu geraku suru," *COM*, no. 55, July 1912, 27.

37. "Geisha o uramen kara mite," *COM*, no. 171, January 1922, 109–115.

38. Sheldon Garon, "The World's Oldest Debate? Prostitution and the State in Imperial Japan, 1900–1945," *American Historical Review* 98, no. 3 (1993): 710–732. Fujime Yuki, *Sei no rekishigaku* [Historiography of sex] (Fujishuppansha, 1997), or in English, "The Licensed Prostitution System and the Prostitution Abolition Movement in Modern Japan," *positions* 5, no. 1 (1997): 135–170.

39. Song Youn-ok, "Japanese Colonial Rule and State-Managed Prostitution: Korea's Licensed Prostitutes," *positions* 5, no. 1 (1997): 175.

40. Song, "Japanese Colonial Rule," 197.

41. Quoted in Gail Hershatter, *Dangerous Pleasures: Prostitution and Modernity in Twentieth-century Shanghai* (Berkeley: University of California Press, 1997), 78.

42. "Keijō karyūkai no konjaku," *COM*, no. 293, April 1932, 101–102.

43. Kimura, *ZaiChō Nihonjin no shakaishi*, 8.

44. For example, "Shokugyō fujin no meianshiki," *COM*, no. 305, April 1933, 91–94.

45. Yasuoka Shōtarō, *Boku no Shōwashi*, vol. 1 (Kōdansha, 1984), 12–13.

46. "Chōsen nyobō no kenkyū," *COM*, no. 55, February 1912, 24–25.

47. "Manzuma Harue no nikki," *COM*, no. 131, May 1918, 107–110, and following issues.

48. "Fujin mondai ni ryūkō suru osoroshii denranbyō," *COM*, no. 91, February 1915, 53–56.

49. "Naichi fujin to Manshū fujin," *COM*, no. 153, February 1920, 67–69.

50. But not Terauchi, who was restrained in his leisure hours, even though his wife refused to live in Seoul. "Sake to onna on ue yori mitaru Keijō no meishi shokun," *COM*, no. 133, July 1918, 64–67.

51. On the *moga* or modern girl, see Barbara Hamill Sato, "*Moga* Sensation: Perceptions of the *Modan Gaaru* in Japanese Intellectual Circles during the 1920s," *Gender and History* 5, no. 3 (1993): 363–381; and Miriam Silverberg, "The Modern Girl as Militant," in *Recreating Japanese Women*, ed. Gail Bernstein (Berkeley: University of California Press, 1991), 239–266.

52. "NisSen danjo tsuya monogatari," *COM*, no. 57, May 1912, 28–29.

53. "Kekkon kara mita naiSen yūwa," *COM*, no. 206, January 1925, 156–159.

54. "Chōsen mondai ni tsuite," *COM*, no. 182, January 1923, 37–40.

55. Oguma Eiji, *Tanitsu minzoku shinwa no kigen* (Shin'yōsha 1995), 241. At least one Korean colonial official was sharply critical of Nazi ideas of pure-bloodedness (243), articulating the often cited mixed racial background of the superior Japanese people as an argument. Oguma's larger argument, that prewar Japanese discourses of race were far more conflicted (or cosmopolitan) than in the postwar era, has had an impact on Japanese scholarship of colonialism.

56. "NaiSenjin no tsūkon jōtai," *COM*, no. 326, January 1935, 32–35.

57. Tessa Morris-Suzuki, "Becoming Japanese: Imperial Expansion and Identity Crises in the Early Twentieth Century," in *Japan's Competing Modernities*, ed. Sharon A. Minichiello (Honolulu: University of Hawaii Press, 1998), 174.

58. "Chōsenjin ni en no aru sei o motsu Keijō zaijū no naichijin," *COM*, no. 109, August 1916, 82–84.

59. Stoler, *Race and the Education of Desire*, 52.

60. Stoler, "Carnal Knowledge."

61. Stoler, *Race and the Education of Desire*, 97. For a relevant example for the French in West Africa, see Alice Conklin, "Rethinking Frenchness: Citizenship, Imperial Motherhood, and Race Regeneration in West Africa, 1890–1940," in *Domesticating the Empire: Languages of Gender, Race and Family Life in French and Dutch Colonialism*, eds., Julia Clancy-Smith and Frances Gouda (Charlottesville: University Press of Virginia, 1998).

62. "NaiSenjin kyogaku wa shinchō no kenkyū o yōsu," *COM*, no. 168, October 1921, 21–22.

63. "Sōtokufu seiji ni okeru Chōsenjin to Nihonjin," *COM*, no. 84, July 1914, 2–6, cataloguing discrimination by the Colonial Government-General against Japanese in favor of Koreans. The residents in various colonial communities were very unhappy after annexation when their Residents' Associations (*kyoryūmindan*) were abolished and both Koreans and Japanese in every locality brought under the same administration by the colonial government. Japanese schools for *naichi* children in these localities preceded the period of annexation, when they received direct financial support funneled through the Foreign Ministry after years of lobbying. See Peter Duus, *The Abacus and the Sword* (Berkeley: University of California Press, 1995), 358–363.

64. "Manshū no joshi kyoiku," *COM*, no. 113, December 1916, 71–73.

65. "Chōsenka ron: Wa ga naichijin o keikoku," *COM*, no. 130, April 1918, 2–9. Similarly, "Chōsenjin no dōka mondai to Nihon," *COM*, no. 133, July 1918, 13–15.

66. "Shoseiji ni taisuru chui," *COM*, October 1932, 81–83.

67. "Zunō no jinshū kaibōgakuteki kenkyu: Daiichi, Zunō taijū to nenrei to no kankei," *COM*, no. 152, February 1912, 27–31. This is the first of a three-part series.

68. "Natsuyasumi to kazoku," *COM*, no. 97, August 1919, 101–110. Also, for example, "Chōsen ni okeru fuyu no mondai: Bōhanhō no undōhō—kakujin iroiro no iken yori," *COM*, no. 139, January 1919, 85–88.

69. "Natsuyasumi to kazoku," *COM*, no. 97, August 1919, 100–110.

70. "Naichijin no ijū oyobi dochaku mondai," *COM*, no. 107, June 1916, 64–77. Numerous features on hot springs demonstrate their importance in making life comfortable.

71. There is much scholarly work in Japanese on the good wife, wise mother model as the mainstream ideal for Japanese womanhood. In English, see Kathleen S. Uno, "The Death of 'Good Wife, Wise Mother,'" in *Postwar Japan as History,* ed. Andrew Gordon (Berkeley: University of California Press, 1993), 293–322. See also Kathleen Uno's chapter in this volume.

72. "Wareware no fujinkan," *COM*, no. 108, August 1916, 89–102.

73. "Keijō no joi," *COM*, no. 132, June 1918, 101–103.

74. "Seikaiichi no onna no satsujin hankoku: onna no jukeisha ga otoko to dōsō no Chōsen," *COM*, no. 116, March 1917, 83–88.

75. Yasuoka, *Boku no Shōwashi*, 7–9.

76. "Denwa kōkanshu," *COM*, no. 103, January 1916, 137–139.

77. "Keijō ni okeru hakama no onna," *COM*, no. 133, July 1918, 85–88.

78. "Naichi fujin to Manshū fujin," *COM*, no. 153, February 1920, 67–69.

79. "Funtō no onna: Otoko yori dokuritsu shita onna," *COM*, no. 100, November 1915, 200–204. Nurses abound in these pages, for example, "Sōtokufu iin no kangofu hyōbanki," *COM*, no. 132, June 1918, 96–100. While many writers disparaged the goals of contemporary women activists in the *naichi,* in the late

1920s *COM* published some pieces favorable to women's rights. For example, "Waga kuni genji no fujin undō ni tsuite," *COM*, no. 207, February 1925, 24–28.

80. "Makoto ni atarashii onna," *COM*, no. 79, May 1913, 147–149.

81. "Manshū no joshi kyoiku," *COM*, no. 113, December 1916, 72.

82. "Shokugyō fujin no meianki," *COM*, no. 305, April 1933, 91–93.

83. For example, "Keijō ni okeru seinen no mondai: Keijō ni okeru seinen no kifū wa warui," *COM*, no. 103, February 1916, 80–88.

84. The best evocation of this process is Carol Gluck, *Japan's Modern Myths: Ideology in the Late Meiji Period* (Princeton, NJ: Princeton University Press, 1985).

9 Women's Deaths as Weapons of War in Japan's "Final Battle"
Haruko Taya Cook

In the Memorial Hall of Yasukuni Shrine in Tokyo hangs a massive oil painting executed in 1944. The collaboration of forty-five women painters on the subject "All Imperial Women Working," the picture shows Japanese women's contributions to the nation in the fall and winter of that fateful year.[1] The viewer can see women—mothers and daughters alike—working at a wide range of tasks. Portrayed are teachers, nurses, farmers, miners, blacksmiths, factory workers, barbers, shopkeepers, streetcar operators, conductors of wood-burning buses, and mail-women. Some of the jobs are ones long assigned to women as nurtur-ers and caretakers. For example, one of the faces shown in close-up is that of a young Red Cross nurse holding a devotional sake cup in her hands, while in the background, a group of nurses in fresh uniforms bows before a Shintō shrine. Men, who in 1944 Japan were presented everywhere as soldiers and fighters, are largely absent from this canvas.

Although the ways Japanese women participated in the war were slowly and gradually defeminized by their work in war-related factories, where they sewed parachutes, collected scrap metal, trained themselves in signaling by semaphore, and wore subdued colors in the midst of the escalating war, women still appeared in the work primarily as nurturers, providers, and supporters of the war physically and spiritually. Some of the activities at which Japanese women and girls are portrayed in the picture were highly gendered before the war, and some remain so in the montage, sustaining the dichotomy between women and men as care-takers and life-givers on the home front vs. soldiers on the front lines.

The painting shows women taking part in important symbolic patriotic activities. In the Shintō shrine and at the train station, mothers, wives, and daughters—armed only with the national flag and tall banners celebrating their loved ones' departure—gather to send their husbands and sons to war. They are represented collecting other women's contributions to the thousand-stitch belts that were believed to protect a man from bullets as they literally enfolded him in the warmth of his family's love, expressed in a cloth stomach wrap he would wear on his person to war. Thereby, women's traditional skill of sewing is upgraded to be an expression of service for their nation. Adolescent girls are shown hard at work sewing parachute silk. We do not see "mere" housewives and mothers anymore. Motherhood alone is not a sanctioned territory in this time of war. Mothers—clothed in flags, white aprons, and *monpe*-pants, their hair often wrapped in a towel to keep it from obstructing their labors—provide moral support for their men on their way to battle.

The painting depicts females of all ages out in the world. In the rural areas we see women working in the field, harvesting rice, herding sheep and cows, and handling rafts of wood down swift rivers, doing the work of the men who were asked to leave to defend the nation. In the towns, mothers and wives manage vegetable shops, act as fish mongers, barbers, and blacksmiths, their peacetime kimono replaced by wartime trousers. All are dressed in khaki or the dark hues of wartime Japan. A breakdown of gender distinctions between the providers and the provided for is already clearly emerging. Women themselves are working to protect their children—who are shown nearby, helmeted in their padded cotton air-raid protection headgear.

The greatest change—in this painting—in the roles assigned to women is that of women training in the skills of battle itself. In the upper right corner, under a soaring Japanese plane, is a line of resolute young women marching to the orders of a uniformed man, spears on their shoulders. In the painting's background, other women are shown thrusting bamboo staves with sharpened points into human-sized straw men, and a row of what seem to be girls in school uniform are shown lying prone in a firing ditch, rifles at their shoulders, engaged in shooting practice. This painting, as rich a visual source as one could hope for in capturing the range of Japanese women's sanctioned activities, omits one crucial dimension of Japanese women's role in the war, which was to be defined in the summer of 1944: We do not see them dying. It is this role of Japanese women that I will address in this chapter.

As I studied the experience of Japanese people during the Fifteen-Year War, 1931–1945, I formed many images of my own. My work on *Japan at War: An Oral History* exposed me to hundreds of personal recollections about the war, and women told me much about how they perceived themselves in it.[2] But when I began to examine the details of the battle on the island of Saipan from June to July 1944, I was truly shocked by what I found. I had undertaken a study of what I expected to be the "Saipan *gyokusai*," one of the strongest images of wartime Japan, that came to signify the apparent preference for death over surrender of nearly all on Saipan. Instead, I came face-to-face with the most callous and cynical exploitation of women's deaths and "sacrifice." Moreover, and perhaps even more horrible, the mythologizing of the events on Saipan has proven profoundly successful and historically persistent.

As I have written elsewhere, the most important point to be made about the "Saipan *gyokusai*" is that it did not occur to the extent or in the way in which it was reported. Nor does what took place on Saipan—especially at Marpi Point and places now called in the tourist trade "Banzai Cliff"—support the conclusion that all Japanese civilians were prepared to die rather than surrender. Despite horrible scenes of suicide and murder, fear and misery, desperation and despair, the facts do not support the stories of mass death on Saipan. In order to grasp the magnitude and meaning of the events on Saipan, we need to ask who killed themselves on Saipan, why the term "*gyokusai*" was applied to that battle, and how that informs our understanding of the final year of death in the Pacific.[3]

In this chapter, I investigate how the concept of "women's deaths" associated with Saipan marked a key departure in the way Japan's wartime leaders and propagandists—and to a great degree, Japanese people themselves—looked at the place of women in Japan's Pacific War. I ask how the deaths of women on Saipan in the summer of 1944 stimulated, by August 1945, a demand that women in Japan conform to a new model of feminine behavior—death. Additionally, I explore what women's deaths meant and what utility women's deaths had for Japanese propagandists. I take a preliminary look at how the propagandists' use of these women's deaths affected the final year of that terrible conflict.

Saipan: Assault on Japan's Southern Frontier

Saipan, in the Marianas, was the jewel in the crown of the Japanese South Seas Mandates at the beginning of the Pacific War. These islands, former German colonies awarded to Japan after World War I, had been developed gradually since the first settlers from the Japanese empire began arriving.[4] Saipan had not been fortified before the war and had a garrison of only about 2,000 men until an army billeting party arrived in February 1944. The largest town on the island was Garapan, often called "the Tokyo of Saipan," located on the coast at the foot of Mt. Tapochau. Home of the South Seas Agency branch for the Marianas before the war, it held some 160 shops, two movie theaters, a post office, schools, an agricultural laboratory, a Catholic church, a Buddhist temple, a Shintō shrine, and the judiciary building of Garapan. Ten miles of roads, 18 feet wide and built from crushed coral reef, ran through the town. Among the shops were 47 brothels, employing as many as 277 women, broken into two classes—31 *geisha* with presumed artistic abilities and 246 "sake servers"—divided by ownership and patronage among the different groups, each serving diverse economic, social, and ethnic clientele.[5] The major industries were moderate-scale sugarcane growing and sugar processing, the catching and drying of tuna, and the mining of mineral phosphates for fertilizer that was increasingly needed in Japan. They occupied a civilian population of approximately 29,000, comprised of 22,000 Japanese, 1,300 Koreans, and 5,000 islanders.[6] The vast majority of the Japanese hailed from Okinawa prefecture; they were themselves seen by main island Japanese as second-tier citizens. One visitor from Japan, the novelist Ishikawa Tatsuzō, described them as "Japanese gypsies."[7] Below the Japanese on the social scale were the Korean subjects of Japan and the Kanaka and Chamorros islanders, who had been the original inhabitants of the Marianas before the coming of European and Asian colonists.

Far from being the "impregnable fortress" Prime Minister Tōjō is reported to have called it, Saipan had few defensive installations. Construction efforts had been drastically limited by shortages in construction materials, especially concrete and lumber. Most of the island's civilians were still on Saipan when the American forces landed, although evacuation efforts had begun in March 1944. The sinking on March 6 of *Amerika maru*—one of the first two evacuation ships—with the loss of all but two of 500 women and children aboard, deterred others from attempting the five-day passage back home until May 31 when both *Chiyo maru* and *Hakusan maru* sailed, only to be sunk a few hundred miles north of the islands. Able-bodied men under 60 and above elementary school age were forbidden from leaving because they became increasingly important in the late efforts to scrape together organized defensive positions despite shortages of building materials for reinforced shelters.[8]

The number of civilians, including settlers, natives, and military employees—extremely difficult to determine accurately—was probably between sixteen and twenty thousand when the American V Amphibious Corps stormed ashore on Saipan on June 15, 1944. In the course of the fighting, the military forces of Japan were given priority in food and water allocation, and were nearly annihilated in fighting with the advancing Americans. The civilians, who had been frightened out of Garapan by the first preliminary bombings, soon found themselves exposed to the full wrath of American and Japanese firepower. Some surrendered upon encountering American forces and were held as captives in camps for survivors established by the Americans at Susupe.[9] So intense was the fighting, and so difficult was the American advance that, at least at first, these camps were little better than enclosed wastelands with little food and medicine.[10] Much of the food needed to sustain life in the camps had to be grown within them, even months after their establishment.

Other civilians were driven along with surviving Japanese troops to the northern part of the island, where nearly four thousand were eventually cornered. It was in this part of Saipan, near Marpi Point, that most of the civilian suicides and killing of civilians by Japanese forces and American close-in assaults took place. Such scenes as those described by Robert Sherrod (discussed below) were given pictorial life by the great Japanese war artist Fujita Tsuguji in his massive painting, "The Day of *Gyokusai* on Saipan Island" ("Saipan-tō gyokusai no hi").

This painting appeared to confirm and actualize the essence of ecstasy in death of the Yamato race we will look at here.

A third group of noncombatants wandered around the mountains of Saipan hiding, searching for food, and seeking any available shelter. Some hid in the hills until well beyond the end of the battle, a few civilians remaining at large until the end of the war, in danger not only from American search parties hunting down still-resisting Japanese soldiers, but also from those Japanese troops as well. In all, at least fifteen thousand civilians survived the battle.[11] Despite the focus in both American and Japanese accounts of this battle on those, especially women and children, who killed themselves or were killed or murdered in the desperate final moments of the battle, in reality, the dead numbered about one thousand, with several thousand others killed in the course of the more than monthlong battle.

As terrible as those last figures are to contemplate, and as awful a human tragedy as each death was, this was not *gyokusai*. Many thousands survived, most of them openly choosing surrender over death. More than ten thousand battered civilians and one thousand military men were captured and returned to Japan after the war. Use of the term *"gyokusai"* allowed the conductors of this war to justify, in glorified terms, the destruction of many lives by combining a sense of tragedy with both lamentation and righteous indignation. While news of *gyokusai* on Saipan spread through the main islands of Japan, wounded and starving soldiers still were wandering in the mountains of Saipan, chased by U.S. strafing until they were made into "war dead" or fell into enemy hands. Thousands of noncombatants were also still roaming until they were captured by or surrendered to the U.S. forces. Back in Japan, all on the island were viewed as "heroic dead." After the end of the war, the first repatriation ship carried about one thousand to the main islands of Japan. In the second stage of repatriation, ten thousand survivors were taken to Okinawa. Noda Mitsuharu, a sailor who was captured after the "final charge" on July 7, found when he returned to his home in Mito, Japan, that his own grave had been erected and his name erased from the family registration.[12] The fate of the Koreans among the internees is still undetermined.[13] All those survivors of the battle on Saipan were made into living ghosts by erasing them from the memory of the living world, and many remain "missing" in most accounts and public memory to this day. The significance of death weighed heavily during the war years and remained unshakable in the postwar era despite shifting meanings of "death" and "dying."

"Women Defend the Imperial Soil"—*First News from Saipan*

News of the American landing on Saipan was not reported immediately in the papers, but when it was, civilians on Saipan, particularly women, began to attract attention as new "courageous Japanese" for the first time during the war. The images of Japanese women who would dare to face the enemy on Saipan occupied considerable space in the *Asahi shinbun* on June 28, 1944, under the headlines, "Splendid: True Nature of Japanese Women!" and "Learn from the Minds of Saipan Sisters!" The introductory paragraph of the main article presented the image of unarmed women standing up against the threatening enemy. Children, too, stand, their teeth tightly clenched against "evil demon American soldiers." The article urged all Japanese women, young and old, to learn from the mind of Japanese women on Saipan and to fight to win this war. Several individual commentators also expressed their opinions. Poet Takamura Kotarō offered "Women and Children Severely Intense," capturing in poetry determined women in a fortification in front of the U.S. forces.[14] The rest of the coverage in the *Asahi shinbun* examined women's deaths (or still, at this time, potential deaths) for the first time in the Pacific War.

The *Asahi shinbun* coverage included comments by observers of the fighting on Saipan. A young brother and sister, born in Saipan and recently returned to Japan from there with their mother, reflected on the time they spent constructing the island's defenses with their classmates and their two other sisters, Kimie, nineteen years old, and Teruko, eighteen, both still on Saipan. In the article, the *Asahi shinbun* reporter quoted their mother expressing her wish that her daughters serve well, assisting soldiers in their service to the nation. Examining this little vignette—the powerful image of a family divided by war—we can see the "mother" image, but it is also clear to us that the mother lacked terminology that might help her express the reality of her daughters' plight. She had recourse only to (or the reporters chose to quote) the overly used, generalized phrase of the war years, "service to the nation."

The reader was then introduced to a Red Cross nurse, Ōtake Yasuko, in her Tokyo office. She recalled her emotional experience watching wounded soldiers and explained that when the battle lines spread into Shanghai (at the start of the "China Incident") in August 1937, the non-commissioned officers' mess in Shanghai had to be made into a field hospital. With bullets flying overhead, she was very busy caring for the injured soldiers brought in. She confessed her chagrin and how, through clinched teeth, she had wished that she was fighting and was not bound by the Red Cross agreement. This nurse then noted that she regretted that she was not a warrior but was "only a caretaker" in China, recalling her fellow Red Cross nurse, Otani Shina from the Shiga Branch, who was machine-gunned and killed by the enemy in the South Seas while attempting to protect a seriously injured soldier in the ocean after the transport ship *Buenosu Airesu maru* was hit.

Ōtake demonstrated and confirmed the power of images of subject and ruler in her choice of a very restricted vocabulary to describe her feelings. She recalled what she referred to as the *"junshi"* of her fellow nurse, directing her rage at the "demon-like enemy." The term *junshi* is most appropriately applied to the feudal practice of senior retainers "following their lord in death" upon the demise of a domain lord. Moreover, it was forever tied at the end of the Meiji era to the *junshi* suicides of General Nogi Maresuke and his wife following the death of the Meiji Emperor. Natsume Sōseki, in his novel *Kokoro,* linked Nogi's *junshi* to the death of the whole Meiji era, and novelist Mori Ōgai (who was also an army general) used *junshi* as the theme of his *Abe Ichizoku;* in both cases, the word *"junshi"* applied to deaths *following* the death of the feudal overlord. Yet when Ōtake used the term the Showa Emperor remained alive in his palace in Tokyo, and the leaders of Japan's military forces and government were actively engaged at the time in planning the next cabinet shake-up.

Ōtake was presented in this mass daily newspaper as arguing that in her experience of war, there were occasions when women showed more strength than men; she said she felt children would assist their mothers on Saipan. Ōtake addressed her Saipan sisters, "Sisters in Saipan, charge!" and urged them to build "the fortress of *nikushin* [flesh and blood]." Ōtake declared, "How courageous [women on Saipan] are! The most beautiful possession of Japanese women has turned out to be fighting power and it prevents the enemy from advancing!" This nurse clearly suggested that women on Saipan should go beyond the dichotomized notion of protected women defended by men and carry the fighting to their foes themselves.[15]

Another recent returnee from Saipan, Tokyo resident Wada Toshiko, wife of an employee of the South Seas Development Corporation, described recent defense activities on Saipan and how women on Saipan conducted the air defense exercises every day after the arrival of the enemy over "the Marshalls." "Thanks to their practice," she explained, "they were able to extinguish the fire at the hospital by their bucket-relay this spring." She said the women's unit volunteered for various activities from early morning through afternoon in order to "defend Japan's soil with their own hands," together with the women's youth group and schoolchildren. Women practiced carrying a stretcher in order to be in charge of nursing, she added. Mrs. Wada wrote that women on Saipan had been wearing *monpe* all day for a long time, while many women in the homeland were not in their air defense clothing. Although Wada was critical of the women's behavior in the homeland, she viewed women's participation in war as caretakers and supporters and not as incipient warriors.[16]

The last major commentator was Takayanagi Mitsuhisa, official historiographer of the Institute for Compilation of Historiographical Materials at Tokyo Imperial University. His remarks seem almost a prologue for what will follow in the exploitation of women's deaths on Saipan; his words were abstract, but at the same time, he put the behavior of Saipan's women into what he represented as the context of Japanese history—"The strong fighting of the Saipan women is a triumphant song of women who build a new generation and a warning that urges the resolution of the national difficulties with body and blood." It was natural that women would also stand on the battlefield in time of war, he argued, listing the example of Tomoe Gozen (late twelfth century), concubine of Minamoto no Yoshinaka, commander of the Minamoto forces in the early stages of the Taira-Minamoto War (1180–1185) who accompanied him when he fled Kyoto in 1184.[17] He also referred to the wife of Kusunoki Masashige (?–1336) in the Yoshino period (when imperial forces tried to seize back power from the feudal barons at the time of the Kenmu Restoration in 1334–1336), who was known historically as a great mother; and the wives of Hosokawa Tadaoki (1563–1646) and Yamauchi Kazutoyo (1546–1605), who were great supporters of their husbands at the end of Japan's Warring States period in the sixteenth century. During the early modern era, Takayanagi emphasized, women also stood face-to-face with the enemy in war and placed themselves within the castle and even fought hard alongside members of the Byakkotai (White Tigers—a band of die-hard supporters of the Tokugawa) in the Bōshin Sensō (or Restoration War) at the time of the Meiji Restoration.[18] Women of the Sengoku (Warring States) period also faced death at the time of the collapse of their castles. Takayanagi went on to explain why there is no documentation of women warriors during the period of the Mongol invasions (Genkō). "That was," he said, "because such behavior was considered natural for women of Japan!"[19] He concluded his remarks by saying, in what no doubt was meant as great praise, "nameless women are proving that they have real strength as 'national women' [*kokuminteki josei*]." It is difficult to tell precisely what he meant by the term "national women," but the implication is clearly that women have achieved something by their dying, and these anonymous women on Saipan were ennobled by dying there.

The messages in the coverage at this stage of the battle, just two weeks after the American landings on Saipan, appear to be mixed, but the images of weaponless women resolutely facing the enemy share some common characteristics. The media depicted these women as spiritually determined to fight, though they had no weapons, not even bamboo staves. Historian Takayanagi implied the impending death of women, citing Japanese history in praising their willingness to die. The Red Cross nurse urged women to be warriors and to fashion a fortress from their very flesh and blood. The returnee woman from Saipan resolutely encouraged women to be caretakers and assistants to soldiers.

The writers in the newspapers on June 28 reflected an expectation of disaster not yet present in official announcements, though the military situation was already well understood and evaluated within the military itself. Where did the idea originate that the garrison on Saipan, and ultimately the entire population of the island, should "destroy themselves"? The Imperial General Headquarters Army Section Confidential War Diary for June 24, 1944, contains the following entry, accompanied by a detailed criticism of why operations on Saipan had not gone as hoped:

The Saipan Defense Force should carry out gyokusai. It is not possible to conduct the hoped for direction of the battle. The only thing left is to wait for the enemy to abandon their will to fight because of the "Gyokusai of the One Hundred Million."[20]

The official notification of the fall of Saipan came in a brief statement on July 18, 1944, from Imperial General Headquarters. It reported that Japanese forces carried out a last attack on July 7 and all attained "heroic death" by the 16th. As for the fate of the civilians on Saipan, the statement was indirect, saying only that they "always cooperated with the military, and those who were able to fight participated bravely in combat and shared the fate of officers and soldiers."[21] Women were not specifically referred to in the military's acknowledgment of the loss of what had seemed to be the critical position in the Central Pacific, as the loss of Saipan meant the collapse of what had been called Japan's "Absolute Defense Zone." Bold headlines in the morning papers of July 19, 1944, told the Japanese public of another major battle fought and lost: "All Members of Our Forces on Saipan Meet Heroic Death/Remaining Japanese Civilians Appear to Share Fate." Few Japanese reading the story or hearing the news whispered among neighbors could have fully appreciated what terrible consequences awaited. But the disclosure that Japan had lost a key outpost in the Mandate territories colonized by Japanese after World War I—trumpeted as a cornerstone of the defensive perimeter girding the empire and only fifteen hundred miles southeast of Tokyo itself—was, for most, a confirmation that the war had entered a new stage. Despite all the assurances of their government, the vaunted defense perimeter that was to have kept at bay American ships and planes had now been deeply pierced, exposing the home islands themselves to attack.

Interested Japanese citizens, tracking the course of the war on maps in their homes and suffering under increasing economic privation due to the accelerated effects of the submarine blockade, could draw for themselves grave conclusions about the war's course. The fall of Saipan did not come suddenly but only after a long series of reversals following the successes of the early stages of the war in China and the Pacific. With the exception of that brief period filled with victory, the Japanese people had heard little good news from the front. War had become a part of the daily routine for them. Some, like Nogami Yaeko (1885–1985), a well-established novelist, had confided their building unease and growing concerns in their diaries. In the spring of 1944, Nogami had written of her odd feelings of acceptance, "The severe enemy air attacks have been repeated and two new [enemy] landing areas were established along the west coast of New Guinea. However, we were calm even when we read this kind of report or article. Nobody seems to care." This seemed to her "an astounding change" from the public attitude of even a year earlier when Attu fell in April 1943, and the whole country had seemed galvanized by the news that the entire garrison had died in battle.[22] In an entry on June 7, 1944, Nogami had noted the invasion of northern France by the U.S. and British forces and followed the news with interest. From mid-June, when she recorded reports of attacks on the Marianas, her attitude toward the conflict seemed to shift from seeing it as a distant war to one in which she was directly involved. According to her diary, she had prepared herself for an air-raid warning.[23] The worst was still to come.

Japanese women in the traditional women's roles of brave mourners and strong mothers re-entered the public discussion of Saipan on the third page of the *Asahi shinbun* on July 19, the day that the fall was reported. Nagumo Riki, widow of Nagumo Chūichi (1886–1944), the Japanese theater commander, expressed her preparedness to accept the news of her husband's death but conveyed her regret about the death of his subordinates.[24] She described her chagrin that Japan did not take back Saipan and added that her children would avenge this, noting her eldest son's entry into the navy. Mrs. Nagumo told the reporter that she would like to serve in a way that would directly affect the fighting. The reporter described how *azuki* bean plants were planted in the family's previously ceremonial garden, and how sand bags for fire extinguishing were neatly lined up. He concluded the story with the comment that now the Nagumo family are fighting at the front lines of the final battle.[25]

Appearing on the same page as the story of the Nagumos was an interview with Saitō Misao, widow of Lieutenant General Saitō Yoshitsugu (1890–1944). Dressed in her kimono bearing the family crest, she greeted mourners at the temporary Buddhist altar that held a photograph of the commander of the Imperial Army forces on Saipan. She told the reporter that she had just learned that her husband had been fighting in Saipan. As a wife of a military man, she said she had been ready for the news. Mrs. Saitō thought her husband had regretted that he had to meet his death before he could serve well at the front, since he had only departed for the battle zone a short time before. She expressed her concerns for the families of his subordinates. She told the reporter that she would bring up her three children to serve their country. The story was illustrated by photographs of these "courageous mourners" and "strong-willed mothers" who would send their sons to the front after their husbands had died. The pictures showed that the widows of the military leaders were now surrounded by sons and daughters, grandsons and granddaughters.

Women's Deaths in Media Imagery

One month after the official news of the fall of Saipan, the *Asahi shinbun*, on August 19, 1944, ran large block-character headlines that riveted the readers' eyes: "The Heroic Last Moments of Our Fellow Countrymen on Saipan / Sublimely Women Too Commit Suicide on Rocks in Front of the Great Sun Flag / Patriotic Essence Astounds the World."[26] The next day, headlines in the *Mainichi shinbun* proclaimed that Japanese women had "Changed into Their Best Apparel, Prayed to the Imperial Palace / Sublimely Commit Suicide in Front of the American Devils" and "Sacrifice Themselves for the National Exigency Together with the Brave Men."[27] The *Yomiuri hōchi*, the country's other major daily, was also emblazoned with the story under the headlines, "Women Combed Their Hair and Put on Make-Up in Departure for Death" and "[They] Purified Their Bodies, Prayed to the Sun Flag, and Committed Group Self-Explosion by Hand-Grenade."[28]

By any account, these were shocking headlines, especially appearing long after the fate of Saipan had been sealed. Where did such stories come from? Why were they appearing across the Japanese press more than a month after the battle on Saipan had died down, after Tōjō had been replaced, and the next grim battles in the Pacific were in the offing? The origin of these stories can be traced to an article by American reporter Robert Sherrod in the August 7, 1944, issue of *Time* magazine.[29] Titled "The Nature of the Enemy," Sherrod's single-page account of events on Saipan, part of *Time*'s wider treatment of the Marianas invasion and campaign, was one of the most stunning pieces of war reportage from the Pacific, filled as it was with graphic, unforgettable images and powerful questions.[30] While at times maudlin and always partisan, Sherrod's account was presented as an investigation into the extraordinary stories he said he had heard of suicides among some of the twenty thousand civilians on the island, of whom the United States had interned some ten thousand.

"The Nature of the Enemy"—a work by an *American* journalist— was to inspire overseas *Japanese* correspondents to file stories on the battle depicted in his description. Passing through the newsrooms and censors in Japan, massaged and replayed, they became the foundation for an unprecedented orgy of glorification of death that was splashed across the front pages of the major dailies. These reports, reactions to them, and the national spiritual mobilization campaigns they fostered established new standards of behavior and commitment for Japan's civilians in the grim wartime conditions their country confronted in the late summer of 1944.

The first story to appear, on page one of *Asahi shinbun* on August 19, was credited to special correspondent Watanabe in neutral Stockholm, Sweden. It began:

The facts that all of our loyal and courageous officers and soldiers defending Saipan Island died in action and that even the Japanese civilians who were able to fight participated in combat and shared the fate of the officers and soldiers, were reported worldwide through the announcement of the Imperial General Headquarters on July 18, and their loyal, courageous, and noble acts have impressed the world. [Now] It has been reported that noncombatants, women, and children have chosen death rather than to be captured alive and be shamed by the demon-like American forces. The world has been astounded by the strength of the fighting spirit and patriotism of the entire people of Japan.[31]

Sherrod's article had been built around a central question, raised in its final section. He first asked:

Death for 80,000,000? What did all this self-destruction mean? Did it mean that the Japanese on Saipan believed their own propaganda which told them that Americans are beasts and would murder them all? Many a Jap civilian did beg our people to put him to death immediately rather than to suffer the torture which he expected. But many who chose suicide could see other civilians who had surrendered walking unmolested in the internment camps. They could hear some of the surrendered plead with them by loudspeaker not to throw their lives away.[32]

Naturally, the last section of Sherrod's piece was not quoted in Japan exactly as written. The *Asahi shinbun* inserted a large headline over the article that covered over half of the front page of the August 19 paper; "Prefer Death to Surrender" replaced Sherrod's "Death for 80,000,000?" "Self-destruction" was translated as "*gyokusai*," and "their own propaganda" was dropped. The third sentence was rendered, "Many Japanese civilians preferred death, rather than capture and torture, and resolutely killed themselves." The last two sentences of the above-quoted paragraph were completely excised. Watanabe's "translation" ended:

Saipan is the first invaded Japanese territory populated with many civilians. Thus, the success of Japanese noncombatants on the islands shows that "Japanese, the whole race, choose death before surrender."

Yomiuri hōchi and *Mainichi shinbun* reported the same news the following day, with a dateline of "Stockholm," and only the addition of a detailed map. Although each paper showed recognizable variations in wording and style, reflecting different reporters or editors and giving the appearance of independent confirmations of the story, both relied on *Time* magazine as their source. The *Yomiuri hōchi* emphasized the death of all on Saipan and called for revenge:

Oh, what heroism and loyalty! Is there anyone who would not pray for the last moment of their noble fellow countrymen without tears and indignation? Look, American demons, we, one hundred million, will become the demons of revenge. The loyal spirits of our brothers on the isolated island in the southern ocean call to us, covered in blood. . . . The children of the Emperor will resolutely crush the American demons. We must respond to their loyal spirits calling to us.[33]

The complete omission in the Japanese accounts of any indication that any Japanese civilians had surrendered stands out as well, despite Sherrod's specific reference to the ten thousand detained civilians being held on Saipan.

Escalation in Exploitation of Women's Deaths

In addition to the sensational and distorted treatment of the article in *Time*, Japan's leading newspapers drew on noted intellectuals to comment on the deaths of civilian women on Saipan, turning their deaths into weapons directed at the Japanese civilian population. In the August 20 issue of *Yomiuri hōchi*, for example, the poet Saitō Ryū wrote how pleased and proud he was of how Japanese women and children had behaved on Saipan. Saitō turned to Japanese history for parallels, identifying one such heroine as Ōbako, a woman whose husband and son were killed by someone from the state of Silla in Korea, an enemy of Yamato–the ancient state of Japan—in AD 562. According to the *Nihongi*, an ancient history of Japan, the wife of the leader Tsukinokishi Ikina became a captive of the forces of Silla, but took her own life. The ancient text states that, standing by the enemy fortress, she composed: "Of the Land of Kara / Ōbako / Waves her head-scarf, / Turning toward Yamato."[34] To Saitō, the women of Saipan stood on the cliff above the Pacific and waved their sleeves praying to the land of the mother country just as Ōbako did fourteen centuries before. Moreover, these "Ōbako of Showa" "held their children firmly in their arms and died together," he reminds the reader.[35] In a concluding paragraph, the poet urged all Japanese women to be prepared for "beautiful death" when the enemy neared the main islands of Japan.[36]

Articles also appeared in the *Yomiuri hōchi*. Dr. Hiraizumi Kiyoshi of Tokyo Imperial University echoed that sentiment:

The women and children of Saipan taught us how splendid the power of blood and tradition was, and they gave us courage that will grow one hundred, no, one thousand times, and will live in the minds of the one hundred million.[37]

Hiraizumi also attempted to find the roots of women's death in history, arguing that the strength of Japanese samurai depended on the strength of their mothers, wives, and children. He argued that the strength of Japanese *bushidō* was the result of mothers' and wives' preference for "honorable death" over "shameful" living. The powerful flow of the moral mind of women, according to Hiraizumi, lay in the foundation of Japanese history. He presented the stories of Uryu Tamotsu's mother (?–1337) and the wife of Nawa Nagatoshi (?–1336) as examples. The story goes that Uryu Tamotsu and his brother met brave deaths during the period of Emperor Godaigo's attempt to reclaim imperial power, when they charged into the enemy in order to rescue two imperial princes who were surrounded by Ashikaga's forces. The majority of Uryu's remaining forces were injured, and Uryu's supporters were gravely dispirited. Then, Uryu's elderly mother encouraged the forces by saying that there was nothing to lament or to be surprised at. When one dares to serve one's lord, she stated, one is prepared for the situation, no matter how many hundred children get killed and how many thousand nephews die. Nawa Nagatoshi (?–1336) intended to "take care of" his family when Emperor Godaigo came from Oki to Senjoyama. His wife stabbed their child and committed suicide so that he would not think of them instead of his emperor. It would seem that these stories forced Hiraizumi to admit that there were differences between the women on Saipan and these samurai women of Japan's past. "It was unprecedented in three thousand years' history that such large numbers of unknown women chose such magnificent deaths."[38]

In the *Mainichi shinbun*, Saitō Fumi, Saitō Ryū's daughter, and a noted poet in her own right, pledged:

I swear to the sisters of Saipan that we will fight to the end with the pride of the women who had fought to the last in the sea of blood, and with the encouragement of death, and with the spirits of the women who had fallen with soldiers.[39]

Other outbursts of emotional praise, accompanied by streaming tears, expressions of pride, and protestations that such acts were the vindication of "the Japanese race," showed "the true nature of Japan," and were "unprecedented in history," filled the pages of newspapers. Commentators emphasized repeatedly that the women of Saipan were not women of samurai families, but just ordinary women. Takayanagi again warmed to his subject as he had when the deaths were only pending and expressed his emotions in the *Asahi shinbun*: "I am deeply moved learning that the blood of the great race would shine with a brilliant light when the time comes."[40]

Not all Japanese accepted these notions uncritically, of course. Critic and foreign policy expert Kiyosawa Kiyoshi's diary recorded his denunciation of such sentiments on August 20, 1944: "Japanese can neither objectively write articles nor read them." He summed up the intellectuals' accounts of the deaths of women on Saipan, as "feudalism—the influence of ancient warriors—in the time of the airplane, a great admiration for *hara-kiri*!"[41] Yet neither Kiyosawa nor any other leading figure publicly questioned the message implicit in the articles about the *"gyokusai* on Saipan,"* that in the face of such praise for the acts of their fellow citizens, all Japanese civilians were now expected to be ready for this kind of death.

Saipan's Inheritance of Gyokusai *from Attu*

The notion of *gyokusai* was first introduced into the Pacific War in May 1943, when American troops retook the outpost of Attu in the Aleutians in the remote Northern Pacific, which had been seized by Japanese forces in the complex operation that had culminated in the Imperial Japanese Navy's disaster at Midway in June 1942. The term—made up from two ideographs with literal meanings of "jewel" and "smashed"— was derived from a sixth-century Chinese classic telling of the morally superior man who would rather destroy his most precious possession than compromise his principles.[42] Rather than the meaningless deaths of a garrison cut off from all hope of reinforcement or escape and overwhelmed by superior numbers and firepower—a description that would accurately fit events on Attu island—the final charge of the Japanese garrison under Colonel Yamazaki Yasuyo (1891–1943) was transmogrified into an act of heroic self-sacrifice and was given the name *"Attu gyokusai."*[43] The phrase had poetic resonance and soon caught on as a euphemism with wide application.[44] It was at Saipan that the term took on its most concrete form in the public mind.

Saipan: Defining the Nature of the Pacific War's Final Stages

Saipan was the battle that defined the character of the Pacific War. Americans—soldiers, policymakers, and the folks on the home front— learned what many took to be "the nature of the enemy" along the sharp coral promontories and the towering cliffs at Marpi Point. After the island's capture by American forces, Japan's leaders and propagandists presented their version of events there to their public as a vision of the nature of the war they were fighting and as a glorification of the national spirit. "I have always considered Saipan the decisive battle of the Pacific offensive," wrote Holland M. ("Howling Mad") Smith, the Marine Corps general who commanded the assault that began on June 15, 1944. As he contemplated the 16,525 U.S. casualties, including 3,426 killed and missing, suffered by the 67,451 men under his command, Smith declared after the war that its seizure made Allied victory absolute.[45] Final figures for Japanese casualties on Saipan vary considerably. American sources identified 23,811 "enemy buried" and 1,780 captured (838 Koreans), with some 14,560 civilians taken into custody.[46] On the other hand, one Japanese source says of the 43,682 military defenders from all units, 41,244 died in the battle for Saipan (June 15 to July 10, 1944), but gives no figure at all for civilian losses.[47] If one were to accept even approximately the U.S. figure for civilians taken into custody, then it was certain that most civilians survived the battle.

Such horrendous military losses are cause enough to remember Saipan, but for the future course of the Pacific War, and for those who made decisions about how Japan, the Japanese, and their leaders would perform, the public deaths of some one thousand civilians at the end of the fighting—multiplied by propaganda, indifference to individual suffering, and desperation—would ultimately prove the most significant statistic of all.

What might otherwise appear to be a matter of journalistic rivalry or jumping on a good story was, in the reporting from Saipan, likely something much more. There is strong evidence that substantial parts of Japan's leadership—not only commanders of the armed forces but members of the so-called "peace group"—were seeking to prepare the Japanese public to carry out such a destiny rather than to surrender their own control of their war and their hold on political leadership and the Japanese people.

Women's Deaths in Political and Strategic Debate

While the military battles between the U.S. forces and Japanese were grinding on and the toll in human lives was mounting at Saipan, political struggles triggered by the defeat of Japanese forces intensified. A battle for political leadership in Japan was fought behind the doors of the Imperial Palace and in the chambers of Tōjō cabinet members and the senior statesmen who were behind Emperor Hirohito.[48] A pessimistic assessment of the war's future course at last had activated statesmen close to the court. Their secret debates were about who should take responsibility for the loss and how blame for defeat in the war could be kept from being affixed to the emperor in whose name the war was fought.

The senior statesmen's primary candidate for full responsibility was General Tōjō Hideki (1884–1948), the Prime Minister. Marquis Kido Kōichi (1889–1977), Lord Keeper of the Privy Seal, believed Tōjō should be left in his position until the last moment. Hosokawa Morisada, son-in-law of Konoe Fumimaro (1891–1945)—who was prime minister during most of the years of the Sino-Japanese War of 1937–1941 but out of government in 1944—quoted Kido as having said to Konoe:

Judging from today's circumstances, the people don't know the [true war] situation at all. After the retirement of the Tōjō cabinet, people might not follow a cabinet that would change a direction even if it were created. Although regrettable, after [the people] have experienced bombings once or twice and received bombings or suffered a landing on the Homeland, the people would move in that direction. Then, we can change to a peace cabinet.[49]

Saipan was to be instrumental in the "peace process." But it would take the Japanese political and military leadership—formal and informal government leaders—more than a year to implement their "plan." I believe Saipan was seized upon as the ideal tool to mobilize the Japanese public. By turning the people's minds toward death, the public might be prepared for several months of struggle, while the "statesmen" would convince the Allies that the Japanese public was indeed prepared to fight to the last, which would serve as a bargaining counter to the American demand for "unconditional surrender" that threatened the position of the Imperial House.

It is vital when considering the consequences of such thinking that we recall that the vast majority of the one million Japanese civilian casualties in the war and perhaps more than half of the military deaths—over one million—occurred in the last twelve months of the conflict. Between July 1944 and August 1945, as Japan's leaders sought to protect themselves and the institutions they claimed to serve, the people of Japan were in fact sacrificed under a national slogan that was eventually refined into "One Hundred Million Die Together," a natural extension of the illusory image of Saipan's civilians embracing death together with their soldiers, in service to their emperor.

The interpretations of major papers came to actualize women's deaths on Saipan in concrete images that would become indelible, indeed would almost become templates for action in the months to come. Headlines claimed women preferred to die rather than be captured by the enemy. The papers described their deaths as beautiful, with women purifying themselves in the sea, combing their long black hair, putting on fresh clothing, praying to the sun flag spread over the rocks, then bowing in the direction of the Imperial Palace before falling into the sea. What seemed at the start of the battle to be a call to arms for women had become, through the calls of intellectuals, propagandists, scholars, poets, and reporters, an elevation of civilian deaths on Saipan. In part due to the clues to American psychology drawn from Sherrod's report, women's deaths came to be presented as "a shield for the emperor" or "the foundation of Greater East Asia." The papers proclaimed repeatedly the ignorance of the Westerners to the "true meaning" of death. These women's deaths took place, according to these commentators, "because of the blood of the Yamato race that flowed in their veins."[50] The most glib commentators were male scholars and literary propagandists historicizing and mythologizing women's horrific dying and creating beautified and glorified images of unrealistic women's deaths. The visual beautification of women's deaths on Saipan became a political and psychological tool during the last stage of Japan's war, which is demonstrated by the words of Imai Kuniko, who offered her poems to "fellow Japanese on Saipan":

At the *extremis* of surrender or death, our fellow Japanese have chosen death.
Having run combs through their hair, women cast themselves out and fall into
  the sea.
Lamenting over these who serenely died, we, the living, will not stop fighting.[51]

Conclusion

What does what we might call "women's death" mean for our understanding of Japan's war? How to exploit women's death seemed to be an issue at the start. It had happened—women did it, that was the claim. The argument went that these women were not left defenseless, they were not slaughtered. They killed themselves. By historicizing their deaths, women's dying became a political weapon. Why were women's deaths necessary? It would seem that men's *gyokusai*—such as at Attu—was not sufficient in order to sustain fighting spirit. Did women have to kill themselves in order to encourage men to die for the sake of the state? Yes, from the propagandists' claims, it would seem so. Indeed, at the very highest levels of Japan's ruling elite, news of what happened on Saipan, when received July 1, 1944, provoked a sense of relief for one of Japan's most prolific observers of events and a man at the core of decision-making. Kido Kōichi, Emperor Hirohito's close confidante in the Imperial Palace, recorded in his diary his comments to Hirohito's chief aide-de-camp, "It was so fortunate that the order [for *gyokusai*] was forestalled thanks to the prime minister's idea."[52] This cryptic reference in his entry for July 1 indicates that an order that all noncombatants should die had been discussed at the highest level of Japan's war leadership. (Saipan was the first "Japanese" territory invaded by the Americans that had a substantial population of civilians.) Apparently Prime Minister Tōjō had intervened to countermand such an order before it could be issued, though we have little clue as to why he did so. Kido's comment shows that events that rendered such an order unnecessary were welcome. The people did it on their own, or so he thought.

And yet, as we list the chronology of "*gyokusai*"—Guadalcanal, Attu, Saipan—and then go on to the frantic battles for the Philippines that gave birth to the Kamikaze and look ahead to Okinawa and what happened to women in Manchuria at the end of the war, we see the images—the pictures of death—multiply. The news of what happened on Saipan, and how civilians were said to have died, spread rapidly not only through the papers, but through personal testimony and documents as well, and became part of the fabric of wartime administration and mobilization. The news was disseminated widely among the village offices in Okinawa prefecture (whence, it should be remembered, a great many of the colonists and workers in Japan's South Seas colonies had come). Nakamura Takejirō, a survivor of a "group suicide" in the Kerima archipelago on March 26, 1945, during the early stages of the American invasion of Okinawa, was twelve years old at the time. He recalled how, with his mother and elder sister, he entered their shelter in the mountains. His sister, twenty years old, asked to die first, with the help of her mother. "On Saipan, all the men were run over by the U.S. tanks [recall the photograph in *Life* and *Time* of a bulldozer pushing

Japanese bodies into a mass grave] and the women were raped," they were told, he said. Half of the one hundred residents of his island successfully committed "group suicide" even before the Americans approached.[53] Prepared by propaganda, the civilians acted.

The escalation in the treatment of women as weapons accelerated as news of death came home to Japan. The first bombing raids on the homeland began at the time of Saipan, and by the late autumn the Americans were using those new bases to attack the major cities. In March 1945 the fire-raids—overwhelming attacks that seemed to allow the destruction of Japan's great cities almost at will—rendered women part of the battlefront. The atomic bombings were merely the final act. Such acts as group suicide in Okinawa were to be repeated on an even grander scale in Manchuria in August when the Soviet Union attacked Japan's colonial "bastion." There, group suicides as they were persistently called—though they were often ordered by local officials or military commanders—involved at times more than 400, sometimes just tens, and occasionally individual families seeking to escape the fate they had been led to expect.[54] There were, of course, many other patterns to be considered in Manchuria, including the hostile local population, the overwhelming sense of abandonment felt by some, and the brutality of the army toward its own civilians by that stage of the war, but it seems clear that the shadow of Saipan was cast that far to the north. In this process, the utility of death emerged as a powerful psychological and political tool targeted on the Japanese people at the same time that it was aimed at the American enemy in a kind of grandiose bluff, threatening to take thousands of lives along in a catastrophic dance of death.

The phenomenon of war has been often depicted in a polarized paradigm, with clear divisions such as home front and battle front, one's own side and the enemy, offense and defense, men and civilians. Gender has been part of this polarized conceptualization of war; the roles assigned to men had been different from those assigned to women. The case of women in Saipan may well mark the point that gendered assignment changed in that war; though sustained in some ways, the introduction of death and dying women forced a greater change than women taking burdens off men in factories or on the fire patrol line or civil defense fronts.

Prior to the last year of the war, when a woman in Japan considered the war she was not likely to see it as a matter of her own death, but would rather view it through her own personal tragedies—deaths or injuries of sons, brothers, husbands, or friends—or on rare, and often public occasions, in more grandiose frames of reference—nation, race, or empire. The Japanese woman experienced the war in geographical areas where dying did not occur to her, personally. Women did not experience the "zone of emptiness" of the military institution and the reality of the killing fields or starvation conditions themselves. Indeed, women were often shielded from those realities by the men who came back from the front who would not talk about the war, and even by those comrades who chose not to visit relatives, even when their loved ones were still alive, fearing that they would have to tell them of the deaths of their loved ones or reveal conditions that surely would lead to their deaths.[55] But after Saipan, these distinctions were broken down, as it was clear to all who manipulated media, set the course of propaganda, and held the political and military reins of power, that women would soon die in great numbers. There is intense contradiction in the image—women pose terrible problems for propagandists. Their "preferred images" might marshal "male" gendered roles and cause women immense anxiety, but from June 1944, very different priorities seem to dictate.

In the year after Saipan's fall in July 1944 and in the subsequent half-century, portrayals and interpretations of the battle for Saipan have helped define how American strategy and victory, Japanese resistance and defeat, and the subsequent horrors of war in the Pacific were justified to history. Saipan—the battle and the mythology of the battle—helped forge an unholy alliance of national stereotypes and self-justifications. America was convinced that unconditional surrender and ruthless willingness to exact the highest possible toll in enemy lives, military or civilian, was the only guarantee of a certain victory. In the end, this conviction was to guide America's policy through the fire-bombings of Japan's cities, the invasion of Okinawa, and the atomic devastation wrought on Japan in lieu of the contemplated invasion. The strategy in Japan that exploited the image of Saipan and the Marianas amounted to a threat of national self-destruction and suicide embraced by Japan's leadership to stave off abject surrender and acceptance of American demands at any cost.

Notes

1. *Kōkoku fujo kaidōno zu* (*Aki to fuyu*) by the Joryūgaka gassaku, 1944 (187.7 cm x 298.5 cm).

2. Haruko Taya Cook and Theodore F. Cook, *Japan at War: An Oral History* (New York: The New Press, 1992).

3. Haruko Taya Cook, "The Myth of the Saipan Suicides," *MHQ: The Quarterly Journal of Military History* 7, no. 3 (Spring 1995): 12–19.

4. See Mark R. Peattie, *Nan'yō: The Rise and Fall of the Japanese in Micronesia, 1885–1945* (Honolulu: University of Hawai'i Press, 1988).

5. Yamada Akiko, *Ianfutachi no taiheiyō sensō*, cited in Suzuki Hitoshi, *Saipan muzan: "gyokusai" ni tsuieta "umi no Mantetsu"* (Nihon hyōronsha, 1993), 180.

6. Suzuki, *Saipan muzan*, 179. See also Hirakushi Takashi, *Nikudan!! Saipan-Tinian sen: gyokusai sen kara seikanshita sanbō no shōgen* (Kyōei shobō, 1979), 266.

7. Ishikawa Tatsuzō, "Kōkai nisshi," in *Ishikawa Tatsuzō sakuhin-shu dai ni-jūsankan* (Shinchōsha, 1973), 405–407.

8. Hirakushi, *Nikudan!!*, 266. Horie Yoshitaka, *Higeki no Saipan tō* (Hara shobō, 1967), 80–81. Those in the northern part of the towns were run by Japanese from the main islands, with one run by a Korean. In southern Garapan they were segregated—one for Okinawans, five for Tokyo people, two from Fukuoka, and one owned by Koreans. See also Bōeichō bōei kenshūjo senshishitsu, *Senshi sōsho*, vol. 6: *Chūbu Taiheiyō rikugun sakusen, 1: Mariana gyokusai made* (Asagumo shinbunsha, 1967), hereafter cited as BBKS. *Mariana gyokusai made* (618) says total evacuees numbered 2,300.

9. See Suzuki, *Saipan muzan*, 198–201.

10. Many American accounts refer to the plight of the Saipan captives in piteous terms and speak of the lessons learned for the coming battle of Okinawa. See e.g., Samuel Eliot Morison, *History of United States Naval Operations in World War II: New Guinea and the Marianas, March 1944–August 1944*, vol. VIII (Boston, MA: Little, Brown, 1953), 339–340. Few speak fully of the truly terrible conditions in the American camps as the battle raged on the island. Many internees died of disease malnutrition, and among the young and old deaths were very common, with more than one thousand documented as dying in captivity.

11. BBKS, *Mariana gyokusai made* (618) gives the total number of civilians on the island at the end of July as about 15,700, "including Koreans." The camp was

divided into four groups: islanders, Japanese, Koreans, and military men and civilian employees of the army.

12. Noda Mitsuharu, interview with the author.

13. Suzuki, *Saipan muzan*, 206.

14. *Asahi shinbun*, June 28, 1944.

15. Ibid.

16. Ibid.

17. Tomoe was one of his last surviving companions. In Barbara L. Arnn's rendition "Tomoe" was urged to flee lest he be embarrassed by the enemy's discovery that a woman was with him; but she refused to go until she had taken the head of an enemy warrior to prove that her prowess was equal to any man's. She then escaped, and is said to have either remarried or lived out her life as a nun. Her exploits are recounted in a Nō play, *Tomoe*, attributed to the great playwright Zeami, in the *Kodansha Encyclopedia of Japan*, vol. 8 (Kodansha, Ltd, 1983), 73.

18. The historian misses the historical irony of these causes all being lost causes, and while sometimes on the imperial side, his last example was of people opposed to the Meiji Emperor.

19. This surely must be an odd way to call for the study and expansion of women's history in Japan!

20. *Rikugun daihon'ei kimitsu sensō nisshi*, quoted in Mikano Hirosuke, *Higeki no Saipan, zettai kokubōken no hōkai* (Futowaaku shuppansha, 1992), 116–118.

21. *Asahi shinbun*, July 19, 1944.

22. Nogami Yaeko, *Nogami Yaeko zenshū: dainiki, daihachikan nikki*, vol. 8 (Iwanami shoten, 1988), 272.

23. Ibid., 316.

24. Vice Admiral Nagumo Chūichi was the operational commander of the aircraft carrier strike force that attacked Pearl Harbor, Hawaii, on December 7, 1941. Present on Saipan when the American forces landed (June 15, 1944), he committed suicide during the final stages of the battle (July 8–13).

25. *Asahi shinbun*, July 19, 1944.

26. Ibid.

27. *Mainichi shinbun,* August 20, 1944.

28. *Yomiuri hōchi,* August 20, 1944.

29. The Marianas campaign was extensively covered. Sherrod's piece "The Nature of the Enemy" appeared on August 7, 1944, in *Time* magazine.

30. *Life* magazine dealt with Saipan and the Marianas in the August 28, 1944, issue and married Sherrod's earlier *Time* article—stated to be an eyewitness account from Saipan—with the strong photographs by *Life*'s own photographers Peter Stackpole and W. Eugene Smith, 75–83. The result was a doubly shocking confirmation of Sherrod's main themes. The four photos of an attempted backing away from "group suicide" by a father, mother, and their four children foiled by a Japanese sniper seemed to confirm stunningly Sherrod's version of the events, 80–81.

Almost as horrifying was the photo captioned "As a JEEP Bears Wounded Yank to Rear, Bulldozer Scoops Graves for Some Saipan Japs" on the page following a photo of a grave marker for an "unknown" U.S. Marine of the 4th Division, 82–83.

31. *Asahi shinbun,* August 19, 1944.

32. *Time,* August 7, 1944, 27.

33. See the front pages of *Yomiuri hōchi* and *Mainichi shinbun* on August 20, 1944.

34. See *Nihongi: Chronicle of Japan from Earliest Times to AD 697,* trans. W. G. Aston (Rutland, VT & Tokyo: Charles E. Tuttle Company, 1972), 85. The *Nihongi* version of the tale would seem to contradict Saitō's evocation of her tale, but Ōbako's preparing herself for death in the poem certainly conformed to the evolving legend of Saipan that he was contributing to creating.

35. See *Egakareta rekishi,* eds., Hyōgoken kindai bijutsukan & Kanagawaken kindai bijutsukan ("Egakareta rekishi"-ten jikkō iinkai, 1993), 100, for a wooden statue of Ōbako.

36. See the August 20, 1944, issue of *Yomiuri hōchi.* The author noted, "Despite the fact that they were neither brought up in the family of warriors, nor the wives of warriors," like Ōbako and the wife of Hosokawa Tadaoki, who stabbed her two children and committed suicide when they were surrounded by the enemy, Saitō declared, the women of Saipan "achieved a sublime and grand last moment, by coloring red the rocks of the South Ocean" with "sublime Japanese blood." Saitō does not bother to provide an explanation of the life of Hosokawa's wife. Her life history is quite complex. She is also known as Hosokawa Gracia (1563–1600). She was a convert to Christianity and is also

known as the very model of the virtuous warrior wife. She was the third daughter of Akechi Mitsuhide, and her husband (Hosokawa Tadaoki) was the eldest son of a daimyo. Her husband refused to support her father when Akechi killed Oda Nobunaga. She was obliged to retire to the countryside and eventually allowed by Hideyoshi to live in Osaka. There she was baptized and became a Christian. Hosokawa Tadaoki later sided with Ieyasu. When Ishida Mitsunari attempted to capture her as a hostage, a retainer of the family executed her on orders of her husband. See *Japan: An Illustrated Encyclopedia,* vol. I (Kodansha, 1993), 567.

37. *Yomiuri hōchi,* August 20, 1944.

38. Ibid.

39. See the front page of the August 20, 1944, issue of *Mainichi shinbun.*

40. See the third page of the August 20, 1944, issue of *Asahi shinbun* for these comments of Takayanagi Mitsuhisa, identified as professor of Kokugakuin University. The institute he headed was located at Tokyo Imperial University.

41. Kiyosawa Kiyoshi, *Ankoku nikki, 1942–1945* (Iwanami, 1990), 221–222. We can also note that Kiyosawa left his diary in his residence in Karuizawa out of fear that its contents might be revealed were it in his Tokyo home (201). He wrote how the reporting director of the Imperial Navy invited the representatives of various circles, including "liberals," in order to discuss "how to heighten the fighting spirits of the people." Such reports were numerous. For example, see also Nogami, *Nogami Yaeko,* 377–379. At the time these articles appeared, Nogami Yaeko was in Kitakaruizawa as part of her regular summer stay. She made no comment in the *Time* article, perhaps because she did not read newspapers regularly, filling her entries of August 19 and 20 instead with details of a barter of ten eggs for some of her children's clothing, her comments on her reading of a work by the Chinese radical writer Lu Xun, the notation that she had completed writing a short piece called "A Memory of Miss Haruko," and her effusive appreciation of her "luxurious" breakfast of bread with butter and a few cups of Indian tea with milk and sugar. But on August 21 she related a story she heard about a woman who had boarded an evacuation ship from Saipan with her three-year-old child after having given birth to a second child just two hours before it sailed. The ship was torpedoed en route and despite an order to abandon the ship without children, she floated in the sea with her two children, hanging to a float until eventually all three were rescued. Rather than write of deaths, of which she may not have heard, she asserted the value of the will to live.

42. John W. Dower, *War without Mercy: Race & Power in the Pacific War* (New York: Pantheon Books, 1986), 231–233 and 352–353, *n*61–64, discusses one interpretation of the origin of *gyokusai* and its development. Dower dates the phrase *"ichioku gyokusai"* (the shattering of the hundred million like a beautiful jewel) from April 1945. Actually, it appeared at least as early as 24 June 24, 1944, when it was used in the *Daihon'ei kimitsu sensō nisshi*. See Mikano, *Higeki no Saipan*, 118.

43. On May 12, 1943, ten thousand American troops assaulted Attu, garrisoned by 2,500 Japanese under Colonel Yamazaki. Americans reported the island "cleared out" by May 28. The final stage of the battle was reached when six hundred Japanese troops made a final assault that, according to some U.S. accounts, nearly reached the American artillery positions. The few troops who survived the attack, realizing they could not breach the new line, committed suicide. Only twenty-eight Japanese were taken prisoner. Colonel Yamazaki, who was said to have led the final assault, received the customary two-rank promotion following his death in battle, and he is usually referred to as Major General Yamazaki. American casualties included 549 Americans killed and 1,148 wounded, while 2,132 became noncombat casualties, in large part because of the harsh arctic conditions. The larger Japanese garrison of Kiska, 200 miles east of Attu, that the Americans had leap-frogged was secretly evacuated in July and more than five thousand survivors of the 5,400 men assigned to defend it were brought out before the impending American invasion. When that blow fell on August 16, the Americans storming ashore found the island abandoned James F. Dunnigan and Albert A. Nofi, *The Pacific War Encyclopedia* (New York: Checkman Books, 1998), 39–40.

44. Kiyosawa, *Ankoku nikki*, 39–40. Yet the phrase did not answer all observers' questions about actions such as Attu, even in Japan. On May 31, 1943, Kiyosawa Kiyoshi noted in his diary that following the previous day's broadcast of the news of the *gyokusai* of Japanese forces on Attu by Imperial General Headquarters, "Today's papers tell us that at the end only a hundred and a few score remained, that the wounded committed suicide, and the healthy charged [into the enemy]." Rather than accept the story, Kiyosawa set down in his diary the thought, "If they were not people related to the military, the following questions would come up and become social problems." Criticizing such events, he asks why headquarters did not dispatch more men although it was reported that Colonel Yamazaki did not request even one more soldier. "Isn't the lack of reflection of their strategy leading to all strategic failures?" he asked. What is the meaning of *"gyokusai*-ism"—a phrase he coined—as seen on Attu? "Next, it will be Kiska," he wrote:

It appears we have one division there. *Gyokusai*-ism will deprive them of their lives. Is this good for the nation? This will be an issue in the future. The general public may not make any inquiry into such things. Oh, stupid general public!

Perhaps he was able to foresee what lay ahead for the people of Japan. While the High Command did eventually evacuate the Kiska garrison prior to an American descent on the island, Kiyosawa remained angry at the Japanese public for their seeming indifference to news he felt should have shocked them into demands for clarification.

45. General Holland M. Smith and Percy Finch, *Coral and Brass* (New York: Scribner, 1949), 181–182, quoted in Morison, *History of United States Naval Operations*, 339–340. Such general views of the importance attached by Tokyo to Saipan may be seen in many official and semiofficial sources, for example Carl W. Hoffman, USMC, *Saipan: The Beginning of the End* (Washington, DC: Historical Division HQ, U.S. Marine Corps, 1950); Jeter A. Isely and Philip A. Crowl, *The U.S. Marines and Amphibious War* (Princeton, NJ: Princeton University Press, 1951); Philip A. Crowl, *United States Army in World War II: The War in the Pacific, Campaigns in the Marianas*, vol. II, pt. 9 (Washington, DC: United States Army, Office of Military History, 1960).

46. Morison, *History of United States Naval Operations*, 339.

47. Kuroha Kiyotaka, *Taiheiyō sensō no rekishi*, vol. 2 (Kōdansha, 1989), 143–146. Also see Cook & Cook, *Japan at War*, 291–292.

48. Bōeicho bōei senshishitsu, *Senshi sōsho, daihon'ei Rikugunbu (8): Shōwa 19–nen made* (Asagumo shinbunsha, 1974), 445–518.

49. Ibid., quoting Hosokawa Morisada, *Nikki*, June 26, 1944, 497.

50. Takayanagi Mitsuhisa, who wrote of the prospects of women fighting in the *Asahi shinbun* back on June 28, now used the term "*junshi*," and described the confirmed deaths as "supreme," or "extremely pure," and claimed that they would lay the foundation of the construction of Greater East Asia. Takayanagi cites the examples of women who "died for their husband and lords" in Japanese history, including Oichi, wife of Shibata Katsuie (1522?–1583), and her thirty servant women, and women who died together with Hideyori at the fall of the Osaka Castle in 1615. According to Takayanagi, it was only common sense that women would also commit suicide when their lord met a sad fate. He explains that women on Saipan "shared the burning blood flowing from the women of the warring states period" and each accepted her own death "as a shield for the Emperor." See *Asahi shinbun*, August 20, 1944.

51. *Yomiuri hōchi*, August 20, 1944. She renders the second line, *Kurogami o kushizukeoete onnarawa, umi o megakete onore o chirikeru.*

52. Kido Kōichi, *Kido Kōichi nikki*, vol. 2 (Tōkyō daigaku shuppankai, 1966), 1114.

53. "Memories of the Okinawa Battlefield," *NHK Special,* August 15, 1997.

54. Jinno Morimasa, *Tairiku no hanayome* (Nashinokisha, 1992), 114–117.

55. Ogawa Masatsugu, "The 'Green Desert' of New Guinea" in Cook and Cook, *Japan at War*, 267–276.

PART IV

Gender,
Work,
Economy

10 *Gendering the Labor Market: Evidence from the Interwar Textile Industry*
Janet Hunter

> Economic progress often brings advances in some aspects of gender differences while frustrating others. Part of the problem lies in social norms and prejudices that impede change; another is in the dictates of profit maximization in a society that until recently allowed restrictions solely on the basis of sex, among other characteristics.
>
> —Claudia Goldin, *Understanding the Gender Gap*[1]

In many industrializing countries women have constituted a major part of the factory work force, and early twentieth-century Japan was no exception. The women who worked in many of Japan's textile mills in the decades up to World War II drew the attention of contemporaries inside and outside Japan. The British Fabian socialist, Beatrice Webb, visiting Japan in 1911, reported in her diary for September 14 a visit to a cotton mill in the city of Nagoya. She seemed struck by the youth of the female workers, but impressed by the quality of the boarding house in which they lived.[2] Nearly twenty years later the American economist John Orchard wrote that "the textile industries . . . are organized to use large numbers of women and children in the operation of the mills."[3] Most of the workers, he noted, were accommodated in dormitories at the mill.

Under the dormitory system, all the needs of the worker are supplied under the supervision of the company. Besides board and lodging, if the girl has not completed her compulsory requirements, and many have not, education is given by company teachers.[4]

Orchard himself went on to caution against blind belief in the benign paternalism such a scenario suggested, and certainly the observations of Japanese contemporaries, and reports from workers themselves, suggested a rather different reality. One silk worker stated that:

From morning, while it was still dark, we worked in the lamplit factory till ten at night. After work, we hardly had the strength to stand on our feet. . . . There was no heat even in the winter, and so we had to sleep huddled together. . . . If we didn't do the job right we were scolded, and, if we did better than others, the others resented it.[5]

Debates over the conditions of female workers in Japan's textile industries might have remained focused at the level of human interest had it not been for the industry's significance in the country's rapidly industrializing economy. By the interwar years the importance of Japanese textile production, in both domestic and international terms, was enormous. In 1930 the textile industry accounted for around one-third of total manufacturing employment in Japan, and the making of thread, cloth, and clothing occupied over 6 percent of the total working population. The value of this production amounted to 30 percent of the total value of manufacturing output, and cloth and yarn exports accounted for over half of the total value of exports throughout these two decades.[6] This giant sector of manufacturing embraced a range of productive activity, from large scale, highly mechanized, capital intensive operations at one end of the spectrum to the individual, highly skilled handicraft worker at the other. Demand for its products came from every level, from luxury to the most basic, from both outside and inside the country.

The young women mentioned above were all employed in the production of raw silk and cotton yarn, and they have rightly been given considerable prominence in the historiography.[7] However, theirs is far from being the only experience of textile work in this period. In fact, the textile labor force was highly diverse in skills, origins, and working environment. It also included significant numbers of men. One purpose of this chapter is to demonstrate the extent of this diversity by looking at the gender division of labor across textile production over the period from 1920 to 1940.[8] Two trends are apparent from looking at this data. One is that these years witnessed an increasing polarization in the textile employment patterns of men and women, that is, an increasing divergence in men's and women's experience of textile work. Secondly, and perhaps more striking, polarization was also evident *within* the female labor market. A growing division became apparent between the work of married and unmarried women, which had little counterpart in patterns of male employment.

This chapter's other concern is to ask the question of why the textile work force was so gendered in the interwar years, and to suggest how developments in these decades were part of a longer term evolutionary process. Such analysis is facilitated by the extensive availability of material left by the employers themselves, and by the existence of numerous surveys of labor in the industry undertaken by government and public bodies (at both national and local levels), independent institutions such as the YWCA, and individual social scientists. Using some of these materials, it will be argued that an element of diversity persisted within textiles, as the different branches of textile production continued to be associated with different imperatives regarding labor, capital, and technology. At the same time, we know that all branches of textile production moved in the interwar years toward a concentration of capital and production, and it is evident that the process of technological and organizational change diminished that diversity. Various sectors of textile production fared differently, but as mechanization and concentration of ownership and capital spread within the industry, other branches seemingly shifted toward the pattern of the more mechanized, more capital intensive and larger scale areas of production, namely cotton spinning and silk reeling. However, technological and organizational changes may have been the occasion of this process of gendering, but cannot necessarily explain it. To understand it more fully we need to take into account a range of other factors—in particular the interwar economic, social, and political environment, and the immense influence wielded by the large textile employers. The net result was that the interwar years reaffirmed and built on the gender division of labor initiated earlier in some parts of textile production. It was also the period that institutionalized the key principles behind the gender division of labor in postwar Japan, in particular the "lifecycle" view of women's work.[9]

The initial part of this essay will give an overview of the gender division of labor in textiles between the wars, using official figures, in particular the decennial national censuses of 1920, 1930, and 1940. While the census data are in some ways problematic,[10] the data are sufficient to provide a reasonably accurate picture of the gender division of labor in textile production, and the extent to which it may have changed during the period under consideration. Consideration will be given not just to the relative numbers of workers of each sex, but also to gender differences in age profiles, marital status, and employment status. It will be shown that while some areas of production, notably silk reeling, spinning, and weaving, consistently employed large numbers of young, unmarried women, other textile-related activities used many more men and older, married or widowed/separated women. Moreover, even in those sectors of production where women were dominant, they were in fact engaged in a limited number of tasks.[11]

The second part of this chapter will seek to analyze why even before World War 1 women had become so numerically dominant in the core areas of large scale and mechanized production. It will be contended that while previously established patterns of work were significant, the relatively low cost of female labor, its supposed docility, and the rapid expansion of the industries pushed employers toward recruiting this kind of labor. The third section considers the extent to which the progress of industrialization—the spread of mechanization and the concentration of capital and ownership—may have offered an opportunity for further gendering of the textile labor force, making textile work more "women's work" than it had been before and heightening the industry's dependence on unmarried women freer to leave their homes and families.[12]

Finally, section four will consider the very specific circumstances of interwar Japan. During these decades alternative employment opportunities for men, and, latterly, mobilization, tended to contribute to the "feminization" of the textile work force. Equally important, though, were the ideologies relating to gender roles in society articulated during these years, and the way in which the large textile employers, particularly in cotton spinning, were able to put forward their own labor policies as the norm not just for the textile industries as a whole, but for patterns of male and female labor force participation in general.

The Gender Division of Labor in Textile Production[13]

As shown in Table 1, in 1920 nearly two million Japanese were engaged in some form of textile production. The number progressively declined over the next two decades, but in 1940 the industry still employed nearly 1.7 million. Table 2 shows that silk reeling employed the most workers, followed by cotton spinning and weaving, dyeing/finishing, and sewing/tailoring, all of which consistently employed well over 100,000 workers throughout these years. Women throughout accounted for the majority of workers in the industry, but their share of the work force fluctuated, declining markedly between 1920 and 1930, and then increasing again during the following decade. This decline to 1930 was in part due to a substantial reduction in the total number of workers in certain major branches of production, notably cotton spinning, thread, knitwear, and braid manufacture, weaving, dyeing, and finishing, which had all employed large numbers of women. Some of these industries recovered, or even grew, in the 1930s, but employment levels overall continued to shrink due to the collapse in silk production and sustained labor rationalization in cotton spinning.

The different branches of production did not show a consistent pattern in terms of their gender division of labor. In 1920 the proportion of the labor force accounted for by women in the major branches of textile production varied from nearly 80 percent in silk reeling down to no more than 44 percent in the dyeing and finishing trades. In all but one case the female proportion of the labor force had declined in 1930, but the fall was greater in those industries that were already employing fewer women. In the case of the dyeing and finishing trades, the fall was dramatic. Silk reeling was the exception. Here an increase in the number of workers was accompanied by an increase in the proportion of the work force accounted for by women, a factor associated with mills taking on more workers to reel the increased cocoon production of Japanese farmers.[14] In all cases except silk, the proportion of women workers then recovered the following decade, increasing the significance of women in the textile work force as a whole. The reduced

Table 1
Textile Workers by Gender 1920–1940

Year	Males (%)	Females (%)	Total
1920	638,600 (32.2)	1,342,900 (67.8)	1,981,500
1930	752,100 (40.5)	1,106,800 (59.5)	1,858,900
1940	641,800 (37.8)	1,057,000 (62.2)	1,698,800

NOTE: Figures to nearest hundred, % to nearest 0.1%.
SOURCE: 1920 census vol. 2, 42 (category 10); 1930 census vol. 2, 144–145, 160–161 (categories 14–15); 1940 census vol. 2, 210 ff. (categories 69–76) [see note 13].

significance of men in textiles may be attributed to a range of factors that will be discussed later. These include the opening up of employment opportunities for men in other, growing branches of manufacturing; the impact of the depression, which may have stimulated more women to try to earn a living as seamstresses, for example; the impact of military preparedness and war; and the increased mechanization of certain production processes. Even so, at the end of the period as at the beginning, the pattern of the gender division of labor still varied considerably between different branches of textile production. In general male workers played a far greater role in the finishing processes and in garment manufacture than they did in the basic processes of thread, yarn, and cloth production.

Age and Marital Status of Textile Workers

In 1920 workers under the age of twenty constituted only a small proportion of the work force in the finishing and sewing trades, but elsewhere they were far more important. This was especially true of the female work force. In some branches of textile production one-half to two-thirds of women workers were under the age of twenty.[15] The proportion of young male workers was far more consistent across the different branches of production. In 1920 a high proportion of these young workers were very young indeed. Around half a million individuals aged fourteen or younger were working in textiles at this time, over 40 percent of them male.[16] Although the number of very young

Table 2
Textile Workers in Major Branches of Textile Production, 1920–1940*

	1920	1930	1940
Silk Reeling	438,900 (82.8%)	480,700 (86.0%)	234,000 (83.9%)
Thread Manufacture	51,200 (58.2%)	30,400 (54.4%)	47,200 (67.2%)
Spinning	297,100 (69.1%)	204,100 (67.8%)	235,470 (72.5%)
Weaving	701,800 (71.8%)	424,300 (69.0%)	480,500 (73.0%)
Knitwear/ Braid	51,700 (51.3%)	59,200 (40%)	68,600 (54.1%)
Dyeing/ Finishing, etc.	300,000 (44.2%)	202,300 (11.5%)	211,200 (20.3%)
Sewing & Tailoring, etc.	213,200 (56.5%)	232,900 (46.0%)	384,400 (53.9%)

* % figure in parentheses = female proportion of the work force
NOTE: Figures include all categories of worker. Figures to nearest hundred, % to nearest 0.1%.
SOURCE: 1920 census vol. 2 (from category 10); 1930 census vol. 2 (from categories 14–15); 1940 census vol. 2 (from categories 69–74) [see note 13].

workers did decline over the interwar years—a trend influenced by the spread of education and the influence of protective legislation—they did not totally disappear. In 1930 girls aged fourteen and under still made up 15 percent of the spinning and weaving work force.[17] More significantly, young workers under twenty continued to play a major part in most areas of production. In most cases there was still a higher proportion of the work force under twenty years of age in 1940 than had been the case in 1920. This was true of both male and female workers, but the major branches of textile production in particular tended to employ large numbers of young women in this age category. In both cotton and silk reeling, for example, 60 to 70 percent of all female workers from 1920 to 1940 were under twenty, but only 25 to 35 percent of male workers were. While the figures for young male workers were broadly in line with those for the nation's occupied male population as a whole, for women, the proportion of textile workers in this age group was way out of line with the national average for women. One feature is consistently apparent: namely, those areas of production in which women workers played the greatest role were also those that tended to employ the youngest women workers.

The other side of the picture of growing dependence on young workers was a decline in the importance of older workers, particularly those over the age of thirty. Some diversity nevertheless persisted. In most branches of the industry, a far greater proportion of male than female workers was likely to be above the age of thirty, but this pattern was reversed in those trades with fewer women—dyeing, finishing, and garment manufacture. The figures also indicate that during the interwar years the age profile for men and women workers in textiles was diverging. Changing employment opportunities for young men, and the move toward war, contributed to a rising proportion of the diminishing number of male workers in all these occupations being over the age of thirty. By contrast, the proportion of female workers in this age bracket declined between 1920 and 1940. The decline was less marked in those branches of production that already had fewer older female workers (mainly silk and cotton spinning), but was very marked in those branches that, at the start of the period, had predominantly employed older women, such as tailoring and sewing. Textile production thus increasingly employed older men and younger women, and in that respect there was some reduction in the diversity of age profiles across branches of production, which can be witnessed at the start of this period.

The marital status of textile workers at this time may be expected to be in part a reflection of the age structure of the work force described above. Almost all adult men and women were, or had been, married during the period with which we are concerned.[18] In as far as textile production was predominantly the province of younger workers, it was also the province of those who were less likely to be married. Trades like finishing, dyeing, and sewing, which had traditionally employed older women, though in smaller proportions, also tended to be the locus of married women. The shift toward the use of younger workers in these industries also reduced the proportion of the work force who were, or had been, married. Across the period, textile workers of both sexes were more likely to be young and unmarried than the average for manufacturing as a whole, and in manufacturing the work force was on average younger and less likely to be married than was the case with the total occupied population.

A further element that sets women workers apart from their male counterparts relates to the role of those who were widowed or separated. We know that while marriage rates for both sexes were extremely high in interwar Japan, men were more likely to marry again if widowed. Their life expectancy was also less than that of women, resulting in the existence within the population of more widows than widowers. The nature of decision making in the area of divorce, and the difficulty with which divorced women achieved a further marriage, contributed to the existence of a larger proportion of women in the divorced/separated category as well. Irene Taeuber's figures indicate that women above the age of thirty-five were more than twice as likely as men to be widowed or separated, and the disparity increased with age.[19] Moreover, such women had a higher labor force participation rate. In 1930, for example, over 12.6 percent of the gainfully employed female labor force consisted of women who were widowed, divorced, or separated, but only 5.6 percent of the male labor force were in that category.[20] This gender difference is shown in the data on textiles. What is also apparent, however, is that women in these categories were not distributed equally across trades. Even allowing for the differing age profiles of different branches of production, it is clear that certain occupations, particularly sewing, were the particular province of widows and separated women. In 1920, for example, 40 percent of the nearly 100,000 female sewing workers were in this category. However, the part played by single (previously married) women in these trades declined substantially between 1920 and 1930. The 1940 census provides us with no comparable figures, but the decline in the relative significance of older women workers in trades formerly populated by older married women highlighted above suggests that it may have become more difficult for widowed or separated women to support themselves through working in textile production.

Work Status and Occupation

A degree of polarization between men's and women's patterns of participation in the textile labor market is further emphasized in data relating to work status and the actual tasks undertaken by men and women within the remit of particular areas of production. The terms for employment status are not consistent across all three censuses, but employers/owners are normally referred to as *jigyōnushi* or *gyōshu*, and workers as *rōmusha* or *rōdōsha*. Other categories include staff, including technicians and supervisors (*shokuin*) and family helpers (*kazoku jūgyōsha*).[21]

Two trends are apparent from looking at this data for the textile industry over the period from 1920 to 1940. Firstly, there was a dramatic decrease over time in the number of individuals categorized as "owners" or "proprietors," but the extent of ownership varied considerably between different branches of production. Even at the beginning of the period, silk reeling and cotton spinning were already demonstrating a high degree of separation of capital and labor, with the proportion of the total work force accounted for by "owners" relatively small. By contrast, in weaving nearly one-third of all females were returned as owners, and half of all men.[22] By 1940 only 8 percent of all workers in weaving were identified as "owners," and only 0.2 percent in the already highly concentrated spinning industry.[23] Within this decline of proprietorship, however, women and men fared differently. While the proportion of male weaving "owners" had sunk to one-quarter of all males in the industry by 1940, for women the figure had collapsed to a mere 1.6 percent.[24] Similar though less dramatic disparities are evident in other branches of production. In particular, those trades where older women had been highly significant, and in which, at the start of the period, many women had been "owners," were no exception to this decline. A further feature is the conspicuously high proportion of widows and separated women in the ownership category. It is likely that female ownership frequently resulted from the death of a husband, and may more often than not have brought with it a caretaker capacity, in which the widow controlled the enterprise until the son or other heir was of an age to take over. As such, it may be suggested, women may have been increasingly lacking any sizable and enduring hold on the ownership of the production process in much of the textile industry.

It should also be noted that the much smaller categories of staff and technicians throughout the period consisted disproportionately of male rather than female workers. Of those female workers who fell into this category, a high percentage were unmarried, but also older.

In general it appears that the ownership patterns developing first in the more mechanized branches of production, with larger production units, such as cotton spinning—significantly those also employing large numbers of young women—were gradually becoming established in other parts of textile production, such as garment manufacture. As the work force shifted even more toward the employment of younger, unmarried women, women workers disproportionately found themselves as "workers" rather than "owners." At the same time, jobs requiring technical, managerial, or supervisory skills were confirmed as mainly the province of men. This aspect of the gender division of labor can be confirmed by analysis of the actual tasks undertaken by men and women within these industries. The 1930 census provides a detailed breakdown of textile workers according to their trade.[25] These data make it immediately apparent that in many branches of textile production the kinds of occupation available to women were far more limited than those open to men. Of the one hundred trades listed for workers employed in the silk reeling industry, for example, fifty-one employed no women whatsoever, whereas only four trades[26] appeared to exclude men. Although in the actual reeling process women had an overwhelming predominance and constituted a significant minority of production workers in one or two other areas, such as baling, their role elsewhere was limited to the domains of cooking, nursing, and office work. A similar pattern is to be found in the other branches of textile production. In silk, wool, flax, and cotton spinning, women dominated the spinning process itself, but few strayed beyond it in any numbers. While the cotton spinning industry claimed to employ over 150,000 workers (104,000 women and 47,000 men), removal of spinning workers[27] from the total leaves a balance of some 53,000 workers, over 70 percent of them men. Of the 124 trades listed for the industry, 56 employed no women. Those women who do appear were again concentrated in medical, welfare, office, and domestic related occupations. In silk weaving 83 percent of all the women employed were weavers, a figure almost matched by the 75.5 percent for cotton weaving production.

It is clear, therefore, that in these areas of reeling, spinning, and weaving, a sharp gender division of labor operated within sectors, which served to exclude women from a significant number of occupations, and men from very few. Women were at the same time enabled to preserve their overwhelming dominance in key parts of the production process. While men were never totally excluded from these core tasks, the numbers involved in them remained small, and if anything showed a tendency to diminish over time. Overall, though, men continued to be employed in a much wider range of tasks in these industries and had a near monopoly on those associated with skill acquisition, technical expertise, and status. In the finishing trades and garment industries that employed fewer women, a similar concentration is apparent. However, the smaller overall role of women meant that the gender division of labor, while still indicating the extent to which women failed to play a role in many trades, was substantially different from that found in the reeling, spinning, and weaving processes.

It is thus apparent that the textile work force was far from homogeneous at the start of the interwar period, and that this diversity was particularly marked if we look at the case of women workers. Part of the explanation for the persistent diversity, and also for the diminution of that diversity, can be found through identifying why the export-oriented textile industries turned to the employment of young women in the first place, and it is this question that will be analyzed in the next section. By the interwar years some other branches of textile production may have faced similar imperatives, and these patterns were, moreover, well enough established to act as models that others could follow, pushing textile producers toward greater uniformity in terms of labor practice.

Why Women?

Despite the failure of the existing historiography to do justice to the diversity that existed within textile employment, it remains the case that young women accounted for a substantial part of the textile work force. Moreover, textile employers with very diverse economic and technological imperatives tended to articulate almost identical reasons for electing to focus on the same labor supply source, namely young women from rural areas. Nevertheless, historians have rarely sought to

analyze the reasons why so many textile employers focused their recruiting attempts on this source of labor.[28]

One particular reason why employers turned to women was furnished by previously established patterns of work. Much textile production during the Tokugawa period had been carried out by women, often
within the context of the farm household. While the household division
of labor differed from region to region, we have many examples of the
women of the household taking the main burden of textile production
by-employment, including working on looms obtained from a putting-
out master. Yamakawa Kikue's memoir of nineteenth-century life in
Mito domain contains the following:

Once the morning chores were done, a housewife would turn to sewing, spinning, or weaving. . . . Throughout the year, any time she had some minutes to
spare, Kiku would turn to spinning the yarn to be used for the family's clothes.
Before she had children Kiku also wove the yarn into cloth. However, as one
child after another was born, and as her husband's social position rose, her
time was taken with other things, and although she continued to spin, she sent
the yarn out to be woven into cloth. Weaving for others on commission was a
standard side job of *bushi* wives and daughters.[29]

In most silk producing areas, the feeding of the silkworms was carried out by women, who subsequently took on much of the task of
reeling the thread off the cocoons.[30] In premodern Japan, as in other
economies, a gender division of labor had developed, and this division
of labor influenced the choices of both employers and employees during the formative years of the mechanized industry. In some cases this
influence was strengthened by an element of skill transference; it is not
surprising to find in the early silk mills young women who had acquired
silk reeling skills at home.

The gender division of labor was not cast in stone. The early years of
industrialization offered ample opportunities for breaking with the past.
The Osaka Cotton Spinning Company, for example, started its operations with more or less equal proportions of male and female workers,[31]
and only later shifted to the female domination of cotton spinning production found in the interwar industry as a whole. However, even
where over time the original rationale for this division may have declined or been lost, it continued to color perceptions, and this remained
true throughout the interwar years. In the minds of many, textile

production was seen to be "women's work." In addition to this assumption, three particular considerations influenced large employers in the pre–World War 1 decades to focus their employment strategies on the employment of young women, mostly from rural areas. Two of these considerations were strictly economic. The third related to employers' perceptions of gender.

A) Reasons of Cost

The argument of labor cost was perhaps the most frequently articulated by employers. In Japan as elsewhere,[32] women were cheaper than men, both for reasons of labor attributes and because they were deemed not to have to support a family. Rural women were cheaper than urban ones; income levels and the cost of living tended to be lower in rural areas, and the Japanese agricultural sector was widely assumed to contain "surplus" labor that could be easily obtained for a low wage. Younger workers could invariably be paid a lower wage than older ones. This was well expressed in a labor management manual for cotton spinners. In Japan, wrote Hashimoto Ryūtarō,

[W]omen have no alternative but to play a supplementary role to men in farming . . . so from the perspective of a girl's parents it has always been thought preferable for her to divert her efforts elsewhere, if there is more lucrative work available, rather than helping with farming, which will scarcely suffice for spending money. . . . It is with this tendency in mind that Japan's spinning companies have established their operations on the basis of women.[33]

A concentration of men in the luxury, craft branches of textile production, where higher value added could support higher labor cost—for example in the Nishijin silk weaving industry[34]—would seem to support this contention.

We have plenty of evidence to show that textile employers from Meiji onward were intensely eager to economize on labor costs, which could amount to a substantial proportion of total production cost. Production costs were often kept high by the need to invest in expensive capital, and raw material and energy costs were often beyond the control of the producer. Much of Japan's textile industry was not internationally competitive. Labor was the one factor of production where employers felt that they had a greater margin of price flexibility. They sought to employ what appeared to be the cheapest labor force available, citing the relatively low productivity of such workers compared with those in more industrialized competitor countries as a reason for trying to push down wages yet further. To employ young rural women, because they were the cheapest possible source of labor, thus became an integral part of employers' strategy.[35]

b) *Reasons of Demand*

A second factor that reinforced the employment of young rural women in these industries was the explosion in the demand for labor that occurred during the 1890s and around the turn of the century. The more mechanized branches of the textile industry, which increasingly catered to the export market, grew rapidly in the years following the Sino-Japanese War of 1894–1895. By 1900 there were already about 125,000 silk operatives, and by 1910 the figure had increased to 190,000. Over the same period the number of female cotton spinners increased from 43,000 to 75,000.[36] The proliferation of new producers meant finding sufficient workers to initiate production, and then perhaps doubling or tripling that number within the space of a few years. Not only did producers increasingly find themselves competing with other employers who might well be offering higher wages or better conditions, but they were hard put to find local workers at any price. In this context, employers felt they had little choice but to look beyond the immediate locality for workers, and given the continuing expansion of the industry it made some sense for them to continue to do so. The result was that in both silk reeling and cotton spinning workers increasingly came from outside the immediate area of the factory.[37] As the Cotton Spinners' Federation wrote as early as 1898:

With the recent establishment and progress of various industries, the demand for workers has suddenly increased, with the result that factories that utilize large numbers for workers, like cotton spinning, regularly face a shortage of workers. They cannot satisfy their demand for labor by recruiting only at the factory location or its immediate vicinity, and have no choice but to go out into the remote mountain districts, and they spend large amounts of money, a huge amount of time, and a great deal of trouble on recruiting workers there. More than twenty of our member spinning companies are now sending out representatives specifically to recruit in places over 100 *ri* [nearly 250 miles] from the factory.[38]

The physical separation of workers from their native places helped to underline the youth of the work force, since domestic responsibilities were likely to make it impossible for married women to leave the farming household. It therefore promoted the female division of labor according to marital status.

c) Docility

Added to these factors of labor cost and labor demand was one that related to gender. Female workers were assumed to be more docile and less troublesome than men when it came to matters of labor management. Youth and rural origins were likely to reinforce this docility. How far these assumptions were the rationalization of already developing recruitment patterns is hard to judge, but there is a great deal of evidence that such perceptions were a powerful influence on the targeting of women in general. This belief in the possibilities of control over the labor force was both cause and justification of the recruitment of female textile labor throughout the prewar years.[39] It first became significant in the context of labor unrest around the turn of the century but was also powerfully articulated against the background of labor discontent after World War I. Hashimoto Ryūtarō, the writer of the labor management manual for cotton spinners mentioned above, commented:

Because it is very difficult to inspire a wilful girl to cease to be wilful, it must not be forgotten that docile girls should be chosen. . . . In general it can probably be said that girls brought up in the mountains tend to be more docile, calmer, and of a simple and honest discipline.[40]

Overall, therefore, pre-industrial work patterns, cost considerations, the rapid increase in the demand for labor, and assumptions about the nature of women workers served as the main arguments for the mass employment of young women workers in the larger scale, export-oriented branches of textile production. In articulating these arguments, employers had adopted a "lifecycle" view of women's work, incorporating in their strategies a belief that manufacturing work was for young women who would work for a brief period before marriage, while men were likely to be older and work through most of their adult years.

It is debatable whether some of the above arguments were as valid as employers presented them as being. Wage levels were certainly relatively low, but wage costs alone do not represent the true cost of labor to the employer. Textile employers bore the brunt of the high transactions costs in the labor market,[41] and invariably subsidized resident workers.[42] While they sought vigorously to pass on to workers the burden of this expenditure, a high proportion was never recouped. Labor productivity was also low, and the idea of increasing it through rewarding labor better was rarely entertained. Nor was female labor as passive as many employers liked to think. A tradition of protest in the core silk reeling areas resurfaced at intervals, while writers like Tsurumi have highlighted cultural forms of resistance, such as the songs sung by textile workers, and the "fleeing" of workers from mills in protest at poor conditions and low wages.[43] Workers' families appeared increasingly willing to back them in going against their employers' wishes.[44]

Through 1914 these arguments were persuasive, but at the end of World War I the strategy was still restricted to silk reeling, cotton spinning, and parts of the weaving industry. That the other branches of textile production had not been exposed to these same imperatives contributed to the diversity of labor that can be seen at this time. What seems paradoxical, however, is that these practices spread in subsequent decades, at a time when the arguments above became increasingly difficult to sustain. Demand for labor in cotton spinning slowed after the boom of World War I, and then declined in the 1920s, while in silk reeling it collapsed in the wake of the depression after 1929. Labor productivity, though still low by international standards, rose remarkably in the wake of technological rationalization in the 1920s, and the cotton industry enjoyed considerable international success in the 1930s, in which the role of "cheap" labor has continued to be debated.[45] Passivity was even further from being total. While an inferior political, economic, and social position for women in prewar Japan was backed up with all the force of the law, and we have evidence showing that overall organized labor protest was less resorted to by women than by men, the interwar period was marked by major disputes involving female workers, for example, the Hayashigumi dispute of 1927, and the Tōyō Muslin dispute of 1930.[46] Women workers obtained increased legal rights and enjoyed a stronger bargaining power vis-à-vis employers.

Not only was much of the rationale for the dependence on high turnover, low wage, low productivity young females gone, the disadvantages of the strategy had become increasingly apparent. It might therefore be expected that the changed circumstances would bring about a change in strategy as well, and that other branches of textile production would be reluctant to use it as a model. As the census data show, however, this does not appear to have been the case. That the already considerable dependence of the silk and cotton industries on young, unmarried women was, if anything, increased in the interwar period, suggests that these industries went out of their way to keep to the same kind of labor.[47] Instead of trying to break out of this cycle of reliance on young women, silk and cotton employers sought instead to refine the existing system and make it work as best they could. They appear to have become locked into a kind of path dependence in which the costs of breaking out of the established system were too high to contemplate and where the relative expense of the labor they employed did not justify their making the attempt. In justifying their position, they became powerful role models for other employers to follow. It required the specific circumstances of interwar Japan, though, to confirm this gendering of the labor market in and beyond the branches of textile production that had initiated it. We need to explain why one particular employment strategy (the use of young females) became the standard that others then followed.

The Persistence of Diversity: Relative Industrialization

As we have seen, the increasing preponderance of young women within the textile labor force as a whole was due to their dominance in the core production activities of those branches that had expanded most rapidly, and moved increasingly toward capital intensive factory operations. The textile industry throughout the interwar decades continued to be marked by different rates of capital intensity and scale of production, but in general there was a move toward greater scale of production and larger concentrations of capital. During the interwar period, weaving, previously dominated by small workshops, expanded its scale of production and export; weaving operations were increasingly undertaken by the large cotton spinning companies through the establishment of integrated spinning and weaving mills.[48] While weaving had always employed large numbers of young women, the process brought it closer to the patterns already established in the other two major branches. Thread production, too, followed this trend as large producers increasingly moved toward vertical integration. The finishing and garment trades were lagging in this respect. Here more local, small scale operations and family businesses persisted. In general, though, the decline in the number of many smaller workshops and family operations contributed both to an increase in the proportion of workers in the industry who were female and to an increase in the proportion of those workers who were young and unmarried. Older, married women, and men, were more and more concentrated in those areas of production that were likely to be smaller in scale, less mechanized, not geared to the export market, or requiring very specific labor attributes.

Associated with this were differing rates of mechanization. Again, some processes were more rapidly mechanized than others, and overall mechanization occurred more quickly in large scale operations with substantial capital at their disposal. The degree of mechanization in turn had an impact on the attributes required of workers, and in the textile industry, technology was invariably regarded as a substitute for labor skills. The corollary of this view was, the greater the use of technology, the greater the dependence on cheaper, less skilled labor.

The relationship between technological change and the nature of a labor force is, in fact, highly complex. The conclusion reached by the historian Nakamura Masanori was that technological innovation in Japan generally created employment opportunities for female workers, but that prewar employers were also reluctant to adopt technological innovations as long as they were faced with a supply of "docile," inexpensive labor.[49] Other studies, however, show that the relationship between technology and women's work is highly diverse and complex. In their book, de Groot and Schrover argue persuasively that "the traditional picture, in which the introduction of new technology led to deskilling, and thus to the employment of unskilled workers, amongst whom were many women, cannot be maintained."[50] It is also clear that the gendering of technology is influenced by a range of factors including alternative job opportunities, the perceived status of work, and the significance of the task, as well as by attitudes to social roles.[51]

It is apparent that in their approach to the gender division of labor, employers in the more mechanized industries largely assigned men to tasks where particular skills or physical strength were required. Engineers and technicians were male, as were workers involved in the parts of the production process more demanding of physical strength, such as unpacking bales of raw cotton or filling. The finishing trades were in general demanding of attributes such as strength or skill, and the slower pace of mechanization here sustained them as areas for male employment. In the employment of women, too, employers paid attention to the physical attributes of workers but from a rather different perspective. Textile employers were devotees of what has been referred to as the "nimble fingers" argument. This reasoning argued that there were certain tasks requiring delicate treatment and manual dexterity that women were better able to perform than men, both because of the smaller size of their hands and fingers, and because their upbringing had tended to instill in them greater skill in carrying out delicate tasks, such as sewing. It was argued in the case of the Japanese silk industry that the reeling and spinning of the fine silk threads were tasks that females were better equipped to undertake. Similar arguments were found when it came to joining breaks in cotton yarn, or in skillful use of a shuttle.[52] The economist Takahashi Kamekichi, writing in 1937, reflected widely held opinions when he pronounced:

Japanese factory girls are skillful with their fingers. They are suited to wherever delicate work is needed, such as in the spinning and weaving processes. Their level of education is such that they have at least completed compulsory education, so they are easily trained in technology and group operation.[53]

To a certain extent, the logic of this argument pointed to the employment of younger workers, who were likely to have smaller, more sensitive and smoother hands than older workers as well as quicker reactions and better eyesight.

The "nimble fingers" argument had a direct bearing on the question of skill, as manual dexterity and the inherent characteristics of female workers were seen as substitutes for skill training. Since many workers were short-term, training seemed uneconomic, and the new breed of management advisors concentrated on ensuring that workers' inherent physical and mental characteristics were such as to make them more or less suited to carrying out particular tasks.[54] Basic aptitude and inherent characteristics of the kind that women were assumed to possess remained a consistent factor in the choice of workers, and shaped the approach to mechanization and shopfloor organization. By having been born with, or acquiring before they entered the mill, the attributes they needed to become productive workers, women were deemed less worthy of any investment in training than their male counterparts, and training as a whole was highly gendered, with men the major beneficiaries as far as technical skills were concerned.[55] It may well be that, as has been argued elsewhere, this "rationalization in terms of the feminine virtues of dexterity and patience only came after a job was feminized,"[56] but the rhetoric was a common one, and its upshot clear. In the case of such female workers, increased efficiency was likely to be generated not by training, but by improved shopfloor organization, or the application of the principles of Taylorism and scientific management. This served further to sharpen the gender division of labor within the industry. Where the use of mechanization spread, these principles could be increasingly implemented.[57]

Finally, we have seen that a desire for control over the labor force was a powerful factor in the employment of young women. This desire remained strong in the years after 1918, and certainly textiles did not experience the extent of unrest to which some other industries were exposed. However, "docility" was less of an imperative for smaller family businesses and workshops. Where labor disputes could do most damage, and hence the control of labor mattered most, namely in larger scale, more capital intensive operations geared to the export market, employers increasingly employed that element of the occupied population that was likely to protest least at what they might do. Where smaller or individual operations persisted, concern over labor unrest came far lower on the agenda.

The persistence of diversity can therefore to some degree be explained through a "relative stage of industrialization" argument. Since different branches of production varied in such respects as degree of mechanization, scale of operation, etc., this diversity was reflected in the composition of their work forces. Even at the end of the interwar period, cotton, dominated by a few huge companies, was located at one end of the spectrum, and sewing, with its myriad individual workshops, at the other. Nevertheless, this argument also points to a gradual diminishing of the diversity, as most branches at some stage moved toward greater capital intensity, scale of production, and use of technology, and the relative importance of small and family workshops tended to decline.[58]

Employment, Mobilization, and Rhetoric

The interwar years as a whole witnessed substantial growth in the Japanese manufacturing sector. The depression proved to be no more than a brief hiatus between the slower growth of the 1920s and the much more rapid expansion of the 1930s. In the process, manufacturing increasingly offered a greater range of employment opportunities outside textiles. Particularly in the 1930s, the expansion of the heavy industries provided an increase in alternative job opportunities for men.[59] While alternative job opportunities for women also increased, particularly with the growth of the service sector,[60] their employment was worse hit by the depression. Moreover, rationalization in cotton spinning in the 1920s and the subsequent collapse in silk employment restricted their opportunities further. Many of the jobs newly available to men were more lucrative than those in textile employment. They were associated with higher value added and greater skills. It therefore became, in general, more difficult and more expensive to procure male workers. While older male textile workers tended to stay, particularly in those occupations that were associated with strength or skill, fewer were occupied as general production workers, particularly in the mechanized branches. The result was a decline in the proportion of men in the textile work force and the "ageing" of those who remained, as shown in the first part of this chapter. These labor market pressures toward feminization of the textile work force were reinforced by the increasing mobilization of men for the purposes of war, particularly after 1937. By October 1940, over 1.69 million men (4 percent of the male population) were in the armed forces, compared to only 243,000 ten years earlier.[61]

Equally important, though, were the ideologies relating to gender roles in society articulated during these interwar years and the labor relations policies formulated by large cotton employers, in particular against the background of these ideologies. These years witnessed a strengthening of the emphasis on domesticity and motherhood as the key to women's social role, and more and more caused that emphasis to become an integral part of the rhetoric of the "family state" (*kazoku kokka*). As industrialization increased the separation of home and work, this rhetoric seemed to threaten the economy's extensive reliance on women's work. The compromise that emerged was one that is found in other economies, namely the growing dependence of manufacturing on young women (future mothers) who could leave their homes and on married women in those areas of the economy where domestic and work responsibilities could be more easily combined, such as home working and agriculture.[62] This ideological emphasis reinforced the division of women workers by marital status identified earlier in the textile industry.

Against this background, the influence of the largest textile producers, particularly in cotton spinning, was immense. As business enterprises, these firms' prime concern was with the generation of profits. That objective was to be achieved in part through the extensive use of female labor, as shown above. These employers were, however, also members of Japanese society, who held views on the roles of the different sexes within that society. In that capacity, and in their capacity as profit-making entrepreneurs, they played a pathbreaking role in formulating and articulating management policies specifically focused around the employment of young, unmarried women and with clear views regarding the gender division of labor.[63] This was also an industry that experienced considerable business success in the 1930s,[64] seemingly providing concrete evidence that such policies paid off. Cotton employers in effect became the mouthpiece for highly influential views representing this particular labor strategy as the ideal norm, not just for the textile industries in general, but for male and female manufacturing employment as a whole.

Conclusion

The initial move toward recruiting large numbers of young, female workers in parts of textile production was stimulated by economic imperatives during the 1890s and around the turn of the century—namely, the rapid expansion in the demand for low cost labor. It was reinforced by the legal and social position of women and widely held perceptions of gender. By 1920 these patterns were still restricted to the large scale, export-oriented areas of production, and the composition of the labor force in textiles as a whole remained far from uniform.

Although large employers in the interwar years recognized many of the deficiencies in their strategy, they opted for marginal improvements in the existing patterns rather than radical change in the composition of the work force. At the same time, the spread of mechanization and the growth of more capital intensive operations exposed other branches of textile production to some of the same imperatives. The pace of manufacturing development and the shift toward war led to greater "feminization" of textile production, pushing the textile work force toward greater uniformity along the lines established by the first mechanized textile industries. All these factors came together to sustain a more formalized division of home and work responsibilities, a shift of males to the "outside" sphere, a growing polarization between the work and social roles of unmarried and married women, and increasing acceptance of the "lifecycle" view of women's work. In this process, there occurred an increasing divergence between the working experiences of men and women and defining of women workers by marital status. The leading textile employers gave a formal voice to these trends, as they sought to define and enhance the efficiency of their own operations against the background of an intensifying rhetoric of domesticity. In doing so they devalued not only the gainful employment of married women, but of women in general.

This preference on the part of employers for young, unmarried women is far from being unique to Japan. Wolf has noted how factory owners in Indonesia in the 1980s and 1990s pushed for a similar profile work force on the grounds that married women were less likely to be regular attenders. "Young women seeking a job sometimes misrepresent their marital status, enlisting the help of the village leader to do so, in order to secure employment."[65] Indeed, this kind of demographic structure of the female work force is typical of many developing economies.[66]

What is also apparent is that the dichotomy between the male and female labor markets and the segregation of the work of married and unmarried women have been perpetuated in the labor force participation of Japanese women in more recent decades. Andrew Gordon's chapter in this volume shows a movement that was focused around the idea of wives being in the home, while Brinton's work shows clearly how even in the 1980s married women, particularly those who were middle-aged, constituted a far higher proportion of part-time and non-regular workers than the unmarried.[67] While, as Gail Bernstein has commented, gender is continuously recreated and reimaged,[68] the continuities are clear. In extending and confirming patterns of employment and labor market participation for men and women in the interwar years, the textile industry helped to lay the basis for the gender division of labor in Japan to the present.

Notes

I wish to acknowledge the support of the British Academy in enabling me to attend the workshop in Santa Clara, California, where the draft papers for this volume were discussed. I would like to thank the participants in the workshop, and in particular the editors of this volume, Barbara Molony and Kathy Uno, for their helpful comments. Some of the material in this chapter was also presented at seminars at the Nissan Institute, Oxford University, and at the Comparative Economic History seminar at the London School of Economics. I am grateful to participants at these seminars, and to Dudley Baines, for their comments.

1. Claudia Goldin, *Understanding the Gender Gap: An Economic History of American Women* (Oxford: Oxford University Press, 1990), 213–214.

2. Beatrice Webb, *The Diary of Beatrice Webb, 1873–1943* (Cambridge: Chadwick-Healey, 1978) (microfiche), vol. 30, 14 September 1911–3 March 1912.

3. John E. Orchard, *Japan's Economic Position* (New York: Whittlesey House/McGraw-Hill, 1930), 340.

4. Orchard, *Japan's Economic Position*, 354.

5. Quotation from Yamamoto Shigemi, *Aa Nomugi Tōge*, in Mikiso Hane, *Peasants, Rebels and Outcastes: the Underside of Modern Japan* (New York: Pantheon, 1982), 182.

6. Employment figures calculated from Naikaku tōkeikyoku, *Shokugyō oyobi sangyō*, vol. 2, *Shōwa 5–nen kokusei chōsa hōkoku* (Naikaku tōkeikyoku, 1935), 150, 160; output from Andō Yoshio, *Kindai Nihon keizaishi yōran* (Tokyo University Press, 1975), 11; export figures from G. C. Allen, *Short Economic History of Modern Japan* (London: Allen & Unwin, 1962), 215.

7. See e.g., E. Patricia Tsurumi, *Factory Girls: Women in the Thread Mills of Meiji Japan* (Princeton NJ: Princeton University Press, 1990); Barbara Molony, "Activism among Women in the Taishō Cotton Textile Industry," in *Recreating Japanese Women, 1600–1945*, ed. Gail Lee Bernstein (Berkeley: University of California Press, 1991); and Janet Hunter, *Women and the Labor Market in Japan's Industrialising Economy* (London: RoutledgeCurzon, 2003) .

8. Textiles here is taken as including the whole range of production processes through reeling and spinning of raw material (e.g., silk cocoons, raw cotton, wool, hemp, etc.) into yarn, the weaving of yarn into cloth (including the manufacture of knitted goods and hosiery), finishing processes such as fulling, bleaching, dyeing and printing, and finally the making of the cloth into gar-

ments, involving individuals such as tailors and seamstresses. The making of other items of apparel, such as hats, gloves, and fans, is excluded.

9. The issue of the postwar gendering of the work force is taken up in Gordon's chapter in this volume.

10. Leaving aside the accuracy of the data itself, categories of occupation and employment changed between censuses. This leads to inconsistencies with other data sources and between censuses. It is also accepted that most data underestimate the extent to which women were gainfully occupied. Effort has been made as far as possible here to achieve comparability between categories, but it is accepted that these may be at best approximate. I believe, however, that the data are sufficient for the nonquantitative analysis attempted here. For a more detailed analysis of the kind of problems raised by this kind of data, see Satō Masahiro, "Shoki kokusei chōsa no shomondai—nōson jūmin no 'ie' ishiki to shokugyō chōsa: Hiroshima-kenka no jirei," *Keizai kenkyū* 48, no. 1 (January 1997).

11. This chapter does not explore the issues raised by the presence of thousands of textile workers from the colonies (mostly Korea), both male and female, since its overriding concern is with gender differences, but the ethnic divide was under some circumstances very important. The chapters in this volume by both Don Smith and Barbara Brooks provide some insights as to how gender may have interacted with ethnicity, and Smith's chapter in particular picks up on some issues that may also have been applicable to textile workers. For example, the Kishiwada Spinning Company strike of 1929–1930 was an example of cooperation between female Japanese and Korean cotton mill operatives (see Michael Wiener, *Race and Migration in Imperial Japan* [London and New York: Routledge, 1994], 171).

12. The process whereby industrialization, by separating home and work, accentuates a division between the work undertaken by married and unmarried women is, of course, well documented for a range of countries. Comment on Britain and France is contained in Louise A. Tilly and Joan W. Scott, *Women, Work and Family* (New York: Methuen, 1978). See e.g., Alice Kessler-Harris, *Out to Work* (Oxford: Oxford University Press, 1982), 25ff.; and Claudia Goldin, *Understanding the Gender Gap*, chapter 2, for the case of the United States. The relatively rapid growth of manufacturing combined with the physical separation of workers from their homes accentuated this process.

13. Except where noted, the information in this section is taken from the three interwar censuses. These are Naikaku tōkeikyoku, *Shokugyō*, vol. 2, *Taishō 9–nen*

kokusei chōsa hōkoku, zenkoku no bu (Naikaku tōkeikyoku, 1929) (hereafter 1920 census); Naikaku tōkeikyoku, *Shokugyō oyobi sangyō*, vol. 2, *Shōwa 5-nen kokusei chōsa hōkoku* (Naikaku tōkeikyoku, 1935) (hereafter 1930 census); and Sōrifu tōkeikyoku, *Sangyō jigyōjō no chii*, vol. 2, *Shōwa 15-nen kokusei chōsa hōkoku* (Sōrifu, 1962) (hereafter 1940 census).

14. During the 1920s many farmers attempted to compensate for declining prices by increasing cocoon production. See Ann Waswo, "Japan's Rural Economy in Crisis," in *The Economies of Africa and Asia in the Interwar Depression*, ed. Ian Brown (London: Routledge, 1989), 115–136.

15. The 1920 census subdivides workers into *hongyōsha* (those for whom it is a main occupation) and *hongyō naki jūzokusha* (dependents [family workers] for whom it is not a main occupation). The more detailed age breakdown is given only for the former, thus excluding nearly 30 percent of the total number working in textiles. Since many young workers, particularly males, were recorded as "dependents," this data seriously underestimates the significance of younger workers in textile production. It can nevertheless give some indication as to how the age profiles of men and women may have varied between the different branches of textile production.

16. 1920 census, 130–133.

17. 1930 census, 140ff.

18. Assessment of rates of marriage is complicated by the existence of both recorded and unrecorded marriages, but Irene Taeuber suggests that "marriage remained the status toward which practically all Japanese moved," with fewer than 5 percent of women and men remaining single into their late thirties. Irene B. Taeuber, *The Population of Japan* (Princeton, NJ: Princeton University Press, 1958), 213.

19. Taeuber, *The Population of Japan*, 213.

20. Calculated from 1930 census, tables 5–6.

21. As mentioned above, the 1920 census subdivides respondents into those claiming a main occupation (*hongyō*) and those claiming to be "dependents" without a main occupation. I have attempted here to incorporate both groups in the consideration of work status, but this subdivision also clearly raises more subjective questions of how individuals viewed their own position in relation to others within the household unit, which lie outside the remit of this chapter.

22. 1920 census, 50–52, 72.

23. 1940 census, 210–11, table 4.

24. Ibid.

25. While this is cross-sectional data, and does not, therefore, give any indication of change over time, it does enable us to identify the extent to which the textile labor market was, or was not, a segmented one at this point in time. In that respect it can shed light on gender bias in different occupations over a longer period. Detailed occupational information on all the major areas of production is given in the 1930 census, table 15, 394ff. All the information in this section is drawn from this table.

26. These were tailoring/sewing, midwifery, stenographer/typist, and a category of "other medical related" persons (*sono ta no iryō ni jūji suru mono*).

27. Those involved in spinning (*sobō* and *seibō*) and operations such as reeling, winding, and doffing (*kasekuri, itogae*, etc.).

28. The reliance on female textile workers is far from unique to Japan, but the methods of recruitment, organization, and the extent of dependence on young, single women had little historical precedent up to the 1930s. In India and parts of Lancashire, men dominated cotton spinning, while elsewhere married women were of greater significance. See e.g., S. D. Chapman, *The Cotton Industry in the Industrial Revolution* (Basingstoke, Hamp.: Macmillan, 1987); Dipak Mazumdar, "Labour Supply in Early Industrialisation," *Economic History Review* 26, no. 3 (1973); and Emily Honig, *Sisters and Strangers: Women in the Shanghai Cotton Mills, 1919–1949* (Stanford, CA: Stanford University Press, 1986).

29. Kikue Yamakawa, *Women of the Mito Domain: Recollections of Samurai Family Life* (Tokyo University Press, 1992), 15.

30. For comment on labor in silk production, see Stephen Vlastos, *Peasant Protests and Uprisings in Tokugawa Japan* (Berkeley: University of California Press, 1986), 96ff. Gail Lee Bernstein's article, "Women in the Silk-Reeling Industry in Nineteenth-Century Japan," in *Japan and the World: Essays on Japanese History and Politics in Honor of Ishida Takeshi,* eds. Gail Lee Bernstein and Haruhiro Fukui (New York: St. Martin's Press, 1988), addresses the issue of why women dominated the factory-based textile industries and discusses the broader development of Japanese silk reeling labor prior to World War I.

31. The history of Tōyōbō reports that Osaka Cotton Spinning Company had 160

female and 133 male workers in December 1883 (Tōyō bōseki kabushiki gaisha shashi henshūshitsu), *Hyakunenshi-Tōyōbō*, 2 vols. (Osaka: Tōyōbō, 1986), 1: 26.

32. See e.g., Goldin, *Understanding the Gender Gap*. There is considerable debate as to the degree to which this is the result of wage discrimination or the lower productivity of female workers. For an illuminating contribution to this debate that focuses on late eighteenth- and early nineteenth-century England, see Joyce Burnette, "An Investigation of the Female-Male Wage Gap during the Industrial Revolution in Britain," *Economic History Review* 50, no. 2 (May 1997).

33. Hashimoto Ryūtarō, *Bōshoku jinji no hanashi* (Osaka: Kōjō sekaisha, 1931), 30–31.

34. For a brief outline of the Kyoto/Nishijin weaving industry, see the introduction to *Kyoto Modern Textiles, 1868–1940* (Kyoto: Kyoto Textile Wholesalers Association, 1995).

35. Japanese textile producers were, of course, not alone in pursuing this strategy. Thomas Dublin, in *Women at Work: The Transformation of Work and Community in Lowell, Massachusetts, 1826–1860* (New York: Columbia University Press, 1979), argues that low wages were initially the basic reason for the preponderance of women in the early Lowell cotton mills, although once a gender division of labor had been established, managers' values tended to sustain it.

36. *Sen'i Sangyō*, ed. Fujino Seizaburō, vol. 11, *Chōki keizai tōkei* (Tōyō keizai shinpōsha, 1981), table 58, 300–301; Takamura Naosuke, *Nihon bōsekigyō shi josetsu*, 2 vols. (Hanawa shobō, 1971), 1: 302ff.

37. For comment on the geographical origins of Japanese textile workers see my "Continuity and Change in the Japanese Labour Market: Rural Impoverishment and the Geographical Origins of Female Textile Workers," in *Japan's Socio-Economic Evolution: Continuity and Change,* eds. Sarah Metzger-Court and Werner Pascha (Folkestone, Kent: Japan Library, 1996).

38. Dainihon menshi bōseki dōgyō rengōkai, *Bōseki shokkō jijō chōsa gaiyō hōkokusho* (Osaka: Dainihon menshi bōseki dōgyō rengōkai, 1898; repr. 1971), 1.

39. See e.g., Dainihon, *Bōseki shokkō*; Fukuoka chihō shokugyō shōkai jimukyoku, *Dekasegi jokō ni kansuru chōsa* (Fukuoka: Fukuoka chihō shokugyō shōkai jimukyoku, 1928); and Niigata-ken dekasegimono hogo kumiai rengōkai, *Chōsa hōkoku* (Niigata: Dekasegimono hogo kumiai rengōkai, 1936).

40. Hashimoto, *Bōshoku jinji no hanashi*, 60, 61–62.

41. Transactions costs here refer to the additional costs of operating in the labor market resulting from factors such as imperfect or distorted information

or poor communications and transport networks. I have discussed the effects of such costs in "Textile Employers and Female Workers in Prewar Japan: Economic Imperatives in an Imperfect Labor Market," Meiji University, *Keiei ronshū* 45, nos. 2–4 (March 1998).

42. For example, one report from Gifu prefecture in the late 1920s showed a silk reeling mill charging female workers 15 sen for three meals a day, when the real cost was 25.2 sen. Shuichi Harada, *Labor Conditions in Japan* (New York: Columbia University Press, 1928), 125. Reports on cotton spinning by Western visitors such as Arno Pearse and Charles Moser indicate equal or greater levels of subsidy. See Arno S. Pearse, *The Cotton Industry of Japan and China* (Manchester, UK: International Federation of Master Cotton Spinners and Manufacturers' Associations, 1929); and Charles Moser, *The Cotton Textile Industry of Far Eastern Countries* (Boston, MA: Pepperell, 1930). This item of employers' expenditure is likely to have risen compared with earlier years due to shifts in management policies and greater pressure to improve workers' conditions of employment.

43. E. Patricia Tsurumi, *Factory Girls: Women in the Thread Mills of Meiji Japan*. Tsurumi also calls attention to the high rate of absconding, which meant that many advances on wages were never repaid, thus causing a considerable loss to employers.

44. This is shown in Tōjō Yukihiko, *Seishi dōmei no jokō tōroku seido: Nihon kindai no hen'yō to jokō no 'jinkaku'* (Tokyo University Press, 1990).

45. There is a vast literature concerning Lancashire and the rise of Japan, and Western economic historians have vigorously debated the sources of Japan's competitiveness and the relative decline of the British cotton industry. For a useful summary, see Alex Robertson, "Lancashire and the Rise of Japan, 1910–1937," *Business History* XXXII, no. 4 (October 1990).

46. The Hayashigumi dispute is discussed in Matsumoto Eiji, *Seishi rōdō sōgi no kenkyū* (Kashiwa shobō, 1991), other protests in Ōkōchi Kazuo and Matsuo Hiroshi, *Nihon rōdō kumiai monogatari-Shōwa* (Chikuma shobō, 1976), 186–192.

47. One seeming paradox is why interwar textile employers, particularly those in urban areas, made little effort to recruit married women from the locality, many of whom had earlier work experience and then settled in urban areas. Such women were cheaper to recruit, would stay longer, would not require residential accommodation, and could be expected to reward investments in training with increased productivity. While women's tenure at textile work, though lengthening in the interwar years, remained on average considerably

shorter than that of men, there nevertheless remained a sizable minority with ten to twenty years' tenure, and these were almost all married women.

48. For the development of cotton weaving during the interwar years, see Abe Takeshi, *Nihon ni okeru sanchi men'orimonogyō no tenkai* (Tokyo University Press, 1989).

49. *Technology Change and Female Labor in Japan*, ed. Masanori Nakamura (Tokyo and New York: United Nations Press, 1994), 211.

50. *Women Workers and Technological Change in Europe in the 19th and 20th Centuries*, eds. Gertjan de Groot and Marlou Schrover (London: Taylor & Francis, 1995), 12.

51. Ulla Wikander, "Periodisation and the Engendering of Technology: The Pottery of Gustavsberg, Sweden, 1880–1980," in de Groot and Schrover, *Women Workers and Technological Change*, 147.

52. Significantly Diane Wolf's study of Java (*Factory Daughters: Gender, Household Dynamics and Rural Industrialisation in Java* [Berkeley: University of California Press, 1992], 114) notes, "The spinning and textile factories administer a dexterity test that consists of quickly distributing spools in bottles and then pulling them out again. In the garment factory, potential applicants are asked to tie knots in single sewing threads."

53. Takahashi Kamekichi, *Nihon sangyō rōdō ron* (Chikura shobō, 1937), 203.

54. One 1929 survey on the efficiency of a group of silk reelers, showing strong evidence of the scientific management movement, suggested that height and weight, rather than the length of the fingers, were broadly correlated with ability. The survey came to the conclusion that the taller workers performed better, Chūō shokugyō shōkai jimukyoku, *Seishi jokō no noryokuteki hōsa* (Chūō shokugyō shōkai jimukyoku, 1929). It was only at this point that writers began to suggest that changing the height of the basins (*kama*), previously always the same level above the floor, might help to make shorter workers more productive.

55. The gendered nature of training in textile production is shown in Hazama Hiroshi, *Nihon rōmu kanri shi kenkyū* (Ochanomizu shobō, 1964), 236ff.

56. de Groot and Schrover, *Women Workers and Technological Change*, 8.

57. In the silk reeling industry, mechanization was slower than in some other parts of textile production. Despite technological change in the interwar years, for example, the spread of the multi-spool reeler, the reeling of thread from cocoons remained highly dependent on the skill of individual workers. Tōjō Yukihiko has suggested that the effects of technological change on ap-

proaches to silk reeling remain ambiguous (*Seishi dōmei no jokō tōroku seido*, 193–220).

58. It should be noted that in the Japanese economy as a whole, small firms and workshops continued to be a crucial part of the manufacturing sector and remained so into the late twentieth century. For a discussion of interwar concentration, see Takafusa Nakamura, *Economic Growth in Prewar Japan* (New Haven, CT: Yale University Press, 1971), chapter 7.

59. The rise of the heavy industries is discussed in Hashimoto Jun, "Kyōdai sangyō no kōryū," in *Nijū kōzō*, eds. Nakamura Takafusa and Odaka Kōnosuke, vol. 6, *Nihon keizaishi* (Iwanami shoten, 1989). Andrew Gordon, *The Evolution of Labor Relations in Japan: Heavy Industry, 1853–1955* (Cambridge, MA: Council on East Asian Studies, Harvard University, 1985), discusses the situation of male workers in this area of manufacturing.

60. See e.g., Margit Nagy, "Middle Class Working Women during the Interwar Years," in Bernstein, *Recreating Japanese Women*.

61. Jerome B. Cohen, *Japan's Economy in War and Reconstruction* (Minneapolis: University of Minnesota Press, 1949), 287–288. The figure rose rapidly thereafter, to around 10 percent of the male population by 1944.

62. See e.g., Yoshiko Miyake, "Doubling Expectations: Motherhood and Women's Factory Work under State Management in Japan in the 1930s and 1940s," in Bernstein, *Recreating Japanese Women, 1600–1945*; and Janet Hunter, "Factory Legislation and Employer Resistance: The Abolition of Night Work in the Japanese Cotton Spinning Industry," in *Japanese Management in Historical Perspective*, eds. Tsunehiko Yui and Keiichiro Nakagawa (Tokyo University Press, 1989). By 1936 there were more women than men working in agriculture, which constituted by far the largest sector of women's employment. These issues are also raised in Kathleen Uno's chapter in this volume, and it is worth noting that many young female factory workers were avid readers of some of the women's magazines propagating the idea of *shūyō* discussed by Barbara Sato in her chapter. Rhetoric implying criticism of married women working outside the home has, of course, been found elsewhere, but in many cases married women's role in the work force was much smaller than in Japan in this period. In England and Wales in 1911, for example, only 13.7 percent of married women were estimated to be in full-time work (Elizabeth Roberts, *Women's Work 1840–1940* [Basingstoke & London: Macmillan, 1988], 45). This compares with nearly half of all married women in Japan in the interwar years.

63. Described in e.g., Hazama, *Nihon rōmu kanri*; Sugihara Kaoru, "Nihon ni

okeru kindaiteki rōdō-seikatsu kateizō no seiritsu," in Sugihara, *Ajiakan bōeki no keisei to kōzō* (Minerva Shobō, 1996), chapter 12. These policies were closely associated with others aimed at securing longer-term commitment from male workers, and it is interesting to note Goldin's comment that in the United States marriage bars for women workers originated in policies that were designed to bond male workers to firms, as well as in a social consensus about the need for married women to remain at home (Goldin, *Understanding the Gender Gap*, 183). Discussion of the relative significance of economic imperatives and gender ideology in formulating these policies lies beyond the scope of this chapter, but this author's view is that while profits were the key objective, gender ideologies constrained and shaped the labor management policies adopted by employers to achieve that objective.

64. For a summary of the development of the cotton industry over the industrialization period, see Ushijima Toshiaki and Abe Takeshi, "Mengyō," in *Nihon keizai no 200–nen*, eds. Nishikawa Shunsaku, Odaka Kōnosuke, and Saitō Osamu (Nihon hyōronsha, 1996). In English, Gary Saxonhouse has a number of articles on labor strategies and productivity change in Japanese cotton spinning. See e.g., "Country Girls and Communication among Competitors in the Japanese Cotton Spinning Industry," in *Japanese Industrialization and Its Social Consequences*, ed. Hugh Patrick (Berkeley: University of California Press, 1976); and "The Supply of Quality Workers and the Demand for Quality Jobs in Japan's Early Industrialization," *Explorations in Economic History* 15, no. 1 (January 1978).

65. Wolf, *Factory Daughters*, 115.

66. For further references, see e.g., *Women and Industrialisation in Asia*, ed. Susan Horton (London: Routledge, 1996).

67. Mary C. Brinton, *Women and the Economic Miracle: Gender and Work in Postwar Japan* (Berkeley: University of California Press, 1993), 135–136.

68. "Afterword," in *Re-Imaging Japanese Women*, ed. Anne E. Imamura (Berkeley: University of California Press, 1996), 329.

11 Sorting Coal and Pickling Cabbage: Korean Women in the Japanese Mining Industry
W. Donald Smith

Early one morning in October 1929, a supervisor berated several Korean women coal sorters for their lackluster work. Since it was 3 AM, it was probably all they could do to stay awake at the conveyor belt where they separated lumps of coal from worthless slag, but they began working with all the enthusiasm they could muster, all except for one young woman. This nineteen-year-old, who worked under the Japanese name Nakajima Masako, was not just tired; she was tired of being bossed around, so she stopped working altogether. The Japanese supervisor, by his account, "pushed" her shoulder twice. "Nakajima," who probably went by a Korean name in her private life, dodged her supervisor's blows, and wrapped herself around his leg. He tried to push her away, and they both fell over.

"Nakajima" went right back to work and that would have been the end of the matter if a male Korean mine worker active in leftist politics[1] had not heard of the incident. He took her to a sympathetic doctor, who said her injuries would require six days' treatment and helped her file an assault charge against the supervisor. The company refused to negotiate or even to apologize, insisting that Nakajima's only injury was a minor scrape on her hand. The police, after conferring with the company, persuaded her to drop the case.

This incident at the Asō company in the Chikuhō coal field of northern Kyushu, while minor in itself, neatly encapsulates the position of Korean women in the mining industry and broader society of prewar Japan. As a coal sorter—a relatively safe but poorly paid

aboveground occupation—Nakajima Masako was typical of Korean
women mine workers, who rarely held the dangerous but well-paid
underground jobs filled by many Japanese women. Nakajima, in her
uneven contest with a violent male supervisor, a hostile corporation,
and the state that colonized her homeland from 1910 to 1945, also typi-
fies the burdens borne by Korean women in Japan because of their
gender, class, and nationality. The odds were against them, but Korean women in prewar Japan were not passive victims of gender and
ethnic discrimination. Like Nakajima, Korean women stood up for
what they thought was right in innumerable encounters with capital
and the Japanese state. They also played a critical supporting role in
the 1932 Asō strike, the most important walkout by Korean miners in
Japanese history.

Most of the little information available on Korean women in the
Japanese coal industry is from the 1930 census[2] and a handful of government and company documents prepared at around the same time,
so this article will focus on that period, at the risk of creating a mis-
leadingly static impression of an industry in the midst of sweeping
change. From about 1928 through 1933 mine operators, seeking to
heighten productivity and increase their control over the labor process, introduced new machinery and new methods of mining, phased
out women underground workers, and moved (especially at mines run
by the *zaibatsu* conglomerates) from a poorly paid, ethnically mixed
work force with high turnover toward a somewhat better paid, exclusively Japanese, and relatively stable work force.

Korean women miners in prewar Japan were a minority within a
minority, never numbering more than five hundred even at their peak
in the mid-1920s, but the questions raised by their presence can help
us see how gender and ethnicity shaped the Japanese coal mine work
force in this period of rapid change. It is well known that the overwhelming majority of workers who hauled coal in the prewar Japanese
mines were women (until the 1933 ban on underground female labor).
Scholars who focus only on gender, however, have assumed that the
predominance of women among coal haulers (*atoyama*) was universally
true in Japan when, in fact, it was true only of ethnic Japanese. As late
as 1930, Japanese women outnumbered Japanese men almost six to
one in this occupation. Among Koreans, however, male coal haulers

outnumbered women almost two to one. Similarly, it is common knowledge that Korean workers were much more likely than Japanese to work underground in the mines, probably because Koreans cost employers less and had fewer employment opportunities. Scholars who focus only on ethnicity[3] mistakenly assume that this was true of all Koreans when it was true only of men. While the majority of Japanese women before 1933 held relatively well-paid but dangerous jobs hauling coal underground in partnership with male hewers, only a minority of Korean women held such jobs.

How can these anomalies be explained? Focusing on the Chikuhō coal field, the region that employed the majority of miners in prewar Japan and even higher proportions of women (of both ethnicities) and Koreans (of both sexes), we will see how the character of Korean migration, the division of labor within the family, Japanese prejudice, and Korean patriarchal ideology made work and life in mining communities so different for Korean and Japanese women and men.

Because of the limited documentation remaining on Korean women mine workers, there is much that we will never know about them. In the case of Nakajima Masako, for example, there is no record of what happened to her after police persuaded her to drop the assault charge she had filed against her supervisor. As stated above, we do not even know her real name. Despite all the gaps in our knowledge of Korean women in the Japanese mining industry, however, their history provides a valuable reminder that ethnicity and gender are just as important as class in shaping the lives of individual workers, even in a seemingly homogeneous country such as Japan.

Women in the Chikuhō Coal Mines

Japanese women played an important role in the Chikuhō coal field, a 787-square-kilometer area between the present-day cities of Fukuoka and Kita-Kyūshū, even before the first modern mines were opened in the late nineteenth century. Men, women, and children had dug coal for centuries in small mines known as badger burrows (*tanuki bori*), as a sideline to agriculture in the densely populated Chikuhō region, so modern mines hired both men and women as a matter of course.

In sparsely populated Hokkaidō, Japan's second most important coal mining region, by contrast, little mining was carried out until after the 1868 Meiji Restoration that put Japan on the path of capitalist industrialization. With no tradition of family-based mining, very few women ever became underground miners in Hokkaidō.[4]

While women had worked in Chikuhō mines from the beginning, in the closing years of the nineteenth century they became structurally indispensable. With the Japanese industrial revolution picking up speed, companies began installing winch engines to speed the hauling of coal out of their mines. These winches had to be operated continuously to maximize profits, but the workers who dug the coal were not provided with any new equipment to help them keep pace. To produce a steady supply of coal for the winches to haul up, the rapidly expanding mines needed large numbers of new full-time workers, and many of these new workers were women. There was more female surplus labor, and women could be paid less, so mining companies sought to use men only in jobs that managers saw as too difficult for women, such as hewing, and to use women for other tasks, such as hauling the coal to a central loading point, from the late nineteenth century until the early 1930s.[5]

Like the women textile workers discussed by Janet Hunter in her essay in this volume, women mine workers were employed in large numbers in Chikuhō because of pre-existing patterns of work, women's relatively low wages, and the need to rapidly expand the labor force in a time of soaring production. Chikuhō mines had an additional reason for hiring women, however. By putting women, most of them married, to work underground along with men, often their husbands, Chikuhō mines found they could improve male retention rates. This was an important consideration in an era when monthly turnover in Chikuhō approached 15 percent.[6] The number of women mine workers continued to increase through the first two decades of the twentieth century, hitting their peak in about 1920. In that year, 66,396 women worked underground in Japan's coal mines, making up 26.6 percent of the underground work force, while 28,474 worked on the surface (30.6 percent of surface workers), for a total of 94,870 women mine workers (27.7 percent of the total).[7]

World War 1 Labor Shortage Brings Koreans to Chikuhō

In addition to residents of Fukuoka prefecture, many of them outcast *burakumin* (members of a group stigmatized for centuries as unclean and still subject to informal discrimination today despite their legal emancipation in 1871), workers from a wide area of western Japan came to work in the Chikuhō mines from midway through the Meiji period (1868–1912). It was not until World War 1, however, that mines recruited large numbers of Korean workers.[8] The war cut off British shipments of coal to Asia, creating new markets for Japanese coal, and drastically reduced shipments of other products from Britain as well, opening new markets for Japanese manufactured goods and, in turn, increasing domestic demand for coal. From late 1916, with little if any surplus labor left in the domestic rural sector and many Japanese miners leaving for more attractive factory jobs, the booming Japanese coal industry turned to colonial Korea as a new source of workers.

National conglomerate Mitsubishi and local company Kaijima were among the first to hire Korean mine workers in Chikuhō. Koreans also went to work at factories and on construction projects, increasing the number of Korean workers in Fukuoka prefecture from under 900 in late 1916 to over 5,000 in May 1919. Only nine of these workers were women at the end of 1916 and 175 in May 1919,[9] and the overwhelmingly male composition of the work force suggests that most Korean migrants in this period saw themselves as sojourners who would return home once they had saved a certain amount of money. Inevitably, however, many stayed on, and the Korean community in Japan, the country's current largest ethnic minority, traces its roots to this period.

It is unclear when the first Korean women went to work in Japan's mines, but the 1920 census counted 65 women among the 5,190 Koreans in the Japanese coal industry.[10] The number of Korean women coal miners grew over the next decade, peaking at around 500 in the mid-1920s.[11] Underground women workers of both ethnicities were then phased out over several years through mechanization of the hauling of coal from the working face whence it was removed to the nearest level shaft, which had been their primary task. Mines began mechanizing this process, known as face transport, for two reasons. First, with the partial mechanization of coal hewing, on the one hand, and the increasing mechanization of transportation along the level shafts leading to the main transport shaft where a winch hauled the coal out of the mine, on the other, manual transport from the face to the level shaft had become a bottleneck.[12] Second, mine operators could see that it was only a matter of time before Japan would give in to international pressure to ban underground female labor, and the government in fact announced in 1928 that such a ban would go into effect in 1933. The ban added momentum to mechanization because the mines knew they would be unable to find men willing to work for the low wages women had received. Mechanization and the resulting reorganization of the labor process were complex, time-consuming processes, so most mines began to replace their underground women workers with men and machinery well before the September 1, 1933, ban on their employment. Some Korean women continued to hold surface jobs in the mining industry, however, and a few were among the several thousand women who went back underground during World War II when restrictions on female labor were eased.

Chikuhō and other coal fields in Fukuoka prefecture employed the majority of coal mine workers in Japan, but accounted for especially high proportions of women and Koreans. The prefecture's mines employed 51.5 percent of all male and 59.7 percent of all female coal miners in Japan in 1930, along with 56.6 percent of Korean men and 69.3 percent of Korean women mine workers.[13] Within Chikuhō, the Mitsubishi conglomerate and the locally owned companies Asō, Arameo, and Kaijima accounted for the majority of Korean employment, both male and female (see Table 1). The Mitsui conglomerate, meanwhile, employed thousands of Japanese women[14] but no Korean workers of either gender until World War II.

Korean Women Overrepresented in Aboveground Jobs

Relatively few Korean women worked underground compared with their Japanese counterparts. The 1930 census, as shown in Table 2, found that 47.3 percent of Korean women in the coal industry were coal sorters, who stood at a conveyor belt some twelve hours a day separating slag from marketable coal, compared with 27.5 percent of

Table 1
Koreans at Selected Chikuhō Mining Companies, March 1928

Company Name	Korean Women	Korean Men	Korean Proportion of Work Force
Mitsubishi	52	3,382	26.8%
Asō	63	297	6.4%
Arameo	50	85	?
Kaijima	28	184	2.2%

SOURCE: Figures for Koreans in 1928 are from Fukuoka Chihō Shokugyō Shōkai Jimu-kyoku, *Kannai zaijū Chōsenjin rōdō jijō* (1929), in *Senji gaikokujin kyōsei renkō kankei shiryōshū*, ed. Hayashi Eidai, vol. 2, part 1, (Akashi Shoten, 1991). Percentages are my calculations based on the above figures and totals for all miners compiled from Nishinarita Yutaka, "Rōdōryoku hensei to rōshi kankei," *Chikuhō Sekitan Kōgyō Kumiai geppō*, in *1920-nendai no Nihon shihonshugi*, ed. 1920-nendaishi Kenkyūkai (Tōkyō Daigaku Shuppankai, 1983), 185. The proportion for Arameo has been left blank because figures for that mine show more Koreans than total miners.

Japanese. Another 10.2 percent were other aboveground workers, compared with 9.7 percent of Japanese. This means that well over half—57.6 percent—of Korean women held relatively safe but poorly paid aboveground jobs, compared with just 37.2 percent of Japanese women. Another 38.5 percent of Korean women worked underground as *atoyama*, compared with 54.4 percent of Japanese, while 3.9 percent were other underground workers, compared with 8.3 percent of Japanese. Women, regardless of ethnicity, were shut out of managerial and technical positions.[15]

Why did so few Korean women work underground? One of the most important reasons is that very few such jobs were available to them. In the room and pillar system employed until the 1920s at most major mines and later at smaller mines, an experienced hewer (*sakiyama*) dug out "rooms" of coal, leaving "pillars" in place to support the roof, while an *atoyama* hauled the coal to a central collection point. The *saki-yama* was almost always a man, but the *atoyama* was commonly a woman,

Table 2
Occupational Distribution in the Japanese
Coal Industry, 1930

Occupation	Korean Men	Korean Women	Japanese Men	Japanese Women
Owners and Operators	3 (0.0003)	0 -	923 (0.0067)	5 (0.0001)
Engineers and Managers	37 (0.0038)	0 -	9,143 (0.0666)	0 -
Hewers	7,681 (0.7892)	0 0	69,898 (0.5090)	0 -
Haulers	148 (0.0152)	79 (0.3854)	3,245 (0.0236)	19,165 (0.5442)
Other in-mine transport	132 (0.0136)	4 (0.0195)	4,984 (0.0363)	61 (0.0017)
Bracers	67 (0.0069)	0 -	6,713 (0.0489)	0 -
Other in-mine workers	780 (0.0801)	4 (0.0195)	16,183 (0.1178)	2,881 (0.0818)
Coal sorters	41 (0.0042)	97 (0.4732)	2,102 (0.0153)	9,674 (0.2747)
Others aboveground	844 (0.0867)	21 (0.1024)	24,133 (0.1757)	3,433 (0.0975)
TOTAL	9,733	205	137,324	35,219

SOURCE: Naikaku tōkeikyoku, *Shokugyō oyobi sangyō*, vol. 2, *Shōwa 5-nen kokuse chōsa hōkoku, zenkoku no bu* (Naikaku tōkeikyoku, 1935), 41–43, 225, 228.

often the *sakiyama*'s wife. Relatively few Korean men were able to become *sakiyama*, whether because of ethnic discrimination or a lack of experience, so there were correspondingly few jobs open to Korean women as *atoyama*. When mines switched from room and pillar to long wall mining, *sakiyama-atoyama* pairs were replaced by larger, usually all-male groups. This created new jobs for Korean men but meant that the number of underground jobs available to women (of either ethnic group) began to decline even before the 1933 ban on their work.

Even when Korean women had the opportunity to work underground, many of them probably turned it down in favor of coal sorting, which was easier to balance with the demands on their time and energy at home. Korean women, most of whom had come to Japan primarily to perform housework for their families, often just did not have the energy required to haul coal for eight to twelve hours a day. *Atoyama* generally carried coal either in bamboo carriers on their backs or by pushing baskets on runners; either way, it was exhausting work. While Japanese women miners also had to cook and clean after a full day's work while their husbands slept or drank sake, the burden of housework may have been even heavier on Korean women in Japan. Unlike Japanese in the colonies, among whom women may have outnumbered men, as Barbara Brooks and Mark Driscoll note in their essays in this volume, men far outnumbered women in the Korean community of prewar Japan. Korean men still expected women to do all the housework, not only for the women's own families but for the boarders many households took in.

Like Koreans, outcast *buraku* women were overrepresented among coal sorters, for similar reasons. Japanese scholar Sakamoto Yūichi argues persuasively that it was not because of discriminatory corporate policies that so many *buraku* women became coal sorters but because coal sorting, while it paid much less than underground work, was also less exhausting. This left *buraku* women in Chikuhō, many of whom commuted to the mines from nearby farming communities, at least minimal energy to do farm work with their families before or after their jobs at the mines.[16]

Cultural factors, while probably less important than the lack of underground jobs available to Korean women and the other demands on their time and energy, may also have discouraged Korean women from becoming coal haulers. Korean working-class women were testing the bounds of patriarchal ideology in this period, taking an assertive role in the 1932 Asō strike, for example, but the Confucian-influenced ideal of sexual separation still had a certain hold on Korean workers, even if far less than on the Korean elite. Underground mining was an exclusively male occupation in colonial Korea, although a few women worked aboveground,[17] so some Korean women (or their husbands) may have rejected underground work as improper for women.

Moreover, women had reason to fear everything from embarrassment to sexual harassment and assault[18] when they went down into the mines, especially considering the style of dress, or lack of dress, common in prewar Chikuhō mines. It was hot in the mines, and exposed skin made it easier for miners to notice the small particles that often provided early warning of an impending roof collapse,[19] so men wore only loincloths and women just short skirts, leaving their breasts exposed. Because women haulers usually worked with their husbands or other family members, nudity was not a particular problem at the working face. When women hauling coal alone through dark mine shafts encountered other men, however, "mistakes could easily occur," as a government report coyly put it.[20]

Workers in the coal sorting plants, by contrast, were fully dressed and almost all of them were women. While coal sorting, like other mine work, was generally off limits to women in the United States, the few males in Japanese sorting plants were either supervisors or boys too young to go into the mines.[21]

It is often assumed that, like coal sorters, almost all the *atoyama* who hauled coal were women before the 1933 ban on most female underground work, but this is a modern oversimplification of a complex situation.[22] In Hokkaidō, almost all underground workers, including *atoyama*, were men, as were the majority of Korean *atoyama* nationwide. The 1930 census counted 19,165 Japanese women and 3,245 Japanese men, along with 148 Korean men and 79 Korean women, working as *atoyama*.[23] There were important differences, however, in the career paths of male and female coal haulers. Most male *atoyama* were young, inexperienced miners. They hoped to eventually advance out of the job, not because they saw hauling coal as a job for women, but because of the higher pay and increased respect accorded to *sakiyama*, according to retired miners interviewed by historian Ichihara Hiroshi.[24] Most men could in fact expect to advance to *sakiyama* status, but women only rarely became *sakiyama*, no matter how skilled or diligent they were.

While Korean women were much more likely to work aboveground than their Japanese counterparts, Korean men were more likely to be hewers or to do other jobs underground than Japanese. Over three out of four Korean male mine workers in 1930 were hewers, as loosely defined by the census. Most of the rest held other jobs underground, while less than 10 percent worked aboveground. Just half of Japanese male coal miners, by contrast, were hewers, and nearly 20 percent worked aboveground. Korean men were excluded from skilled jobs and management almost as entirely as were women of either ethnic group; just 0.4 percent of Korean men were engineers or managers, compared with 6.6 percent of Japanese men.[25]

Aboveground workers were on the whole paid less than those inside the mines, but gender was just as important as the location of work in determining wages. Coal sorters, almost all of whom were women, were paid about half the wages of workers in male-dominated aboveground occupations at the mines. Underground, women *atoyama* were paid some 20 to 30 percent less than workers in male-dominated specialties. *Atoyama* received high pay, however, compared to other women in prewar Japan: some 70 percent more than that of female factory workers and double that of coal sorters.[26] Underground work meant not only higher wages but much higher rates of death and injury, however, so it is difficult for an outside observer to say whether it was better for a woman to take a relatively well paid but dangerous job underground or a poorly paid but safer job aboveground. (Men, by contrast, could earn almost as much in many jobs aboveground as they could underground.) Women could earn much more for their families by going underground, especially if they formed teams with their husbands, because this would ensure that the men actually went to work most days instead of drinking and gambling. Many women felt great pride in doing difficult, dangerous jobs alongside men,[27] but many others hated underground work and were relieved when the government banned women from most work inside the mines.[28]

Wages for women mine workers were well below those of men, as we saw above, and the evidence suggests that Koreans as a whole were paid less than Japanese.[29] Were Korean women, then, paid less than either Korean men or Japanese women? Specific wage data for Korean women miners are lacking, but anecdotal evidence suggests that they were at the bottom of the wage hierarchy. Officials at one Hokkaidō coal mine, for example, said during World War II that they hoped to hire Korean women as coal sorters because of their low wages.[30]

Despite women's lower wages, many Korean men were hired, in effect, to replace women, most of whom were Japanese. This was especially true in the 1920s as companies, especially Mitsubishi, mechanized face transport and laid off women coal haulers of both nationalities in anticipation of a ban on female underground labor. The new mechanical face conveyors still had to be loaded by hand, so companies hired Korean men to perform the combined tasks of hewing and loading coal.[31] When Japanese women miners were laid off, their husbands often left with them to seek higher-paying work because of the difficulty of supporting a family on the pay of one miner. Life was no cheaper for Koreans, but they had little chance of finding better jobs, so Korean men filled the positions vacated by many male Japanese miners as well.

What little we know about the recruitment of Korean women miners, meanwhile, comes from a roster of workers at one mine operated by the major local company Kaijima. Women on this roster were from villages scattered across southern Korea, suggesting that they were not recruited directly by the company but came to the mine with husbands or other family members.[32]

The roster, compiled by the Kaijima Oonoura colliery's No. 7 mine, lists 1,388 Korean workers employed from 1928 through 1943, of whom 26 are clearly identifiable as women. All 26 women on the roster were hired in 1938 or later, although it is known that women worked at the mine before 1938.[33] Kaijima hired the women at ages ranging from sixteen to thirty-nine. Occupations are specified for just three women: two coal sorters, one hired at sixteen and the other at twenty-five, and a "hewer" (probably an *atoyama*) hired at eighteen. It can be inferred that a fourth woman, aged thirty-seven, was also an *atoyama* or other underground worker because she was fired for smoking in the mine, a serious safety violation.

The Kaijima roster does not give us a clear picture of Korean women workers' marital status, but this does not appear to have been as important as it was for Japanese women in determining where in the mine compound they worked. Among Japanese women, coal sorters were younger and less likely to be married than were *atoyama*,[34] possibly because coal sorters were paid so little that they could not support themselves on their wages alone, much like the young female office workers who live with their parents in Japan today. Korean women in Japan as a whole married much younger than Japanese, so Korean coal sorters were much more likely to be married than were Japanese in the same occupation, and probably were not much different from Korean *atoyama* in this respect. In 1920, for example, 64 percent of Korean women aged fifteen to nineteen in Fukuoka prefecture were married, compared with just 18.3 percent of Japanese women in that age group. The proportion increased to 92.7 percent for Korean women aged twenty to twenty-four, compared with 65.5 percent of their Japanese counterparts in Fukuoka[35] and, as Driscoll notes, an even smaller percentage of Japanese women in the colonies.

Limited Participation in Formal Economy

Korean women were not only less likely than their Japanese counterparts to work underground but less likely to work in the mining industry as a whole. In 1930, for example, while there were 3.9 Japanese men in the industry nationwide for every Japanese woman, there were 47.5 Korean men for every Korean woman.[36] Coal and metal mining combined occupied just 0.3 percent of Korean women in Japan, compared with 6.3 percent of Korean men.[37]

Where were the other Korean women workers in Japan? In broad sectoral terms, 11.9 percent of Korean women worked in manufacturing (mostly textiles) and 2.6 percent were involved in commerce. The most prevalent occupation among Japanese women, by contrast, was agriculture (20 percent), followed by commerce (4.6 percent) and manufacturing (4.4 percent). Surprisingly, perhaps, to Americans used to seeing minority women working as maids in white households, 2.2 percent of Japanese women were household servants, nearly double the 1.2 percent of Korean women engaged in this occupation. Altogether, just 17.6 percent of Korean women were formally employed, compared with 33.1 percent of Japanese women. (The comparable figures for men were 79.5 percent for Koreans and 58.5 percent for Japanese.)[38]

Why did so few Korean women work outside the home? Many Japanese, who saw Koreans as unclean and inattentive to detail, were probably reluctant to bring Koreans into their households as servants or into their shops as employees. Moreover, the minimal educational attainment and limited Japanese language skills of Korean women meant that many jobs were closed to them. Despite Japan's claims that it was bringing enlightenment to Korea, over half—56 percent—of all Koreans arriving in Japan in 1927 had no formal education whatsoever,[39] and

Korean women and mine workers had even less education. Out of 151 Korean women at one Chikuhō mine in 1928, 149 (98.7 percent) had no formal education, while the other two had "elementary school level" educations. As for Korean men at the mine, 816 (90.3 percent) had had no schooling, 87 (9.6 percent) had had "elementary school level" educations, and one was a middle school graduate. Only 19.2 percent of the Korean women at the mine understood Japanese, compared with 44.9 percent of the men.[40] Japanese miners were well educated compared to Koreans, but not by the standards of a nation that claimed to have implemented universal, compulsory education. Among Japanese female miners, 35.5 percent had no schooling in 1924, as did 15.7 percent of Japanese male miners. Educational attainment was considerably higher among other groups of Japanese workers; only 6.5 percent of female textile workers and 2.7 percent of male metal or machine workers, for example, had no formal education.[41]

An even more important reason why so few Korean women worked for wages was their primary motive for coming to Japan in the first place: to work for their families. The first wave of Korean migration to Japan was predominantly male, but women played a key role in making this migration possible. Women staying in Korea made clothes for men going to Japan as laborers[42] and replaced them in the fields,[43] continuing, of course, to cook and clean for children and elderly family members. Men, in turn, sent part of their wages home to Korea. As men became settled in Japan, they began to send for their families, and toward the end of the 1920s families began to migrate together, so the male-female ratio among Koreans in Japan narrowed from 7.6 to 1 in 1920 to 2.4 to 1 in 1930 and 1.5 to 1 in 1940.[44]

Official figures confirm that, in contrast to Japanese women going to the Asian continent, many of whom, as Brooks and Driscoll report elsewhere in this volume, were unmarried sex workers, the vast majority of Korean women in Japan were married and primarily engaged in housework for their families. In 1928, for example, 69.9 percent of newly migrating women reported that they had been sent for by family members,[45] and most Korean women in Japan—76.6 percent in 1930—were classified as "dependents."[46] Once women migrated, they were much less likely to return to Korea than were men,[47] suggesting that their continued residence in Japan did not depend on their personally finding and holding paid employment. Just because women were classified as dependents did not, of course, mean that they did not bring money into the family. Women worked outside the formal economy, cooking and cleaning for boarders and making everything from the spicy pickled cabbage known as *kimch'i* to black market liquor, in addition to performing the myriad tasks of household production and reproduction that allowed other family members to work for wages.

Korean women's lesser participation in the formal sector meant they had fewer contacts with Japanese people than did Korean men and, perhaps as a result, they were less "Japanized." Partly because so many of them were married when they arrived in Japan, Korean women were much less likely than Korean men to marry Japanese; from 1938 to 1942, for example, 96 percent of "mixed marriages" involved a Korean man and a Japanese woman.[48] Women were also less likely to learn to read or speak Japanese, an affront to Japanese officials trying to extinguish the Korean language. Women held on fiercely to gendered cultural norms in the face of official attempts to "improve" the Korean lifestyle through imposition of Japanese mores. They rejected the Japanese *kimono* in favor of the traditional Korean skirt (*ch'ima*) and blouse (*chŏgori*), even as Korean men quickly adopted Western or Japanese clothing. In addition to promoting Japanese clothing, Japanese officials encouraged Korean women to sit and walk like Japanese,[49] and to learn Japanese flower arrangement (*ikebana*) and the ceremonial preparation of tea. Training in these skills was intended to make Korean women into proper "Japanese" wives[50] and loyal imperial subjects who would, like the "good wives and wise mothers" discussed in Kathleen Uno's essay in this volume, provide a solid foundation for the Japanese state's mobilization of civilian resources and, like the postwar Japanese housewives targeted by the New Life Movement discussed in Andrew Gordon's essay, encourage their husbands to be diligent and docile workers. Unlike the government's efforts to train "good wives and wise mothers" and the corporate-led New Life Movement, however, attempts to assimilate Koreans (of both genders) were a dismal failure. Far from making Koreans want to emulate Japanese, the government's programs, especially heavy-handed wartime policies such as the forced Japanization of Korean names and compulsory worship at Shintō shrines, left a legacy of bitterness that will last well into the 21st century.[51]

Major Role in 1932 Asō Mine Strike

Korean women miners, unlike textile workers,[52] may never have walked off the job themselves in Japan, but they did play a major supporting role in the 1932 Asō strike, the biggest in Chikuhō that year and the largest strike ever by Korean miners in Japan. Some four hundred strikers, all men, showed courage and determination in taking on capital and the state for twenty days in the harsh anti-union, anti-Korean atmosphere of the times, but their struggle would have been much harder without the support of Korean women.[53]

Locally owned Asō, a major employer of Koreans of both sexes in the 1920s, had apparently laid off all its underground women workers by the summer of 1932.[54] That is when it sparked the strike by laying off or transferring three hundred male miners, the majority of them Koreans, in the face of slumping demand for coal. Workers demanded severance pay for laid-off miners, along with better conditions and the reversal of earlier wage cuts for remaining workers.

To win converts to the strike and put pressure on the company, squads of strikers passed out fliers and copies of a strike newspaper almost every day at both Asō and nearby Mitsubishi mines. Despite police roundups resulting in at least 271 workers being taken into custody,[55] strikers were able to steadily increase their ranks. The walkout, which began August 15 with 80 Korean miners, doubled in size within the first two days. The number of strikers more than doubled again to 365 as of August 25 before leveling off in the last few days of August at around 400, some 40 percent of the Korean work force at Asō.[56] In addition, some 200 Korean miners from outside Asō, mostly from Mitsubishi mines, flocked to Asō to support the strike.[57] In contrast to this display of solidarity among Korean workers, not a single Japanese worker joined the walkout, despite handbills appealing to them as "brother miners" whose own fate depended on the outcome of the strike.[58]

Despite the strikers' determination, their tactics failed to put much pressure on the company. Asō, already trying to cut output because of the depressed coal market, was hardly worried about lost production, and it could count on the police to keep strikers from blocking mine entrances or attacking company property.

The actions of Korean women protesters, most of them the wives of Korean miners, were another matter, however. The women staged sit-ins and "visits" to the company to discuss the strikers' demands, leaving both Asō and the pro-Japanese Korean organization Sōaikai "extremely angry,"[59] according to the Kyōchōkai, a semi-official organization devoted to promoting harmonious labor relations. When the women barged into company offices, Korean miner Hwang Haksŏng recalled, they would spring at company officials, scratching and clawing, while yelling out their grievances. They also attended demonstrations, often, according to Hwang, with each woman carrying a baby on her back and holding another child by the hand,[60] underscoring their roles as mothers while showing that mothers are not necessarily passive observers of events outside the household. Company officials were clearly unsure how to deal with this "unladylike" behavior, while the police hesitated to beat women and children.

Two weeks into the strike, with the company still refusing to negotiate, over fifty women arrived at company headquarters in Iizuka, Fukuoka prefecture, on August 29 to find their way blocked by police. Some fifteen of the women managed to rush past the police into the office, but the company refused to meet with them.[61] On the same day, thirty-three male strikers arrived at company president Asō Takichi's second home in Fukuoka City after walking all night across Yakiyama Pass from Iizuka. The president was not home, however, so the strikers left a petition with the butler and delivered copies to prefectural officials as well.[62]

With the dispute becoming more heated, prefectural authorities on the same day sent the head of the Fukuoka Special Higher Police to urge company officials to work toward a settlement,[63] probably fearing that the unrest would spread to the seven thousand Koreans working at other Chikuhō mines. In response, negotiations began August 31 and a settlement was reached September 3. The settlement provided for severance payments to dismissed workers but did not address most of the remaining miners' demands for higher pay or improved conditions.[64]

There is no evidence that the women's actions on August 29 led directly to prefectural intervention in the strike, but government officials probably saw continued clashes between women and the authorities as a greater threat to public order (or at least to public perceptions of the police) than the male strikers' petitioning and leafleting. Prefectural officials were not the only contemporary observers to recognize the importance of women's role in the Asō strike. An organization that specialized in monitoring social movements, for example, put participation in the strike at over one thousand people, counting strikers' wives and children as full participants.[65]

Unfortunately for labor, male strike leaders do not seem to have recognized either the potential or the interests of women. The Asō strike committee did organize at least some of the visits by "family members" to company headquarters. It seems to have viewed women as strictly an auxiliary force, however, and not as workers with ideas and energy of their own, even though some of the women protesters had probably worked underground themselves, and many no doubt still worked in sorting plants or other aboveground facilities at Asō. The strikers' demands also included nothing specifically geared to women's concerns. Postwar chronicles of the strike, moreover, fail to treat women as an important force in their own right.[66]

Women at the Wartime Mines

For some Japanese women, like those in the United States, World War II brought new (if temporary) opportunities to advance into jobs previously held by men. For the vast majority of Korean women, however, the war brought little change at best.

In the prewar coal mines, it was almost unheard of for a woman of any ethnicity to become a *sakiyama* and the 1933 ban on most underground work by women further restricted their opportunities. Women were limited to working in the narrow, dangerous seams known as "low coal" or in small mines overlooked by government inspectors.

After the ban was lifted and women went back into most mines in August 1939, however, some Japanese women became *sakiyama* responsible for supervising Korean male *atoyama*. Coal companies reasoned that putting Korean men, who were regarded as reluctant to raise their fists against women, under female supervisors would result in a more orderly and productive workplace than would be possible under male supervisors, and Japanese women in fact reported few problems working with Korean men.[67]

Oota Yuki was one such Japanese female *sakiyama*. She had followed her father into Shinoka mine in Chikuhō when she was fourteen, taking her ailing mother's place hauling coal on a bamboo sled. In 1943, at age seventeen, she became a *sakiyama* in charge of Korean miners, and in 1944 received a commendation for staying on the job despite a head injury, inspiring her Korean subordinates. As she later told local historian Idegawa Yasuko, however, Oota was not concerned with inspiring anyone; she continued working to make sure her family would be fed.[68]

Some of these new women *sakiyama* were *burakumin*,[69] and the war opened up new opportunities for male *burakumin* as well, sometimes at the expense of Koreans.[70] Even some long-term Korean resident men became supervisors in charge of Korean conscript workers.

Korean women were one of the few groups for whom no new opportunities, no matter how short-lived, opened during the war. There is no record of even a single Korean woman becoming a *sakiyama*, although they did continue to work at Kaijima, Meiji,[71] and other Chikuhō collieries. As of June 30, 1944, there were 369 Korean women and 140,419 Korean men working in Japan's metal and coal mining industry.[72] Korean women also worked as nurses and interpreters at mine hospitals and as cooks at mine mess halls.[73]

While their numbers pale next to the 200,000 young Korean women forced to become "comfort women" for the Japanese military, Korean women were also pressed into sexual servitude at mining and construction sites in Japan. At least one hundred Korean women were sent to "comfort centers" set up for male Korean forced laborers near at least eighteen coal and metal mines in Hokkaidō,[74] for example, and at least ten such centers were set up near Chikuhō mines. Mining companies, probably seeing sexually satisfied men as less likely to stage work stoppages or flee the mines, were intimately involved in establishing, supervising, and subsidizing the comfort centers. In Chikuhō, for example, mine supervisors reportedly rewarded diligent Korean men with visits to these establishments, many of which accepted company scrip, normally worthless outside mine compounds, in payment.[75]

The Japanese government used coercion and deceit to supply young women for sex in coal-producing areas, just as it sent women to military encampments throughout Asia and the Pacific. Shim Mija, for example, was sixteen when the police called her in for decorating a map of Japan as part of a school project with Korean roses of Sharon rather than the officially prescribed cherry blossoms. When she resisted a policeman's attempt to rape her, he inserted bamboo skewers under Shim's fingernails, branded her shoulder with a red-hot iron, and sent her to a comfort center in Fukuoka prefecture.[76] Most or all of the girls and women sent to the centers were apparently, like Shim, young and unmarried. According to a former Chikuhō mine foreman, they were supplied as members of a women's volunteer corps (*joshi teishintai*), which enrolled single girls and women aged twelve to forty for factory work and sexual slavery.[77] Korean brokers also provided women, however, as in Hokkaidō, where they set up comfort centers at the request of companies such as Mitsui, Mitsubishi, and Sumitomo, staffing them with girls as young as fourteen.[78]

Conclusion

With Japan's defeat in August 1945, colonial conscript laborers left the mines as quickly as they could, although many longtime Korean residents stayed in Japan, where they and their descendants today number around 700,000, down from a peak of 2 million in 1945. The ships carrying workers home to Korea and China returned full of demobilized Japanese soldiers asking for their old jobs back, so most women quickly left the coal pits. The exclusion of women from underground work was then formalized by the U.S. authorities who oversaw the 1945–1952 Allied Occupation of Japan, and the last officially authorized women were gone by March 1947,[79] although some women continued to work illegally in small, rarely inspected mines as late as 1961.[80] Women kept working as coal sorters, but they were phased out as mechanization transformed sorting from a labor-intensive, largely female occupation into a relatively capital-intensive and almost entirely male occupation beginning in the 1950s.[81] The Japanese coal industry itself is all but gone now,[82] with even the giant slag heaps left behind by the mines being leveled to build shopping centers and golf courses. Even after the last mine disappears, however, the Korean men and women who supplied the coal that built much of modern Japan will continue to be important to our understanding of gender and ethnicity.

The occupational distribution of women miners in Japan described in pioneering studies by Japanese economic historian Nishinarita Yutaka and German scholar Regine Mathias[83] holds true only for ethnic Japanese, while the characteristics of Korean miners in Japan described in innumerable studies apply only to men, suggesting that the key features of any labor force often become visible only when that work force is analyzed in both gender and ethnic terms. This essay has suggested some factors contributing to the lower proportion of Korean women working underground compared with Japanese. The small number of Korean men able to become *sakiyama* meant that there were correspondingly few jobs available for Korean women as *atoyama*. Moreover, cultural factors and the heavy burden of household labor borne by Korean women probably discouraged them from taking relatively well paying but exhausting underground jobs in the mines, resulting in the overrepresentation of Korean women in coal sorting and other aboveground occupations.[84]

The gendered occupational distribution of ethnic Japanese mine workers is beyond the scope of this chapter, but the basically descriptive accounts of Nishinarita and Mathias need to be supplemented by analytic research explaining segmentation of the work force by gender, age, and marital status. Comparative research, both international and interindustry, is also needed. How did coal sorting become "women's work" in Japan and a task for men in many other countries? Why did Japanese mines, which recruited male workers from distant areas of Japan and Korea, not recruit groups of young women from rural areas, as did the textile mills? These are just two of the many questions that need to be answered.[85]

The statistical sketch of Korean women miners presented here provides only the broadest outlines of the complex lives led by these women. It is likely, for example, that some women felt empowered by doing jobs just as difficult as those done by men while others dreaded each new day at work. The scarce documentary evidence remaining sheds no light on these issues, making it crucial for researchers to locate any retired Korean women miners who may still be alive while there is time to fill in the gaps in our knowledge of their experiences.

Notes

I would like to thank Hayashi Eidai, Ichihara Hiroshi, Niizuma (formerly Nagao) Yuri, Sakamoto Yūichi, Tanaka Naoki, Yokogawa Teruo, and Nishida Hideko for supplying valuable materials, and Hwasook Nam Bergquist, Morris Linan Bian, Kim Sunjoo, W. Donald Burton, the participants in a workshop at the University of Washington, and the editors of this volume, Barbara Molony and Kathleen Uno, for their helpful comments on earlier versions of this essay.

1. The description of the incident here and in the previous paragraph is drawn from *Asō rōmu gakari nisshi,* October 19 and 26, 1929, reproduced as "Chikuhō ni okeru rōdō undō shiryō: Taishō 14-nen-Shōwa 12-nen," in *Chikushi jogakuen tanki daigaku kiyō,* ed. Doi Taira, no. 6 (March 1971): 7, 9–10. The male mine worker, a coal car handler for Asō, was a member of the Nihon Taishūtō (Japan Masses' Party).

2. Naikaku tōkeikyoku [National Statistics Bureau], *Shokugyō oyobi sangyō,* vol. 2, *Shōwa 5-nen kokusei chōsa hōkoku, zenkoku no bu* (Naikaku tōkeikyoku, 1935).

3. This refers primarily to specialists in the Korean minority, as most Japanese scholars still take Japanese ethnicity as a given.

4. Women miners are not unique to Japan, of course. Britain and France employed women until the nineteenth century, and many thousands play key roles in mining across the developing world today. See Kuntala Lahiri-Dutt and Martha McIntyre, eds., *Women Miners in Developing Countries: Pit Women and Others* (Aldershot, UK: Ashgate Press, 2006), which also contains two essays on women miners in prewar Japan. In the United States, a few women worked in mines early in the twentieth century, and thousands more went underground in the 1970s as affirmative-action policies and a booming market eroded barriers to their employment. See Marat Moore, *Women in the Mines: Stories of Life and Work* (New York: Twayne Publishers, 1996).

5. Nishinarita Yutaka, "The Coal Mining Industry," in *Technology Change and Female Labour in Japan,* ed. Nakamura Masanori (Tokyo: United Nations University Press, 1994), 60–62. Due to the poor quality of this translation, those who read Japanese are advised to consult the original version, published as "Sekitan kōgyō no gijutsu kakushin to joshi rōdō" in *Gijutsu kakushin to joshi rōdō,* ed. Nakamura Masanori, 71–105, (Kokuren Daigaku, 1985).

6. Nōshōmushō Kōzankyoku, *Kōfu taigū jirei* (1908), cited in Ogino Yoshihiro, *Chikuhō tankō rōshi kankeishi* (Fukuoka: Kyūshū daigaku shuppankai, 1993), 21.

Chikuhō had a monthly average turnover of 14.9 percent in 1906, compared with 7.1 percent for Hokkaidō.

7. Nōshōmushō Kōzankyoku, *Honpō kōgyō no sūsei* (1920), in Nishinarita, "The Coal Mining Industry," 87.

8. For an abortive 1897–1898 experiment with Korean labor at a mine in Saga prefecture, see Tōjō Nobumasa, "Meijiki Nihon ni okeru saishō no Chōsenjin rōdōsha: Saga-ken Chōja tankō no tankōfu," in *"Kankoku heigō" mae no zai Nichi Chōsenjin*, eds. Komatsu Hiroshi, Kim Yŏngdal, and Yamawaki Keizō (Akashi Shoten, 1994), 131–175.

9. *Fukuoka nichinichi shinbun*, June 27, 1919.

10. Naikaku tōkeikyoku, *Shokugyō*, vol. 2, *Taishō 9-nen kokusei chōsa hōkoku, zenkoku no bu* (Naikaku tōkeikyoku, 1929), 249.

11. A June 1928 survey found 320 Korean women miners in Fukuoka prefecture. Fukuoka chihō shokugyō shōkai jimukyoku, *Kannai zaijū Chōsenjin rōdō jijō* (1929), in *Senji gaikokujin kyōsei renkō kankei shiryōshū*, ed. Hayashi Eidai, vol. 2, part 1 (Akashi shoten, 1991), 125. Assuming that Fukuoka accounted for 69.3 percent of Korean women miners in Japan, as it did in the 1930 census, this would produce a national total of about 462. Assuming even minimal undercounting, the 1928 total could easily have approached 500.

12. Tanaka Naoki, *Kindai Nihon tankō rōdōshi kenkyū* (Sōfūkan, 1984), 379, 395.

13. Calculated from Naikaku tōkeikyoku, *Shokugyō oyobi sangyō*, vol. 2, *Shōwa 5-nen kokusei chōsa*, 41–43, 225; and *Fukenhen*, vol. 4, *Fukuoka-ken*, 118.

14. In December 1917, for example, Mitsui employed 3,237 women out of 11,170 miners at its Tagawa coal mine, all of them apparently Japanese. Chikuhō sekitan kōgyō-shi nenpyō hensan iinkai, *Chikuhō sekitan kōgyō-shi nenpyō* (Fukuoka: Nishinihon bunka kyōkai, 1973), 285. Despite the company's reliance on female labor, Mitsui titled an official company history "A Century of Men." *Otokotachi no seiki: Mitsui Kōzan no hyakunen*, ed. Mitsui kōzan kabushiki kaisha (Mitsui kōzan kabushiki kaisha, 1990).

15. Calculated from Naikaku tōkeikyoku, *Shokugyō oyobi sangyō*, vol. 2, *Shōwa 5-nen kokusei chōsa*, 41–43, 225, 228. Figures for Japanese calculated by subtracting those for Koreans and Taiwanese from totals.

16. Sakamoto Yūichi, "Chikuhō sekitan kōgyō to hisabetsu buraku: Nihon shihonshugi to 'hisabetsu rōdō' o megutte," *Buraku mondai kenkyū*, no. 140 (August 1997): 101.

17. Women and girls accounted for 954 of the 30,093 workers in the Korean coal and metal mining industry in June 1931. Nine female workers were Japanese and the rest Korean. Minami Manshū tetsudō keizai chōsakai dai-ichibu, *Chōsenjin rōdōsha ippan jijō* (Dairen: Minami Manshū Tetsudō, 1933), 82–83.

18. Mining was neither the only industry nor Japan the only country, of course, in which women had (and have) to endure sexual harassment and assault to earn a living. For examples from the Japanese textile industry, see E. Patricia Tsurumi, *Factory Girls: Women in the Thread Mills of Meiji Japan* (Princeton, NJ: Princeton University Press, 1990), 89, 119, 144, 165–167, 196.

19. Interview with Idegawa Yasuko, May 16, 1995, Kurate-machi, Fukuoka prefecture.

20. Osaka chihō shokugyō shōkai jimukyoku, *Chikuhō tanzan rōdō jijō* (Osaka: Osaka chihō shokugyō shōkai jimukyoku, 1926), 76.

21. Retired miner Nagaoka Iwao, for example, was a coal picker as a boy at Mitsubishi Hōjō mine, while his father was a coal sorting supervisor, the highest job available, according to Nagaoka, to *burakumin*. Interview, Hōjō-machi, Tagawa-gun, Fukuoka prefecture, May 25, 1995.

22. This is a common misconception, shared by Regine Mathias, for example, who writes that "*atoyama* . . . became a synonym for women miners in general." Mathias, "Female Labour in the Japanese Coal Mining Industry," in *Japanese Women Working,* ed. Janet Hunter (London and New York: Routledge, 1993), 101.

23. Naikaku tōkeikyoku, *Shokugyō oyobi sangyō,* vol. 2, *Shōwa 5-nen kokusei chōsa,* 41–43, 225, 228. Figures for Japanese calculated as in n. 15.

24. The division of miners into *atoyama* and *sakiyama* was not, in general, a matter of company rankings, but something left up to the miners themselves. Personal communication from Japanese mining historian Ichihara Hiroshi, September 4, 1997.

25. Calculated from Naikaku tōkeikyoku, *Shokugyō oyobi sangyō,* vol. 2, *Shōwa 5-nen kokusei chōsa,* 41–43, 225, 228. "Hewers" (*saitanfu*) and *atoyama* are treated as separate categories in census reports, but *atoyama* are included in a broader category of "hewers" in some other documents, such as the Kaijima roster cited above.

26. At the Mitsubishi Shinnyū mine in June 1928, for example, coal sorters were paid an average of 16.54 yen a month, compared to 26.67 yen for male miscellaneous workers, 28.32 yen for porters, 35.90 for operatives, and 39.16 yen for drivers. The only workers paid less aboveground than coal sorters were female

miscellaneous workers, at 15.32 yen a month. Underground, by comparison, women "hewers" (probably *atoyama*) averaged 33.20 yen a month, compared to 35.15 yen for porters, 36.39 yen for drivers, 38.75 yen for "miners" other than hewers, 39.84 yen for miscellaneous workers, 41.36 yen for male hewers, and 44.70 yen for operatives. Tomigashi Fumiya, "Shinnyū tankō dai-6-kō jisshū hōkoku," collection of Tokyo University Engineering Library (1928), cited in Ogino, *Chikuhō tankō rōshi kankeishi*, 304. For a comparison of average wages by gender in mining and factory labor, see *Nihon rōdō undō shiryō*, ed. Rōdō undō shiryō iinkai, vol. 10 (Rōdō undō shiryō kankō iinkai, 1959), 284–285.

27. Kubo Umeno, for example, recalled in a circa 1990 interview that she had "really liked the work," adding that she was a "much more skilled and dedicated worker" than her husband and contributed more to supporting their four children. After her husband left her, she worked alone, doing both the hewing and hauling until she left the mines in about 1942 after some 30 years of underground work. Tajima Masami, *Tankō bijin: yami o tomosu onnatachi* (Tsukiji shokan, 2000), 23–29.

28. Harada Tsuma, for example, said she was glad when female underground labor, which "was no kind of work for women," was banned during the 1945–1952 U.S. occupation of Japan. Tajima, *Tankō bijin*, 15.

29. According to a secret Home Ministry report, for example, Japanese workers in mining and metallurgy in Fukuoka prefecture had "maximum" daily wages in May 1924 of 3.4 yen, compared with 2.9 yen for Koreans; "minimum" wages of 0.9 yen, compared with 0.8 yen for Koreans; and "normal" wages of 2.0 yen, compared with 1.5 yen for Koreans. Japanese and Korean workers in the same industrial category in Hokkaidō reportedly had the same "normal" wage, 2.5 yen. The Japanese "minimum" of 1.6 yen trailed the Koreans' 1.8 yen, but the Japanese "maximum" of 3.97 yen was well ahead of the Koreans' 3.0 yen. Naimushō shakaikyoku dai-ichibu, *Chōsenjin rōdōsha ni kansuru jōkyō* (unpublished report, 1924), in *Zai Nichi Chōsenjin kankei shiryō shūsei*, ed. Pak Kyŏngsik, vol. 1 (San'ichi Shobō, 1975–1976), 492.

30. Rōdō kagaku kenkyūjo, *Hantō rōmusha kinrō jōkyō ni kansuru chōsa hōkoku* (1943), in *Chōsen mondai shiryō sōsho*, ed. Pak Kyŏngsik, vol. 1 (San'ichi shobō, 1982), 39.

31. For the example of Mitsubishi Shinnyū mine in 1923, see Okada Hideo, "Shinnyū tankō dai-rokkō hōkoku," (1929), collection of University of Tokyo Engineering Library, cited in Chung Jin Sung [Chŏng Chinsŏng], "1920-nendai no Chōsenjin kōfu no shiyō jōkyō oyobi shiyō keihi: Chikuhō chihō no Mitsubishi-kei tankō o chūshin to shite," *Nihon shigaku shūroku*, no. 10 (1990): 32.

32. Fifteen women were from South Kyŏngsang, six from North Kyŏngsang, one from South Chŏlla, two from North Chŏlla, one from North Ch'ungch'ŏng, and one from South Ch'ungch'ŏng province.

33. "Kaijima tankō dai-nanakō Chōsenjin kōfu iroha meibo," collection of Arirang Bunko, Tagawa, Fukuoka prefecture. The roster, covering workers hired from August 31, 1928, through October 22, 1942, does not specify the sex of workers, but relationship to the head of household is listed for all but 164 workers, making it possible to identify these 26 women. The first identifiable woman was hired September 19, 1938, but it is clear from other sources that Korean women worked at Oonoura mine No. 7 before then, so it is likely that many of the 164 workers for whom no relationship is listed were also women. I am indebted to Hayashi Eidai, whose papers comprise the Arirang Bunko, for providing me with a copy of this document.

34. Nishinarita, "The Coal Mining Industry," 69–70.

35. Calculated from Naikaku tōkeikyoku, *Taishō 9-nen kokusei chōsa hōkoku, fuken no bu,* vol. 40, *Fukuoka-ken,* 286–287.

36. Calculated from Naikaku tōkeikyoku, *Shokugyō oyobi sangyō,* vol. 2, *Shōwa 5-nen kokusei chōsa,* 41–43, 225, 228.

37. Ibid., 224. The broad occupational categories enumerated here and in the next paragraph technically refer to Japanese and colonials (*gaichijin*), but Koreans comprised over 99 percent of colonial women and almost 99 percent of colonial men.

38. Ibid., 224.

39. Yamaguchi-ken Keisatsubu Tokubetsu Kōtōka, *Raiou Chōsenjin tokubetsu chōsa jōkyō,* (1927), in *Zai Nichi Chōsenjin kankei shiryō shūsei,* ed. Pak Kyŏngsik, vol. 1, cited in Kim Kwangyŏl, "Kyōiku teido kara mita 1920, 1930-nendai tonichi Chōsenjin no tokushitsu," *Ikkyō ronsō* 115, no. 2 (Feb. 1996): 470.

40. Calculated from Fukuoka chihō shokugyō shōkai jimukyoku, *Kannai zaijū Chōsenjin rōdō jijō,* 109. These figures for Mitsubishi Hōjō mine apparently include both mine workers and family members. The criteria for whether a person "understood" Japanese are not indicated.

41. Naikaku tōkeikyoku, *Rōdō tōkei jitchi chōsa hōkoku* (1924), cited in Nishinarita, "The Coal Mining Industry," 73.

42. Clark W. Sorensen, *Over the Mountains Are Mountains: Korean Peasant Households and Their Adaptations to Rapid Industrialization* (Seattle and London: University of Washington Press, 1988), 140.

43. In one hamlet in South Chŏlla, for example, so many men had left by the late 1920s that women did all the farm work. "Katei fujin manpyō," *Higashi*, January 25, 1928, cited in Kim Chŏngmi, "Chōsen nōson josei ni taisuru Nittei no seisaku," *Chōsen shisō*, no. 3 (June 1980): 115.

44. Calculated from census figures in Morita Yoshio, *Sūji ga kataru zai Nichi Kankoku Chōsenjin no rekishi*, ed. Kim Yŏngdal (Akashi shoten, 1996), 41.

45. Fukuoka chihō shokugyō shōkai jimukyoku, *Kannai zaijū Chōsenjin rōdō jijō*, 70. The report quotes this figure from a survey conducted by South Kyŏngsang Province.

46. Calculated from Naikaku tōkeikyoku, *Jinkō hoka*, vol. 1, *Shōwa 5-nen kokusei chōsa hōkoku, zenkoku no bu*, 135; and vol. 2, *Shokugyō oyobi sangyō*, 228.

47. Among men, 76.6 returned to Korea in 1928 for every 100 who went, while the return ratio among women was 55.1 percent. Calculated from Fukuoka chihō shokugyō shōkai jimukyoku, *Kannai zaijū Chōsenjin rōdō jijō*, 65.

48. Calculated from Chōsen Sōtokufu, *Chōsen jinkō dōtai tōkei* (various years), cited in Morita, *Sūji ga kataru zai Nichi Kankoku Chōsenjin no rekishi*, 76. Korean-Japanese marriages made up 42 percent of all marriages involving at least one Korean from 1938 to 1942.

49. Fukuoka chihō shokugyō shōkai jimukyoku, *Kannai zaijū Chōsenjin rōdō jijō*, 138; and Shihōshō Chōsabu, "Fukuokakenka zaijū Chōsenjin no dōkō ni tsuite," *Setai chōsa shiryō*, no. 26 (1939), in Hayashi, *Senji gaikokujin kyōsei renkō*, 419.

50. For one example, see *Fukuoka nichinichi shinbun*, April 11, 1943.

51. The Japanese assault on Korean culture imbued that culture, including traditional gender norms, with a nationalist significance it would not have had otherwise. The identification of traditional Korean gender norms with nationalism, and the subsequent subordination of women's interests to "larger" political causes, continues today, especially among Koreans in Japan. Symbols of Korean identity also continue to be targets for racist Japanese. In a series of attacks since the 1990s, for example, Japanese men have used razors to slice the *ch'ima* and *chŏgori* worn by Korean schoolgirls on trains in Tokyo and other major cities.

52. Korean and Japanese women joined forces in the spring of 1930, for example, in a strike against the Kishiwada Cotton Spinning Company. See Michael Weiner, *Race and Migration in Imperial Japan* (London and New York: Routledge, 1994), 171–174.

53. For a detailed account of this strike, see W. Donald Smith, "The 1932 Asō Coal Strike: Korean-Japanese Solidarity and Conflict," *Korean Studies*, no. 20 (1996): 94–122.

54. The five Asō mines involved in the strike—Sannai, Kamimio, Tsunawaki, Akasaka, and Yoshikuma—stopped using women underground sometime between February 1930 and March 1932. Asō's sixth mine, Mameta, still employed women underground as of March 1932 and it is unclear when they were dismissed. Moji tetsudōkyoku unyuka, *Ensen tankō yōran*, March 1930 and March 1932, cited in Ogino, *Chikuhō tankō rōshi kankeishi*, 401m.

55. Arrest figures compiled from incidents cited in Kyōchōkai Fukuoka Shutchōjo, "Kabushiki kaisha Asō shōten Chōsenjin kōfu rōdō sōgi gaikyō," (Kyōchōkai Fukuoka shutchōjo, 1932), 16, 18, 19, 34; and Chikuhō sekitan kōgyō-shi nenpyō hensan iinkai, *Chikuhō sekitan kōgyō-shi nenpyō*, 367. The number arrested in these incidents could be anywhere between 271 and 285 due to the ambiguity in one Kyōchōkai account.

56. Kim Ch'anjŏng, *Hi no dōkoku: Zainichi Chōsenjin kōfu no seikatsushi* (Tabata Shoten, 1980), 25, 30, 44, 53, and Kyōchōkai, "Kabushiki kaisha Asō," 1, 11, 16, 19. Kim cites a figure of 426 on August 29, while the Kyōchōkai puts the overall number of Asō strikers at 396.

57. Kim Ch'anjŏng, *Hi no dōkoku*, 36–44, 53.

58. The Nihon sekitan kōfu kumiai, or Japan Coal Miners' Union, an affiliate of the moderate Sōdōmei labor federation, provided organizational support, however.

59. Kyōchōkai, "Kabushiki kaisha Asō," 20–21.

60. Kim Ch'anjŏng, *Hi no dōkoku*, 62.

61. Kyōchōkai, "Kabushiki kaisha Asō," 19, 20.

62. Ibid.

63. Ibid., 22.

64. Ibid., 32–35.

65. Kyūshū shakai undō tsūshinsha, *Kyūshū shakai undō nenkan* (Iizuka, 1933), in Tanaka, *Kindai Nihon tankō*, 476.

66. See, for example, Kim Ch'anjŏng, *Hi no dōkoku*, 13–78, and Hayashi Eidai, *Kyōsei renkō kyōsei rōdō: Chikuhō Chōsenjin kōfu no kiroku* (Gendaishi shuppankai, 1981), 43–69.

67. Interview with Idegawa Yasuko. Idegawa has interviewed dozens of retired Japanese women miners.

68. Idegawa Yasuko, *Hi o unda hahatachi* (Fukuoka: Ashi shobō, 1984), 207–209.

69. Interview with Idegawa.

70. Nagaoka Iwao, for example, said he is sure that, except for the war, he would never have become a labor supervisor. His duties included traveling to Korea to obtain workers for forced labor. Interview, June 14, 1995.

71. For three Korean women coal sorters at Meiji's Akaike mine from June 1944 through June 1945, see Meiji kōgyōsho Akaike tankō, *Rōmu geppō*, vol. 2, part 2, June 1944–October 1945, in Hayashi, *Senji gaikokujin kyōsei renkō*, 1153, 1173, 1177, 1192, 1204.

72. Labor Ministry statistics, cited in Kang Chaeŏn, "Zai Nichi Chōsenjin no rokujūgonen," *Kikan sanzenri*, no. 8 (Winter 1976): 27.

73. *Fukuoka nichinichi shinbun*, June 20, 1940; Rōdō kagaku kenkyūjo, *Hantō rōmusha kinrō jōkyō ni kansuru chōsa hōkoku* (1943), in *Chōsen mondai shiryō sōsho*, ed. Pak Kyŏngsik, 74, 113, 155.

74. Nishida Hideko, "Senjika Hokkaidō ni okeru Chōsenjin 'rōmu ianfu' no seiritsu to jittai," *Joseishi kenkyū Hokkaidō* 1 (August 2003): 16–36.

75. For the rediscovery of the Chikuhō centers, see *Nishinippon shinbun*, *Yomiuri shinbun*, and *Asahi shinbun*, February 21, 1992, evening editions. I am indebted to local historian Yokogawa Teruo for information on this topic, on which he and other local scholars and activists have conducted groundbreaking research.

76. Nishino Rumiko, *Jūgun ianfu: moto heishitachi no shōgen* (Akashi shoten, 1992), 117–118. The rose of Sharon is a symbol of Korean nationalism, although it is not clear from this account whether Shim consciously used the flower in this way. Nishino quotes Shim as using the Japanese term *asagao*, normally translated as morning glory, for the flower, but *asagao* is also an archaic term for the rose of Sharon, known in Korean as *mugunghwa*.

77. *Yomiuri shinbun*, February 21, 1992. The *teishintai* was not formally established until 1943 but Shim's dispatch to Fukuoka prefecture in 1940 demonstrates official involvement from an early stage. For a brief introduction to the *teishintai*, see *Sengo hoshō handobukku*, eds. Utsumi Aiko et al. (Nashi no kisha, 1992), 38, 41.

78. As of 1940, the age range was fourteen to thirty-one. Nishida, "Senjika Hokkaidō ni okeru Chōsenjin," 26.

79. "The Coal Fields of Kyūshū," Supreme Commander for the Allied Powers, General Headquarters, Record Group 331, Box 2494, Folder 1, "Records of Allied Operational and Occupation Headquarters, World War 11" (Suitland, MD: Washington National Records Center, 1948), 21.

80. Chikuhō sekitan kōgyō-shi nenpyō hensan iinkai, *Chikuhō sekitan kōgyō-shi nenpyō*, 589, cited in Iwaya Saori, "Nihon kingendai no sekitan kōgyō ni okeru josei rōdōsha," undated graduation thesis, Osaka University of Foreign Studies, 14.

81. For a study of this phenomenon at two Hokkaidō mines, see Hokkaidōritsu rōdō kagaku kenkyūjo, *Tankō ni hataraku fujin no rōdō jittai* (Sapporo: Hokkaidōritsu rōdō kagaku kenkyūjo, 1961).

82. Japan's last underground coal mine closed in 2002, but a few strip mines remain in production.

83. See n. 5 for Nishinarita and n. 22 for Mathias.

84. The explanation offered here is not meant to minimize the reality of ethnic discrimination. Koreans' lives clearly were made more difficult by racist attitudes on the part of both Japanese workers and managers, although there is no hard evidence that women from different ethnic and status groups were steered into different jobs at the mines as a matter of policy.

85. Janet Hunter's essay on the textile industry in this volume is a model of the kind of research on the gendering and racialization of jobs needed regarding the mining industry in Japan and around the world.

12 Managing the Japanese Household: The New Life Movement in Postwar Japan

Andrew Gordon

In a memoir of his twenty-five years as a personnel manager at a major steel mill, Orii Hyūga included the following anecdote:

> One day [in 1953], an accident occurred at the Kawasaki mill [of Nippon Kōkan (NKK)]. Upon investigating, Vice-Superintendent Komaki discovered that the accident resulted from the employee's exhaustion from staying up all night to care for his daughter, who was in the NKK hospital with a serious illness. Komaki was shocked at this fact, and he resolved that, just as he had long maintained, the company's welfare policy would have to be turned around 180 degrees to focus not only on the employee and the workplace, but to involve housewives and families, to increase the housewives' cultivation, to systematize daily life, and to serve as an advisor or counselor to realize the fruits of family health.[1]

This puzzling statement is worth pondering.[2] As in this translation, the wording in the Japanese version obscures the "fact" that so upset Komaki. Was he simply shocked that the daughter was so sick? That is unlikely. Was he shocked that a family member needed to stay over-night at the hospital? Perhaps, but if so, why not focus on the shortage of nurses that forced the family to provide around-the-clock care? But insofar as a wife is entirely absent from the anecdote, yet wives were the object of the resulting new policy, a more likely interpretation is the following: Komaki was upset that this man's wife was not keeping watch in the hospital, thus allowing her husband to replenish his energies at home for work the next day.

Soon after this accident, NKK (Japan's second largest steelmaker with 24,000 employees at two major mills) became the first corporation in Japan to initiate its own in-house, or more precisely, "outreach," version of something called the New Life Movement.[3] Komaki, Orii Hyūga, and their colleagues clearly believed that to insure efficient use of labor in the workplace, a particular division of gender roles in the family had to be reinforced, if not created. The New Life Movement was one means to this end.

The New Life campaign began in the late 1940s as a set of loosely connected initiatives of government ministries and women's organizations. These built on various prewar and wartime campaigns to "improve daily life," and they included programs to heighten morality, frugality, and efficiency; democratize social relations; redesign kitchens; and improve domestic hygiene. The New Life Movement was most widespread in farm villages, where the prominent concern with kitchen design and hygienic handling of garbage prompted critics to joke that the movement was just a bunch of women swatting flies. Beginning in 1953 with NKK, major corporations also joined the campaign, and two years later the prime minister offered his support by creating and funding a "New Life Movement Association" (Shin seikatsu undō kyōkai) to coordinate and promote such activities. The movement thus addressed a range of issues and took place in a variety of settings. In this chapter, I focus on its corporate, primarily urban incarnation. As in the countryside, and perhaps even more so, a chief concern of the movement was to "engender" postwar society by articulating and reinforcing ideal patterns of behavior for women and men.

After telling the story of Komaki and the exhausted worker's accident, Orii went on in his memoir to reflect on the campaign's philosophy. As he understood it, the New Life Movement was based on the belief that

in any human being's life, workplace and home are intimately and inseparably related. Life in the home is the barometer for the next day's life [at work]. In principle the housewife is in charge of home life, and we can say that the husband both takes his rest and builds his energy under her initiative. Thus, we wished to elevate the housewives who played this role and thereby establish the foundation for a bright, cheerful home, a bright society, and beyond that, a bright, cheerful workplace.[4]

By the end of the 1950s, at least fifty of Japan's most prominent corporations had initiated New Life Movement programs with similar goals. This campaign is distinctive in its location at the intersection of the histories of labor management and the family and gender relations in postwar Japan. Komaki and Orii were two of many men and women promoting a society where efficient, modern, "professional" housewives were essential to the operation of the postwar industrial economy. The New Life Movement is thus a chapter in the history of the ascendance of the "corporate-centered society" (*kigyō shakai*) in Japan. By this term, I mean a society where meeting the needs of the corporation is understood to be social common sense and to be congruent with meeting the needs of all society's inhabitants: women and men, employees and their families.

In this essay, I examine what the New Life Movement meant for the gender division of labor in workplace, home, and society, and for the women it addressed. The movement spoke of rationalizing the role of housewife, the life of the family, and the home as both physical and social space. But its greater impact was in naturalizing a certain model of gender relations—of proper roles for men as well as for women. A society where women of all social strata managed the home, while their men managed the workplace, came to be understood as the natural way things were and ought to be.

To describe the New Life Movement as a noteworthy episode in twentieth-century Japanese history should contribute as well to our understanding of the recent histories of gender, family, and work around the world. A growing literature on the twentieth-century history of these topics for the most part focuses on Western Europe and North America, exploring comparable processes through which the role of housewife was defined and redefined.[5] These studies reveal that the situation of the housewife as household manager and consumer, and her husband's status as producer in the workplace, were connected intimately. They show us, in other words, the close links between discourses of "rationalization" of home and of industry. They also make it clear, as will this essay, that there were important local variations on this global theme of contemporary history. Modernity everywhere has been marked by gender difference reconstructed through politics and culture and presented as natural destiny. Without arguing for an exceptional exceptionalism, I hope to show some particular inflections in the social dynamics and cultural contours of the Japanese case.

Reforming Daily Life in Prewar Japan

A tradition of state and grassroots reformism dating back to the Meiji era sought to "improve" the quality of daily life in Japan, making the work of middle-class wives in particular more "rational" and "modern."[6] These prewar endeavors to reform domestic life were diverse and wide-ranging in their concerns. Like the post–World War II New Life Movement, they combined great enthusiasm over the potential of modern science and rationality to improve women's domestic lives with a moralism rooted in the austere world view of Edo-era Japanese Confucianism. The vision behind such activity, in the words of one bureaucratic supporter, was one of "scientific diligence and thrift," directed from on high.[7]

During World War II, ongoing state activities served as a precursor to the New Life Movement. The Welfare Ministry started the Campaign to Renovate Daily Life (*Seikatsu sasshin undō*) in 1939. The change in terminology from "improve" to "renovate" was accompanied with a new stress on austerity and a new anti-Western tone.[8] The term "renovate" (*sasshin*) also implied a greater degree of state intervention, but in practice these wartime campaigns appear to have had little organizational energy or impact, and few *direct* ties to the postwar New Life Movement.[9] Much of the wartime frugality in Japan was probably a necessity borne of scarcity more than a response to exhortation. The Ministry's efforts *were* responsible, however, for introducing one new element that exerted a powerful, if ironic, influence on the postwar movement: state concern with population and women's reproductive role. The Welfare Ministry founded a state-funded Population Problem Research Institute (*Jinkō mondai kenkyūjo*) in 1939. During the war this institution was a vehicle for pronatalist policies; in the postwar New Life Movement, the institute's successor organizations in the ministry promoted family planning and birth control.[10]

The New Life Movement and the State

Soon after the end of World War II, the prewar and wartime supporters of New Life activities turned their attention once more toward housewives and the home. They sang an old tune in a newly democratic key.

Both the continuities and the new departures are important, and assessing their balance is difficult. The Ministries of Agriculture, Education, and Welfare launched parallel and overlapping initiatives, and as before and during the war, women's organizations cooperated with enthusiasm. At the same time, a new concern with democratic form and substance led all participants to proceed cautiously in rhetoric and in practice. While the political arena was intensely polarized as a resurgent Japanese left challenged conservative political hegemony, programs to reform domestic life won support that cut across ideological positions of "left" and "right."

In 1947 the coalition cabinet led by Socialist Party Prime Minister Katayama Tetsu introduced one of the first such efforts, the "Campaign to Construct a New Japan." One component of this drive was government support for groups of youth or of women who organized locally for the purpose of the "renovation of new life" (*shin seikatsu no sasshin*); this was probably the first official postwar use of the expression "new life." Although an emphasis on "democratizing" the family was new, as before and during the war this 1947 campaign spoke simultaneously of establishing "rational" family life and promoting austerity.[11]

Over the following years, women's organizations, such as the National Coordinating Committee of Regional Women's Groups, actively supported a variety of endeavors on behalf of their vision of a New Life Movement.[12] In addition, state ministries climbed on the New Life bandwagon in the late 1940s.

In 1948, the Ministry of Agriculture and Forestry launched the Movement to Reform Daily Life to fulfill the provisions of the recently passed Law to Promote Agricultural Reform. The "reform" in the law's title was not the dramatic land reform program that put an end to tenant farming in Japan; it referred to reform of family life in farming villages. At the behest of U.S. occupation authorities, in 1948 and 1949 the ministry set up the Daily Life Reform Division and staffed it with Extension Officers for Daily Life Reform. The program was modeled on the system of extension officers of the U.S. Department of Agriculture. Upon its inauguration in 1949, the ministry appointed 288 extension officers for the Daily Life Reform program. They made the rounds of villages nationwide, both working with existing organizations of women and helping to found new groups as well.[13]

In the Ministry of Education, the staff of the Social Education Section took on responsibility for a variety of regional and local activities aimed at women and the family, in cooperation with the Women's Associations and teachers of home economics in the public schools.[14] American practices of educating women in "modern" domestic science inspired these initiatives as well. These reformers combined the rhetoric of modern household management with that of traditionalistic austerity, with some increase in the weight of the former. The social education bureaucrats were among the chief promoters of the 1947 New Life programs of the Katayama cabinet, sending officials out to survey conditions in villages and convening study groups and lectures around the country.[15]

The third major bureaucratic supporter of the New Life Movement was the Welfare Ministry; actually, its concern was to lower the rate at which new lives joined the nation and regulate the methods used to control that rate. Insofar as the state had outlawed and condemned both abortion and birth control from the Meiji period through the end of the war, this aspect of the New Life Campaign requires some explanation. Beginning in 1947, mortality rates started a long, steady decline and birth rates skyrocketed. Official thinking of these years came to be marked by a profound fear that overpopulation would choke off any hope of economic recovery. With the prewar option of promoting emigration to the colonies no longer possible, the government gradually moved toward support of family planning and birth control.[16]

The legacy of prohibition remained significant. As early as 1946, the Welfare Ministry had set up a Population Problem Discussion Group with seventeen expert members. Its initial statement of November 1946 was cautiously calling for "appropriate" birth control. "Birth control can cause a decline in feelings of moral responsibility in marriage and invite the decay of sexual morality. We must therefore strive to raise the level of sexual morality and moral ideals, and promote proper sex education. We must take special care to prevent a 'reverse selection effect.'"[17] This last expression was eugenic jargon for "reverse" natural selection; many politicians, bureaucrats, and state advisors feared that the superior classes would rush to take advantage of liberalized birth control, while the genetically inferior lower classes would not be able or willing to follow suit. The result would be decline in the quality of the race.

Yet the first breakthrough toward population control was not a campaign for contraception. Apparently, the state viewed abortion as less threatening to sexual morality than contraception, and it legalized abortion in the 1948 Eugenics Protection Law. As Table 1 makes clear, women took immediate advantage of this new freedom, and abortion played a major role in reducing the number and rate of births. But then, as the annual number of abortions soared to well over half the number of births by 1953, the state shed its reluctance to promote other forms of birth control. In 1953 the Welfare Ministry established a standing Advisory Council on Population Problems with an unambiguous mandate to encourage contraception.

One year later, the conservative government of Hatoyama Ichirō moved to pull these several threads together into a national New Life Movement.[18] Hatoyama's version of the movement was strongly moralistic. Under his first cabinet, formed in December 1954, he won public support with a promise of "austere government" (cutbacks on entertainment expenses). In the course of the election campaign of February 1955 he promised to extend this movement, and he asked the Ministry of Education's Advisory Council on Social Education to make specific proposals. Its report, which was to guide planning for the movement, suggested the state coordinate and nurture the efforts of existing organizations, especially private ones, so as to avoid oppressive bureaucratic domination.[19] The council called for a campaign in villages, schools, and workplaces. The government was to provide material support and publicize designated "model" endeavors. The council divided prospective activities into two categories. "External" activities were to improve people's food, clothing, and shelter; this was the "rationalization" aspect to the movement. "Internal" reforms addressed the democratic dimension, as the council spoke of "raising the people's consciousness of their lives and realizing democracy through a national movement," but internal self-improvement also focused prominently on frugality and self-discipline. To implement this agenda, Hatoyama's government allocated fifty million yen for the 1955 fiscal year to found the New Life Movement Association.[20]

Table 1
Abortions and Births in Japan, 1949–1957

Year	Number of Abortions	Ratio of Abortions/ Births (%)	Number of Births
1949	246,000	9	2,697,000
1950	489,000	21	2,338,000
1951	638,000	30	2,138,000
1952	806,000	40	2,005,000
1953	1,068,000	57	1,868,000
1954	1,143,000	65	1,770,000
1955	1,170,000	68	1,731,000
1956	1,159,000	70	1,665,000
1957	1,122,000	72	1,567,000

SOURCE: Kōseishō, *Yūsei hogo tōkei hōkoku* (annual reports) and *Nihon no jinkō kakumei*, ed. Mainichi shinbunsha (Mainichi shinbunsha, 1970), 239.

The reactionary ideological stress in Hatoyama's movement is striking. Numerous commentators criticized the campaign themes of nationalism, moral education, and austerity, seeing in them a return to the oppressive social politics of prewar and wartime Japan.[21] These certainly were major themes of the New Life Movement as promoted by the Ministries of Agriculture, Education, and Welfare, by women's groups, and by Prime Minister Hatoyama. But the government's New Life Movement was not simply a traditionalistic reaction to postwar democracy. The movement also stressed rationalizing domestic life and applying to it a scientific spirit, implicitly of Western origin; in so doing it harked back to a spirit of the 1920s that had been downplayed during the war. In addition, advocates of the movement, including bureaucrats, consistently proclaimed their desire not to promote a top-down movement along prewar lines, and discussion of the movement constantly invoked a new era of "democracy and culture." While it would be wise to doubt that government officials (or middle-class reformers, male or female, for that matter) had abandoned an elitist mentality of social management, the democratic themes of this movement should not be dismissed as window dressing.

The New Life Movement activities sponsored by these three ministries, promoted by the central government, and joined by both old guard women's groups and new clusters of younger, less prominent villagers throughout the Japanese countryside were part of a complicated early postwar social and cultural process: the reconstruction of the ideology and role of "good wife, wise mother."[22] In towns and villages throughout Japan, the role of the housewife was, in a certain sense, "professionalized." By this, I do not mean that women were now paid wages for previously unpaid household labor, for they were not. But through participation in movement activities and through proliferation of movement rhetoric, they were trained in a discrete set of skills, and their work at home was granted public legitimacy and credentials as scientific, rational, modern, and even democratic.

To be sure, much about the movement was hardly new. The sometimes heavy hand of bureaucratic guidance, frequently in league with established village leaders, is one link to the past evident in accounts of the New Life Movement in the countryside.[23] The rhetoric of austerity in weddings and funerals and frugality in cooking with inexpensive materials is another such link, part of a Japanese inflection that places the case closer to that of Germany than the United States.[24] And the undeniable enthusiasm of many participants for what they called a new "cultural" role in a new "democratic" age had precedents in the 1920s.

But the postwar movement was different in several ways. At a time of widespread eagerness for ideas and behaviors seen to be democratic, women played active roles in defining a movement of broad reach. In villages the movement spread well beyond the rural upper class. It offered previously forbidden, empowering knowledge of birth control. It encouraged women's implicitly political involvement in household and family issues, paving the road toward the surge of "citizen's movements" of the 1970s. Finally, rather than serving as a base for military mobilization as in the 1930s, and despite the fact that millions of women worked as producers on farms and in factories in the 1950s, especially in textile and electronic firms, the movement facilitated the ascendance of a gender-divided ideology of economic mobilization: men were defined as producers and women as (modest) consumers and newly rational household managers.[25]

The New Life Movement and the Corporation

While most Japanese who still can remember the New Life Movement associate it with the dusty countryside, it also had an urban, corporate face in a nation whose population was shifting from countryside to cities and suburbs, while suburbs grew out toward the countryside.[26] In its corporate incarnation, the New Life Movement played two related roles at the intersection of the histories of gender and of work. First, it involved corporations directly in professionalizing the urban housewife's role as a part of a broader drive by businesses to rationalize the economy and raise productivity. The corporate campaign made rationalizing the household a project parallel to rationalizing the workplace. It identified the enterprise-dominated society with a particular structure of gender roles.[27] Second, the campaign worked to pre-empt or prevent the possibility envisioned by some unions that home and family would support alternative values to those of the enterprise. Like the state initiatives focused mainly on the countryside, corporate programs that focused on city dwellers were effective. Although they told women what to do or be, they offered space where women could participate in defining the role of modern household manager.

In December 1953, Japan's four major business associations organized their own New Life Movement Association, more than a year before the Hatoyama government created its body of practically the same name.[28] The corporate New Life campaign originated in a 1951 drive to restrain corporate spending on entertainment. This campaign initially reflected a panic that the economic recovery stimulated by American procurement for the Korean War would be frittered away in bars and nightclubs. Thus, one executive called the movement the "backbone of increased productivity," and he compared the extravagance and gaudy living of Japan, "drunk on the sweet liquor of the war boom," to the admirable austerity being practiced in England and Germany where the postwar economies were recovering splendidly and "already advancing overseas into Southeast Asia."[29]

The Japan Industrial Club coordinated the association's activities and published a monthly newsletter filled with examples from various companies. On its inauguration, the New Life Association had already enrolled two hundred corporate members. After one year, membership had reached four hundred, reported to be 50 percent of the target population of all companies in Japan with over one thousand employees. The association promoted two basic types of activities. The first sought to eliminate waste within companies. This cluster of activities paralleled the drive for frugality promoted among housewives by the state and women's groups. Movement advocates called on managers to exercise "self-restraint" (*jishuku*) in business entertainment, as well as in company-sponsored funerals, New Year and mid-year (*o-chūgen*) gift-giving, and dress. They cited models such as the admirably restrained corporate funeral of the president of an insurance company.[30] The association also promoted savings and a "buy Japanese" campaign.

Such concerted business activity did little in the long run to restrain extravagant executive patronage of hostess bars.[31] But it did reflect an orientation toward production and consumption that characterized the rhetoric and to some extent the operation of Japan's postwar political economy. As articulated by bureaucrats and businessmen, the New Life Movement self-consciously resisted the "Fordist" logic of mass industrial production. Under "Fordism," the engine of economic growth is domestic demand generated by surging consumption enabled by high wages.[32] While domestic demand was in fact an important stimulus to Japan's postwar economic boom, the virtuous cycle of accumulation and growth envisioned by the New Life campaigns began with moderate consumption, high rates of savings, and high investment in industrial production to meet overseas demand.

The second realm of association activity reached beyond the company to rationalize the life of the family, especially the behavior of the wife as consumer and reproducer. While the push for self-discipline within the corporation was the main stream of New Life Association endeavors, with virtually all the four hundred corporate members engaged in it, this second "outreach" dimension was also extensive. A 1959 survey of the Welfare Ministry's Population Problem Research Center listed forty-nine companies with a total of 1.16 million employees that had launched their own New Life programs, all with some degree of emphasis on "family planning" (i.e., birth control), while another forty were said to be considering the matter (Table 2).[33]

We thus find two sets of parallels between the corporation and the household. First, the activity of corporate leaders ran parallel to that of the state; business leaders calling for frugality within the corporation

Table 2

Corporations with New Life Programs for
Employees' Wives as of 1960

Year Founded	Corporation Name
1953	Nippon Kōkan / Jōban Coal Mining Co.
1954	Asō Industries
1955	Tōshiba Electric / Toyota Automobile / Nippon Light Metals
	Nippon Ceramics / Hitachi Shipbuilding / Honshū Paper
	Mitsui Coal Mines
1956	Ebara Engineering Works / Chūbu Electric Power Co.
	Shōwa Denkō / Tokyo Kyūkō Railway / Yūbetsu Coal Mining
	Keihin Kyūkō Railway / Hitachi Engineering Works
	Japan National Railways / Nagoya Railway / Tōhoku Pulp Co.
	Nippon Glass / Tōbu Railway
1957	Harima Shipbuilding / Fuji Steel / Nihon Seikō / Nippon Express
	Ishikawajima Heavy Industries / Shin Nippon Chissō
	Tōyō Kōatsu / Keihanshin Kyūkō Railway / Nippon Mining
	Fujikura Electric Wire
1958	Denden kōsha / Jūjō Paper / Mitsubishi Mining
	Tokyo Electric Power Co. / Nippon Victor / Kubota Metal Works
	Nippon Wireless / Fujikoshi Iron Industries / Keio Teito Railway
1959	Japan Steel Co. / Sumitomo Chemicals / Chichibu Cement
	Japan Airlines / Mitsubishi Rayon / Nisshin Textiles
	Nissan Automotive / Tokyo Gas Co. / Sumitomo Metals
	Teikoku Oil Co. / Railway Benevolent Association
1960	Onoda Cement

SOURCE: "Kigyōtai renraku kyōgikai no genjō," *Shin seikatsu* 6, no. 6 (June 1959): 9; *Shin seikatsu* 7, no. 8 (August 1960): 8–10; and *Shin seikatsu* 7, no. 9 (September 1960): 6–8. The 1960 report lists four companies not mentioned in the 1959 Welfare Ministry survey.

mirrored agriculture or education officials pleading for frugality within the village or the household. Second, the enterprise itself took a similar stance toward both work and home; corporate calls for rational households echoed managerial drives to rationalize the workplace. Together, the corporate movement offered prescriptions to men at work and women at home that defined gender-based roles in society and economy.

The effort at NKK, whose manager was quoted at the beginning of this chapter, was the most frequently cited of any corporation's New Life campaign for employee wives. In the details of the movement at NKK, its major aspects emerge in clear relief: "rationalizing family life" by giving a sort of professional training to the housewife, and consolidating corporate hegemony in the workplace by insuring that home and family would not support radical unions and alternative values to those of the enterprise.

Within two or three years of its founding, NKK's New Life program had gone beyond a primary initial focus on family planning. It grandly aspired to "rationalize daily life." Specifically this meant teaching women to do better jobs at managing household budgets, using their leisure time, rearing their children, and "cultivating" themselves (by writing poetry, for example). NKK set up a New Life Movement office in the Welfare Section of the personnel division, and the company hired women with relevant backgrounds (social worker, home economics teacher, midwife) to work as "counselors" and run the program.

Activities began with women in the company's family housing blocks, where a residents' organization was already in place to handle chores such as tidying up public spaces. In other cases, the New Life counselors recruited employee wives whom they identified as potential leaders, typically the wives of senior foremen or crew bosses. They explained the movement's goals to these women and urged them to form and lead groups of five to fifteen housewives.[34] These small groups were to serve as the basic units of the entire project. NKK initially chose 5,366 households (about one-fourth the total) as the targets of the campaign, dividing Kawasaki into 20 districts of 300 households, with a "counseling center" in each district staffed by a company counselor. As well as organizing group activity out of the centers, the counselors used them as bases for making home visits to individuals. They decided that by waiting for people to come to the center, they would learn of family problems only after a crisis had erupted.[35]

In addition to the group meetings and outreach crisis intervention, the counselors organized a wide array of classes and cultural activities open to all employee wives. These included cooking, sewing and knitting classes, instruction in futon repair as well as flower arranging, and showings of movies or *kami-shibai*.[36] According to a 1955 report, cumulative annual attendance at a given course ranged from five hundred to two thousand women.[37] The counselors also arranged special lectures by prominent experts in various fields. In 1955 these included lectures on health, clothing, savings, mutual aid, simplifying funerals and weddings, family planning, childrearing, and family recreation. A woman who attended every talk would be enlightened on how to manage her entire existence and that of her family, literally from cradle to grave.

The most distinctive aspect of the New Life Movement in comparison to similar corporate initiatives in other countries was surely the use of small groups as the core of the movement.[38] The New Life campaigns in villages relied upon such groups. The oral testimony of one of the NKK counselors offers a rich picture of the corporate version. Ōshima Ai worked briefly during World War II in a factory, and she then served for over a decade as an elementary schoolteacher in Niigata city. In 1958, she saw a newspaper ad recruiting women for a school of social work in Tokyo. Tired of teaching and ready for a change, Ōshima enrolled, and after a six-month course of study, she was hired by NKK as a New Life counselor.[39]

Ōshima recalls that the staff was divided into an original cadre of "family planning counselors," mainly midwives, and "life planning counselors," such as herself. Her understanding of her mission reflected the rhetoric of Orii Hyūga and other promoters precisely. If the New Life Movement nurtures trust and consensus in the family, and "teaches women to lead rational lives, the worker will provide high quality labor to the company and will be able to live a fulfilling life."[40] When she joined the New Life staff, a complex structure was already in place to carry out this mission. The basic neighborhood groups of ten women were organized into "blocks" that were further grouped into regions. The leaders of each neighborhood group in a given block would meet in a "leader's group" monthly with a counselor who acted as community organizer, case worker, and even labor manager.

As community organizer, Ōshima would discuss topics that the groups might address, solicit ideas, and offer her suggestions. Her self-described goal was to push the groups to be independent and set their own agendas, but she describes her fellow counselors as quite varied in the extent to which they sought or achieved this goal. As case worker, Ōshima heard from the leaders about problems of troubled families, which might require her intervention in a home visit. And as labor manager, she solicited comments on work-related problems that were disrupting family life, and she reported these to the company personnel office.

Nearly forty years later, when asked what sorts of issues were addressed by the groups that she oversaw, Ōshima promptly reeled off the following impressive list of topics of edification or self-cultivation: family health, cooking, nutrition, childrearing, sewing, tea and flower arranging, haiku writing, travel, sports, folk dance, factory visits, singing the company song, bazaars to exchange household goods, household budget keeping, survey of eating habits, saving to own a home. As in the village New Life Movement, groups that set particular goals (reform family eating habits, for example) and met them successfully would present their results in elaborate detail to an annual company-wide convention. NKK's champion groups would go on to present at similar regional meets of multiple companies or write up their results for publication. Ōshima felt these events were an exciting new experience for most women, a delightful source of "psychological and social recognition and reward."

Detailed reports are available for numerous other companies. These make it clear that the methods of staffing and organizing the outreach programs of the corporate New Life campaign, as well as the issues addressed, were basically the same at the roughly fifty major corporations that joined the movement. Publications and conferences allowed various corporations to exchange information and led them to develop more or less identical programs.[41]

The Tōshiba initiative aspired to be distinctive. Managers renamed its program a "Good Life Movement" to convey their sense of an independent agenda.[42] In fact, the campaign at this booming electronics firm did include a few interesting twists. To make sure that wives could walk to the meetings, the company's Welfare Section staff mapped the residences of employees and chose meeting places at the center of circles with no more than a twenty-minute walking radius. The manager in charge of the program negotiated a bulk discount from local condom makers, and Tōshiba sold these to the wives of its male workers at one-third to one-fifth the retail price. After an initial purchase through her Good Life group, a woman could avoid possible embarrassment and reorder by mail.[43]

In an unusual parallel to movements to promote household efficiency in prewar America, and in contrast to the German case analyzed by Mary Nolan, the Tōshiba program included classes to encourage the use of electricity and electric appliances in daily life, and the company rewarded group leaders with company appliances.[44] Although I should stress that I have found no discussion of comparable initiatives in accounts of New Life activities at other Japanese companies, at this company, at least, the movement served to promote the buying habits of modern consumer capitalism among housewives.

Perhaps the most interesting twist at Tōshiba is that the Good Life Movement drew on management tools originally developed for the workplace in the United States. Housewives serving as group leaders were taught the American import called "TWI" (Training-Within-Industry), a method of problem solving that was simultaneously in use in Tōshiba's factory where foremen were being taught how to work with their subordinates to increase productivity.[45] The use of TWI for wives neatly implied that the home was a woman's workplace.

In addition to rationalizing the household in these manifold ways, corporate New Life campaigns aided managers in the 1950s who were locked in an often bitter contest with activist unions for hegemony in the workplace.[46] In his memoir quoted at the outset, Orii Hyūga presented a dramatic picture of the kinds of antagonism the New Life Movement could possibly soften. He described a bargaining session from 1949 or so, in which

union members would shout at the top of their voices: "Take a look at the workers' dining hall. We haven't seen a grain of rice in days. Do you think we can do heavy labor to rebuild the nation's industry drinking soup that doesn't even taste of miso, with maybe four or five dumplings in it? Prices are going up. Even rationed goods have doubled or tripled in price. We want a cup of rice a day! We want the money to buy it!"[47]

Implicit in this quote is anger at the difficulty of sustaining a household, and it is no surprise that the company's labor strategists hit on the idea of helping employee wives to manage the home. But because of new postwar sensitivity to "undemocratic" intervention in people's lives, not to mention labor laws adopted during the American occupation that banned company intervention into union affairs, this aspect was usually submerged beneath the surface of the movement.

While both NKK and Tōshiba managers denied that the New Life activity had anything to do with policy toward the union, Tōshiba's man in charge of the Good Life Movement, Hongo Takanobu, allows a glimpse of this subtext in a 1957 article. The Good Life Movement, he wrote, was a form of "service" to employees and their families, a manifestation of the company's goodwill and caring feelings for them. It will be only "natural" if such service generates trust and intimacy between the employees and the company.[48]

In some cases the connections were more obvious. The New Life Movement at the Nikkō refinery of the Furukawa Denkō company (the infamous Ashio copper mine) focused much attention on helping housewives do more with less, a skill that of course helped reduce employee pressure for pay increases. Thus, New Life counselors taught wives how to "avoid unnecessary expenditures" and how to prepare meals with inexpensive but nutritious ingredients. The company also encouraged wives to supplement family incomes, arranging for the women to make artificial flowers in their homes for export. A reported 500 women were making flowers, earning an average of 1,000 yen per month (a typical husband in the refinery brought home about 15,000 yen). In addition, Furukawa set up a program of factory visits for employee wives, bringing roughly 2,500 women to visit the refinery in small groups. The model compositions written by some women after the visit, and later published, nicely reflect the company's expectations. These women reported they gained a new understanding of the company's situation: "I felt like the factory and the family were directly linked together"; "Now that I know about my husband's workplace, I understand what a big impact the family has on production"; "Efforts to conquer the factory's current crisis must begin at home."[49] Such wives were unlikely to put up with strike-happy husbands.

As intense confrontations between unions and companies continued throughout the 1950s, managers at NKK and other firms were well aware that some of the strongest and most radical unions in Japan, for instance in the auto industry and in the Kyūshū coal mines, had orga-nized wives and families into powerful support groups. Hongo at Tōshiba admitted in his 1957 report that many unions opposed New Life programs on grounds that such activities should be the responsibility of public institutions of education, that corporate programs intervened excessively into the private lives of employees, and that managers were trying to win employee loyalty in anticipation of labor disputes. Hongo denied any such intent of course, but the terms of his denial made clear his engagement in a contest to win the loyalty of workers. The New Life Movement, he concluded, was a company service in which participation was voluntary. And these days, "in any case it is always the union, not the company, that tries to draw families into labor struggles. The reverse is unheard of."[50]

The left wing of Japan's labor movement in the 1950s stood staunchly against the so-called productivity movement and "rationalization" in the workplace as devices either to speed up the work pace or eliminate jobs.[51] From this perspective, rationalization of the home under the movement was also suspect. One union activist, Nagano Junzō, writing in 1955, blasted the New Life Movement as an austerity campaign cast in the wartime mold, the household version of the newly launched industrial productivity campaign. Reflecting the anti-imperialism of the union movement's left wing, he attributed both these campaigns to capitalism's need to generate profits for military investment and remilitarization, as before 1945. Such movements never benefit workers, he claimed, because they seek to restrict consumption and make workers get by with less. They encourage people to be satisfied with modest lifestyles and devote time saved by rationalizing the household to increased work hours. The proper way to both improve standards of living and productivity, he concluded, was to use unions to realize a New Life through higher wages, better working conditions, and shorter hours.[52]

The fact that this critique was written by a male activist is worth noting. While numerous women worked in factories and belonged to unions, many were young and unmarried, so less likely to care about the New Life programs. Further, women were vastly underrepresented among union leaders, and critiques of the New Life Movement by female union activists were rare.

At NKK the most pointed criticism of the New Life Movement came from the Communist Party cell on the left wing of this company's diverse and vigorous union movement. In a book on conditions at the mill, published in 1955, the party authors accurately assessed the movement as just one of a number of activities ranging from sports clubs to poetry writing or music appreciation clubs through which the company was competing with "autonomous" (often party-sponsored) circles.[53] In this context, the party criticized the New Life Movement as the effort of personnel managers to limit the family size of workers in the belief that large families caused workers' poverty. The authors blasted a lecturer at the company who had reportedly boasted in the fall of 1954 that the New Life Movement had saved NKK 706,000 yen a year in birth allowances, medical expenses, and child allowances. Company spokesmen did, however, publicly justify the considerable expense of movement activities in these terms.[54] The authors concluded that the real problem was low wages. While poverty led many worker families to desire knowledge of how to control births, these men and women were reported to be deeply unhappy at their inability to afford to have children.

The party's book was published as a collective endeavor. No individual authors are listed, but one may suspect that the writers were men. The concluding suggestion that better paid workers would gladly have large families, one can imagine, did not reflect the feelings of many Japanese women (and perhaps many men) who, with such alacrity, took advantage of access to abortions and contraception not only in the impoverished early postwar years but in more affluent later decades.

The mainstream of the NKK union in the 1950s supported the left wing of the Socialist Party and militant workplace activism, so one might expect the union to have opposed the movement in similar terms. In fact, though the union viewed the New Life Movement with some suspicion and responded with initiatives of its own, it did not object vigorously. Within a year of the start of the New Life Movement, NKK's Kawasaki mill union started publishing a family page in its newspaper. The union at NKK's Tsurumi mill started the Housewives' Association in 1955, and the Kawasaki mill's union followed suit. In 1956 the Kawasaki union designated one of its (male) paid staff members a "family" organizer, a position parallel to its three "workplace organizers."[55] His function was to canvass opinions of employee wives and families and bring their problems to the attention of union leaders.[56]

The union movement at NKK and in many large private corporations in the 1950s was assertive. Through the union, the mill's workers consistently opposed company policy, going well beyond questions of pay. This was a point in Japan's postwar history when the corporation had not yet consolidated a firm hegemony as the unquestioned normative institution of society. A "common sense" consensus that the needs and the good of the enterprise were the needs and the good of all was emerging in this decade, but it was still sharply contested by many unions. In such a context, the New Life Movement at dozens of major corporations around Japan was part of an intense multifaceted contest for the hearts and minds of workers and their families. The company used the movement to reinforce a profoundly gender-divided social order in which men, both white- and blue-collar, were to offer a strong professional commitment to efficient work, while their wives would devote an equally professional energy and commitment to managing the home. The union promoted parallel activities that sent almost identical messages to women about their proper roles, with the slight twist that the husband with the well-managed home would be free to support the union: "[T]he housewife, at the center of the household, should understand her husband's labor union activities, wish for the improvement of all aspects of his work conditions, and build a happy home."[57]

Making "New Lives" at the Grassroots

How did women respond to the corporate New Life activities? Whether the messages of this movement were convincing or not, without question they reached many women, over one million nationwide and nearly 20,000 at NKK. In September 1963, the tenth anniversary year of the New Life Movement at NKK, 63 percent of employee households (17,242 of 27,296) belonged to New Life groups; at the main

Kawasaki mill the total was 72 percent.[58] Although counting members is a crude measure of impact, other evidence suggests that NKK's New Life Movement was well received.

First, it is important to recognize how many women were "ready" to hear the movement's messages by virtue of their place in the social structure. While the number of Japanese women employed as wage earners outside the home increased sharply in the 1950s, two-thirds of female employees were single.[59] Only in later decades did large proportions of urban married women with children begin to take paid jobs outside of farms or family businesses. The great majority of women married to either blue-collar production workers or white-collar salarymen were full-time housewives. Two 1950s surveys of neighborhoods with many NKK and Tōshiba families show how few of the women married to factory workers themselves worked outside the home. They also reveal that the issues addressed in the New Life Movement closely fit with the structure of these women's daily lives.

A 1951 survey of Kawasaki and Yokohama found that only 4 of 250 wives in working-class families worked for wages outside the home. The 246 full-time housewives spent roughly ten hours a day on housework and child care, a commitment that was the same for both "holidays" and "work days" (weekdays). They spent a full three hours daily on sewing, 50 minutes each on shopping, cleaning, and washing.[60] A similar portrait is drawn by a sharply focused survey of 1957 that examines 77 families in a working-class neighborhood in Kawasaki. The men in this neighborhood are characterized as relatively skilled, senior workers. Twenty-one of them worked at NKK, seven at Tōshiba, six at the Hitachi shipyard, and 61 of the 77 households included one union member (presumably the husband). In only 6 of the 77 households did both husband and wife work outside the home. The women handled household finances; fully 79 percent of the men handed over their wage envelopes unopened to their wives, who typically doled out the husband's weekly allowance.[61]

These women, it seems reasonable to conclude, would be likely to appreciate New Life messages promising to make their work more efficient, more "modern," more scientific, and by implication, more respected. This promise would have resonated with other messages they had access to, in particular that of the so-called "housewife debate" that raged in women's magazines of the mid-1950s. In these publications, defenders of the modern housewife claimed that while men typically worked under capitalism, and their wives were economically dependent on this labor, the wife nonetheless performed household labor comparable in value to the husband's since it helped reproduce his labor power.[62] Anticipating this spirit, the 1951 Kawasaki-Yokohama survey argued:

> While the hours spent by the wives on housework cannot in themselves be evaluated as social labor [*shakaiteki rōdō*], they are indispensable for the maintenance of a family's life and the reproduction of labor power. . . . In this sense, hours spent on housework have a primary importance for a woman that is comparable to the wage-earning work hours of the husband.[63]

Some of the best evidence of the grassroots response comes from Ōshima Ai.[64] When she started her job in 1959, the veteran counselors initiated her with war stories of the chilly initial response of many women who resented intrusive meddling in the private matter of birth control. Her seniors were told "it's none of your business how many kids we have, or when we have them," and doors were occasionally slammed in their face. NKK men clearly felt threatened by women's reproductive rights. Angry husbands yelled at counselors that "the New Life Movement is union busting," or that they "hear gossip that NKK wives work nights along the banks of the Tama river" (a place where unlicensed prostitutes plied their trade).[65]

Gradually the counselors won the trust first of potential group leaders, then members. In this process, Ōshima reveals, the workplace status of the husbands played a key role. Wives of supervisors "were often relatively sophisticated, aware of workplace issues, and took a leadership role . . . they got less social respect than management wives and saw more benefits from participation in the movement."[66] Not all of these women embraced the movement immediately, and many no doubt joined in response to social pressures tied to a husband's work relations; once a foreman's wife was a group leader, it would be difficult for his subordinates' wives to resist invitations to join.

But positive attractions also drew participants. Counselors experimented with a variety of meeting venues, and discovered that homes, while cramped, worked better than the neighborhood association's clubhouse. Ōshima learned that many women were drawn by the chance to enter the homes of other wives and see how they were organized. Over time she noticed a clear change in attitudes toward family size, as more women chose to have just two or three children upon whom they could lavish attention and resources. She credits the movement with encouraging this change, and she also attributes to their New Life experience that in later years NKK women were active in citizens' movements, and were often community leaders.[67]

But her most telling testimony concerns the constant tension she observed between goals of encouraging women to be independent-minded and to serve family or company. Workplace supervisors would report to company staff that during breaks their men griped that New Life groups had turned their wives into know-it-alls. Ever sensitive to tiny hints of trouble, managers then referred these reports back to the counselors, and Ōshima would rejoin that in the long run stronger women would produce better families, and the husbands would come around. This tension was not trivial; the problem of handling resistant husbands who could not accept more self-reliant women was a common item for discussion in the New Life groups. The movement was contributing to a changing social dynamic among NKK families.

Documentary sources confirm this oral testimony of widespread support for NKK's New Life Movement. Eighty percent of the married women responding to the NKK Welfare Section's own survey in 1963 claimed the movement was "a good thing."[68] The independent 1957 survey of Kawasaki working-class residents reveals that all twenty-one NKK housewives belonged to neighborhood groups that met about once a month. The practice of birth control was reported to be spreading. Women enthusiastically were joining classes and activities such as a "low cost shopping field trip" or an outing to the famous Asakusa Temple in Tokyo. The monthly meetings were said to be enjoyable social events, occasions for "well-side gossip."[69]

The survey also placed NKK's New Life Movement squarely in the center of labor-management struggles:

That the union has no strong grasp over the community is shown in the fact that not one of the twenty-one women are critical of the New Life Movement. In terms of community policy, clearly the company is several steps ahead of the union at NKK. . . .

The company began mailing a family edition of its PR magazine directly to all the wives in the movement, in their names, and all twenty-one women claim to read this. A bit later, the union also established a "family page" in its newspaper, but it has the workers carry this home to wives, and its penetration is not as great: six of twenty-one don't usually see it, and there is a tendency to confuse it with the company paper. Without question, these two family-oriented publications are sites of an ideological battle tied to the union-company struggles.[70]

Oral testimony of union activists tells a similar story. The union at the Kawasaki mill only created its own Housewives' Association after the New Life Movement had been under way for two years. Its structure of neighborhood discussion circles, whose leaders were often wives of union officers, mirrored that of the New Life Movement circles often led by wives of foremen. While the man who organized the union's association, Kawakami Hideji, claims that its members became energetic supporters of the union, especially during strikes, another union man, Nakao Yasuji, recalls that when the company purposely scheduled New Life meetings to coincide with those of the union group, most women chose the New Life gatherings, even though the union meeting provided train fare and food.[71]

The outcome of this contest between union and company organizations for wives is no surprise. Indeed, these union activities arguably reinforced the New Life Movement more than they competed with it. The union and the company visions of the proper role for a housewife were essentially the same. Both wanted her to be a competent household manager who would nurture the husband to function effectively, whether at work or in the union. The earlier start and vastly superior resources of the company's program put the union at a great disadvantage.

Finally, multiple sources credit the New Life Movement with sharply reducing birth and abortion rates and increasing the use of contraception among NKK families. According to a Welfare Ministry survey, the rate of pregnancy among NKK employee wives fell by two-thirds from 1952 to 1955, the birth rate fell in half, and the rate of abortion dropped by 80 percent. Meanwhile, the proportion of NKK wives using contraceptives rose dramatically from 41 to 74 percent, well over the national rate of 52 percent. Since one assumes some of the remaining 26 percent were trying to conceive, the true proportion of women practicing family planning was even higher. In addition, a shift in preferred methods of birth control reflected greater awareness and control on the part of the women. In 1952, condoms, rhythm, and withdrawal were the methods used in 73 percent of the families who practiced birth control. In 1955, diaphragms and contraceptive gel were being used by 62 percent of NKK employee wives.[72] While the corporate leaders of the New Life Movement undeniably adhered to a conservative view of morality and gender roles, they also offered appropriately "scientific" and "democratic" knowledge and means (including condoms and diaphragms) that could give new confidence and control to women.[73]

Closing Shop

The corporate New Life Movement was most extensive and energetic in the 1950s and early 1960s. By the end of the 1960s, it faced an identity crisis. The role of the full-time housewife was so well established, and so many young girls studied home economics in middle school, high school, and junior college, that corporate programs to teach women to cook and shop hardly seemed necessary.[74] Some companies sharply curtailed their programs at this point, declaring their mission accomplished. At NKK in the 1970s and 1980s the Welfare Section continued to publish a handbook for group leaders, and the groups were encouraged to continue meeting on their own, but the company severed its direct link to the groups by disbanding the counseling staff. Ōshima shifted to a position as social worker in the company hospital.[75]

The national office of the corporate New Life Movement Association looked for new problems to solve. For a time, the degenerate youth of the day, both radical students and those equally selfish "my-home" types committed to the pursuit of private, individual, or family pleasure over company profit, provided a convenient focus.[76] The movement then won a new lease on life with the oil crises of the 1970s. Calls for conservation by Ministry of International Trade and Industry ministers dovetailed nicely with the "rational frugality" of the New Life Movement, whether promoted by state ministries and women's groups or by companies seeking to cut internal waste.

But in the 1980s, in the face of ever greater international pressure, the conception of Japan's political economy into which the New Life

Movement so neatly fit (restrained consumption, high savings, high investment, high output for export) was no longer viable. The corporate New Life Association recognized this and finally folded its tents in 1985. Its closing declaration clarifies the awareness in corporate Japan that the national and global context had shifted, that business needed a new vision linking consumers and workers to corporations and the outside world:

The economic environment has changed completely from the time of our movement's founding. . . . Leaders in the corporate world are hardly concerned these days with an austere New Life Movement of rationalization and self-denial. . . . At a time of severe trade friction and demands that we increase our imports, for our nation's business leaders to wave the flag of conservation and rationalization will only draw more foreign criticism . . .

At the time our movement started, we sought to accumulate capital through rationalization and frugality, but today we are seeking to increase profits through increased sales; thus, the focus of management has changed and support for our movement has naturally weakened.[77]

Comparative Reflections

By the time the corporate New Life Association closed its doors, a broad array of official and private-sector programs to "rationalize" the home and the job of homemaker had been operating for nearly four decades. From one perspective, the impact was paltry. In 1979, a confidential European Community report caused a sensation when its brutally frank assessment that Japan was a nation of "workaholics living in rabbit hutches" leaked to the public. Reporters at home echoed this view in some detail:

With the spread of electric appliances, living standards certainly rose. But the living environment changed to something extremely unnatural, as the kitchens of so-called 2DK [two bedroom, plus dining/kitchen area] apartments were crammed with appliances. Kitchens no longer had back doors, so air circulation worsened. Stainless steel counters offered decreased space to prepare food. Small plastic chopping boards replaced substantial wooden ones. They were more slippery and caused injuries.[78]

Even discounting for this writer's nostalgia for roomy (but dark and drafty) old farmhouse kitchens, the results of rationalizing the home were surely mixed.

More important than its material impact on the condition of being a housewife was the impact of the multiple facets of the New Life Movement in naturalizing gender roles. The visible hand of the government makes it clear that the Japanese state acted vigorously to guide processes of social change in accord with a vision of proper gender roles and a political economy of recovery and growth in which consumption ought to be restrained. The movement played a part in the "metropolitanization" of the countryside, a process in which norms of rural and urban society converged in the realm of gender roles and expectations, as in other areas. And business managers climbed on the campaign bandwagon to help make the corporation a hegemonic institution whose interests were seen by most people as naturally congruent with the national interest as well as the personal interests of all Japanese, women as well as men. Dozens of elaborate company programs offered training and recognition to modern, rational housewives who would superintend the realms of consumption and reproduction while their husbands did their part at work to raise productivity and bring prosperity to the firm.

On a general but significant level, this story is hardly unique to Japan. In Germany, industrial corporations supported national campaigns to rationalize housework beginning in the 1920s, and, of course, education of housewives was a central component.[79] In Chile, at least one major copper mine in the 1920s ran an extensive campaign in which a staff of company social workers taught cleanliness, hygiene, nutrition, and child-rearing techniques—the entire gamut of Japan's New Life activities—to the miners' wives.[80] In the United States, the founders of the home economics profession, together with government officials in the Department of Agriculture and civilian missionaries of scientific management such as Lillian Gilbreth, led a drive to professionalize the job of housewife that anticipated (and influenced) the concerns of similar prewar and postwar Japanese reformers.[81] And some American corporations, with Ford the most famous but not the only example, involved themselves directly in helping the wives of workers manage their homes.[82]

But several aspects of the Japanese story are worth noting in order to begin mapping a comparative analysis of the varied interactions of working women and men with governments, corporations, and social reformers in this century. First, gender ideologies have linked home, workplace, and the broader society with differing shades of emphasis in the history of capitalist economies around the world. Widespread and profound fear of profligate consumption characterized Japan's New Life Movement. While such fear can be found in American cultural history as well, a powerful American domestic ideology in the twentieth century has exalted the housewife for supporting the economy in her role as "Mrs. Consumer" more than in Japan.[83] If one were to construct a scale of national measures of the relative virtue of frugality and enthusiastic consumption, Japan would be at the austere end, close to both prewar and postwar Germany where similar fears of excessive consumption have been prominent themes of state and business.[84]

In a related contrast to the United States, Japan's New Life Movement honored and nurtured the skills of the housewife, from cooking and sewing to childrearing, while the mid-century American housewife-as-consumer lived in a society which, in Glenna Matthews's telling of the story, denigrated those skills.[85] In its affirmative view of her activity and the stress on training and teaching of skills, the New Life Movement presented the work of homemaker as a "professional" (albeit unpaid) activity to a greater degree than in the United States.

Second, the explicit and ambitious role of not only government agencies but also private corporations in Japan is without parallel. To be sure, the Sociology Department at the Ford Motor Company hired social workers to visit employee homes and help solve domestic "problems," as the company defined them, as early as 1915.[86] A scattered array of major American firms followed suit, as did the El Teniente mines in Chile, and a fair number of postwar German corporations offered social services to employee wives. But none of these efforts were as extensive and sustained as those of Japan's major corporations. In no other nation did the national business community with state encouragement organize a campaign to orchestrate training for over one million wives of the nation's male industrial workers.

Finally, the Japanese case is without parallel in its reliance on small groups, or circles, as the unit of social mobilization and education of housewives. The resemblance between the New Life Movement activities described above, and the famous Quality Control (QC) Circles in Japanese workplaces, is uncanny. About fifteen years after the rural circles of the early postwar New Life Movement began in 1947, and a decade after the corporate version organized NKK women into small groups, the QC Circle movement took off throughout Japan. By the 1970s, millions of men, and a fair number of women, had joined small groups at work to solve problems of daily work life, just as some women had done at home twenty years earlier. The men in the 1970s triumphantly reported reductions in cycle time and the like at company, then regional, then national conferences, as farm women and city housewives had done with kitchen redesign in the 1950s. It is doubtful the similarity is a coincidence. Both movements reflect a distinctive pattern of social action and mobilization. While the social pattern of circle activity did not *originate* with the women of the New Life Movement, at some level of latent or manifest awareness their endeavors surely informed the quality control projects of managers (some, such as Hongo Takanobu at Tōshiba, were involved in promoting both movements) and workers. Both in concept and in practice, the organization of home and work in recent Japanese history has been marked by the *concerted* pursuit of efficiency, productivity, and rationality.

More digging into other national cases may reduce the extent of these contrasts. But if these comparative claims are sustained, they help explain two phenomena that remained noteworthy in the 1990s. On one hand, despite longstanding predictions of dramatic change, and some significant signs of shifting behavior such as increased divorces, later age at marriage, and declining birth rates, for better or worse the continued commitment of many women in Japan to a primary job as household manager remains impressive. On the other hand, despite legal changes and challenges and predictions of more to come, the gendered division of labor in Japan, both between work and home, and within persistently discriminatory workplaces, remains truly tenacious.[87]

Notes

In preparing this essay, I benefited from the comments of students and faculty attending seminar presentations in February 1992 at Columbia's Institute for East Asian Studies and Princeton's East Asian Studies Colloquium, organized by Carol Gluck and Sheldon Garon, respectively. I also benefited from the close readings and comments offered by Jordan Sand, Barbara Molony, Kathleen Uno, and a reader for the journal *Social Politics*. A longer version of this essay appeared in *Social Politics* in summer 1997, and I am grateful for permission to reproduce the overlapping portions here. Finally, Ms. Takizawa Mayumi prepared a seminar paper on the New Life Movement in a course I taught at Hōsei University in 1992–1993, which provided much valuable information. Her specific contributions are mentioned in various notes.

1. Orii Hyūga, *Rōmu kanri 20 nen* [Twenty years of labor management] (Tōyō keizai shinpōsha, 1973), 111.

2. Orii cited this statement from Kanda Michitoku, *Nippon kōkan, Matsushima tankō*, vol. 3, *Akarui shokuba zukuri jireishū* [Nippon Kōkan and Matsushima coal mine, vol. 3, Case studies in building a bright workplace] (Shinseikatsu undō kyōkai, 1964), 5. This was a handbook prepared in 1964 by the national office of the New Life Movement. Unfortunately, the original handbook contains in it nothing to clarify the paragraph's opaque logic.

3. The Japanese term is *shin seikatsu undō*. The final word, *undō*, can be translated as either "movement" or "campaign." It is used in expressions such as "labor movement" or "peace movement," as well as to describe all sorts of state-led mobilizing campaigns. To convey the breadth of the term, I will use both translations in this chapter.

4. Orii, *Rōmu kanri*, 113. For a similar view of the NKK movement in a business magazine, see "Seisansei kōjō no bakkubōnu: tejika no gōrika no michi, shin seikatsu undō" [The backbone of productivity increase: The close-at-hand path to rationalization, the New Life Campaign], *Maneijimento* 14, no. 5 (September 1955): 21.

5. For example, Robert G. Moeller, *Protecting Motherhood: Women and the Family in the Politics of Postwar West Germany* (Berkeley: University of California Press, 1993); Glenna Matthews, *"Just a Housewife": The Rise and Fall of Domesticity in America* (New York: Oxford University Press, 1987); Mary Nolan, "'Housework Made Easy': The Taylorized Housewife in Weimar Germany's Rationalized Economy," *Feminist Studies* 16, no. 3 (Fall 1990): 549–577; and Karen Offen, "Body Politics: Women, Work and The Politics of Motherhood in France,

1920–1950," and Irene Stoehr, "Housework and Motherhood: Debates and Policies in the Women's Movement in Imperial Germany and the Weimar Republic," both in *Maternity and Gender Policies: Women and the Rise of the European Welfare States, 1880s–1950s*, eds. Gesela Bock and Pat Thane (London: Routledge, 1991). See also Renate Bridenthal, "Professional Housewives: Stepsisters of the Women's Movement," in *When Biology Became Destiny: Women in Weimar and Nazi Germany*, eds. Renate Bridenthal, Anita Grossman, and Marion Kaplan (New York: Monthly Review Press, 1984).

6. See Sheldon Garon, *Molding Japanese Minds: The State in Everyday Life* (Princeton, NJ: Princeton University Press, 1997), chapter 4. Also see Barbara Sato's essay in this volume, which discusses the related concept of "self-cultivation" or "self-improvement" (*shūyō*) among Taishō-era housewives and magazine readers.

7. Sheldon Garon, "Rethinking Modernization in Japanese History," *Journal of Asian Studies* 53, no. 2 (May 1994): 356.

8. Ibid., 357.

9. *Kōseishō 20 nen shi,* ed. Kōseishō [Welfare Ministry] (Kōsei Mondai Kenkyū-kai, 1959), 141, 213.

10. Ibid., 213–214, 527–536.

11. On the national movement's themes, *Shakai kyōiku jū nen no ayumi,* ed. Kanagawa-ken kyōiku iinkai (Kanagawa, 1957), 21–22, held in the Kanagawa Prefectural Women's Center library. On activities of the local government and women's organizations in Kanagawa and Tochigi prefectures in 1947–1948, see "Zadankai: shin seikatsu undō no hansei to kadai," *Shakai kyōiku* 13, no. 12 (December, 1958): 21.

12. The National Coordinating Committee of Regional Women's Groups (Zenkoku chiiki fujindantai rengō kyōgikai) was founded in July 1952. Its major goals were to prevent tuberculosis, promote birth control, support moral education for youths, and eliminate backroom money politics.

13. Kon Wajirō, "Seikatsu kaizen fukyūin no tōjō," *Kasei dokuhon* (1951), cited in *Nihon fujin mondai shiryō shūsei,* vol. 7 (Domesu shuppan, 1981), 628–629. See also Nōrin suisan shō, *Nōrin suisan shō 100 nen shi* 3 (1981), 113–116.

14. The "social education" program of the Ministry of Education was elaborated in the years after World War I, and a Social Education Section was created in the ministry in 1924, part of the interwar push to bolster social morality and "reform" daily life. See *Gakusei 100 nen shi,* ed. Monbushō (Monbushō,

1972), 528–529. Also see Jordan Sand, *House and Home in Modern Japan:* Architecture, Domestic Space, and Bourgeois Culture, 1880–1930 (Cambridge, MA: Harvard University Asia Center, 2004), 286; and Kobayashi Yoshihiro, "Taishō ki ni okeru shakai kyōiku seisaku no shintenkai: seikatsu kaizen undō o chūshin ni," *Kōza Nihon no kyōiku shi* 3, *Kindai* II (Dai ichi hōki, 1984).

15. On these activities in Kanagawa prefecture, see Kanagawa-ken kyōiku iinkai, *Shakai kyōiku jū*, 388–389.

16. Although emigration was not allowed by the Allied Occupation authorities, the government did begin a program to subsidize travel expenses of Japanese willing to emigrate to Latin America as soon as the Occupation ended in 1952. By 1958, only thirty thousand people had made use of this program. *Jinkō hakusho,* ed. Kōseishō jinkō mondai kenkyū jo (Kōseishō jinkō mondai kenkyū jo, 1959), 111. I am indebted to Takizawa Mayumi for this citation. For English language discussion of birth control in postwar Japan, see Samuel Coleman, *Family Planning in Japanese Society: Traditional Birth Control in a Modern Urban Culture* (Princeton, NJ: Princeton University Press, 1983); and Tiana Norgren, "Abortion before Birth Control: The Interest Group Politics behind Postwar Japanese Reproduction Policy," *Journal of Japanese Studies* 24, no. 1 (Winter 1998): 59–94.

17. See Kōseishō, *Kōseishō 20 nen shi*, 527, on the founding of this group, and 531 for the citation from its report. The Japanese for the term "reverse effect" is *gyaku sata genshō.*

18. Prime Minister Hatoyama had been struggling with Yoshida Shigeru for leadership of Japan's conservative political forces since his "depurge" in 1951 by the Occupation authorities. An adroit career politician first elected to the Diet in 1915, Hatoyama's politics ranged widely over time, but despite some noteworthy prewar stands in favor of constitutional and parliamentary government, Hatoyama before, during, and after the war was consistently nationalistic in foreign policy and conservative in matters of political ideology, education, and gender. In 1955 his government initiated a determined (ultimately failed) drive to amend the postwar constitution along prewar lines. For Hatoyama's politics, see John Dower, *Empire and Aftermath: Yoshida Shigeru and the Japanese Experience* (Cambridge, MA: Council on East Asian Studies, 1979), 249–252. Hatoyama's interest in the New Life Movement might have had an inspiration very close to home. His mother, Hatoyama Haruko, was well known in the prewar years as an author of popular texts on childrearing, in which she described her own exacting methods of raising her sons. See Hatoyama Ichirō, *Watakushi no jijō den* (Kaizōsha, 1951), 21–25, for his recollection of his mother's childrearing phi-

losophy, and Donald Roden, *Schooldays in Imperial Japan* (Berkeley: University of California Press, 1980), 133–135.

19. *Asahi shinbun*, March 24, 1955, 1.

20. Information in this paragraph provided by Takizawa Mayumi, "Shin seikatsu undō to kazoku keikaku," seminar paper, Hōsei University, 1992.

21. For example, Nagano Junzō, "Shin seikatsu undō to rōdō kumiai," *Rōdō keizai junpō* (September 1955).

22. For another discussion of this reconstruction process, see Kathleen S. Uno, "The Death of 'Good Wife, Wise Mother'?" in *Postwar Japan as History*, ed. Andrew Gordon (Berkeley: University of California Press, 1993).

23. For a more detailed presentation of the rural side to the movement, see Gordon, "Managing the Japanese Household," *Social Politics* 4, no. 2 (Summer 1997), 245–283.

24. Compare Matthews, *The Rise and Fall of Domesticity*, chapter 7, 188 and *passim*, to Nolan, "'Housework Made Easy,'" 552, where she speaks of the "austere vision of modernity" in Germany.

25. Perhaps because the majority of wage-earning women in these years were young and unmarried, and the New Life Movement never addressed the situation of women in their role as producers.

26. On the "metropolitanization" of the countryside, see William Kelly, "Finding a Place in Metropolitan Japan: Transpositions of Everyday Life," in Gordon, *Postwar Japan as History*.

27. See the Hunter essay in this volume, which analyzes the complementary creation of a gendered (female), but *unmarried*, labor force in the textile industry.

28. The four organizations were Nihon kōgyō kurabu, Keidanren, Nikkeiren, and Keizai dōyūkai. The business group was called Shin seikatsu undō no kai. The body created by the Hatoyama cabinet was called Shin seikatsu undō kyōkai.

29. "Seisansei kōjō no bakku bōn: tejika na gōrika no michi, 'shin seikatsu undō'" *Manejimento* 14, no. 5 (September 1955): 13.

30. Ibid.

31. On this general phenomenon in later years, see Anne Allison, *Nightwork* (Chicago, IL: University of Chicago Press, 1994).

32. On Fordism, see Robert Boyer, *The Regulation School: A Critical Introduction* (New York: Columbia University Press, 1990), or Michel Aglietta, *A Theory of Capitalist Regulation: The U.S. Experience* (London: New Left Books, 1979).

33. "Kigyōtai renraku kyōgikai no genjō," *Shin seikatsu* 6, no. 6 (June 1959): 9. Another list of forty-eight companies that have implemented New Life programs for worker families is printed in *Shin seikatsu* 7, no. 8 (August 1960): 8–10, and vol. 7, no. 9 (September 1960): 6–8.

34. Interview with Ōshima Ai, September 26, 1991.

35. The most complete account of the NKK movement is offered by Kanda Michitoku, "Kigyōtai shin seikatsu undō no 'umi no oya': Nippon kōkan kabushiki gaisha," *Akarui shokuba zukuri: jireishu (3)*, (Shin seikatsu undō kyōkai, 1964), 3–29. This paragraph also draws on "Kōjō, jigyōjo ni miru shin seikatsu undō no jirei," *Rōsei jihō*, December 23, 1955 (no. 1358): 29–34.

36. *Kami-shibai* was a form of theater in which a narrator told a story using colorful posters to illustrate the progress of the plot. For more on this form, and the displacement of such local cultural practices by centralized media such as television, see Marilyn Ivy, "Formations of Mass Culture," in Gordon, *Postwar Japan as History*.

37. "Kōjō, jigyōjo," 31. For example, sewing classes met 62 times in 1954 with a cumulative total of 1,499 women in attendance.

38. I have found descriptions of similar corporate programs to train housewives and offer social work services to families in the United States, Chile, and Germany. Rather than encourage the women to run their own small groups, the programs relied on individual outreach or adult education classes. See Stephen Meyer, *The Five Dollar Day: Labor Management and Social Control in the Ford Motor Company, 1908–1921* (Albany: SUNY Press, 1981), 134–140; Sarah Deutsch, *No Separate Refuge: Culture, Class and Gender on an Anglo-Hispanic Frontier in the American Southwest, 1880–1940* (New York: Oxford University Press, 1987), 97–98; Thomas M. Klubock, "Class, Community, and Gender in the Chilean Copper Mines: The El Teniente Miners and Working Class Politics, 1904–1951," PhD dissertation, Yale University, 1993, chapter 2; and Mary Nolan, "'Housework Made Easy,'" 566.

39. Interview with Ōshima Ai, September 26, 1991.

40. Ibid.

41. On Tōshiba, see Hongo Takanobu, "Tōshiba 'jyōzu na kurashi no undō' no

ikikata," *Rōmu kenkyū* 12, no. 10 (December 1957): 30–34. On Hitachi, see "Kōjō, jigyōjo," 34–37. Also, the series of booklets published by the government New Life Movement Association in the 1950s and 1960s, titled *Akarui shokuba zukuri*, contains numerous detailed profiles of activities at mines, shipyards, factories, and offices around the country. Likewise, the monthly issues of *Shin seikatsu* (New life), the publication of the business federations' New Life Movement Association, contain briefer, but even more numerous, accounts.

42. Hongo, "Tōshiba," 31, and interview with Hongo Takanobu, March 11, 1991.

43. Hongo, "Tōshiba," 33–34, and interview. As did all electric companies in the 1950s and 1960s, Tōshiba employed thousands of unmarried young women in their teens. Condom distribution was for married women only, and the requirement that a woman first place an order through a local unit would have insured these young girls did not have access.

44. Hongo, "Tōshiba," 32–33. See Mary Nolan, "Rationalization," 564–565; and Stuart Ewen, *Captains of Consciousness: Advertising and the Social Roots of the Consumer Culture* (New York: McGraw Hill, 1976), chapter 6, on the comparison of consumerism (or its repudiation) in German and American movements to rationalize the household. In America it appears that to some extent a stance of relatively uninhibited consumption replaced frugality as the primary virtue of the housewife.

45. Hongo, "Tōshiba," 34.

46. The present essay is part of an ongoing study of this contest. For analysis of labor-management relations at NKK in the 1950s, and the impact of rationalization at the workplace on company-union relations, see Andrew Gordon, "Luttes pour pouvoir dans l'atelier," *Annales* (Mai-Juin, 1994).

47. Orii, *Rōmu kanri*, 5.

48. Hongo, "Tōshiba," 30–31.

49. "Katei ni chokketsu shita shin seikatsu undō" [New Life Movement ties up directly with families], *Manejimento* 14, no. 9 (September 1955): 20–21. On the history of Ashio, site of Japan's first major pollution case at the turn of the twentieth century, as well as a major riot in 1970, see *Journal of Japanese Studies* 1, no. 1 (1974); and Nimura Kazuo, *Ashio bōdō no shiteki bunseki* (Tokyo University Press, 1986).

50. Hongo, "Tōshiba," 31.

51. Hyōdō Tsutomu, *Gendai no rōdō undō* (Tokyo University Press, 1981), 25–30; and Andrew Gordon, "Contests for the Workplace," in Gordon, *Postwar Japan as History*, 378–383.

52. Nagano, "Shin seikatsu undō to rōdō kumiai," 20, 23.

53. *Keihin no kōro kara: tekkō rōdōsha no tatakai,* ed. Nihon kyōsanto kawasaki saibō (Gogatsu shobō, 1955), 143, 146–147.

54. *Asahi shinbun,* August 25, 1956, "Keikaku shussan de shigoto no nōritsu kōjō," for an example. I am indebted to Takizawa Mayumi for this citation.

55. On the workplace organizers, who circulated among the mills' various shops to hear and act upon worker complaints and build support for the union's positions, see Gordon, "Luttes," 531–533.

56. Interview with Kamimura Hideji, October 14, 1992, and *Tatakai no ayumi: Nippon kōkan Kawasaki rōdō kumi ai undō shi,* ed. Nippon kōkan Kawasaki seitetsujo rōdō kumiai (n.p., 1970), 146–150, on union outreach to housewives at the Kawasaki mill; and *Tsurutetsu rōdō undō shi,* ed. Nippon kōkan Tsurumi seitetsujo rōdō kumiai (Tsurumi, 1956), 466–468, on union outreach to housewives at the Tsurumi mill.

57. Nippon kōkan Kawasaki, *Tatakai no ayumi,* 147.

58. Orii, *Rōmu kanri kanri 20 nen,* 112.

59. Kumazawa Makoto, *Portraits of the Japanese Workplace* (Boulder, CO: Westview, 1996), 160.

60. *Kawasaki rōdō shi: sengo hen,* ed. Kawasaki shi (Kawasaki, 1987), 425.

61. Ibid., 428. See also the Hunter essay in this volume, which notes that the marital division of labor in the interwar period laid the basis for this preponderance of single women among female wage laborers and, conversely, the small numbers of married women wage laborers.

62. On the housewife debate, see Maruoka Hideko, *Nihon fujin mondai shiryō shūsei,* vol. 9 (Domesu shuppan, 1981), 191–222; and *Shufu ronsō o yomu: zen kiroku I, II,* ed. Ueno Chizuko (Keisō shobō, 1985).

63. Kawasaki, *Kawasaki rōdō shi,* 423.

64. The following is from an interview with Ōshima Ai, September 26, 1991.

65. Licensed prostitution existed in Japan until 1958 (the law ending the system was passed in 1956 but was gradually enacted). See Yuki Shiga-Fujime, "The

Prostitutes' Union and the Impact of the 1956 Anti-Prostitution Law in Japan," in the *U.S.-Japan Women's Journal*, English Supplement, no. 5 (1993): 3–27.

66. Interview with Ōshima Ai, September 26, 1991.

67. Ibid.

68. Orii, *Rōmu kanri*, 112.

69. Kawasaki, *Kawasaki rōdō shi*, 512–513.

70. Ibid.

71. Kawakami Hideji interview, October 14, 1992; Nakao Yasuji interview, October 15, 1991.

72. Aoki Hisao, "Jitchi shidō ni yoru kazoku keikaku fukyū no sokushin to kōka ni tsuite: Nippon kōkan Kawasaki seitetsujo no chōsen," Kōseishō, *Jinkō mondai kenkyūjo nenpō*, vol. 1 (n.p., 1956), 20; and Mainichi shinbun jinkō mondai kenkyū kai, *Nihon no jinkō mondai* (Shiseidō, 1976), 334. Both these sources are cited in Takizawa, "Shin seikatsu undō to kazoku keikaku." Even more impressive figures are presented in a report on NKK in a management publication in 1955. The report claims that in the first year of the program, pregnancies and births fell 70 to 80 percent, while abortions fell by 65 percent. By the next year (1955), 80 percent of families were reported as practicing birth control. See "Kōjō, jigyōjo," 32–33.

73. Work in the history of women in the United States shows that some political women in the 1970s and 1980s began this activity in the PTA and other stereotypically female positions. Essays by Tocco, Sato, and Molony in this volume also offer examples of similar empowerment through activities that appear at first glance to be "traditional."

74. For a comprehensive account of the housewife's role in the 1970s, the endpoint of this essay, see Suzanne Vogel, "Professional Housewife: The Career of Urban Middle Class Japanese Women," *Japan Interpreter* 12, no. 1 (Winter 1978): 16–43.

75. Interview with Ōshima Ai, September 26, 1991; interview with Okuda Kenji, November 27, 1992.

76. This is evident from a survey of the issues of the movement's publication, *Shin seikatsu*, in the 1960s and 1970s.

77. *Shin seikatsu* 32, Final number (August 1985), 2–3.

78. Kawasaki, *Kawasaki rōdō shi*, 797–798.

79. Nolan, "'Housework Made Easy.'"

80. Klubock, "Class, Community, and Gender," chapter 2.

81. Matthews, *The Rise and Fall of Domesticity*, chapter 6.

82. Meyer, *The Five Dollar Day*, 134–140; and Deutsch, *No Separate Refuge*, 97–98.

83. Matthews, *The Rise and Fall of Domesticity*, 188. According to Daniel Horowitz, *The Morality of Spending: Attitudes toward the Consumer Society in America, 1875–1940* (Baltimore, MD: Johns Hopkins University Press, 1985), xxi, American history has been marked by a "complicated, uneven and long-term process" in which the United States "became a nation of modern consumers." In this process, the relative virtue or vice of consumer desires and expanded consumption has generated much controversy.

84. On postwar German attitudes, which recognized the positive economic impact of expanded consumption but worried over the negative social consequences, see Moeller, *Protecting Motherhood*, 139–141.

85. Matthews, *The Rise and Fall of Domesticity*, 192–193, 222 and *passim*.

86. Meyer, *The Five Dollar Day*, 123–149.

87. Mary Brinton, *Women and the Economic Miracle: Gender and Work in Postwar Japan* (Berkeley: University of California Press, 1993), 29, shows that in 1987 Japan still had the deepest M curve of any advanced industrial country. Her book is an important attempt to explain this and other related phenomena. For an upbeat work that links this commitment to the high morale of housewives, see Iwao Sumiko, *The Japanese Woman* (New York: Free Press, 1993). For a work that stresses discrimination, see Alice Lam, *Women and Japanese Management: Discrimination and Reform* (London: Routledge, 1992).

PART V

Theorizing Gender

13 The Quest for Women's Rights in Turn-of-the-Century Japan

Barbara Molony

[W]e should take up . . . this discussion of equal rights for men and women only after we have first considered the nature of men and women and become well informed on what rights are.

—Fukuzawa Yukichi, "The Equal Numbers of Men and Women"[1]

Responding to a fussy diatribe by Katō Hiroyuki that denounced, eponymously, "Abuses of Equal Rights for Men and Women," Fukuzawa Yukichi published these words in 1875. Though Fukuzawa believed that debate about "rights" should occur only after the meaning of "rights" was better understood, his words were not heeded. "Rights" remained a central issue in a wide variety of intellectual and political discussions, including feminist ones, in the late nineteenth and early twentieth centuries.[2]

To be sure, Fukuzawa was correct in asserting that "rights" did not have a singular meaning clear to all. And his suggestions that men's and women's natures were worthy of analysis sounds more postmodern than Fukuzawa would ever have intended. That is, Fukuzawa was not interpreting "gender," but rather was attempting to state what he viewed as naturalized gender roles as the basis for men's and women's complementary rights.

The Japanese were not alone in perceiving "rights" to have multiple meanings.[3] Rights discourse in Japan was lively and diverse, particularly because it surfaced in a variety of contexts and blended notions of Tokugawa anti-authoritarianism[4] with a tidal wave of often conflated "Western" rights discourses. In addition, the terms for "rights" (*kenri*), "women's rights" (*joken*), "male-female equality" (*danjo byōdō*), male-female equal rights (*danjo dōken*), and other concepts in the lexicon of rights were themselves neologisms. (These terms were, at times, used interchangeably, though their meanings were actually distinct.) It should be pointed out that late nineteenth-century politically motivated activists in Japan were not entirely to blame for the conflation of Western philosophers' terms. The works of Rousseau, Mill, Spencer, Locke, and other theorists of the state, civil society, and rights, differing in time and nationality though they did, entered Japanese discourse within a decade of each other.[5] In addition, state, nation, nationality, ethnicity, gender, and so on were all in the process of mutual construction around the same time, and in some cases, rights advocacy was used selectively to resist the emerging structure of one or another of these categories. Conversely, the language of rights could also be employed to help reify any of these categories or institutions, either in a positive, supportive way or through a Foucaultian type of negotiation. That is, as Foucault noted: "Where there is power, there is resistance, and yet, or rather consequently, this resistance is never in a position of externality to power. . . . [T]he strictly relational character of power relationships . . . depends upon a multiplicity of points of resistance."[6]

Meiji-era (1868–1912) *joken* can be seen as a way of conceptualizing relations of power. Other than People's Rights advocate Ueki Emori, who claimed that resistance to unresponsive government was a people's right and duty and that men and women were entitled to equal rights, Meiji-era advocates for women did not call for women's resistance to the state or society that might lead to its overthrow.[7] Resistance always occurred in relation to the institutions of power it called into question. At the end of the nineteenth century, women's rights constituted a quest, undertaken through a "multiplicity of points of resistance." To put it a bit more simply, women's rights called for *inclusion*, not *revolution*. This chapter suggests two reasons: first, the fundamental nature of rights themselves, and second, the identification, for some 1890s women's advocates, of rights with recognition and rewarding of female self-cultivation as a marker of a woman's personhood.

Rights discussions in the late Meiji era, whether by advocates for men or for women, developed in a context of iconoclastic rejection of past (Tokugawa) relations of power and of engagement with foreign ideas. That power (e.g., a state, social norms, laws, customs) would exist was not questioned; rather one's relationship to power was under discussion. And the most important way to frame questions about one's relationship to power was through discussion of rights. Rights at that time, in Japan and elsewhere, were strictly gendered, however, and so women's quests for rights involved—as feminist theorist Wendy Brown writes—"a longing to share in power rather than be protected from its excesses."[8]

Any quest for rights, then, might seem rather ironic. One of the purposes of rights is protection from something—such as from encroachment by another person, from encroachment by the state, or from being limited in one's expression. (The various notions of rights are frequently in conflict—one's freedom of expression, for example, might conflict with another's right to protection—but that is beyond the scope of this chapter.) Notions of rights as protection from encroachment were clearly held by some Meiji rights advocates; but to what extent were they applied to women? I would argue that the idea of rights as protection *from* the state was a very minor thread in women's rights talk—instead the main focus was on inclusion *in* the state and equality in both the private domain of the family and the public domain of civil society.[9] Admittedly, a "public/private" dichotomy does not quite work here, where women sought to empower themselves in the family ("private") through means of the law ("public") and through public recognition of their intellectual accomplishments. The notion of protection was not absent from Meiji discourse but it arose more in connection with the idea of "liberation" (*kaihō*) than with rights. "Liberation" was not used in discussing women's political rights until Socialists began using the term in 1907. *Kaihō* was first used to discuss the liberation of prostituted women and girls from contractual bondage after the 1872 *Maria Luz* affair in which unfree sex workers escaped from a ship of that name, and came to include, by the end of the century, liberation of wives, through divorce, from oppressive marriages.[10]

"Civil society" is a term commonly used in Western social and political discourses—like all such terms, it has no single, stable meaning—but did it exist in Japan in the Meiji period? It is clear that it did by the 1920s when rights of participation in civil society were understood to be related to *kōminken* (variously interpreted as civic and civil rights).[11] Though "civil society" was not named in the late nineteenth century, it was in the process of development and its existence was understood, even if prematurely, by rights advocates. Some critics, taking civil participation for granted, lamented what they viewed as Japanese women's limited involvement in social and philanthropic endeavors.[12] Yet, as early as the late nineteenth century, women and men working to improve the status of women were instrumental in the development of civil society through the creation of institutions like schools and welfare organizations as well as ideas disseminated in cities and towns throughout Japan by speeches, newspapers, and magazines. Even if unnamed, a concept or institution may exist, and borrowing language from one context to apply to an analog elsewhere can be illuminating.[13]

As Carole Pateman has shown, the term "civil" has had shifting meanings in Western discourse. Before the creation of the social contract, "civil" was seen as the opposite of "natural"; thereafter, it was seen as the opposite of "private."[14] Thus, by the nineteenth century in the West, civil society came to be viewed as standing in opposition to the family (the private).[15] But such an opposition was not assumed by women's rights advocates in turn-of-the-century Japan. While some rights advocates in the early Meiji period did assume the family was a warm private haven from a cold public world, others believed the official policy of gender inequality in the early modern Japanese family offered little comfort to women.[16] Later Meiji images of the family may not have been so gloomy for women, but again, the family was not seen as something separate from the public sphere. Indeed, many Meiji advocates for women believed women deserved a public role not *despite* their family status but *because* of it. Thus, for instance, the mother who kept her family healthy could be seen, during the first Sino-Japanese War (1894–1895), as serving her nation publicly.[17] The ideological opponents of the women's rights advocates—gender conservatives who opposed any concept of inherent (natural) rights or even earned rights based on service in the public sphere—also argued that the family was the basis of the state.[18] But their idea of "family" was a patriarchy with no thought of rights or even equality among its members. So where did rights advocates start their quest for women's rights?

Although the earliest discussions of rights in the 1870s and 1880s often did not explicitly correlate rights with male gender, the Japanese discussants frequently employed the ideas of Rousseau, whose vision of a social contract was founded on the rights of men in a fictive fraternal relationship.[19] Those men and (the smaller group of) women who clamored for rights in the 1870s demanded the rights of political participation or inclusion. By 1890, a tiny minority of men had been awarded the right of inclusion in the state and civil society, but women were pointedly excluded from political participation.[20] The modern state was gendered as "male" by 1890—maleness was required of all government officials, including the emperor—and the state itself was seen as a fraternity under a patriarchal emperor.[21] Indeed, when political rights were extended in 1890 to some of the men who had earlier demanded rights of fraternal inclusion, many of those activists followed up on their demands by joining parties and entering the government in some capacity.[22] The prior state and society were male dominated as well, and it required no imagination for many in the late nineteenth century to take male gender for granted as a requirement for political participation.

But though it was a necessary condition, male gender was not a sufficient condition of inclusion. Large numbers of men were outside the political arena, excluded either because of their occupation or because of lower-class status. Many men continued to work for inclusion but perhaps cared as much about gaining the respectability that was implied by their participation in civil society and the state as about casting ballots.[23] Male gender as a barrier to inclusion in politics was not at issue for them, class was; and unenfranchised men were seeking to claim the rights of fraternal inclusion that were enjoyed by other men.[24]

This chapter will discuss the goals of women's rights advocates and the meaning of their demands in the context of turn-of-the-century state and society formation. It examines women's rights discourses in late nineteenth-century periodicals, some of them directed to a female readership and some directed to a general, often male, audience. Sources include journals like *Meiroku zasshi, Jogaku zasshi, Joken, Tōkyō fujin kyōfukai zasshi,* and some regional publications.[25] Nineteenth-century advocates for women were, of course, of varying minds about the definition of "women's rights," but all agreed that women did not have rights at that time. Some argued for a communitarian inclusiveness reminiscent of the Rousseauian ideas espoused in the 1870s when neither ordinary men nor women had political rights. Others, inspired by Mill, stressed improved education as a way for women to gain the subjectivity (personhood or identity) that would make them eligible for rights. There were also those who believed inclusion must follow the elimination of patriarchal sexual privileges, such as those implied by polygamy, prostitution, and patrilineality.[26] This chapter examines these different positions and their similarities and differences with late nineteenth-century arguments for expanding men's inclusion in the state.

Meiji-Era Engagement with Western Rights Theories

In its formulation and its legal applications, the concept of rights is one that separates the individual from his or her community rather than embracing the notion of community. People struggle for rights on behalf of an oppressed identity group (a class, a gender, and ethnicity), but when rights are granted they are applied to individuals.[27] This type of thinking was discussed in the West by philosophers as divergent as Jefferson and Marx. Japanese commentators on Meiji civil law, both before and after the implementation of the Civil Code of 1898, rightly argued that this concept of rights was at odds with the notion, codified in the Constitution of 1889, that women, and especially wives, were under the jurisdiction of the patriarchal family head, and thus had no individual rights within the community of the family nor the independent right of contract that would permit rights in the larger society.[28] The Civil Code, therefore, explicitly excluded the idea of rights held equally by separate individuals (irrespective of household membership).[29]

Nevertheless, Japanese supporters of improving the lot of women brought rights in as a means to elevate women's status. Many saw rights in terms of inclusion in state and civil society rather than as a basis for continuing resistance and separation from power. This view of rights had many parallels with Western notions in the eighteenth and nineteenth centuries. Under the social contract, which had come to be understood in the West as occurring after the defeat of the metaphorical father (the patriarchal king), individuals voluntarily gave up some rights in return for the protection of civil law and inclusion in the fraternity of citizens—liberty, equality, and fraternity were the ideal of the civil, or public, sphere.[30] The "state" that was constructed of this public sphere could define the terms of inclusion or citizenship, according to Rousseau, though Mill championed the rights of individuals against this "tyranny of the majority." Mill and Rousseau were particularly important sources for the creation of Japanese thinking about rights.

The problem with this construct was that its theorists supposed that only "individuals" could enter into this contract; because of their putative weakness in strength and intellect, women were not entitled to ownership of property in the person, and were therefore not individuals. For Mill, women were thus not in the public sphere, and where they were—the home—was to be "private" or off limits to the state and dominated by the home's own patriarch, who was part of the civil, egalitarian "fraternity." Not surprisingly, women's rights advocates (including Mill) reckoned that education was one key to making women deserving of being "individuals" and therefore improving their status, but even Mill did not know what to do with a husband's right to dominance in marriage. Rousseau, male-centered though his writings often appear, did, in fact, suggest that women had a publicly important role—that is, as mothers. Men could not be "brothers" if they were not ethical fathers and sons, and the mother was the key to preserving the moral and ethical family. This idea resonated with women's rights thinking in turn-of-the-century Japan, one of whose key components was moral and intellectual cultivation and its connection with social respect.

Historians of Japan have traditionally raised concerns about "state intrusion in the family," but that formulation ignores the fact that patriarchal dominance may have felt more confining to many women in the Meiji era than state authoritarianism. (In fact, one component of state authoritarianism was the reification of male dominance in family law.) Patriarchal problems in the "private" sphere seemed so debilitating in Meiji Japan that issues surrounding marriage and sexuality became a major early concern of women's rights advocates. Inclusion in the state, which must be preceded or accompanied by inclusion in the public sphere, was thus a goal (though one fraught with problems) of many feminist political activists, in Japan as it was in Western countries as well.

Though concepts of rights and participation in civil society as they developed in eighteenth- and nineteenth-century Western thought were central to the mid- to late-Meiji discourse on rights, the political context was quite different. Most significantly, the metaphorical patriarch (the emperor) was not defeated in Japan but rather was used as the center-piece of a male-gendered (and upper-class-centered) polity. When male sex was made a requirement for emperorship in 1890, many women's rights advocates were surprised and disheartened.[31] Neverthe-less, though the emperor had to be male, he co-existed with a slowly expanding participatory society, a scenario that led many advocates of rights, both civil and women's rights, to continue to look, in varying degrees, to Western discussions of rights as desirable and perhaps even normative. Rights discourse was a big tent that accommodated a variety of opinions, and Japanese thinkers—male and female, radical and lib-eral—drew on what appealed to them in this diverse body of thought.

Even though rights might be problematic, based as they were on as-sumptions—masculinist, Western, individualistic—that presented sig-nificant drawbacks, there were feminists in the Meiji period who advo-cated women's rights.[32] Looking back at her activist career, Fukuda Hideko noted in 1913 that while she and other women in the Freedom and People's Rights movement of the 1880s may have wanted equal rights with men, by the end of the Meiji period women on the left (like herself) wanted liberation from men.[33] Historian Sotozaki Mitsuhiro notes that nonsocialist feminists in the Taishō period reinvigorated talk about equal rights in reaction to the socialists' focus on liberation, creating a varied and sophisticated discourse on rights.[34] The extremely lively discussions and activism around women's rights in the 1910s, 1920s, and 1930s had historical antecedents.[35]

Nor were the issues raised by women's rights advocates *sui generis*; they developed in the context of men's political rights. The concept of male fraternity, so central to Rousseauian rights discourse, was deeply embedded in Japanese social culture, even in contexts in which rights were not at issue. Donald Roden's study of elite male education in im-perial Japan, for instance, describes a fraternal communalism that vio-lently resisted even the suggestion of a womanly presence in its hal-lowed manly halls.[36] Some women who used notions of rights to advocate elevating the status of women would have agreed with the gender essentialism implied in the fraternity concept while rejecting the notion that it might presume male superiority; others leaned toward the notion of rights inherent in individuals irrespective of gender. But because women's rights implied women's inclusion in the state and civil society—which would erode a sense of fraternity of male citizens—and because most advocates for women recognized that equality first required the destruction of patriarchal family practices, women's rights talk eventually diverged from (male) rights discourse after the 1890s, when some men had become enfranchised citizens.

Discussing women's rights primarily in terms of politics, however, overlooks a significant part of the discussion about women in Meiji Japan. At that time, discussions of women's rights were closely related to discussions of women's education, particularly education beyond the elementary level. Cultivating a good, moral, ethical, responsible character capable of manifesting agency—through being an exemplar or even a leader—was a goal of Confucian education as well as the recently introduced Western-style learning.[37] Intellectual and moral cultivation produced a person worthy of respect, worthy of having a recognizable subjectivity. The centrality of education in rights discourse at the turn of the century suggests that rights at that time were closely connected to the desire for respect for women's subjectivity. Talk of rights takes persons' subjectivity for granted; talk of education as self-cultivation advances the cause of women as subjects or persons. In Meiji Japan, even the type of education that claimed to train women who did not need *political* rights was to mold ethical wives and mothers who led by example in the family and in civil society. These women would be active not in electoral politics but, as individuals or as members of organizations, in public activities such as relief for the poor or more controversial reforms like those calling for regulation of sexuality.[38]

Some scholars suggest that 1890s discussions about women, which focused more on educated women's managing a warm, loving family and home (*katei*) or on playing a leadership role in legal reification of moral reform (especially reform of the patriarchal family), was a shift away from earlier discourses focusing on political rights.[39] But I would argue that there is no real gulf between the 1880s and the 1890s when viewed from the perspective of respect for women's personhood. Before 1890, discussions focused on the equality between men and women (*danjo byōdō*)—a concept used both as the foundation for women's rights (*joken*) and equal rights (*dōken*) and as the justification for the attack on polygamy. Unlike *joken* advocates, advocates of monogamy did not necessarily wish women to be active in politics, but they did view women as fully realized individuals deserving equality and respect. Both types sought women's inclusion in society—one through political, civil, or civic participation on a par with men, the other through the use of law to improve familial relations, which would further dissolve the barriers between public and private spheres. The theme of respect for women's subjectivity also undergirded the 1890s focus on moral reform and on "creating a warm home." These discussions were supplemented by those on equal rights and, most noticeably, on education. Ethical and well-trained women were worthy of respect and were, therefore, integrated with society, a necessary step toward inclusion in the state and possession of rights.

Women's Rights and Women's Education

Decades after its inception in the 1870s, at the height of the pre–World War II feminist political movement, women's education—at least elementary education—had become so normalized that it was viewed as both a right and a duty. Although as late as the 1920s many farm families and others disputed the need for any education for their daughters beyond the sixth grade, others, particularly those who contributed to the public discourse on the elevation of women's status either through "rights" or through "liberation," took it for granted that women's education was both a prerequisite for and a result of that elevation. Feminist Hiratsuka Raichō (1886–1971) argued, from Meiji precedents, that education helped to advance the rights and powers of wives in marriage[40]—a liberatory discourse—while Ichikawa Fusae (1893–1981) tied women's education to social and political participation[41]—a rights discourse.

From the beginning of the Meiji period, what later came to be called *fujinron* (discourse on womanhood) occupied the attention of quite a few commentators, many of whom discussed education, especially in the context of morality in the family and, by extension, in the whole nation. *Meiroku zasshi* (founded 1873, circulation 3,000) was an early venue for these discussions.[42] Mori Arinori, who later became education minister, noted in a series of articles in *Meiroku zasshi* in 1874 that girls should be educated, that educated women could better protect their chastity as well as their husbands' morality, and that mothers should instill moral values in their children.[43] Moreover, Mori argued, as had Mill, that education was not only a right but a prerequisite for rights; thus, Mori nimbly combined gender, rights, and education.[44] He called attention to women's weakness, however, when he added that oppression of the weak by the strong was a sign that righteousness did not prevail.

Tsuda Mamichi, another contributor to *Meiroku zasshi*, who vehemently rejected the idea of keeping women out of the public eye,[45] was, however, less enthusiastic about women's rights in his argument for otherwise representative government, taking as natural that women and other incompetents should be excluded from the electorate.[46] Tsuda recognized the disjunction in Western law between the civil rights of unmarried and married women. Since husbands possessed their wives, he wrote in 1875, married women had unequal personal, property, and contract rights. While it was "evil" to shut women up entirely, Tsuda wrote, why should Japan go so far in the other direction and grant women rights not yet enjoyed in the West?[47] Sakatani Shiroshi, decrying bigamy in 1875, went on to say that equal rights should be limited to the bedroom, as it was far worse for a wife to have more rights than her husband than for a husband's rights to surpass his wife's.[48] The previous year, he had argued that preventing women from cutting their hair, as men were encouraged to do, was unjust; though he added that haircuts would mainly be beneficial because they would promote women's virtue.[49] Sakatani's influential discussion of women, then, focused mainly on private matters. Nakamura Masanao, who had called for educating "wise mothers, good mothers" (*kashikoi haha, yoi haha*) in an influential speech at the opening of Tokyo Women's Normal School in 1874, continued his discussion, in the pages of *Meiroku zasshi* in 1875, of the role of compassionate and educated mothers in giving birth to good children and then educating them in spirituality, morality, and arts and sciences.[50] Fukuzawa Yukichi, perhaps the most famous early participant in the "*fujin ronsō*" (dispute about women), and author of the influential *Nihon fujinron* in 1885, stressed monogamy as the basis of equality (*byōdō*).[51] Elsewhere, Fukuzawa linked "equality" closely to education.

Like Fukuzawa, female advocates for women also linked education, monogamy, and respect. Moving beyond the printed word alone, women advocates took the feminist message to the public through political speeches, like those of (Nakajima) Kishida Toshiko and Fukuda Kageyama Hideko, or through organizing civic groups and thereby moving into and helping to develop civil society in Meiji Japan. Kishida gave scores of speeches between 1882 and 1884. Her talks were pointedly political, calling for equal rights for men and women, decrying the stultifying effects of repression of freedom of thought, denouncing the equating of personhood with male gender alone[52] and, above all, calling on women to develop the mental strength (*seishin ryoku*) to be confident public persons.[53] Kishida rhetorically connected the development of women's subjectivity—their existence as persons in society—both to national strength and to People's Rights politics. Because "[e]quality, independence, respect, and a monogamous relationship are the hallmarks of relationships between men and women in a civilized society," she stated, women's rights would elevate Japan in international esteem and thereby aid in its defense against a possible Western threat.[54] Kishida also gave sexual inequality a political twist her colleagues in the People's Rights movement should not fail to grasp when she equated male supremacy with the government's dominion over the people—as in her speech entitled "The government is the people's god; man is woman's god" ("Seifu wa jinmin no ten; otoko wa onna no ten").[55]

Kishida inspired women all over Japan.[56] Women's groups sprang up in cities and towns, large and small—many of them to welcome speakers like Kishida. There were women's friendly societies (*joshi konshinkai*), women's freedom parties (*fujin jiyūtō*), women's rights associations (*jokenkai*), women's societies (*fujin kyōkai*), and at least one women's freedom hall (*joshi jiyūkan*).[57] Whether these groups continued to exist long after they sponsored Kishida and others is unclear. Yet they did have specific goals, and they did participate in feminist debates that continued in later decades. Their role in disseminating ideas of rights and reforms is as significant as their role in involving women in nongovernmental advocacy groups outside the home. Moreover, they helped set the stage for the growth of larger and more influential feminist groups, such as the Japan Christian Women's Reform Society (Nihon Kirisutokyō fujin kyōfukai) or the Women's Morality Association

(Fujin tokugikai) in the next half decade, and they created a context for the expansion of women's rights discourses in magazines and journals in the 1890s.[58] These groups dealt with political advocacy on behalf of monogamy and women's sexual dignity, political discussion, and collaborative feminist efforts to set up schools for girls and women.[59] "*Joseiron*" (discourse on femininity) carried out by these groups meant discourses on ways to improve women's lot through politicizing the private by means of education, marital respect, and the relationship of these to public voice and self-cultivation.

Educator Fukuda Hideko followed in Kishida's footsteps.[60] Inspired by Kishida, the young Hideko founded a community women's group that brought in speakers on natural rights, equality, and freedom.[61] Though her school was closed by the government and she herself jailed, her efforts were lauded by feminists who celebrated her release in 1889.[62] The following year, Fukuda petitioned the Diet to permit women's political participation—a clear use of what she viewed as her right to address the government.[63] In 1891, Fukuda caught the attention of the mainstream media with her proposal to establish a newspaper for women run entirely by women.[64] Like Kishida, Fukuda tied women's rights and political involvement to strengthening the nation.[65] Though more famous than most of their contemporaries, Fukuda and Kishida were not alone among women who translated into notable political action their desire for the right of inclusion, for education, and for respect that came with personhood.

Thus, a wealth of commentary on education and rights, in print and in speeches of the People's Rights advocates and embedded in the structure and philosophy of separate educational institutions for boys and girls,[66] informed thinking in the late 1880s when new publications directed at educated women began to be published. Women's rights discourse in the late nineteenth century took many forms, of course. But fundamental to all discussion was the connection between *joken* and *jogaku* (women's education). While the content of rights discourse had changed by the middle of the 1880s, the examination of rights within the family continued in the pages of magazines like *Jogaku zasshi*, discussed in the next section. There was no simple unidirectional trajectory in the development of ideas of women's rights and education. For example, Tsuda Umeko, who taught for a while at Meiji Jogakkō before founding her own school, eschewed political rights for women while fighting tenaciously for their right to prove their worth through educational accomplishment.[67] Positing a polarization between the state and society, Tsuda argued that women's responsibilities to serve society meant that they must be educated as good mothers,[68] but that they had no obligations to the state.[69]

Discourses on Education, Morality, and Rights in Late Meiji

The most important of the new journals for women in the 1880s was *Jogaku zasshi* (Women's education journal), co-founded by Iwamoto Yoshiharu (Zenji) in 1885, and edited by him for most of its eighteen years. *Jogaku zasshi* employed the talents of numerous writers, including at least eight women known in their day as advocates of rights, both women's rights and people's rights; the most famous of these were probably Shimizu Toyoko, Kishida Toshiko, and Wakamatsu Shizu (who married Iwamoto in 1889).[70] All were influenced by the readily accessible thought of the Freedom and People's Rights polemicists as well as lively intellectual discourse in other publications like the *Meiroku zasshi* of the previous decade and *Kokumin no tomo*, a journal that shared a readership with *Jogaku zasshi*.[71] From these sources, the writers were influenced by a diverse body of thought on rights.

Jogaku zasshi, as a journal that took women's education seriously, treated the issues of *jogaku* and *joken* in numerous editorials and articles. These two terms were used extensively over the entire period, but their meanings kept shifting, and therefore their intersections shifted as well. Writing in *Jogaku zasshi*'s predecessor, *Jogaku shinshi* (New women's education journal), in 1884, Iwamoto defined the term *jogaku* as a type of education that concerned the body and soul, the future, and the status of women;[72] until the day when there was human education, *jogaku* would be necessary, he added.[73] His working with the term *jogaku* became more sophisticated four years later when, in a response to economist Taguchi Ukichi's questioning of the neologism "jogaku" in an article in *Tokyo Keizai zasshi*—a journal founded by Taguchi—Iwamoto felt compelled to clarify his thinking. Taguchi wondered why there should be *jogaku* (literally "female education") if there were no *dangaku* (literally "male education").[74] Iwamoto replied, in an article entitled "Jogaku no kai," that *jogaku* had multiple meanings—the education of women (*joshi no kyōiku*) and education for or about women (*joshi no gakumon*); thus it could mean either a type of education geared to women or women's studies.[75] Moreover, he wrote, *jogaku* was the key to women's rights in that it would raise the position of women, extend their rights, and promote their welfare.[76]

Raising women's status had particular and changing meanings to Iwamoto. In 1885, Iwamoto stressed that women's human character must be recognized.[77] He argued for the fundamental equality of men and women although he rejected male/female equal *rights*.[78] The phrase "respect the male, despise the female" (*danson johi*) was particularly odious to Iwamoto.[79] Christianity, which permeated Iwamoto's thinking, emphasized the equal humanity of men and women in the eyes of God.[80] That women must not be seen as less than human, he wrote in 1885, did not imply that men and women must be granted equal rights; servants are human, too, but they do not have the same rights as their employers.[81] Though Iwamoto believed in gender equality before God, he—as did many contemporary social contract theorists in the West whose grounding was also in Christianity—took social stratification by gender as perfectly natural.[82]

From the mid-1880s to the early 1890s, when Iwamoto fervently espoused education for women, he also believed that the purpose of women's education should differ from men's. Women must be trained to be good wives and mothers—but he called for a "modern" type of wife and mother.[83] Christian, modern (*kirisutokyōteki, kindaiteki*) thinking would respect men and women for the particular roles each fulfilled. It would elevate women's status. It would create mothers who were intelligent and wives who were good persons, and not merely mothers who were wise educators of their children and wives who served their husbands well.[84] But it would not require political rights.[85] Such a concept of rights, which would set a woman apart from the community constituted by her family, was alien to Iwamoto's communitarian construction of rights at that time. To counter opponents' criticism that educated women made bad wives, *Jogaku zasshi* extolled the virtues of an educated wife.[86]

By 1887, editorials in *Jogaku zasshi*, which reflected Iwamoto's views, asserted that women's rights, women's work and economic independence, and equal respect in marriage would be enhanced by women's education. The editorials conveyed a sense of optimism that the course of Japan's modernization would be progressive if the need to investigate the true nature of men and women based on concepts of equality were recognized; if correct education, understanding of rights discourse, and interactions between men and women were developed; if prostitution was eliminated; if monogamy was fostered; if a modern home based on the human bond between husband and wife was created; and if other reforms were undertaken.

· Iwamoto was bitterly disappointed in the 1889 Constitution. His sense of betrayal when he read that gender determined imperial succession[87] comes across as surprising naiveté. But interestingly, it was after this shock that Iwamoto adopted a new approach to women's education and to women's rights. In a June 1889 article entitled "100-Year Chronic Disease" ("Hyaku-nen no koshitsu"), Iwamoto presented a stinging criticism of sexism in education.[88] If Japanese opposed women's high schools, objected to women voting, objected to monogamy, insulted the morality of female students, and failed to regard men and women as equally human, then Japan would never cure its century-long chronic disease. The ruler would be separated from the people, the people from the officials, the slave from the master, the rich from the poor. It is remarkable how advocacy of the education of women, of Christian moralism, of religious egalitarianism, and of women's civil rights are all brought under one discursive umbrella. Moreover, the article's rhetorical device of equating the disease with standard symbols of Tokugawa authoritarianism like the separation of the ruler and the ruled or the people and the officials is a powerful one.

Jogaku zasshi published a number of criticisms of the denial of women's right of political inclusion in 1890. In an unsigned article, *Jogaku zasshi* called for women to take part in political discussions in order to promote "political harmony among men and women" (*seijijō danjo kyōwa*).[89] Shimizu Toyoko wrote in August 1890, condemning the recent passage of legislation barring women from political meetings, that "if individual rights are to be protected, and the peace and order of society secured, laws should not be discriminatory, granting advantage to men only, and misfortune only to women."[90] In another article two months later, Shimizu considered it irrational that "one part of humanity arbitrarily controls . . . the other part."[91] These articles indicate Shimizu's individual rights based concept of women's rights as well as her displeasure with the denial of women's agency.

Iwamoto, two years later, expanded on some of these aspects of rights discourse and added education to the mix. In an important article that seemed to completely reject his earlier stress on men's and women's fulfillment of their naturally defined duties, he called for a much freer and more unfettered education for the girls at Meiji Jogakkō and other schools. In an 1892 installment of the series of articles entitled "Gotō no joshi kyōiku" (Our side's women's education), he considered the gender essentialism increasingly dominating the higher schools for women to be a violation of "true womanhood" (*makoto no josei*). Though the terminology was the same as that used in Western discourse, "true womanhood" had specific meanings for Iwamoto. Gender essentialism was slavery, he wrote, because long-term discrimination against women had constructed a womanly nature that was probably unreal, so no one knew women's true nature. Until women's true nature could be determined, it was imperative to allow girl students the freedom to develop their minds. Conversely, too, education that permitted an individual's development would also free women's true nature from the shackles of discrimination, thereby permitting it to be observed. When and if differences between men's and women's nature were discovered, moreover, those differences must not become the basis of discriminatory treatment.[92]

Elsewhere in the "Gotō no joshi kyōiku" series Iwamoto revisited the issue of marriage and motherhood. Not only was education the key to a more egalitarian marriage, Iwamoto also wrote that women did not need to marry at all if they so chose. Along with other Japanese advocates of women's rights, Iwamoto had earlier problematized the marital relationship, attempting to insert rights in where several Western theorists had ignored them, although he argued from the same Christian viewpoint those theorists had originally used to deny full humanity to women. By 1892, Iwamoto was opening up a space for a respectable unmarried status. Although it was true, Iwamoto wrote, that women were the ones who bore children, that fact alone was not what made one a woman. Women and men were "psychologically, mentally, and socially" constructed.[93] Based on this notion, he expanded the definition of motherhood. Queen Victoria was mother of her nation, Heloise was the mother of love, and so on. Thus, girls' education should create mothers who are intelligent and wives who are able to do good deeds in the public arena.[94] At the height of the Sino-Japanese War, however, Iwamoto appeared to be adopting a view that naturalized women's separate status in the family when he advocated the equation of their domestic role with national service for wives: that is, that the home is equivalent to the battlefield.[95]

Many advocates of women's rights focused on sexuality issues in their struggle for developing women's personhood and dignity. The heterosexual relationship was problematized early on in the discussions on womanhood, as seen in the early discussions by *Meiroku zasshi* writers. These articles stressed the damage done by polygamy to Japanese ethical values and Japan's resulting weakness in the face of the West. Feminists expanded these ideas and discussed control of sexuality— that of men and of some women—as a way of improving women's conditions and helping their development as full, equal human beings.

Sexuality issues were increasingly politicized after the founding of the Tokyo (later Japan) Christian Women's Reform Society by Yajima Kajiko in 1886.[96] The society's views on monogamy—as good for Japan, as respecting nature's gender balance, and as a move away from evil customs of the Confucian past—emerged in articles by and about the society's political activities in *Shinonome shinbun* and *Tōkyō fujin kyōfukai zasshi* in the late 1880s.[97] *Jogaku zasshi*, another source of information about the Reform Society, also stressed control of male sexuality through the banning of polygamy in an 1887 article by Iwamoto entitled "The Atmosphere of Adultery" ("Kan'in no kūki"), for which the entire issue in which it was to appear was banned by the government.[98]

Women's advocates viewed polygamy as a denigration of women's rights. For that reason, Yajima and others were passionate in their struggle against it—this was no abstraction to them. In 1889, Yajima delivered to government officials a petition with 800 signatures, demanding an end to concubinage. She took a dagger on this mission, prepared to commit suicide if she were unable to hand over her petition.[99] *Tokyo nichi nichi shinbun* reported that in November 1891, the Reform Society planned to submit a petition to the Diet for legislation banning polygamy. Thus, the Reform Society recognized the use of the power of the state in influencing equality in the marriage relationship.[100] Male morality was often at stake in these discussions; Shimizu, for instance, wrote "Discussing Japanese Males' Moral Character" ("Nihon danshi no hinkō o ronzu").[101]

Discussions about controlling all men's sexuality were accompanied by those concerning the control of some women's sexuality. Reform Society goals included the elimination of prostitution as well as concubinage as two sides of the same coin.[102] The sex trade denigrated wives by supporting husbands' adultery, and thus was seen as a women's rights issue that focused on legitimate wives. As for women in the sex trades themselves, Reform Society attitudes were often unsympathetic. The Reform Society's journal, *Tōkyō fujin kyōfu zasshi*, called for shaming women into leaving sex work: "Succumbing to the easier life of prostitution . . . they brazenly walk the streets in broad daylight. . . . There is no way to stop them other than to shame them into reforming!" Overseas prostitution, moreover, shamed Japan as a whole, the journal noted, and may have contributed to anti-Japanese discrimination in the United States.[103] The Reform Society's concern about prostitution was, in these types of comments, less connected to saving fallen women—which was, in fact, another goal of the organization—as it was to supporting the human dignity and equal personhood of wives.

Gaining subjectivity was an important requirement for eligibility for rights; and rights discourse was a well-used way of discussing subjectivity. The two were often elided. The issue of "morality" was essential to women's subjectivity. This can be seen, for instance, in the journal *Joken* (Women's rights). Established in September 1891, *Joken* included articles by leading feminists such as Fukuda Hideko and reported extensively on the activities of the Women's Morality Association throughout Japan.[104] The goals of various branches of this association called for freedom (*jiyū*), equality, women's rights, and morality (*tokugi*). [105] The Women's Morality Association's stated goal was "the expansion of women's rights and the elimination of the evil of 'respect the male and despise the female.'"[106] Like *Jogaku zasshi*, *Joken*, in an 1891 article entitled "People's Rights or Men's Rights?" (*Minken ka danken ka?*) strongly criticized the exclusion of women from the political world, arguing that "rights" should not be gendered.[107]

The Women's Reform Society and the Women's Morality Association attempted to push their agendas in the political arena. That venue was quite restricted, however. Even before the revisions of the Police Security Regulations of 1890, with its infamous "Article 5"—which banned women from all political participation, including political speaking and assembly—the City Code and Town and Village Code of 1888 pointedly excluded women from such participation.[108] Feminists submitted petitions to the Diet to eliminate these restrictions, but failed.[109] In response, feminist Shimizu Toyoko contributed her important article in *Jogaku zasshi*, "Why Are Women Not Permitted to Take Part in Political Meetings?" ("Naniyue ni joshi was seiden shūkai ni sanchō suru to o yurusarezaru ka?").[110] One response by the government, in turn, was a Diet member's assertion that women should not have political rights because they should focus on their work in the home—the first such assertion in the Diet.[111] Failing to gain a political voice, women's rights advocates did not abandon their causes, but turned even more attention to the issues of sexuality, which were now redefined as "social" rather than the banned "political." Economic independence became yet another part of feminists' quest for sexuality-based marital respect as social reforms.

Shimizu (and others) connected the rights of citizens (*kokumin*) with social and moral issues.[112] Women needed to be citizens—to have the right of participation—because they should educate their children as citizens and support their husbands in the exercise of their citizenship. Thus, Shimizu posited that women's political rights arose from their relationship with those who had (some) rights. This resonated with Kishida Toshiko's 1884 article, "Appeal to My Sisters" ("Dōhō shimai ni tsugu").[113] Women's advocacy groups, then, restructured the political to be more like the social or moral. Advocacy of improving women's conditions did not end with Article 5; concerns about morality, the home, economic conditions, and other issues took center stage as women moved increasingly into public realms of advocacy, or civil society. And women's education was essential to this ability to penetrate civil society, in its creation of a woman's personhood or subjectivity.

Conclusion

Notions of women's rights in late Meiji discussions of women's education encompassed marital equality, economic independence, overcoming denigration—as exemplified in the phrase "respect the male, despise the female"—and supporting women's dignity and subjectivity, as well as rights of societal or state participation. Discussion of *jogaku* could encompass a wide variety of meanings, each of which could be rhetorically used in different ways to improve the status of women and/or women's rights. Most importantly, they supported the notion of women's potential personhood, a necessary prerequisite for rights. The education arguments were revived by Taishō activists, and the parallels with Meiji thinking are strong.[114]

Was there any danger, however, in the quest for rights? Perhaps—because of the nationalistic meanings of political participation. As Carol Gluck notes in *Japan's Modern Myths*,

Ethical, national, and historical values were gradually intertwined in various renderings, the ideological amalgam of which was a catechism of citizenship that joined code and country in a newly generalized civil morality.[115]

If the type of morality catechized as the foundation for "citizenship" was derived from ethical, national, and historical values, that left much less room for the kinds of values espoused by advocates of women's rights. Under those circumstances, either women's rights advocates would become marginalized—which is exactly the opposite of their goal of inclusion—or they would be forced to compromise. The legacy of Meiji-era rights advocacy is, thus, quite complex. It left as unfinished business the meaning of inclusion if the family-state were left even marginally intact. The quest for women's rights must be applauded, but it must be viewed as part of the larger context for rights in an emperor-based system, a matter of continuing concern to prewar feminist-suffragist movements.

Notes

Parts of this essay have appeared in my essay, "Women's Rights and Japanese State, 1880–1925," in *Public Spheres, Private Lives in Modern Japan, 1600–1950: Essays in Honor of Albert Craig*, eds. Gail Bernstein, Andrew Gordon, and Kate Nakai (Cambridge, MA: Harvard University Asia Center, 2005), and my article "Women's Rights, Feminism, and Suffragism in Japan: 1870–1925," in *Pacific Historical Review* 69, no. 4 (2000): 639–661.

1. Fukuzawa Yukichi, "The Equal Numbers of Men and Women," *Meiroku zasshi* 31 (March 1875), in *Meiroku zasshi: Journal of the Japanese Enlightenment*, trans. William Reynolds Braisted (Cambridge, MA: Harvard University Press, 1976), 385.

2. Although the term "feminism" (*feminizumu*) was introduced in Japan after the period under consideration in this chapter—in a 1910 article in *Hōgaku kyōkai zasshi*—I shall use the term to refer to a broad range of discourses supportive of women's rights or the improvement of women's condition or status. See *Nihon josei no rekishi*, ed. Sōgō joseishi kenkyūkai (Kadokawa shoten, 1993), 192–193, for more on the introduction of the term "feminism."

3. Susan Mann has written persuasively that "contemporary Western feminism may remain parochial in its insistence that its own *telos* of freedom and agency be at work in every record of women's lives." See Mann, "The History of Chinese Women before the Age of Orientalism," *Journal of Women's History* 8, no. 4 (Winter 1997): 174. In the case of discussions about rights, writers were explicit about the quest for women's rights; the historian need not project her own feminist hopes of finding calls for agency.

4. George M. Wilson, *Patriots and Redeemers in Japan: Motives in the Meiji Restoration* (Chicago, IL: University of Chicago Press, 1992), offers an insightful treatment of Tokugawa anti-authoritarianism.

5. Mill's *On Liberty* was translated very early—in 1868. This translation was followed in the 1870s and early 1880s by translations of works by other Western political theorists. Rousseau's *Social Contract*, though translated later (1882) than Mill's work, was highly esteemed by People's Rights advocates. See *Japanese Thought in the Meiji Era*, ed. Masaaki Kosaka, vol. 8, *Japanese Culture in the Meiji Era* (Tōyō Bunko, 1969), 115, 146.

6. Michel Foucault, *History of Sexuality: An Introduction*, vol. 1 (New York: Vintage Books, 1980), 95.

7. Ueki Emori, cited in Roger W. Bowen, *Rebellion and Democracy in Meiji Japan: A Study of Commoners in the Popular Rights Movement* (Berkeley: University of California Press, 1980), 205. *Shisō, seiji: josei kaihō shisō no tenkai to fujin sanseiken undō,* ed. Suzuki Yūko, vol. 1, *Nihon josei undō shiryō shūsei* (Fuji shuppan, 1996), 23, notes that other than Ueki, whose writings about women's rights were inspired by the demand for voting rights by Kusunose Kita, few of the leading male People's Rights advocates discussed women's rights in their writings. Women like Fukuda and Kishida were, therefore, particularly important. See also Sharon Sievers, *Flowers in Salt: The Beginnings of Feminist Consciousness in Modern Japan* (Stanford, CA: Stanford University Press, 1983), 28–29.

8. Wendy Brown, *States of Injury: Power and Freedom in Late Modernity* (Princeton, NJ: Princeton University Press, 1995), 4.

9. See also Noriyo Hayakawa, "Feminism and Nationalism in Japan, 1868–1945," *Journal of Women's History* 7, no. 4 (Winter 1995): 111.

10. Sotozaki Mitsuhiro, *Fujin kaihō ronsō,* vol. 2, *Nihon fujinronshi* (Domesu, 1989), 22–24.

11. Kevin M. Doak notes that "civil society" (*shimin shakai*) came to be used in Japan in the 1920s, but the Japanese translation's urban implication (*shimin*) made it unpopular with rural folk. Doak, "What Is a Nation and Who Belongs? National Narratives and the Ethnic Imagination in Twentieth-Century Japan," *American Historical Review* 102, no. 2 (1997): 290.

12. One critic, in an 1897 *Chūō kōron* article, blamed Buddhism for this. See Muta Kazue, "Images of the Family in Meiji Periodicals: The Paradox Underlying the Emergence of the 'Home,'" *U.S.-Japan Women's Journal: English Supplement,* no. 7 (1994): 63.

13. Gad Prudovsky, "Can We Ascribe to Past Thinkers Concepts They Had No Linguistic Means to Express?" *History and Theory* 36, no. 1 (February 1997): 15–31.

14. Carole Pateman, *The Sexual Contract* (Stanford, CA: Stanford University Press, 1988), 11.

15. Brown, *States of Injury,* 151.

16. See Martha Tocco's essay in this volume.

17. Iwamoto Yoshiharu, in *Taiyō,* "Katei" column, cited in Muta, "Images of the Family," 64. See also Kathleen Uno's chapter in this volume.

18. See e.g., Hozumi Yatsuka, quoted in Kosaka, *Thought*, 381, 383. "Family" was not seen in the same light by conservatives and by feminists. For feminists, the family was made up of loving members whose sexually differentiated but complementary roles were to be equally valued. Conservatives found that definition of the family threatening, believing that it could undermine the foundation of the Japanese authoritarian state. That is, as the influential conservative legal scholar Hozumi wrote in 1896, "The obedience to . . . the headship of the family is, inferentially, what we confer on the Imperial House as the extant progenitor of the nation"; or, in 1898, "The family expanded becomes the country . . . we cannot be indifferent to whether the family institution is maintained or abolished!"

19. For more on Rousseau's ideas, see e.g., Carole Patemen, *Sexual Contract.*

20. See e.g., Sievers, *Flowers in Salt,* 52; and Yasukawa Junosuke and Yasukawa Etsuko, *Josei sabetsu no shakai shisōshi* (Akaishi shobo, 1993), chapter 1.

21. On "fraternity" see e.g., Donald Roden, *Schooldays in Imperial Japan: A Study in the Culture of a Student Elite* (Berkeley: University of California Press, 1980).

22. Suzuki, *Shisō, seiji,* 18.

23. See e.g., Andrew Gordon, *Labor and Imperial Democracy in Prewar Japan* (Berkeley: University of California Press, 1991).

24. Most men, regardless of social or economic class, were included in the electorate by *fusen* (universal suffrage) legislation passed in 1925. The first national (Diet) election in which this expanded electorate could vote was the 1928 election.

25. As well as commentary by Sotozaki, *Fujin kaihō ronsō*; Fujita Yoshimi, *Meiji jogakkō no sekai* (Shōeisha, 1984); Aoyama Nao, *Meiji jogakkō no kenkyū* (Keiō tsūshin, 1982); and Noheji Kyōe, *Josei kaihō shisō no genryū* (Azekura shobo, 1984).

26. Patrilineality is effectively problematized by Kathleen Uno in "Questioning Patrilineality: On Western Studies of the Japanese *Ie*." *positions* 4, no. 3 (Winter 1996): 569–594. She argues convincingly that scholars have often distorted the historical roles of patrilineality. Meiji women's rights advocates also strongly contested what they saw as continuing patterns of women's subordination through patrilineality and its ties with the other "p's" of patriarchy, prostitution, and polygamy.

27. Brown, *States of Injury,* 98.

28. For an extended discussion of Meiji Civil Code, see *Japanese Legislation in the Meiji Era,* ed. Ryosuke Ishii, vol. 10, *Japanese Culture in the Meiji Era* (Tōyō Bunko, 1969), 601–692.

29. Ironically, critics of the individual rights basis of the first draft of the Civil Code complained that the code smacked of "European" civil rights ideas.

30. Pateman, *The Sexual Contract, passim,* and Yasukawa and Yasukawa, *Josei sabetsu,* chapter 1.

31. Noheji, *Josei kaihō shisō,* 14.

32. Pioneering work in English on Meiji-era feminists was done by historian Sharon Sievers, whose often used and cited classic, *Flowers in Salt,* was the first English language book to take Meiji feminism seriously.

33. Fukuda Hideko, quoted in Sotozaki, *Fujin kaihō ronsō,* 44. Some socialists moved away from talking about rights because women did not have the freedom to make contracts, on which political rights were based. Since rights were meaningless in that context, many socialists turned to other forms of social and labor reform to improve women's conditions and status.

34. Sotozaki, *Fujin kaihō ronsō,* 28.

35. Works treating early twentieth-century feminist activism are numerous. For a sampling in English, see Sharon H. Nolte and Sally Ann Hastings, "The Meiji State's Policy toward Women, 1890–1910," in *Recreating Japanese Women: 1600–1945,* ed. Gail Lee Bernstein (Berkeley: University of California Press, 1991); Mikiso Hane, *Reflections on the Way to the Gallows: Rebel Women in Prewar Japan* (Berkeley: University of California Press, 1988); Sharon H. Nolte, "Women's Rights and Society's Needs: Japan's 1931 Suffrage Bill," *Comparative Studies in Society and History* 28, no. 4 (1986): 690–714; Sheldon M. Garon, "The World's Oldest Debate? Prostitution and the State in Imperial Japan," *American Historical Review* 98, no. 3 (1993): 710–732, and "Women's Groups and the Japanese State: Contending Approaches to Political Integration, 1890–1945," *Journal of Japanese Studies* 19, no. 1 (1993): 5–41; Helen Hopper, *A New Woman of Japan: A Political Biography of Katō Shidzue* (Boulder, CO: Westview Press, 1996); Kathleen Molony, "Feminist Ideology in Prewar Japan," in *Proceedings of the Tokyo Symposium on Women,* eds. Merry I. White and Barbara Molony (Tokyo: International Group for the Study of Women, 1979); and Vera Mackie, *Creating Socialist Women in Japan* (Cambridge: Cambridge University Press, 1997).

36. Roden, *Schooldays in Imperial Japan,* 146, 139.

37. See chapters by Martha Tocco, Donald Roden, and Barbara Sato.

38. See e.g., Sievers's discussion of the Women's Reform Society in her *Flowers in Salt*, 87–114.

39. See e.g., Muta, "Images of the Family," 62–63, who offers important evidence that articles on "women's rights" peaked in 1886, to be replaced by those focusing on *katei*.

40. Hiratsuka Raichō, "Yo no fujintachi ni," *Seitō* 3, no. 4 (1913), quoted in Noheji, *Josei kaihō shisō*, 157.

41. Barbara Molony, "Ichikawa Fusae and Japan's Prewar Women's Suffrage Movement," in *Japanese Women: Emerging from Subservience, 1868–1945*, ed. Hiroko Tomida and Gordon Daniels (Folkestone, UK: Global Oriental, 2005).

42. Yamaguchi Miyoko, *Meiji keimōki no fujin mondai ronsō no shūhen* (Domesu, 1989), 186.

43. See Kathleen Uno's discussion of the "good wife, wise mother" ideal in this volume.

44. See Mori Arinori, "On Wives and Concubines, Part Three," *Meiroku zasshi* 15 (August 1874), in Braisted, *Meiroku zasshi*, 189–191, and also his "On Wives and Concubines, Part Four," *Meiroku zasshi* 20 (November 1874), in Braisted, *Meiroku zasshi*, 252–253.

45. Tsuda Mamichi, "The Distinction between Husbands and Wives," *Meiroku zasshi* 22 (December 1874), in Braisted, *Meiroku zasshi*, 277.

46. Tsuda Mamichi, "On Government, Part Three," *Meiroku zasshi* 12 (June 1874), in Braisted, *Meiroku zasshi*, 155–159.

47. Tsuda Mamichi, "Distinguishing the Equal Rights of Husbands and Wives," *Meiroku zasshi* 35 (April 1875), in Braisted, *Meiroku zasshi*, 435–436.

48. Sakatani Shiroshi, "On Concubines," *Meiroku zasshi* 32 (March 1875), in Braisted, *Meiroku zasshi*, 392–399. Sakatani may have been betraying his class snobbery, as he took as his example of excessive women's rights the spectacle, which he found distasteful, of a lower-class Tokyo wife yelling at her husband for cruelly selling her clothes.

49. Sakatani Shiroshi, "Female Decorations," *Meiroku zasshi* 21 (November 1874), in Braisted, *Meiroku zasshi*, 271.

50. Yamaguchi, *Meiji keimōki*, 194. Nakamura was the first president of Tokyo Women's Normal School.

51. Ibid., 199. For an extensive treatment of the philosophical basis for Fuku-zawa's thought on equality and on education, see Yasukawa and Yasukawa, *Josei sabetsu*, 36–104.

52. Suzuki, *Shisō, seiji*, 56–85, offers a wealth of information about Kishida and her public activities. Newspaper articles, reprinted here, show that Kishida had an extraordinarily busy schedule, rushing from city to city to speak out—with occasional censorship by the police—on women's rights.

53. Kishida Toshiko, "Dōhō shimai ni tsugu," reprinted in Suzuki, *Shisō, seiji*, 74–85.

54. Kishida, "Dōhō," quoted and translated by Sievers, *Flowers in Salt*, 38.

55. Suzuki, *Shisō, seiji*, 57.

56. Ibid., 56.

57. Ibid., 71–73, has articles describing the founding of several of these groups.

58. Hirota Masaki, "Kindai eriito josei no aidentiti to kokka," in *Jiendaa no Ni-honshi*, eds. Wakita Haruko and S.B. Hanley, vol. 1 (Tōkyō daigaku shuppankai, 1994), 203, is not impressed with the Okayama Women's Friendly Society, not-ing that its members were merely wives and daughters of men in the People's Rights movement. He contrasts this group with those formed by women not related to male activists.

59. Suzuki, *Shisō, seiji*, 98.

60. Sievers, *Flowers in Salt*, 36.

61. Hane, *Reflections on the Way to the Gallows*, 36.

62. Suzuki, *Shisō, seiji*, 95.

63. Ibid., 127.

64. Ibid., 98.

65. Hirota, "Kindai eriito josei," 202.

66. Sōgō joseishi kenkyūkai, *Nihon josei no rekishi*, 195–197. See also the chapters by Kathleen Uno and Martha Tocco in this volume.

67. Barbara Rose, *Tsuda Umeko and Women's Education in Japan* (New Haven, CT: Yale University Press, 1992), 103.

68. Rose, *Tsuda Umeko*, 102.

69. Ibid., 134.

70. Fujita, *Meiji jogakkō no sekai*, 35, 79, and Noheji, *Josei kaihō shisō*, 24. The others were Tanabe Hanaho, Ogino Ginko, Yoshida Nobuko, Andō Tane, and Kojima Kiyo.

71. Noheji, *Josei kaihō shisō*, 68.

72. Aoyama, *Meiji Jogakkō no kenkyū*, 676.

73. Noheji, *Josei kaihō shisō*, 108.

74. Aoyama, *Meiji Jogakkō no kenkyū*, 676.

75. Noheji, *Josei kaihō shisō*, 105.

76. Ibid., 9.

77. Ibid., 129.

78. Ibid., 128.

79. Ibid., 133.

80. Aoyama, *Meiji Jogakkō no kenkyū*, 7.

81. Noheji, *Josei kaihō shisō*, 129.

82. Rebecca L. Copeland finds Iwamoto less encouraging of women. Indeed, she writes, he trivialized women writers. See Copeland's "The Meiji Woman Writer 'Amidst a Forest of Beards,'" *Harvard Journal of Asiatic Studies* 57 (1997): 388.

83. Noheji, *Josei kaihō shisō*, 155, notes that the four characters—*ryō, sai, ken,* and *bo*—were used throughout "Gotō no joshi kyōiku." Iwamoto's use of "good wife, wise mother" (*ryōsai kenbo*), Noheji notes, differed from that of his contemporaries in his stress on Christianity as the basis for that type of education.

84. Iwamoto Yoshiharu, "Gotō no joshi kyōiku," a short collection, which first appeared as articles in *Jogaku zasshi* from 1890 to 1892, cited in Noheji, *Josei kaihō shisō*, 82–83, 131–32, and 139–158.

85. Noheji, *Josei kaihō shisō*, 131.

86. Ibid., 112.

87. Ibid., 14.

88. Iwamoto Yoshiharu, "Hyaku-nen no koshitsu," *Jogaku zasshi* no. 167 (June 22, 1889), cited in Noheji, *Josei kaihō shisō*, 137.

89. Suzuki, *Shisō, seiji*, 125–126.

90. Shimizu, quoted in Sievers, *Flowers in Salt*, 52–53, and Suzuki, *Shisō, seiji*, 127.

91. Shimizu, quoted in Sievers, *Flowers in Salt*, 101.

92. Noheji, *Josei kaihō shisō*, 139, 143, 145.

93. "Gotō no joshi kyōiku," cited in Noheji, *Josei kaihō shisō*, 151.

94. Ibid., 151–152.

95. Muta, "Images of the Family," 64. See also Kathleen Uno's chapter in this volume.

96. "Fujin kyōfukai," in *Asano shinbun*, December 12, 1886, reprinted in Suzuki, *Shisō, seiji*, 85. See also Sumiko Otsubo's chapter in this volume.

97. See Suzuki, *Shisō, seiji*, 86–94, who cites several articles from these journals.

98. Aoyama, *Meiji Jogakkō no kenkyū*, 4.

99. Yukiko Matuskawa and Kaoru Tachi, "Women's Suffrage and Gender Politics in Japan," in *Suffrage and Beyond: International Feminist Perspectives*, eds. Caroline Daley and Melanie Nolan (New York: New York University Press, 1994): 174.

100. "Ippu ippu no seigan," *Tokyo nichi nichi shinbun*, November 26, 1891, reprinted in Suzuki, *Shisō, seiji*, 92.

101. Shimizu Toyoko, "Nihon danshi no hinkō o ronzu," in *Shinonome shinbun*, May 8–10, 1889, reprinted in Suzuki, *Shisō, seiji*, 111–114.

102. Muta Kazue, "Senryaku to shite no onna," *Shisō* (February 1992): 220–227, and Sievers, *Flowers in Salt*, 95.

103. *Tokyo fujin kyōfu zasshi*, September 20, 1890, cited in Sievers, *Flowers in Salt*, 214n.

104. Suzuki, *Shisō, seiji*, 132–142, cites several articles about the Women's Morality Association in various locations.

105. At the same time, the Ministry of Education, in its compendium of regulations, stated that the goal of women's education was "womanly morality" (*jotoku*). Womanly morality required that the focus of girls' education be the fostering of "docility" (*wajun*) toward one's husband and "chastity" (*teisō*). This morality theme, which contrasted with the goals of the Women's Morality Association, was reiterated in another journal established in 1891, *Jokan* (Women's mirror). See Sōgō joseishi kenkyūkai, *Nihon josei no rekishi*, 197.

106. Women's Morality Association goals, stated in "Fujin tokugikai kaisoku," *Joken*, September 29, 1891, reprinted in Suzuki, *Shisō, seiji*, 141–142. The organization limited membership to women.

107. "Minken ka danken ka," *Joken*, 29 September 1891, reprinted in Suzuki, *Shisō, seiji*, 141.

108. Suzuki, *Shisō, seiji*, 26.

109. Petitions and reactions, cited in Suzuki, *Shisō, seiji*, 126–131.

110. Entire article reprinted in Suzuki, *Shisō, seiji*, 127–129; excerpted translations in Sievers, *Flowers in Salt*, 52–53.

111. Suzuki, *Shisō, seiji*, 26–27, and Hayakawa, "Feminism and Nationalism," 111.

112. "Citizenship" is a complicated term in this period. See Atsuko Hirai's insightful commentary on terms translated as "citizen" in "State and Ideology in Meiji Japan—A Review Article," *Journal of Asian Studies* 46, no. 1 (1987): 89–103.

113. Hirota, "Kindai eriito josei," 202.

114. Hiratuska Raichō was one of many who picked up on Iwamoto's themes. Noheji, *Josei kaihō shisō*, 85.

115. Carol Gluck, *Japan's Modern Myths: Ideology in the Late Meiji Period* (Princeton, NJ: Princeton University Press, 1987), 102.

14 Womanhood, War, and Empire: Transmutations of "Good Wife, Wise Mother" before 1931

Kathleen Uno

Western historians have begun to explore diverse aspects of gender policy during Japan's modern era (1868–1945). This quest began in the 1980s with research focused primarily on policies toward women rather than men or both women and men. As Sharon Sievers considered the roots of Japanese feminism, she also illuminated issues of state policy and women's political rights; meticulous research by Sharon Nolte analyzed policies that blocked women's efforts to attain formal political participation. Sally Hastings, Gregory Pflugfelder, Mariko Tamanoi, Sheldon Garon, and I have analyzed efforts by government officials and institutions to mobilize women for nonpolitical participation in national affairs. Sandra Wilson has discussed the wartime mobilization of women, while Vera Mackie has explored aspects of socialist women's interactions with the prewar state.[1] At the present time, studies in modern Japanese women's history on a wide range of topics continue to proliferate as investigations of developments in the history of masculinity are beginning to flourish.[2]

In making the socialization of "good wife, wise mother" (*ryōsai kenbo*) the aim of the new higher girls' schools (*kōtō jogakkō*),[3] in 1898, the Education Ministry (Monbushō) intervened conspicuously in the process of gender construction on the heels of the first Sino-Japanese War (1894–1895). The creation of a separate secondary education track for girls as well as its emphasis on moral education and homemaking skills channeled young women toward a domestic destiny rather than wage employment, cultural and intellectual pursuits, or political activities in the public sphere. Yet a growth of educational opportunities, capitalist development, urbanization, waves of popular social and political activism, and above all the growth of Japan's formal and informal overseas empire brought changes to Japanese society, including the worlds of Japanese women, as the twentieth century progressed. What, if any, modifications of *ryōsai kenbo* took place as Japan's empire expanded, increasing numbers of women attended the higher girls' schools, the ranks of employed women swelled, publications for female readers proliferated, and women participated in public affairs in fields ranging from relief and charitable projects to feminist, labor, and socialist movements?

The intent of this chapter is to interrogate the development of "good wife, wise mother," a central concept in the state's vision of womanhood, from the late nineteenth century to the beginning of the Pacific War in 1931. In general, Western studies of Japanese women, gender, and society have taken for granted the existence of strong or state-prescribed norms of womanhood, with *ryōsai kenbo* most commonly described as an unchanging, oppressive ideology. For example, studies published since the 1980s by Sievers, Robert J. Smith, Sharon Nolte and Sally Hastings, Yoshiko Miyake, Kuniko Fujimura-Fanselow, Shizuko Koyama, Ulrike Woehr, and I contain limited discussions of *ryōsai kenbo*. While some of these works sketch aspects of its historical evolution, a comprehensive study of its prewar evolution has yet to appear.[4]

The Japanese language scholarship is extensive. Earlier works present *ryōsai kenbo* as a lynchpin in the ideology of the prewar emperor system, the repressive, militaristic state that led Japan into the disastrous Pacific War (1931–1945). Although in this literature *ryōsai kenbo* is often linked to early modern (1600–1867) and imported Western notions of womanhood, there has been relatively little concern with tracing its twentieth-century shifts. Most later works by younger Japanese scholars have tried to recuperate *ryōsai kenbo,* emphasizing its modernity, especially the greater domestic and social agency that it awarded to women as mothers. Again, the principal contrast is between early modern and modern notions of womanhood. A few recent works by writers in each camp, most notably Nakajima Kuni, Tachi Kaoru, and Koyama Shizuko, discuss changes in *ryōsai kenbo* over time.[5]

In starting to track the twentieth-century trajectory of "good wife, wise mother," this essay takes these Japanese revisionist works as a point of departure. Yet this chapter diverges somewhat from recent

Japanese scholarship in attempting to root changes in *ryōsai kenbo* in the dynamics of empire and war, without neglecting such other important factors as the growth of female education and employment, diffusion of Western notions of romantic love, companionate marriage, and the influences of feminism and the mass media. During the first three decades of the twentieth century,[6] overseas expansion in times of war and peace was a crucial engine of growth, and Japan's participation in three successive wars sparked fresh consideration of women's responsibilities toward state and society. Between the first Sino-Japanese War and the 1931 Manchurian Incident, prewar nationalism, the guiding star of the quest for empire and power, influenced reconceptualizations of *ryōsai kenbo* and the formulation of other notions of women's possible service to state and society, even among educators and social observers located outside the institutional structure of the state.

This study, based on preliminary research, offers a working hypothesis rather than a definitive statement or interpretation of *ryōsai kenbo*'s evolution before the Pacific War. More extensive investigation is needed to analyze comprehensively changes in this crucial early twentieth-century notion of the feminine and to explore more fully the linkages between women, gender, and state in prewar Japan. Pending further research, this essay argues that shifts in *ryōsai kenbo* were more than simply a response to rising educational levels or the progress of industrialization in Japan during the opening decades of the twentieth century. Widespread nationalism as well as official and nonofficial reactions to overseas expansion, foreign confrontations, and war—the wellsprings of empire—exerted a profound influence on the genesis and subsequent reformulations of *ryōsai kenbo* as private Japanese citizens and the state sought to cope with pressing social, economic, and political issues before 1931.

Late Nineteenth-Century Origins of "Good Wife, Wise Mother" and Educated Motherhood

On the whole, from the 1868 Meiji Restoration to the end of the nineteenth century, the Japanese state lacked an explicit, consistent gender policy, even though its leaders implemented many military, economic, and political reforms to enhance national security. The creation of loyal citizens who would serve the new nation was a major concern. Founded in 1872 to mold children into sound citizens, the modern educational system mandated compulsory education for both genders.[7] Yet despite the gender blindness of the new school policies, there were noticeable gender asymmetries in other early state policies. In the 1870s, women were not allowed to cut their hair short, and, as Theodore Cook discusses in this volume, "universal" conscription required only male youths to serve emperor, country, and later empire in its newly constituted armed forces. Although excluded from this form of national service, some Japanese women responded to calls to save the nation. Influenced by study and exposure to Western political ideas, as early as the 1880s, a handful of Japanese women sought direct participation in public affairs for their gender. Promulgation of the constitution in 1889 rudely dashed their hopes to gain the vote. Also during the 1880s, women were banned from the academic middle and high schools as well as the civil service exams, greatly diminishing their opportunities for careers in the professions and government service. Yet as Janet Hunter explains in this volume, at lower levels of the public world, female blue-collar workers in the textile industry became the mainstays of the modern sector and remained so until 1930 when heavy industry began to dominate the economy. While a negative definition of womanhood—defined by what women could not do—gradually emerged from the prohibitions of the first three decades of the modern era, until the final years of the nineteenth century, the Japanese state lacked a *positive* vision of modern womanhood.

After mobilization for the nation's first modern conflict, the first Sino-Japanese War, Japanese leaders, especially Education Ministry officials, began to reconsider the state's de facto woman policy. Building on ideas formulated earlier by prominent educators, including a past education minister, the ministry adopted *ryōsai kenbo* as its prescription for Japanese womanhood. It also established a separate educational track for girls that included a nationwide network of public higher girls' schools, and added lessons explaining gender roles to its moral education textbooks in the elementary and middle schools. In the aftermath of the Russo-Japanese War (1904–1905), insights from the war and political turmoil, as well as concern over the moral fiber of citizens and economic distress during the postwar recession, led to renewed consideration of women's wartime role, the impact of war on women, and optimal womanhood in general. Participation in a third major armed conflict, World War I, again prompted re-evaluation and modifications of *ryōsai kenbo*. While the Japanese state's gender policies included more than just the Education Ministry's regulation of female schooling, as primary school enrollment rates of Japanese boys and girls had reached 98 percent by the late 1890s, *ryōsai kenbo* emerged as a key element. However, the vast educational establishment encompassing ministry officials, public schoolteachers, and principals was never the sole arbiter of this ideal. Throughout the era, private school educators, intellectuals, journalists, feminists, and young women themselves also contributed to the transmutation of *ryōsai kenbo* by creating competing notions of womanhood.[8]

Reassessment of women's social roles began shortly after the 1868 Meiji Restoration. Besides the structural innovations in the government, economy, and military organization, changes in social customs, including some aspects of early modern gender roles and gender relations, were proposed. Mixed bathing, public nudity, lack of consideration toward women, and other forms of public behavior were unpalatable to Westerners. Internationally minded Japanese realized that as long as their society and people were perceived as uncivilized, the great powers would not renegotiate the unequal treaties relegating Japan to an inferior position in the world order. In addition, some leaders came to cherish a vision of Japanese mothers as the socializers of the next generation of citizens needed to build and defend a strong Japanese nation-state. Education of girls to become wise mothers would ensure their future role as positive agents of national change. This re-evaluation of womanhood was part of the new regime's proposals for sweeping reforms to defend the country against the threat of Western imperialism. In this way, social as well as economic and political reforms became part of the agenda to strengthen Japan in the modern age.

Changes in motherhood for the sake of the nation gained imperial support very early in the new era. Embedded in the edict establishing the new school system was the notion that women as mothers merited a solid education. The Meiji Emperor (1852–1912) himself encouraged the education of women in a rescript encouraging nobles to travel abroad, stating that:

We still lack an established system of education for women in this country, and they are generally deficient in the power of judging and understanding things. How children grow up depends on how their mothers bring them up, and this is a matter of supreme importance. It is commendable that those who go abroad from now onward should take with them their wives and daughters or their sisters. These women would then see for themselves how other women receive their education in the lands they visit and would also learn the way to bring up their children.[9]

Likewise, two leading educators who were also strong nationalists strongly endorsed educated motherhood for the sake of the nation. With war as the catalyst, their ideas later crystallized into the *ryōsai kenbo* education policies after the first Sino-Japanese War. In "Creating Good Mothers" (1875), Nakamura Masanao (1832–1891), principal of Japan's first public higher girls' school in the 1870s, outlined the significance of motherhood for the advancement of Japanese culture, society, and state. He wrote that:

we must invariably have fine mothers if we want effectively to advance the people to . . . enlightenment and to alter their customs and conditions for the good. If the mothers are superb, they can have superb children, and Japan can become a splendid country in later generations. . . . Now to develop fine mothers, there is nothing better than to educate daughters.[10]

In 1876, Mori Arinori (1847–1889), Japan's first education minister from 1885 to 1889, also exalted motherhood, but lumped Japan together with other Asian countries in its lack of respect for women:

The position ordained for woman to occupy is one of the highest and most sa-cred ever created by the will of the Supreme Being. It is that of the mother of mankind in general, and of a country and family in particular. Women are the mothers of human beings; they are the mothers of the country and nation. Throughout Asia, women are looked down on . . . clearly it will take Asia several hundred years to reach [the position/situation of women in] Holland.[11]

A decade later, Mori's views on the significance of motherhood for the Japanese nation remained unchanged. In 1887, he elaborated on his earlier views:

The foundations of national prosperity rest on education. We must remember that the safety or peril of the state is related to the success or failure of women's education. It extremely important to foster consciousness of the nation in our education of women.[12]

Mori also emphasized the overriding importance of women's education in a speech to district administrators in Hyogo prefecture, advancing some startling arguments in an attempt to bolster support for girls' education among the skeptical local officials.

Regarding the sequence of education, girls' education should take precedence over that of boys. After all, girls differ from boys. When they bear children, immediately home education falls entirely into the hands of one compassionate mother whose calling [*tenshoku*] is to be a teacher. If women can acquire proper credentials as natural [*tennen*] teachers, [we educators] have achieved a complete victory.[13]

In that year, he also defined the purpose of women's education as "nurturing *ryōsai kenbo*" in one of his speeches, very likely employing the term for the first time in Japan.[14]

The Meiji Emperor, Nakamura, Mori, and Western advocates of educated motherhood agreed that Japan would benefit from training women to effectively exercise their innate capacity to instruct their children. The nationalism permeating their arguments for women's education reflects the preoccupations of the 1870s and 1880s—the drive to escape Western imperialism by implementing far-reaching reforms. Later, nationalism as well as national security concerns led Japan to pursue territorial imperialism, as did the Western powers. Anxiety about the nation's future led Meiji men in power to advocate the Western idea of educated motherhood in order to train the mothers who would shape the next generation of citizens. In a nutshell, their view was that "great mothers equal great children, and great children equal a great nation." That is, women's private labor in the home had public implications, and this seemingly private labor could contribute to national strength and development. However, because a vast number of leaders and ordinary Japanese still tended to view childrearing and housework as private labor in the private world of the home, there was little enthusiasm for girls' education beyond the elementary level until after the Sino-Japanese War.

In the 1890s, the educated motherhood of early Meiji combined with early modern notions of wives' responsibility for household management to form *ryōsai kenbo*. The notion of wives' authority over some forms of domestic and productive labor had strong roots in the household ideals and practices of all classes in early modern Japan, although actual tasks supervised and performed differed somewhat by economic status, occupation, and region.[15] Wealthy women did some household labor themselves in addition to supervising servants, while ordinary women did productive labor that contributed to the household livelihood in addition to housework and child care. While the Western notion of educated motherhood had less resonance with native traditions, it appealed to many policymakers and other proponents of modern reforms for two major reasons: it promised that Japanese children could be shaped into sturdy, patriotic adults who would contribute to the progress of the nation; and it was also compatible with the familiar Confucian dictum "the family is the root of the state." The novel element in *ryōsai kenbo*, then, was its stress on the significance of women's, especially mothers', role in the upbringing of children more than its prescriptions for wives.

Ryōsai Kenbo and the First Sino-Japanese War

The trials of war led to a new recognition of the contributions that women could make to the nation, and led as well to the incorporation of older ideas of wifehood and newer ideas of motherhood into a state prescription for womanhood. Victory over Asia's largest empire in the Sino-Japanese War, its first modern conflict, greatly magnified Japan's international prestige, but the war severely strained the nation's resources. As the battles raged, Japan's leaders became aware that success in modern warfare depended on a state's ability to mobilize its entire population, including its women, to unprecedented tasks for the duration of the conflict. New awareness of the value of mobilizing civilians on the home front brought forth a new educational policy for women with *ryōsai kenbo* at its core.

Neither Nakamura's "good mother" nor Mori's "compassionate mother" or "good wife, wise mother" had exerted widespread influence on norms or behavior before the first Sino-Japanese War. However, at the close of the war in spring 1895, officials in the Education Ministry and private educators began to support *ryōsai kenbo* in their publications and speeches.

Hosokawa Junjirō, a noted educator, pinpointed women's education as a source of national strength and military power in the May 1895 issue of *Dai Nippon kyōikukai zasshi* (Journal of the educational association of the Japanese empire). He also remarked on the difference between Japan and weaker Asian countries, and compared Japan favorably to strong Western nations.

[In] Korea it is not necessary to elaborate on the fact that . . . women's condition is most lamentable and . . . [their] educational facilities incomplete. . . . China is a great country . . . but beyond [schools teaching about] aspects of morality and clothing and food, one does not hear about educational facilities. . . . In India, it is said that women's education is almost nonexistent. The only girls who receive an education are from certain poor families who are offered to serve at temples . . . because some of the children attached to priests learn reading, writing, arithmetic, music, dance, etc. In Persia, it is said that . . . Western ways are diffusing and there are nationally established schools, but there is no system to educate girls in schools. . . . In Egypt, although it is said that women's position is high and that more than in other Eastern countries they have a spirit of independence [*dokuritsu kishō*], to the extent that they supervise trade, there has been no establishment of women's education . . . . When countries do well in developing their strength, they are never scorned by other countries. We hear from certain gentlemen about Korea and China's political affairs and customs, and we also hear from them that their military strength is inferior to ours. India has not been able to throw off British rule. . . . Persia was formerly a strong country, but now it is in decline and can barely maintain its territory. . . . This is sufficient to demonstrate the poverty and weakness of countries where women's education is not flourishing. In contrast, the Western nations that are said to be wealthy and powerful, that is, England, France, Germany, Austria, Russia, and the U.S.A., are places where women's education prospers. This is sufficient to demonstrate that wealthy and powerful countries have flourishing women's education. . . . In a word, can one not use women's education as the measure to rank the nations in terms of wealth and power?

 . . . If women are cut off from the world outside the home and don't venture outside, their vision is narrow; their outlook is limited to home and village; and they lack patriotism. It is as though half of the people [*kokumin*] do not exist. Although there are constraints on men who engage in national affairs, women receive almost no encouragement to participate in national affairs. Thus it is as if . . . [the nation] has lost the strength of half its population.[16]

In Hosokawa's view, educating women would strengthen Japan by augmenting its national strength, which, following the nation's success in armed conflict overseas, increasingly included the capability to wage war effectively. Through women's education, Japan could increase its competitive edge over other countries in terms of wealth, power, and military capacity.

Unlike Nakamura and Mori who admired Western models of womanhood, some conservative educational officials placed as much emphasis on "good wife" as "wise mother," largely because they cherished conceptions of womanhood such as those found in the early modern advice books for women, including dedication to household (*ie*), continuity, self-sacrifice, modesty, obedience to husband and in-laws, and frugality. However, one of the virtues of *ryōsai kenbo* was its ambiguity. Nationalists of liberal or conservative stripes could support it. Those more open to Western models could support "wise mother," derived from the notion of educated motherhood, while those who looked to Japan's own tradition could emphasize woman's role as "good wife," a frugal manager and hard worker in the enterprise household (*ie*).[17]

As shown in this chapter, after 1895 discussion of the positive contributions that women could make to national affairs surfaced frequently in the speeches of successive education ministers, and by the late 1890s, the term *ryōsai kenbo* itself appeared in official discourse. In 1895, Education Minister Saionji Kinmochi (1849–1940) stated, "We must without fail rely on the inner strength of ladies [*fujin*] in order to educate [*yōsei suru*] nationals. This is the reason that the Western countries apply the greatest effort to women's education."[18] Then in 1898, Minister Kabayama Sukenori (1937–1922) justified the ordinance mandating higher girls' schools as follows:

A sound middle-class society cannot be nurtured by educating boys alone. In cooperation with "wise mothers and good wives," they order the home well. Only then can the welfare of society be advanced. [The education at girls' high schools] is to nurture "wise mothers and good wives." Therefore in addition to nurturing dispositions of characters of grace and refinement and dispositions of gentleness and chasteness, they teach knowledge and virtues of the letters, sciences, and crafts needed in the daily life of the higher classes.[19]

Later, Education Minister Kikuchi Dairoku (1855–1917) expressed even stronger support for education fostering *ryōsai kenbo*. In June 1901 during his initial address as minister, he expounded at length on the goals of women's education. At the same time, he also reiterated the benefits the state derived from such education. He began by observing that girls and boys had separate but complementary duties, and should refrain from infringing on the duties of the opposite sex. According to Kikuchi, countries with many good homes (*katei*) flourish, while those with many bad homes decline. The home is the root of the state, but the quality of the housewife (*shufu*) determines the quality of the home. Since girls' mission was to marry and become "good wives and wise mothers," the purpose of girls' education was to prepare them fully for their calling. Therefore the presumption was that girls did not require vocational education.[20]

The Education Ministry's support for "good wife, wise mother" was not simply rhetorical; the concept became the philosophical foundation of girls' education, first at the secondary levels and finally at the elementary level as well.[21] To cultivate good wives and wise mothers, moral education and domestic science, rather than foreign languages, natural sciences, mathematics, or social sciences, became the core of girls' higher education.[22]

"Good Wife, Wise Mother" in the Aftermath of the Russo-Japanese War

The experience of war again brought about a reconsideration of Japanese notions of womanhood among educators, policymakers, and intellectuals. Within a decade of its inception, *ryōsai kenbo* underwent the first of a series of transformations. The Russo-Japanese War, even more than the first Sino-Japanese War, was a watershed in modern Japanese history. Japan had once more won a major victory in a modern war, this time defeating one of the Western powers. But the consequences of victory went beyond the achievement of great power status and increased opportunities for imperial expansion. A rethinking of *ryōsai kenbo*'s domestic destiny for women and concerns about national values came to the forefront due to the social problem of supporting widows and children of dead and disabled soldiers, as well as the psychological letdown after decades of striving to catch up to the West, many months of wartime privation, and the postwar economic reces-

lso contributing to the impetus to re-evaluate *ryōsai kenbo* was the
ve growth of female enrollments in secondary education, the entry of women into new occupations, and declining student interest in
the narrowly domestic curriculum of the public girls' schools. Discussions on women's paid employment outside the home, including such
issues as the pros and cons of wage work for women, women's calling,
and the role of vocational courses in girls' schools' curricula were central to the debates over *ryōsai kenbo* in this period.

The establishment of *ryōsai kenbo* as the cornerstone of the girls'
higher educational track had had an impact on moral education at the
elementary school level during the opening decade of the twentieth
century. The ethics textbooks used in the primary schools stressed gender difference after implementation of the Higher Girls' School Ordinance in 1899. Ethics lessons that youngsters read just before graduation
attempted to instill precepts that would guide them later in life. Until
1907, pupils encountered these lessons in the fourth grade but thereafter
in the sixth grade, because compulsory schooling was lengthened from
four to six years in that year.[23] In 1903 the second to the last lesson in
the fourth year ethics textbook taught that,

The man [*otoko*] becomes the master of the house and works at the household
occupation [*kagyō*]. The woman [*onna*] helps the man and takes care of the
household [*ie o sewa suru*]. Therefore their purpose [*kokorogake*] must differ. . . .
Because knowledge is important to both men and women, they must polish
the knowledge necessary to do their respective tasks. It is a mistake to think
that women are inferior to men.[24]

Although the differing responsibilities and tasks of men and women
were emphasized, as "master" of the house, the husband was given authority over his wife in the household, and the role of the wife in the
household's livelihood was minimized. Yet inequality in gender roles
was mitigated by the assertions that women were equal to men and that
men and women alike needed to continue to learn even after graduation from school. The textbook focused on optimal performance of the
tasks of everyday life by individual men and women.

As the century progressed, elementary school ethics lessons disseminated a crucial aspect of the notion of educated motherhood—the social or public significance of women's care for children in the home—
to the Japanese masses, a far broader segment of the population than

the elite Japanese women attending the higher girls' schools. By 1910, a vision of Japan as a world power and of the contribution that its nationals, even women, could make to its greatness, had infused elementary school textbooks. The next to the last lesson in the sixth year ethics textbook once more explained the respective duties of men and women, and then continued,

Girls' [*joshi*] being inside caring for a household [*ikka*] and planning the peace and happiness of the home is one of the good manners and beautiful customs of the country [*ikkoku no ryōfu bizoku*]. As mothers, girls' rearing of children badly or well readily influences the kind of persons they become and in the long run is related to the prosperity or decline of the state.[25]

The 1901 and 1911 ethics textbooks for the higher girls' schools also asserted the complementarity of male and female gender roles and the relation of gender difference to the national weal. At this time, although the number of women engaging in wage labor outside the textile industry was clearly rising and the distaste of many young women for a narrowly domestic curriculum in the higher girls' schools was becoming clear, women's work outside the home was not mentioned in most textbooks. The plight of war widows in financial distress, however, was an issue that nationalist educators, policymakers, and intellectuals could not easily sweep under the rug. Thus in a handful of lessons, references to women's wage work and vocational training appeared. In permitting women to venture from the confines of domesticity, the watchword in these texts was "if need be" (*man'ichi no baai*).[26]

In the post–Russo-Japanese War years, the eminent, conservative female educator Shimoda Utako was critical of both *ryōsai kenbo* education and character or personality (*jinkakushugi*) education.[27] The latter she considered equal education for men and women and therefore undesirable, while the former was not thoroughgoing enough in its nationalism. For Shimoda, training women to be "good wives, wise mothers" was insufficient. In her view, the aim of female education was to nurture "the complete woman as a national." Shimoda assumed the complementarity of gender roles, but she also assumed the inferiority of women. For that reason, men should work outside the home, earn income, and manage state and society, while women's natural calling was to stay at home building the economic foundation of the nation through hard work and thrift. They should also, for the sake of national progress, stay a half step behind men. Although women themselves were not equal to men, she wrote, their function in society was a crucial one because "'the foundations of both the state and society' were built on the family and 'managing the home and regulating the family build the foundation of the nation and society.'"[28]

Yet despite the prescriptions of Education Ministry regulations, the school regulations enforced by many rank-and-file teachers and administrators, and the abundance of writings presenting dedication to wifehood and motherhood as women's calling in life, the higher girls' schools harbored ideas and practices that contradicted *ryōsai kenbo*. Around 1910, students Yamakawa Kikue and Tokunaga Yuki shared with other female pupils Christian Socialist Kinoshita Naoe's novel *Pillar of Fire*,[29] banned by the school authorities for its portrayal of youthful involvement in social activism on behalf of urban workers. In this volume, Gregory Pflugfelder analyzes discourses on intense, intimate "S" relationships that developed between young women at the higher girls' schools. In opposition to the notions of teachers, administrators, and other authoritative figures, womanhood was contested terrain even in the higher girls' schools, just as it was in the larger society.

Ryōsai Kenbo in the Aftermath of World War 1

After 1914, debates over women's paid employment continued to be central to contests over definitions of womanhood, including *ryōsai kenbo*, but the lessons of World War 1 gave new urgency to the issue. Once again, notions of womanhood in the domains of the Education Ministry followed shifts in state strategies to maintain the nation's international power and its empire. A major strategic lesson of World War 1—the réalization that civilians' performance on the home front was as crucial to modern warfare as the armed forces' actions in battle—suggested to some leaders that a purely domestic role for women would impede future military success. With defense of nation and empire at stake, even conservatives who were loath to endorse a public role for women had to grapple with the relationship between women's work and their social participation and national progress. The outcome was a shift in *ryōsai kenbo* that, on the one hand, accepted greater participation by women in work outside the home and, on the other, upheld their domestic responsibilities. According to Koyama Shizuko, there was an intensification of gender difference at the same time that work outside the home gained legitimacy. Koyama claims that a dual transformation evolved that emphasized the power of women's love, a companionate spousal relationship, and the family as a place of love, perceived as a refuge from the stresses of the greater world, far more than contributions of women to the public world as employees.[30]

Yet surprisingly, in contrast to its predecessor the Deliberative Council on Education (Kyōiku chōsakai; 1915), the Special Deliberative Council on Education (Rinji kyōiku kaigi; 1916–1919) did not affirm women's work outside the home. Rather, it gave priority to moral and ideological concerns—the nurturing of women who would uphold the family system (*ie seido*), serve the emperor, and be aware of the national polity (*kokutai*). Woman's fundamental role was "good wife, wise mother," a calling that required neither specialized nor vocational education. The state then should not provide higher or specialized education for girls (except teacher training), nor should it in principle open the universities to women. In the immediate aftermath of World War I, moral and ideological concerns outweighed the newly discovered exigencies of strategic planning in the formulation of educational policy for women. Yet the voices supporting higher education and vocational training for women continued to chorus loudly and the number of employed women continued to climb, setting the stage for more positive evaluations of women's work to emerge in the 1920s.[31]

Koyama argues that after 1920 virtually all the girls' higher school ethics textbooks "began to express opinions on women's work [*shokugyō*], and there was a sudden shift away from explaining occupational preparation as needed in case of the unforeseen." Some authors cited the progress of the times (*jisei no shimpo*) or changes in recent economic conditions as reasons for their altered stance on female employment. Others expanded the notion of *ryōsai kenbo* education, arguing that employment outside the home would provide women a better basis to be more helpful to their husband and children. To them, life experiences could also be considered education. Another justification for the endorsement of women's work was the development of women as human beings, especially the fostering of independence and self-reliance,[32] but Koyama argues that the most compelling reason of all was the assertion that women's work was valuable to society and state.[33]

Other factors such as the diffusion of notions of mothers' special responsibilities for childrearing, the growth of women's education and employment, the exposure to new models of family life, the decline of three-generation households in the cities, the growth of the new middle class, and the formation of a mass culture of consumption in the cities reinforced the need to consider *ryōsai kenbo*. Most conspicuous was the rise of companionate ideals of husband-wife relationships and family life, which highlighted the desirability of mutual affection and de-emphasized to some extent the male role as "master" of the household. In the growing new middle class of the cities, a young bride was more likely to live in a two-generation household and less likely to fall under the daily authority of a mother-in-law. Despite the state's efforts to instill its version of female domesticity in ordinary girls, economic necessity, past practices of farm and merchant wives' economic participation, increasing opportunities for wage labor, and the new aspirations in popular culture worked against acceptance of *ryōsai kenbo* among lower-class rural and urban women.[34]

The Army Ministry's attitudes toward women in tandem with a militarized outlook toward national affairs help explain support for the status quo in educational policy; that is, the failure to augment vocational training and higher education for women. In the mid-1920s, even though there was an increased recognition of the need to mobilize women for unprecedented production and leadership roles in modern warfare, key educators of women seem to have continued to regard women primarily as the moral trainers of the next generation of Japanese soldiers and citizens. This single-minded view of adult women as socializers of children apparently overrode alternative visions of women as direct participants in the world of paid labor and public affairs. The 1904 views of Military Inspector General Tanaka Yoshitoshi, circulating in the 1920s, epitomize this view. While describing at length how rural and urban French women were thrust into unaccustomed productive work during World War 1 and how their valiant and capable efforts were admired by men as they returned from the front, Tanaka reminds Japanese women that educating their children is of vital importance to the Japanese state. He does not discuss how Japanese women might prepare for wartime work or leadership roles or how they would perform wartime feats like the women of France. He seems to assume that they will rise to the occasion, as French women did, but his greatest concern is to enlist women in the current ongoing battle against moral decay. He claims that one symptom of current moral weakness is the failure of young women to dedicate themselves to national aims. Should the next generation lack an ethos of patriotism, self-sacrifice, and service, he asserts, grave difficulties would lie ahead for the state in the future.[35] Tanaka's focus on the morality and patriotism of women and citizens upheld older notions of *ryōsai kenbo*, rather than supporting one of the 1920s variations that proposed expansion of the social participation of women. The concern of Tanaka and his supporters lay with alleviating current moral problems rather than gaining strategic advantages during a future mobilization.

An Ending or a Beginning?

Transmutations of *ryōsai kenbo* during the Taishō era (broadly defined) were closely related to strategies of war and empire that aimed to increase Japan's international status and power than to any other single factor. Of course, this assertion does not deny the role of other trends such as the development of industrial capitalism, florescence of mass consumer culture, women's rising educational attainments, the diffusion of companionate family values, the emergence of "the woman question," and the growth of the new middle class in the cities. Since Education Ministry officials made *ryōsai kenbo* the cornerstone of women's education from 1899, the intimate link between state goals and shifting conceptions of *ryōsai kenbo* is hardly surprising. In one sense, under the centralized system of educational administration, not only bureaucrats in the national and provincial capitals but all teachers and principals employed at public schools in the empire were state officials.

Yet by the post–World War 1 era, the perspectives of teachers, principals, and higher officials were not monolithic, nor were the views of other public commentators on *ryōsai kenbo*, including the host of educators at private educational institutions. The following remarks suggest the wide-ranging views on *ryōsai kenbo*, which could not all be explored in this brief essay. All along, there were criticisms nearly as blunt as the one by this anonymous writer in 1925, who boldly remarked that "'oppressive/restrictive [*kyūkutsu na*] *ryōsai kenbo*, which says that women should not take one step outside the home is the notion of olden times.'"[36]

In the final chapter of *Fujin mondai no hanashi* (1929), Suzuki Bunshirō, the chief of the social department of the *Asahi shinbun* (Asahi newspaper), presented some late Taishō–early Showa views of *ryōsai kenbo* in an attempt to revitalize its popularity among contemporary young women. He argued that it is unfairly labeled as "feudal" and "old-fashioned," which made it unappealing to young women and feminists. As had others in the past, Suzuki emphasized the public significance of *ryōsai kenbo* and declared it the key to the advancement of the country and society. And surely not for the first time, *ryōsai kenbo* exhibited racial overtones: while the virtues of Japanese women were compared favorably to those of women from the powerful Western nations, when compared to the virtues of women from some other Asian countries, Japanese women's virtues were presented as superior.

Some Japanese who are self-styled new thinkers call it *ryōsai kenbo*, a "remnant of the feudal era." . . . There are many who are eager to abolish it, especially among those women who call themselves "feminists" [*fujin no joseishugisha*, or feminists]. . . . I do not agree. Why is *ryōsai kenbo* mistaken? If it is a product of Japan's feudal era, one can ask then what else in the feudal era Japan should be thankful for. . . . Probably many of the opponents of *ryōsai kenbo* interpret this phrase as the woman's way of absolute obedience to her husband, expounded by Kaibara Ekiken Sensei and others. But . . . why is only this term equated with . . . Confucian commentaries of the feudal era . . . and taken literally? . . . Because there are no young women who read Kaibara Ekiken's and other [early modern] advice books for women . . . naturally they interpret *ryōsai kenbo* literally, denounce it as old-fashioned, and its influence is probably not what one would expect. . . . Without *ryōsai kenbo*, can the women's movement itself truly develop and progress? Can it not be said that only with *ryōsai kenbo* is human progress possible. . . . Is there anywhere in the world a flourishing nation or sound society without *ryōsai kenbo*? . . . The difference between countries that flourish and countries that decline is the difference between the *ryōsai kenbo* of their nationals.

If you compare women shut up in harems, and mothers from India and other small Asian countries who give birth at age ten, to the mothers of Japan and the great countries of Europe and America, you will understand. The problem is the content of the 'good' of good wife and the 'clever' of clever mother. Thus, in this, racial character [*minzokusei*] is strongly revealed. The contemporary Japanese *ryōsai kenbo* must be appropriate to the times and at the same time must of necessity be the same as the *ryōsai kenbo* of Europe and America. The way of the feudal era *ryōsai kenbo* has been transmitted to the way of Japan's Showa period *ryōsai kenbo*, and if it has a feature that is superior to the way of *ryōsai kenbo* of other countries, it probably is the spirit of sacrifice and service for the sake of the household, husband, and child. Even if in the past, this was the result of the despotic morality of males, the fact that this spirit of sacrifice has been cultivated remains the most precious aspect of Japan's way of *ryōsai kenbo*.

Probably . . . socialists and feminists [*joseishugisha*] would say that such sacrificial sprit of Japanese women [at the time of the Russo-Japanese war] was a product of the subordinate morality anaesthetized by imperialism. But if so, were the women of imperialist Russia also at that time the same as Japanese women? This was probably not the case, as a letter from a Russian official reveals that he was extremely surprised [by Japanese women during that war.] . . . This kind of spirit of sacrifice of Japanese women—as mothers and as wives . . . has come to be their magnificent special characteristic . . . can there not be one more aspect of a new Japanese women's movement that will add still more new spirit and broaden and deepen the object of sacrifice?[37]

As Suzuki's impassioned, patriotic appeal reveals, despite the chorus of voices demanding advanced education, paid employment, and full political participation for women, an opposing melody with a familiar refrain also sounded in the 1920s. The song of the past tied the welfare of the nation to women's central role in the home and to their moral virtues rather than broad social participation. The notes of national and racial superiority can be clearly heard in Suzuki's refrain: "good wives and wise mothers" are essential for national (and also for human) progress. In his comparisons, Suzuki asserted the superiority of Japanese women over women of other Asian countries and Russia, and their parity with women from the most powerful Western countries. For the sake of their nation, Japanese women should cultivate a "spirit of sacrifice—as mothers and wives," their "most magnificent special characteristic," rather than their self-interest and independence as workers or independent political agents. These tensions remained unresolved until the crises of the Manchurian Incident (1931), the second Sino-Japanese War (1937–1945), and the war against the Allied powers (1941–1945) shifted the balance in favor of the nationalist song.

The primary concern of this brief essay is to chart shifts in the notion of *ryōsai kenbo*, a conception of Japanese womanhood that emerged in the 1890s and that became the bedrock of state educational policy for women. Many other aspects of *ryōsai kenbo* could not be explored in this essay—for example, the implementation of *ryōsai kenbo* in the classrooms of girls' secondary schools by teachers and principals; class differences in expectations of women as "good wife, wise mother"; the response of students and parents to educators' initiatives; the role of *ryōsai kenbo* in women's education in the colonies; and its place in the social education in state-sponsored women's and girls' associations (*fujinkai* and *shōjokai*). The evolution of *ryōsai kenbo* in the turbulent eras after Taishō—during recession from 1927 to 1934, national emergency of 1931–1937, and wars in mainland Asia and the Pacific from 1937 to 1945—is beyond the scope of this study, but worthy of study in its own right.[38]

In closing, I will raise one more significant issue: To what extent did Japanese women accept *ryōsai kenbo*, the state's definition of womanhood? The answer is as complex as the diversity of Japanese women whose lives and outlooks were influenced by factors such as class, age, and rural or urban residence. A glimpse at the possibilities moves this essay away from the realms of institutional and cultural history and closer to the social history of modern Japanese gender. Already by 1909 female enrollments at professional schools (*senmon gakkō*),[39] practical schools (*jitsugyō gakkō*), and other higher schools (*kakushu gakkō*) surpassed those at the higher girls' schools and normal schools (*shihan gakkō*), indicating young women's deepening interest in the world of work. In the late 1910s, even Kaneko Fumiko, a penniless and unsophisticated yet smart and ambitious lower-class girl, disdained the girls' schools; she enrolled in a boys' school, in the hopes of receiving a "real" education that would allow her to eventually attend a girls' medical school. In the late 1920s, teachers and other working women presented a petition with fourteen thousand signatures to the House of Peers requesting the opening of universities to women and the expansion of vocational education in the curricula of the secondary girls' schools. These actions reveal women's determination to assert their voices in public affairs to change state policies. But the Education Ministry turned a deaf ear to their pleas. In the 1930s, the prevalence among farm women in one southwestern village of verbal and sexual frankness, smoking, drinking, hard labor in the fields, and willingness to divorce, suggests that they had transmuted the Japanese state's conceptions of womanhood according to their own logic.[40]

The establishment of *ryōsai kenbo* has implications for modern Japanese gender and social history beyond the world of women. The assertion that household affairs and childrearing constituted a special female domain had the potential to reshape the identities of the majority of Japanese men—not only urban working-class and new middle-class men whose workplace was separate from the home, but the majority of men who still lived and worked in farm, merchant, and perhaps artisan enterprise households. Andrew Gordon's chapter in this volume suggests that the transformation of working-class Japanese men into dedicated workers who abandoned children and household affairs to their wives' management was not complete until the 1950s, and that this redefinition of male identities was accomplished in part by the intervention of their employers. While the focus of this chapter is primarily on the recasting of female gender, in the end, the Meiji construction and Taishō transformations of the notion of *ryōsai kenbo* also created reverberations in the domains of men throughout the twentieth century. The establishment of new norms, ideas, and behaviors for men and women in the decades following the Meiji Restoration of 1868 reveals that gender construction was an integral part of the genesis of Japanese modernity, whether or not the process of constructing femininity, masculinity, or the relationship of the genders was consciously undertaken.

Notes

1. Sharon Sievers, *Flowers in Salt: The Beginnings of Feminist Consciousness in Modern Japan* (Stanford, CA: Stanford University Press, 1983); Sharon Nolte, "Women, the State, and Repression in Imperial Japan," Michigan State University Working Papers on Women in International Development No. 33 (Sept. 1983); Sally Hastings, "From Heroine to Patriotic Volunteer: Women and Social Work in Japan, 1900–45," Michigan State University Working Papers on Women in International Development No. 106 (November 1985); Sharon Nolte, "Women's Rights and Society's Needs: Japan's 1931 Suffrage Bill," *Comparative Studies in Society and History* 28 (1986): 690–714; Gregory Pflugfelder, "Politics and the Kitchen: The Women's Suffrage Movement in Provincial Japan," paper presented at the Association for Asian Studies Annual Meeting, Chicago, Illinois, April 7, 1990; Sharon Nolte and Sally Hastings, "The Meiji State's Policy toward Women, 1890–1910," in *Recreating Japanese Women, 1600–1945*, ed. Gail Lee Bernstein (Berkeley: University of California Press, 1991), 151–174; Mariko Tamanoi, "Songs as Weapons: The Culture and History of *Komori* (Nursemaids) in Modern Japan," *Journal of Asian Studies* 50, no. 4 (1991): 793–817; Sheldon Garon, "Women's Groups and the Japanese State: Contending Approaches to Political Integration, 1890–1945," *Journal of Japanese Studies* 19 (1993): 5–41; Sandra Wilson, "Mobilizing Women in the 1930s," *Gender and History* 7 (1995): 295–314; Vera Mackie, "Engaging with the State: Socialist Women in Imperial Japan," in *Feminism and the State in Modern Japan*, ed. Vera Mackie (Melbourne, Australia: Japanese Studies Centre, 1995); and my *Passages to Modernity: Motherhood, Childhood, and Social Reform in Early Twentieth Century Japan* (Honolulu: University of Hawaii Press, 1999). Treatments of state repression of women's activism include Sievers, *Flowers in Salt*, and Mikiso Hane, *Reflections on the Way to the Gallows: Rebel Women in Prewar Japan* (Berkeley: University of California Press, 1988).

2. Recent English language studies on Japanese women's history include E. Patricia Tsurumi, *Factory Girls: Women in the Thread Mills of Meiji Japan* (Princeton, NJ: Princeton University Press, 1990); Bernstein, *Recreating Japanese Women*; Yoshiko Furuki, *The White Plum: A Biography of Ume Tsuda* (New York: Weatherhill, 1991); Yamakawa Kikue, *Women of the Mito Domain*, trans. Kate Wildman Nakai (University of Tokyo Press, 1992); Barbara Rose, *Tsuda Umeko and Women's Education in Japan* (New Haven, CT: Yale University Press, 1992); *Japanese Women Working*, ed. Janet Hunter (New York: Routledge, 1993); Mackie, *Feminism and the State*; Helen M. Hopper, *A New Woman of Japan: A Political Biography of Katō Shidzue* (Boulder, CO: Westview Press, 1996); and Vera Mackie, *Creating Socialist Women in Japan* (New York: Cambridge University Press, 1997). Classic older works include: Mikiso Hane, *Rebels, Peasants, and Outcastes: The*

Underside of Modern Japan (New York: Pantheon Books, 1982); Robert J. Smith and Ella Lury Wiswell, *The Women of Suye Mura* (Chicago, IL: University of Chicago Press, 1982); and *Women in Changing Japan*, eds. Joyce Lebra, Joy Paulson, and Elizabeth Powers (Stanford, CA: Stanford University Press, 1976).

English books shedding light on the still newer field of Japanese men's history include: Donald Roden, *Schooldays in Imperial Japan: A Study in the Culture of a Student Elite* (Berkeley: University of California Press, 1980); Roger S. Keyes, *The Male Journey in Japanese Prints* (Berkeley: University of California Press, 1989); Ihara Saikaku, *The Great Mirror of Male Love*, trans. Paul Gordon Schalow (Stanford, CA: Stanford University Press, 1990); Tsuneo Watanabe and Jun'ichi Iwata, *The Love of the Samurai: A Thousand Years of Japanese Homosexuality*, trans. D. R. Roberts (London: GMP Publishers Ltd., 1989); Gary Leupp, *Male Colors: The Construction of Homosexuality in Tokugawa Japan* (Berkeley: University of California Press, 1995); and Gregory Pflugfelder, *Cartographies of Desire: Male-Male Sexuality in Japanese Discourse, 1600–1950* (Berkeley: University of California Press, 1999). Except for the studies by Roden and Pflugfelder, the above works illuminating male gender construction focus primarily on the early modern rather than the modern period.

3. Although they were called "higher girls' schools," female students enrolled in these institutions following graduation from elementary school. Thus they were the equivalent of middle schools (*chūgakkō*) rather than high schools (*kōtō gakkō*) in the male educational track. However, since at this time girls were barred from high schools and colleges, the *kōtō jogakkō* established a separate track of public secondary education for girls and was intended to be the highest educational institution for females. A few young women attended public normal schools (*shihan gakkō*), including two girls' normal schools. Regarding women's education in late Tokugawa and early Meiji, see Martha Tocco's chapter in this volume and "School Bound: Women's Higher Education in Nineteenth-Century Japan," PhD dissertation, Stanford University, 1994.

4. Discussions appear in Sievers, *Flowers in Salt*, 11, 22–24, 107–113; Robert J. Smith, "Making Village Women into 'Good Wives and Wise Mothers,'" *Journal of Family History* 8, no. 1 (Spring 1983): 70–77; Kathleen Uno, "Death of 'Good Wife, Wise Mother'?" in *Postwar Japan as History*, ed. Andrew Gordon (Berkeley: University of California Press, 1993), esp. 296–303; Shizuko Koyama, "The 'Good Wife and Wise Mother' Ideology in Post–World War I Japan," *U.S.-Japan Women's Journal*, English Supplement, no. 7 (December 1994), 31–52; Ulrike Woehr, "Between Revolution and Reaction: The Japanese Women's Movement in the Taishō Era," in *War Revolution & Japan*, ed. Ian Neary (Sangate, Great Britain: Japan Library, 1993), 50–73; and Kathleen Uno, "Origins of

'Good Wife, Wise Mother,'" in *Japanische Frauengeschichte(n),* eds. Erich Pauer and Regine Mathias (Marburg, Germany: Förderverein Marburger Japan-Reihe, 1995), 31–46. See also Keiko Fujimura-Fanselow, "The Japanese Ideology of 'Good Wives and Wise Mothers': Trends in Contemporary Research," *Gender and History* 3, no. 3 (1991): 247–248; Kathleen Uno, "Women and Changes in the Household Division of Labor," in Bernstein, *Recreating Japanese Women,* 35–39; Nolte and Hastings, "The Meiji State's Policy," 158–159; and Yoshiko Miyake, "Doubling Expectations: Motherhood and Women's Factory Work under State Management in Japan in the 1930s and 1940s," in Bernstein, *Recreating Japanese Women,* 269–271.

5. Classic works in Japanese are Fukaya Masashi, *Ryōsai kenboshugi no kyōiku* (Nagoya: Reimei shobō, 1981), and Koyama Shizuko, *Ryōsai kenbo to iu kihan* (Keisō shobō, 1991). See also Komano Yōko, "Ryōsai kenboshugi no seiritsu to sono naiyō," in *Josei kaihō no shisō to kōdō, senzen hen,* ed. Tanaka Sumiko, vol. 1 (Jiji tsūshinsha, 1975), 142–143; Katano Miyako, "Ryōsai kenbo no genryū," in *Onnatachi no kindai,* ed. Kindai joseishi kenkyūkai (Kashiwa shobō, 1978), 32–57; Nakajima Kuni, "Ryōsai kenbo kyōiku no seiritsu," *Joshi kyōiku mondai,* no. 2 (Winter 1980): 140–152; Nagahara Kazuko, "Ryōsai kenboshugi kyōiku ni okeru 'ie' to shokugyō," in *Kindai,* vol. 4, *Nihon joseishi,* ed. Joseishi sōgō kenkyūkai (Tōkyō daigaku shuppankai, 1982), 149–184; and Katayama Seiichi, *Kindai Nihon no joshi kyōiku* (Kenpakusha, 1984). Fine works by a younger generation of scholars include Tachi Kaoru, "Ryōsai kenbo," in *Onna no imēji, Joseigaku kōza 1,* ed. Joseigaku kenkyūkai (Keisō shobō, 1984), 184–209; Nakajima Misaki, "Ryōsai kenbo shugi kenkyū no genjō to kadai," *Sōgō joseishi kenkyū,* no. 6 (August 1989): 24–41; Haga Noboru, *Ryōsai kenbo ron* (Yūzankaku, 1990); and Tomono Kiyofumi, "Ryōsai kenbo shisō no hensen to sono hyōka," *Rekishi hyōron,* no. 517 (May 1993): 56–67.

6. Although in its narrowest political sense, the Taishō period falls between the years 1912 and 1926, I had planned to follow the lead of Japanese and American historians who define the period in broader terms as the period between the Russo-Japanese War (1904–1905) and the beginning of the Showa recession in 1927. Since the other contributors have not adopted it, I abandoned this periodization. See Nakajima Kuni, "Taishō no joshi kyōiku," in *Taishō no joshi kyōiku,* ed. Nihon joshi daigaku joshi kyōiku kenkyūjo (Kokudosha, 1975), 6, 45*n,* and Andrew Gordon, *Labor and Imperial Democracy in Prewar Japan* (Berkeley: University of California, 1992), 3, 5–7.

7. Regarding initial developments in women's education in the modern era and their early modern antecedents, see Martha Tocco's chapter in this volume.

8. Regarding the influence of men's self-improvement literature and the emerging mass media on women's sense of self, see Barbara Sato's chapter in this volume.

9. Jinzō Naruse, "The Education of Japanese Women," in *Fifty Years of New Japan*, ed. Shigenobu Okuma, vol. 2 (1910; reprint, New York: Kraus Reprint Co., 1970), 206–207.

10. Nakamura Masanao, "Creating Good Mothers," in *Meiroku zasshi*, trans. William Braisted (Cambridge, MA: Harvard University Press, 1976), 402. Regarding Nakamura's and Mori's early Meiji ideas on women, see also Sievers, *Flowers in Salt*, 16–25.

11. Ivan P. Hall, *Mori Arinori* (Cambridge, MA: Harvard University Press, 1973), 245, and Katano, "Ryōsai kenbo," 37.

12. Hall, *Mori Arinori*, 423.

13. Katayama, *Kindai Nihon*, 117.

14. Katano, "Ryōsai kenbo," 39.

15. Naruse, "The Education of Japanese Women," and Atsuharu Sakai, "Kaibara Ekiken and 'Onna Daigaku,'" *Cultural Nippon* 7, no. 4 (December 1939): 43–56.

16. Hosokawa Junjirō, "Kokuryoku to joshi kyōiku to no kankei," *Dai Nippon kyōikukai zasshi*, no. 195 (May 1, 1895), cited in *Kyōiku*, vol. 4, *Nihon fujin mondai shiryō shūsei*, ed. Mitsui Tametomo (Domesu shuppan, 1977), 246–248.

17. See, for example, Martha Tocco's essay in this volume, and my "Women and the Household Division of Labor," in Bernstein, *Recreating Japanese Women*, 1–18.

18. Fukaya, *Ryōsai kenboshugi*, 158. Saionji's terms as education minister were: Oct. 3, 1894–Sept. 28, 1896, Jan. 12, 1898–April 30, 1898, and Jan. 7, 1906–July 14, 1908, under Prime Ministers Itō Hirobumi (second cabinet) and Matsukata Masayoshi, and in his own first cabinet. *Concise Dictionary of Modern Japanese History*, comp. Janet Hunter (Berkeley: University of California Press, 1984), 269–273.

19. Katayama, *Kindai Nihon*, 116. Kabayama headed the Education Ministry in Yamagata Aritomo's third cabinet, from Nov. 8, 1898 to Oct. 19, 1900. Hunter, *Concise Dictionary*, 271.

20. Katayama, *Kindai Nihon*, 121.

21. Fukaya, *Ryōsai kenboshugi*, 153–157, 173–227, and Tomono, "Ryōsai kenbo shisō," 61.

22. Fukaya, *Ryōsai kenboshugi*, 188–209, and Katayama, *Kindai Nihon*, 119.

23. Byron Marshall, *Learning to Be Modern* (Boulder, CO: Westview Press, 1996), 93.

24. Nagahara, "Ryōsai kenboshugi kyōiku," 157. The title of the lesson was "The Duties of Men and the Duties of Women" ("Otoko no tsutome, Onna no tsutome").

25. Nagahara, "Ryōsai kenboshugi kyōiku," 158.

26. Ibid., 160–163, 171; and Koyama, *Ryōsai kenbo to iu kihan*, 201–208.

27. Regarding *jinkaku* (character) and women's self-improvement, see Barbara Sato's chapter in this volume.

28. Nagahara, "Ryōsai kenboshugi kyōiku," 175.

29. An English translation of this novel is Naoe Kinoshita, *Pillar of Fire*, trans. Kenneth Strong (London: Allen and Unwin, 1972).

30. Koyama, "'Good Wife, Wise Mother' Ideology."

31. Nakajima Kuni, "Taishō no joshi kyōiku," 17; Nagahara, "Ryōsai kenboshugi kyōiku," 162, 171–175; and Koyama, "'Good Wife, Wise Mother' Ideology," 40–44. See also Barbara Sato's chapter in this volume regarding young women's employment as self-cultivation (*shūyō*).

32. Barbara Sato discusses work as preparation for modern wifehood and motherhood, self-cultivation, and autonomy in women's magazines and the attitudes of young women in both her chapter in this volume and in her *The New Japanese Woman: Modernity, Media, and Women in Interwar Japan* (Durham, NC: Duke University Press, 2003).

33. Koyama, *Ryōsai kenbo to iu kihan*, 218–226.

34. Despite a generation of promotion in the schools and media, internalization of the state's pronouncements on womanhood, including *ryōsai kenbo*, by nonelite Japanese women in the prewar period is open to question. See for example, Smith and Wiswell, *The Women of Suye Mura*.

35. Tanaka Yoshitoshi, *Gunkoku no fujin*, reprinted in *Kindai josei bunken shiryo sosho*, ed. Nakajima Kuni, vol. 2, *Onna to sensō* (Ōzorasha, 1992), 232–234.

36. Fukaya, *Ryōsai kenboshugi*, 233.

37. Suzuki Bunshirō, *Fujin mondai no hanashi* (Osaka: Asahi shinbunsha, 1929), 269–273.

38. Haruko Cook's essay in this volume sheds some light on conceptions of womanhood in wartime Japan.

39. Marshall indicates that *senmon gakkō* encompassed a variety of schools, and has been translated as "colleges," "vocational," "technical," "professional," "specialized," or "specialty" schools. *Learning to Be Modern*, 68.

40. Nagahara, "Ryōsai kenboshugi kyōiku," 163, 183; Kaneko Fumiko, *The Prison Memoirs of a Japanese Woman*, trans. Jean Inglis (Armonk, NY: M.E. Sharpe, 1991); and Smith and Wiswell, *The Women of Suye Mura*, esp. chapters 4–7.

15 *Toward a Critique of Transhistorical Femininity*

Ayako Kano

This essay is an attempt to describe and thereby debunk a particular set of arguments that have congregated in late capitalist Japanese intellectual space around the idea of femininity. It is an attempt to stress a point that historians may find obvious, but that literary critics have had greater trouble acknowledging: that categories such as "woman" and "femininity" are historically constructed. The failure to acknowledge the historicity of gender categories leads too easily to an assumption of a transhistorical and essential continuity about women and femininity, which has troubling consequences for gender relations within Japan as well as for the gendered relationship of Japan to other nations.

In the late 1980s and early 1990s, three prominent contemporary literary critics, Karatani Kōjin, Yamashita Etsuko, and Suga Hidemi, theorized the relationship between gender, language, and subjectivity, and all three associated some kind of unchanging continuity with femininity in Japan. This continuity, they alleged, makes Japan unique. According to Karatani, it was the persistence of "matrilinearity" that had supported the emperor system as well as the writing of literature. According to Yamashita, it was the repeated return to "Japanese subjectivity" based on the merging of mother and child that had limited Japanese feminism. And according to Suga, it was the maintaining and obscuring of "femininity" that had characterized the process of literary vernacularization. In the theorizing of Karatani, Yamashita, and Suga, an assumption of continuity about gender—"some things about Japanese women never change"—operated together with an assertion of national uniqueness—"Japan is uniquely different from the West"—as two wheels on a perpetual motion machine, driving and reinforcing each other. The arguments of these three critics were symptomatic of a larger discursive formation in late twentieth-century Japan that made these kinds of theories possible, plausible, and popular. The purpose of my essay is to expose the logic of these arguments and thereby aid their demise.

The emergence of a discourse of transhistorical femininity at this point in history might be attributed to a number of factors and their combination. First, we might consider the tremendous blossoming of feminism in 1980s Japan, which the conclusion of the United Nations Decade for Women and the passing of the Equal Employment Opportunity Law in 1985 both fueled and epitomized. In 1983, the percentage of married women employed in wage-earning work outside the home exceeded 50 percent for the first time, and underscored the increasing significance of women as wage earners and consumers. The "age of women" (*onna no jidai*) became a slogan for activists as well as advertising agents. More women were insisting that their voices be heard in the political arena, as women candidates metaphorized as "Madonna Whirlwinds" (*senpū*) swept through the elections. The government began sponsoring community centers and lectures aimed at women under the slogan of "women and men living together in harmony" (*kyōsei*). At the same time, feminism as intellectual discourse sprang into the limelight, popularized by a few prominent and controversial academic feminists, such as Ueno Chizuko. Within a few years, books on feminism multiplied like the proverbial bamboo shoots after spring rain.[1] As the presence of feminism grew in the academy and on the bookshelves, so did the space for critique of feminism, preparing ground for the gender theories of Karatani, Yamashita, and Suga.

Second, what also characterized the 1980s was the dissemination of certain strains of poststructuralism, aided by the translation of Foucault, Lacan, and Derrida, and by the publication of popular guidebooks. The antifoundationalist and antihumanist critique of ideas, such as "woman," "equality," and "liberation," obviously put into question many of the ideals of feminism. While many feminists have always engaged in critical reflection about the universality of "woman," the desirability of "equality," and the content of "liberation," and while a few feminists, such as Kanai Yoshiko, have worked vigorously to reformulate feminist goals along poststructuralist lines, the encounter left enough room for an antifeminist backlash. To see this backlash as enough room for an antifeminist backlash. To see this backlash as the *ressentiment* of those left out of the "feminist whirlwind" of the 1980s would be too simple, though it would be a satisfying retort to precisely those who insist on dismissing feminism as an expression of *ressentiment*. What remains notable is the use of Foucaultian, Lacanian, Derridean, and other poststructuralist vocabulary in the gender theories of Karatani, Yamashita, and Suga, and the way the idea of a diachronically constant femininity remains in their theorizing even after the synchronic unity of the category of "woman" has been deconstructed.

Third, we might consider the economic and political climate of the 1980s and 1990s that generated and supported a discourse of "reverse Orientalism." Reverse Orientalism is not anti-Orientalism, which opposes Orientalism. Neither is it Occidentalism, which specularizes the West as exotic. In some ways it is an internalization of the Orientalist paradigm by the Orientalized. In other words, whereas the Western Orientalist would look at Japan and see an exotic Other that is fundamentally different from the West, a reverse Orientalist would be a Japanese looking at Japan as fundamentally different from the West. The late 1980s and early 1990s might be remembered as the "age of women" by feminists and as the "age of poststructuralism" by intellectuals; many more Japanese citizens will remember it as the "age of the bubble economy." It was the advent of a call for "a Japan that can say no," supported by the mighty yen. *Nihonjinron*, or the discourse of Japanese uniqueness, became popular as a way to explain Japanese economic strength (or threat) and political debility (or irresponsibility). While Japan-bashing and revisionism raged in the United States, in Japan the idea of national uniqueness became so popular that it seems to have become a naturalized part of the intellectual landscape.

The arguments of Karatani, Yamashita, and Suga were representative of the way in which the idea of an ahistorical feminine essence—what might be called a "fallacy of transhistorical femininity"—operated in this kind of intellectual climate. Its rhetorical power was bound up with the mechanisms of insisting on Japan's unique difference from the West—what might be called reverse Orientalism.[2] The consequences were a denial of Japan's masculine aggression toward its neighbors, past and present, as well as an antifeminist affirmation of the status quo of gender relations in Japan, past and present.

Karatani Kōjin's Matrilinearity

I would like to consider Karatani Kōjin's theory first, for two reasons: first, his is the only one of the three that has been translated into English up to now; and second, the influence of his theorizing is recognized by both Yamashita and Suga. Karatani, along with Hasumi Shigehiko, was probably the most consequential literary critic in 1980s Japan. Like Hasumi, Karatani was influenced by poststructuralism, and like Hasumi, his intellectual interest extended beyond literary criticism to social and philosophical criticism. To an extent hard to imagine in the United States, "critics" (*hyōronka*) in Japan cut across conventional academic disciplines, and effortlessly slip across the boundary between academic and journalistic discourse. To see Karatani as just a "literary critic" is thus a mistake; it would be more accurate to call him a "public intellectual."

I would first like to consider Karatani's argument in *Origins of Modern Japanese Literature*, a book originally published in Japan in 1980 as *Nihon kindai bungaku no kigen* and translated into English in 1993.[3] Gender is conspicuously absent from the argument in the 1980 Japanese edition. In the 1993 English edition, Karatani supplements each chapter with an appendix, and the appendix to what was originally the sixth and last chapter appears to rectify the lack of attention to gender issues in the original. Yet rather than engage in a discussion of gender, this appendix displaces it into a discussion of a reactionary "return to Japan." A careful analysis of the two editions reveals what is at stake in Karatani's way of discussing gender issues in the context of his conception of language and subjectivity.

In her "Introduction" to the English edition, Brett de Bary characterizes Karatani's agenda in this book as "one of ideology critique, of an aggressive defamiliarization" (*Origins*, 1):

Not unlike Western studies stimulated by the reconceptualization of issues of ideology and culture in the 1960s by writers such as Louis Althusser, Michel Foucault, and Roland Barthes, Karatani's text made that which seemed most natural and self-evident—the categories by which textbooks and newspaper columns, bookstore shelves and university departments were identified—the object of analysis. (*Origins*, 1–2)

Karatani himself has written in the afterword to the first Japanese edition that each of the words of its title, "Japanese," "modern," "literature," and especially "origins," should be bracketed (*Kigen*, 218).

In bracketing and questioning the categories "Japan," "modernity," and "literature," Karatani avoids the twin monsters of universalism and particularism: on the one hand, a eurocentrism disguised as universalism that would claim that these categories are the same as, or an imitation of, categories in the West; on the other hand, an essentialism disguised as particularism that would claim that Japan's case is utterly different. In his "Foreword: In the Mirror of Alternate Modernities," Fredric Jameson takes note of this aspect of Karatani's argument. Jameson points out how Karatani describes Japan's modernization process as an extreme condensation of what took place over many centuries in the West. The whole process from the Enlightenment to postmodernity was condensed in Japan to a single century, from the 1860s to the 1960s. Because of this, says Jameson, "it is as though that great laboratory experiment which was the modernization of Japan allows us to see the features of our own development in slow motion, in a new kind of form" (*Origins*, ix). In other words, the process by which certain categories and institutions of modernity were established in Japan is more dramatic and more clearly visible because it was more rapid. Therefore, it allows a reader like Jameson to see Western modernity with new eyes. It might be noted here that Jameson is performing a significant role for legitimizing Karatani's argument in American academia: through Jameson's mediation Karatani is positioned as a "third-world" theorist capable of "post-contemporary interventions."[4] Jameson draws attention to Karatani's method of uncovering "inversions," which turns "the historical into the natural, and generates an illusion of temporal depth and continuity" (*Origins*, x–xi). This model of condensation and inversion allows Karatani to look at Japan's modernity and modern literature in a way that avoids the problems of universalism and particularism.

One of Karatani's strongest arguments in this book is that a new mode of writing, which was established around the 1890s and perceived to be a closer approximation of speech, produced a new kind of subjectivity in Japan: the isolated and inner self. This mode of writing is customarily called "unification of speech and writing" (*genbun itchi*), and

Karatani adopts the phrase with the important caveat that it was not so much a case of "writing like you're speaking" but that of "writing in a way that came to seem as if you're speaking."

Borrowing Sigmund Freud's formulation in *Totem and Taboo* of the emergence of "abstract language and thought" that makes separation of the internal and external possible, Karatani writes:

[W]hat I find most significant in Freud's thought is the notion of the simultaneous emergence in the human being of the capacity for "abstract thought and language" and of "interiority" (accompanied by an awareness of the external as external). What does "abstract thought and language" correspond to in the Japanese context? Perhaps to the conception of writing which evolved in the Meiji period, known as genbun itchi. For genbun itchi was a manifestation in the linguistic realm of the establishment, around 1890, of the various institutions of the modern state. (*Origins*, 39)

This formulation draws on a poststructuralist understanding of how subjectivity is constituted in language, as well as on the Derridean critique of phonocentrism, which regards written rather than spoken language as primary—hence the formulation that writing produces subjectivity and that a new mode of writing produces a new kind of subjectivity. As an example, Karatani discusses the writer Kunikida Doppo (1871–1908), known for his lyrical descriptions of natural scenes:

For Doppo the "inner" was the word (the voice), and expression was the projection outward of that voice. In Doppo's work the concept of "expression" came into being for the first time in Japanese literature. Before this time, no one spoke of literature in terms of expression. It was the identification of writing with speech which made such a concept possible. (*Origins*, 40)

Karatani's argument about the connection between a modern mode of writing (*genbun itchi*) and a modern subjectivity is brilliantly argued and has become widely accepted among scholars of modern Japanese literature. Yet the question of how gender might inflect this argument is entirely absent from Karatani's text.

Within Karatani's theory, the new inner self, or interiority (*naimen*), is ungendered, but/and/therefore assumed to be male. All the examples Karatani gives are of male writers and their male protagonists: Kunikida Doppo, Futabatei Shimei, Tayama Katai, Uchimura Kanzo, Shiga Naoya, etc.[5] By not discussing female writers and/or female fictional characters, Karatani avoids the question of how language and writing might construct subjectivity differently for women.

A similar blindness to gender difference characterizes Karatani's brief discussion of the various social institutions that produced a new kind of "subject" of the nation-state in the 1890s. Karatani lists the school and the military as institutions that molded "human beings," i.e., (national) subjects with certain homogeneous qualities, out of peoples that had previously belonged to diverse social classes:

For example, it is said that the military was formed for the purpose of defense and resistance against the Western powers. Its actual effect, however, was to cultivate in human beings that had hitherto belonged to diverse classes and modes of production a certain group discipline and functional mode of existence. The military was an organ of "education." . . . "Human beings," in a word, were produced by both the school system and the military. (*Origins*, 131)

Karatani also links the function of the factory to those of the military and the school in its production of homogeneous human beings: "If the factory is a school and the military a school, the modern school system itself may be seen as a factory. . . . The modern nation-state itself is an educational apparatus that produces 'the human being'" (*Origins*, 132).

In these statements, the "human being" is ungendered and/therefore/nonetheless assumed to be male. Karatani avoids the question of how these institutions might have molded women differently from men, and thus skips over the question of whether or not women were considered "human beings." Yet, as I have suggested elsewhere, the modern nation-state produced the category of "woman" as quite separate from that of "man = human."[6] The military, the schools, and the factories were all sites for the production of gendered "human beings"—men and women separate from each other and the first superior over the second. Only men were drafted for military service, and the military produced specifically male subjects predicated on a particular mode of gender and sexuality.[7] Separate schools were set up for men and women beyond the elementary school level, and the curriculum for women was intended to produce "good wives, wise mothers."[8] Young women were employed in factories in great numbers, and their marginal status within society and their exploitation at a lower wage justified each other in a vicious circle.[9] Karatani's argument about the production of the homogeneous human subject, whether in the realm of writing or in institutions such as schools and factories, is fundamentally blind to gender difference and gender asymmetry.

In response to the challenge from feminists pointing out his blindness to gender, Karatani has elaborated a theory of matrilinearity in Japanese society.[10] It is a bizarre theory, but it has gained a conceptual sophistication and rhetorical momentum that asks to be taken seriously. It has been repeated in many publications and has been quoted and further expanded by other intellectuals. The implications, which are distressing, show clearly how the assumption of a transhistorical essence about womanhood can combine with a stance of reverse Orientalism to produce a highly masculinist and antifeminist argument.[11] It is for this reason that I would like to examine this theory in some detail.

In the afterword to chapter six in the English translation, Karatani sketches a theory of matrilinearity to justify the absence of women in his text. He claims that "until very recently Japanese society maintained a matrilineal structure" (*Origins*, 169), and that the "Japanese emperor system itself has roots in a matrilineal system" (*Origins*, 169). The emperor system during the Heian period (from the eighth to twelfth centuries) depended on a system in which the patriarchs of the powerful Fujiwara clan would marry off their daughters to the emperor (which was not too difficult since the practice of polygyny prevailed). The aim of these patriarchs was to have one of their daughters bear the emperor's first son and legitimate heir. They would thus seek to become the maternal grandfathers of future emperors. This is what Karatani calls the basis of the emperor system in matrilinearity (*Origins*, 170). I hardly need to point out that the position of the "woman" in this scheme is significant only in that she mediates between men: the emperor and the Fujiwara patriarchs. The term "matrilineal," however, gives the impression that the mother was somehow in charge of the proceedings.

Some feminists have attempted to challenge Karatani's theory of matrilinearity by noting that he misuses the anthropological term "matrilinearity,"[12] or by demonstrating that Japanese society was, historically speaking, not "matrilineal" in any sense of the term.[13] Yet such lines of attack do not work against Karatani's argument, since he insists that he is not making a historical or anthropological argument. He is not really talking about kinship systems in Japanese history but about operations of "cultural ideology."[14] Thus, he attempts to shield his argument from challenge on the basis of historical or anthropological evidence.

Karatani claims that patriarchal structures have always come from foreign countries: China in premodern times, the West in modern times. In Japan, patriarchy has not entirely displaced matrilinearity, but has worked together with it in a kind of "bilinearity."[15] For this reason, says Karatani, it is dangerous to critique patriarchy as feminists have done. A critique of patriarchy is a critique of what is foreign, and only adds to the legitimacy of the indigenous, the matrilineal. Since matrilinearity is the basis of the emperor system, feminism leads to a valorization of the emperor system and to a reactionary return to Japaneseness (*Nihon kaiki*). In the context of Japanese history, Karatani claims, feminism leads back to fascism.[16]

Karatani's claim is that some forms of Japanese feminism have had a troubling association with the emperor system and fascistic ideology through a valorization of motherhood. Yet Karatani is making a larger claim that goes beyond a historically specific instance: the claim of the matrilineal underpinnings of Japanese culture as something that is continuous through history and keeps returning to the surface. The obvious problem with this theory of matrilinearity is that it falls precisely into the kind of ahistorical essentialism that Karatani usually and rightly criticizes. It is a move away from the genealogical critique that the rest of *Origins of Modern Japanese Literature* performs so effectively.

In the early 1990s, Karatani further elaborated on the idea of matrilinearity, connecting it to the Japanese writing system and the structure of the Japanese psyche. In his serialized essay "Nihon seishin bunseki" (Psychoanalysis of Japan),[17] Karatani identifies the Japanese writing system, which uses three different scripts, as a unique apparatus that has enabled Japan to neither reject nor internalize foreign elements. Karatani claims that foreign words are imported into Japanese, yet maintain their foreignness through a separate script. This system of writing that marks "words of foreign origin" (*gairai go*) enables Japan to import such foreign systems as Confucianism, Buddhism, Christianity, Marxism, etc., without fully internalizing them.

To import foreign ideas through the kanji or katakana script is to neither reject it nor internalize it. Historically an apparatus was created that would neither resist nor internalize foreign elements. This apparatus is none other than this writing system. . . . To import foreign script is to be "castrated" in the Lacanian sense. What the duality of the Japanese writing system shows is the experience of the foreclosure of "castration" through the script.[18]

This is what Karatani means by "duality" (*nijūsei*): the dual use of "Chinese" characters (*kanji*) and the indigenous syllabic system (*hiragana*) in modern Japanese writing.

Karatani's theory continues: *kanji* have been coded as masculine and foreign, while the *hiragana* have been coded as feminine and Japanese. Historically, women have been more closely associated with the *hiragana*. Thus, the Japanese writing system shows clearly the persistence of a feminine element alongside the masculine element. The dual use of masculine and feminine script on the level of *écriture* parallels the dual structure of patriarchy and matrilinearity on the level of social ideology.

Karatani would not claim that we are conscious of using masculine *kanji* and feminine *hiragana*, or that in using a mixture of scripts in writing we are keeping foreign words foreign. He would claim that these matters do not operate on the level of awareness; they might be called structures of the Japanese unconscious, which explains the need for a "Psychoanalysis of Japan" to uncover this mechanism. He takes Lacan's claim that the unconscious is structured like language and tries to show that the unconscious of Japan is structured like the Japanese writing system. Yet by relying on a psychoanalytic model, Karatani ends up replicating psychoanalysis' ahistorical assumptions about sexual difference.

The assumption of a transhistorical femininity in Karatani's argument here goes hand in hand with a discourse of reverse Orientalism. As I mentioned earlier, in the main argument of *Origins of Modern Japanese Literature* Karatani avoids the problem of universalism versus particularism. Yet in the appendix to the English translation and in "Psychoanalysis of Japan," Karatani has made a clear turn toward insisting on the peculiarity of Japan.[19] Why this sudden turn toward reverse Orientalism?

One answer lies in Karatani's desire to point out why postmodernism has failed to have a critical function in Japan. Karatani claims that

while a postmodern and poststructuralist critique of the subject has a political significance in the West, this is not the case in Japan. This is because Japan has not fully achieved modernity, has never had a solid symbolic structure, and has never consolidated the masculine Oedipal subject.
In this context, a postmodern critique is not critical at all but only serves
to legitimate the status quo. Thus, we might see how Karatani's desire to
critique present-day Japan entices him into a rhetorical stance of arguing
for Japanese uniqueness. What remains problematic, however, is that
such an assertion of Japanese uniqueness moves in tandem with a
transhistorical assertion about femininity in Japan. Although Karatani's
critical assessment of present-day Japan and his warnings against the uncritical celebration of postmodernity offer some valuable insights, they
also are imbricated with arguments that only serve to discredit feminism
and to strengthen the masculine symbolic order.

Some of Karatani's disciples joined him in combining a reverse Orientalist assertion of Japanese uniqueness with an assumption of a transhistorical category of femininity. It is their arguments to which we now turn.

Yamashita Etsuko's Postfeminism

In *Origins of Japanese Women's Liberation Ideology: A Postfeminist Essay*,
Yamashita Etsuko uses Karatani Kōjin's strategy of uncovering the historical "origins" of what has supposedly come to seem natural,
self-evident, and ahistorical.[20] Yet her argument ultimately relies on an
ahistorical notion of subjectivity, which goes hand in hand with an assertion of Japanese uniqueness. The entire argument about the uniqueness of Japanese subjectivity, moreover, is deployed in the service of a
vehement attack against what the author sees as the dangers of feminism in Japan.

The title of the book, containing the words "women's liberation"
and "feminism," gives the false impression that this is a profeminist
text—the book is indeed found in the "feminism and women's studies"
section in bookstores and libraries. A closer reading of the title, however, alerts the reader to a very different possibility. The term "feminism" (*feminizumu*) is used with the specific connotation of the Western
liberal capitalist modernizationist feminism advocated in the 1980s by a
few deluded Japanese feminists; this is juxtaposed with "women's liberation" (*josei kaihō*), which carries the connotation of that which was

there before "feminism" but which has always been caught in the modern, Western, and therefore seemingly universal hypothesis that women are oppressed and need to be liberated. Thus both "women's liberation" and "feminism" are bracketed, questioned, and finally dismissed in the book's argument. Even more telling is the subtitle; "postfeminism" seems a code word for an attitude that might be summarized as: "we are tired of talking about feminism; it's passé; let's move on to something else."

What a reader needs to understand, then, is that this text is an attack against feminism rather than a feminist analysis. While the book purports to present a critical analysis of what is wrong with current Japanese feminism, it does not offer a viable proposal for a better kind of feminism. Yamashita's proposal for an alternative to current Japanese feminist practice reveals the bias of her position:

Whether we are talking about women's rights or about motherhood, the trap lies in discussing them as generalities. There are no women's rights and no motherhood reducible to generalities, or graspable as universalities common to all women. We can only discuss the way various individuals, each one differing in birth, socialization, and environment, choose certain things and live in certain ways, within the network of relationships on which they depend. . . . The only solution is for each individual to deal with the various problems that arise at the various stages of life, and to go on living without ressentiment. (*Nihon*, 221)

This position is a complete denial of collective politics, feminist or otherwise. It refuses to acknowledge either the existence of shared experience, or the possibility of coalition among people with different but communicable experience. Moreover, this is no more than a brand of individualism that is virtually indistinguishable from the bourgeois capitalist liberalism Yamashita attacks in the rest of her book. The difference, Yamashita would argue, lies in the "authenticity of desire" in her individualist utopia. Each woman should do what she really wants to do and not imitate what others are doing. Whether such authenticity is at all possible for human beings is a question not asked by Yamashita.[21] The irony of a proposal of isolationist individualism as a solution to the problem of liberal capitalism alerts us to the possibility that the writer might be confused about the nature of the problem she analyzes.

Yamashita's agenda is to "examine Japanese feminist thought from a viewpoint that is free from the 'repressive hypothesis' [*yokuatsu no kasetsu*]" (*Nihon*, 6). The notion of "repressive hypothesis" alludes to, but does not equal, Michel Foucault's formulation—i.e., the common idea that sexuality is something that earlier periods repressed and that modernity has sought to liberate.[22] Using the polysemy of the Japanese word "*yokuatsu*," which may denote either (sexual, psychological, psychoanalytical) repression or (economic, political, legal) oppression, Yamashita proposes the argument that it was modernity that created the consciousness that "I am oppressed," i.e., that one is suffering from "*yokuatsu*." Thus Yamashita is not only able to strike a fashionably Foucaultian gesture of spurning the repressive hypothesis, she can also dismiss the whole notion of women's oppression as nothing more than hypothesis, a state of mind one can choose to snap out of.

According to Yamashita, not only would it be an epistemological mistake to look at premodern Japanese women through the lens of the repressive hypothesis; it would be misguided and arrogant of feminists to suppose that women past and present are suffering from oppression. Yamashita's aim to "liberate" (*kaihō suru*) history from the assumptions of *yokuatsu* is most fruitful when it allows her to uncover facts that, in her mind, contradict the dominant paradigm of feminist historiography. It is most odious, in my mind, when it is used to argue for the need to "liberate" Japanese women today from "women's liberation."

Much of the rhetorical and ethical force of Yamashita's historiographical project is derived from her critique of what she considers the problems caused by contemporary Japanese feminism. This feminism is defined as liberal, capitalist, eurocentric, and modernizationist, advocating women's entry into the work force and men's participation in housework. This form of feminism, Yamashita claims, is espoused by the government, the industries, the mass media, and a few elite feminists who have become celebrities in the 1980s (*Nihon*, 3–29). According to Yamashita, the central problem of this brand of feminism is its eurocentrism, disguised as universalism:

In the minds of Japanese feminists, "women" of Europe and the United States always exist as the universal model. Japan is compared with this model, and its women are judged to be low in status. It is thought that women living in Japan, Asia, and Africa will—and should—progress along with the development of their societies, and to reach the level of women in Europe and the United

States. We must point out, however, that such a way of thinking is in itself Eurocentric. (*Nihon*, 7)

Yamashita's strategy in the introductory chapter of her book is to align this dominant school of feminism with everything that is wrong with Japan and the world today: with capitalism and its proclivity to reduce everything to monetary value (*Nihon*, 12); with neocolonialist exploitation of third-world nations as the basis of Japanese prosperity (*Nihon*, 12–13); and with a mass consumer society based on endless desire for imitation and differentiation (*Nihon*, 18–21). This makes it possible for her to deny any critical function to feminism while accusing feminism of collaborating with institutions of power.[23]

Yamashita's frustration with the current situation is certainly shared by myself and by other Japanese feminists. Many of her dissatisfactions are precisely those voiced by feminists whom Yamashita attacks: Ueno Chizuko, for example, critiques Japanese capitalism from a Marxist feminist position; Kanai Yoshiko calls for a global feminism that refuses to make the exploitation of Asian women a condition for the liberation of Japanese women; and Ehara Yumiko analyzes how the mass media manipulates women's desires.[24] Yet Yamashita chooses to identify feminism as a part of the problem of contemporary society, rather than as a part of its potential solution—hence her attempt to liberate Japanese women from women's liberation.

Her blaming of Japanese feminism for various contemporary social ills serves as both conclusion and premise of her historical analysis. This creates a circular argument: her thesis is that the current opportunistic marriage between feminism and state power is a repetition of what happened in the 1920s, as a prelude to Japanese fascism and colonial expansion that led to World War II. The current deplorable state of Japan is one indication that history repeats itself and feminism remains trapped within this repetition. The argument becomes circular when the conclusion is turned into a premise: the current state is deplorable and shows that history repeats itself; yet it is because history repeats itself that the current state must be considered deplorable.

The thesis that history repeats itself is a popular but dangerous one: it tends to ignore specificities of historical situations, perceiving homologies without differences. We notice, for example, how Yamashita's argument does not allow her to perceive much difference between the situation of the 1920s and that of the 1980s, and between prewar and postwar feminist thought. Indeed, her argument is predicated on the homology between the two:

During the war, almost all elite women were active as trustees of [organizations supporting the war effort, such as] "Taisei Yokusan Kai" and "Dai Nihon Fujin Kai," yet after the war the same women, without self-examination or self-awareness, became trustees of ladies' organizations and members of the House of Councilors. We must change the attitude of resorting to uncritical complicity with the ruling powers in our desperate efforts to improve women's social status. Both the motherhood ideology [*bosei shugi*] of Takamure and the women's rights ideology [*joken shugi*] of Kaneko Shigeri became active participants in fascism—we need to look hard at that fact, as a trap of women's liberation thought [*josei kaihō shisō*]. (*Nihon*, 163)

Yamashita condemns feminist thought past and present without historical grounding in the complex, and often contradictory, interrelationships between feminism, nationalism, fascism, and capitalism. Historians of the era do analyze feminist complicity in the war effort without identifying feminism with "everything that went wrong." The main chapters of Yamashita's book do contain much useful information, pointing to possible areas for historical research. Too often, however, her prejudice in favor of historical continuity leads her to "discover" exactly such continuity. In the process, any evidence that feminism has contributed to the improvement of women's lives in Japan is swept under the rug.[25]

Yamashita applies Karatani Kōjin's strategy of ideological critique to the idea of "repression/oppression" of women. In the process Yamashita also borrows Karatani's argument about *genbun itchi*, the modern mode of writing that offers the appearance of more closely approximating speech. It is this mode of writing that creates the consciousness of an interior self and a consciousness that one is "repressed/oppressed." Yamashita situates the first feminist movement in Japan, the Bluestockings (Seitō), and the movement's publication of the same name, as caught within this mode:

Seitō can be characterized as a literary movement expressed in the genbun itchi style by women. . . . It is in Seitō that women speak frankly of their "interiority" through literary works written in a vernacular style. These women sought to establish themselves as subjects [*shutai*] within the system of genbun itchi. (*Nihon*, 71–72)

However, it is when she starts describing the new kind of subjectivity that was produced by this new kind of writing that she departs from Karatani's paradigm. According to Yamashita, the subjectivity expressed through *genbun itchi* by feminists such as Hiratsuka Raichō was quite different from the Cartesian cogito of the West. It was instead a kind of return to a primordial self (*kongen teki jiko*) that was at once modern and postmodern and, we are made to assume, premodern as well. In other words, it was a transhistorical constant rather than a new dimension that revealed itself in the new mode of writing.

While Karatani's conceptualization of "interiority"—the internal self isolated from the external world and therefore able to describe it— stresses the process of its historical and linguistic production, Yamashita's concept of Japanese subjectivity is an ahistorical essence, a uniquely Japanese subjectivity that is distinguished from the Western, Cartesian cogito (*Nihon*, 94). This Japanese subjectivity is variously referred to as "naturality" [*jinen*],[26] "self-differentiation/*différance*" (*jiko sai ka*),[27] "becoming" (*seisei*),[28] and is alternately described as that which precedes or transcends the differentiation of subject and object (*shu-kaku goitsu*),[29] and a soft subject arising from a soft triangle based on the merging of the mother and child (*boshi yūgō*),[30] rather than on the Oedipal struggle between father and son.[31] Yamashita mixes and matches the vocabulary of Buddhism, poststructuralism, and Nishida philosophy, also alluding to familiar tenets of *Nihonjinron* discourse—a uniquely Japanese subjectivity that is fluid and relational rather than rigid and autonomous, group-oriented rather than individualistic, feminine rather than masculine, and so on.

The nature of such a Japanese subjectivity has been the topic of much essentialist debate since the prewar period, by feminists as well as by Japanese cultural theorists whose interests have little to do with feminism.[32] What is yet to be undertaken is a historical investigation of how this "uniquely" Japanese subject is produced through various discursive practices. Yamashita, too, leaves the nature and production of such a subjectivity unexplained and unquestioned. She gives one possible cause for the formation of the soft Japanese subject: the great status and substantial power given to the mother in the traditional family structure (*Nihon,* 55–57). Yet she gives little evidence for this great power, which supposedly transcends even that of the patriarch, and simply concludes that this was the structure of the Japanese household (*ie*), in which the woman was oppressed by her mother-in-law, rather than by her husband (*Nihon,* 187).[33] Because of the lack of sufficient explanation, the uniquely Japanese subject in her argument remains posited as an ahistorical essence that has characterized and limited Japanese feminism (*Nihon,* 186–187), and that has shaped Japanese history in a profound way.

Significantly, Yamashita avoids the question of what exactly shapes history. At times she reduces all "feminist" progress to the logic of capitalist pursuit of profit (*Nihon,* 16–22); at other times, she dismisses capitalist expansion as a cause, pointing to the independent periodic oscillation between women's liberation and return to the family (*Nihon,* 155–156). Nationalist ideology of motherhood and wartime need for female workers seem to compete as historical forces defining women's roles (*Nihon,* 157–181). The relationships between Japanese subjectivity, the logic of capitalism, and the ideology of the nation-state remain rather unclear, although Yamashita borrows Asada Akira's theories concerning the nation-state to try to account for some of the complexities of historical change and continuity (*Nihon,* 190–191; 198–199).[34]

Yamashita's position toward this uniquely Japanese subjectivity is one of ambivalence: at times she seems to value it as a postmodern alternative to the modern Western cogito (*Nihon* 92–94), at other times she also emphasizes its connection to fascism (*Nihon,* 186–187; 219–220). A feminism based on the modern individualist subject should logically call forth a similar ambivalence from her—a recognition of its value as well as a critique of its limitations. Yet this ambivalence is forcibly resolved in the direction of "postfeminism"; this forced resolution causes much of the tension and the circularity of the book's argument. Because the text cannot acknowledge what is positive in feminism, it must bend over backwards, producing an ahistorical and circular account of how things never change. Thus in Yamashita's argument, the assumption of a transhistorical essence is aligned with an assertion of the uniqueness of Japanese society: the result is an antifeminist argument.

Yamashita's book can be read as the precursor of the backlash against feminism in 1980s and 1990s Japan. Yamashita's writing might well have started initially as a positive move to diversify feminist scholarship and to venture an unorthodox historical interpretation of Japanese feminist thought. Yet it was quickly seized by the masculinist media, eager to see a good fight, eager to champion the idea of "postfeminism."[35] Her stance vis-à-vis Japanese feminism remains conflicted and contradictory: much of her research draws on scholarship influenced by feminism, yet her conclusion is resolutely antifeminist.

Suga Hidemi's Femininity

In a series of articles published in the early 1990s entitled "The Structure of Novelistic Modernity,"[36] the literary critic Suga Hidemi traced an argument about the modernization process in Japanese literature, a process that he summarized by the term "vernacularization."[37] Vernacularization is the equivalent of Karatani's *genbun itchi*: the forging of a new mode of writing that seems to better represent speech. According to Suga, vernacularization repressed and obscured "femininity," even while maintaining and utilizing it.[38]

If this sounds vague, it is symptomatic of Suga's argument as a whole. The problem begins with Suga's definition of "femininity":

I define femininity as a kind of alterity [*tasha sei*] that is both maintained and obscured in the process of the establishment of modern literature; it does not directly refer to natural sexual difference.[39]

This definition threatens to make his argument tautological; the process of vernacularization maintained/obscured femininity, which is defined as that which vernacularization maintained/obscured. Or, to rephrase, vernacularization repressed that which it repressed.

The ambiguity of what exactly vernacularization does to femininity—maintaining and utilizing, on the one hand; obscuring and repressing, on the other hand—is never clearly explained. What happens to femininity under vernacularization is left unclear; but what is clear is that it parallels what happens to matrilinearity under patriarchy, according to Karatani's theory. In other words, Suga here is relying on Karatani's theory, borrowing the idea of the transhistorical femininity that has structured Japanese society. This allows him to leave the definition and status of femininity itself unclarified.

What anchors Suga's argument and prevents it from becoming completely circular is his discussion of several female writers, such as Higuchi Ichiyo, Wakamatsu Shizuko, and Tanabe Kaho. He also pays attention to what he considers the marks of gender in various modes of writing: he is especially concerned to point out what happens to sentence endings and punctuations in *genbun itchi*. He considers certain types of sentence endings and punctuations to be coded as feminine; consequently, they are shown to be maintained/obscured in the process of vernacularization.

Yet even here, the problem of tautology persists. Suga's reading of short stories by women writers relies on a simplistic interpretation of Lacanian theory, according to which woman is defined as lacking the phallus and therefore perpetually seeking to obtain the phallus. Consequently, Suga ferrets out hints in these stories that the female characters are in search of the phallus. Anything that might be vaguely linked to the phallus is indeed interpreted to be the phallus: a child, a husband, a father, the name of the father = family name, God, a mirror, a cloth collar sold by a male merchant. Any hint of desire for these phallic symbols is interpreted to be a sign of phallocentrism. Suga's definition of the "phallus" proves to be as tautological as his definition of "femininity":

> The phallus, like the "name of the father" = surname [*sei*] is an exterior Other [*gaibu teki tasha*] that guarantees the identity of the self. If the genbun itchi writing style is an attempt to make the "writing" [*bun*] match the interior Truth of the self—imagined as "speech" [*gen*]—then there is a need for a new exterior Other to be posited, in order to guarantee the Truth of the "writing."[40]

In other words, the phallus is that which guarantees vernacularization; femininity is that which is repressed/maintained/obscured in vernacularization. Since most female writers followed the process of vernacularization, they turn out to be phallic rather than feminine. On the other hand, a male writer may turn out to be much more feminine than a female writer, since femininity has less to do with the sex-gender of a writer than with his or her mode of writing.[41]

Suga's analysis of modes of writing, however, suffers from a further level of tautology. He alleges that certain sentence endings (such as "*desu, masu*" now conventionally considered a formal style showing respect toward the addressee) and certain punctuations such as dashes and ellipses are marked as feminine. These sentence endings and punctuations become repressed in the process of vernacularization. However, no persuasive support is given for the allegation that "*desu, masu*" are feminine endings, or that dashes and ellipses are "marks of female illogical-ness" (*josei teki hironri*).[42] Indeed, I would argue that Suga's categorization of certain modes of writing as feminine can only be the result of, rather than the premise for, the argument that vernacularism's repression of these modes constituted repression of femininity: It is only because Suga defines femininity as that which is repressed in vernacularization that he can ascribe femininity to certain sentence endings and punctuations that did not make it into the dominant mode of writing. There is nothing intrinsically feminine about them.

Where does this circular argument lead? Or, to invert the direction of inquiry, what drives this circular argument? To answer these questions, we need to look at how reverse Orientalism operates together with an assertion of transhistorical femininity, which requires a detour through a different strand of argument that Suga makes in a book entitled *Novelistic Force*. There, through a critique of Edward Said's formulation of Orientalism, Suga takes up the position of the reverse Orientalist. Gender operates in his argument in complex ways, but what emerges clearly is the tandem movement of reverse Orientalism and a claim that "women have always been close to the center of power in Japan."

Reverse Orientalism

In a formulation that has become classic by now, Edward Said points out the sexist dimension of Orientalism.[43] The Orient, according to Western representations, suggests "not only fecundity but sexual promise (and threat), untiring sensuality, unlimited desire, deep generative energies" (*Orientalism*, 188). The Orient is associated with sexual availability; that is, the availability of Oriental women to Western men:

We may as well recognize that for nineteenth-century Europe, with its increasing embourgeoisement, sex had been institutionalized to a very considerable degree. On the one hand, there was no such thing as "free" sex, and on the other, sex in society entailed a web of legal, moral, even political and economic obligations of a detailed and certainly encumbering sort . . . the Orient was a place where one could look for sexual experience unobtainable in Europe. (*Orientalism*, 190)

Orientalism ascribes characteristics of femininity to the Orient, emphasizing "its eccentricity, its backwardness, its silent indifference, its feminine penetrability, its supine malleability" (*Orientalism*, 206). Orientalism and sexism go hand in hand: "[W]omen are usually the creatures of a male power-fantasy. They express unlimited sensuality, they are more or less stupid, and above all they are willing" (*Orientalism*, 207). Orientalism feminizes the Orient.

There is no doubt that Orientalism feminizes Japan, as one of the Oriental nations. Yet Japan's position vis-à-vis Orientalism becomes complicated because of its semi- and double-colonial position: Japan, under the threat of being colonized by the West, became a colonizing nation itself. Orientalized Japan Orientalized other Asian nations in turn.[44] Within the double movement of Orientalized-Orientalizer, the position of the feminine becomes equally complicated.

In his book *Novelistic Force*, Suga Hidemi criticizes Said's formulation of Orientalism, because it perceives the West-Orient relationship as a static one.[45] Instead, he proposes to understand the relationship in Hegelian terms, as a dialectic of Master and Slave. According to Hegel, says Suga, the Slave eventually overcomes the Master, because the Master is dependent on the Slave.[46] If the Orient (Slave) is an object that must be represented by the West (Master) as subject, the way for the Slave (Japan) to become a subject is to imitate and eventually transcend the Master (the West). Suga shows how "the decline of the West" in the early twentieth century signaled Japan's chance to become a subject:

The problem, as ironic as it may seem, is that there actually existed a certain period during which the Orient could recognize itself as a subject, capable of performing a critique of the West. This period was characterized by the arguments [in Japan] about "overcoming the modern," which coincided with "the decline of the West," and by the ideals of "the Greater East Asian War" (*Shōsetsu*, 16).

For Japan as a Slave of the West to become a subject, it had to imitate and surpass Western imperialism; for Japan to become the Master, it had to force other Asian nations to take on the position of the Slave. As the disastrous results leading up to Japan's defeat in World War II showed, however, Japan should never have tried to "overcome" its status as Slave.[47]

The "Orientalism" that Said criticizes is in this sense analogous to Hegel's "Master-Slave" dialectic. We may say that Said analyzes and points out the hegemonic domination of the "Slave" by the "Master." Yet Said's theory of hegemony remains within the simplistic pattern of the Master unilaterally dominating the Slave. . . According to Said's theory of power, the Master remains perpetually the Master, and the Slave remains perpetually the Slave. Of course, according to Said, the domination of the Slave by the Master depends on the Slave's internalization of the Master's consciousness (i.e., the Orient made to imitate the West). That is, the Orient must accept its status as "Orient." According to Hegel's dialectic, however, the Slave, through fear and service to the Master (i.e., work), at some point realizes the Master's intention. This is the point at which the Master declines and the Slave becomes the Subject.

Said's perspective of criticizing "Orientalism" is unable to come to terms with this moment in which the hierarchy of Master and Slave is reversed. . . . It is impossible to discuss "Orientalism" today without critiquing the moment in which the Slave becomes (Master) Subject.[48] To repeat, this is what is taught to us by the "overcoming the modern" argument of 1920s and 1930s Japan, as well as by the numerous variations on this theme that keep returning to us to this day. (*Shōsetsu*, 17–18)

The Master-Slave dialectic, then, is responsible for a vicious cycle in which the colonized and Orientalized nation seeks to overcome that condition of slavery by becoming a Master who colonizes and Orientalizes other nations. According to Suga, in order to avoid the destructive dialectical logic of the Slave plotting to overcome the Master, we must think of a different kind of logic.

It is at this point in the argument that Suga launches into the question of gender in order to show the complexity of Japan's status as Slave. First, he points out that in the Hegelian dialectic, both the Master and the Slave are conceived as men, while the woman is posited as the object of desire for which the two men must compete; it is the woman who causes the Master-Slave relationship to come into existence.[49]

Suga insists that the "universal" Hegelian paradigm does not apply to Japan, and cites Orikuchi Shinobu (1887–1953), an influential scholar and poet writing in the early twentieth century, in order to prove the particularity of Japan. Orikuchi deduced from the women-centered culture and literature of the Heian court in tenth- and eleventh-century Japan that the position of women during this time had been close to the most important source of power—the emperor. Orikuchi notes that the literary dominance of women in Japan had its origins in ancient social structures:

In large clans or tribes, the oral declarations announcing the chief's wishes or commands came to be communicated formally through various complex processes. Informal announcements, however, were dictated to high-class ladies-in-waiting—attending the chief in the capacity of shamans—and were communicated through their words. . . . This was the original cause that gave rise to the court literature of the Heian period, centered on the ladies-in-waiting.[50]

According to Orikuchi, women in ancient Japan had served the center of power as shamans, attendants, and educators of emperors, and this was the origin of women-centered literature in the tenth and eleventh centuries. Suga extends Orikuchi's notion of the "literature of ladies-in-waiting" (*nyōbo bungaku*) to present-day Japan, drawing an analogy between the position of women in the emperor system with that of the Slave in relation to the Master in Hegel's dialectic:

In Hegel, both Master and Slave are posited as male, and woman is doubly oppressed by being objectified. According to Orikuchi, however, the Slave in ancient Japan is posited as female. Orikuchi's perspective is quite useful in measuring the differences and commonalities between the West and Japan. . . . The peculiarity of the [Japanese] emperor system as a mode of rule lies in its use of women, not as part of the mechanism of alienation and oppression, but as attendants (i.e., Slaves) in direct contact with the gods (i.e., Masters) (*Shōsetsu*, 145–146).

Suga goes on to say that the sexual difference between the male Master and the female Slave in Japan prevented the overthrow of the Master that would have been possible in the male-centered Hegelian dialectic. Suga does not explain why a female Slave cannot overthrow a male Master, and his logic is not supported by anything except the sexist and heterosexist assumption that a woman will remain devoted to her man. Hence, Suga moves on to formulate a logic of "noise" which he associates with femininity, the novel, the fetish, and a possible solution to the problem posed by the Hegelian dialectic. I will not attempt to trace Suga's argument any further, except to say that it, too, is paradigmatic of an intellectual move that connects reverse Orientalism and transhistorical femininity. The recognition that Japan has played the role of Woman to the West as Man leads to a perverse valorization of woman's role in mythical or ancient Japan, and to the conclusion that Japan is different from the West in that women have been the pillars of the ruling system. This kind of argument is characterized by shaky historical evidence and circular logic: in order to prove that women were close to power, appeal is made to women's literature, but in order to prove that women's literature is a sign of power, appeal is made to women's proximity to the center of power.

Furthermore, if femininity was indeed repressed by vernacularization, i.e., "modernization" of literature in Meiji Japan, as Suga argues, this creates a dilemma for feminism. There would be two options for feminism, neither of them satisfactory: feminism either must become antimodernist (and therefore potentially reactionary) in its effort to recover lost femininity; or it must suppress femininity altogether in its effort for further modernization.[51] Either way, feminism is doomed to fail. And if women have always been powerful in Japan, Japan has no need for feminism to begin with.

Antifeminism

Thus far I have shown how Suga Hidemi and Yamashita Etsuko have elaborated on Karatani Kōjin's theory on language and subjectivity, feeding the gender question into Karatani's ungendered schema of *Origins of Modern Japanese Literature*. As we have seen, Karatani himself has recently elaborated a theory about matrilinearity in response to criticism that his earlier schema was blind to gender. The result of these elaborations has been a highly complex and problematic set of theories, all of which explicitly, as in the case of Yamashita—or implicitly, as in the case of Karatani and Suga—attack Japanese feminism.

It should be stated that most feminists in Japan, like most other people in Japan, did cooperate both socially and ideologically with the state during World War II. It is also true that this remains a major problem that Japanese feminism must confront. Debates within the feminist community in Japan show that most present-day feminists are fully aware of this problem, and that they consider this issue to be crucial in theorizing about all aspects of women's lives.[52] There is, in other words, much internal critique about this aspect of Japanese feminism. What is exemplified by the arguments of critics such as Karatani, Suga, and Yamashita, however, seems less like a critique of feminism than feminist-bashing.

On the other hand, it would be too simplistic to say that a critic like Suga Hidemi is antifeminist. Suga's statements and writings suggest that he would like to present himself as a sympathizer, not a basher, of Japanese feminism: this is why he would bother to point out the shortcomings and potential pitfalls of Japanese feminists. In this regard, he seems to differentiate himself from someone like Yamashita Etsuko, who refuses to acknowledge either the material accomplishments or the critical functions of feminism in Japan. Interestingly, Suga has even been called a "feminist critic in drag" (*dansō josei hihyōka*), a critic who is actually a woman inside but merely looks like a man outside. Putting aside the fascinating question of transvestism and performativity in gender and criticism, we might note how a discourse of "Suga Hidemi is a better feminist critic than most female feminist critics" operates to dismiss these other female feminist critics.[53]

The theorizing of the relationship between language, subjectivity, and gender by all three critics remains problematic in that they all locate some transhistorical essence to which feminism returns as a reaction against modernity. For Karatani this is "matrilinearity"; for Yamashita it is the "Japanese self" under various aliases; for Suga it is "femininity." Whereas a "Western" feminist philosopher like Luce Irigaray would define femininity as something that has not yet been represented in the phallic order,[54] these Japanese thinkers link femininity with something that used to exist in close proximity to political power in ancient times in Japan, something that was repressed yet somehow maintained and utilized in modernity, and something that continues to return in the form of fascism.[55]

This idea of a persistence of something that makes Japan unique in its gender arrangement through all of its history is certainly questionable. Elsewhere I have shown that categories such as "woman" and "femininity" only come into being with modernity, and that the formation of woman is a modern phenomenon, inseparable from the process of building a modern nation-state.[56] Many of the essays in this present volume also trace this modern formation of categories of gender and sexuality.

The Unacknowledged Masculinity of Japan

Antifeminism is not the only consequence of the perpetual motion machine that combines reverse Orientalism with transhistorical femininity. The discursive operation that links an essentialist Japan with an essentialist femininity serves to make us forget the numerous ways in which Japan is, in fact, "masculine."

Orientalism feminizes the Orient. Let us, for purposes of this argument, grant that this formula is valid: "West : Orient = Man : Woman." The West is to the Orient as Man is to Woman. What this formula represents is a process of Orientalizing and feminizing, a dynamic making of non-Western and nonmasculine categories to shore up the Western and masculine subject. These uses of "West," "Orient," "Man," "Woman" are all relational; these terms are constructed in and through the process of Orientalizing and feminizing. What the formula does not represent, in other words, are fixed entities, such as "the West," "the Orient," "Man," and "Woman." To read the formula as representing fixed positions, categories, or entities is to arrive at false conclusions. Most often what happens is a metonymic slide from the status of the abstract term "Woman" denoting a process of feminization to the status of "women" as historical agents. This slide can then be used against feminism: if Japan is Woman, then women in Japan are central to the nation, and therefore need no further strengthening in the form of feminism.[57]

Moreover, this formula of "Japan = Woman" also can be used to mask another formula, according to which "Japan = Man." To insist on the femininity of Japan as a nation obstructs recognition of the "masculinist" role Japan played, and continues to play, vis-à-vis other nations. Reverse Orientalism would affirm the formula "Japan : West = Woman : Man" in which the first term of each half of the equation is considered superior to the second half. But this reverse formula obscures the formula that would logically follow from Japan's semi- and double-colonial position: "Japan : Asia = Man : Woman." This is an obvious fact: in the light of Japan's colonial aggression toward Asia, the claim that Japan is a feminine nation sounds utterly ludicrous. Yet this aspect of the gendered relationship between Japan and Asia is precisely what is hidden by the tandem movement of reverse Orientalism and transhistorical femininity.

Ueno Chizuko eloquently expresses her exasperation with the perpetual tandem motion of reverse Orientalism and gender essentialism:

Under the oppositional schema of West versus Orient, Japanese feminism is under the cultural injunction to distance its arguments from Western thought, in order to prove that it is not an importation from the West. However, according to this schema, the Orient, defined as a difference from the West, has always already been "Woman." Thus the masculinist discourse of "We have always been 'Woman'" functions to delegitimate women's feminist discourse. What we hear is a masculinist chorus in unison: "The land of the rising sun has always been a nation that celebrates 'sister's power' [imo no chikara], with a goddess called Amaterasu Oomikami at the very origins of the nation; women have always been strong so they don't need to become any stronger." The discourse of the "motherly emperor"—the idea that the emperor was really a mother figure—is an extension of this line of argument.

Whenever one raises the question of gender, one is inevitably trapped into this mode of reverse Orientalism. This stupefying intellectual climate is extremely irritating. Why everyone keeps falling into such an obvious trap is beyond me, but unless a third way is presented to us, the pendulum movement between the two poles of Orientalism and reverse Orientalism will keep swinging for a while.[58]

Like Ueno, I believe that there must be a way out of the two poles of Orientalism and reverse Orientalism. This essay's critique of the three theories of Karatani Kōjin, Yamashita Etsuko, and Suga Hidemi has been an attempt to show how a "third" way is also needed between the pole of "Japanese women have always been oppressed" and the pole of "Japanese women have always been powerful."

It is my contention that the tandem operations of reverse Orientalism and the assumption of transhistorical femininity in the discursive space of late capitalist Japan continues to serve two mutually enabling purposes: First, it serves as a defense against the threat of feminism, contributing to the maintenance of the sexist status quo of gender relations within Japan. Second, it serves to obscure the masculinity of Japanese society, especially in its gendered colonial relationship to the rest of Asia. The arguments exemplified by Karatani, Yamashita, and Suga may have been symptomatic of the intellectual climate of the late 1980s and early 1990s, but unless we expose and dispose of the persistent underlying assumptions, we are doomed to remain trapped in this "extremely irritating" and "stupefying" intellectual climate.

Notes

The arguments in this essay were initially formulated in the early 1990s. Nonetheless, the recent recrudescence of "feminism bashing" in Japan—in which conservative politicians have argued for the maintenance of naturalized and ahistorical definitions of "masculinity" and "femininity," and have attacked the notion of a "gender-free" society—leads me to believe that the logic discussed in this essay is still alive, and its critique still relevant. An earlier version of some parts of this essay has been published as part of my "Japanese Theater and Imperialism: Romance and Resistance," *U.S.-Japan Women's Journal*, English Supplement, no. 12 (1997): 17–47. All translations from the Japanese are mine unless indicated otherwise.

1. Symbolically, these books were shelved in some bookstores in the "women's books" section alongside guidebooks to marriage and childrearing, and in other stores in the "contemporary thought" section alongside translations of French poststructuralism.

2. To complicate matters slightly, Karatani, Yamashita, and Suga are all quite critical of Japan and would not readily assert that Japan is *superior* to the West. They do agree, however, that Japan is more "advanced" and more "postmodern" than the West. The difference of their position from that of a nationalist version of reverse Orientalism is that they see Japan's postmodern condition as a deplorable phenomenon.

3. Karatani Kōjin, *Nihon kindai bungaku no kigen* (Kōdansha, 1980); *Origins of Modern Japanese Literature*, trans. Brett de Bary et al. (Durham, NC: Duke University Press, 1993). Subsequent citations of these works will be referred to in the text as *Kigen* and *Origins* along with the relevant page numbers.

4. "Post-Contemporary Interventions" is the title of the series edited by Fredric Jameson and Stanley Fish, under which the English translation of Karatani was published by Duke University Press.

5. The one exception is Higuchi Ichiyō, a woman writer whom he discusses as part of the "discovery of the child." Karatani sees Higuchi as writing about children in a way that precedes the production of the homogeneous human being (*Origins*, 133). In the English appendix, which I discuss below, he further valorizes Higuchi's writing as not conforming to the logic of *genbun itchi*. See Karatani, *Origins*, 135.

6. See Ayako Kano, *Acting Like a Woman in Modern Japan: Theater, Gender, and Nationalism* (New York: Palgrave, 2001).

7. See, for example, the essays by Mark Driscoll and Theodore Cook in this anthology.

8. See the essays by Martha Tocco and Kathleen Uno in this volume. See also Mitsuda Kyoko, "Kindaiteki bosei kan no juyō to hen'yō: 'Kyōiku suru hahaoya' kara 'ryōsai kenbo' e," in *Bosei o tou: rekishiteki hensen*, ed. Wakita Haruko, 2 vols. (Kyoto: Bunkōsha, 1985) 2: 100–129.

9. See Janet Hunter's essay in this volume. See also Murakami Hatsu, "Sangyō kakumei ki no joshi rōdō," in *Kindai*, vol. 4, *Nihon josei shi*, ed. Joseishi sōgō kenkyūkai (Tōdai shuppankai, 1982), 77–114; and Patricia E. Tsurumi, *Factory Girls: Women in the Thread Mills of Meiji Japan* (Princeton, NJ: Princeton University Press, 1990).

10. Initially, Karatani used the term "matriarchy" (*boken sei*); he later modified the term to "matrilinearity" (*bokei sei*). He also uses the term "bilinearity" (*sōkei sei*) to counter historical evidence in favor of patrilinearity by insisting that patrilineal and matrilineal systems coexisted. After the publication of the English translation of *Origins of Modern Japanese Literature*, Karatani modified the term further, referring to "mixed use" (*kōyō sei*), and most recently, "duality" (*nijū sei*). The change in terminology reflects a gradual abstraction of the level of argument: from the level of women's political power (matriarchy) to the level of women's status in hereditary succession (matrilinearity), to the level of écriture (duality). This is discussed further below.

11. Ueno Chizuko formulates the problem as "the problem that an essentialist theory of Japan [*nihon honshitsuron*] arising from reverse colonialism-Orientalism always comes bound up with an essentialist theory of woman [*josei honshitsu ron*]." Ueno Chizuko et al., "Nihon bunka to jendā," *Hihyō kūkan*, 2nd ser., no. 3 (1994): 6–43. This is a roundtable discussion with Mizuta Noriko, Asada Akira, and Karatani Kōjin. The quote is from p. 39.

12. Ueno, "Nihon bunka to jendā," 9–10.

13. Ibid., 13–14.

14. Ibid., 8–14. After struggling in vain to pin down Karatani's definition of terms such as matrilinearity and bilinearity, Ueno ends up telling Karatani to stop using these terms because they are confusing. Karatani agrees but does not alter his theory.

15. See also Karatani Kōjin, "Sōkei sei o megutte," *Senzen no shikō* (Bungei shunjū, 1994), 157–183.

16. Karatani uses the example of Motoori Norinaga (1730–1801), a nativist scholar who advocated a return to the feminine mode (*taoyame buri*) of writing as properly Japanese, defined over and against the masculine mode (*masurao buri*) of imported Chinese systems of writing and thought. See Karatani, *Origins*, 170–171. For a critique of Karatani's reading of Motoori Norinaga's advocacy of femininity, see his roundtable discussion with Harry Harootunian, *Hihyō kūkan*, Tetsuo Najita, Naoki Sakai, and Koyasu Nobukuni, "Edo shisōshi e no shiten," 1st ser., no. 5 (1992): 6–36. See especially 24–27.

17. Karatani Kōjin, "Nihon seishin bunseki," *Hihyō kūkan*, 1st ser., no. 4 (1992): 271–281; 1st ser., no. 5 (1992): 336–345; 1st ser., no. 7 (1992): 246–261; 1st ser., no. 8 (1993): 241–255; and 1st ser., no. 9 (1993): 242–251.

18. *Hihyō kūkan*, 1st ser., no. 5 (1992): 344. Note that Karatani has more recently published a book titled *Nihon seishin bunseki* (Bungei shunjū, 2002), but the argument about the feminine and masculine elements of the Japanese writing system is not included in the book version.

19. He would call it "singularity." This is another point on which there is a spirited exchange between Karatani-Asada and Ueno-Mizuta in the roundtable discussion published in *Hihyō kūkan*, 2nd ser, no. 3 (1994): 37–39.

20. Yamashita Etsuko, *Nihon josei kaihō shisō no kigen: posuto feminizumu shiron* (Kaimeisha, 1988). The title echoes that of Karatani Kōjin's *Origins of Modern Japanese Literature*, and Yamashita explicitly acknowledges her debt to his ideas. Subsequent citations of this work will be referred to in the text as (*Nihon*), along with the relevant page numbers.

21. We might consider René Girard's argument that all desire is mediated and imitative: *Deceit, Desire, and the Novel: Self and Other in Literary Structure*, trans. Yvonne Freccero (Baltimore, MD: Johns Hopkins University Press, 1965).

22. Michel Foucault, *The History of Sexuality: An Introduction*, trans. Robert Hurley, vol. 1 (New York: Vintage Books, 1980), 10–13.

23. The accusation against current Japanese feminism is more fully developed as a personal attack in *"Josei no jidai" to iu shinwa: Ueno Chizuko wa onna o sukueru ka* (Seikyūsha, 1991). The title is a parody of a book by Ueno Chizuko, *Onna wa sekai o sukueru ka* (Keisō shobō, 1986).

24. See Ueno Chizuko's *Shihonsei to kaji rōdō* (Kaimeisha, 1985) and *Kafuchō-sei to shihon-sei: Marukusu shugi feminizumu no chihei* (Iwanami shoten, 1990); Kanai Yoshiko's *Tenki ni tatsu feminizumu* (Mainichi shinbunsha, 1985) and *Posuto modan*

feminizumu: Sai to josei (Keisō shobō, 1989); and Ehara Yumiko's *Josei kaihō to iu shisō* (Keisō shobō, 1985), *Feminizumu to kenryoku sayō* (Keisō shobō, 1988), and *Radikaru feminizumu saikō* (Keisō shobō, 1991).

25. Note, for example, her entirely negative evaluation of increased sexual freedom in the prewar period (*Nihon*, 150–157) and of the increased participation of women in the work force (*Nihon*, 204–208). While it would be foolish to regard these developments as unequivocal feminist advances, a complete dismissal makes us suspicious of Yamashita's basic assumptions.

26. Yamashita, *Nihon*, 76, 106–107.

27. Ibid., 105.

28. Ibid., 105, 150.

29. Ibid., 76.

30. Ibid., 56, 161.

31. Ibid., 127, 190.

32. The work of Takamure Itsue is an example of the former; those of Nishida Kitaro and Watsuji Tetsuro are examples of the latter. Ōgoshi Aiko, Minamoto Junko, and Yamashita Akiko are a few of the contemporary feminists exploring the subject from a nonessentialist perspective. See their *Sei sabetsu suru Bukkyō: feminizumu kara no kokuhatsu* (Hōzōkan, 1990), and their *Nihon-teki sekushuariti: feminizumu kara no sei fūdo hihan* (Hōzōkan, 1991).

33. This thesis is also used in Yamashita's *Mazakon bungaku-ron: jubaku to shite no "Haha"* (Shin'yōsha, 1991). Her *Takamure Itsue-ron: 'Haha' no arukeorogi* (Kawade shobō shinsha, 1988) also uses much of the same terminology of Japanese subjectivity and has been criticized by Ochiai Emiko as essentialist and protofascist. See Ochiai Emiko, *Kindai kazoku to feminizumu* (Keisō shobō, 1989).

34. See Asada Akira, *Kōzō to chikara: kigōron o koete* (Keisō shobō, 1983).

35. On the phenomenon of the younger generation of feminists critiquing the older generation, see Mizuta Noriko's comments in *Hihyō kūkan*, 2nd ser., no. 3 (1994): 42–43. Yamashita's subsequent frontal attack on feminists such as Ueno Chizuko seems to have been fully supported by male editors and intellectuals, as her acknowledgments indicate. See her *"Josei no jidai" to iu shinwa*.

36. Suga Hidemi, "Shōsetsu-teki modaniti no kōzō," *Hihyō kūkan*, 1st ser., no. 3 (1991): 52–76; 1st ser., no. 5 (1992): 108–128; 1st ser., no. 6 (1992): 213–233; 1st ser., no. 7 (1992): 148–169; 1st ser., no. 10 (1993): 232–250; 1st ser., no. 11 (1993): 229–248;

and 2nd ser., no. 3 (1994): 141–160. Most of the argument about femininity is made in 1st ser., no. 6 and no. 7. The series was published with a few revisions and an additional chapter as *Nihon kindai bungaku no "tanjō": genbun itchi undō to nashonarizumu* (Ōta shuppan, 1995).

37. The Japanese word he uses is *"zokugo kakumei"* (vernacular revolution), but he glosses it in *katakana* as "vernacularism." The context of his argument suggests that "vernacularization" is a better translation. This is the term I will use to translate *zokugo kakumei*.

38. Throughout this essay, Suga uses the Japanese word *"josei sei"* glossed in *katakana* as "femininity."

39. *Hihyō kūkan*, 1st ser., no. 6 (1992): 214.

40. *Hihyō kūkan*, 1st ser., no. 7 (1992): 160.

41. Suga cites Higuchi Ichiyō as an exceptional writer who exemplifies femininity in her rejection of the vernacularized *genbun itchi* style in favor of a more arcane style of writing (that harks back to the Heian women writers). See *Hihyō kūkan*, 1st ser., no. 7 (1992): 160–168. In a separate essay, Suga also claims that the bisexual male writer Nakagami Kenji exemplifies true femininity while the feminist writer Tomika Taeko is "phallocratic." See Suga Hidemi, "'Sōshitsu' no jimeisei: Hachiju-nendai feminizumu to bungaku," *Gunzō* 47, no. 11 (October 1992): 296–318.

42. *Hihyō kūkan*, 1st ser., no. 6 (1992): 224.

43. Edward Said, *Orientalism* (New York: Vintage, 1978). Subsequent citations of this work will be referred to in the text as *Orientalism*, along with the relevant page numbers.

44. See, for example, Stefan Tanaka, *Japan's Orient: Rendering Pasts into History* (Berkeley: University of California Press, 1993).

45. Suga Hidemi, *Shōsetsu teki kyōdo* (Fukutake shoten, 1990). Subsequent citations of this work will be referred to in the text as *Shōsetsu*, along with the relevant page numbers.

46. "Man became a Slave because he feared death. To be sure, on the one hand this fear [*Furcht*] reveals his dependence with respect to Nature and thus justifies his dependence with respect to the Master, who *dominates* Nature. But on the other hand, this same fear—according to Hegel—has a positive value, which conditions the Slave's *superiority* to the Master." Alexandre Kojève, *Introduction to the Reading of Hegel: Lectures on the Phenomenology of Spirit*, ed. Allan Bloom (Ithaca, NY: Cornell University Press, 1969), 47.

47. Takeuchi Yoshimi wrote after World War II: "The 'most painful thing in life,' awakening from a dream, occurs when the *slave* rejects his status as *slave* while at the same time rejecting the fantasy of liberation, so that he becom es a *slave* who realizes that he is a *slave*." Takeuchi Yoshimi, "Kindai to wa nani ka," *Takeuchi Yoshimi zenshū,* 17 vols. (Chūō kōronsha, 1980), 4: 155. The translation is from Richard F. Calichman, *What is Modernity? Writings of Takeuchi Yoshimi* (New York: Columbia University Press, 2005), 71. Takeuchi and other intellectuals involved in the prewar debate on "overcoming the modern" are discussed in Sakai Naoki, "Modernity and Its Critique: The Problem of Universalism and Particularism," in *Postmodernism and Japan,* eds. Masao Miyoshi and H. D. Harootunian (Durham, NC: Duke University Press, 1989), 93–122.

48. The Japanese word for "Subject" (*shutai*) is written with the character for "Master" (*shu*). This makes possible a complicated pun on subject = master and subjection = slavery, which Suga exploits fully. On the distinction between *shutai* = agent of action, *shukan* = epistemological subject, *shugo* = propositional subject, *shudai* = thetic subject, see Sakai Naoki, *Voices of the Past: The Status of Language in Eighteenth-Century Japanese Discourse* (Ithaca, NY: Cornell University Press, 1991).

49. For example, René Girard in his *Deceit, Desire, and the Novel* (cited above), points out that Hegel's Master-Slave dialectic is most often a relationship between two men, with a woman as the object over which the "fight to the death" takes place, which determines the Master-Slave relationship: the one who did not risk death becomes Slave to the Master. Girard understands this triangular relationship to be the most prevalent example in the European context. In his view, however, the three points in the triangle can be taken by either men or women; they can even be taken by books, ideas, things, or God. In *Between Men,* Eve Sedgwick takes over where Girard had left off. She argues it is not merely a historical coincidence that the most prevalent form of the triangular relationship is that of the two Men fighting over a Woman as desired object. It is bound up with how communities are formed. The two Men create a homosocial bond, a relationship of rivalry and desire, which is relayed, mediated, and made possible through the Woman as desired object. Woman has no position in society except as the third term that is the object of desire and rivalry between two Men. Only Men can be the subjects of desire. See Eve Sedgwick, *Between Men: English Literature and Male Homosocial Desire* (New York: Columbia University Press, 1985).

50. Orikuchi Shinobu, "Nyōbo bungaku kara inja bungaku e," *Orikuchi Shinobu zenshū,* 31 vols. (Chūō kōronsha, 1965), 1: 266. See also 265–320.

51. Suga accuses feminist critics such as Ueno Chizuko, Ogura Chikako, Tomioka Taeko, and Ehara Yumiko of precisely this fault. See Suga, "'Sōshitsu' no jimeisei," 296–318. Ueno, Ogura, and Tomika published a series of roundtable discussions in which they tore apart canonical Japanese male writers for their sexism: See Ueno Chizuko, Ogura Chikako, and Tomioka Taeko, *Danryū bungaku ron* (Chikuma shobō, 1992). Suga criticizes the feminist critics for discussing only the content of the novels, and for ignoring the issue of novelistic *écriture.*

52. See, for example, the various collections of debates on the issue of motherhood and the state: *Shiryō: bosei hogo ronsō,* ed. Kōuchi Nobuko (Domesu shuppan, 1984); *Shiryō: Sengo bosei no yukue,* ed. Suzuki Naoko (Domesu shuppan, 1984); and *Shiryō: Josei-shi ronsō,* ed. Koshō Yukiko (Domesu shuppan, 1984). See also the various works by Suzuki Yūko, including her *Tennōsei, "ianfu," feminizumu* (Inpakuto shuppankai, 2002); *Feminizumu to sensō* (Marujusha, 1997); and *Feminizuuu to chōsen* (Akashi shoten, 1994).

53. See Watanabe Naomi, "Deai sobireta danjo: 'bungei jihyō' to 'feminizumu,'" *Gunzō* 48, no. 4 (April 1993): 330–335.

54. Luce Irigaray, *This Sex Which Is Not One,* trans. Catherine Porter and Carolyn Burke (Ithaca, NY: Cornell University Press, 1985).

55. Karatani, for example, claims that Irigaray's theory (as well as other Western poststructuralist theories) loses its critical edge in Japan. He claims that the Symbolic has not been as totally masculine in Japan as Irigaray claims it has been in the West; therefore, a critique against the masculine Symbolic does not work as a critique against the status quo, but actually serves to strengthen the "feminine" emperor system. See his interview with Brett de Bary, "Feminizumu to kindai hihyō," *Subaru* 13, no. 11 (November 1991): 214–235.

56. See chapter 2 of my *Acting Like a Woman in Modern Japan.*

57. This is the way reverse Orientalism and the assumption of the continuity of gender operate together with antifeminism: if one thinks there is something continuous and unchanging about women in Japan (continuity), and if one is inclined to show that Japan is different from the West (reverse Orientalism), one may do so by claiming Japanese women have traditionally not been oppressed by patriarchy and therefore feminism does not work in Japan (antifeminism). Or, if one does not like feminism (antifeminism) and if one thinks Japan is different from the West (reverse Orientalism), one can easily conclude that feminism does not work in Japan because Japanese women have always had access to power and writing (continuity). And if one assumes continuity

for Japanese women (continuity) and if one does not like feminism (antifeminism), one can conclude that Japan is different from the West because women have been valorized in Japan (reverse Orientalism). Thus, the three wheels reinforce and perpetuate each other's motions, locking themselves into a circular trajectory from which they cannot be easily dislodged.

58. Ueno Chizuko and Nakamura Yūjiro, *"Ningen" o koete: idō to chakuchi* (Seidosha, 1989), 207–209. This is a collection of letters exchanged between Ueno and the philosopher Nakamura Yūjirō.

16 Feminism and Media in the Late Twentieth Century: Reading the Limits of a Politics of Transgression

Setsu Shigematsu

This essay explores the intersections of feminist discourse, women, and the mass media in Japan during the last three decades of the twentieth century to inquire how certain feminist discourses have been accommodated, incorporated, and repudiated by various sectors of the media industry. By examining how feminist discourses have been produced and disseminated through the circuits of mass cultural production, I will attempt to map out some important shifts in feminist politics since the 1970s.[1] Taking the emergence of the women's liberation movement in 1970 as a point of departure, I explain how the radical feminist politics of this movement contrast with the liberal feminist discourses that were promoted through the media industry. In contrast to the radical feminism of the women's liberation movement, the government and corporate interests began promoting their own versions of liberal feminism in the mid-1970s. These corporate and state versions of liberal feminism emphasized a discourse of equality and individualism that was compatible with late capitalist consumerism. As I trace several points of intersection between feminist discourses and the mass media, I contextualize these crossings in relation to the changing socioeconomic conditions between the 1960s and 1990s.

In the first part of this essay, I outline a genealogy of feminist criticism and its relation to the mass media by providing an overview of the different ways that grassroots women's groups and feminist scholars have critically engaged with the media industry (*masu komi*). In particular, I discuss how the women's liberation (*ūman ribu*) movement sought to fundamentally redefine women's identities, and introduce several of its key concepts germane to this discussion, such as the liberation of sex. By examining some key criticisms and distinctions that feminists have made about the media industry regarding its male-dominated structure and the commercialization of sex, I attempt to show how the production of feminist discourses across Japan have simultaneously been attempts to redefine women's subjectivities and their political interests.

In the second part of this essay, I trace some of the changes in women's magazines since the 1970s, examining the ways that feminist discourses have been incorporated into a discourse that promotes individualist consumerism. In this section, I also explore the potential feminist significance of the mass production of women's pornographic comics as one of the ways that sex has been commercialized for women. Finally, in the third part of this essay, as a way to illustrate the complex imbrications of feminist discourse, the mass media, and women's cultural production, I discuss the life and work of one mass culture icon and artist—Uchida Shungiku. In the last part of this essay, I elaborate how women like Uchida market their sexuality as transgressive public performances, and in so doing I question the ramifications and limits of a politics of transgression.

Feminist Criticism and Women's Culture

Inoue Teruko, a prominent feminist scholar and critic of the media, has stated that the ideology and thought (*shisō*) of contemporary women in Japan cannot be discussed without addressing the media industry.[2] Since the early 1970s, Inoue has been a pioneering feminist critic of the media industry.[3] Feminist critics like Inoue make a distinction between what they refer to as "mainstream" (*shuryū*) mass media and "women's culture" (*josei bunka*). The term women's culture is used to distinguish media that consciously targets women as its audience, in contrast to mainstream mass media, which generally refers to newspapers and commercial radio and television broadcasting that target mixed audiences and employ mostly men. "Women's culture" refers to commercial print media such as women's magazines, comics for girls (*shōjo manga*), ladies' comics (*redisu komikkusu*), romance novels, as well as television programming aimed at women. Although there are many ways in which there is an overlap between mainstream mass media and women's culture, especially in the realm of television—since women overall watch more television than men—both these terms have functioned as useful analytic categories for feminist analyses.[4]

Feminist scholars such as Suzuki Midori, Inoue Teruko, Mizuta Noriko, and Funabashi Kuniko have described mainstream mass media as a sphere that men dominate.[5] By making this claim, they refer to the fact that men predominantly own and manage the industry, despite women's various forms of participation as employees, directors, journalists, artists, and consumers. The following statistics concretely indicate what male dominance of the media industry means, providing a clear picture of the gendered division of labor of the mass media. Although women comprise approximately 40 percent of the labor force, throughout the 1990s the percentages of women employed in the mainstream sectors of the industry remained low; for example, women made up less than 10 percent of the total number of employees in newspapers companies in 1998.[6] In the early 1990s, 4 percent of newspaper reporters were women, reaching only 9.5 percent by 1998.[7] Throughout the 1990s, women comprised less than 10 percent of NHK (*Nippon hōsō kyōkai;* Japan's public broadcasting corporation) employees, and less than 2 percent of its management positions by the late 1990s.[8] In private broadcasting companies, women made up approximately 20 percent of the total number of employees from the early to the late 1990s, with less than 4 percent in management positions by the late 1990s.[9] Women's significant underrepresentation in these mainstream sectors of the mass media evidences how overwhelmingly male dominated this industry has remained.[10]

In spite of the structural male dominance of the media industry overall, the manufacturers of women's culture depend on women as potential consumers, and therefore strive to create products that women will identify with, desire, and select. The media industry has shaped and produced women's culture, which as part of a larger market system, driven by a capitalist profit-making logic, must produce commodities that women desire to purchase. The industry must then also reproduce women as desiring subjects in this continuous circuit of production and consumption.

Many feminist scholars have discussed how the socioeconomic conditions since the 1960s have made women key targets as consumers in a hyperadvanced consumption-orientated capitalist society. As competition intensified during the 1960s and 1970s, competing publishing companies diversified their print media and thereby sought to create various market niches of women. In the process of the competition to generate higher levels of consumption, the media industry employed more women as new producers of women's culture, especially in the sector of print media and publishing.[11] The production of women's culture as a part of the machinery of the media industry has involved the marketing of particular idealized images of womanhood, and the dissemination of a complex assemblage of discourses about women's identities and sexualities, comprising a competing field of discourses.

The Women's Liberation Movement

In the wake of the anti–Vietnam war and student movements of the late 1960s, a new kind of women's liberation movement exploded in 1970, launching a radical critique of the gender politics of Japanese capitalist imperialism.[12] Inaugurating what many feminist scholars have described as the beginning of the second wave of feminism in Japan, this radical feminist movement—known as *ūman ribu*—signaled a break from the New Left and existing women's movements.[13] In the process of redefining the terms of liberation from a "woman's position," this movement made women's subjectivity and sexuality central to their political concerns. By emphasizing how the marriage-family system was an ideological apparatus that functioned to reproduce and regulate women's identities and sexualities, *ūman ribu* distinguished itself from former postwar women's movements that had never rejected the family system or questioned the sex-role division of labor.[14]

Ūman ribu's fundamental reconceptualization of women's identity was connected to its analysis of the family system and the prescription that a woman must become a man's wife and reproduce *his* children. The equation that woman = housewife (*shufu*) = mother (*haha*) has functioned as the modern prescription of "womanhood," a teleological prescription directing women toward the regulatory ideal of *ryōsai kenbo* (good wife, wise mother).[15] In her analysis of the regulatory function of *ryōsai kenbo* in the postwar period, Kathleen Uno writes that a "transmuted vision of women that often emphasized their difference from men as homebound wives and mothers continued to influence state

policies toward welfare, education, employment, sexuality and reproduction at least until the late 1980s."[16] *Ūman ribu* argued that a capitalist
and patriarchal family system positioned women against each other, and
articulated how crucial it was for women to realize their *collective identity*
and their relationship to other oppressed peoples. In order to struggle
in solidarity with others against oppressive systems, it was necessary to
grasp both one's individual complicity and the importance of collective
action.[17]

The sexual revolution that was part of the First World countercul-
ture movements of the 1960s and early 1970s overlapped historically and
conceptually with *ūman ribu*, but it was not synonymous with *ūman ribu*'s
notion of sex liberation. For *ūman ribu*, the liberation of sex meant liberation from the existing ways that women and their sexuality had been
defined through masculinist ideologies of sex, and asserted that liberation required knowledge about and control over their own bodies and
their sexuality. Sex liberation for *ūman ribu* also meant women's freedom
to choose to marry or give birth.[18] According to many women of *ribu,*
sexual liberation would be meaningless without the concomitant dis-
mantling of the family system, which was rejected as an institutional
and ideological key to multiple interlocking systems of oppression that
reproduced Japan's patriarchal capitalist and imperialist nation.[19]

Along with their critique of the family system, *ūman ribu* advocated
and affirmed women's expression of their sexuality and sexual agency.
As an extension of their critique of the family system under capitalism,
many women of *ribu* chose to give birth outside the marriage system,
and established alternative communes where women and their children
could live, as part of their collective struggle to create a different society. *Ūman ribu*'s liberation of sex involved an articulation of their own
discourse about their bodies, their sexuality, and subjective desires,
which they spoke and wrote about and practiced as one aspect of their
movement.

The women of *ūman ribu* strategically engaged the mass media from
the inception of the movement, and organized and published their own
alternative media.[20] *Ūman ribu*'s alternative media thoroughly and playfully criticized the media industries' multiple forms of sexism and constituted the beginning of a legacy of feminist media criticism. Like other
grassroots movements, *ūman ribu* groups produced their own alternative

media, known as *minikomi*. This small-scale, not-for-profit, printed matter included newsletters, zines, pamphlets, and bound journals, comprising a massive corpus of self-published feminist literature that circulated through women's networks. *Minikomi* was produced as a deliberate alternative to circumvent the male-dominated, capitalist logic of the media industry in order to maintain self-determination and autonomy in terms of its form, content, production, and distribution.

Following the rise of *ūman ribu*, grassroots women's groups spoke out against the gender politics of the mass media in several ways, forming community-based action groups that have continued activities throughout the 1980s and 1990s.[21] One of the most active and long-standing feminist groups organized in 1975 called themselves Women's Action Group (Kōdōsuru onnatachi no kai).[22] In 1975, this group began criticizing the sexist practices of the mass media, launching a series of protests against NHK, major newspapers, *manga* (comics), and weekly magazines, as well as the sexist advertising of large corporations such as *House*.[23]

Women's Studies and Feminism

Beginning in the late 1970s, in response to the women's liberation movement, women who were invested in academic and scholarly endeavors worked toward the establishment of women's studies (*joseigaku*), and created another expansive body of literature. Unlike the small-scale production and distribution of *minikomi*, academic feminist publications were printed through universities and publishing houses (like Keisō shobō) to be marketed to a wider reading audience and distributed through commercial bookstores. Part of the work of women's studies has been directed toward a critique of the media, and the work introduced in this essay draws on both *minikomi* and this academic feminist literature. There has been a contentious relationship between some proponents of women's studies and certain *ribu* activists who criticized women's studies scholars for distancing themselves from grassroots activism and for not challenging the masculinist epistemologies and modes of production of the academic establishment.[24]

The International Women's Year in 1975 marked a historical shift toward the mainstreaming of a reformist and liberal feminist discourse that gained ascendancy in contrast to *ribu*'s more radical demands. The

International Women's Year became a rallying point for existing women's groups to reorganize to form the "Liaison Group," representing a coalition of over forty women's groups that would cooperate with government initiatives.[25] The government responded to the ramifications of the UN initiatives for women by establishing local women's centers and forming the Headquarters for the Planning and Promoting of Policies Relating to Women.[26] By giving support to "women's initiatives" that were not too subversive, the government could appear "pro-woman," without endorsing any substantive challenges to the family system or the sex-role division of labor. A dramatic event that marked this conservative shift in 1975 was a government-sponsored rally that commemorated the International Women's Year that was attended by the Emperor Hirohito and the Empress Nagako.[27] This event symbolized how the government realigned the terms of the International Women's Year with its own imperial symbols and made alliances with moderate women's groups that were willing to accept the state's political terms.

Large capital and corporate advertisers also recognized the commercial advantages of promoting a new consciousness about the status of women. In 1979, for example, Seibu Department Store embarked on a new marketing campaign called "The Era of Women" (*onna no jidai*). One of their posters that promoted this slogan featured two "seductive looking" Caucasian models, bent over mopping the floor of a ship's deck.[28] This poster aptly illustrates how Caucasian women typically symbolized both the "sexual" and the "liberated" woman and at the same time cynically mocked the notion that work outside the home would actually liberate women. This cynical projection and exoticization of the white woman as a model of the "sexually liberated individual" would continue to characterize the way that advertising and the media attempted to associate feminist sentiments with foreign women, creating the false impression that the organic formation of feminism in Japan was a foreign infiltration.

The appropriation of feminism by the mass media and advertising has been calculated and selective, deploying what could be seen as profitable to a corporation's image. This selective appropriation and dilution of feminism was well captured by an advertisement by Tokyo Gas Company, whose advertisers coined the slogan, "City gas is feminist, isn't it?"[29] According to this marketing logic, anything helpful to women, or anything women consume, can be called feminist. In this way, advertisers divested their feminism of any anticapitalist elements and critical substance in order to make it more conducive to these kinds of commercial schemes.

In 1977, a new magazine named *Feminisuto* was published by a group of Japanese feminists who sought to produce media from "the viewpoint of independent women" with an "international perspective."[30] As part of an attempt to disseminate feminist discourse to a larger audience, this feminist publication moved away from a *minikomi* format to a more mass market oriented distribution.[31] What is striking about this publication is that it received funding from companies such as Shiseido, Max Factor, and Seibu Department Store, signaling a feminist rapprochement with corporate interests.[32] In 1980, on the back cover of its second English-language issue, a white male model in a three-piece suit stands smiling with his head cocked to one side, under a slogan, "We men dream of wings, too!" This slogan playfully inverts the common reference to liberated women as "women with wings," suggesting that this well-dressed "white man" also wants to be liberated so that he too can fly. Unlike previous forms of feminist *minikomi* that rejected a capitalist logic of production and did not seek corporate financing, this feminist accommodation of corporate interests was symptomatic of a shift in feminist discourses during the late 1970s.

Commercializing Sexual Liberation

Many feminists have argued that the aftermath of the sexual revolution did not make sex "free," instead, it resulted in a more liberal and explicit commodification of sex.[33] From the mid-1960s, the marketing of pornographic media expanded beyond the confines of sex shops, and the gratuitous circulation of nude or seminude female models in men's weekly magazines became an integral part of mass print media aimed at men. For example, in 1964, the publisher Magazine House launched *Heibon Punch,* a popular men's weekly magazine that typically featured nude Caucasian women as centerfolds and pin-up girls. Mark Schilling describes *Heibon Punch* as a "seminal publication that brought sex out of the dirty bookstore and into the mainstream," making it a magazine that would later become a target of *ūman ribu*'s and feminist derision.[34] A year later in 1965, the publisher Shuiesha came out with its weekly edition of *Playboy* magazine, which became a top-selling magazine throughout the 1990s. The mass marketing of particular racial and class-specific images of female bodies normativized the visual consumption of a particular racialized taxonomy of female sexuality in the name of "free sex." And, as described below, the marketing of these racialized images would continue to shift in the 1970s through the 1990s.

Although *ūman ribu*'s brand of sexual liberation sought to affirm women's assertion of their sexual subjectivity, the media industries' version of sexual liberation became a mandate to expand the commercialization of sex. By appropriating a rhetoric of freedom of expression to justify the ubiquitous marketing of sex, sexual liberation became a double bind for women, making it appear as if it was a matter of individual freedom to buy and sell sex. The inaugural issue of the Japanese monthly edition of *Playboy International* in 1975 coincided with the inauguration of the UN Decade for Women, marking the simultaneity of the official recognition of women's issues and the international expansion of the pornography industry.[35] With its format of glossy pull-out centerfolds, this magazine increased both the quantity and the photographic quality of its predominantly nude white models. The concurrent dissemination of more explicit sexual images of women and the expanded diffusion of feminist discourses illustrates how the media industry commodified sexual liberation and diluted feminist discourses to further capitalist ends.

During the high economic growth period more Japanese women became housewives (*sengyō shufu*), but at the same time more housewives were sought as a cheap and flexible labor supply, effecting a chiasmatic movement of women from the workplace to the home as "full-time" housewives, and from the home to the workplace as "part-time" workers.[36] During the 1960s, the percentage of nuclear family households increased to 60 percent, and the average number of family members dropped from five to three.[37] According to Mizuta Noriko, an important marker of Japan's transition toward a postindustrial society has been the shift in emphasis of the role of the family from that of a system of reproduction to a site of consumption.[38] With the general economic stability and the shrinkage of the family, the government and industry promoted an ideological shift from concern about "quantity" to a promotion of "quality" of lifestyle, predicated on more leisure and consumption.[39] During this period, publishing companies launched an increasing number of mass seller weekly women's magazines that promoted consumerism and a cosmopolitan image, with titles such as *Shopping, Misesus* (Misses), and the two top-selling weeklies, *Josei jishin* (1958) and *Josei seven* (1963). These weeklies employed more *katakana* and addressed their readers with the newer and more generic term "*josei*" (woman), instead of "*shufu*" (housewife) and "*fujin*" (lady).[40]

From the 1960s onwards, advertising became a larger and more visible presence in the mass media, and along with mass culture, women's culture was also transformed into an image-based visual culture.[41] The mass media functioned as a conduit for commercial advertising interests that sought to redefine feminine identity based on the imperatives of a model of consumption that promoted idealized images of independent and cosmopolitan women. Although the images of an independent, cosmopolitan lifestyle did not correspond with the vast majority of women's reality, it was precisely the slippage and contradiction between the image and reality that generated the desire for mobility and freedom of choice and the products that symbolized this lifestyle.

Despite the rising number of women entering the labor force and their increasing levels of education, women's decision-making power and wages were not commensurate with men's.[42] Government policy and industries' practices reinforced the dominant discourse that women's proper place was in the home and thereby maintained the sex-role division of labor. By maintaining that women *were supposed to be* full-time housewives, industries justified paying women as "part-time" workers no matter how many hours they worked. In spite of the gains in women's purchasing power, women's labor has been used as a source that is complementary and supplementary to male labor, but has remained subordinate to men's labor in terms of wages and career opportunities. By the mid-1990s, women comprised less than 10 percent of managerial positions in the work force.[43] From 1985 to 2000, excluding part-time work, working women earned approximately 60 percent of men's wages.[44] This remained the general reality of the gendered division of labor despite the implementation of the Equal Employment Opportunity Act (EEOA) in the mid-1980s. Most feminists opposed the act, since it stripped women of their existing protections and held no penalties for companies violating the law.[45] Rather, by using the rhetoric of "equality," this "procorporate" legislation placed the onus on individual women to choose a corporate career track just like men if they wanted to secure their economic independence.

However, since the rise of *ūman ribu*, as Ueno Chizuko has repeatedly stated, many feminists in Japan have remained critical of a discourse of equality with men, and have insisted on the recognition of feminine difference and systemic social change. In 1994, the government established the Headquarters for the Promotion of Gender Equality and the Office for Gender Equality as part of the Prime Minister's Offices, which was a further bureaucratic expansion of state feminism. Many feminists have been critical of how a version of state feminism that promotes "cooperation and equal participation by men and women in society" reveals the government's disregard for the history of feminist criticism in Japan that has rejected the paradigm of equality with men.[46]

Magazines for the Individual Woman

Concurrent with the socioeconomic changes discussed above, the production of women's magazines underwent a paradigm shift in the early 1970s.[47] There was a fundamental shift away from the general women's magazine geared toward either unmarried or married women, to a proliferation of specialized magazines based on age, hobbies, and interests.[48] From the 1970s onwards, women's magazines continued to increase in number and diversity, producing an expansion of consumer choices meant to generate and reflect consumer desire.

The manufacturers of women's magazines made major changes, not only in terms of the variety, number, and content of the magazines, but transformations that might best be described in terms of a new ideology or logic that organized the world of women's magazines. Women's magazines served as a space where many of the maxims and concerns of feminism were integrated and modulated, becoming another formative space for the dissemination of liberal feminist discourse. These magazines were referred to as the "new woman" magazines, focusing on the development of women as individuals. These "new woman" magazines marketed individuality (*kosei*), independence (*jiritsu*), new-ness (*atarashisa*), and freedom (*jiyū*) as key concepts of their contents and images. Although the stress on women as individuals was certainly not a new feminist concept (but paradigmatic of modern subjectivity), this assertion of woman's individuality offered an alternative feminine ideal to the woman = good wife, wise mother formula. Summarizing this shift in the redefinition of woman through women's culture, Inoue Teruko writes:

Since the 1970s in Japan, whether it be *shōjo manga* [girls' comics], popular songs, or women's magazines, regardless of their motives, they have all func-tioned to dissolve the binary sex-role model and urge the progress of dissemi-nating the emergence of woman [*onna*]—not as a mother, housewife, or wife—but as an individual [*kojin*].[49]

Four general characteristics of these new magazines have been: (1) the diminishing emphasis on marriage as a primary factor in defining women; (2) the encouragement of consumption for self-enhancement; (3) the increase in visual images shifting the activity of consumption from reading to looking; and (4) a cosmopolitan image symbolized by foreign titles, products, and Caucasian models or models with a "Cau-casian look."

The publication of a new magazine in 1977 called *Croissant* signaled a shift to a more mainstream marketing of feminist discourses that be-came more prevalent across the new women's lifestyle magazines. Its inaugural issue printed a feature article on baby hotels, promoting a woman's choice to pay for child care as a commercialized service. In its first few years, this magazine featured articles such as "The World of Lesbians" (1978), "Liberation from Marriage" (1979), and "Marriage is a Danger for Women" (1980), and thereby gained a reputation for dis-couraging women to marry.[50]

Inoue has also described how the distinctions between housewife (*shufu*), mother (*haha*), prostitute (*shōfu*), and girlfriend (*koibito*) began to diminish during the 1970s, marking the diffuse effects of sexual libera-tion. For example, formerly the qualities of being "beautiful" (*utsuku-shii*) and sexually attractive (*seiteki miryoku*) were not emphasized as im-portant for housewives, but this view changed with the emergence of the "new woman" magazines.[51] Rather than defining a woman's self-identity in terms of being a housewife—by her ability to perform domestic duties, raise children, organize the family budget, and get along with the in-laws—the emerging values for the "new woman" were associated with how a woman makes herself attractive through fashion and beautification techniques such as cosmetics, weight control, and skin care. The traditional housewife magazines had devoted a high proportion of advertising to food products, medicine, and domestic appliances, but the new women's magazines sold a much greater proportion of advertising for leisure and travel, as well as cosmetics and other "artificial beautification" products (*seikei biyō kigu*).[52]

While feminist discourses attempted to dismantle this chain of equivalence between woman = wife = mother, the media and advertising industry incorporated certain aspects of feminism to promote a more individualized form of consumerism. The advertising industry transformed this emphasis on woman's individuality into the notion of woman as individual consumer, who consumes for her self-enhancement, and whose identity is defined through the products she selects. Although feminist discourses promoted women's economic independence and freedom to choose (marriage or motherhood), the media and advertising industry deployed these key concepts within a consumerist logic to mean the "freedom to choose" one's own products and value one's desires about leisure and self-enhancement. Rather than actually liberating women from the social obligations of wife and mother, this intensified emphasis on a woman's looks and her body would help naturalize women's patterns of consumption and willful participation in the increasingly costly and invasive practices of the beauty industry.

According to Inoue's research, during the 1950s, despite the influx of American Hollywood movies, a minority of Caucasian models appeared in women's magazines. But by the 1960s the number of Caucasian models increased, and in the 1970s, this shifted to an upsurge in "half" models (part Japanese) and *Nihonjinbanare*—Japanese who had a Caucasian look, especially in the new women's magazines such as *non no*.[53] This last change coincided with the increasingly explicit sexualized images of women's bodies, combining the former image of the sexualized Caucasian female with a Japanese look. One of the best-known icons of this trend during the early 1990s was Miyazawa Rie, a "half" model of

Russian and Japanese descent, who increased her social capital exponentially by marketing her own nude photo collection called *Santa Fe*.[54]

Several Japanese critics have described the apparent cosmopolitanism in Japanese women's magazines as the "unknown nationality" (*kokuseki fumei*) or the "nationless culture" (*mukokuseki bunka*) of these magazines. However, what is characteristic of this nationless cosmopolitanism is the appropriation of symbols of white European and American upper middle-class culture. Hence, rather than being an eclectic mélange of cultures and races, this nationlessness reinscribes whiteness as a sign of privilege and cultural capital, re-marking the existence of a global hierarchy of race. The racialized hierarchies that have been the legacies of Euro-American imperialism are also naturalized through the idealization and promotion of whiteness as a beauty ideal. With the increased use of Caucasian models, this promotion of white beauty may appear to be a benign form of aestheticism; however, the cultural capital of whiteness reproduces a racialized beauty hierarchy with effects that are hardly benign. The boom in cosmetic surgery in Japan and Korea since the 1990s is one example of how the ideology of white beauty has translated into a highly profitable body industry, making it possible for non-white women to look more Caucasian if they are willing to pay the price.[55] The naturalization of such a costly devotion to white beauty is encoded through the logic of capitalist consumerism as an individual woman's free choice.

From Girls' Comics to Ladies' Pornography

The *manga* within women's culture offers a fertile field to rethink the different ways that women's participation as producers and consumers in the print media industry has mediated the commercialization of sexuality as a form of mass cultural production. By tracing how sexuality has been commercialized for women, particularly with the emergence of the subgenre of pornographic comics for women since the mid-1980s, I will discuss how this particular form of women's cultural production manifests certain feminist sentiments but functions as a commercialized version of sexual liberation.

Since the early 1970s, the *manga* industry has undergone what Matthew Thorn has called a "gender revolution." Thorn is referring to the dramatic influx of female artists who entered this trade in the late 1960s and early 1970s and proceeded to change the form and content of *shōjo manga*.[56] Subsequent to the entrance of female artists into what had previously been a male-dominated field, the popularity of *shōjo manga* boomed.

Many commentators have noted how *shōjo manga*'s exploration of sexuality is one of its most notable features. Throughout the 1970s, *shōjo manga* expanded in terms of genres and diversified into subgenres such as science fiction, fantasy, and homoerotic romance, which were distinct from the dominant genre of heterosexual love-comedies. Various forms of sexual ambiguity, crossdressed heroines and homoeroticism between beautiful young boys (*bishōnen*) have been characteristic features of *shōjo manga*.[57] *Shōjo manga* thus became a space for sexual exploration that provided alternative configurations of love and sexuality other than heterosexual love and marriage. The diversification and overall increase in *shōjo manga*'s publications parallel the changes in the women's magazines seen above. Within the genre of heterosexual love-comedies, Fujimoto Yukari argues that by the 1980s *manga* artists created story lines that promoted a clearer recognition of the heroine's own desires and a greater realism about the limitations of cross-sex relationships, challenging the monopoly of heterosexual love as the singular ultimate fantasy.[58]

As the market niche of *shōjo manga* readers of the 1970s came of age through the 1980s, publishing houses appealed to adult readers with "ladies' comics" forming a new genre. In 1980 there were only two publications, but by 1989 the market expanded, offering forty-two different titles on the market, comprising a diverse range of ladies' comics.[59] The production of ladies' comics during the 1980s forged another significant transformation in the publishing sector of women's culture. Following the proliferation of pornography throughout the 1970s and 1980s, a subgenre of erotic ladies' comics emerged in the late 1980s that rivaled the graphic detail of pornographic comics for men.[60] The boom in ladies' comics peaked in the early 1990s, but in 1996, the *Mainichi Daily* reported that there were approximately thirty erotic women's comic magazines on the market, with the highest-selling magazine, *Comic Amour,* boasting an annual circulation of over five million issues.[61] By 2000, there were still approximately twenty-five different titles of erotic ladies' comics on the market.[62] In addition to its sheer mass circulation, the audience of ladies' comics—though still associated with a low-brow form of entertainment—challenges the assumption of a readership that is determined by age or marital status. For example, the readers of *Comic Amour* range from women in their late teens to their fifties, and include high school and college students, office ladies, housewives, mothers, and other working women.[63]

The emergence of this genre of pornography for women has been driven by diverse forces and charged with conflicting implications. This comic form of sexual entertainment challenges common conceptions about pornography by reconstituting what gets eroticized and for whom. Fujimoto Yukari's feminist analyses explore how this subgenre of *manga* draws out the complexities of feminine desire.[64] Fujimoto has stated that this mass production of women's pornography for and by women is truly epoch-making, not only in Japan, but worldwide.[65] The gradual expansion of sexual explicitness from within the genre of *shōjo manga* indicates that the boundaries of pornographic entertainment and women's culture have gradually disintegrated as a result of the exploration of sexual themes by women *manga* artists, and was not simply a mimicry of pornography for men. Thus, rather than being a sudden imitation of pornography for men, this new field of erotic entertainment developed, in part, from an existing trend within *shōjo manga* and demonstrated what sexual fantasies drawn by women for women can entail.

This mass market provides a space for female *manga* artists to design their own versions of erotica and vie for more creative control within an industry that remains predominantly male-owned and managed. In this competitive commercial arena, women artists have displayed a tremendous variety of sex fantasies. The fantasies range from extramarital affairs to stories of incest, and themes of sadomasochism and "prostitute" fantasies abound, as do "first time" stories and narratives of lesbian love. Sometimes stories of sex with gangsters (*yakuza*) and transsexuals are also featured, as well as a motley mix of quasi-rape scenarios and orgies—all of which are meant to facilitate autoerotic pleasure for the reader. While detailed drawings of body parts and orifices are par for the course, the illustrations repeatedly focus on images of diverse types of women posing seductively, touching themselves, being touched, taking control, being ravaged, and enjoying multiple forms of ecstasy, page after page, making women's bodies both the object and subject of the gaze.[66]

The effect of making the images of women's bodies the primary object of the gaze for women readers in many ways minimizes the role of male characters. Fujimoto has commented that in heterosexual encounters, the face of the man, or men, are often masked, or left undrawn, which she interprets as illustrative of the relative insignificance of the identity of the man. In other words, the male characters are created only to enhance the pleasure for the women characters and readers. As I have argued elsewhere, ladies' comics have a pedagogical function, teaching women to explore the possible meanings of sexual fantasies and experiment with erotic desire.[67]

Although pornographic comics for women did not derive from a purely feminist impulse—nor do they garner unanimous feminist support[68]—this form of exotica appears to advocate and encourage the expression of female sexual desire, which, as mentioned before, *ūman ribu* affirmed as only one aspect of women's sexual liberation. By providing a forum where women can explore new sexual frontiers, women's pornography creates a space where sexual fantasies are shared, circulated, and sold as entertainment. Although most of these sexual fantasies fly in the face of conservative ideals about conjugal sex, if sexual freedom only takes place within the *personal* domain of sexual fantasy and practice, the question this raises is whether the production and reading practices of these texts is transgressive or libratory in any societally transformative manner, or does this limited transgressiveness enhance its entertainment function?

This production process functions to package, commodify, and circulate particular representations of sex within a commercial industry that remains owned and managed by men. Thus, rather than directly challenge this male-dominated structure, women's pornography allows for a symbolic economy of sexual transgression, where sexual liberation becomes a privatized endeavor instead of a broader political agenda for substantive social change. While it is possible to interpret women's pornography as a commodity compatible with a feminist sentiment, capitalism's historical advancement has not been gender-blind.[69] Rather, corporate practices in Japan (and elsewhere) have consistently relied on gendered and racialized divisions of labor, mobilizing and reinscribing these differences to extract and commodify labor.

Uchida Shungiku's Body of Transgression

The above discussion of women's pornographic comics and sexual transgression provides an appropriate prelude into a discussion of Uchida Shungiku. Uchida's work is often predicated on transgressions of modern notions of femininity, sexuality, motherhood, and family, which are all issues that resonate and overlap with feminist concerns. Her work provides an indication of how feminist contentions surge through the circuits of mass culture and demonstrates the ways that artists like her can challenge the limits of various feminist discourses. As a female artist in the media industry whose work explicitly participates in the production of potentially subversive discourses of gender and sexuality, Uchida's various forms of cultural production provide compelling examples of the limits and possibilities of a feminist politics of transgression.

Uchida was born in the port city of Nagasaki in 1959. In her works, Uchida describes girlhood memories of her father leaving the family, and living in dilapidated apartments, marking her class upbringing. Her mother worked as a hostess trying to make ends meet.[70] Uchida was a teenage runaway by the age of sixteen. She writes about her teenage years sleeping in public parks and getting by with various odd jobs, including working as a hostess like her mother. At the age of twenty, Uchida moved to Tokyo and pursued her childhood dream to become a *manga* artist. Four years later in 1984, Uchida debuted as a professional *manga* artist, and she quickly became known as a "hot-seller." Within a few years she began appearing in women's magazines such as *an an* (1986), *More* (1986), *Bishō* (1988), and the "high-brow" *Fujin kōron* (1990),[71] giving interviews about her life and viewpoints on sex, womanhood, and gender relations.

Uchida's work cannot be confined to the world of women's culture; she has published across a wide range of magazines: men's erotic *manga,* the avant-garde magazine *Garo,* women's periodicals, men's news weeklies, music magazines, and her own *manga* series, which are read by an audience of mainly young adult men and women. Uchida is prolific. She has created over forty different *manga* series for different publishing houses, several of which have been transformed into television programs and films.[72] Her talents are multiple. She is also an award-winning fiction writer, an essayist, a novelist, a performing vocalist with her own band, and a television and film actress. As a celebrity, she makes regular appearances on TV talk shows and has appeared in dozens of women's and men's magazines. In the same way that Uchida's modes of cultural production cannot be confined to the domain of women's culture or the genre of *manga,* the strength of her work and singularity of her style are forged through the way Uchida transgresses the boundaries of art, public performance, erotica, comedy, and social criticism.

What has set Uchida apart from many other celebrities has been her self-conscious production of a publicly transgressive subject. Uchida has made a name for herself by publicly transgressing the codes of marriage and fidelity and mocking the *ryōsai kenbo* ideal. The other salient characteristics of Uchida's work have been her provocative integrations of sexuality, power, and violence and her synthesis of an autobiographical subtext in her *manga* and fiction. These aspects of Uchida's work resonate with feminist concerns about sexuality, women's bodies, and subjective experience, but also push the limits of certain feminist discourses. The feminist assertion that the personal is political is extended and challenged by the way that Uchida exposes and recreates herself through the machinery of the mass media. Uchida makes her most "personal experiences" objects of the public gaze, and thereby attempts to manipulate the voyeuristic desire of the audience. In what follows, I will demonstrate how Uchida works within the media industry to create a publicly transgressive subject.

Uchida works *with* and *against* taboos, divisions, and institutions that are constructs of modernity.[73] In other words, her transgressive capabilities that generate the "shock value" of her work rely on a perpetuation of the very modern mores and boundaries she seeks to breach. Her transgressive public acts call attention to the general cultural sedimentation of various social taboos that encode and regulate sexuality by deploying sexualized stigmas according to a heterosexist logic—stigmas that function differently for men and women. While Uchida undoubtedly profits from her transgressive acts, she also performs as a "survivor" of sexual abuse who can violate social taboos.

Feminist Miya Yoshiko has stated, "In a society where women have for so long accepted silence as the only response to rape . . . We are beginning to recognize that rape is not something that happens out on the street, but . . . it is located within the family. This only adds to the problem of silence."[74] Miya's statement implicitly refers to three taboos— the taboo for women to talk about rape, the taboo for women to talk about their own rape, and the taboo to speak out about rape within the family.

In 1993, Uchida published her first autobiographical novel (*jidenteki shōsetsu*), a bestseller, which she called *Fazza Fakka*, or *Father Fucker*.[75] With *Father Fucker*, Uchida transgressed all the above taboos at once. Through this novel Uchida exposes the extent of the potential violence within the family system. The book is marketed as "a shocking autobiographical novel" about a high school girl who is continually raped by her stepfather with her biological mother's permission.

Uchida's strategy of self-presentation is to transgress taboos, thereby making herself a spectacle of the gaze, but unlike other idealized models of femininity, this spectacle talks back. Uchida's story gives the "raped girl" a public voice, maneuvering from private experience to the public of a reading audience. Maneuvering in this direction underscores the "private" domestic struggle over the female body that feminist discourses have made a political struggle. Uchida's subjective experience is mediated through the character of Shizuko, her own (re)creation. Shizuko is the protagonist who narrates the story of her childhood to adolescent years. When Shizuko is a teenager, she is sexually active and becomes pregnant by her high school boyfriend. When her stepfather finds out he flies into a rage and after beating her severely, he prepares to sew up her genitals so that she cannot have sex anymore. It is from this point in the story that the stepfather begins raping Shizuko, instead of sewing her up (201). According to Uchida, it is normal (*futsū*) for teenagers to be sexually active. Her mother, however, tells Shizuko that the reason why her stepfather forces her to have sex on a regular basis is because she was doing "abnormal" things (*futsū dewa nai koto*) with her boyfriend (234–235). In published interviews, Uchida finds fault with the use of the terms "normal" and "abnormal" as devices to regulate women's sexuality and behavior, and she frequently contests the underlying assumptions about what is normal behavior, criticizing society's regulation of women's sexuality.[76]

Though the story is dramatic and shocking, the author stated that she consciously avoided producing a victim's narrative and sought to make the story "entertaining and interesting" (*omoshiroi*) for her readers. The production of the tone of Shizuko's voice foregrounds the fact that Shizuko's "private experience" is mediated by the author's narrational style. The tone of the story, while dark and depressing, in many passages has elements of comic relief and irony. The novel begins with Shizuko speaking, saying that her home was a "brothel" (*baishun juku*), that her only customer was her stepfather and her mother was her boss or madam.

I was a prostitute. . . . I actually tried it, but I was no good at it. . . . But even to say that I was a prostitute, I was the absolute worst material for the job. . . . My madam [*okami-san*] was always getting angry with me. . . . My madam was the person who raised me until I was sixteen—my own mother. My customer was her lover and the father who raised me. (4–5)

Uchida's authorial ability to use various literary devices, such as metaphor, ironic distance, and humor, marks the fact that she is not the "traumatized rape victim" who cannot respond adequately to what happened to her, nor the pitiful subject of a victim's narrative; she is a survivor who packages and markets her own story of sexual violence.

Uchida's strategies of presenting herself in this way prevent her from bearing the typical stigma of the "rape victim." Rather than reproducing a sense of "shame" about it, Uchida repeatedly refers to her rape in her interviews in a straightforward manner, as one of the many elements of her life story. This repeated reference to her rape creates a kind of overexposure of rape and domestic violence, practically rendering them her trademarks. Thus, rather than trying to avert social stigma, Uchida appropriates the stigmatized position in order to gain public recognition of what happened to her and to subvert the typical view that a raped woman should remain a silenced and powerless victim.

The multiple agendas that infuse Uchida's desire to tell her story complicate a straightforward feminist reading of her story as a survivor's narrative. In this case, Uchida—after coming into her success as a *manga* artist—markets her private sexual experiences and thus turns them into a commodity for entertainment. By speaking out through the mass media, Uchida sought to expose how her mother treated her. Uchida has publicly stated that her story is an indictment of her mother because her mother refused to apologize or even remember their past. Uchida has also said that her decision to write *Father Fucker* was informed by her critical stance toward the taboo to speak out against one's family and parental authority.[77] Uchida has stated that *she* challenges the family system because blood lines are left unquestioned as the fundamental and legitimate basis for socioeconomic obligations and relations. Uchida's view on this point resonates with that of *ūman ribu*, insofar as she calls into question its fundamental legitimacy. Uchida expresses her desire to defy certain taboos and normative codes regulating the nuclear family; however, what makes her call different from *ūman ribu* is that her personal imperative to indict her own family—while being made public—falls short of a collective call to question the politics of the family system. In spite of being approached by members of the domestic violence movement to join their cause during the 1990s, Uchida has declined to become a representative figure of the movement, and has retained her stance as an "individual" who speaks on her own behalf.[78]

Uchida predicates much of her work on a subversion of the norms and ideals of the family system and makes a mockery of its dominant logic. In Uchida's novel, for example, Shizuko is made to call her rapist "honorable father" (*otōsama*). The shock value of Uchida's work comes from her ability to bring together that which dominant ideology seeks to juxtapose as mutually exclusive. By calling herself a prostitute in her own home, Uchida figuratively collapses the ideological framework that idealizes the family and the home as a private and safe space. In her case, the home becomes the brothel, the stepfather the customer, the daughter the prostitute, the mother the madam and procurer. This collapse subverts the ideological ideals that support the modern family system, such as *ryōsai kenbo,* the sex-role division of labor, and the private/public division. However, to reverse perspectives, this taboo-breaking narrative, which appears to be a drastic deviation from the norm, is not unheard of. Rather, daughters working as prostitutes and mothers who are madams are the normal conditions for those who make their living in the sex industry, which is a reality not often written about from the perspective of the sex worker.

Contra–Ryōsai Kenbo

According to Uchida, the zenith of her public recognition dovetailed with the mass media's coverage of her as an "unwed mother." A year after Miyazawa Rie's *Santa Fe* nude photo collection had successfully triggered a frenzy in the mainstream media, Uchida decided to publish a different kind of nude photo exposé. In October 1992, *Josei seven,* one of the highest-selling weekly women's magazines, published two feature articles on Uchida along with nude photo exposés, over two consecutive weeks.[79] Unlike other nude female spectacles, the images of the eight-month pregnant Uchida displayed a sensual and eroticized pregnant body, demonstrating how the media participates in producing select women as transgressive icons.

In this case, through this public performance Uchida embodies a different kind of maternal figure who takes pleasure in being provocative. The caption beneath Uchida's photo published on October 8, 1992, states: "Giving birth and taking off my clothes are things I do because I want to do them. The form of a pregnant woman's body is fun and interesting, isn't it?" By exposing herself Uchida manages to maintain her visibility and work in a public domain by distinguishing herself through the very act of transgressing social norms. By posing her maternal body as an aestheticized and sexual spectacle for a female audience, the glamorous images of Uchida celebrating her own "transgressiveness" make her a new kind of maternal icon.[80]

By 2002, Uchida had been married and divorced three times, and was on to her fourth marriage. During her previous marriages she had three children, and all three times Uchida impregnated herself by having relations with men who were not her legal husband at the time of her pregnancy. During this time, Uchida publicized her position on mothering and decoupling marriage, and the concept of motherhood, "From the outset I've thought that to have a child is a fundamentally unrelated thing to whether or not one gets married. . . . As for my own pregnancy, I didn't need a marriage relationship."[81] Although Uchida speaks against the injunction to be a man's "good wife" and have her "husband's child," unlike most single mothers, her economic power enables her to move in and out of the marriage system and still financially provide for her children without having to rely upon the largesse of her husbands.

According to Uchida, a woman's self-identity and sexuality should not to be lost in the performance of mothering. She says, "Although for my child I may be 'mother,' as for myself, I am who I am [*watashi wa watashi da.*] . . . although I now have a child, I can still say that I haven't changed at all in any way."[82] Uchida thus promotes a different kind of synthesis between womanhood and motherhood, which ultimately values her individuality over motherhood. Uchida refuses the old *ryōsai kenbo* ideal, making publicly visible a kind of motherhood that affirms the expression of feminine sexuality.[83] In such instances, the media has served as a stage for displaying a more diverse array of feminine ideals, alongside new and modified incarnations of *ryōsai kenbo*.

The life and work of Uchida Shungiku provides a provocative example of the imaginative openings and possibilities created through and across the continually shifting sites of mass culture. Due to her success as a *manga* artist, Uchida has been able to use her cultural capital to circulate her ideas and create mass visibility of a different paradigm of womanhood, adding another option to the pre-existing and predominant reincarnations of *ryōsai kenbo*. At the same time, feminine icons like Uchida have come to signify the extent to which media industries have incorporated certain women to market their individual expression, including their own experiences of sexual abuse. Uchida's publicized acts of transgression thus gesture toward the convergence between the profitable production of a transgressive feminine icon and liberal feminism that promotes token women to serve as emblems of individuality, ingenuity, hard work, and success.

While Uchida's public persona revels in being maverick, the very transgressiveness of her actions (re)marks the deeply sedimented regulatory ordering of sex. The act of transgression does not dismantle or destroy a social institution but relies on a reinscription that marks the insurgent moment and the boundaries that are crossed.

Through this discussion, I have attempted to map out several major shifts in feminist politics and its modes of production since the 1970s, focusing on the divergences between the radical feminism of *ūman ribu* and subsequent versions of state-sponsored and commercialized liberal feminist discourse. By examining the changes in women's magazines and women's active participation in the commercialization of sex, I have elaborated how liberal feminism promotes woman as an individual who consumes and transgresses for her own advancement. This politics of individual transgression not only is symptomatic of the contradictions of the mass production of woman as an individual, but also points to the likely significance of the individual as the conceptual limit that prevents the imaginings and formations of other subjectivities and collectivities as forces of collaborative movement and change.

Notes

I wish to express my thanks to Barbara Molony, Kathleen Uno, and to my colleagues at Cornell University and friends who read and commented on earlier drafts of this essay. This essay was originally drafted in 1997.

1. Marilyn Ivy has provided a cogent account of the historical formation of mass culture and the mass media in modern Japan in "Formations of Mass Culture," in *Postwar Japan as History,* ed. Andrew Gordon (Berkeley: University of California Press, 1993), 239–258.

2. Inoue Teruko, "Masu komi ga tsukuridasu josei, kekkon, katei," in *Joseigaku to sono shūhen* (Keisō shobō, 1980), 111. Inoue has been a pivotal figure who has participated in both the *ūman ribu* movement and women's studies, theorizing their relation to each other.

3. Before women's studies (*joseigaku*) was established or the term feminism became more commonly used during the late 1970s and early 1980s, Inoue was a pioneering feminist critic of the media industry. Terms such as "feminism" (*feminizumu*) and "feminist" (*feminisuto*) began to be popularized during the late 1970s through publications such as *Feminisuto* and *Croissant,* which are cited in this essay. This is not to say, however, that the production of "feminist discourses" did not predate this popularization into mass culture. See, for example, Sharon Sievers, *Flowers in Salt: The Beginnings of Feminist Consciousness in Modern Japan* (Stanford, CA: Stanford University Press, 1983); and *Feminism and the State in Modern Japan,* ed. Vera Mackie (Melbourne: Japanese Studies Center, 1995).

4. Inoue, "Masu komi," 111. The boundaries of mainstream culture, women's culture, and girls' (*shōjo*) culture are often crossed and ambiguous, and the phenomena of cross-reading (i.e., girls reading boys' *manga*) further complicates assumptions about the gender(ing) of readers.

5. Suzuki Midori, "Media mondai ni torikumu kusa no ne no joseitachi," in *Josei to media,* eds. Katō Harueko and Tsuganezawa Toshihiro (Kyoto: Sekai shisōsha, 1992); Inoue Teruko, "Media ni taisuru feminisuto apurōchi," in *Hyōgen to media,* vol. 7, *Nihon no feminizumu,* ed. Ueno Chizuko et al. (Iwanami shoten, 1995); Mizuta Noriko, "Josei no jikō hyōgen to bunka: jo ni kaete," in *Josei no hyōgen to bunka,* ed. Mizuta (Tabata shoten, 1993); and Funabashi Kuniko, "Pornographic Culture and Sexual Violence," in *Japanese Women: New Feminist Perspectives on the Past, Present, and Future,* eds. Kimiko Fujimura-Fanselow and Atsuko Kameda (New York: The Feminist Press, 1995), 255–264.

6. Muramatsu Yasuko and Hilaria Gössmann, *Media ga tsukuru jendā* (Shin'yōsha, 1998).

7. Muramatsu and Gössmann, *Media ga tsukuru jendā*, 20–31; *Sōgō jānarizumu*, no. 156 (Spring 1996): 110–111; and *Sōgō jānarizumu*, no. 168 (Spring 1999): 68–69.

8. *Sōgō jānarizumu*, no. 168 (Spring 1999): 68–69.

9. Ibid.; Inoue Teruko and Ehara Yumiko, *Josei no dēta bukku*, 3rd. ed. (Yūhikaku, 1999), 201.

10. *Fujin rōdō no jitsujō*, ed. Rōdōshō fujin kyoku (Ōkurashō insatsu kyoku, 1986), and Ueno Chizuko, "Women and the Family in Transition in Postindustrial Japan," in *Women of Japan and Korea: Continuity and Change*, eds. Joyce Gelb and Marian Lief Palley (Philadelphia, PA: Temple University Press, 1994), 23–27.

11. In contrast with the mainstream media (newspaper, television, and broadcasting companies) discussed above, publishing houses have employed a significantly higher percentage of women. For example, women comprised an approximate average of 45 percent of new incoming employees among ten major publishing companies in 1991. Among established publishing companies such as Kōdansha, Shōgakukan, Kōbunsha, and Bungeishunjū, an average of 25 percent of the editors were women in 1991. Morohashi Taiki, *Zasshi bunka no naka no joseigaku* (Meiroku shoten, 1993), 294.

12. *Shiryō Nihon ūman ribu shi*, ed. Miki Sōko et al., vol. I (Kyoto: Shokado, 1992); *Shiryō Nihon ūman ribu shi*, ed. Miki Sōko et al., vol. II (Kyoto: Shokado, 1994); *Seisabetsu e no kokuhatsu: ūman ribu ha shuchō suru*, ed. Aki shobō henshū bu (Aki shobō, 1971); *Onna no shisō*, ed. Saeki Yōko (Sanpo, 1972); and Tanaka Mitsu, *Inochi no onnatachi e: torimidashi ūman ribu ron* (Tabata shoten, 1972).

13. Ueno Chizuko, "Nihon no ribu: sono shisō to haikei," in *Ribu to feminizumu*, vol. I, *Nihon no feminizumu*; Inoue Teruko, "Masu komi to josei no gendai," in *Onna no imēji*, ed. Josei kenkyūkai hen (Keisō shobō, 1980), 42; Tanaka Kazuko, "The New Feminist Movement in Japan, 1970–1990," in Fujimura-Fanselow and Kameda, *Japanese Women*, 343–352; and Tanaka Kazuko, *A Short History of the Women's Movement in Modern Japan* (n.p., 1977).

14. *Women's Movements in Postwar Japan*, selected articles in *Shiryō: sengo nijūnen shi*, ed. Tsuji Seimei, trans. Wake A. Fujioka (Honolulu, HI: East-West Center, 1968); and Tanaka, *A Short History*, 47.

15. My use of "regulatory ideal" implies that the ideal of *ryōsai kenbo* has a regulatory function precisely because women do not live up to or according to this

ideal. But because of its historical institutionalization and general cultural intelligibility, it functions as an ideal standard against which the reality of women's lives are often evaluated, even though not all women consciously desire to become a "good wife, wise mother." See Kathleen Uno's essay in this volume.

16. Kathleen Uno, "Death of 'Good Wife, Wise Mother'?" in Gordon, *Postwar Japan as History,* 294; and Tachi Kaoru, "Ryōsai kenbo," in Josei kenkyūkai hen, *Onna no imēji,* 184–209.

17. *Ūman ribu* argued that sex discrimination, as well as other forms of discrimination, was not only structural and institutional but had become a part of one's internalized consciousness and was reproduced by women themselves. This internalized consciousness had thus far prevented women from confronting the roots of their oppression and their own complicity in supporting systems of discrimination. Following from this argument, women's liberation would therefore require collective action to transform social conditions and one's own consciousness.

18. Sōko et al., *Shiryō Nihon,* vol 1; Ueno, "Nihon no ribu"; and Ueno Chizuko, *Onna to iu kairaku* (Keiso Shobo, 1986), 245–269.

19. I further examine the history, philosophy, and practice of *ūman ribu* in my PhD dissertation, "Tanaka Mitsu and the Women's Liberation Movement in Japan: Toward a Radical Feminist Ontology," PhD dissertation, Cornell University, 2003, and forthcoming book.

20. Saito Masami, "Feminizumu riron ni yoru hihanteki disukōsu bunseki no tenkai: uman ribu undō no media gensetsu wo jirei to shite," PhD dissertation, Ochanomizu Women's University, 2000.

21. The Group of Fighting Women against Mass Media's Sex Discrimination was a group that organized in 1975 to take action against sexism in newspapers, magazines, and commercials. "Ribu hōkoku: gonenme no watashitachi," ed. Onna erosu henshūin kai, in *Onna erosu,* no. 7 (1976): 135; *Media ni egakareru josei zō,* ed. Media no naka no sabetsu wo kangaeru kai (Chushobo, 1991); *Media ga tsukuru jendā,* 9–103; Suzuki Midori, "Women and Television," in Fujimura-Fanselow and Kameda, *Japanese Women,* 75–90; Suzuki, "Media mondai," 57–70; and Inoue, "Media ni taisuru," 19–30.

22. The original full name of Women's Action Group was International Women's Year Action Group (Kokusai fujin nen wo kikkaketoshite kōdō wo okosu onnatachi no kai). For a record of their activities from 1975 to the mid-1990s, see *Kōdōsuru onnatachi ga hiraita michi,* ed. Kōdōsuru kai kirokushu kenshu iinkai (Miraisha, 1999).

23. This group effectively stopped a sexist commercial by *House*. See "Watashi tsukuru hito, boku taberu hito," in Kōdōsuru kai, *Kōdōsuru onnatachi,* 34–36.

24. Many *ribu* women still resist or refuse to identify with the newer term "feminist," and make a political distinction between the terms "ribu" and "feminism." Ehara Yumiko, *Feminizumu Ronsō 70 nendai kara 90 nendai* (Keisō Shobō, 1990), 17, and also her "Japanese Feminism in the 1970s and 1980s," trans. Yanagida Eino and Paula Long, in *U.S.-Japan Women's Journal,* English Supplement, no. 4 (1993): 49–69. In this essay, Ehara notes the differing and at times negative opinions toward *ūman ribu* by some founders of women's studies and points out that other founding scholars like Inoue Teruko conceived and theorized women's studies as a direct extension of the principles of *ūman ribu*. Miki Sōko, "Ribu tamashi no nai joseigaku nante," in *Onna erosu* 11, no. 11 (1978): 145–149. Interviews with *ribu* members such as Saeki Yōko, Miki Sōko, Tanaka Mitsu, Inoue Teruko, Akiyama Yōko, Yonezu Tomoko, Wakabashi Naeko, and others, 1999–2002.

25. In 1975, the Liaison Group for the Implementation of the Resolutions of the International Women's Year Conference of Japan was established and has continued to work with the government, holding national conferences every five years. This group formulated the Plan of Action Toward the Year 2000, regarding women's issues. The Bureau for Gender Equality now offers a home page, listing governmental activities with this Liaison Group: www.gender.go.jp/index2.html.

26. Vera Mackie, "Feminist Critiques of Modern Japanese Politics," in *Mapping the Women's Movement,* ed. Monica Threlfall (London: Verso, 1996), 272, and Jan Bardsley, "Spaces for Feminist Action: National Centers for Women in Japan and South Korea," in *National Women's Studies Association Journal* 11, no. 1 (Spring 1999): 136–149.

27. Many *ribu* women and anti-imperialist women's groups protested this rally. See *Onna ga tennōsei ni tachi mukau toki,* ed. Shinryaku ikuaruzu sabetsu to tatakau ajia fujin kaigi (n.p., 1977). Muto Ichiyo also describes this change in the women's movements in greater detail in "Women, Women's Movements, and Japanese Society in the 80s" (unpublished manuscript).

28. Ueno Chizuko, "Imēji no shijō," *Sezon no hasso,* ed. Ueno Chizuko (Libro Port, 1991), 41.

29. Citation from Tokyo Gas Company's 1984 advertisement. Lise Skov and Brian Moeran, "Introduction: Hiding in the Light: From Oshin to Yoshimoto

Banana," in *Women, Media, and Consumption,* eds. Skov and Moeran (Honolulu: University of Hawai'i Press, 1995), 29.

30. "A Brief History of 'Feminist,'" *Feminist International* 2 (1980): 104.

31. Its first issue, which had Yoko Ono's face on its cover, sold a record high number of twenty thousand copies. Thereafter, the magazine faced financial difficulties.

32. "A Brief History of 'Feminist,'" 128.

33. Funabashi Kuniko has argued that the sexual revolution was harmful for women because the increasing availability of sexually stimulating media promoted, in her opinion, "violence and exploitation of the female sex." Funabashi, "Pornographic Culture and Sexual Violence," 257; Kawashima Yōko, "Nihon no taishū poruno bunka no jendā ideorogī," in *Nichi Bei josei jānaru,* no. 20 (1996), 3–30; and Ueno, *Onna to iu kairaku,* 245–269.

34. Mark Schilling, *The Encyclopedia of Japanese Pop Culture* (New York: Weatherhill, 1997), 65.

35. *Playboy International* (Dec. 1975).

36. Yoko Kawashima, "Female Workers: An Overview of Past and Current Trends," in Fujimura-Fanselow and Kameda, *Japanese Women,* 275; and Ochiai Emiko, *The Japanese Family System in Transition* (Tokyo: LTCB International Library Foundation, 1996), 9–35. During this period, the number of employed women doubled from 5.31 million to 10.95 million, and Japan's GNP increased eight-fold. While women have always worked at home, for family businesses, and in agriculture, it was in 1965 that the proportion of women working for wages for the first time exceeded 50 percent of the total female labor force. Kazuko, "The New Feminist Movement," 343.

37. Ueno Chizuko, "The Japanese Women's Movement," in *The Japanese Trajectory: Modernization and Beyond,* eds. Gavan McCormack and Yoshio Sugimoto (Cambridge: Cambridge University Press, 1988), 167–168.

38. Mizuta, "Josei no jikō hyōgen," 9.

39. Ivy, "Formations of Mass Culture," 239–258. Ueno Chizuko describes this as a new form of consumption that was packaged as a "lifestyle" that included home improvement, hobbies, leisure, fashion, culture, tradition, and convenience. See Ueno, "Imēji no shijō," 5–136.

40. Inoue, "Masu komi to josei," 48–49; and Morohashi, *Zasshi bunka no naka,* 29.

41. According to surveys cited by Inoue, in 1973 advertisements comprised approximately 25 percent of women's magazines, and this figure rose to 30 percent by 1980. See Inoue, "Masu komi to josei," 54–61; and Inoue and Ehara, *Josei no dēta bukku,* 1st ed. (Yūhikaku, 1991), 210–211.

42. Hara Kimi, "Challenges to Education for Girls and Women in Modern Japan: Past and Present," in Fujimura-Fanselow and Kameda, *Japanese Women,* 104; Ueno, "The Japanese Women's Movement," 174–176; and Inoue and Ehara, *Josei no dēta bukku,* 1st ed., 96–97.

43. *Nihon no josei deitā banku,* ed. Bandō Mariko (Ministry of Finance Publishers, 2001), 46.

44. Ibid., 48–49.

45. Vera Mackie, "Equal Opportunity and Gender Identity: Feminist Encounters with Modernity and Postmodernity in Japan," in *Japanese Encounters with Postmodernity,* eds. Johann Arnason and Yoshio Sugimoto (London: Kegan Paul, 1995), 95–113. See also Ueno Chizuko, "The Impact of Industrialization and Post-Modernization from the Gender Perspective," in *The Predicament of Modernization in East Asia,* eds. Eric Wu and Yun-han Chu (Taipei: National Cultural Association, 1995), 139–152.

46. The women of *ribu* did not seek equality with men because they saw the male-centered/masculinist (*dansei chūshin shakai*) organization of society as a structure of exploitation, and therefore to become like men would only add to the oppression of others. Sōko et al., *Shiryō Nihon,* vols. I and II; Tanaka Mitsu, *Doko ni iyou to riburian* (Shakai hyōronsha, 1983); Ueno, "Nihon no ribu"; and "Ueno Chizuko," in *Broken Silence: Voices of Japanese Feminism,* ed. Sandra Buckley (Berkeley: University of California Press, 1997), 280.

47. Inoue, "Masu komi to josei," 43; and Morohashi, *Zasshi bunka no naka,* 13.

48. According to the 1971 Publishers Yearbook there were twenty-one titles listed under the category of women's magazines; by 1982, there were forty-six magazines listed under this category, twenty-eight of which had begun since 1970. Inoue, "Masu komi to josei," 45–47. These new magazines of the 1970s streamlined their focus by specializing in fashion for a particular age group, or a particular interest such as interior design, childrearing, sports, sex, cooking, travel, and job hunting.

49. Inoue, "Media ni taisuru," 10; and Inoue, "Josei zasshi ni miru feminizumu," in Katō and Tsuganezawa, *Josei to media,* 111–119.

50. In *Croissant*, see August 25, 1978, 72–75; March 10, 1979, 27–33; and June 25, 1980, 4–11. The June 1980 article introduces the work of Simone de Beauvoir. Sakamoto Kazue has also written that *More*, a popular women's magazine, "drew on feminist thinking" during the late 1970s and sought to help its readers deal with the tensions of being a "career woman" and the pressure on women to marry. See Kazue Sakamoto, "Reading Japanese Women's Magazines: The Construction of New Identities in the 1970s and 1980s," in *Media, Culture and Society* 21 (1999): 183–185.

51. Inoue, "Masu komi to josei," 64–65; and Ochiai Emiko, "Bijuaru imēji to shite no onna: sengo josei zasshi ga miseru sei yakuwari," in *Hyōgen to media*, 105–107.

52. Inoue, "Masu komi to josei," 58; and Nancy Rosenberger, "Antiphonal Performances? Japanese Women's Magazines and Women's Voices," in Skov and Moeran, *Women, Media, and Consumption*, 146.

53. Ochiai, "Bijuaru imēji," 105–107; Inoue, "Masu komi to josei," 52–71; and Morohashi, *Zasshi bunka no naka*, 120–123.

54. Mark Schilling, "Worshipping the Naked Goddess: The Media, Mores and Miyazawa Rie," *Japan Quarterly* (April–June 1992): 218–224.

55. Shirley Geok-lin Lim, "The Center (Can)not Hold: American Studies and Global Feminism," *American Studies International* 39, no. 3 (Oct. 2000): 25–35.

56. Matthew Thorn, "Unlikely Explorers: Alternative Narratives of Love, Sex, Gender, and Friendship in Japanese 'Girls'' Comics," Available at *Shōjo Manga Home Page* at www.matt-thorn.com/shoujo_manga/sexual_ambiguity/index.html

57. Thorn, "Unlikely Explorers."

58. Inoue summarizes Fujimoto Yukari's analysis of *shōjo manga* in "Media ni taisuru," 7–8.

59. Inoue and Ehara, *Josei no dēta bukku*, 1st ed., 214. By 1993, there were over fifty different magazines on the market, with a combined circulation of 120 million. Frederik Schodt, *Dreamland Japan: Writings on Modern Manga* (Berkeley, CA: Stone Bridge Press, 1996), 124.

60. Some ladies' comics deliberately stay away from sexual topics. Schodt, *Dreamland Japan*, 19. The popularity of ladies' comics reached its peak in the early 1990s.

61. "Ladies' Comics Reflecting Repressed Sexual Desires," *Mainichi Daily News*, June 30, 1996, and July 1, 1996, and Schodt, *Dreamland Japan*.

62. *Zasshi shinbun sōkatarogu* (Media risōchi senta, 2001), 354–369.

63. Schodt, *Dreamland Japan*, 127; "Women Seeking Security," *Asahi News Service*, Nov. 2, 1994; and "'Josei muke poruno' wa teichaku shita ka," in *Tsukuru: tokushu josei to media* 12 (1994): 72–79.

64. Fujimoto Yukari, *Watashi no ibashō wa doko ni aruno* (Gakuyō shobō, 1998); Fujimoto Yukari, *Kairaku denryū: onna no yokubō no katachi* (Kawade shoten, 1999); and Erino Miya, *Redīsu komikku no joseigaku* (Seikyūsha, 1990).

65. Fujimoto Yukari, "Redīsu komikku to iu hyōgen," in *Asahi gurafu* (Asahi shinbun shuppansha, 1995).

66. Yamada Toyoko, "Mōdo to poruno no ayaui kankei," in *Porunogurafī*, vol. 3, *New Feminism Review* (Gakuyō shobō, 1992), 101–111. Yamada discusses the ambivalence and pleasure women derive from looking at beautiful women's bodies and how such looking is constitutive of women's sexual identity and desire. According to a survey conducted in 1986, the amount of visual images in the new woman's magazines, such as *JJ*, *non no*, *with*, *More*, *an an*, *Elle*, and *Olive* was on par with *Playboy* and *Penthouse*. See Inoue and Ehara, *Josei no dēta bukku*, 1st ed., 211.

67. Setsu Shigematsu, "Dimensions of Desire: Sex, Fantasy, and Fetish in Japanese Comics," in *Themes and Issues in Asian Cartooning*, ed. John Lent (Bowling Green, OH: Popular Press, 1999), 127–163.

68. There are significantly different opinions about pornography among feminists in Japan. For an example of different feminist views of pornography, see *Porunogurafī*, vol. 3, *New Feminism Review*, and Fujimoto, *Kairaku Denryū*.

69. See, for example, Stuart Hall, "The Local and the Global," in *Culture, Globalization and the World-System: Contemporary Conditions for the Representation of Identity*, ed. Anthony D. King (Minneapolis: Minnesota University Press, 1997), 19–40.

70. Uchida Shungiku, *Atashi ga umi ni kaeru made* (Bungei shunjū, 1996). A hostess is an occupation in the *mizushobai* industry, broadly understood as the entertainment-sex industry. Anne Allison has written about the role of the hostess in her analysis of the production of masculinity. See *Nightwork: Sexuality, Pleasure, and Corporate Masculinity in a Tokyo Hostess Club* (Chicago, IL: University of Chicago Press, 1994).

71. *an an* (April 18, 1986); *More* (Feb. 1996); Bishō (Nov. 27, 1993); and *Fujin Kōron* (Jan. 1990).

72. The best-known adaptation of her *manga* was the television series *Minami-kun no koibito* made in 1990. In 1996, *Me o tojite daite* and *Monokage ni ashibyōshi* were made into films. Her novel *Father Fucker* was also adapted into the film *Girl of Silence* and has been screened at international film festivals. It was directed by Arato Genjirō and distributed by Film Makers, Inc.

73. Ueno has argued that what is considered "traditional" by most Japanese are modern concepts constructed in the Meiji period. For example, "The marriage considered traditional for a Japanese woman, in which she is married as a virgin to an unknown man," has become traditional only since the fourth decade of the Meiji period. See her "Genesis of the Urban Housewife," *Japan Quarterly* 34 (April–June 1987): 130–142.

74. "Miya Yoshiko: Interview," by Buckley, in her *Broken Silence*, 164.

75. *Fazza Fakka* (Bungei shunjū, 1993). Subsequent page numbers in text refer to this title. According to the publisher, by 1998, *Father Fucker* (*Fazā Fakka*) had sold over half a million copies: 354,000 in hard cover, 270,000 in paperback. Correspondence with Bungei shunjū, March 16, 1998.

76. *Maboroshi no futsu shōjo* 2 (Futaba sha, 1989), and telephone interview with Uchida Shungiku, Jan. 7, 1997.

77. Uchida has also stated that she wrote her story because, according to current law, her mother would automatically inherit her estate. Telephone interview conducted with Uchida Shungiku on Jan. 7, 1997.

78. Telephone interview with Uchida, Jan. 7, 1997, and interviews in March 2002 with feminists involved with the domestic violence movement.

79. In 1992, *Josei seven*'s weekly circulation was between 746,000 and 840,000, according to ABC Hōkoku. As one of the highest-selling women's weekly magazines, *Josei seven*'s circulation dwarfs the circulation figures of traditional monthly housewife magazines such as *Shufu no tomo,* which in 1992 was approximately 177,000.

80. In 1997–1998, when Uchida was pregnant with her second child, she published her second nude photo exposé in the magazine *Flash* (Jan. 27, 1998), and as part of her book, *Anata mo ninshin shashin wo torou* (Parco shuppan, 1998). She published photos of her fourth pregnancy in *Kingyoku*, ed. Uchida Shungiku (East Press, 2001).

81. Uchida Shungiku, *Watashitachi wa hanshoku shite iru I* [We are reproducing 1] (Bunka Comics, 1994), 84. Uchida states that unlike most other women, she can afford to have a child outside of a marriage relationship.

82. Ibid., 177.

83. Ueno Chizuko, "Collapse of 'Japanese Mothers,'" in *U.S.-Japan Women's Journal,* English Supplement, no. 10 (1996): 17.

Index

Abortion, 169, 429, 430, 446–447, 459*n*72

Abstinence, in *Eisei shinpen,* 200–201

Advertisements, 77, 192–193, 561–562, 564

Agriculture, women in, 371, 386*m*4, 391*n*62, 419*n*43, 512

Akagawa Manabu, 174

All-female educational institutions. *See* Girls' schools

All-Japan Women's Self-Cultivation Society, 116, 118

Alternative media, *ūman ribu* and, 559–560

Ambition, as masculine, 71–72

American education, 49, 59*n*34–35, 138

American family life, 127*n*42

American gender ideology, women's education and, 51

Amerika maru, evacuation ship, 330

An Encouragement of Learning, 70, 72, 77–78, 80, 85

Anglo-Japanese Alliance, 283

Anti-V.D. marriage restriction law petition, 230–232, 233–240, 236, 241, 256*n*80

Antifeminism, 536–537, 543–544, 545

Antifeminists, 169, 522

Arai Tsuru, 243

Arakawa Gorō, introduction of petition for marriage restriction to Diet, 240, 245

Army, Imperial Japanese, 261–275, 270, 271, 272, 277, 278–279, 285, 508, 526; and hygiene, 198, 199, 206, 218*n*4

Asahi shinbun (newspaper), 332–335, 337–338, 339 340

Asaka Chōbei, representative, on marriage restriction petition, 235

Asō mines, 393, 394, 398, 408–410, 420*n*54

Assimilation, 295–296, 308–309, 316

Association for Asian Studies, session on Japanese women, 30*m*0

Association of Race Hygiene, 244, 245

Atomi Girls' School, terms of endearment used in, 134

Atoyama (coal hauler), 399–400, 402, 410, 416*n*24

Attu, 354*n*43, 347

Autoeroticism, Tanaka on, 205. *See also* Masturbation

Battle of Saipan. *See* Saipan
Bigamy, women's rights and, 473
Birth control, 244, 255*n*76, 428, 429, 431, 433, 446–447
Birth rates, New Life Movement and, 446–447, 459*n*72
"Blood tax," 262–263, 276
Bluestockings, 534. *See* also Bluestocking movement
Bluestocking movement (Bluestocking Society), 187*n*114, 165–168, 227, 241
Boxer Rebellion, 283
Boys' schools, 147–148
Brothels, 225
Burakumin, 397, 401, 411
Burke, Edmund, 62–63, 65, 86
Bushi, portrayal of, 262
Butler, Judith, 9–10, 210, 220–221*n*4

Carpenter, Edward, 168–169, 171–172
Caucasian women, 561, 567. *See also* White beauty
Censorship, 147, 183*n*54, 192, 297, 319*n*8, 340
Chastity, 117, 177, 473
Chesterfield, Lord, 64–65, 84
Chikuhō coal mines, 393–394, 395, 396, 397
China, 197, 217, 251*n*24, 276–277, 279, 283, 296–305
Chinese, characterization of during Sino-Japanese War, 275–276
Chiyo maru, evacuation ship, 330
Chōsen kōron (magazine), on colonial women, 211–212

Chōsen oyobi Manshū (*COM*) (magazine), Seoul-based journal. *See* COM.
Christianity, 62–63, 234, 477
Chūma Okimaru, presentation of petition to restrict marriage, 238–239
Citizens, creation of loyal, 495–496
Citizenship, 51, 307, 379, 394, 482, 483; and military service, 260, 270–275, 284–285; and gender, 469, 472, 492*n*112
Civil Code, 468, 487*n*29
Civil rights for women, married compared with unmarried, 473
Civil society, 466, 485*n*11
Civil sphere. *See* Public sphere
Civilian deaths, images of, 345–346
Class, 46–47, 85, 106, 108, 136, 155, 241–242, 401, 413–415, 513. *See also Bushi;* Middle-class identity; Warrior class
Coal haulers, gender and ethnicity of, 394–395. *See also Atoyama*
Coal industry, 394–395, 397–405, 422*n*82
Coal miners, government ban on underground work for women in mines, 410
Coal sorters, 393–394, 398–399, 401, 403, 412
Coeducation, 51–52, 144
Colonial areas, 193, 220*n*13, 299, 307, 318*n*3, 385*n*11. *See also* Expatriate communities; *particular communities*
Colonial community, 299, 315
Colonial government, 297–298
Colonial imperialism, sexological discourse in Japan and, 196
Colonial monthlies. *See* Magazines
Colonial newspapers, 192–193, 218*n*4

Colonial relationship, Japan with rest of Asia, 546

Colonial women, 210, 211, 220–221*n*14, 300–310. *See also* Women

Coloniality, sexological modernism in Japan and, 195

COM *(Chōsen oyobi Manshū)*, 296–297, 308–309, 310, 311, 320*n*17, 324–325*n*79; content, 298–299, 304, 305, 306–307, 312, 315

Comfort women, 199, 218*n*4, 411–412

Communist Party, New Life Movement criticism, 441

Companionate marriage. *See* Marriage

Condoms, distribution of, 457*n*43

Confucian gentleman, 66, 72, 74–75

Conscript army, 264–265, 281

Conscription, 189*n*26, 262–263, 264–266, 272, 273, 274, 280–281, 290*n*39, 293*n*70; empowerment as a result of, 267–268, 270

Conscription law, 266, 268–269, 286*n*4

Conscripts, 189*n*31, 267–269, 270, 282

Consumerism, 101, 119, 120–121, 457*n*44, 460*n*83

Contraception. *See* Birth control

Corporate programs for training housewives, 456*n*38

Corporations, 432–442 *passim*

Cotton industry, 376, 379–380, 381, 420*n*52

Cotton Spinners Federation, 373–374

Cotton spinning, 362–363, 368, 381, 387–388*n*31

Cult of manliness, 88

Cultural differences, in Korean coal mines, 20

Cultural norms, gendered, 407

Cultural variance, cultural construction of more than two genders, 29–30*n*9

Daily life, prewar efforts to reform, 426–442 *passim*

Daily Life Reform program, 427

Dalian, colonial newspapers in, 192–193

Danshi, defined as imperial male, 280

De Bary, Brett, on Karatani's *Origins of Modern Japanese Literature,* 523

Death, as wartime propaganda weapon, 328, 331, 332, 339, 341–342, 343, 352–353*n*36

Democracy, power in primitive, 209

Desire, 208, 531. *See also* Sexual desire

Disease, 16, 311–312

Divorce, 223*n*37, 230–235, 314, 367, 451, 465

Domestic woman. *See* Private woman

Dormitories, 182*n*40, 359–360

Draft dispensations, for men in public institutions of higher learning, 97*n*64

Duty to country, 271, 276

Economic independence, 482

Economic miracle, Japan seen as enjoying fruits of, 19

Education, 71, 100–113, 108, 125*n*18, 144, 151, 285, 405–406, 428, 468, 471, 474; during Tokugawa period, 39–48; gender boundaries and, 47–48; restriction for women's, 48–49; moral/religious foundations of, 51–52, private academies, 68–69; for military, 260, 278–279, 280; Japanese schools for *naichi* children, 323*n*63; for Korean girls, 405–406; for women, 498. *See also* Education for girls; Education for boys; Women's education; Meiji women's education; Gentleman, education of

Education for boys, 42–43, 260, 269, 278–280, 282, 285

Education for girls, 55*n*4, 101, 126–127*n*38, 172, 310–311, 378, 497–498, 515*n*3. *See also* Girls' schools; Women's education

Education Ministry. *See* Ministry of Education

Educational policies, prewar prohibition of girls in middle schools, 101

Educational system, 110, 282–283, 293*n*71, 496

Educators, early Meiji period, 83–84. *See also* Fukuzawa Yukichi

Ehara Yumiko, manipulation of women by mass media, 533

Eisei shinpen, 198–202

Elections in Japan, candidates from Korea, Manchuria, 299

Ellis, Havelock, 136–137, 143, 167, 169, 188*m*28

Emperor, military connection with emphasized, 282

Empire, 17, 212, 295–296, 509; sex workers in, 193, 197, 218–219*n*4, 300, 303–304, 406

Employment, 117, 380, 386*m*5, 386*n*21, 387*n*25, 405–406

English gentleman, 62–63

Equal Employment Opportunity Law (1985), 521, 564–565

Erotica. *See* Ladies' comics; Pornography

Erotophobia, 203, 207

Ethics textbooks, 504–505, 507

Ethnic discrimination, 20, 422*n*84

Ethnic division of labor, coal mining, 413

Ethnic identity, role of colonies in shaping, 315

Ethnic National Eugenics Protection Bill, 245

Eugenics, 17, 226, 227, 228, 233, 235, 241, 242–245, 246–247, 250*m*10; public awareness raised, 236–237; sex education and, 428–429

Eugenics Protection Law, 247, 429

European colonies, 306–307, 309–310, 316, 321*n*24

Expatriate communities, 301–302. *See also* Colonial areas

Factory workers, 123*n*2, 228–229, 359–392 *passim*, 439–440

Family, 115–116, 424–425, 433, 445, 466–467, 486*n*18, 535–536, 563, 572

Family law, 469

Family planning. *See* Birth 8control

Father Fucker (Uchida Shungiku), 574–575, 588*n*75

Female education. *See* Education; Education for girls; Women's education

Female employment. *See* Women workers

Female-female sex, new formulation, 140–141, 146–147, 157

Female labor. *See* Women workers

Female literacy, 11, 56*m*10

Female self-cultivation, women's right and, 464–465

Female sexuality, 16–17, 21, 207–208, 225

Female writers, Suga on, 538

Feminine essence, ahistorical, 522
Feminine writing, 538
Femininity, 520–521, 537, 539, 544, 572
Feminism, 484*n*2, 530–531, 532–533, 536–537, 547. *See also* Liberal feminism; Women's rights
Feminist(s), 139–140, 163, 170, 174, 176–177, 228, 254–255*n*65, 470, 562, 583*n*24; thought, 534, 536–537; discourse, 555, 560–561; politics, shifts in, 578–579
Feminizumu. See Feminism
Fifteen-Year War, experience of Japanese people, 328
Fordism, New Life Movement and, 433
Foreign threat, faced by Meiji leaders, 265
Foucault, Michel, 191–192, 198, 201, 217, 218*n*3, 464, 532
Frühstück, Sabine, 195
Fujin kurabu (magazine), self-cultivation in, 110
Fujin sekai (magazine), 99, 111, 112, 114, 115
Fujinron, discourse on womanhood, 472
Fujita Tsuguji, Japanese war artist, 330
Fujo shinbun (magazine), Itoigawa *shingū,* 156
Fujokai (magazine), 99–100, 116–117, 118
Fukuchi Gen'ichirō, 85
Fukuda Hideko, 470, 475
Fukushima Shirō, founder of *Fujo shinbun,* 162–163
Fukuzawa Yukichi, 70–72, 73–74, 82–83, 85, 103, 274, 282, 463, 473–474; on the gentleman, 61, 70–86

passim, 74, 75, 76, 80, 86; Keiō Academy and, 75, 77; prescriptive literature of, 77, 78, 79–80; Kuroda Kiyotaka and, 89–90. *See also An Encouragement of Learning.*
Fundamental Code of Education, Fukuzawa and, 71
Furuya English Academy for Girls, 170
Furuya Toyoko, on same-sex love, 170–171, 172, 190*m*42
Futabatei Shimei, on Japanese women on Russian frontier, 301

Gaikotsu, Miyatake, 192, 193–194
Garapan, town in Saipan, 329
Garon, Sheldon, on history of Japanese women, 240–241
Geisha, attention of *COM,* 304
Genbun itchi, 525, 551*n*41
Gender, 56*m*11, 90, 104, 111–120, 143, 245, 478, 496, 520, 544; difference, 50–51, 425; norms, 225–226, 419*n*51; essentialism, 479, 546; assumption of continuity, 553–554*n*57; blindness, Karatani's, 525–526, 527
Gender division of labor, 361–362, 363–370, 371–372, 397–405, 385*m*10, 413, 425, 431; in textile industries, 360–361, 369–370, 382–383
Gender issues, discussion in *Origins of Modern Japanese Literature,* 523–526, 527
Gender politics, of postwar mass media, 560
Gender roles, 53, 100–101, 260, 362, 380–381, 424, 449, 496, 505–506
Gentility, 63, 66, 67, 68, 72–73, 75, 76–86 *passim,* 83, 88, 89; of essence, 64,

65, 69–70, 72, 74. *See also* English gentleman; Gentleman

Gentleman, education of, 61, 62–63, 64, 65, 66–67, 70, 76–77, 91–92*n*1; of civilization, 74, 75, 76, 86, 87, 88, 89–90. *See also* English gentleman

German army, 270, 271, 286*n*3

Girls' education, 42–43, 310–311, 493–495

Girls' schools, 16–17, 133, 134–136, 142, 164, 170, 178–179*n*4, 504, 506

Good Life Movement, 437–439

Good wife, wise mother, 210, 220*n*14, 242, 312–313, 407, 431, 477, 503, 507; applicability of policy, 222–223*n*31; model, 324*n*71; socialization as aim of girls education, 493–494; origins, 495–500

Guadalcanal, 347

Gyokusai, 330–333, 343, 346–347. *See also under* Saipan

Habuto Eiji, on same-sex love, 143

Hakusan maru, evacuation ship, 330

Hamao Shirō, on gender difference in same-sex love, 149

Harbin, Japanese women in, 301

Hashimoto Ryūtarō, on docility of rural girls, 374

Hatoyama Ichirō, Prime Minister, 429, 430, 454–455*m*8

Headquarters for the Planning and Promoting of Policies Relating to Women, 561

Headquarters for the Promotion of Gender Equality, 565

Hegel's Master-Slave dialectic, 540–541, 542–543, 552*n*42

Heibon Punch (magazine), sex in mainstream, 562

Hereditary military class, 262. *See also Bushi*; Samurai class

Heterosexual ferocity, 201–202

Higashikuni Naruhiko, Prime Minister, national morality and, 102

Higher Girls' School Ordinance (1907), 504

Higuchi Ichiyō, 547*n*5

Hiraizumi Kiyoshi, glorification of death, 341–342

Hiratsuka Raichō, 165–168, 225, 226–229, 231, 239–240, 241, 242–243, 472

Hirohito, Emperor, 344–345, 347, 561

Hirosawa Ei, soldier images of, 259–260

Hiroshima incident, suppression of NWS, 236

Historical interpretation, of Japanese feminist thought, 536–537

Hokkaidō, 395–396, 402

Home, concept of, 448, 503

Homoeroticism, 196, 216. *See also* Same-sex love

Homophilia, tradition of Japanese, 194

Homophobia, imported from the West, 219*n*5

Honda Masuko, on schoolgirls, 150–151

Honda Noboru, 87–88

Hongo Takanobu, 439, 440

Hosokawa Junjirō, on education for women, 501–502

Household, rationalizing, 432, 435

Household labor, 443, 444

Housewives, 112, 425, 435, 443, 500, 563; New Life Movement and, 426–427, 431, 439–440

Housewives' Association, 442

Hozumi Shigetō, 229–230, 236

Husband, ideal, 110

Hysteria, 205, 207, 208, 209, 212, 220–221*n*14, 224*n*43; category of sexological modernism, 196, 197, 220*n*14

Hysterical women, 209, 211–212

Ichikawa Fusae, 228–229, 240, 472

Identity, 68, 122, 408, 558–559, 564–567, 587*n*66

Images, 337–338, 339, 345–346, 347–348, 558, 563, 567; Japan and Japanese soldier, 275–277; "All Imperial Women Working" painting, 326–328; painting of *gyokusai,* 330–333

Imperial General Headquarters Army Section Confidential War Diary, on operations on Saipan, 335–336

Imperial Japanese Army and Navy, 261, 268, 271, 277. *See also* Army, Imperial Japanese

Imperialism, 284, 297, 299

Individual, significance of, 578–579

Industrialization, 362, 385*n*12. *See also* Mechanization

Inner Mongolia, Japanese women living in, 302

Inoue Teruko, 556, 566, 567, 588*n*3

Intermarriage, Kyokuhō on, 308–309. *See also* Marriage

International Women's Year (1975), 560–561, 582*n*22, 583*n*25

Ishikawa Ken, on women's education, 45, 57*n*23, 57*n*24

Itō Noe, critic of marriage rejection alliance, 237

Iwamoto Yoshiharu, 476–477, 478, 479–481

Japan Industrial Club, New Life Movement and, 432–433

Japan Society for the Popularization of Eugenic Marriage, 244

Japan Society for the Prevention of Venereal Disease, 243

Japan Women's College, 242–244

Japanese colonialism, 295, 309–310, 316. *See also* Colonial women

Japanese concubines, in Manchuria, 302–303

Japanese propagandists, women's deaths and, 328–329

Japanese public, loyalty to government, 263

Japanese soldiers, 275–277, 283

Japanese textile production, economic importance of, 360

Japanese uniqueness, 522, 530

Japanese women, 223*n*34, 317, 321*n*26, 334–335, 337–338, 394, 405–406, 451. *See also* Colonial women

Japan's Pacific War. *See* Saipan; World War II

Jitsugyō no Nihon (magazine), 106, 107, 109

Jitsugyō no Nihonsha (publisher), 105–106

Jogaku, 476–479

Jogaku sekai (magazine), 99

Jogaku zasshi (journal), 476, 478–479

Joint suicide. *See* Suicide

Joken, 83, 464, 467, 472, 475–476. *See also* Women's rights

Joken (journal), 467, 481–482

Jokun, 43–44, 45–48, 57*n*21, 58*n*25

Josei dōmei (magazine), NWA publication, 236

Joshi, 320*n*19

Joshi yō ōraimono. See Ōraimono

Journalism, 139–140, 152–153, 154–156, 158, 169, 176. *See also* Media
Junshi, 355–356*n*50

Kabayama Sukenori, Education Minister, on education for women, 502
Kaibara Ekiken, 42–43
Kaijima (mine), 397, 398, 404
Kamichika Ichiko, 163–165, 168–169, 265
Kamikaze, *gyokusai* and, 347
Kanai Yoshiko, 521–522, 533
Kaneda Ai, suicide of, 160–161
Karatani Kōjin, 520–521, 522, 523–526, 527, 528, 535, 547*n*2, 549*n*16; matrilinearity theory of, 523–530 *passim*, 543; terms used by, 548*n*10, 548*n*14
Karayuki-san, voices of, 300–301. *See also* Sex workers
Katayama Tetsu, Socialist Party Prime Minister, Campaign to Construct a New Japan, 427
Kawamura Kunimitsu, on Western sexology, 194
Kawasaki Mill union, New Life Movement and, 442, 446
Keiō Academy, 75, 76, 77, 80–82, 83, 85, 86, 95*n*35
Key, Ellen, ideas of, 227, 228
Kingu (magazine), 110, 111
Kiriyama Benroku, 87–88
Kishida Toshiko, 474–475, 489*n*52
Kiyosawa Kiyoshi, 342–343, 353*n*41, 354–355*n*44
Kōdansha (publishing company), 105–106, 110, 111

Korea, 18, 295–296, 299, 315, 318*n*3, 320*n*7; Japanese women living in, 210, 302, 304–305. *See also* Seoul
Korean coal miners in Japan, 393–394, 397–398, 403, 405–406, 413
Korean colonial government, intermarriage promoted by, 307–308
Korean women in Japan, 398–400, 401, 405–406, 407, 411
Korean women miners, in Fukuoka prefecture, 415*n*1
Korean women protesters, Asō mine strike and, 409
Koreans, as colonials, 418*n*37
Koreans in Japan, male-female ratio, 406
Kure Shūzū, on same-sex love, 149–150
Kuroda Kiyotaka, 89
Kyōyō, expression of self-cultivation, 103–104

Labor, 380–381, 410, 440, 445–446; age and marital status, 364, 368, 382–383, 404; costs, 372–374, 388*n*35; force, control over, 374, 379; disputes, 375–376, 379. *See also* Wages
Ladies' comics, 569–570, 587*n*60
Language, 524–525, 544
Law to Promote Agricultural Reform, 427
Liberal feminism, 555, 578–579. *See also* Feminism; Women's rights
Life magazine, images of Saipan, 352*n*30
Literacy, 44, 45–46, 48–49
Love and friendship, forms of, 133

Maeda Ai, on appeal of *shūyō* for women, 105

Magazines, 105–111, 123*n*1, 137, 211–212, 562, 586*n*59. *See also titles of specific magazines and journals*

Male bodies, pure/impure undecidability of, 216

Male-female sexual relationships, 23, 141, 151, 232, 237–239, 469, 480–481

Male homoeroticism, 212, 214, 215, 216–217

Male-male sex, 140–141, 142–143, 166, 212, 219*n*5

Manchuria, 18, 296, 302–303, 348; Japanese women in, 210, 302, 321*n*26

Manchurian Incident, 298–299, 302–303, 511

Manga industry, gender revolution in, 568

Manhood, 13–14, 17, 18, 63, 86, 271–272

Manliness, gendered ideal of, 63

Manufacturing sector, 367, 380, 391*n*58

Marianas. *See* Saipan

Marital status, 364–368, 381, 382–383, 385*n*12, 404–405, 413, 473

Marriage, 114, 117, 128*n*45, 173–174, 208, 228, 229, 306–308, 508; premarital tests, 17, 225; restriction laws of different countries, 229–242; petition for restrictions, 230–232; rejection alliance, 236–237; rates, 386*n*18; and work, 391*n*62–63; Iwamoto on, 479–480; Uchida on, 577–578. *See also* Marital status; Marriage restriction laws; New Woman Association (NWA)

Marriage regulation laws, 244, 251*n*25. *See also* Marriage restriction laws

Marriage rejection alliance, 236–238

Marriage restriction laws, 231–236

Masculine ideal, 75, 77–78, 83, 90, 103

Mass media, 557, 561–562. *See also* Media; Journalism; Women's magazines; Magazines

Mass women's magazines. *See* Women's magazines

Master-Slave dialectic, 540–541, 551–552*n*46

Masturbation, 193, 196, 197, 200, 204–205, 207. *See also* Autoeroticism

Masuda Giichi, 107–109, 111–114, 119

Maternal Body Protection Law, 247

Matrilineal structure: of Japanese society, 527–528

Mechanization: in coal mines, 361, 362, 371, 377, 379, 397–398, 404. *See also* Technology

Media, 100, 211, 236, 238, 533, 555, 556, 557, 558; stereotype of flamboyant revue star, 161–162; images of Japanese soldier in, 275–277; on military expansion, 292*n*64; depictions of fighting women in Saipan, 335–336; women's studies and, 560. *See also* Alternative media; *Asahi shinbun* (newspaper); Japanese press; Mass media; Propaganda

Meiji Civil Code, wives' rights limited under, 118

Meiji educational reforms, 53–54. *See also* Meiji women's education; Girls' schools; Women's education

Meiji educators, Fukuzawa Yukichi, 61, 76
Meiji Emperor, on education for women, 497–498
Meiji gentleman, 61–62, 85, 86. *See also* Gentleman
Meiji women's education, 39, 48–51
Meiroku zasshi (magazine), 472, 473
Metropole, 295, 299
Middle-class identity, 41, 101, 117. *See also* Identity; Class
Military, 260, 262, 274–275, 278–279, 292*n*64, 272, 282; service, 270, 271, 285, 291*n*52
Militia, not conscription army, 273–274
Mill (John Stuart), 469
Minakata Kumagusu, 197, 212–217
Mine workers, 406, 418*n*33, 421*n*70. *See also* Coal miners; Korean coal miners in Japan; Korean mine workers; Korean women miners
Minikomi, alternative media, 559–560
Ministry of Agriculture, initiatives of, 427
Ministry of Education, 426, 427, 428, 453–454*m*4, 493, 496
Mitsubishi, 397, 398, 404, 408, 416–417*n*26
Miyatake Gaikotsu. *See* Gaikotsu, Miyatake
Miyazawa Rie (model), 567, 576–577
Modanizumu, 297
Modern hygiene, 113, 198–199, 237–245
Modernist texts, desire for empire in, 198
Modernity, 4, 7, 15, 17, 20–22, 269–270, 297, 314–316
Modernity studies, 4–7, 32*n*17

Modernization of Japan, 5–6, 19, 524
Modernization studies, 4–5, 6
Moral guides, 42, 43–45. *See also* Jokun; Ōraimono
Moral guides for girls. *See Jokun*
Morality, 46, 65, 79, 102–103, 115–120, 244, 310, 428, 472–483, 504; popular (*See also Risshin shusse*), 100, 101, 110
Mori Arinori, 78–79, 472–473, 498–499
Mori Ōgai, 82, 197–207, 221*n*9, 333
Motherhood, 138, 228, 242, 479–480, 498–499, 504–505, 572, 577–578
Motherhood Education Association, 244
Mothers, 23, 209, 327, 497, 535–536
Mount Mihara, 159–160, 186*n*94, 186*n*97
Mount Mihara disease, rash of suicides, 159
Movement to Reform Daily Life, 427

Nagako, Empress, International Women's Year commemorated by, 561
Nagamine Hideki, translation of Lord Chesterfield's *Letters to His Son,* 84
Nagana Junzō, union activist, attack on New Life Movement, 440–441
Naichi children, 310, 323–324*n*63
Naichi community, Manchuria context, 318*n*7
Naichi women, 304–305, 314–316, 324–325*n*79
Nakae Chōmin, 273–274
Nakajima Kenzō, reconfiguration of gender roless, 100–101

Nakamura Masanao, 84, 86, 473, 498

National Coordinating Committee of Regional Women's Groups, 427

National Eugenics Law, 240, 244–247

National identity, 92*n*1, 315, 316

National Marriage Guidance Society, 244

Nationalism, 17, 90, 194, 430, 495, 499, 505, 534. *See also* Citizenship

Nationality, 13, 18

Nemoto Shō, gender issue for VD restriction, 234

Neo-Confucianism, 39–40, 41–42, 121

New Life Association, 432–433, 435–436, 442–443

New Life Movement, 11–12, 20, 407, 423–425, 429, 430, 431, 439, 444, 449; NKK and, 424, 443; housewives and, 426–427; influence of New Life Movement on Ōshima Ai, 436–437; Ōshima Ai's stories about, 444–445; end of, 447–448; reliance on small groups, 450–451

New Woman Association (NWA), 17, 172, 225, 226–227, 229, 251*n*25; petition for marriage restriction, 233–234, 235, 238–240; Police Regulation Law and, 229, 239–240

"New woman" magazines, 565–568

Newspapers, 340, 341–343

Nimble fingers argument, 378–379, 390*n*52

Nishi Amane, 265–266, 271–273, 290–291*n*44

Nitobe Inazō, 66–67, 106–107

NKK, 423–424, 435, 441, 442–443, 445–446

Nogami Yaeko: diaries of, 337, 353*n*41

Noma, Seiji, 109–110, 111

NWA. *See* New Woman Association (NWA)

Office for Gender Equality, 565

Ogyū Sorai, 67

Okayama Women's Friendly Society, 489*n*58

Okinawa: group suicide, 216–217, 347, 348

Onna daigaku, 45–46, 58*n*267. *See also* *Jokun*

Ōraimono: 43–44, 45, 57*n*23

Orient, Western association with sexual promise, 539–540

Orientalism, Western association with sexuality, 539–541, 545. *See also* Master-Slave dialectic; Reverse Orientalism

Origins of Japanese Women's Liberation Ideology: A Postfeminist Essay, 530–537

Origins of Modern Japanese Literature, 523–526, 528

Orii Hyūga, 423–424, 438–439

Otake Kōkichi, 165–167, 168, 188*n*19

Ōsawa Kenji, 243, 253*n*48

Ōshio Heihachirō, rebellion, 267–270, 288*n*23

Ōshima Ai, stories about New Life Movement, 436–437, 444–445

Paternalistic system, harmonious home under, 113

Patriarchal values, 113, 162, 192, 235, 395, 467, 471, 528, 536–537, 559

Patriotic activities, symbolic of women, 327

People's Rights Movement, 267–268, 271–273, 481

Pflugfelder, Gregory, 212, 280

Philippines, *gyokusai* at, 347

Poetry. *See* Takamura Kotarō; Yosano Akiko

Police Regulation Law, 226, 235–236, 239–240, 247, 253–254*n*59

Political participation, 226, 229, 291*n*52, 467, 482, 483

Polygamy, 480–481

Population Problem Discussion Group, 428

Population Problem Research Institute, 426

Population statistics, Japanese women in colonies, 302

Pornography, 562, 563, 569–570, 571, 587*n*66, 587*n*68

Port Arthur, 283, 294*n*78

Postfeminism, 531

Postmodernism, 12, 529–530

Poststructuralism, 196–197, 521–522

Power, 7–8, 11, 16, 465

Propaganda, 347–348, 349

Prostitutes, 142, 241–242, 301, 302, 304, 320*n*21. *See also* Sex workers; Geisha; Comfort women

Prostitution, 16, 82–83, 206, 314–315, 458*n*65, 465, 481

Public sphere, ideals of, 468–469

Publishers, 105–106, 122, 562–568

Race: efforts to distinguish Japanese from Korean and Chinese, 226, 312

Racial poisons, eugenics and, 246

"Racial stock," 228

Racism, 309–310, 313, 323*n*63, 510, 568

Rape, 573–574, 575

Reader participation, 116, 118–119

Reading, 101, 120–121

Red Thought Society, 172

Reform Society. *See* Tokyo Christian Women's Reform Society

Repatriation, after World War II, 331

Repression, sexual, 194–195, 200–203, 218*n*3, 532

Reproductive function, compared with erotic drives, 208

Reverse Orientalism, 522, 529–530, 539, 542–543, 545, 546, 553–554*n*57, 583*n*24

Rights, 463–464, 465, 468

Risshin shusse, 103, 104

Rousseau, 467, 469

Rural communities, changes in, 279–280

Russia, Japanese women living in, 302

Russo-Japanese War, 100–101, 283, 496–497, 503

Ryōsai kenbo, 21, 254*n*63, 500–504, 506–509, 512, 513; education for girls, 493–494, 495, 506; gender policies of state, 496–497; origins of, 499–500; public significance of, 510–511; regulatory function of, 581–582*n*15. *See also* Good wife, wise mother; Motherhood

"S": in mass media, 137, 140, 176; term, 133, 136, 174–175

Said, Edward, on sexist dimension of Orientalism, 539–541

Saipan, 329–330, 331–332, 334, 335–336, 343–344, 345, 350*n*8, 350–351*n*10–11, 355*n*45; evacuation efforts, 330, 353–354*n*41; *gyokusai* at, 328, 347; women and, 333–335; fall of, 336–337, 349

Saitō, 233, 352–353*n*36

Sakiyama (coal hewer), 399–400, 410, 411, 416*n*24

Same-sex attachments, 12, 23, 143

Same-sex love, 142, 143, 144–146, 147, 148, 150, 163–165, 168, 169–171, 172–173; terms, 140–141, 157–158, 174–175; as idealistic and altruistic loyalty to own gender, 189–190*m*40; as part of trajectory of modernity, 190*m*42. *See also* Same-sex suicide; Male homoeroticism

Same-sex suicide, 153–154, 155, 157–159, 160, 185*n*89, 186*n*99. *See also* Suicide

Samurai class, education of, 68, 72

Samurai warrior, compared with soldier, 260

Schoolgirl culture, 142–143, 176–177

Schoolgirl intimacy, 133, 134–136, 138, 139, 146–147, 153–154, 175, 176

Schoolgirls, 133–134, 135, 137, 150–152, 158–159, 164, 175, 177; same-sex suicide and, 153–154, 158–159

"Seiiku," sexological hygiene in Japanese Imperial Army, 199–205

Seitō (journal), founding of, 227. *See also* Bluestocking Society

Seitō movement, founding of, 227, 534–535. *See also* Bluestocking movement

Self-cultivation, 101, 102–104, 106–107, 109–111, 116, 437, 465, 471, 475

Self-Cultivation Society for *Fujokai*'s Beloved Readers, 118–119

Self-development, in women's magazines, 99–100

Self-reliance, as masculine, 71–72

Selfhood. *See* Self-development

Seoul, 313, 314

Sex, commercialization of, 556, 563. *See also* Prostitution; Prostitutes; Geisha; Sex workers

Sex education, eugenics and, 428–429

Sex fantasies, variety of women's, 570–571

Sex roles, 11, 564

Sex workers, 10, 193, 197, 208, 218–219*n*4, 220*n*13, 300–301, 305–306. *See also* Comfort women; Geisha; Prostitutes

Sexologists, 12, 139–140, 143–144, 145–146, 148–149

Sexology, 140, 141, 156, 157, 167, 193–195, 196, 197, 199, 206, 210–211, 223*n*36

Sexual abstinence, 202. *See also* Abstinence

Sexual desire, 207–208, 237, 571

"Sexual Development." *See* "Seiiku"

Sexual exploitation, in Japanese empire, 17. *See also* Comfort women

Sexual hygiene, in Japanese Imperial Army, 199

Sexual intercourse, 203–204

Sexual liberation, commercializing, 562–568

Sexual perversion, 146–148, 163, 205–207, 208, 235

Sexual privileges, patriarchal, 468–471

Sexual repression, as basis of all sexual dysfunction, 200–201

Sexual revolution, 559, 562, 584*n*33

Sexuality, 12–14, 22, 82, 140–146, 193, 208–217, 559, 568, 572; power and,

16, 218*n*3; control of, 16, 242, 309,
    471, 481. *See also* Female sexuality
Sexuality issues, politicized, 225, 480
Sexually transmitted disease, pre-
    marital tests for, 230
Shakuo Kyokuhō, 297, 308–309, 311,
    319*n*8
Sherrod, Robert, 338–340, 346,
    352*n*29
Shimizu Ichitarō, representative,
    on marriage restriction petition,
    235
Shimizu Toyoko, on women barred
    from political meetings, 478–479,
    482
Shimoda Utako, on women's educa-
    tion, 505–506
Shinjū, joint suicide and, 153–154
Shishi, as inversion of Fukuzawa's
    gentleman, 73
Shōchiku Revue, 161
Shōjo manga, sexual exploration and,
    569
Shufu no tomo (magazine), readership
    of, 119
Shūyō, 103–104, 105, 107–109, 112–113,
    116, 118–119, 120, 121–122; for
    women, 114–116, 117–118, 122
Shūyō (book), publication of, 106
Sievers, Sharon, 487*n*32, 493
Silk industry, 360–380, 386*m*4
Silk reeling, 363, 368, 375, 390*n*54,
    390–391*n*57
Sino-Japanese War, 268, 275–276, 279,
    406, 480, 496, 500
Sisterhood, 133–134, 138–139
Slang terms, 180*m*5. *See also* Terms of
    endearment
Smiles, Samuel, 65, 84, 103

Social prominence, craving for, 108–
    109
Socialist Party, New Life Movement
    and, 441–442
Sociopolitical problem of inequality,
    208–209
Soldiers, 18, 186*m*, 259–270, 277–278,
    279–280, 289*n*33. *See also* Con-
    scripts
Sone/Okamura suicides, 153–157
Speech, implications of in schoolgirl
    intimacy, 134–135
State, women's inclusion in, 466–467,
    496
State activities, as precursor to New
    Life Movement, 426
Steel mills, 423–424. *See also* NKK
Stereotypes, 19, 317, 459*n*73
Sterilization laws, 244
Subjectivity, 468–472, 481–483, 525,
    530, 535–536, 544. *See also* Identity
Success, 109, 122
Suga Hidemi, 520–521, 522, 537–543,
    544, 547*n*2, 551*n*41
Suicide, 153–154, 155, 159–160, 333,
    347–348. *See also* Mount Mihara
    disease; Same-sex suicide
Suicides, 160–161, 184*n*73, 330. *See also*
    Sone/Okamura suicides
Suzuki Bunshirō, 510–511

Taiwan, 210, 263, 276, 295–298
Taiyō (magazine), contents and circu-
    lation, 106
Takamura Kotarō, poetry about
    Japanese women in Saipan, 332
Takarazuka Revue, 161
Takayanagi Mitsuhisa, examples of
    women's suicides, 355–356*n*50

Tanaka Yoshitoshi, Military Inspector General, 508–509

Tanaka Kōgai, 205–210, 222*n*22

Tsuda Mamichi, on women and electorate, 473

Teachers, 40–41, 52, 55*n*6, 108, 173, 236, 260, 280, 499, 509

Technology, 361, 377. *See also* Mechanization

Terms of endearment, 134–136, 148, 174–175

Textile employers, 361, 390*n*47

Textile industries, 359–360, 361, 362–363, 368, 371, 372, 376–380, 387*n*28, 389*n*42s; gender division of labor in, 369–370, 383. *See also* Cotton industry; Cotton spinning; Silk industry; Women's work

Textile production, 361, 363–370, 365, 371, 372, 382

Textile workers, 20, 359, 360–361, 362–363, 364–366, 367, 368, 385*n*11

Time magazine, story on suicides in Saipan, 338–340, 341

Tōjō Eikyō, 278–279, 292–293*n*65

Tōjō Hideki, General, battle for political leadership and, 344–345

Tokugawa shoguns, 261

Tokyo Christian Women's Reform Society, control of male sexuality and, 480

Tōshiba, Good Life Movement, 437–438, 439

Toyama Shōichi, 266–267, 288*n*17

Tozuka Matsuko, 172, 173–174

Tsuda Umeko, on women's education, 475–476

Tsurumi mill union, New Life Movement influence on, 442

Uchida Shungiku, 12, 21, 556, 573, 574–576, 577–578, 588*n*78; life of, 572, 577, 588–589*n*80–81; work of, 572–573, 578, 579, 588*n*72

Ueki Emori, 464, 485*n*7

Ueno Chizuko, 521, 533, 546, 548*n*11, 565, 584*n*39

Ūman ribu, 558–559, 563, 582*n*17

Unions, 440, 441, 438–439, 446

United Nations initiatives for women, 561; Decade for Women, 521, 563

Universal military service, 268. *See also* Imperial Japanese Army and Navy

University, nationally funded in Japan, 60*n*38

Uno, Kathleen, analysis of regulatory function of *ryōsai kenbo*, 558–559

Upton, Emory, on new Japanese army, 263–264

Venereal diseases, 225, 229–242, 245, 248*n*1, 251*n*24, 281, 311–312

Vernacularization, 537, 538–539, 543, 551*n*37

Voting, not for women, 496. *See also* Women's rights

Wages, 375, 388*n*32, 388*n*35, 389*n*43, 441; coal mining, 396, 403–404, 416–417*n*26, 417*n*29; textiles, 373–375

War, 265–266, 275, 348, 509. *See also* Imperialism; Sino-Japanese War; World War I; World War II

War songs, 275–276

Watanabe, "translation" of Sherrod's story, 339–340

Welfare Ministry, 426, 428, 429, 433,
    446, 453*n*9
White beauty, ramifications of, 568
White women. *See* Caucasian women
Widows, 338, 367, 368–369, 503–505
Wives, 110, 114, 118, 209, 230–242, 306,
    400, 423, 446, 473, 478. *See also*
    Good wife, wise mother
Woman, as category, 10, 20, 31*n*2, 520,
    521, 522, 526, 527, 544. *See also*
    Women
Womanhood, 13–14, 21, 86, 113–114,
    500, 506–507, 512–513, 518*n*34, 558;
    state vision of, 496–497. *See also*
    Ryōsai kenbo; Women's education;
    Women's rights
Womanly morality, women's educa-
    tion and, 491*n*105
Women, 22, 44, 79, 175, 328, 361, 494,
    565, 567; proper place in the home,
    23, 113–114, 564; status of, 41–42,
    561; relationships among, height-
    ened profile of, 175–176; as men's
    plaything, 208–209; right to vote,
    261; colonial imperialism experi-
    ence of, 300–310; ideal in colonies,
    312–313; agents of modernity, 316–
    317; images of, 326–328; wartime
    role, 327, 496–497; history of
    fighting, 334–335; war and, 348–
    349, 508–509; rural, 372–376; nim-
    ble fingers argument, 378–379;
    jobs available to, 380, 399–400;
    political involvement, 431; in Meiji
    Japan, 471; role of good wife,
    wise mother, 507; lower-class ru-
    ral and urban, *ryōsai kenbo* not ac-
    cepted by, 508; Japanese com-
    pared with others, 511; in ancient
    Japan, 541–542; objects of desire

and rivalry, 552*n*42; as targets and
    consumers, 557–558; identity, 558–
    559; power of, 564; redefinition of,
    566; working for wages, 585*n*36.
    See also Colonial women; Women
    workers
Women workers, 300–301, 313–317,
    326, 372, 375, 377–379, 398, 506, 507;
    stereotypical positions, 19, 459*n*73;
    textile workers, 359–360, 362, 369–
    370, 370–376, 377–379, 387*n*28; coal
    miners, 403, 410–412, 414*n*4; mine
    workers, 413, 417*n*27–28; wages of,
    505, 564
Women's Action Group, 560, 582*n*22
Women's advocacy groups, 482
Women's culture, 556–557, 566
Women's deaths, 328–329, 341–343,
    344–348
Women's education, 39, 48–51, 52–
    54, 83, 104, 243, 428, 499–509, 512;
    Tokugawa period, 41, 46–47, 58–
    59*n*29; higher education, private
    initiative and, 52–53; rural
    women's access to, 56*n*10; stabil-
    ity of state and, 56*n*12; goal of,
    57*n*23, 491*n*105; purpose of, 105,
    477; women's rights and, 468–
    476; womanly morality and,
    491*n*105. *See also* Education for
    girls; Meiji women's education
Women's liberation, 237–238, 465,
    530–531
Women's liberation movement, 209,
    555, 558–560
Women's magazines, 99, 101, 104, 156,
    556, 564, 585*n*41, 586*n*50, 588*n*79;
    British, 126*n*36, 130*n*68; American,
    130*n*68; specialized, 565–568,
    585*n*48

Women's movement, 225–226, 232–238, 472–481; connected to rise of same-sex love, 169–170

Women's organizations, New Life Movement and, 427. *See also* Seitō movement

Women's pornography, 570, 571, 587*n*66

Women's rights, 20–21, 23, 314, 464–465, 466, 468–472, 475, 483, 555, 578–579; political, 465, 467, 468, 469, 470–471, 475, 477, 478–479, 487*n*33. *See also* Joken; Rights; Feminism; Women's Movement

Women's roles, 53, 327, 380–381, 431, 497, 511, 536

Women's sexuality, Tanaka Kogai's obsession with, 207–208

Women's status, 228, 468–469, 477

Women's work, 372, 377–379, 506, 507

Woodblocks. *See* Images; Media

Work, 326–327, 425, 507. *See also* Women workers

World War I, reconfiguration of gender roles after, 100–101

World War II, 326–356 *passim*; wartime atrocities, 296, 543–544

Writing, 524–525, 528, 538–539. *See also* Genbun itchi

Yabe, Hatsuko, Red Thought Society and, 172

Yamashita Etsuko, 520–521, 522, 530–537, 547*n*2, 550*n*35

Yasuda Tokutarō, 147, 149, 150, 162

Yokuatsu, 532

Yomiuri hōchi (newspaper), exploitation of women's deaths in Saipan, 341–342

Yosano Akiko, poem addressed to brother in army, 284, 294*n*80

Yoshiya (writer), 163–165, 187*n*113, 265

Harvard East Asian Monographs
(*out-of-print)

*1. Liang Fang-chung, *The Single-Whip Method of Taxation in China*

*2. Harold C. Hinton, *The Grain Tribute System of China, 1845–1911*

3. Ellsworth C. Carlson, *The Kaiping Mines, 1877–1912*

*4. Chao Kuo-chün, *Agrarian Policies of Mainland China: A Documentary Study, 1949–1956*

*5. Edgar Snow, *Random Notes on Red China, 1936–1945*

*6. Edwin George Beal, Jr., *The Origin of Likin, 1835–1864*

7. Chao Kuo-chün, *Economic Planning and Organization in Mainland China: A Documentary Study, 1949–1957*

*8. John K. Fairbank, *Ching Documents: An Introductory Syllabus*

*9. Helen Yin and Yi-chang Yin, *Economic Statistics of Mainland China, 1949–1957*

*10. Wolfgang Franke, *The Reform and Abolition of the Traditional Chinese Examination System*

11. Albert Feuerwerker and S. Cheng, *Chinese Communist Studies of Modern Chinese History*

12. C. John Stanley, *Late Ching Finance: Hu Kuang-yung as an Innovator*

13. S. M. Meng, *The Tsungli Yamen: Its Organization and Functions*

*14. Ssu-yü Teng, *Historiography of the Taiping Rebellion*

15. Chun-Jo Liu, *Controversies in Modern Chinese Intellectual History: An Analytic Bibliography of Periodical Articles, Mainly of the May Fourth and Post–May Fourth Era*

*16. Edward J. M. Rhoads, *The Chinese Red Army, 1927–1963: An Annotated Bibliography*

17. Andrew J. Nathan, *A History of the China International Famine Relief Commission*

*18. Frank H. H. King (ed.) and Prescott Clarke, *A Research Guide to China-Coast Newspapers, 1822–1911*

19. Ellis Joffe, *Party and Army: Professionalism and Political Control in the Chinese Officer Corps, 1949–1964*

*20. Toshio G. Tsukahira, *Feudal Control in Tokugawa Japan: The Sankin Kōtai System*

21. Kwang-Ching Liu, ed., *American Missionaries in China: Papers from Harvard Seminars*

Harvard East Asian Monographs

22. George Moseley, *A Sino-Soviet Cultural Frontier: The Ili Kazakh Autonomous Chou*

23. Carl F. Nathan, *Plague Prevention and Politics in Manchuria, 1910–1931*

*24. Adrian Arthur Bennett, *John Fryer: The Introduction of Western Science and Technology into Nineteenth-Century China*

25. Donald J. Friedman, *The Road from Isolation: The Campaign of the American Committee for Non-Participation in Japanese Aggression, 1938–1941*

*26. Edward LeFevour, *Western Enterprise in Late Ching China: A Selective Survey of Jardine, Matheson and Company's Operations, 1842–1895*

27. Charles Neuhauser, *Third World Politics: China and the Afro-Asian People's Solidarity Organization, 1957–1967*

28. Kungtu C. Sun, assisted by Ralph W. Huenemann, *The Economic Development of Manchuria in the First Half of the Twentieth Century*

*29. Shahid Javed Burki, *A Study of Chinese Communes, 1965*

30. John Carter Vincent, *The Extraterritorial System in China: Final Phase*

31. Madeleine Chi, *China Diplomacy, 1914–1918*

*32. Clifton Jackson Phillips, *Protestant America and the Pagan World: The First Half Century of the American Board of Commissioners for Foreign Missions, 1810–1860*

33. James Pusey, *Wu Han: Attacking the Present Through the Past*

34. Ying-wan Cheng, *Postal Communication in China and Its Modernization, 1860–1896*

35. Tuvia Blumenthal, *Saving in Postwar Japan*

36. Peter Frost, *The Bakumatsu Currency Crisis*

37. Stephen C. Lockwood, *Augustine Heard and Company, 1858–1862*

38. Robert R. Campbell, *James Duncan Campbell: A Memoir by His Son*

39. Jerome Alan Cohen, ed., *The Dynamics of China's Foreign Relations*

40. V. V. Vishnyakova-Akimova, *Two Years in Revolutionary China, 1925–1927*, tr. Steven L. Levine

*41. Meron Medzini, *French Policy in Japan During the Closing Years of the Tokugawa Regime*

42. Ezra Vogel, Margie Sargent, Vivienne B. Shue, Thomas Jay Mathews, and Deborah S. Davis, *The Cultural Revolution in the Provinces*

*43. Sidney A. Forsythe, *An American Missionary Community in China, 1895–1905*

*44. Benjamin I. Schwartz, ed., *Reflections on the May Fourth Movement.: A Symposium*

*45. Ching Young Choe, *The Rule of the Taewŏngun, 1864–1873: Restoration in Yi Korea*

46. W. P. J. Hall, *A Bibliographical Guide to Japanese Research on the Chinese Economy, 1958–1970*

47. Jack J. Gerson, *Horatio Nelson Lay and Sino-British Relations, 1854–1864*

48. Paul Richard Bohr, *Famine and the Missionary: Timothy Richard as Relief Administrator and Advocate of National Reform*

49. Endymion Wilkinson, *The History of Imperial China: A Research Guide*

50. Britten Dean, *China and Great Britain: The Diplomacy of Commercial Relations, 1860–1864*

51. Ellsworth C. Carlson, *The Foochow Missionaries, 1847–1880*

52. Yeh-chien Wang, *An Estimate of the Land-Tax Collection in China, 1753 and 1908*

53. Richard M. Pfeffer, *Understanding Business Contracts in China, 1949–1963*

54. Han-sheng Chuan and Richard Kraus, *Mid-Ching Rice Markets and Trade: An Essay in Price History*

55. Ranbir Vohra, *Lao She and the Chinese Revolution*

56. Liang-lin Hsiao, *China's Foreign Trade Statistics, 1864–1949*

*57. Lee-hsia Hsu Ting, *Government Control of the Press in Modern China, 1900–1949*

58. Edward W. Wagner, *The Literati Purges: Political Conflict in Early Yi Korea*

*59. Joungwon A. Kim, *Divided Korea: The Politics of Development, 1945–1972*

*60. Noriko Kamachi, John K. Fairbank, and Chūzō Ichiko, *Japanese Studies of Modern China Since 1953: A Bibliographical Guide to Historical and Social-Science Research on the Nineteenth and Twentieth Centuries, Supplementary Volume for 1953–1969*

61. Donald A. Gibbs and Yun-chen Li, *A Bibliography of Studies and Translations of Modern Chinese Literature, 1918–1942*

62. Robert H. Silin, *Leadership and Values: The Organization of Large-Scale Taiwanese Enterprises*

63. David Pong, *A Critical Guide to the Kwangtung Provincial Archives Deposited at the Public Record Office of London*

*64. Fred W. Drake, *China Charts the World: Hsu Chi-yü and His Geography of 1848*

*65. William A. Brown and Urgrunge Onon, translators and annotators, *History of the Mongolian People's Republic*

66. Edward L. Farmer, *Early Ming Government: The Evolution of Dual Capitals*

*67. Ralph C. Croizier, *Koxinga and Chinese Nationalism: History, Myth, and the Hero*

*68. William J. Tyler, tr., *The Psychological World of Natsume Sōseki*, by Doi Takeo

69. Eric Widmer, *The Russian Ecclesiastical Mission in Peking During the Eighteenth Century*

*70. Charlton M. Lewis, *Prologue to the Chinese Revolution: The Transformation of Ideas and Institutions in Hunan Province, 1891–1907*

71. Preston Torbert, *The Ching Imperial Household Department: A Study of Its Organization and Principal Functions, 1662–1796*

72. Paul A. Cohen and John E. Schrecker, eds., *Reform in Nineteenth-Century China*

73. Jon Sigurdson, *Rural Industrialism in China*

74. Kang Chao, *The Development of Cotton Textile Production in China*

75. Valentin Rabe, *The Home Base of American China Missions, 1880–1920*

*76. Sarasin Viraphol, *Tribute and Profit: Sino-Siamese Trade, 1652–1853*

77. Ch'i-ch'ing Hsiao, *The Military Establishment of the Yuan Dynasty*

78. Meishi Tsai, *Contemporary Chinese Novels and Short Stories, 1949–1974: An Annotated Bibliography*

*79. Wellington K. K. Chan, *Merchants, Mandarins and Modern Enterprise in Late Ching China*

80. Endymion Wilkinson, *Landlord and Labor in Late Imperial China: Case Studies from Shandong by Jing Su and Luo Lun*

*81. Barry Keenan, *The Dewey Experiment in China: Educational Reform and Political Power in the Early Republic*

*82. George A. Hayden, *Crime and Punishment in Medieval Chinese Drama: Three Judge Pao Plays*

*83. Sang-Chul Suh, *Growth and Structural Changes in the Korean Economy, 1910–1940*

84. J. W. Dower, *Empire and Aftermath: Yoshida Shigeru and the Japanese Experience, 1878–1954*

85. Martin Collcutt, *Five Mountains: The Rinzai Zen Monastic Institution in Medieval Japan*

86. Kwang Suk Kim and Michael Roemer, *Growth and Structural Transformation*

87. Anne O. Krueger, *The Developmental Role of the Foreign Sector and Aid*

*88. Edwin S. Mills and Byung-Nak Song, *Urbanization and Urban Problems*

89. Sung Hwan Ban, Pal Yong Moon, and Dwight H. Perkins, *Rural Development*

*90. Noel F. McGinn, Donald R. Snodgrass, Yung Bong Kim, Shin-Bok Kim, and Quee-Young Kim, *Education and Development in Korea*

91. Leroy P. Jones and Il SaKong, *Government, Business, and Entrepreneurship in Economic Development: The Korean Case*

92. Edward S. Mason, Dwight H. Perkins, Kwang Suk Kim, David C. Cole, Mahn Je Kim, et al., *The Economic and Social Modernization of the Republic of Korea*

93. Robert Repetto, Tai Hwan Kwon, Son-Ung Kim, Dae Young Kim, John E. Sloboda, and Peter J. Donaldson, *Economic Development, Population Policy, and Demographic Transition in the Republic of Korea*

94. Parks M. Coble, Jr., *The Shanghai Capitalists and the Nationalist Government, 1927–1937*

95. Noriko Kamachi, *Reform in China: Huang Tsun-hsien and the Japanese Model*

96. Richard Wich, *Sino-Soviet Crisis Politics: A Study of Political Change and Communication*

97. Lillian M. Li, *China's Silk Trade: Traditional Industry in the Modern World, 1842–1937*

98. R. David Arkush, *Fei Xiaotong and Sociology in Revolutionary China*

*99. Kenneth Alan Grossberg, *Japan's Renaissance: The Politics of the Muromachi Bakufu*

100. James Reeve Pusey, *China and Charles Darwin*

101. Hoyt Cleveland Tillman, *Utilitarian Confucianism: Chen Liang's Challenge to Chu Hsi*

102. Thomas A. Stanley, *Ōsugi Sakae, Anarchist in Taishō Japan: The Creativity of the Ego*

103. Jonathan K. Ocko, *Bureaucratic Reform in Provincial China: Ting Jih-ch'ang in Restoration Kiangsu, 1867–1870*

Harvard East Asian Monographs

104. James Reed, *The Missionary Mind and American East Asia Policy, 1911–1915*

105. Neil L. Waters, *Japan's Local Pragmatists: The Transition from Bakumatsu to Meiji in the Kawasaki Region*

106. David C. Cole and Yung Chul Park, *Financial Development in Korea, 1945–1978*

107. Roy Bahl, Chuk Kyo Kim, and Chong Kee Park, *Public Finances During the Korean Modernization Process*

108. William D. Wray, *Mitsubishi and the N.Y.K, 1870–1914: Business Strategy in the Japanese Shipping Industry*

109. Ralph William Huenemann, *The Dragon and the Iron Horse: The Economics of Railroads in China, 1876–1937*

110. Benjamin A. Elman, *From Philosophy to Philology: Intellectual and Social Aspects of Change in Late Imperial China*

111. Jane Kate Leonard, *Wei Yüan and China's Rediscovery of the Maritime World*

112. Luke S. K. Kwong, *A Mosaic of the Hundred Days:. Personalities, Politics, and Ideas of 1898*

113. John E. Wills, Jr., *Embassies and Illusions: Dutch and Portuguese Envoys to K'ang-hsi, 1666–1687*

114. Joshua A. Fogel, *Politics and Sinology: The Case of Naitō Konan (1866–1934)*

*115. Jeffrey C. Kinkley, ed., *After Mao: Chinese Literature and Society, 1978–1981*

116. C. Andrew Gerstle, *Circles of Fantasy: Convention in the Plays of Chikamatsu*

117. Andrew Gordon, *The Evolution of Labor Relations in Japan: Heavy Industry, 1853–1955*

*118. Daniel K. Gardner, *Chu Hsi and the "Ta Hsueh": Neo-Confucian Reflection on the Confucian Canon*

119. Christine Guth Kanda, *Shinzō: Hachiman Imagery and Its Development*

*120. Robert Borgen, *Sugawara no Michizane and the Early Heian Court*

121. Chang-tai Hung, *Going to the People: Chinese Intellectuals and Folk Literature, 1918–1937*

*122. Michael A. Cusumano, *The Japanese Automobile Industry: Technology and Management at Nissan and Toyota*

123. Richard von Glahn, *The Country of Streams and Grottoes: Expansion, Settlement, and the Civilizing of the Sichuan Frontier in Song Times*

124. Steven D. Carter, *The Road to Komatsubara: A Classical Reading of the Renga Hyakuin*

125. Katherine F. Bruner, John K. Fairbank, and Richard T. Smith, *Entering China's Service: Robert Hart's Journals, 1854–1863*

126. Bob Tadashi Wakabayashi, *Anti-Foreignism and Western Learning in Early-Modern Japan: The "New Theses" of 1825*

127. Atsuko Hirai, *Individualism and Socialism: The Life and Thought of Kawai Eijirō (1891–1944)*

128. Ellen Widmer, *The Margins of Utopia: "Shui-hu hou-chuan" and the Literature of Ming Loyalism*

Harvard East Asian Monographs

129. R. Kent Guy, *The Emperor's Four Treasuries: Scholars and the State in the Late Chien-lung Era*

130. Peter C. Perdue, *Exhausting the Earth: State and Peasant in Hunan, 1500–1850*

131. Susan Chan Egan, *A Latterday Confucian: Reminiscences of William Hung (1893–1980)*

132. James T. C. Liu, *China Turning Inward: Intellectual-Political Changes in the Early Twelfth Century*

133. Paul A. Cohen, *Between Tradition and Modernity: Wang T'ao and Reform in Late Ching China*

134. Kate Wildman Nakai, *Shogunal Politics: Arai Hakuseki and the Premises of Tokugawa Rule*

135. Parks M. Coble, *Facing Japan: Chinese Politics and Japanese Imperialism, 1931–1937*

136. Jon L. Saari, *Legacies of Childhood: Growing Up Chinese in a Time of Crisis, 1890–1920*

137. Susan Downing Videen, *Tales of Heichū*

138. Heinz Morioka and Miyoko Sasaki, *Rakugo: The Popular Narrative Art of Japan*

139. Joshua A. Fogel, *Nakae Ushikichi in China: The Mourning of Spirit*

140. Alexander Barton Woodside, *Vietnam and the Chinese Model: A Comparative Study of Vietnamese and Chinese Government in the First Half of the Nineteenth Century*

141. George Elision, *Deus Destroyed: The Image of Christianity in Early Modern Japan*

142. William D. Wray, ed., *Managing Industrial Enterprise: Cases from Japan's Prewar Experience*

143. T'ung-tsu Ch'ü, *Local Government in China Under the Ching*

144. Marie Anchordoguy, *Computers, Inc.: Japan's Challenge to IBM*

145. Barbara Molony, *Technology and Investment: The Prewar Japanese Chemical Industry*

146. Mary Elizabeth Berry, *Hideyoshi*

147. Laura E. Hein, *Fueling Growth: The Energy Revolution and Economic Policy in Postwar Japan*

148. Wen-hsin Yeh, *The Alienated Academy: Culture and Politics in Republican China, 1919–1937*

149. Dru C. Gladney, *Muslim Chinese: Ethnic Nationalism in the People's Republic*

150. Merle Goldman and Paul A. Cohen, eds., *Ideas Across Cultures: Essays on Chinese Thought in Honor of Benjamin L Schwartz*

151. James M. Polachek, *The Inner Opium War*

152. Gail Lee Bernstein, *Japanese Marxist: A Portrait of Kawakami Hajime, 1879–1946*

153. Lloyd E. Eastman, *The Abortive Revolution: China Under Nationalist Rule, 1927–1937*

154. Mark Mason, *American Multinationals and Japan: The Political Economy of Japanese Capital Controls, 1899–1980*

155. Richard J. Smith, John K. Fairbank, and Katherine F. Bruner, *Robert Hart and China's Early Modernization: His Journals, 1863–1866*

156. George J. Tanabe, Jr., *Myōe the Dreamkeeper: Fantasy and Knowledge in Kamakura Buddhism*

157. William Wayne Farris, *Heavenly Warriors: The Evolution of Japan's Military, 500– 1300*

158. Yu-ming Shaw, *An American Missionary in China: John Leighton Stuart and Chinese-American Relations*

159. James B. Palais, *Politics and Policy in Traditional Korea*

160. Douglas Reynolds, *China, 1898–1912: The Xinzheng Revolution and Japan*

161. Roger R. Thompson, *China's Local Councils in the Age of Constitutional Reform, 1898– 1911*

162. William Johnston, *The Modern Epidemic: History of Tuberculosis in Japan*

163. Constantine Nomikos Vaporis, *Breaking Barriers: Travel and the State in Early Modern Japan*

164. Irmela Hijiya-Kirschnereit, *Rituals of Self-Revelation: Shishōsetsu as Literary Genre and Socio-Cultural Phenomenon*

165. James C. Baxter, *The Meiji Unification Through the Lens of Ishikawa Prefecture*

166. Thomas R. H. Havens, *Architects of Affluence: The Tsutsumi Family and the Seibu-Saison Enterprises in Twentieth-Century Japan*

167. Anthony Hood Chambers, *The Secret Window: Ideal Worlds in Tanizaki's Fiction*

168. Steven J. Ericson, *The Sound of the Whistle: Railroads and the State in Meiji Japan*

169. Andrew Edmund Goble, *Kenmu: Go-Daigo's Revolution*

170. Denise Potrzeba Lett, *In Pursuit of Status: The Making of South Korea's "New" Urban Middle Class*

171. Mimi Hall Yiengpruksawan, *Hiraizumi: Buddhist Art and Regional Politics in Twelfth-Century Japan*

172. Charles Shirō Inouye, *The Similitude of Blossoms: A Critical Biography of Izumi Kyōka (1873–1939), Japanese Novelist and Playwright*

173. Aviad E. Raz, *Riding the Black Ship: Japan and Tokyo Disneyland*

174. Deborah J. Milly, *Poverty, Equality, and Growth: The Politics of Economic Need in Postwar Japan*

175. See Heng Teow, *Japan's Cultural Policy Toward China, 1918–1931: A Comparative Perspective*

176. Michael A. Fuller, *An Introduction to Literary Chinese*

177. Frederick R. Dickinson, *War and National Reinvention: Japan in the Great War, 1914–1919*

178. John Solt, *Shredding the Tapestry of Meaning: The Poetry and Poetics of Kitasono Katue (1902–1978)*

179. Edward Pratt, *Japan's Protoindustrial Elite: The Economic Foundations of the Gōnō*

180. Atsuko Sakaki, *Recontextualizing Texts: Narrative Performance in Modern Japanese Fiction*

Harvard East Asian Monographs

181. Soon-Won Park, *Colonial Industrialization and Labor in Korea: The Onoda Cement Factory*

182. JaHyun Kim Haboush and Martina Deuchler, *Culture and the State in Late Chosŏn Korea*

183. John W. Chaffee, *Branches of Heaven: A History of the Imperial Clan of Sung China*

184. Gi-Wook Shin and Michael Robinson, eds., *Colonial Modernity in Korea*

185. Nam-lin Hur, *Prayer and Play in Late Tokugawa Japan: Asakusa Sensōji and Edo Society*

186. Kristin Stapleton, *Civilizing Chengdu: Chinese Urban Reform, 1895–1937*

187. Hyung Il Pai, *Constructing "Korean" Origins: A Critical Review of Archaeology, Historiography, and Racial Myth in Korean State-Formation Theories*

188. Brian D. Ruppert, *Jewel in the Ashes: Buddha Relics and Power in Early Medieval Japan*

189. Susan Daruvala, *Zhou Zuoren and an Alternative Chinese Response to Modernity*

190. James Z. Lee, *The Political Economy of a Frontier: Southwest China, 1250–1850*

191. Kerry Smith, *A Time of Crisis: Japan, the Great Depression, and Rural Revitalization*

192. Michael Lewis, *Becoming Apart: National Power and Local Politics in Toyama, 1868–1945*

193. William C. Kirby, Man-houng Lin, James Chin Shih, and David A. Pietz, eds., *State and Economy in Republican China: A Handbook for Scholars*

194. Timothy S. George, *Minamata: Pollution and the Struggle for Democracy in Postwar Japan*

195. Billy K. L. So, *Prosperity, Region, and Institutions in Maritime China: The South Fukien Pattern, 946–1368*

196. Yoshihisa Tak Matsusaka, *The Making of Japanese Manchuria, 1904–1932*

197. Maram Epstein, *Competing Discourses: Orthodoxy, Authenticity, and Engendered Meanings in Late Imperial Chinese Fiction*

198. Curtis J. Milhaupt, J. Mark Ramseyer, and Michael K. Young, eds. and comps., *Japanese Law in Context: Readings in Society, the Economy, and Politics*

199. Haruo Iguchi, *Unfinished Business: Ayukawa Yoshisuke and U.S.-Japan Relations, 1937–1952*

200. Scott Pearce, Audrey Spiro, and Patricia Ebrey, *Culture and Power in the Reconstitution of the Chinese Realm, 200–600*

201. Terry Kawashima, *Writing Margins: The Textual Construction of Gender in Heian and Kamakura Japan*

202. Martin W. Huang, *Desire and Fictional Narrative in Late Imperial China*

203. Robert S. Ross and Jiang Changbin, eds., *Re-examining the Cold War: U.S.-China Diplomacy, 1954–1973*

204. Guanhua Wang, *In Search of Justice: The 1905–1906 Chinese Anti-American Boycott*

205. David Schaberg, *A Patterned Past: Form and Thought in Early Chinese Historiography*

206. Christine Yano, *Tears of Longing: Nostalgia and the Nation in Japanese Popular Song*

207. Milena Doleželová-Velingerová and Oldřich Král, with Graham Sanders, eds., *The Appropriation of Cultural Capital: China's May Fourth Project*

208. Robert N. Huey, *The Making of 'Shinkokinshū'*

209. Lee Butler, *Emperor and Aristocracy in Japan, 1467–1680: Resilience and Renewal*

210. Suzanne Ogden, *Inklings of Democracy in China*

211. Kenneth J. Ruoff, *The People's Emperor: Democracy and the Japanese Monarchy, 1945–1995*

212. Haun Saussy, *Great Walls of Discourse and Other Adventures in Cultural China*

213. Aviad E. Raz, *Emotions at Work: Normative Control, Organizations, and Culture in Japan and America*

214. Rebecca E. Karl and Peter Zarrow, eds., *Rethinking the 1898 Reform Period: Political and Cultural Change in Late Qing China*

215. Kevin O'Rourke, *The Book of Korean Shijo*

216. Ezra F. Vogel, ed., *The Golden Age of the U.S.-China-Japan Triangle, 1972–1989*

217. Thomas A Wilson, ed., *On Sacred Grounds: Culture, Society, Politics, and the Formation of the Cult of Confucius*

218. Donald S. Sutton, *Steps of Perfection: Exorcistic Performers and Chinese Religion in Twentieth-Century Taiwan*

219. Daqing Yang, *Technology of Empire: Telecommunications and Japanese Imperialism, 1930–1945*

220. Qianshen Bai, *Fu Shan's World: The Transformation of Chinese Calligraphy in the Seventeenth Century*

221. Paul Jakov Smith and Richard von Glahn, eds., *The Song-Yuan-Ming Transition in Chinese History*

222. Rania Huntington, *Alien Kind: Foxes and Late Imperial Chinese Narrative*

223. Jordan Sand, *House and Home in Modern Japan: Architecture, Domestic Space, and Bourgeois Culture, 1880–1930*

224. Karl Gerth, *China Made: Consumer Culture and the Creation of the Nation*

225. Xiaoshan Yang, *Metamorphosis of the Private Sphere: Gardens and Objects in Tang-Song Poetry*

226. Barbara Mittler, *A Newspaper for China? Power, Identity, and Change in Shanghai's News Media, 1872–1912*

227. Joyce A. Madancy, *The Troublesome Legacy of Commissioner Lin: The Opium Trade and Opium Suppression in Fujian Province, 1820s to 1920s*

228. John Makeham, *Transmitters and Creators: Chinese Commentators and Commentaries on the Analects*

229. Elisabeth Köll, *From Cotton Mill to Business Empire: The Emergence of Regional Enterprises in Modern China*

230. Emma Teng, *Taiwan's Imagined Geography: Chinese Colonial Travel Writing and Pictures, 1683–1895*

Harvard East Asian Monographs

231. Wilt Idema and Beata Grant, *The Red Brush: Writing Women of Imperial China*

232. Eric C. Rath, *The Ethos of Noh: Actors and Their Art*

233. Elizabeth Remick, *Building Local States: China During the Republican and Post–Mao Eras*

234. Lynn Struve, ed., *The Qing Formation in World-Historical Time*

235. D. Max Moerman, *Localizing Paradise: Kumano Pilgrimage and the Religious Landscape of Premodern Japan*

236. Antonia Finnane, *Speaking of Yangzhou: A Chinese City, 1550–1850*

237. Brian Platt, *Burning and Building: Schooling and State Formation in Japan, 1750–1890*

238. Gail Bernstein, Andrew Gordon, and Kate Wildman Nakai, eds., *Public Spheres, Private Lives in Modern Japan, 1600–1950: Essays in Honor of Albert Craig*

239. Wu Hung and Katherine R. Tsiang, *Body and Face in Chinese Visual Culture*

240. Stephen Dodd, *Writing Home: Representations of the Native Place in Modern Japanese Literature*

241. David Anthony Bello, *Opium and the Limits of Empire: Drug Prohibition in the Chinese Interior, 1729–1850*

242. Hosea Hirata, *Discourses of Seduction: History, Evil, Desire, and Modern Japanese Literature*

243. Kyung Moon Hwang, *Beyond Birth: Social Status in the Emergence of Modern Korea*

244. Brian R. Dott, *Identity Reflections: Pilgrimages to Mount Tai in Late Imperial China*

245. Mark McNally, *Proving the Way: Conflict and Practice in the History of Japanese Nativism*

246. Yongping Wu, *A Political Explanation of Economic Growth: State Survival, Bureaucratic Politics, and Private Enterprises in the Making of Taiwan's Economy, 1950–1985*

247. Kyu Hyun Kim, *The Age of Visions and Arguments: Parliamentarianism and the National Public Sphere in Early Meiji Japan*

248. Zvi Ben-Dor Benite, *The Dao of Muhammad: A Cultural History of Muslims in Late Imperial China*

249. David Der-wei Wang and Shang Wei, eds., *Dynastic Crisis and Cultural Innovation: From the Late Ming to the Late Qing and Beyond*

250. Wilt L. Idema, Wai-yee Li, and Ellen Widmer, eds., *Trauma and Transcendence in Early Qing Literature*

251. Barbara Molony and Kathleen Uno, eds., *Gendering Modern Japanese History*